CW00832339

The Secret History of PWE

The Political Warfare Executive 1939–1945

The Secret History of PWE

The Political Warfare Executive 1939–1945

David Garnett

With an Introduction and Notes by Andrew Roberts

A *St Ermin's Press* Book

First published in Great Britain in 2002
By St Ermin's Press
In association with Little, Brown

The Public Record Office is the custodian of David Garnett's
original manuscript, reference CAB 102/610.

ISBN 1 903608 08 2

A CIP catalogue for this book is
available from the British Library.

Typeset in Imprint by M Rules
Printed and bound by
Clays Ltd, St Ives plc

St Ermin's Press
In association with Little, Brown
An imprint of Time Warner Books UK
Brettenham House
Lancaster Place
London WC2E 7EN

www.TimeWarnerBooks.co.uk

Contents

Illustrations

Introduction

The Political Warfare Executive is the final draft of the official history of one of the nine secret services of the Second World War, written by a distinguished author who served as its Director of Training.[1] It was fully in keeping with the rather bohemian and experimental nature of PWE for its leadership to chose the Bloomsbury Group novelist David Garnett as their chronicler, and still more in keeping with the ethos of Bloomsbury that they got so uninhibited and honest a critique that it had to be classified 'Secret – For Official Use Only' for over half a century, and can only now be published.

We can for the first time now know the whole truth about the British (and later Allied) propaganda effort in the Second World War, and much of it makes for pretty uncomfortable reading. The tale of inter-departmental wrangling and Whitehall empire-building that Garnett unflinchingly relates is little short of shameful, and shows how various government departments seemed to expend far more energy in outwitting and undermining one another than in trying to confuse and demoralise the enemy. Even Graham Greene's coruscating short story on the wartime Ministry of Information, *Men at Work*, does not convey half the wasteful pointlessness of British propaganda in the early part of the war. That things improved so dramatically after 1941 was largely due to the work of PWE.

The intended template of PWE was the efficient propaganda organisation set up at Crewe House during the Great War, whose deputy director was the Canadian-born former military attaché Sir Campbell Stuart. During the Munich Crisis of September and October 1938, various forward-thinking people in the British Civil Service and the BBC, principally Sir Stephen Tallents, the director-general designate of what was to become the Ministry of Information (MoI), suggested the creation of another such single body with responsibility for co-ordinating British foreign propaganda. Incredibly, and due largely to departmental territory squabbles, it was to be a full three years before that body – PWE – was finally to come into being.

During the Munich Crisis Tallents wished to inundate Germany with tens of millions of anti-Hitler leaflets, spread right across the country by small balloons and the RAF, but his plan came up against the appeasers in government

(Notes: Files are to be found at the Public Records Office unless otherwise stated.)

1. The other eight were MI5, MI6, SOE, the Government Code and Cipher School, Radio Security, MI9, London Controlling Section, and the Auxiliary Units.

and Whitehall and was dropped. On 4 October 1938 he wrote a memorandum about how the Czech crisis had 'taught us various lessons, but the sharpest and most urgent of them was the need for properly coordinated arrangements for the conveyance of information to enemy countries'.[1] To achieve this he recommended that when the Ministry of Information was brought into being on the outbreak of war, it ought to contain a special department immediately ready to put out publicity material to enemy countries.

Another of Tallents' suggestions was for a department of MoI that would be specifically committed to the study of public opinion in enemy countries, but this idea quickly ran foul of both the Foreign Office (FO), which saw one of its traditional areas of expertise being encroached upon, and the Treasury, on the inevitable grounds of cost. Throughout the long and hard-fought story of the creation of a British propaganda arm these two most powerful departments of state played blinding hands in what one historian has dubbed the 'interdepartmental game of beggar-my-neighbour'.[2] The point at which the Foreign Office started to come round to the idea of PWE was when the head of its News Department, Reginald 'Rex' Leeper, was offered a major role in the new Executive.

Meanwhile, in a move that very significantly complicated matters, the Prime Minister Neville Chamberlain asked the veteran Great War propagandist Sir Campbell Stuart to set up his own clandestine propaganda department, without the seemingly obvious precursor of even informing Tallents. Stuart's operation centred on Electra House, the building on the Victoria Embankment from where he already chaired the Imperial Communications Committee, which served as its 'front' for a while. The official title of Electra House was the Department of Propaganda in Enemy Countries, and there were plans for it to move to Woburn Abbey in Bedfordshire on the outbreak of war. Although its operations were wound down after Munich, they were beefed up again in the spring of 1939 when Hitler's invasion of the rump of Czechoslovakia made it clear that war was the most likely outcome after all.

After war broke out in September 1939, and Tallents inevitably found out about Electra House, its operations first came under the auspices of the first Minister of Information, Lord Macmillan, but then in October 1939 overall responsibility for it was transferred to the Foreign Office. In another about turn, in June 1940, it was placed under the new Minister of Information, Churchill's friend Alfred Duff Cooper, who had resigned over Munich but was now back in the Cabinet.[3] Succeeding Chamberlain as Prime Minister that May, Churchill cast a series of depth charges into what were already very choppy Whitehall waters. On 16 July 1940 he approved the charter of a Special Operations Executive (SOE), 'to co-ordinate all action by

1. FO 898/1.
2. Charles Cruickshank, *The Fourth Arm* (1977), p. 15.
3. PREM 1/374.

way of subversion and sabotage against the enemy overseas'. On so doing he famously charged its director, the energetic Minister of Economic Warfare and Labour politician Dr Hugh Dalton, to 'Set Europe ablaze!'

The scramble for the right to formulate and distribute propaganda to foreign countries certainly set Whitehall ablaze. As Stuart quitted the scene altogether, one of Dalton's first acts was to split the roles of SOE between SO1, which took over the secret propaganda role of Electra House and was placed under Leeper's immediate control, and SO2, which dealt with sabotage. Although Dalton also had plans to try to appropriate Electra House's 'open' propaganda role, in the meantime it was left under Duff Cooper's control at the Ministry of Information.

By the end of 1940, however, departmental warfare had broken out between SOE and MoI over the control of 'open', 'white' or 'non-subversive' propaganda, i.e. that type of propaganda – mainly BBC broadcasts – which made no secret of the fact that they originated from the United Kingdom. This was specifically differentiated from the 'secret', 'black' or 'subversive' propaganda that SO1 put out from Woburn Abbey and elsewhere, which purported to originate from resistance groups in occupied Europe.

In attempting to defend his departmental ground, Duff Cooper tried to argue that there was no real difference between the subversive and non-subversive propaganda activities, whilst Dalton wrote counter-memoranda arguing that the BBC's broadcasts to enemy and enemy-controlled countries – by then half of Europe – should be transferred in their entirety to SOE. 'I think these two papers make quite a pretty debate!' he wrote of his and Duff Cooper's submissions to the Cabinet.[1]

To adjudicate between the two combative and influential ministers, both of whom had a large number of important backers and impeccable anti-appeasement credentials, a busy Churchill appointed the Lord President of the Council, Sir John Anderson, whose compromise formula – based roughly on the status quo – managed to please no one. Duff Cooper personally suspected, as he wrote in his autobiography *Old Men Forget*, that Churchill had farmed out the decision to Anderson 'because he knew [propaganda] could not win the war', and was thus not much interested in it.[2]

In order to come up with a workable solution, a meeting was held on 16 May 1941 between the Foreign Secretary Anthony Eden, Duff Cooper, Dalton and Anderson. They decided that a Ministerial Committee should be set up with each of the first three ministers sending a senior official to represent their departments. Duff Cooper had therefore effectively kept control of 'open' propaganda, Dalton of its 'secret' counterpart. Yet within a month Duff Cooper was complaining to Churchill that the compromise was not working, and that if it did not control all Britain's propaganda output there was no point in the MoI's continued existence.

1. INF 1/859.
2. Alfred Duff Cooper, *Old Men Forget* (1957), p. 288.

The somewhat exasperated Prime Minister had many more pressing and dangerous problems on his hands in May 1941 than ministerial wrangling over propaganda. In the real war that month – as opposed to the Whitehall turf war – Iraq had declared for Germany, the House of Commons had been destroyed in London's heaviest air raid, Rudolf Hess had parachuted into Scotland, Vichy had endorsed an important agreement with Hitler, the Germans had invaded Crete and HMS *Hood* had been sunk off Greenland. It was therefore understandable if Churchill asked his friend the former Great War Minister of Information Lord Beaverbrook to look into the propaganda issue for him.

Unfortunately, and in a move quite alien to his nature, Beaverbrook seems to have slightly ducked the thorniest issue – the future control of foreign propaganda – thereby forcing Churchill to step in with a minute written on 21 June 1941, the day before the Germans invaded the Soviet Union. The War Cabinet's deliberations on the minuted views of Churchill, Beaverbrook and Duff Cooper were then taken a few days later, just as Churchill removed Duff Cooper from the MoI and sent him to the Far East to report on the military situation there. The upshot was that the *status quo ante* of 16 May – the tripartite Standing Ministerial Committee – came into force, which by 8 August had a charter readily approved by the (presumably somewhat relieved) Prime Minister.

The reason that this blatantly compromise solution eventually succeeded was that it was so obviously the result of so much give and take between the principally interested parties, including the BBC, SOE, the MoI, the War Cabinet, Number Ten, the FO, the Chiefs of Staff and the Service Ministries. Furthermore, the three officials appointed were perfectly suited to their difficult task. Representing the FO was Robert Bruce Lockhart, who knew the secret service well from his days as a British agent during the Russian Revolution but was also popular in Fleet Street from being a long-standing editor of the Londoner's Diary gossip column in Beaverbrook's *Evening Standard*. Rex Leeper represented the MoI, but having been a diplomat most of his life was amenable to the FO point of view, while Major General Dallas Brooks, a former soldier, represented Dalton's Ministry of Economic Warfare (MEW) and SOE, but was not afraid to stand up to his master when the occasion demanded. It was agreed that together these men would act 'as a General Staff for the conduct of political warfare'.[1]

The first man to be tested was General Brooks, for no sooner had Dalton realised that the PWE had its eye on his SO1 operations than he put up a stiff rearguard action against the Ministerial Committee, in defence of what amounted to half of his domain. In the face of this fierce resistance the Committee had to complain in September 1941 that: 'For twelve months the energy of our whole propaganda effort, which should have been directed

1. FO 898/1.

against the enemy, has been largely dissipated in inter-departmental intrigues and strife.' If anything they underestimated the timeframe: Munich had taken place three years previously.

An angry Dalton finally admitted defeat, not least because the incoming Information Minister Brendan Bracken, who was an equally close and old friend of Churchill's as Duff Cooper had been, was not about to allow SOE a completely free hand in political warfare. For all his fury and sarcasm directed at Bruce Lockhart, Leeper and Brooks, Dalton acquiesced in a situation that allowed the PWE to get on with the job of fighting the political and psychological war against Germany largely free from too much ministerial interference. As one historian has described the continuing relationship between PWE and SOE: 'For the rest of the war the two bodies were forced to live together, suffering all the discomforts of a close union, and enjoying none of the blessings.'[1] The formation of PWE was publicly announced on 11 September 1941 in a ministerial answer to a parliamentary question put by Commander King-Hall MP, after not less than two whole years had elapsed since the outbreak of war. It had not been bureaucratic Britain's finest hour.

Although David Garnett's history of PWE does chronicle many of the 'discomforts' referred to above, it also tells us far more about the operational existence of this extraordinary body, which recruited some of the most exceptional, unusual and talented people of any of the nine secret organisations of the Second World War. It goes into much detail about the operations that PWE undertook to demoralise Germany and her allies, sowing rumours, deceiving the population and promoting anti-Nazi activity throughout occupied Europe. In the surprising absence of an accessible, definitive, single-volume biography of PWE, this is the most important document we have concerning the multifarious activities of this vital branch of Britain's wartime propaganda arm.

Napoleon once said that in warfare there was only the smallest of gaps between the sublime and the ridiculous; this was certainly true in PWE, which along with its American counterpart OWI dropped no fewer than 265 million anti-Nazi leaflets on Germany, and broadcasted hundreds of thousands of hours of black propaganda of all kinds. On the ridiculous side, PWE also promoted rumours such as the one that the British Government had imported 200 man-eating sharks from Australia, which had been released in the English Channel to eat Germans whose invasion boats had been sunk.[2]

As the Cold War heated up in the spring of 1952, especially over the issues of German rearmament and Korea, the Foreign Secretary Anthony Eden and the Chiefs of Staff approved a paper to establish a new PWE, 'if war appears imminent'. It was thought useful to disinter the history of PWE that Garnett had written sometime after 1945, as it was hoped that it

1. Cruickshank, *ibid.*, 27.
2. See Garnett p. 215.

might at least contain some helpful recommendations in the struggle against Communism. Two of Garnett's key conclusions were that he was 'convinced that Political Warfare will play a larger part in future both in peace and war', and that PWE's work 'was hindered by the semi-independent status of the BBC services to the enemy and enemy-controlled countries over which it had only partial and intermittent control. During war, the department should be given executive and administrative powers over BBC services to enemy countries.'

Sometime in the summer of 1952, therefore, Mr D. D. Brown of the Information Research Department 'unearthed a draft official history, which had got buried in the Historical Section of the Cabinet Office'.[1] Such documents rarely get 'buried' by mistake, and it became very clear why Garnett's book had suffered such a fate. As Mr Brown minuted to Mr A. B. Acheson, an official in the Cabinet Office, on 6 August, the number of copies made of Garnett's history should be kept strictly limited because it amounted to 'a *chronique scandaleuse*', which, he said, 'abounds in somewhat unmeasured judgements on persons still in the public service or in public life'. Brown went on to give no fewer than fifteen examples, complete with accompanying page numbers, in which Garnett had made remarks about organisations or PWE officials that might be regarded as libellous if ever it was published. The briefest perusal will show readers that he was rather spoiled for choice, and that he could quite easily have provided another score or so without over-taxing himself.

In the seven years since Garnett wrote his history, several of the people criticised in it had risen to high positions in the Diplomatic Service and HM Opposition. Hugh Dalton had been Chancellor of the Exchequer in the Attlee Government, Ivone Kirkpatrick had been knighted and was then UK High Commissioner in Germany, Rex Leeper had also been knighted and had held two ambassadorships before becoming a director of De Beers, and Richard Crossman had become an MP and sat on the Labour Party's Executive. The history even went so far as to quote a very negative SOE report on the PWE mission to the United States headed by David Bowes-Lyon, the brother-in-law of King George VI, which concluded that as a result 'Great Britain stands in grave danger of losing the peace' that would come after victory, which was a very serious (if unsustainable and slightly hysterical) charge. These luminaries were not men whom the Civil Service were about to offend by making Garnett's history widely available, and accordingly only four copies were made, and sent to the four service officers at the Ministry of Defence, War Office, Admiralty and Air Ministry who were members of the Group set up by Eden and the Chiefs of Staff to look into resuscitating PWE.

Furthermore, attached after the title page of Garnett's history was an official disclaimer stating that 'the opinions and judgements which it contains are

1. FO 1110/353.

his alone and should not be regarded as having official authority or endorsement'. Mr Brown also felt that if somehow a copy were to leak into the public domain, a contingency he judged 'extremely unlikely', a 'defence of qualified privilege would be available even if any of the persons unfavourably mentioned by Mr Garnett were to attempt to bring a libel action'.

Yet to cover themselves still further there is evidence to suggest that some doctoring of the original copy took place before it was copied. For example, Mr Brown warned Mr Acheson that comments that Garnett had made on page 221 (page 244 in this volume) about Colonel (but by then Brigadier Sir Richard) Gambier-Perry were 'somewhat unmeasured', which is Civil Service-speak for potentially embarrassing and/or libellous. Yet when one turns to that page there is no mention of the Colonel by name, but merely a sentence or two of gaps created by an unseen, post-Garnett hand. Fortunately this does not seem to have been widespread, and if a culprit is needed I would point to a note in the relevant FO file made in April 1953 by Mr Brown to his superior in the Information Research Department (a cover for an offshoot of the secret service) which states that 'I have already passed the Library [copy of Garnett's] paper to the Security Dept.'[1] Whoever was responsible, the excisions seem to be light, and with all the major figures in PWE now dead, and the threats of both Nazism and Communism having been seen off, it is only right that this important and fascinating document should now become publicly available.

David Garnett was always likely to have been an odd choice for bureaucrats to make if they wanted a safe, banal official history written, let alone a whitewash that left every major figure in PWE happy with the verdict. Born in 1892, he was a member of the Bloomsbury Group through birth, conviction and two marriages. The son of the publisher Edward Garnett, through whom he knew D. H. Lawrence and Joseph Conrad, David Garnett became friendly with J. Maynard Keynes, the Strachey family and Duncan Grant. Quaker-educated, he spent the Great War working for the Friends' War Victims Relief Mission in France. He won the Hawthornden and Tait Black prizes in 1923 for his debut novel *Lady Into Fox*, the first of many works of fiction, and in 1939 became literary editor of the *New Statesman*. 'Bunny' Garnett was good-looking, fair-haired and blue-eyed, and in 1942, two years after the death of his first wife Rachel Marshall (the sister of Frances Partridge), he married Angelica, the daughter of Duncan Grant and Vanessa Bell.[2] (For what it is worth I believe that Garnett might have been the model for Nick Jenkins, the narrator of Anthony Powell's *Dance to the Music of Time*.)

David Garnett was a pacifist, a successful and well-connected literary man of left-leaning political views, and thus probably the last man the Widmerpools of Whitehall should have chosen if they wanted an easy time. Yet I believe that the modern reader will discern beneath Garnett's acerbic

1. *Ibid.*, ref PR 102/17/G & PR 68/46/G.
2. *Who Was Who* lists her as the daughter of Clive Bell, but see Garnett's *DNB 1981-85* entry, p. 159, by his sister-in-law Frances Partridge.

asides an essential objectivity, and also shafts of that subtly ironic humour at which the Bloomsbury Group excelled. There are some moving passages, too, as when he reports the murder of two anti-Nazi Germans in an Allied prisoner-of-war camp, but there is also humour, as when the journalist Mr Vernon Bartlett MP claimed that while working at Woburn Abbey he was 'butted by a llama and bitten by a rhea' in the Duke of Bedford's zoo.

Any organisation that called upon the diverse but undeniable talents of as varied a *galère* as Noël Coward, Raymond Mortimer, Freya Stark, Denis Sefton Delmer, John Wheeler-Bennett, Leonard Miall, Robert Byron, Jock Bruce Lockhart, Quentin Bell, E. H. Carr, Dick Crossman, 'Bomber' Harris and Joanna Scott-Moncrieff could never have been a dull place to work, especially as some of the operations which they devised were often so bizarre. What is one to make, for example, of the dropping of large numbers of dead carrier pigeons into Germany with messages attached to their legs, in the hope of deceiving the Gestapo into thinking that the German resistance was in close touch with British Intelligence? (Of 330 live pigeons also dropped, five flew home with messages written by their German finders.) German ration books were forged to create confusion, as well as stamps bearing Himmler's face in the hope that people would revolt at the idea of his becoming the next Führer. Just as devious was the fact that PWE regularly used to broadcast pornography as a way of attracting radio audiences, something Sir Stafford Cripps predictably much disliked.

One refreshing contrast with today is the names chosen for various operations. Whereas nowadays public relations reasons dictate that they have to boast heroic, uplifting titles such as Operation Desert Sword or Operation Hope, in the Second World War they were called by more homely nouns. This book abounds with operations called such names as Matchbox, Dartboard, Periwig, Market Garden and Husky. Weird as it may seem in the circumstances, they seem to speak of a gentler era. (Given his priapic tendencies, few would have cracked PWE's codename for Duff Cooper – 'The Vicar'.)

We know from Sefton Delmer's autobiography, *Black Boomerang,* that a large number of PWE's files were destroyed after the war. That makes this book, saved from the oubliette of history by St Ermin's Press, all the more valuable. Sir Winston Churchill once said that in war the truth needed to be protected by 'a bodyguard of lies'. This is the story of the men and women who constituted that bodyguard.

Andrew Roberts
www.andrew-roberts.net
[December] 2001

Glossary

The intelligence and special operations world is notorious for its plethora of acronyms. Here are some of the most frequently used ones in David Garnett's secret history of the Political Warfare Executive (PWE).

ABSIE	American radio station built up in Britain by OWI
BEF	British Expeditionary Force
BSC	British Security Co-ordination
C	Head of Secret Intelligence Service
CIO	Chief Intelligence Officer
CHQ	Woburn Abbey, country headquarters of British propaganda effort
'D' Section	SIS's sabotage branch
DNI	Director of Naval Intelligence
DDMI	Deputy Director of Military Intelligence
DMI	Director of Military Intelligence
DPW (E & S)	Director of Political Warfare for Enemy and Satellite Countries
DPW (O)	Director of Political Warfare for Occupied Countries
DPWI	Director of Political Warfare (Intelligence)
EH	Electra House, Victoria Embankment. Sir Charles Stuart's Department of Propaganda in Enemy Countries
FFI	Free French (Gaullists)
FO	British Foreign Office
GSI	*Gustav Siegfried Eins*, a PWE radio station
INC	Information News Censorship
IP1	interdepartmental amalgam (see p. 9)
IP2	see above
ITF	International Transport Federation
JIC	Joint Intelligence Committee
LF	Larchfield; from which PWE Black propaganda was broadcast
ME	Middle East
MEIC	Middle East Intelligence Centre
MEW	Ministry of Economic Warfare
MoI	Ministry of Information
NSDAP	Nazi Party
OSS	Office of Strategic Services (USA)

OWI	Office of War Information (USA)
PID	Political Intelligence Department, FO (SOE's cover organisation)
Ps/W	Prisoners of War
PW	Political Warfare
PWB	Psychological Warfare Branch (USA)
PWD	Political Warfare Department
PWE	Political Warfare Executive
RUs	Research Units, i.e. broadcasting stations
SAS	Special Air Service
SFHQ	Special Forces Headquarters
SHAEF	Supreme Headquarters Allied Expeditionary Force
SIS	Secret Intelligence Service
SOE	Special Operations Executive
SO1	SOE's covert propaganda department
SO2	SOE's sabotage department
SO/M	Special Operations Mediterranean

'This history was prepared by Mr David Garnett on instructions from the Director-General of the Political Warfare Executive given under the authority of the Foreign Secretary. Mr Garnett, who was during the war a member of the staff of the Executive, was allowed a free hand in writing it, and he is responsible for its contents, the accuracy of the facts stated, and the method of presentation. In particular, the opinions and judgements which it contains are his alone and should not be regarded as having official authority or endorsement.'

Introduction

Character of this Record

The following history deals with the most important Political Warfare activities carried out from this country from the time of Munich until the German surrender. The work in connection with enemy prisoners of war is briefly recorded up to the autumn of 1946. My terms of reference did not include Political Warfare to Japan and the Far East.

While many branches of the work have been recorded in very great detail, others receive only a brief mention; this is in part due to incomplete departmental records, in part to my belief that more can be learned for the future from a very full record of the difficulties encountered in carrying out certain important operations than from a brief sketch of a wider field.

Perhaps the most serious omission is that I have not dealt with the finances of the department. But a post-mortem on the cost of PWE would have been an almost impossibly difficult task, and though I have little doubt that I should have unearthed many extravagances and some examples of a penny-wise, pound-foolish policy, I have no faith that any lessons for the future could have been deduced from them.

Conclusions and Recommendations

The present Director General of PID [Political Intelligence Department], Major General Strong,* asked me to include my conclusions and recommendations as he believed that the chief value of this record would be if a department of Political Warfare were reconstituted.

Future of Political Warfare

I am convinced that Political Warfare will play a larger part in future both in peace and in war.

The increase of popular education, the development of wireless broadcasts and television, of advertising and the study of mass psychology, make

---

* [Major-General Sir Kenneth William Dobson Strong (1900–82) was Chief of Eisenhower's Intelligence staff for the Sicily landings of 1943; joined SHAEF 1944; was criticised for underestimating the Ardennes offensive 1944–5, succeeded Sir Robert Bruce Lockhart as Director-General of PWE 1945–7: Director-General, Ministry of Defence Intelligence, 1964–6.]

it probable that psychological pressures of various kinds will be increasingly applied by one country to another. Indeed, these pressures are today being applied particularly in the form of 'wars of nerves'.

USA and USSR Are Committed to Political Warfare

In any *war* in which the USSR or the United States are involved, Political Warfare is almost certain to play a large part, for the Russians will wish to make full use of the Communists in every country as agents for propaganda and subversion, and the Americans believe in Psychological Warfare, if only as a variety of advertising.

Allegiance Is Shifting to Party Loyalty

There will be larger disloyal minorities in most countries during the next war as the spread of international and class movements and the disappearance of monarchical institutions is producing a change of allegiance in every country, patriotism being replaced by loyalty to parties or ideologies.

A British victory would be the only alternative to Communism and in many countries the only hope of survival for those groups which value personal freedom, property, religion and similar legacies from the past.

Britain should therefore be prepared to carry out Political Warfare before or immediately on the outbreak of another war and not have to build up an organisation for it after war has begun.

If reconstituted only at the outbreak of war, a Political Warfare department is too likely to be regarded as a 'new boy', a nuisance which is crippled and fighting for its life, instead of a department to which the Army, Navy and Air Force turn for specialised services.

There should therefore be at least a shadow department of Political Warfare in existence which should deal with social, diplomatic and political trends.

Requisites for Political Warfare Should Be in Readiness

It is also recommended that FORD should make it a responsibility to keep

a. In constant readiness a library and files with the documentation for political warfare both by black and white media. This should include recordings of speeches by all probable enemy leaders and material suitable for television – i.e. films of banquets, conferences and public and private occasions.

b. A constantly revised list of persons qualified to carry out Political Warfare and subversive tasks either from Britain or abroad.

c. A study and analysis of all political and social groups and developments in other countries.

Transmitter Strength Must Be Ensured

Transmitters have been proved to be essential weapons both of war and of Political Warfare.

In 1940, Britain was in an inferior position with regard to transmitters compared with Germany. This was partly overcome by purchases in the United States. In the event of another war, the United States is unlikely to part with transmitters necessary for her security.

The services are no doubt responsible for the maintenance of the transmitter strength of this country at a point adequate for defence purposes.

They should ensure an adequate margin of transmitter strength for Political Warfare also.

Overlapping Organisation of Political Warfare

The work of Political Warfare during the last war was handicapped in the first place by an overlapping of functions between several departments and throughout the war by the organisation of the department itself. As a result, the same kind of Political Warfare was carried out by different authorities in the same area and some kinds of Political Warfare were not done at all.

Organisation Should Be under One Minister

There should be one department only charged with all forms of Political Warfare and Subversion to enemy and enemy-controlled countries, under one Minister who should be a member of the War Cabinet.

The failure of SO1 and SO2 to co-operate in 1940–1, and the experience of PWE itself, has shown that Political Warfare and Subversion should be organised regionally and not functionally.

Regional Organisation Required

The department for Political Warfare and Subversion should be organised in directorates for each country to which Political Warfare is carried out, and the Regional Director should be responsible to the Director General for all Political Warfare and subversive activities within his region.

It is recommended that each Regional Director should have under him a chief executive responsible for organisation, so as to leave him free to deal with policy, planning and co-ordination with other regions.

Relations with BBC

The work of PWE was hindered by the semi-independent status of the BBC services to enemy and enemy-occupied countries over which it had only partial and intermittent control.

During war, the department should be given executive and administrative powers over BBC services directed to enemy-controlled countries.

The name BBC should be retained for purposes of goodwill, and as cover, but the BBC staff should become PWE staff, should be paid by PWE and have no right of appeal to the Governors or the Minister of Information.

The BBC should be required to continue to provide services such as intelligence, monitoring, access to library of records, etc., for the transferred services.

Importance of Political Warfare Agents

The use of agents for Political Warfare in the field was insufficient in the last war and will offer increased possibilities in any future war in Western Europe. The selection and training of agents for Political Warfare will therefore be a matter of importance.

The experience of the 'Hackett' school should therefore be preserved in the form of a study on the training, selection and motivation of agents. This should be, if possible, a joint paper by Major Hackett and Major Gallie, the successive commandants of the school.

Leaflet Dissemination

The dissemination of leaflets and printed matter could not be carried out efficiently by the RAF as a secondary task, incidental to bombing.

Provision should be made for leafleting as a special service by the RAF either by a bomber squadron or by other means.

Need for Technical Research

PWE suffered from the lack of technical research on propaganda media.

A study of Political Warfare media should be made and kept under review in time of peace.

A directorate of technical research to study such subjects as leaflet dissemination by means of rockets, gliders and robot planes, and of such matters as television, inserting matter into the enemy's Hellschreiber news-service, etc., etc., should form part of any department for Political Warfare in the future, and should be formed now as part of the shadow Political Warfare organisation.

Allied Refugee Governments

The task of Political Warfare to occupied countries was complicated by powers given to certain refugee governments.

No carte blanche authority should be given to any ally in any future war to control Political Warfare to its own population from British soil.

Importance of Contingency Planning

Contingency planning was of great value to Political Warfare. A Political Warfare department should include a staff of planners, who should prepare plans for probable contingencies.

Propaganda to Prisoners of War

Political Warfare played an important part in propaganda to enemy prisoners of war. Such propaganda was of value in assisting to solve the problems of manpower during the period of their captivity.

Secondary results were to exploit a valuable medium of Political Warfare to the enemy, to prevent plans for enemy resurgence being made in Ps/W [prisoner-of-war] camps, and to influence public opinion favourably to Britain after their return.

This work was hampered by a lack of continuous and uniform policy, by shortage of trained staff and by misunderstandings with the military authorities.

I recommend that a study of propaganda to enemy prisoners of war, during the last war and after it should be made primarily from the point of view of manpower and secondarily from that of Political Warfare, and that an agreed policy for the application of such lessons in any future war should be formulated by the War Office and the Foreign Office. This should include a definition of the status of prisoners of war retained as a labour force after the conclusion of hostilities.

Political Warfare Training

The value of Political Warfare training was proved by the training given at Woburn and Brondesbury.

Political Warfare training is a function of the department which should provide training for officers and other ranks carrying out Political Warfare functions in the field.

Training should be made widely available to allies, civil affairs officers, etc.

Political Education of our Troops

Political Warfare carried out useful functions in the political education of our own troops.

The department should be responsible for providing political education for British and Dominion troops in the form of lectures, booklets, etc.

In time of peace as in time of war, the value of such political education to our troops in Palestine, India and the Middle East, Malaya, etc., is self-evident. It should be a function of the shadow Political Warfare Department.

David Garnett
February 1947

PART I

Departments EH and SO1 till the Formation of PWE

Pre-War Views on Political Warfare

A belief in the importance of propaganda to the enemy was a legacy of the 1914–18 World War, which was reinforced by many currents of opinion in the years which followed.

The work of the British Propaganda Department, afterwards described by Sir Campbell Stuart* in [*The*] *Secrets of Crewe House*, had been seized upon by Field Marshal Lüdendorff as one of the explanations of the defeat of Germany. In point of fact in 1918 the German Armies were defeated in the field and the German Government sued for an armistice in order to save the territory of the Reich from invasion. Lüdendorff sought to convince the world that he and his armies had not been defeated because they had not utterly disintegrated and he invented various myths to explain away the facts. The German Army had been 'stabbed in the back' by the civilian population; the simple German soldiers had been hypnotised by propaganda, 'the traditional British weapon', and by Bolshevik poison; Germany had agreed to an armistice on the basis of the Fourteen Points.

As Lindley Fraser has pointed out in a book[1] based on the work of the German Region PWE,[2] these were myths. But they were widely accepted in the twenties and thirties, and played an important part in bringing about the

---

1. *Germany between two Wars*, Oxford University Press.
2. The subject of the book German Political Mythology was included in the syllabus of PWE School Brondesbury and the lectures on this subject were given first by Mr Koeppler and later by Mr Fraser using Mr Koeppler's notes. Mr Stirk also provided considerable material.

* [Sir Campbell Arthur Stuart (1885–1972). Canadian-born, Campbell was assistant military attaché at the Washington Embassy 1917; deputy director of propaganda in enemy countries 1918; a director of *The Times* from 1919 to 1960. Published *The Secrets of Crewe House* in 1920.]

Second World War. If it could be proved that Germany was not defeated by force of arms, it was far more reasonable for the Germans to embark on a second world war after eliminating the spiritual weaknesses which had led her to abandon the struggle in 1918. The myths of Lüdendorff were therefore the foundations of National Socialist Militarism. Nor were they only acceptable to Germans whose self-respect found the fact of military defeat intolerable. They were widely believed in Britain and in America. Not unnaturally the myth of the role played by British propaganda found ready credence among those who had been responsible for it and passages from Lüdendorff[1] were frequently quoted by British propagandists in tributes to themselves.[2]

The views of Lüdendorff were accepted and reinforced by Hitler, and the effectiveness of Hitler's propaganda methods in building up the Third Reich and in dividing and triumphing over Germany's neighbours, one by one, confirmed the belief that Political Warfare was a weapon of the first importance – 'a fourth fighting arm'.

Even without German political mythology or the spectacular object lessons of Hitler's propaganda triumphs, far greater interest would inevitably have been paid to propaganda in 1939 than in 1914. Not only had the political struggles of European nations for power taken on an increasingly ideological aspect, but there was an immense growth of interest in psychology as a science in the twenties and thirties, and an immense technical exploitation of mass psychology in advertising. The highest hopes were thus held in many diverse quarters of the success likely to attend our efforts once we were able to turn Hitler's propaganda weapons upon the German people.

A Memorandum on Propaganda to Germany sent to R. A. Leeper* by Vernon Bartlett** of the *News Chronicle* on 27th September, 1938, contained the following passages:

> One may take it for granted – and every visitor to Germany brings back impressions to confirm it – that Germany could be defeated on the Home Front even while her armies were still winning victories over those of less prepared and more happy-go-lucky States.
>
> Fear of reprisals will probably cause both sides to hesitate before they take to dropping bombs. Every day of this hesitation should be a British victory since it should be devoted to flooding enemy territory with propaganda.

---

1. Lüdendorff, *My War Memories*.
2. e.g. in Sir Campbell Stuart's *The Secrets of Crewe House* and Air Commodore Groves' lecture on Political Warfare to Staff Officers of the Southern Command.

* [Sir Reginald Wildig Allen 'Rex' Leeper (1888–1968) joined the Intelligence Bureau, Department of Information, 1917; entered FO 1918, First Secretary, Warsaw, 1927–9; Assistant Under-Secretary 1940; assistant to Sir Robert Bruce Lockhart at PWE 1941–3; Ambassador to Greece 1943–6 and the Argentine 1946–8; director, De Beers, 1950–6.]

** [(Charles) Vernon Bartlett (1894–1983), foreign correspondent, *The Times*, 1919–22; diplomatic correspondent, *News Chronicle*, 1934–54; opposed appeasement 1938; Independent MP 1938–50.]

Much the same views were held in the Services. Thus certain 'bright ideas' originating from MI3-a were forwarded to Sir Stephen Tallents,* Director-General Designate of the Ministry of Information during the Munich crisis by Colonel W. J. Turner from the War Office and included the proposal that following the precedent of the Congress of Vienna, after the escape of Napoleon from Elba, Hitler should be outlawed as a disturber of the peace of Europe, and that war should be declared, not against the German people but against Hitler and the Nazi leaders. The officer concluded: 'The effect of such a declaration would not only be good propaganda as far as the world is concerned but might have results in Germany which could prove decisive.'

The belief in the importance of propaganda to Germany was accompanied by certain assumptions which were a measure of the peaceful mentality of almost all sections of the British people at the time.

It was assumed that our propaganda should be addressed to the 'good Germans', who were believed to form an overwhelming majority of the inhabitants of the Third Reich and who were assumed to be willing to listen to the voice of reason and to be capable of action to stop a war if Hitler started one.

Thus the conception was not of political *warfare* to an enemy so much as an appeal, over the heads of the Nazi leaders, to people we persisted in regarding as our friends. This state of mind was partly 'wishful thinking', partly the influence of the large numbers of 'good German' refugees in Britain, who refused to despair of their countrymen.

The myth of the 'good German' was accompanied by a belief that the most effective medium of propaganda would be the printed word – for print alone could present reasoned argument in a permanent form. Broadcasting was recognised as invaluable for spreading news quickly, but the printed leaflet was regarded as the most important weapon of propaganda.

These views were held in the Air Ministry – a matter of great importance, since the RAF would be the agency of disseminating leaflets in a war.

A Most Secret Note on the Employment of Aircraft for dropping leaflets in Enemy Countries, prepared in the Air Ministry and dated 25th September, 1938, contains the following passage:

> There is little doubt that the dropping of propaganda in thickly populated areas would be of great value. Used in conjunction with wireless it may have a most marked effect. . . . The Air Staff regard

---

* [Sir Stephen George Tallents (1884–1958), entered Civil Service 1909; severely wounded with Irish Guards 1915; Chairman, Milk Control Board, 1918; British Relief Commissioner Poland and Baltic Provinces 1919–21; Imperial Secretary, Northern Ireland, 1922–6; Secretary, Empire Marketing Board, 1926–33; controller, public relations, BBC, 1935–40; controller Overseas Service, BBC, 1940–1; principal assistant secretary, Ministry of Town and County Planning, 1943–6.]

> propaganda as a weapon. In view of the well-known and widespread opposition in certain quarters in Germany to the present regime, and of the vital importance of securing neutral and especially American opinion on our side, it might well pay us to put up with some small delay before we take effective counter actions, even if the enemy's taking such action first would undoubtedly justify reprisals in kind.

The conviction that there was a powerful anti-Nazi party in Germany which might be expected to take action against Hitler persisted in Department EH and its successors for years – indeed it persisted in certain minds until in course of time it became true.

It was strong enough in the first months of the war to make the task of building up resistance in Poland, Czechoslovakia and Austria appear quite a secondary one. And this scale of values lasted for a long time after Germany had overrun Europe. Indeed it was never explicitly acknowledged that building up and sustaining the spirit of resistance among our friends would produce greater political and military advantages than any open propaganda directed to our enemies.

The Crisis before Munich

On 9th November, 1938, Sir Stephen Tallents, Director General Designate of the Ministry of Information submitted a Memorandum to the *Standing Sub-Committee to prepare plans for the Establishment of a Ministry of Information* of the Committee of Imperial Defence which stated that the 'partial mobilisation of the Ministry of Information, ordered on 26th September (the time of the Munich crisis) disclosed a number of points requiring decisions or adjustments'.

'The outstanding lesson . . . was the lack of machinery for securing the prompt, wide and efficient conveyance of British news and views to potentially enemy peoples.'

The remainder of the paper was devoted to the steps taken during the crisis before Munich to improvise the requisite machinery.

'Authority to approach Sir Campbell Stuart was given[1] and acted on in the week ending 24th September, and he devoted himself to the problem, making his private house available for the purpose.'

On the previous day, the possibilities of leaflet dissemination over Germany had been discussed at a meeting between Sir Hughe Knatchbull-Hugessen* of the Foreign Office with Wing Commander A. L. Fiddament

1. Sir Campbell Stuart informs me that he was sent for by 'C', then Admiral Sinclair, who asked him to undertake the work.

* [Sir Hughe Montgomery Knatchbull-Hugessen (1886–1971), member of British delegation to Paris Peace Conference 1919; head of Chancery, Paris, 1924–5; Ambassador to China 1936–8, where he was badly injured by Japanese aeroplane fire; Turkey 1939–44, where he was spied upon by his Albanian valet 'Cicero'; and Belgium 1944–7.]

of the Air Ministry. The discussion was resumed the following day at the FO with Sir Stephen Tallents, Mr Todd of the Stationery Office and Mr Robert Byron also present, and rough estimates were given that twelve Whitley bombers could disseminate ten million leaflets, on one trip, or twenty million if they could do two trips in one night. Mr Todd stated that the Stationery Office could deliver twenty million leaflets in a week.

The note on the Employment of Aircraft for dropping leaflets in Enemy Countries which has been quoted above concluded with the request that the leaflets should all be printed and held ready in advance as they would be required for immediate use.[1] Leaflets were thereupon drafted by Mr Robert Byron.

Under the stimulus of the threat of immediate war much urgent work was done. On 27th September, W/Cdr Fiddament reported[2] that: 'the Chief of Air Staff had spoken to General Gamelin* who agreed that it would be desirable to broadcast a joint announcement of policy by British and French stating that no attack would be made on populous civil areas except as reprisals'. The FO approved but believed that authority for such an announcement would be necessary from the Cabinet. If any broadcast were undertaken it should be reinforced by leaflets. At the same meeting the FO approved the texts of a general leaflet and a warning to the civil population to evacuate a selected area.

By 29th September, W/Cdr Blackford had taken over from W/Cdr Fiddament and the Air Ministry had modified the views put forward four days earlier in certain respects. Blackford was able to state that the Air Ministry had that day bought 200 alarm clocks and had set on foot a special balloon unit of fifteen men for the dissemination of leaflets by hydrogen balloons with clockwork release. It was planned that the unit should operate from the neighbourhood of Nancy.

Besides these preparations for dropping leaflets over Germany, the importance of other forms of printed propaganda was fully realised during the Munich crisis. In a paper by Robert Byron dated 5th October, 1938, reviewing the needs revealed by the crisis, not only are questions of German Gothic type and of Germanic layout discussed but paragraph 3 is headed *Pseudo-documents*.

'There will come a stage when it is desired to circulate documents which look as if they were of official, or at least of domestic, origin. To give these the proper aspect needs a careful study of Nazi methods of presentation and

---

1. The views in this paper were modified four days later when W/Cdr Blackford informed A. P. Ryan that the DCAS did not feel that the use of aircraft detailed for dropping leaflets would be justified unless the Government ordered it.
2. Minutes of a meeting in Mr Leeper's Room, FO, 27th September, 1938.

* [Maurice Gustave Gamelin (1872–1958), a French general who in 1935 became Chief of the General Staff by seniority and by 1940 was, briefly but disastrously, Commander-in-Chief. He was hurriedly replaced by General Weygand after his inability to deal with Blitzkrieg was apparent. His defining phrase: 'To attack is to lose.']

use of symbols. Designs of swastikas, wreathed, tilted and straight; of the eagle cum swastika, and of Hitler's personal standard, should be ready for blockmaking.' Mr Byron then stressed the importance of collecting stocks of photographs of Hitler, of badges of Nazi organisations and of having the right qualities of paper.

The existence of overlapping [was] also revealed by the Munich crisis though its disastrous effects in producing inter-departmental strife were not realised until long afterwards. On 5th October, Major Grand[1]* informed A. P. Ryan that on 26th September his chief had ordered him to form immediately a section for the dissemination through all channels *outside this country* of material to enemy and neutral countries. He proposed to do so through the following media: broadcasts from stations outside Britain such as Radio Luxembourg, inserting suitable material into the neutral press adjacent to enemy territory, leaflets disseminated by 'balloons, carrier pigeons, special democrats, communists, commercial travellers and seamen, by whispering campaigns'.

Major Grand's projects with regard to balloons were co-ordinated with those of the Air Ministry. The others remained. Indeed Mr Walmsley states that Sir Campbell Stuart's organisation and that of Major Grand were definitely parallel. Mr Walmsley had offered his services at the time of the Munich crisis and had been given an interview by Sir Campbell Stuart.

After the German occupation of Prague, Major Grand invited Mr Walmsley to send him suggestions for propaganda. Mr Walmsley proposed forging Nazi party literature passing between Germany and branches of the NSDAP [Nazi Party] in foreign countries through the British mails. Mr Walmsley regards it as 'a matter of great regret that Grand never put this proposal through, though he promised to do so, as it would have started black propaganda two years earlier than actually happened'.[2]

The proposal is interesting because it shows that Mr Walmsley was thinking of Nazi Party members as a target at a time when practically everyone concerned regarded the 'good Germans' as the objective of our political warfare.

Major Grand's chief project was the production of a regular news-sheet, 'a very crude affair by later standards',[3] to be smuggled into Germany and distributed as from an oppositional organisation. The 'good German' was the target in this case.

The lessons of the crisis before Munich and the steps which needed to be

1. Head of the 'D' organisation.
2. That this statement is completely inaccurate is shown by Mr Walmsley's next remark.
3. Information from Mr Walmsley.
* [Major-General Laurence Douglas Grand (1898–1975) was educated at Rugby, Woolwich and Cambridge. A sapper, Grand was appointed by Admiral Sinclair of SIS to head the sabotage special unit 'Section D' in March 1938 under the cover title of the Statistical Research Department of the War Office. CBE 1943; Director of Fortifications and Works, War Office, 1949–52.]

taken were set out at considerable length by Sir Stephen Tallents in a document (MIC 15).

This paper was circulated to those concerned and provoked a letter from the DCAS Air Ministry (Air Marshal R. E. C. Peirse)[1] and a reply to it from Mr Leeper of the Foreign Office.[2] The gist of Air Marshal Peirse's letter was the need for a permanent body charged with the duty of studying public opinion in Germany and with framing propaganda – as unsuitable propaganda could do infinite harm. Such a body should have up-to-date material constantly ready.

Mr Leeper stated that certain proposals which had been made would be laid before the meeting, but that he thought the preparation of material which continually got out of date was unnecessary, in any case the study of public opinion in foreign countries was entirely a matter for the Foreign Office.

The proposals referred to by Mr Leeper dealt entirely with 'the presentation of the British point of view to the German public' *in time of peace*.

No organisation was proposed even for this but only four methods: that of broadcasting, personal contacts between British and German businessmen, a British organisation in Germany, and literature. There was no hint in the Foreign Office proposals of the need to prepare for propaganda during war.

At a meeting of the Ministry of Information Sub-Committee held on 14th December, 1938,[3] Sir Campbell Stuart pointed out that there were two problems, propaganda in war and information in peacetime. As a result of discussion a sub-committee was appointed under the chairmanship of Sir Campbell Stuart with the following terms of reference:

> In the light of existing arrangements concerning British publicity in foreign countries, to report on the possible methods of conducting propaganda in such countries in the event of war, and on the machinery required for the purpose.

As a result plans for setting up an Enemy Publicity Section were outlined by Sir Campbell Stuart on 16th January, 1939,[4] which should be separately housed and in time of peace should consist of a head of the section, a liaison officer with the services, and a liaison officer with the BBC.

In the event of war a Foreign Office man would be required and three experts, one on Germany, one on Italy and one on 'other countries'.

Meanwhile the Secretary of the Sub-Committee was investigating such practical matters as German type and the layout of leaflets in the war of 1914–18.

1. MIC 17 dated 28th November, 1938.
2. MIC 18 dated 7th December, 1938.
3. MIC Fifth Meeting.
4. Note of a Meeting in the Public Trustee's Room.

A considerable degree of overlapping of functions between Sir Campbell Stuart's Department and that of a section of the Overseas Department of the Ministry of Information was later to be revealed. This is perhaps therefore the place to point out that while Sir Campbell Stuart and Major Grand were both planning to carry out Political Warfare, the Ministry of Information was making preparations which resulted in its undertaking functions defined as: 'To watch and check enemy news and propaganda in all countries and to undertake counter-propaganda and counter-news service to ensure that the British position and case is fully understood.'[1] To carry out this function, a Division for Enemy and Enemy-Occupied Countries was set up under the Controller Overseas Publicity with regard to which the following statement is made:[2]

> It is concerned with the collection of news and information from these countries, the distribution of news and information to them, and the conduct of propaganda and counter-propaganda necessary to meet enemy statements and mis-statements.

There was thus a Director Enemy Division in the Ministry of Information Duty Room Committee, responsible for guidance, as well as a Liaison Officer Department EH.

By June 1940, the Enemy and the Enemy-Occupied Division was organised in four sections to deal with: France and French Colonies, Belgium and Holland, Italy, Czechoslovakia and Poland and Germany.

'The Enemy Division was responsible for watching and checking all enemy propaganda and for taking all necessary steps for countering and defeating such propaganda.'

While Department EH was not concerned with countering German propaganda in Britain or neutral countries there was a clear overlap of function with regard to the collection of intelligence on propaganda which was the special function of the Intelligence Section of Department EH.

The overlap of functions between Department EH and the 'D' organisation was not brought to an end by the transfer of the small 'D' propaganda team concerned with 'Black' printed material to Department EH. For the 'D' organisation and its successor SO2 claimed to control all propaganda disseminated through agents outside Britain and to operate its own broadcasts from abroad, and did in fact carry out such work without any co-ordination with Department EH or its successor SO1.

The inter-departmental strife which led to frequent reorganisations of Department EH and in which PWE was itself forced to engage would seem to be traceable to the creation of at least *three separate* organisations for

1. Memorandum on MoI Organisation circulated to members of MoI.
2. *Ibid.*

carrying on propaganda or Political Warfare to the enemy with overlapping functions and animated by diverse points of view.

Moreover a fourth body claiming the right to carry out propaganda functions was recognised by the amalgamation of PR and MI7 under DPR at the War Office.

The duties of IP1 in the enlarged directorate were: The preparation of military propaganda in conjunction with the Directorate of Military Operations and Intelligence. The study of enemy and neutral press and wireless propaganda.[1]

The functions of IP2 were: Military propaganda in conjunction with the Foreign Division of the Ministry of Information. Liaison with the BBC through Broadcasting Division, MoI.[2]

The establishment of IP1 and IP2 led to a claim, which was agreed for Department EH by Brigadier Brooks, that front-line propaganda against the enemy was not a PWE responsibility.

Similarly, as we shall see there was a section set up later under DNI [Director of Naval Intelligence] at the Admiralty for carrying out operational propaganda to the German Navy.

In addition to these bodies, the main instrument of propaganda, the BBC European Services, remained a separate organisation with its own hierarchy and outlook throughout the war and for long periods pursued its own policy little influenced by the various departments which nominally controlled it.

Pre-War Organisation of a Shadow Enemy Propaganda Department

The months succeeding the setting up of Sir Campbell Stuart's shadow Department were devoted to earmarking suitably qualified staff, choosing suitable premises, studying the possibilities of various media of propaganda and laying in the necessary material, reference books, documents, etc.

Mr Valentine Williams, the author and journalist, who had been recruited in January 1939, served as a 'talent scout'. Among others he suggested the name of Mr Cyrus Brooks in April 1939.

Mr Leo Russell and Colonel R. A. D. Brooks visited the late Duke of Bedford* and came to a 'gentleman's agreement' with him on the conditions upon which the Department could use the Riding School at Woburn Abbey as their Country Headquarters. After the Duke's death the whole of Woburn Abbey was taken over by the Department.

Sir Campbell Stuart's Department was conveniently given rooms in

1. Kite No. 1507.
2. *Ibid.*
* [Herbrand Arthur Russell, 11th Duke of Bedford (1858–1940), succeeded brother 1893; President, Zoological Society, 1899–1936; FRS 1908.]

Electra House, Victoria Embankment, the offices of the Imperial Communications Advisory Board of which Sir Campbell was chairman. It thus became known as Department EH and its cover and notepaper was naturally that of the organisation which had provided it with accommodation.

Mr Valentine Williams was concerned with[1] the investigation of German, Austrian and Czechoslovak press conditions; of the *Deutschland Freiheit Sender*; locating and obtaining information from refugees and neutrals arriving in Britain; the foundation of a library using 'Mr Walmsley's invaluable list' as a basis; making a list of German periodicals which would be useful to EH. Mr Kirkpatrick* was consulted on the latter subject.

In addition, Mr Kirk and Count de Salis were investigating the possibilities of propaganda through Roman Catholic channels in Germany.

Mr Valentine Williams attended meetings of the *International Propaganda and Broadcasting Enquiry* held at 32, Chesham Place, under the chairmanship of Mr Ivison Macadam.

This body was chiefly concerned with preparations for Ministry of Information functions, but matters such as the foreign press, a report on German, Italian and Russian propaganda and propaganda through missionaries, concerned Department EH.

All was to be in readiness for war by 1st August.[2]

By the 19th August, Mr Williams had received his 'Mobilisation Instructions'.

'D' Propaganda Unit

Meanwhile the 'D' organisation which was concerned with the introduction of propaganda and subversive material into Germany through neutral countries had formed a small unit of seven persons which had begun production of propaganda material which purported to be of German or Austrian origin, some of which was actually introduced into the Reich before the outbreak of war.[3]

The BBC Weapon

While these preparations were being made, the importance of broadcasting the British case to the world through the BBC had been realised.

In January 1938, at the request of the Cabinet, the Arabic service had been started in order to counter Axis propaganda to the Arab world. It was the first BBC foreign-language programme.

---

1. Observations on a meeting held 1.5.39.
2. Mr Ivison Macadam. Meeting held 13.6.39.
3. Mr A. W. Parker's information.

* [Sir Ivone Kirkpatrick (1897–1964) entered FO 1919; head of Chancery, Berlin, 1933–8; foreign advisor to BBC 1941; controller of BBC European Services 1941–4; identified Rudolf Hess 1941; Assistant Under-Secretary in charge of information work 1945–7; Permanent Under-Secretary, FO, 1953–6.]

The inception of the European Service of the BBC was the Munich crisis when on 27th September Mr Neville Chamberlain's speech was broadcast in French, German and Italian. These services were continued from that date as news services.

It was planned that in the event of war the BBC should retain control of them under the general direction of the Ministry of Information.

Summary of Expansion of BBC European Services

German

Started 27th September, 1938, as a daily service. Up till 23rd March, 1943, there were Austrian transmissions at irregular intervals included in this service, when German for Austria was established as a separate service. Service expanded considerably throughout the succeeding years; by April 1945, the average period was 4 hours 42 minutes daily.

Italian

Service started 27th September, 1938, with a daily broadcast. By April 1945 broadcasts were 3 hours daily.

French

Service started on 27th September, 1938, with one daily transmission. The service was expanded and by April 1945 was 5 hours 45 minutes daily.

Spanish

Started 4th June, 1939, with one 15-minute period daily. Service expanded throughout and by April 1945 was 1 hour 45 minutes daily.

Portuguese

Started 4th June, 1939, with one 15-minute period and expanded until by April 1945 was 1 hour 45 minutes daily.

Hungarian

Service started 5th September, 1939, with one 15-minute period daily. By April 1945 was 1 hour 45 minutes daily.

Polish

Service started 7th September, 1939, with a 15-minute period. By April 1945 was 2 hours 40 minutes daily.

Czech (Czech and Slovak)

Started on 8th September, 1939, with one 15-minute period daily. On 31st December, 1941, Slovak was included in the Czech Service at irregular intervals. By April 1945 was 2 hours 25 minutes daily.

Roumanian

Service started on 15th September, 1939, with one 15-minute period daily. Service expanded throughout. By April 1945 was 1 hour 10 minutes daily.

Serbo-Croat (and Slovene)

Started 15th September, 1939, with one daily 15-minute period and irregular broadcast in Slovene. On 22nd April, 1941, a regular daily Slovene period was introduced. By April 1945 was 1 hour 35 minutes daily.

Greek

Service started 30th September, 1939, with one 15-minute period weekly. By April 1945 was 1 hour 26 minutes daily.

Bulgarian

Service started 7th February, 1940, with one 15-minute period daily. By April 1945 was 1 hour 15 minutes daily.

Swedish

Service started 12th February, 1940, with a daily bulletin of 15 minutes. By April 1945 was 30 minutes daily.

Finnish

Started 18th March, 1940, with one 15-minute period daily. By April 1945 was 1 hour daily.

Danish

Service started 9th April, 1940, with Danish news summary included in the Norwegian news bulletin transmission. On 12th April, 1940, Danish was given a separate news time. By April 1945 was 1 hour 15 minutes.

Norwegian

Service started 9th April, 1940, with a 15-minute transmission. By April 1945 was 2 hours per day.

Dutch

Service started 11th April, 1940, with two 15-minute periods, and one 8-minute period, and was expanded at intervals including Dutch Government Period 'Radio Orange'. By April 1945 was 2 hours 15 minutes daily.

Swiss

Started 13th April, 1941, with a 15-minute period daily in German, French, Italian and English. Continued until 7th May, 1941, when the service was withdrawn.

Belgian

Started 28th September, 1940, with programmes for Belgium in French and Flemish consisting of a 10-minute period for 'Radio Belgique', and a Belgian Government programme. During 1943 and 1944, the service was re-shuffled. By April 1945 was 30 minutes daily.

Luxembourg Patois

Service started 13th November, 1940, with a 5-minute talk on Sundays only. On 29th March, 1943, it was extended to a 15-minute period on four days a week. On 4th October, 1943, there was a daily period of 15 minutes introduced, which was in force in April 1945.

Albanian

Started 13th November, 1940, with a transmission of 5 minutes' duration. The service was enlarged on 2nd November, 1942, to 15 minutes. From 15th August, 1943, until 10th December, 1944, was increased to 25 minutes daily. In April 1945 was 15 minutes daily.

Icelandic

Started 1st December, 1940, with a weekly newsletter of 15 minutes and continued until 25th June, 1944, when Icelandic was withdrawn.

Russian

Started 7th October, 1942, with a weekly news review of 15 minutes on Wednesdays only and discontinued on 26th May, 1943.

Austrian

Started 29th March, 1943, with one 15-minute period. By April 1945 was 2 hours daily.

Department EH

War appeared imminent the last week in August and Department EH was mobilised at 10 a.m. on 1st September. Germany had invaded Poland that morning. Orders were to proceed to the Sugarloaf Hotel, Dunstable, and ask for a Mr Gibbs Smith which was an alias for a member of Sir Campbell Stuart's staff.

The organisation of Department EH was as follows: Sir Campbell Stuart, his personal staff, his chief printing officer, and the Military Wing responsible for liaison with the Services, were in London at Electra House. Captain Shaw, Sir Campbell Stuart's Deputy, with the Planning, Editorial and Intelligence sections were at Woburn Abbey Riding School, which, following the practice of that time, will be referred to as Country Headquarters or CHQ. The Political Intelligence Department of the Foreign Office, of which Mr R. A. Leeper was head, was in the close vicinity, at Marylands. Mr Leeper and Foreign Office experts were thus able to attend meetings of Department EH in the country, in a consultative capacity, and to approve matters of propaganda policy.

The work of Department EH was divided into: planning; editorial functions including drafting leaflets; secret activities through a department in neutral countries (these were the placing of agents for the collection of intelligence and dissemination of propaganda); intelligence, including editing and issuing intelligence documents; liaison duties with the Political Intelligence Department of the Foreign Office and the Foreign Office; with MoI and the BBC with particular reference to the guidance of the BBC German Service; with the Services including liaison with the Air Ministry in regard to leaflets; with the Secret Service Departments, i.e. with 'C' and 'D'; with the MEW and the Refugee Organisations through a sub-department set up at the beginning of October 1939 under Mr Leonard Ingrams;* with French Departments responsible for propaganda to Germany through EH Paris office under Mr Noël Coward.**

The 'D' propaganda unit had also received instructions to proceed to Woburn, but they found no provision had been made to co-ordinate their activities with those of EH. They were not invited to meetings, and after a few days of waiting returned to London. Soon afterwards 'D''s organisation found premises for them at Hexton, not far from the country headquarters of D himself. A favourable report was made on their work by an investigator[1] at the request of Sir Campbell Stuart and they finally became incorporated with Department EH.

Much the greater part of the work of Department EH was carried out at CHQ. Work done exclusively in London was that of the Military Wing as regards liaison with the Services, for Intelligence and with the Air Ministry in connection with leaflets. Details regarding the printing and delivery of leaflets were arranged with the Stationery Office and were usually handled in London. Apart from this, Sir Campbell Stuart and Lt Colonel Brooks in the interests of the Department had to carry out propaganda to highly placed officers in the Services, to keep the goodwill and interest of Ministers, and of British newspaper proprietors and to keep a watchful eye on any developments likely to prejudice the work, or even the existence of the Department itself.

Close liaison between London and Country was maintained by the habit, early initiated by Sir Campbell Stuart and Lt Colonel Brooks, of going down to Woburn for long weekends starting on Friday evening and returning on Sunday afternoon. The value of this contact was increased by their taking

---

1. He had no knowledge of printing, or of German type, layout and paper sizes, or of the German language, so he could make no real judgement regarding their work.

* [Leonard St Clair Ingrams (1900–53), banker connected with the Baring family who served in MEW, SOE and PWE. Sefton Delmer referred to him as 'A star operative on the British side of the secret war of wits.']

** [Sir Noël Coward (1899–1973), actor, playwright, composer, producer, patriot; see in particular *Cavalcade* (1931), *This Happy Breed* and *In Which We Serve* (1942).]

with them visitors from the Foreign Office and the MoI and of inviting visitors from the BBC. Saturday thus became the busiest day for the Department.

Intelligence

No arrangement had been made for Intelligence.[1] An Intelligence Department of EH[2] was set up and held its first meeting on 3rd September. The next day, Lt Colonel Brooks was requested to arrange for all Intelligence Reports from the Fighting Services to be sent to Mr Vernon Bartlett, its head.

The Intelligence Department issued a daily Intelligence bulletin compiled from Service Reports and the world press. This, the 'News Digest', became one of the most widely useful documents issued by the Department and was continued throughout the war, see [pp. 224–3].

Besides reading the world press and issuing the News Digest the Intelligence Department at that time drafted leaflets which were later submitted to the Planning Committee.

Mr Walmsley states:

> As regards intelligence productions . . . there were two major developments apart from the Daily Digest. The first was the beginning of systematic propaganda analysis. This began in November 1939 when I made a tentative quantitative analysis of German propaganda (BBC monitoring) under set themes. When this was shown to Campbell Stuart he immediately commissioned a fortnightly analysis of German propaganda based on the system of quantitative analysis. These dealt with German Home Propaganda, propaganda to Britain, propaganda to France and propaganda to Neutrals. From 22nd December till 9th July, 1940 these analyses were issued as a Foreign Office print. They continued to be produced till at least 25.2.41. These were the first analyses of propaganda in this country (and possibly any other) to rely on quantitative analysis. Their initial fault was to underestimate the importance of secondary implications. These faults were corrected in due course. The second major development (after the German conquest of Western Europe) was also in the field of propaganda analysis. This was the deduction of enemy strategic intentions from analyses of enemy propaganda. I believe the initial request came to me from Colonel Brooks, who said that all possible information was needed on German intentions about the invasion of Britain. On 16th July I produced the first analysis of German propaganda with this end in view and regular documents were produced until 31.5.42. After the invasion threat had passed the study

1. Mr Walmsley's evidence.
2. It consisted of: Mr Vernon Bartlett (Head), Mr Kirk, Mr Walmsley, Mr Colvin, Mr Joffe.

> extended to all possible theatres of German operations . . . it was the one field of intelligence in which PWE made an original contribution to the study of enemy military strategy and recognition of this fact was helpful to PWE. The principle of analyses [was], when established, very simple . . . to discover how German propaganda to different audiences had behaved in certain situations in the past and see whether the pattern was repeating itself. . . . The abandonment of invasion was deduced from propaganda with a margin of error of not more than 48 hours . . . though I am sure there was a lot of luck in this.

Another side of Mr Walmsley's work which came later was to 'provide a general picture of Germany either politically or in the way of listener research. In the first year . . . there would not have been resources to do this, but the matter was at least discussed. On 3.8.40 the German Sub-Committee recommended that a series of notes be written on the character of the classes of person whom we are addressing in Germany. . . . This would describe the sensitive and insensitive points of each class.'

Mr Valentine Williams did not, however, think the idea a practical or useful one and the proposal was not taken up till March 1941.

Leaflets

Department EH was, at the outset, greatly influenced by the experience of its Chief in the war 1914–18. It was therefore natural that its members should concentrate on the production of leaflets and the collection of intelligence. It is perhaps indicative of this preoccupation with the printed word that it was not until nearly a year after the beginning of the war, and after Department EH itself had been transformed into another Department, that any British leaflet dropped in Germany advertised the times and wavelengths of the BBC German-language broadcasts.[1]

The first leaflets consisted of: warnings to the German people which were in effect indictments of German aggression; reminders of the great potential strength of Britain and France; affirmations of Anglo-French unity; attacks on Germany for her alliance with Godless Bolshevik Russia[2] and attacks on the plutocratic nature of the German ruling classes.

Printing was by HM Stationery Office and was plain and bold; sometimes the leaflets gained from the urgent stop-press appearance.

Apart from speeches and statements by Mr Neville Chamberlain and Allied leaders, the leaflets were the work of many hands. All the leading

1. This suggestion was first brought to the attention of the Planning Committee, 16.10.39, by Mr Duncan Sandys but it was considered to be 'impracticable' for reasons not recorded.
2. Following the directive of PID. On 4th October, 1939, Mr R. A. Leeper stressed that the emergence of Russia was the unexpected event of the first months of the war and that by his pact with Stalin, Hitler had '*given the Allies the strongest propaganda weapon that could have been forged*'.

members of the Department contributed suggestions and ideas and the leaflets themselves were vigorously criticised at meetings. Nor was the criticism confined to members of the Department. The Air Ministry in the person of Wing Commander Blackford claimed the right to reject any leaflet, either on legalistic grounds that its subject matter might provoke the enemy into carrying out reprisals on captured pilots or because the leaflet might injure Air Force morale, or on grounds of taste alone. These claims were never directly combatted and the claims of the Royal Air Force to exert an influence upon leaflet wording and policy were tacitly accepted until late in the war. Owing to the existence of the Military Wing of EH, co-operation or contact between the leaflet writers and officers in the Air Ministry was not possible though many of the latter were keenly interested in the work. On one occasion, Mr Valentine Williams visited the Air Ministry to discuss leaflets with officers in the German section of Air Intelligence[1] but contacts were discouraged.

Mr Walmsley states that 'the leaflets were written in English and then translated by a German mining engineer called Schmidt. The results were not good. Among the leaflets produced in the first winter was a weekly newspaper *Wolkiger Beobachter*. There was also the "Londoner Post", an objective news-sheet of four small pages sent to selected German addresses in neutral countries.'

Mr Walmsley is of the opinion that some of the early leaflets were by no means worse than the later ones. Be that as it may, British Political Warfare to Germany during the EH period can only have been of negative value since its principal themes were German responsibility for the war, the complete accord and mutual trust of the British and French, the strength of the French Army and the Maginot line, the imminent economic collapse of Germany.

The German people as a whole was indifferent to the first argument, and it was only a few months before the second, third and fourth were falsified.

Planning in Department EH

The formation of a Broadcasting Committee at CHQ on 11th September, 1939, was followed, after two meetings, by that of a Joint Planning and Broadcasting Committee, which, for the first few months, met daily. The senior member of Department EH took the chair. It was attended not only by the principal officers of the Department but also by one or sometimes two representatives of the BBC and usually by two or more members of PID.

At this daily meeting the 'Sonderberichte' or Special Reports given in the German programme of the BBC and the texts of leaflets were discussed and approved. In later months, through the pressure of other duties, Captain Shaw and Mr Valentine Williams were often called away and full meetings were only held twice a week. But after the full daily meeting was discontinued, its place was filled to some extent by the meetings of a discussion

---

1. The present writer took part in the discussion.

group which consisted of those junior officers of the Department who were chiefly concerned with originating propaganda ideas. One result of this habit of frequent meeting and constant discussion was to build up a fairly consistent attitude to most of the problems of propaganda among the leading members of the Department at CHQ.

Planning in Connection with BBC

On 23rd January, 1940, the Planning Committee agreed that Mr Murray's *General Directive to the BBC*[1] should be circulated to the Committee and discussed at Saturday's meeting. Shortly afterwards the *Weekly Directive to the BBC for the German programmes* became an established routine document. On 27th January, the Committee approved Mr Murray's *Directive to the BBC for the Austrian programmes*. On 30th January, 1940, Mr Bruce Lockhart* of PID undertook to provide a *Directive to the BBC for Czech broadcasts*.[2]

In addition to the weekly directives, a *General Directive for Propaganda* was discussed at a Special Meeting on 4th February and, after modifications, was issued as a Memorandum from Department EH to the BBC on 25th February, 1940. It was followed up by a list of EH Do's and Dont's which summarised the practical points which Department EH was trying to alter in the BBC German programmes.

The Planning Committee wished to increase the scope of BBC broadcasting to Germany which was based upon news bulletins and insisted that personality speakers were needed – men who would build up a following among the German public. The first proposal for a BBC 'Uncle', who was referred to as 'Uncle Caractacus', was on 11th October, 1939. Names considered in January 1940 include Mr Sefton Delmer,** Professor Lindley

1. Mr Murray claims both the invention of the Directive as the instrument for controlling propaganda and of the word itself. This obsolete substantive is stated, however, to have been in current use by the British Communist Party before 1939.
2. Minutes of Planning and Broadcasting Committee.

* [Sir Robert 'Jock' ('Bertie') Bruce Lockhart (1887–1970), diplomat and author. Educated at Fettes, Berlin and Paris; scandalous rubber planter in Malaya; Vice-Consul, Moscow, 1912; acting Consul-General 1914–17; headed special mission to Russia 1918, but imprisoned and exchanged for Litvinov; left foreign service 1922. Editor Londoner's diary, *Evening Standard*, 1928–37; re-joined FO 1939; British representative to the Czech government-in-exile, 1940; Deputy Under-Secretary of State in charge of PWE 1941–5. Author of *Memoirs of a British Agent* (1932), *Retreat from Glory* (1934) and *Comes the Reckoning* (1947). Despite his excellent autobiographical writings, he badly requires a modern biography.]

** [(Denis) Sefton Delmer (1904–79), born in Berlin of Australian parents and educated in Germany and later at Oxford. Worked on Lord Beaverbrook's *Daily Express* from 1927 and head of that paper's Berlin bureau 1928–33; friendly with Ernst Röhm and first British reporter to interview Hitler, travelling in his plane and walking beside him through the burnt-out Reichstag. Reported Spanish Civil War 1936–8; recruited by SOE to spread false rumours in enemy-occupied territories 1940; chief foreign affairs reporter, *Daily Express*, from 1945 until 1959 when he was sensationally sacked by Beaverbrook. See autobiography: *Trail Sinister* (1961) and *Black Boomerang* (1962).]

Fraser, Mr R. H. S. Crossman* and Mr Patrick Gordon Walker,** all of whom later distinguished themselves at the microphone, as well as such names as that of Mr Max Beerbohm.***

The BBC, however, was slow to take up the idea. EH papers record considerable impatience with this dilatoriness. Eventually Professor Lindley Fraser was selected[1] and, when he had become familiar with broadcasting technique in German, developed into the leading member of a team of personality speakers.

On 20th April, 1940, Mr Ogilvie, Director General of the BBC,† visited CHQ and attended a meeting in which EH criticisms were ventilated. Less than a month later, following what Sir Campbell Stuart regarded as a gross mishandling of Mr Chamberlain's speech although he had personally rung up Sir Stephen Tallents and made suggestions as to how it should be used, a statement of EH complaints against the BBC included unwillingness to co-operate evinced by delay in replying to suggestions; unwillingness to carry out weekly directives; complete lack of direction of BBC bulletins and Sonderberichte as a whole; insufficient attention to BBC news bulletins: foolish items being included with downright inaccuracies on many occasions.

Examples of BBC unwillingness to co-operate with Department EH included: A list of potential speakers had been handed in on 11th March. By 11th March not one had been approached. Although the BBC stated two of them had been approached, this was untrue. No reply had been received by the Planning Committee on the subject. Sonderberichte submitted by members of the Department had not been acknowledged, not used and not returned. An arrangement with the TUC for speakers had taken three months to complete. Suggestions for a new speaker for Austria had been made, and a name had been suggested but no action had been taken. Suggestions for the use of Hitler recordings had been ignored for weeks. A Planning Committee had made recommendations about forms of announcement, 'trailing' times of

---

1. Professor Lindley Fraser made his first broadcast as Caractacus on 15.2.40.

* [Richard Howard Stafford Crossman (1907–74), journalist, politician and diarist. After Winchester and New College, Oxford, he became a fellow of the latter in 1930 and assistant editor of the *New Statesman* in 1938. Joined MEW 1940, and was assistant chief of the Psychological Warfare Department at SHAEF from 1944 to 1945. Labour MP for Coventry East 1945–74; Minister of Housing 1964; Leader of the House of Commons 1966; four volumes of controversial diaries published posthumously 1975–81.]

** [Patrick Chrestien Gordon Walker, Baron Gordon-Walker (1907–80), was a student and history tutor at Christ Church, Oxford. BBC European Service (German workers) 1940–4; assistant German Service Director, BBC, 1945; Labour MP, Smethwick, 1945–64 and Leyton 1966–74; Secretary of State for Commonwealth Relations 1950–1; Secretary of State for Foreign Affairs 1964–5; Secretary of State for Education and Science 1967–8.]

*** [Sir Henry Maximilian 'Max' Beerbohm (1872–1956), author and cartoonist. Artistic, fashionable and highly cultivated, 'the incomparable Max' was the *Saturday Review*'s dramatic critic 1898–1910. Wrote *Zuleika Dobson* (1911) and *Seven Men* (1919). Knighted 1939.]

† [Sir Frederick Wolff Ogilvie (1893–1949), economist. Served in army 1914–19; fellow of Trinity College, Oxford, 1920; President and Vice-Chancellor, Queen's University, Belfast, 1934–8; Director-General, BBC, 1938–42; undertook special war duties for British Council 1943–5.]

bulletins and precautions against Gestapo activities. The recommendations had been largely ignored. Recommendations on the simplification of translators' language had been made without result. When broadcasts by Mr F. A. Voigt had been suggested, it had been objected that he must have a voice test though he was a practised broadcaster. Continual obstacles had been put in the way of his being given a voice test.

Mr Walmsley states: 'I do not think it is an exaggeration to say the relation of Electra House to the BBC was an organisational disaster. In the early months there was as good as no control whatever. . . . By the time Crossman came on the scene EH had fairly effectively gained control over talks to Germany. Over the next twelve months he established pretty good control over the German news output of the BBC as well as greatly strengthening EH's hold on talks. . . . By the time Crossman left Bush House . . . the BBC was effectively independent of PWE (EH) in both news and talks.'

The reasons for the difficulties arising between Department EH and the BBC may be found partly in the dual control of the BBC. As early as 22nd September, 1939,[1] Mr Ryan had complained that the BBC received instructions from two conflicting authorities: Department EH and the Overseas Branch of the MoI. In part it was due to the conditions under which the BBC was carrying out work and which was to be fully described a year later.[2]

The European Services of the BBC had expanded with little regard to the accommodation available and working conditions were largely responsible for inefficiencies and failures. But even had the conditions been perfect, the attempt by an outside body, situated at a distance, to carry out the control of certain regions of a hierarchical organisation by directives was a matter of the greatest difficulty. This had been clearly perceived by the only member of the Planning Committee[3] with BBC experience who, as early as 10th February, 1940, stated that the ideal system would have been to have a studio at CHQ with a line to the BBC. 'This would enable the Country to control German news broadcasts.' Such a system would have taken authority for the European Services completely out of the hands of the BBC and would have placed responsibility for execution as well as policy on Department EH and its successors, by no means an impossible task as was later proved by Mr Delmer's creation of the Atlantik and Calais services. Department EH, however, did not at any time seek such powers. Owing to no radical alteration occurring in the relations of Department EH and the BBC, matters continued to be unsatisfactory and the Planning Committee Minutes record a melancholy list of complaints.

The use of the word Nazi is an example and EH protests were vain. Thus on 3rd August, 1940,[4] it was reported to have been employed seven

1. Minutes of Planning and Broadcasting Committee.
2. Organisation of the German Service on BBC by R. H. S. Crossman, 25.5.41.
3. Mr Ralph Murray. Minutes of a meeting held on 10.2.40.
4. Planning Committee Minutes, 3.8.40.

times in one talk although it did not appear in the original text provided. Again Department EH demanded regional treatment of news and the BBC was unable or unwilling to provide it. Thus Mr Bruce Lockhart[1] complained that there were not enough Czech items in the BBC news bulletins though plenty of material was available. And this senior member of PID had to 'vet' the Czech programmes himself.

It was only by such expedients, by providing or suggesting speakers, by demanding reforms, by writing scripts, by continual interference and supervision, that Department EH was able to impose its wishes, and then imperfectly, upon the BBC. Sometimes the views it sought to impose were proved later to be wrong. Thus in February and March, Department EH sought to impose a ban on the use of music in European broadcasts[2] on the grounds that it was particularly easy for the Gestapo to overhear and identify musical items. No doubt Department EH was correct in assessing the musical gifts of the Gestapo highly, but experience showed that the risk was worth running and the value of music as a propaganda weapon was later proved up to the hilt, not only on the BBC. Nor does EH insistence on presenting Hitler as a puppet in the hands of others (particularly of Stalin until Hitler attacked Russia) seem in retrospect to have been a very fruitful device and it is at least arguable that the later method of stressing Hitler's personal responsibility not only for the war but for all Germany's defeats and difficulties would have been more convincing.

Although there are many signs that EH interference was often exasperating to responsible officials of the BBC, Department EH was often useful to them. Thus Department EH was able to protest on a high level when the Services put out false news for short-term operational reasons[3] which was most damaging to the reputation for truth on which our overt propaganda was based. Against such abuses the BBC found a powerful defender in the Military Wing of Department EH. But the greatest service which the Department was able to perform was thanks to the confidence placed in it by the Chiefs of Staff. The officers of the Military Wing obtained foreknowledge of the military situation and they could therefore give strategic guidance to the BBC European Services which was more accurate than that which could be supplied by the MoI. On the discretion with which they used such knowledge the future of the Department as well as the quality of our propaganda to Europe depended.

Indirect Propaganda. The Londoner Brief

An early activity of Department EH was the attempt to influence opinion in Germany through Germans in neutral countries or through business circles

1. Minutes of Planning Committee, 10.9.40.
2. Minutes of Planning Committee, 4.3.40, item 19.
3. Minutes of Planning Committee, 11.5.40, item 4, and again 26.7.40.

in neutral countries which were in close contact with Germany. With this object, a fortnightly series entitled *Der Londoner Brief* was written by members of the staff of Department EH, printed on particularly good paper and dispatched through Crawford's Agency to an address list of Germans and neutral firms in close contact with Germany, in Belgium and Holland. By March 1940, 3,000 copies of this periodical were dispatched.

This overlapped similar forms of publicity to neutral countries by the Overseas Publicity Division of the MoI. On 30.12.39 the MoI proposed that they should distribute 250,000 copies of *Der Londoner Brief* to S. America at a cost of £100,000 p.a. In May 1940, the British Library of Information to [the] USA applied for and were sent fifty copies of an English version. Certain Belgian firms which were annoyed by receiving *Der Londoner Brief* made complaints which eventually came up at the EH-MoI Co-ordination Committee. This medium of propaganda came to an end soon after the German occupation of Western Europe though plans to continue it for circulation to S. America and the Far East were discussed and a flimsy was sent by bag to Zagreb for stencilling early in July 1940. No example of *Der Londoner Brief* has been seen by the present writer.

In a report to the War Cabinet, Sir Campbell Stuart stated[1] that preparations were in an advanced stage to produce another newsletter in German, which would be printed in the neutral countries bordering on Germany, and posted into it. It seems probable that the German invasions of Norway, Denmark and the Low Countries occurred before this instrument of propaganda had come into existence.

Department in Neutral Countries

In his report to the Cabinet, Sir Campbell Stuart frequently referred to his 'Department in Neutral Countries'. Sir Campbell Stuart expressly stated that he had no intention of developing an extensive and redundant secret service of his own; but he had placed, and was arranging to place, a few well-chosen agents at points at which the intelligence which Department EH needed was likely to emerge from Germany. These agents were in Switzerland and Belgium as is shown by a later report which records that a member of Department EH had visited Denmark, Sweden and Norway and inaugurated a more regular service of intelligence which should supplement that of the agents in Switzerland and Belgium. These agents were to be employed in introducing propaganda material into Germany as well as collecting intelligence. The placing of agents in the field was to become the subject of bitter controversy later on, as in spite of Sir Campbell Stuart's explicit statement that he had no intention of creating his own secret service, the placing of EH agents was so regarded by the D organisation, the functions of which they were duplicating. It was not, however, until

---

1 WP(R)105, 29.3.40.

Department EH and the D organisation had been merged into SOE as SO1 and SO2 that friction between the two branches came to a head.

Liaison with the French

Liaison with the French broadcasting authorities was established by Sir Campbell Stuart some months before the war with the twofold object of ensuring that French broadcasting stations should be arranged so as not to assist the navigation of German raiding aircraft, and to co-ordinate the news and policy of British and French programmes.

The vital importance of the first of these problems had been long appreciated in Britain and a system of synchronisation had been worked out by Air Commodore Nutting and the BBC engineers. By this, British transmitting stations were grouped and every programme was transmitted from four stations using the same wavelength. Thus, on the night of 31st August the BBC was able to pass from the normal system to that of a synchronised service.

No such plans had been worked out by the French, who welcomed British technical advice and, with the help of British equipment, the French northern stations were synchronised as rapidly as possible.

On the outbreak of war, Sir Campbell Stuart established a branch office of Department EH in Paris, which was staffed by Mr Noël Coward, Colonel Sinclair, (replaced by Lord Strathallan on 18th September) and Squadron Leader Wilson.

A report by Lt Colonel Brooks on his visit to Paris on 17th September reveals that the organisation of the French 'opposite number' of Department EH rendered it largely ineffective. It consisted of a civilian organisation including M. André Maurois,* Professor Tonnelat, Professor Vermeil and Capitaine de Vaisseau Lecompte. But though leaflets were drafted by its members and printed by its authority, and forwarded to the Grand Quartier General, the Committee had no knowledge of what subsequently became of them and no authority to ensure that they were disseminated. Admiral Fernet informed Lt Colonel Brooks that Capitaine Schuls, who was responsible for leaflet dissemination at GQG, disbelieved in the use of aircraft for that purpose and was hostile to the organisation. It seems probable that the shortage of French bombing aircraft[1] was not unconnected with this attitude.

An offer made by Capitaine Schuls, through the EH Paris Office, of facilities for delivery of 50,000 letters a month to neutral countries may be regarded as an indication of the propaganda methods contemplated by the

1. At the outbreak of war, the French first-line strength was approximately 300 bombers with 100 in reserve. The German was approximately 2,500 first-line with 4,500 in reserve, not counting 1,200 troop carriers and the Lufthansa fleet.

* [André Maurois, *nom de plume* of Emile Herzog (1885–1967), French novelist, biographer and intellectual. Liaison officer between French and British armies in the Great War; wrote lives of Disraeli (1927), Voltaire (1935) and Proust (1949) amongst many other fine works.]

French authorities at the outset of the war. The offer was refused.[1] An enquiry from the French as to whether the British could disseminate leaflets prepared by the French[2] was favourably considered. During the early months of 1940, a concertina leaflet, designed to demonstrate Anglo-French unity by sea, on land, and in the air, through the medium of photo-montage, was prepared and printed in France and disseminated by the RAF.

Fécamp Broadcasting Station

Towards the end of October 1939 a complication arose which temporarily undid the results of the good work of Air Commodore Nutting and the British wireless experts in synchronising the French radio transmissions. This was the starting up of the hitherto silent Fécamp Broadcasting Station, which was the property of the International Broadcasting Company of which Captain Plugge, MP,* was chairman, carrying programmes in English for the benefit of the BEF [British Expeditionary Force] and propaganda addressed to Austria,[3] Czechoslovakia and Poland in German, Czech and Polish.

A request from Air Commodore Nutting that Fécamp be closed down, addressed to General Jullien, was passed to the French civilian authorities with a strong recommendation that action be taken. This, however, had no result. Sir Campbell Stuart in two reports to the War Cabinet[4] referred to the serious situation caused by this 'obsolete station' which had been allowed to reopen 'under pressure from interests in this country and in France'. Until the station was closed down it would be difficult to continue the discussions on Anglo-French co-operation in propaganda broadcasts to Germany or for the French to discuss broadcast propaganda in a spirit of full mutual confidence.

A complication mentioned by Mr Ryan of the BBC was that Lord Gort** had broadcast on Fécamp Station before its dangerous character had been explained to him.

---

1. Planning and Broadcasting Committee Minutes, 30.11.39.
2. *Ibid.*
3. The propaganda to Austria was paid for by supporters of a Hapsburg restoration and presumably was authorised by the French Foreign Office.
5. WP(R)(39)58, 26.10.39, and WP(R)(39)95, 27.11.39.

* [Captain Leonard Frank Plugge (1889–1981) was a captain in the RAF 1918; Inter-Allied Aeronautical Commission of Control in Berlin 1919–20; Conservative MP, Chatham, 1934–45; Chairman, parliamentary science committee, 1939–43; part-owned and operated many continental broadcasting stations; general committee, Radio Society of Great Britain, 1923–5; created first radio programme for BEF in France.]

** [Field Marshal John Vereker, 1st Viscount Gort (1886–1946), commanded 4th battalion, Grenadier Guards, 1917–18, MC, DSO and two bars, VC. Chief of the Imperial General Staff 1937–9. Commander-in-Chief of the BEF from September 1939, he was outflanked by German invasion of Belgium and Low Countries in May 1940 and withdrew to Dunkirk, from where the army was evacuated. Became Governor of Gibraltar 1941–2 and Malta 1942–4.]

Captain Plugge also controlled a station at Antibes which he offered to the MoI for a period of 100 days at a cost of £600 per diem. While this station was not dangerous as a navigational guide to German aircraft raiding Britain, it would have been of great assistance to aircraft raiding Toulon or Marseilles. There was a possibility that the chief naval base of our ally might be endangered by a programme sponsored by a British Government Department and put out by a British company.

The question of closing Fécamp Station came before the War Cabinet.[1] The Secretary of State for Air stated that M. Daladier* apparently wished to shelter behind General Gamelin's decision not to close the station, and asked that Lord Gort should press for the immediate closing down of the station.

The Secretary of State for War (Mr Hore-Belisha)** thought it was important we should not be put in the position of pressing for the closing down of this particular station but agreed that General Gamelin should be approached by Major General Howard Vyse.*** The Prime Minister said he would take the matter up with Mr Daladier if this approach did not have the desired result. The station was in fact closed down.

Two important suggestions for means of carrying out Political Warfare were made by the French to officers of Department EH. One was the specification of a leaflet bomb,[2] the other of a leaflet shell.

German Refugees

On the declaration of war, the possible value of German refugees was fully realised and many hundreds of them offered their services in various ways, first to one Government Department and then to another. If their ideas found favour they were often subsidised and during the early months of the war cases occurred of refugees drawing independent subsidies from several British Government sources for the same, or for much the same, work. It

---

1. WM(39)11, 11.12.39.
2. See leaflets, p.189.

* [Edouard Daladier (1884–1970), French Prime Minister for a few weeks in 1933 and 1934; War Minister in the Popular Front Government of 1936. A left-wing pacifist-sympathiser and enthusiastic appeaser, he signed the Munich Pact as Prime Minister in 1938. Resigned in 1940, became War and then Foreign Minister, and was arrested and interned on the fall of France until 1945.]

** [(Isaac) Leslie Hore-Belisha, Baron Hore-Belisha (1893–1957), President of Oxford Union 1919; Liberal MP, Davenport, 1923–45; supported National Government 1931; Financial Secretary to the Treasury 1932–4; as Minister of Transport, 1934–7, he introduced the eponymous traffic safety beacons; reforming Secretary of State for War 1937–January 1940, when he was forced to resign after clashing with Gort and other senior generals over the BEF's defences; Minister of National Insurance, Churchill's caretaker ministry, 1945.]

*** [Major-General Sir Richard Granville Hylton Howard-Vyse (1883–1962) entered the army in 1902; captain 1908; served in Europe 1914–17, Palestine 1917–18; colonel 1926; major-general 1933; head of military mission with French High Command 1939–40; Chairman, POW department of Red Cross and St John, 1941–5.]

was obviously important to co-ordinate the work of refugees. Mr Leonard Ingrams was instructed to carry out this work, and as a result the activities of German refugees were made available through various channels. A refugee organisation which must be mentioned at this period was the De Muth Committee. Another of value to Political Warfare Intelligence was the Wiener Library.

Department EH Liaison with Services

In so far as this was concerned with day-to-day details, such as the approving of a leaflet by the Air Ministry, the instructions to the printers and the arrangements for delivery and the necessary liaisons were dealt with by the officers under Lt Colonel Brooks in the Military Wing. Besides such routine matters, liaison with the Services involved:

1. Eliciting intelligence from three Service Intelligence Directorates.
2. Eliciting information regarding the strategy of the war and military plans based on it.
3. Obtaining service approval for propaganda projects and plans put up by Department EH.

A Service Consultative Committee was formed with the *main object of co-ordinating propaganda policy with the strategical plan*. Members included Sir Campbell Stuart, Captain Shaw, Lt Colonel Brooks, Mr Leeper (Head of the Political Intelligence Department, FO), Major General Beaumont Nesbitt, Admiral Hallett,* Air Commodore Groves, Wing Commander Blackford, and Mr E. H. Carr** (Director of Foreign Publicity, Ministry of Information).

The minutes reveal that the strategical plan of the war, or military plans for forthcoming operations, were seldom touched upon. Such matters as the need for an Anglo-French policy in regard to jamming were discussed, but the greater part of the Committee's time was given up to comparatively trivial details such as particular rumours, the possibility of using searchlights playing on low clouds as instruments of front-line propaganda, and such questions as releasing the names of members of U-Boat crews, or interned German seamen. An important policy point recorded is an extract from a

---

* [Vice-Admiral John Hughes-Hallett (1901–72), educated at Osborne, Dartmouth and Gonville and Caius College, Cambridge; served in battle cruiser *Lion* 1918, secretary to Anglo-German naval conference 1935; captain 1940; on defence division of naval staff 1940; naval advisor to combined operations 1941; naval commander of disastrous Dieppe Raid 1942; responsible for initial naval plan for Normandy landings; major role in Mulberry harbours scheme 1944; retired from RN 1953. Conservative MP, Croydon East, 1955–64.]

** [Edward Hallett Carr (1892–1982), historian, diplomat, journalist. Double first from Trinity College, Cambridge, classical tripos; served in foreign service in Riga, Geneva and London 1916–36; assistant editor, *The Times*, 1941–6. A notorious Soviet sympathiser and fellow-traveller whose many publications include the fourteen volume *A History of Soviet Russia* (1950–78).]

letter from Major General Beaumont Nesbitt opposing the re-education of German prisoners of war, 'If we segregate the Nazis from anti-Nazis, may not there be a tendency to enhance the feeling, which to my mind is already too prevalent, that Nazi and Germans are two different people?'

EH Co-ordination with the Ministry of Information

Co-ordination between EH and the MoI on various matters was rendered absolutely essential owing to the overlap between the functions of the Enemy Division of the MoI and Department EH described on pages 7 and 8 and meetings with the Foreign Publicity Department of the Ministry were arranged. All the items on the agenda of the first meeting on 28.12.39 were put up by Department EH. They were:

1. Propaganda among Germans in neutral countries.
2. Closer co-operation between Department EH and MoI on specific propaganda themes, e.g. inflation.
3. Co-operation with MoI representatives abroad (press attachés, etc.).
4. German propaganda in Sweden.

Of these subjects the most important to the work of Department EH was item 3, in order that a system by which the chief contents of German newspapers could be telegraphed as early as possible and the telegrams forwarded to EH with minimum delay should be inaugurated.

Fortnightly meetings were arranged. Discussions at these meetings ranged over a wide variety of topics but the practical question of obtaining German newspapers through Holland, and of securing telegraphed news-summaries which arrived before the newspapers themselves, cropped up frequently. Another constant theme was the supposed imminent economic collapse of Germany and the subject of inflation.

The meetings resulted in decisions being made on points in which co-operation was essential though much time was taken up with unrealities. Thus on 17th May, 1940, the first item on the agenda was a proposal which reveals the amateurishness of the period.

'That we should keep on attacking Nazidom with a view of goading Hitler to fury. He should be irritated and driven to doing something desperate.'

The debate on this proposal had to be deferred owing to Sir Walter Monckton's* absence – which may conceivably have been due to the fact

* [Walter Turner Monckton, 1st Viscount Monckton of Brenchley (1891–1965), lawyer and politician. President of the Oxford Union 1913; served in France 1914–18; called to Bar 1919; Attorney-General and friend to the Prince of Wales 1932–6; confidant of Edward VIII during the Abdication Crisis 1936; Director-General, Ministry of Information, 1940–1; Solicitor-General 1945; Conservative MP, Bristol West, 1951–7; Minister of Labour 1951–5, where he appeased the trade unions; Minister of Defence 1955–6; privately opposed Suez and became Paymaster-General 1956–7; Chairman, Midland Bank, 1957–64.]

that the German Army, having broken through on the Meuse, was rapidly overrunning France.

With the imminent danger of the invasion of Britain, a more realistic tone appeared in the minutes of what then became the Policy Committee of the MoI and the representatives of EH took part in useful discussions on such wide matters as home morale, provision of news for French refugees in Britain and methods of mitigating the injustice of the indiscriminate treatment of enemy aliens who had recently been interned. With regard to the latter, Department EH was responsible for suggesting and drafting a letter which was signed by the Prime Minister which was handed to every internee and which ended with a reference to 'this temporary loss of freedom for the sake of our final victory over the enemy'.

Mr Valentine Williams remained an energetic member of the MoI Policy Committee until June 1941, shortly before his departure for the USA.

Early Criticism of Department EH inside the Services

It was not unnatural that Department EH should have aroused criticism in the early days of the war. 'It is, I think, generally agreed that the organisation of propaganda in its role of auxiliary to Britain's effort by sea, land and air, leaves much to be desired,' wrote Brigadier L. R. C. Penney for DMI [Director of Military Intelligence] in a minute of 24th November, 1939, which called for the setting up of a small inter-Service committee to review the situation. The minute proposed a committee of D [Deputy] DMI (O) representatives of NI and AI and the GSO1, MI7 (Colonel Aylmer Vallance). 'I am also inviting Colonel R. A. D. Brooks representing Sir Campbell Stuart's organisation.' This invitation was apparently not sent[1] and Colonel Brooks was not present at the first meeting, but in his absence the critics of Department EH met with unexpected opposition on the part of the Air Ministry representative, Air Commodore P. R. C. Groves. Air Commodore Groves, who was DDI4 at the Air Ministry, had great faith in the propaganda weapon and had been favourably impressed by the work of Department EH.

At the first meeting, he pointed out that Sir Campbell Stuart's Department had been set up by the War Cabinet to carry out propaganda to the enemy and that no other arrangements could be made without that decision being rescinded, which was in his opinion unlikely.

He urged also that Colonel Brooks must be invited to subsequent meetings. As a result of Air Commodore Groves' intervention the Inter-Services Committee on Propaganda proved short-lived. At a subsequent and final meeting at which Air Commodore Groves took the chair in the absence of Brigadier Penney, he tore up the secretary's minutes of the previous meeting, after challenging their accuracy. The events described above were

1. Information from Air Commodore P. R. C. Groves.

followed three months later by Air Commodore Groves accepting an invitation to join the staff of Department EH in which he became Colonel R. A. D. Brooks' Deputy in the Military Wing.

Criticism of Department EH in the Press

A corollary of the widespread belief that British propaganda might play a decisive part by unifying the 'good Germans' in opposition to the Nazis, was the demand in Parliament and the press to know the details of our propaganda in order to criticise it vigorously. The public was unused to war controls and suspicious of military mentality.

The demand showed itself particularly in regard to leaflets. To the man in the street and the ordinary journalist it appeared fantastic that the text of a leaflet which had been scattered in millions over enemy territory should be withheld on the pretence that its publication would assist the enemy. Only Colonel Blimp, it was felt, could have conceived so ridiculous an idea. But in this case Colonel Blimp would have been right, for the publication of leaflets would inevitably have provoked hostile criticism, both in Britain and in neutral countries, which would be quoted by the enemy so as to ridicule British propaganda from British sources.

Considerable pressure was required to maintain the secrecy of our leaflets. Lord Halifax,* the Secretary of State for Foreign Affairs, addressed a personal letter to each of the leading Editors. This was not enough and Sir Campbell Stuart's knowledge of Fleet Street led him to pursue what was probably the only course which, in the prevailing state of public opinion, at that stage of the war, could successfully muzzle the press. He took the newspaper proprietors into his full confidence and a meeting held on 2nd November at Electra House was attended by Major the Hon. J. J. Astor, MP** (*The Times*), the Hon. Rupert Beckett (*Yorkshire Post*), Mr Esmond Harmsworth*** (Chairman of Associated Newspapers Ltd), Sir Roderick

* [Edward Frederick Lindley Wood, 1st Earl of Halifax (1881–1959). Conservative MP, Ripon, 1910–25; Under Secretary, Colonial Office, 1921; Viceroy of India as Lord Irwin 1925–31; succeeded as Viscount Halifax 1934; Lord Privy Seal and Leader of the Lords 1935–7; negotiated unsuccessfully with Hitler at Berchtesgaden 1937; Foreign Secretary 1938–41; Ambassador in Washington 1941–66; OM 1946.]

** [John Jacob Astor, 1st Baron Astor of Hever (1886–1971), was born in New York but educated at Eton and New College, Oxford, after his father naturalised in 1891. Served in Household Cavalry 1914–18, severely wounded and right leg amputated. Inherited vast fortune on father's death in 1919. Unionist MP, Dover, 1922–45; joint-owner of *The Times* 1922–66; member BBC's advisory council 1937–9. Philanthropist and owner of Hever Castle.]

*** [Esmond Cecil Harmsworth, 2nd Viscount Rothermere (1898–1978), educated at Eton, commissioned into Royal Marine Artillery 1917; Conservative MP, Thanet, 1919–29, Chairman, Associated Newspapers, 1932; Chairman, National Newspapers Association, 1934–61; Chairman, Newsprint Supply Company, 1940–59; suggested morganatic marriage for Edward VIII 1936; succeeded father 1940; retired 1971.]

Jones (Reuters), Sir Walter Layton* (*News Chronicle*), Mr J. R. Scott (*Manchester Guardian*), and Lord Southwood** (*Daily Herald*). Only Lord Beaverbrook's group of newspapers was unrepresented and the following week Sir Campbell Stuart entered, with consummate tact, upon the appeasement of that section of the press.

A second meeting of the newspaper proprietors was held on 3rd January, 1940, and a third on 18th March. All recent British leaflets were handed round, and Sir Campbell Stuart then delivered an address on the developments which had taken place since the previous meeting. The following points from the address given on 18th March, 1940, are of interest as an indication of Sir Campbell Stuart's outlook three weeks before the Germans brought 'the phoney war' to a close by the invasion of Norway and Denmark.

Though the snow lying for a month over Britain had grounded our heavy bombers, and periods of east wind had made dissemination by balloon impossible, altogether twenty-five million leaflets had been dropped since the previous meeting. Sir Campbell Stuart then told a little story intended to show the value of our leaflets: a newly trodden path, obviously used by numbers of people, had been discovered by the German authorities in a forest. It led to a tree on which a leaflet had been pinned.

The BBC were giving five talks in German daily. Professor Lindley Fraser had been discovered as a personality speaker. Two BBC officials spent their time between the BBC and CHQ.

The growth of propaganda had needed an increase of staff. Mr F. A. Voigt had been selected as a key-man. Two liaison officers with the MoI had been appointed.

Department EH had recently been given the task of propaganda to Russia and Sir Campbell Stuart was surveying the formidable problem. Relations with the French were close and with refugee organisations were smooth.

Living Conditions at Woburn. Food and Recreation

The establishment of a body of persons, which soon came to number some hundreds, in close contact with each other, working long hours in the country, raised social problems for many Government Departments and private

---

* [Sir Walter Layton, 1st Baron Layton (1884–1996), economist, editor and newspaper proprietor. Fellow, Gonville and Caius College, Cambridge, 1909–14; Ministry of Munitions 1914–18; member of Milner mission to Russia and Balfour mission to USA 1917; Editor, *The Economist*, 1922–38; Chairman, *News Chronicle*, 1930–50 and *Star* 1936–50; Director-General, programmes, Ministry of Supply, 1940–2; chief advisor on programmes, Ministry of Production, 1941–3; head of Joint War Production Staff 1942–3.]

** [Julius Salter Elias, Viscount Southwood (1873–1946), printed *John Bull* for Horatio Bottomley, 1906, from whom he bought it 1920; acquired *People* (1925), *Daily Herald* (1929), *Illustrated News Review*, *Sporting Life*, *Woman* and several others. Chairman, Illustrated Newspapers Ltd.]

businesses evacuated from London during the war. The problem was more acute for Department EH than for most, owing to the work of its members being secret in its nature and largely concerned with the enemy. Later on the problem was to become more complicated in the special case of the persons employed in houses for secret broadcasting.

The provision of amenities at Woburn was tackled in the typical British fashion – by the formation of a committee. A Recreation Committee, meeting first in October 1939, busied itself with such matters as finding a squash court and a football field, subscription to a nearby golf club, the hiring of horses and attempting to obtain permission to ride them in Woburn Park, obtaining books from the Times Book Club and elsewhere to form a library, the institution of a weekly cinema show in the Abbey, the establishment of a canteen with a bar, the laying of a dance floor and the providing of Christmas lunch, and the laying out and care of two lawn tennis courts, table tennis, billiards and clock golf. The formation of a choral society and the organisation of lessons in German all followed.

This Committee did much to render life at CHQ tolerable. After six months or so it seems to have died, only to be revived again when new conditions called for further amenities.

Mr Walmsley gives the following impression of Woburn 1939–40:

> Work was apt to go on until the early hours of the morning. This was not quite as arduous as it sounds, since the Lyons canteen was supplemented by an excellent small bar in which you could have five sherries or a reasonable bottle of French claret for half a crown: I was told that one-tenth of the salary bill of the whole Department passed through this bar. Those were also the days in which gallon jars of sherry and bottles of gin enlivened the evening working hours of secretaries and others, somewhat to the surprise of regular civil servants who visited us from time to time. It was not unusual, also for people to take two or three hours off in the afternoon, encouraged in this by Valentine Williams himself. There was wonderful skating on the lakes and the Duke of Bedford's beautiful park was full of interest to the zoologically inclined (Vernon Bartlett used to allege that he had been butted by a llama and bitten by a rhea).

The maintenance of good morale among the staff working at CHQ was a difficult matter, and required continual adjustments. It arose partly from the conditions of enforced secrecy and segregation; partly from the strain of continual preoccupation with enemy conditions which combined to generate a rather unreal mental atmosphere. It grew more difficult as the years went by and was always one of the problems facing the Security Officer.

Those who did not belong to CHQ were inclined to believe that its atmosphere had a damaging effect on the work of the department as a whole. They felt that those indigenous to CHQ tended to regard themselves as the elect and suspected those in London of interfering with, or sabotaging, matters which they were not subtle enough to understand. As nothing in the shape of a combination room had been provided, visiting members of the London staff had nowhere to go between meetings and nowhere to work in the Abbey and consequently felt unwelcome. Apart from this, the atmosphere of Woburn Abbey was one of the strangest that the writer has ever experienced. There was more than a touch of madness about it.

Secret Broadcasting

Sir Stephen Tallents, in his report on lessons of the Munich Crisis,[1] wrote:

> There may be lessons to be deduced from the success with which the apparently mobile Deutsche Freiheitsender,[2] the secret opposition radio station, continued its operations in spite of the vigilance of the Gestapo.

There were many things to be learned, the most fundamental being that the Freiheitsender was not, as it purported to be, in Germany, which was the reason why the Gestapo was unable to do anything about it. The range of a relatively low-powered short-wave transmitter, if properly beamed according to the time of the year, extends to several thousand miles and may extend all over the world. It is directed towards the stratosphere at an angle and follows its original path until it reaches the Heaviside layer from which it is deflected. A short-wave transmission emitted in the heart of England, beamed so as to be audible in Bulgaria, will be audible within a short distance of the transmitter owing to the 'ground wave', but it will be inaudible at a hundred miles away even though it is clearly audible at a 1,000. This was not immediately apprehended by those directing our propaganda and unnecessary schemes for putting short-wave transmitters on to boats were frequently put forward and seriously considered. Short-wave transmitters can be placed wherever is most convenient and, provided the intelligence Service is sufficiently good, can broadcast programmes which bear every mark of local origin. Owing to the likelihood of making such errors, based on faulty intelligence, it is difficult to preserve the illusion that such a broadcasting station is secretly operating among its audience for a long period. Almost inevitably mistakes are made and suspicion begins to be aroused that the broadcasts are not what they appear. As an instrument of subversive propaganda secret broadcasting of this kind is a most potent weapon. So long as the audience believes that the station is operating secretly in its midst, its existence is a symbol of resistance. The Freedom Station is a subject about which thrilling speculations and rumours are perpetually rife; its listeners tend to regard themselves as initiates; to be

1. MIC 15 para., 15, 9.12.38.
2. Probably that operated by Willy Muenzenberg from Paris was meant.

indulgent and uncritical and they are likely to identify themselves with the views expressed, for Resistance is psychologically infectious.

There are few drawbacks from the point of view of those operating the station. Responsibility cannot be brought home and must always be denied; the speakers can take any line, can incite to murder or anything else in safety. As all transmissions can be made from previous recordings, it is simple to take security precautions. Moreover the secret station lends itself to wide variations in type.

It may kindle resistance, of whatever type is required among our friends; it can service the clandestine press and resistance movements after they have come into existence; it can incriminate the enemy or sow dissension among his satellites; it can spread rumours; it can corrupt and debauch the discipline of the enemy's troops, or of certain services. With all this, it is astonishingly cheap to operate compared with long- or medium-wave transmissions. Perhaps the chief limitation during the years 1939 to 1945 was that only a minority of listeners possessed short-wave sets capable of receiving such broadcasts in some countries and that minority belonged to the wealthier sections of society. In those countries where short-wave sets remain a rather expensive luxury, secret broadcasts addressed to the haves are likely to be more successful than those addressed to the have-nots. This does not apply in cases in which the broadcasts are designed to service a Resistance movement or the clandestine press.

In the first six months of the war when there was considerable faith in the opposition within Germany, it was natural for those in EH to wish to set up a Freedom Station which would carry on the good work of the 'apparently mobile Freiheitsender' which had successfully defied the Gestapo from the neighbourhood of Paris.

The first of the RUs, Research Units, or secret broadcasting stations, was started in May 1940. Mr Terry Harman, on Sir Campbell Stuart's instructions, visited France and through the 2e Bureau was able to meet Herr Spieker, or 'Mr Turner' as he was known during his stay at Woburn. Mr Turner's career had been chequered and included having been the leader of a German Frei Korps, a friend of the brothers Strasser, and Polizei-Präsident of Danzig. He may be classed therefore among the unsuccessful gangsters who had fallen foul of the National Socialist Party instead of joining it. For some months he was provided with the means of broadcasting his opinions to Germany on short-wave from what was commonly known as the 'Bahnhof'. Mr Turner, however, did not feel comfortable after the Nazis had reached the channel ports, and by the end of 1940 had transferred himself to the USA.[1]

The engineering side of the work, installation, operation and upkeep of the transmitter was undertaken by the SIS [PASSAGE DELETED ON THE GROUNDS OF NATIONAL SECURITY]. The existence of this station was not without influence on the future of the Department.

1. Information on Herr Spieker was obtained from Mr Harman and Mr Murray.

Department EH becomes SO1

The German conquest of Holland, Belgium and France and the French request for an armistice were to transform the character of British propaganda and it was inevitable that the machinery set up in the hopes of [furt]hering a revolution in Germany would have to be radically overhauled.

At a critical moment, ten days after the fall of France, Sir Campbell Stuart was called away to Canada by his duties as Chairman of the Imperial Communications Advisory Board and took with him his deputy, Captain Herbert Shaw, leaving Mr Valentine Williams as his deputy at CHQ and Colonel Brooks in charge at Electra House. He did not depart, however, without making provision for being secretly consulted on confidential matters, by means of a personal code containing the names of those Cabinet Ministers and departmental officials of the FO, MoI, MEW, etc., whose views were likely to affect the future of Department EH.

On 23rd June, 1940, Sir Campbell Stuart had addressed a letter to Mr Duff Cooper,* Minister of Information, announcing his immediate departure. He had arrived at an agreement with the Minister in which the relations of Department EH, the Ministry of Information and the Foreign Office were clearly defined for the future. Department EH was to retain its separate identity, with Sir Campbell directly responsible to the Minister of Information, and to conduct propaganda into Germany, Poland and Czechoslovakia and propaganda to the German Armies. Department EH was to remain on the Secret Service vote. But the definitions did not deal with the changed aspect of affairs. There was no hint that Department EH should be concerned with propaganda to our allies under German occupation. Difficulties, moreover, arose which made it appear that the 'charter' subscribed to by Sir Campbell Stuart and Mr Duff Cooper would require drastic modifications.

Sir Walter Monckton, Director General of the Ministry of Information, had become aware that Department EH was engaged in secret broadcasting to Germany, or, in the language of Sir Campbell Stuart's code, 'that Father kept a farm', of which he had been kept in ignorance. Sir Walter had up till then believed that under the Charter he was himself responsible for all broadcasts to Germany and 'Topsy' (as he was referred to in the code) was unquestionably angry.

On 10th July Mr Valentine Williams wrote to Sir Walter Monckton offering to explain to him in confidence the nature of these broadcasts, but Sir Walter Monckton was not appeased and replied next day that he would

---

* [Alfred Duff Cooper, 1st Viscount Norwich (1890–1954), entered FO 1913; served Grenadier Guards 1917–18; married Lady Diana Manners 1919; Conservative MP, Oldham, 1924–9; St George's Westminster 1931–45; Secretary for War 1935–7; First Lord of the Admiralty 1937–8, when he resigned in protest at the Munich Agreement; unsuccessful Minister of Information 1940–1; resident Cabinet Minister, Singapore, 1941–2; Chairman, Cabinet committee on security, 1942–4; successful Ambassador to France 1944–7; wrote sublime *Talleyrand* (1932), and autobiography *Old Men Forget* (1953).]

have no further concern with the work of Department EH an that he was explaining to the Minister of Information and to the Secretary of State for Foreign Affairs his reasons for refusing to co-operate in future. This would produce a deadlock. Sir Campbell Stuart was apprised of the turn of events by code in a telegram which ended: 'Family very worried situation generally. Surmise attempt to break Father's (Sir Campbell Stuart's) lease.' In another cable Sir Campbell Stuart was warned that 'the vicar' (Mr Duff Cooper) might seize upon the situation to force through a plan affecting Father's personal position. Sir Campbell Stuart cabled back that Mr Williams was to consult Gladwyn Jebb.* But it was clear from a further cable that Sir Campbell Stuart was fully occupied with his other activities.

During the weeks when these exchanges were taking place, Britain was passing through the greatest moments in her history. The German conquests of Norway and Holland, by a combination of airborne troops and a fifth column of traitors, had revolutionised the outlook of statesmen whose limitation had been an incapacity to believe in what they had not experienced. It is peculiarly fitting, therefore, that the Cabinet memorandum on the organisation of the Home Defence (Security) Executive, set up under Lord Swinton to co-ordinate action against the Fifth Column in Britain, and the setting up of a new organisation to co-ordinate all action by way of subversion and sabotage against the enemy overseas, should have been drawn up and circulated by Mr Neville Chamberlain, who, after giving place to Mr Churchill, had become Lord President of the Council. In this document[1] Mr Dalton,** Minister of Economic Warfare, is nominated chairman of the Special Operations Executive with authority to co-ordinate Sabotage Service 'D', MI(R) and Department EH. Any departmental difficulties which might arise were to be referred to the Lord President of the Council.

Dr Dalton, who had become Minister of Economic Warfare on 15th May, had visited CHQ early in July and had been favourably impressed by what he had seen, and he realised that 'Black' activities, such as secret broadcasts, might play a large part in helping to prevent Germany from

1. Home Defence (Security) Executive, Special Operations Executive. WP(40)271, 19.7.40.

* [Hubert Miles Gladwyn Jebb, 1st Baron Gladwyn (1900–96), entered FO 1924; served in Teheran, Rome and FO; Private Secretary to Permanent Under-Secretary of State 1937–40; acting Assistant Under-Secretary of State, MEW, August 1940; acting Counsellor, FO, 1941; Head of Reconstruction Department 1942, in which capacity he attended conferences of Quebec, Cairo, Teheran, Dumbarton Oaks, Yalta, San Francisco and Potsdam. Acting Secretary-General of UN February 1946; Ambassador to France 1954–60.]

** [(Edward) Hugh Dalton, Baron Dalton (1887–1962), son of Canon John Dalton, chaplain to King George V; Eton, King's College, Cambridge, and friend of Rupert Brooke; served in France and Italy 1914–18; lecturer LSE 1921; reader, London University, 1920–36; author: *Practical Socialism for Britain* (1935); Labour MP, Peckham, 1924–9, Bishop Auckland 1929–31 and 1935–59; refused office in National Government 1931; Minister of Economic Warfare 1940; President of Board of Trade 1942; Chancellor of the Exchequer 1945; nationalised Bank of England 1946; resigned in 1947 after inadvertently giving a budget leak. Life peerage 1950.]

fully exploiting the economic resources of the countries she had recently occupied. On 22nd July the Cabinet approved the memorandum of the Lord President and SOE came into existence with Dr Dalton as chairman and Sir Robert Vansittart* as his principal adviser. Mr Gladwyn Jebb was appointed Dr Dalton's Chief Executive Officer with the rank of Under-Secretary.

It is hardly necessary to say that these changes involved the resignation of Sir Campbell Stuart which took place at the beginning of August.

The new body, SOE, was to consist of two branches. Department EH was to become SO1 and 'D''s organisation and MI(R), both under new direction, were to become SO2. SO1 was to preach subversion and SO2 was to practise sabotage and provide the means for carrying it out.

This dichotomy was to prove disastrous. As we have seen Department EH and Section D overlapped at many points and friction was bound to arise between them. The one method to overcome this would have been to merge them into one Department and this was indeed what had been recommended. But in practice they were never merged. EH was perpetuated as SO1 and Section D was perpetuated as SO2 and friction between the two branches increased, all the more since the heads of the two branches had separate access to the Minister.

Mr Leeper was brought in as the new head of SO1 and was to retain his position as head of the Political Intelligence Department of the Foreign Office. On 13th August Mr Leeper informed Mr Valentine Williams that 'anything to do with propaganda that concerns Dalton and not Duff Cooper under the new agreement is to go to him through myself and Vansittart and not through Jebb'.

Mr Duff Cooper had circulated a document on 18th July to the Prime Minister, the Lord President, the Foreign Minister and Dr Dalton[1] in which he attacked the distinction between propaganda to enemy and enemy-occupied countries (EH) and that to the rest of the world (MoI) and proposing that the distinction should be between European and non-European countries and that the propaganda side of EH should be fused with the Foreign Policy Department of the MoI in order to take care of Europe, and secondly that all broadcasting and leaflet propaganda should be done by the MoI.

Had this been accepted the 'Ministry of Subversion' would have been destroyed before it had been created.

A meeting took place on 1st August, 1940, between Dr Dalton and Mr Duff Cooper which led to an agreement[2] that the dividing line should be

1. In SOE Archives (AD/SI) File CD/I, 10/2a.
2. Dr Dalton's letter of 2.8.40 and Memorandum of Agreement in SOE Archives same file as above.
* [Robert Gilbert Vansittart, Baron Vansittart (1881–1957), entered FO as attaché in Paris 1903; Private Secretary to Secretary of State 1920–4; Private Secretary to Prime Minister 1928–30; Permanent Under-Secretary, FO, 1930–8; opposed appeasement of Germany and so was 'kicked upstairs' to powerless post of chief diplomatic advisor 1938–41.]

between those activities which might be discussed in Parliament and those on which the Government would refuse to allow discussion.

Thus broadcasting would be controlled by Mr Duff Cooper, leaflets and the Country House by Dr Dalton. Mr Duff Cooper was free to establish sections or Departments dealing with all foreign countries and Dr Dalton could do the same, even in neutral territories.

On 17th August the Minister of Economic Warfare informed Mr Valentine Williams that the London headquarters would be shifted from Electra House to Lansdowne House and that the staff would be increased to deal with the enemy-occupied countries of Europe. He also informed Mr Williams that he had appointed Mr Leeper to be Director of subversive propaganda for the whole area, and that he would rank on an equality with Mr Jebb, who would be his Chief Executive Adviser under Sir Robert Vansittart for SO activities. The Minister then formally invited Mr Williams to act as head of the establishment in the country, responsible to Mr Leeper, who in turn would be responsible to Sir Robert Vansittart and himself.

Difficulties with MoI

The formation of SO1 accentuated the difficulties between the Department and the Ministry of Information rather than ended it, since the agreement reached between Dr Dalton and Mr Duff Cooper had put the Department in an impossible position.

A Cabinet decision of 18th November to set up a committee under the Chancellor of the Exchequer (Sir Kingsley Wood)* 'to examine what changes, if any, were necessary in the constitution and management of the BBC in order to ensure its effective control by HMG'[1] gave Dr Dalton an opportunity to raise the issue again.

A battle of memoranda followed. Mr Leeper pointed out[2] that the distinction drawn by the Minister of Information between overt and covert propaganda cut across the intention behind the charter giving Dr Dalton control over subversive propaganda. The MoI in their BBC propaganda to Germany and Italy were animated by subversive motives. The distinction between activities about which parliamentary questions might be asked was artificial as questions might be asked about leaflets.

Shortly afterwards Mr Leeper put forward the further powerful argument that printed and broadcast propaganda were supplementary and must

1. WM290(40) of 18.11.40, item 4.
2. Minute by Mr Leeper on subversive propaganda, 26.11.40.
* [Sir (Howard) Kingsley Wood (1881–1943), solicitor 1903; Conservative MP, West Woolwich, 1918–43; Parliamentary Secretary, Ministry of Health, 1924–9; reforming Postmaster-General 1931–5; Minister of Health 1935–8; Secretary of State for Air 1938–40; as Lord Privy Seal 1940 he was instrumental in effecting the change of PM from Chamberlain to Churchill; Chancellor of the Exchequer 1940–3.]

be under the same control.[1] For example, leaflets were most wanted when our transmissions had to be faded out owing to air raids.

The MoI Case for Control

The questions at issue between the Ministry of Information and the Ministry of Economic Warfare were taken up to a Special Committee of the War Cabinet in December 1940. The Minister of Information submitted[2] that there had grown up in the last few months a division in the control of propaganda. He pointed out that if MEW took over broadcasts it would do away with the distinction between overt and covert propaganda, and that in the case of Holland, Norway, Belgium and Poland control of the BBC involved consultations with the exiled Governments, which would make it difficult for MEW to maintain secrecy. From every point of view the control of leaflets should be 'returned to the MoI'. It was impossible to prevent British newspapers from publishing them. All foreign propaganda should be controlled by one department which might be the MoI or MEW, but if by the latter, the activities of the MoI would be so reduced as hardly to justify its continuance.

The SOE Case

The Minister of Economic Warfare's case was[3] that Department EH had been established at the outbreak of war to conduct all propaganda to the enemy. This followed the experience of the last war when a special department for such propaganda, separate from the Ministry of Information, had also been set up. Germany's conquests in Western Europe and the entry of Italy into the war had in the early summer enlarged substantially the area of enemy territory. But control of propaganda to the occupied territories and even to Italy had not been at once transferred to Department EH. It remained under the MoI. Experience had shown, however, that this arrangement was not only anomalous, but also unsatisfactory. Since propaganda to enemy and enemy-occupied territories was a form of warfare it must be subordinated to a war-strategy associated intimately with anti-Fascist revolutionary activities and planned in closest co-operation with the Chiefs of Staff. Such work must be done by a secret department.

All propaganda against the enemy wherever he is must be subversive. All subversive propaganda must be under one direction, whether its channel of dissemination be open or secret. All propaganda to enemy countries should therefore come under the control of the existing subversive organisation, namely, the SOE.

1. Minute by Mr Leeper on BBC broadcasts to enemy and enemy-occupied countries, 4.11.40.
2. Memorandum dated 14.12.40 (VII a 19).
3. Material for a paper to the Cabinet Special Committee dated 15.12.40.

The paper proposed that responsibility for BBC broadcasts to enemy-occupied countries should therefore come technically under the Foreign Office, which could answer any questions on the subject in Parliament. The result of the enquiry merely confirmed the status quo for a time and the Lord President of the Council did not meet the two Ministers until 16th May, 1941.

The transfer of Department EH to the jurisdiction of the Minister of Economic Warfare had thus not settled the outstanding difficulties of the Department with the Ministry of Information which it is almost superfluous to point out were due to the overlapping functions of Department EH and the Enemy Division of the Overseas Directorate of the MoI. But although the old difficulties with MoI remained, new difficulties had been introduced by its intimate association with SO2.

SO2 Claims

The relationship of SO1 and SO2 as conceived by the latter organisation[1] was that SO2 should be responsible for all activities in the field which were divided into Political Subversion, Sabotage and Underground Propaganda. The two first were no concern of SO1 which, however, supplied SO2 with directions regarding the third, either in the form of actual copy for leaflets, or directives. SO2 would not claim any exclusive right to dissemination of SO1 propaganda and SO1 could arrange for dissemination by other agencies, such as the RAF, provided they had no organisation of their own in the field. Any SO1 specialist sent out would automatically come under SO2. Though SO2 channels of communication were inadequate to carry SO1 material, SO2 claimed that all communications sent out by SO1 through the FO or other channels must pass through the office of SO2.

The SO1 Case

The claims made in this paper by SO2 to control SO1 were vigorously rebutted. In the first place, underground propaganda was only a small and not the most important part of SO1 activities; in the second,[2] 'for SO1 to give a directive to SO2's people is not enough. Those who carry out a directive, which can only be telegraphed, can only do so adequately if they are trained and think along the same lines as those who give it. . . . Moreover, many of the directives can best be conveyed through other channels than SO2's communications. The personal links established over a long period between SO1's Military Wing and the Service Departments cannot be transferred to SO2 without serious loss of efficiency.' Mr Leeper pointed out that though SO1 would not wish to have a 'field force' of its own, it

1. Minute from Lt Colonel Taylor to Gladwyn Jebb, 17.11.40.
2. Comments on paper by Mr Taylor to Mr Jebb by R. A. Leeper, 25.11.40.

would require representatives responsible for the whole field of propaganda directed against the enemy. In a covering letter to the Minister of Economic Warfare,[1] Mr Leeper coupled the lack of control of the BBC and the lack of comprehension of the scope of SO1 by SO2 as factors which he found increasingly disturbing.

> In SOE propaganda and activities are linked, but the main propaganda links are outside SOE altogether and the link with SO2 is quite secondary. So far as SO1 is concerned SO2 is merely part of the machinery (and only a part of it) for carrying out our propaganda. The machinery of other Government Departments, especially the Service Departments, and of the BBC is very much more important. We must be free to use all the machinery available both at home and abroad for our propaganda purposes and it is to my mind a complete misreading of the positions to lay down a rule that abroad SO2 should operate for SO1 and that our representatives abroad should be under SO2.

No action was taken, however, by the Minister to reconcile his warring Departments (for they had in fact remained separate).

In retrospect, it became apparent to many of the officers of both PWE and SOE, particularly those on the level of Director, that so long as the Departments remained separate, an important part of the work of organising resistance in German-occupied Europe would not be properly carried out. The original plan for a single department of subversion and special operations was sound. It is difficult not to believe that had its constituents been fused on its formation and regional directors appointed responsible for all forms of political warfare and subversion and special operations within their areas, the work of both of what became PWE and what remained SOE might have been carried out more efficiently on a larger scale. Certainly there would have been none of the jealousies and disputes in the field, and in the council chamber, which form the subject of many tedious pages in this history.

Developments in Secret Broadcasting

By the summer of 1940, the value of the secret transmitter was realised and immediately after the formation of SO1, plans were discussed for setting up German, Italian and French teams which were to be lodged in separate houses and kept as far as possible apart. The history of some of these RUs will be dealt with separately.

The emergence of the secret broadcast, as a weapon of propaganda, compensated, to some extent, for the disappointment which was felt at the results of the early EH leaflets and the refusal, on the part of the Air Ministry, to undertake leafleting except as incidental to bombing.

---

1. Minute by R. A. Leeper to the Minister of Economic Warfare, 25.11.40.

At the first meeting held after the formation of SO1, a project for starting an international Communist station to broadcast in German was mentioned.[1] During the following weeks, offers were made to Mr Darsie Gillie to take control of a French Freedom Station which it was hoped could be done without interfering with his work on the BBC.

By 28th September, 1940, the proposed Communist German station had been transformed into a left-wing station but had not begun operations owing to the difficulty of recruiting staff.

Several RU speakers were obtained from internment camps in the Isle of Man.

By the middle of November 1940, the *Das Wahre Deutschland* was closed and the Neu-beginn RU started with Mr Crossman as housemaster. By the same date a Roumanian and an Italian RU, both of the Freedom Station type, were started.

Sefton Delmer

David [in fact Denis] Sefton Delmer had spent years of his boyhood in Berlin and he spoke German perfectly, with a special knowledge of Berlin slang. Like many leading members of the Department, he had been a journalist writing for Lord Beaverbrook's newspapers in the years before the war. As such he had lived again in Berlin and had become a personal friend of leading members of the Nazi Party; as such [he] had been in Madrid during the siege in the Spanish Civil War. In the early part of 1940, he had broadcast frequently in the BBC German service, but he found the atmosphere of the BBC uncongenial and, in November and December, he visited Lisbon in order to renew personal contacts with enemies of the Nazi regime who would assist him to carry out his ideas. He found his own views on political warfare to Germany were shared by these men.

'For talks, one of the best subjects[2] is corruption of leaders. We should serve up inside dope which is new and true. Talks should strike a tough note frequently, should be rude and robustly abusive.'

Delmer's conception of the possibilities of secret broadcasting, strongly supported by Leonard Ingrams, was revolutionary. Delmer and Ingrams had always favoured the kind of propaganda which aims at inducing action on the part of the listener. What he believed seemed to them of quite secondary importance if he could be made to act in the desired manner. The kinds of action which they regarded as desirable were those subversive to the German Reich and damaging to the German war machine and they thought that such action might be produced by the listener's self interest. The method of imparting news items designed for this purpose was to be that of such newspapers as the *Daily Mirror*, which, by denouncing vice, secure a large circulation among those who wish to read about it.

---

1. Meeting held by Mr Leeper, 31.8.40.
2. Letter to Leonard Ingrams, 8.12.40.

Delmer proposed therefore to denounce the corruption and morals of the Nazi leaders, to relate with the virtuous airs of an upright Party man, the abominations practised by the corrupt. Interspersed with scandals and open pornography, he would put out news items which led the listener to believe that it was easy to behave in an anti-social way and to escape the consequences.

Hitler's famous dictum that propaganda should be couched so as to be understood by the members of the audience with the lowest intellectual level, was interpreted in terms of emotional appeal – that is to say that the emotional appeal was to those with the lowest instincts.

Delmer's ideas were not immediately welcomed in the German region of SO1, where Mr R. S. Crossman was devoting much of his time to the Neu-beginn RU for which he acted as housemaster and for which Mrs Crossman acted as housekeeper. The policy of 'Neu-beginn', which was the only one compatible with HMG policy of 'toughness' to Germany and with the refugee personnel available, appealed to their political idealism. Its appeal was still to the 'good German'. But it occurred to Leonard Ingrams that an RU of a different character might be wanted to send code messages in German for SO2 and, when SO2 backing [had] been secured, Delmer's plans went ahead.

Delmer's Assistants on GS1

To help run his station Delmer brought in two men: Ernst Adam (also known as Bedam), who had been adjutant to Kléber, the defender of Madrid, and later Chief of Staff to General Duran. In the early months of the present war Adam had worked for Willy Muenzenberg's Freedom Station which broadcast from Paris. The second man selected by Delmer was Alexander Mass, who had started life as an actor and then became a broadcaster in the Moscow German propaganda programme. During the Spanish Civil War Mass had been a captain in the International Brigade when he first met Delmer. In the early months of the war he was the chief speaker and scriptwriter in Willy Muenzenberg's Freedom Station. Delmer had, however, to wait for these assistants. Adam's arrival was delayed as he had been put by SO2 on board a British cruiser which took part in the pursuit of the *Bismarck*, and landed him in West Africa on his way to Woburn. Alexander Mass, who had escaped from a concentration camp in Oran, was on his way to Mexico before he could be intercepted at Bermuda. Meanwhile, the Minister of Economic Warfare was anxious that the new RU should start operations at once. It was begun on 16th May by Delmer with the assistance of Peter Secklmann, a corporal in the Auxiliary Pioneer Corps, at Larchfield. The house therefore bore the initials LF. Later Mr and Mrs Reinholz joined the team, but after a trial of a few months were got rid of.

After the new station, Gustav Siegfried Eins, had been broadcasting for perhaps a fortnight, its purpose was outlined by Mr Leeper in the following terms:

> The station aims to strike at the roots of totalitarianism with individualistic sentiments, the appeal of which is reinforced by the very nature of man. . . . In order to accelerate the corruption of Germany it seeks to poison the souls of individual Germans by guiding their attention, under the pose of right-mindedness, to the pleasures and benefits of avarice, crime, greed, the lusts of the flesh and all the rest. It seeks to foment envy, suspicion, hatred and so on by indirect comment . . . it is hoped more and more it will be issuing actual instructions in the service of SO2.[1]

On the same date Delmer defined the aims of his station as follows:

> 1. The objective of LF is subversive. We want to spread disturbing and disruptive news among the Germans which will induce them to distrust their government and disobey it, not so much from high-minded political motives as from ordinary human weakness (for which, however, we shall be delighted to supply a high-minded political excuse).
> 2. We are making no attempt to build up a political following in Germany. We are not catering for idealists.
> 3. Our politics are a stunt. We pretend we have an active following to whom we send news and instructions. The purpose of this is to provide ourselves with a platform from which to put over our stuff.
> 4. We therefore make no attempt to provide our listeners with a political programme.
> 5. Our listeners are intended to feel they are eavesdropping on the private wireless of a secret organisation, whose members presumably know what the programme of the organisation is. What the listener learns of this programme he picks up by studying the news that we put over. He finds that we are anti-communists who once thought Hitler pretty good, fought alongside him in fact, but are now appalled at the corruption, godlessness, profiteering, place-hunting, selfishness, clique rivalries, party-above-the-law system, which the party has instituted.
>
> Gustav Eins is appalled at the left swing in social politics which is coming under the aegis of the Hitler-Stalin hook-up and which is going to give the party bureaucrats even greater power.
> 6. GS1 by its organisation is able to get plenty of news from everywhere inside Hitler Europe, news which all tends to show directly, or (preferably) indirectly, that every man for himself is the axiom every intelligent German should be following.
> 7. We have already put over directly and by implication
>
> That Wehrmacht soldiers, the best element in the Volk, are being bumped off in Himmelfahrtskommandos, while the SS party police are being given cushy jobs at home to make Germany safe for the Partei.

1. Leonard Ingrams to R. A. Leeper, 8.6.41.

That party Blockwaerte and such people are keeping back the news of soldiers' relatives killed in air raids.

That it is ridiculous to fire-watch in factories while your own home is burning down through lack of a fire-watcher and your children burned to death.

That while the party bosses go off to Dubrovnik and other nice safe places for their holidays, they ask us ordinary Germans to stay at home and be bombed during our holidays.

And masses of stuff proving the corruption of the machine, the selfishness of its leaders. We concentrate our attacks on the lesser known local leaders.

We shall be putting over a line on food racketeering which is intended to make people buy and sell even more in the Black Markets than at present.

We have told of the passive sabotage the population of Vorarlberg has been carrying on against the unpopular Nazi leaders, in the hope that this undetectable sabotage may appeal to some of our listeners and be carried out by them.[1]

Pornography as Listeners' Bait

Delmer did not scruple to introduce passages of extreme indecency which undoubtedly did much to attract an audience quickly. But, unfortunately for the peace of the Department, the 'ground-wave' of the beamed broadcasts could be picked up easily near Woburn, and sometimes in London, and programmes intended to attract the thugs of the SS had their British eaves-droppers. There were repeated protests from the Foreign Office, and Mr Leeper had to become the unwilling apologist for matter which was extremely distasteful to him.

Sir Stafford Cripps'* Scruples and Views

[1941]
A year after GS1 had been broadcasting, the Secretary of PWE was greeted by Sir Stafford Cripps, then Lord Privy Seal, with the words, 'I am sorry you belong to that beastly pornographic organisation' and stated that he intended to take up the matter of GS1 with the Secretary of State for Foreign Affairs or if necessary with the Cabinet. 'To what sort of audience could it possibly appeal?' demanded Sir Stafford. 'Only to the thug section

1. Delmer to Leonard Ingrams forwarded to R. A. Leeper, 8.6.41.

* [Sir (Richard) Stafford Cripps (1889–1952), son of Lord Parmoor, nephew of Beatrice Webb; devout Christian Socialist; Labour MP, Bristol East, 1931–50; proposed Popular Front 1936; expelled from Labour Party 1939–45; Ambassador to Russia 1940–2; Leader of the House of Commons and Lord Privy Seal 1942; Minister of Aircraft Production 1942–5; President of the Board of Trade 1945–7; Chancellor of the Exchequer 1947–50.]

of the Nazi Party who are no use to us anyway.' In Sir Stafford's opinion, our RUs should concentrate on giving messages of hope and sympathy to the 'good Germans' on whom we should rely to rebuild Germany after the Nazis were defeated.[1]

Fortunately, however, GS1 had acquired such a large audience that Delmer was able to omit grosser indecencies, while continuing to employ abusive and coarse language. The programme proved to have an immense appeal for German listeners and its single speaker 'Der Chef' became a famous figure, remembered in Germany and discussed, to the present time, three years after the station closed down.

The US Berlin Embassy on GS1

Most listeners to GS1 took for granted that the station was inside Germany, and the US Embassy in Berlin devoted considerable attention to it as indicating the existence of a powerful opposition group.

> The illegal broadcasting station Siegfried 1 supposedly transmitting inside Germany, operates daily on the 31.5 metre band taking the air at 7 minutes to the hour. Using violent and unbelievably obscene language, this station criticised the actions of the Party and certain party-favoured officers, especially the SS. Superficially it is violently patriotic and is supposed by many German officers to be supported by the German Wehrmacht in secret. A very large number of Germans listen to this station, and often names, dates, and addresses are given in such detail that it may be assumed that the statements could be quickly discredited if no background existed. When there is no air-raid warning, the station is heavily interfered with, but during alarms, it comes in very clearly. Various explanations are given as to the ability of this station to continue operating. The most reasonable is that it is worked automatically with records and has been found several times in odd places wholly unattended. When found and destroyed a similar set is put up elsewhere. The station has been operating for about four months.[2]

Method of Operating GS1

The possibility of producing a programme such as GS1 depended upon a constant flow of detailed intelligence, particularly of a scandalous sort – the kind of gossip in which high-ranking officers of the Wehrmacht and the SS might be expected to indulge when they were perfectly secure from being overheard. Such intelligence was to be found in the Top Secret CSDIC reports on prisoners of war and the success of GS1 was assured when General Rawlinson realised that it was perfectly safe for him to supply Sefton

1. Private information.
2. Report from US Embassy in Berlin to Washington, dated 8.9.41.

Delmer with the essential material of these reports which were scrambled and made anonymous before they were seen by any of the German staff working for Delmer. Censorship intercepts, captured mail and letters and diaries found on German casualties and prisoners of war were also invaluable sources supplying authentic details on which Delmer could build up a story. All such intelligence supplied to Black was exclusive and the greatest care had to be exercised in its use. For example, an American woman, Mrs Geneva Stribling Wolff-Limper, married to a German and herself an ardent pro-Nazi, was in the habit of writing to her sister in the USA through an intermediary in Switzerland. This correspondence was found to provide a rich mine of material for 'Gussie'. Unfortunately a request to allow this correspondence to continue addressed to the American censorship passed through the hands of Mr James Warburg, Director of OWI [Office of War Information] in Great Britain. As Mr Warburg also saw the monitored broadcasts of GS1 it was thought that it might jeopardise the cover of GS1 if this material were used.

Co-operation of the Service Departments

The co-operation of the Service Departments in the provision of Intelligence of every sort and kind was not one-sided as GS1 provided them with exactly the cover they required in order to put out the kind of rumours which they wished German soldiers, sailors and airmen to believe. The Admiralty were particularly quick to realise the importance of Delmer's work and Lieutenant Commander McLachlan was authorised to put the resources of the operational propaganda unit in the Admiralty at Delmer's disposal. This marked the beginning of attempts to use Black propaganda for operational purposes and to promote a free flow of all grades of secret information to Delmer and his staff. Out of this collaboration grew Atlantik and Calais and Radio Livorno. The example set by the Director of Naval Intelligence, Rear-Admiral Godfrey,* was gradually followed by the Air Ministry Intelligence with enthusiasm and complete confidence, by the War Office with cautious and limited interest. The experience gained was to make possible the complete and intimate collaboration of 'Black' with the highest level of SHAEF [Supreme Headquarters Allied Expeditionary Force].

Mr Walmsley's Sketch of Delmer

As there can be no question that Sefton Delmer made the largest personal contribution to Political Warfare during the war, a sketch of the man and of his methods of work, from the impartial hand of Mr Walmsley, will not be out of place.

* [Rear-Admiral John Henry Godfrey (1888–1971) served in Gallipoli campaign 1917–19; commanded battle cruiser *Repulse* 1936–8; Director of Naval Intelligence 1939–42; flag officer commanding Royal Indian Navy 1943–6; admiral 1945. After clashes with Churchill as DNI, he was the only officer of his rank to receive no official recognition for his war service.]

'I hope the history of Delmer's unit is being written separately and given as much importance as at least the whole of the rest of PWE.

'I think Delmer joined in May 1941. At that time there were weekly meetings in Leeper's room attended by Delmer, Crossman, Voigt and myself and (I believe) Adams, Barry and Ritchie Calder.* These meetings often degenerated into long tirades by Voigt against the methods of British propaganda. He was, however, totally unsympathetic to the idea of anything but the whitest of white propaganda and seemed unable to distinguish between propaganda to different audiences. At these meetings Delmer used to assume an attitude of innocence and modesty. It was fairly clear from the outset that Delmer and Crossman were incompatibles, not only in character but in their approach to propaganda. Delmer, however, never gave Crossman (his titular superior) any reason for suspecting "disloyalty", and the only effect of the incompatibility (I believe) was to slow down the taking over by Delmer of all black propaganda. In case it is not recorded elsewhere, it is easy to forget that at first Delmer controlled only one small black station and that his control of black leaflets and of Crossman's "European Revolution" station (really the BBC in sheep's clothing) came at rather a late stage. Delmer never asked to control anything extra until it seemed not only ripe but overripe.

'Although Delmer almost at once set up his own intelligence section in the country, I myself was a regular visitor at his house. He was not only an indefatigable but an unceasing worker, and after dinner, from nine until one or two in the morning, discussions on new projects and new themes were broken only by intervals of listening to his own station or even to rival ones.

'On the use of refugees, Delmer always had the greatest contempt for the BBC staff, but maintained that there were excellent refugees to be used if you knew where to find them. In support of this he had indeed acquired an astonishingly good team from the point of view not only of talent but of character. Even so, in spite of anything he may say himself, it was his training which made them what they were. Even the "Corporal", probably one of the most successful radio voices in Europe, filled Delmer with such despair that on the twelfth day he was on the point of giving him up altogether. The more one reflects the more one appreciates Delmer's complete singleness of purpose and untiring application to work. I have seen him squatting on his vast settee at RAG reading through a paragraph of a talk, not once or twice but literally dozens of times, muttering crossly to himself as he did so, then sending the wretched composer off to change a few words and repeating the same process with the same talk about once an hour for three or four hours

* [Peter Ritchie Calder, Baron Ritchie-Calder (1906–82), was a socialist author and journalist who worked on the *Daily News* (1926–30), *Daily Chronicle* (1930) and *Daily Herald* (1930–41); vividly covered the Blitz 1940; appointed to PWE 1941; life peer 1966.]

on end. Stopping, in the middle of a sentence, a worried wrinkle would appear on his large brow, and, retrieving at least one of his shoes and giving his braceless trousers a heave, he would stump rapidly out of the room to impart a new brilliant idea to one of his writers, probably by that time in bed. I do not know whether his hold on his refugees was strengthened or shaken by exhibiting in his sitting room a trophy – a shield bearing the words: "Hier sind Juden unerwünscht", allegedly captured in Germany by C. E. Stevens and smuggled out in a side-car.'

SO1 Political Warfare to France

[June, 1940]
The rejection of Mr Churchill's offer of common citizenship, the refusal to carry on the fight from North Africa, and the appeal to Hitler for an armistice produced an almost pathological shock on many Englishmen, and in the moments of French collapse there were few in Britain who could set themselves at once to the immense task of rehabilitating the morale of the French people because they never despaired of them. The realisation of that need was present in the MoI and in those who expanded the BBC news service in French into 'Ici la France', as the programme of 'Les Français parlent aux Français' was originally called. Although Mr Ralph Murray had urged the need to stress the evacuation of French Divisions at Dunkirk in order to forestall German allegations that the British had run away and left the French in the lurch, such a realisation was not generally present in Department EH. With despairing and unbalanced views in the ascendant, it was fortunate that overt propaganda to France during this critical period was an MoI responsibility.[1]

The BBC French Service

During the whole of the SO1 period the BBC French European Service was under the control of the MoI and there was a weekly meeting with Sir Maurice Peterson in the chair attended by Oliver Harvey,* Raymond

---

1. Mr Leeper stated: 'French Anglo-phobia is increasing and will increase as time goes on,' and Monsignor Vance stated that: 'The French must be regarded definitely as enemies.' Minutes of Planning Committee, 29.6.40. Nor was the latter aberration momentary as the Monsignor returned to the charge: 'The French in England have become the most dangerous enemies with which this country has to deal.' Minutes of Planning Committee, 13.7.40, and followed this up by attacks on the BBC programme 'Ici la France'. Minutes of Planning Committee, 3.8.40.

* [Oliver Charles Harvey, 4th baronet and 1st Baron Harvey of Tasburgh (1893–1968), diplomat and diarist. Served in France and Palestine 1914–18; entered FO 1919; Private Secretary to Anthony Eden 1936 and to Lord Halifax 1938; Minister in Paris 1939; Private Secretary to Eden 1941–3; Assistant Under-Secretary, FO, 1943; Deputy Under-Secretary 1946; Ambassador to Paris 1948–54. Diaries published posthumously: *Diplomatic Diaries 1937–1940* (1970) and *War Diaries 1941–1945* (1978).]

Mortimer,* Darsie Gillie (Head of BBC French Region) and after his appointment in September 1940, Dr Beck (SO1), at which a directive was drafted.

Staff of the BBC French Service

At that time and throughout the remainder of the war, a main factor dominating the character of the BBC French Service was that many of its members were experts many of whom brought great professional talent to the microphone. There were thus never any of the technical difficulties in 'building up' personality speakers without broadcasting experience or perfect linguistic qualifications which so hampered the output of the BBC Service to Germany. Practically all the speakers were French and most of them were either famous actors or broadcasters. One and all were inspired by the greatness of their mission and had complete faith in their ultimate success. The French programme was therefore from its inception, in July 1940, technically a first-class programme of high artistic merit, and passionately sincere.

The BBC French Service had also the immense advantage of being staffed by Frenchmen, many of whom had just returned from the field.[1] It was thus able to rely for several months on their past experience and their intuition as regards the future. It did however, from very early on, find it necessary that the line of policy, intuitive though it might be, should be set down in black and white and rigidly adhered to. Thus a fortnightly directive for the French BBC Services was written in the French Region of the BBC itself – it was a detailed document which often amounted to fourteen pages. The fact that this was found necessary is a clear proof that the MoI directive was not adequate.

The period during which the BBC French Service was a responsibility of the MoI was a time of great strain. But the editor, Darsie Gillie, was a courageous man and a born fighter, and the output during this period remained at a very high level and no major mistakes of policy were made. Thanks very largely to the BBC French Services, the population of France realised that Britain was not going to be defeated and would carry on the struggle indefinitely, if necessary, until victory. Once this had been appreciated the majority of Frenchmen became strongly pro-British, and incidents like Mers-el-Kebir did little to shake their support.

In the period under review, the BBC French Services were handicapped by the lack of transmitter time available. In January 1941[2] the BBC French Services consisted of:

---

1. Jacques Duchesne (Michel Saint Denis) was one of the French troops evacuated from Dunkirk.
2. Annex to Z 488/244/17 Memorandum on French propaganda from London prepared in the FO, 27.1.41.

* [(Charles) Raymond (Bell) Mortimer (1895–1980), literary and art critic. Cipher clerk, FO, 1918; literary editor, *New Statesman*, 1935–47; Ministry of Information 1940–1; chief reviewer, *Sunday Times*, 1952–80.]

Seven news bulletins daily, prepared by the British staff of the BBC French section.
Talks and features following on the news including bulletins addressed to Catholics, to women, to doctors and chemists and to youth.
A five minutes' labour talk given with the early morning news bulletin prepared by M. Henri Hauk, and vetted by the MoI.
A bi-weekly programme of 'Les Français parlent aux Français' prepared by the French staff of the BBC and vetted by the British staff of the BBC but not by the MoI.
A bi-weekly programme by Les Forces Français Libres, prepared and broadcast by General de Gaulle's organisation and submitted to the MoI.
Broadcasts in Moorish Arabic for French North Africa.

The Foreign Office memorandum quoted above raised objections to the Labour talks since they might lead to the view that a British victory would mean a return to the *Front Populaire*. The memorandum also stressed the need for censoring General de Gaulle's propaganda including his own speeches.

Requests for the services of Mr Darsie Gillie first in a consultative capacity, and secondly as the SO1 French Regional Director, were made to the BBC in September 1940 by Mr Leeper but without success. Professor Denis Brogan was accordingly appointed Regional Director in October 1940, but only held the post for four or five months. In a letter on his removal[1] he complained that he had no direct access to the Free French authorities, that he was not informed of SO1 policy and that a member of the Planning Committee had usurped his authority. But he paid the following tribute to the work of the BBC French Services.

Professor Denis Brogan on the BBC French Service

'The French BBC broadcasts have been extremely successful, the most successful of all our foreign broadcasts because they have not been too obviously tendentious, because they have given news and because they have allowed the creation of a personal relationship between broadcasters and listeners. A broadcaster is, and must be, a personality to be effective. The French broadcasters for the BBC, Duchesne, Bourdan, etc., have their own fans.'

Lack of French Intelligence

The BBC French Service, however, met with great difficulties during its first year. These were principally owing to an absence of an adequate supply of intelligence, and guidance of the right kind. This lack was not due to neglect by the MoI since no Government Department after the fall of

1. From Mr Denis Brogan to Mr Valentine Williams, 27.3.41.

France had any adequate supply of intelligence on France; indeed there were no sources except monitoring. The first task after the formation of SO1 French Region was to obtain intelligence and supplies of material from the French press were laid on through Lisbon. But no preparations had been made to lay in documents and reference books. There was nothing comparable to what had been done for the German Department as far back as the autumn of 1938. For example, no copy of the Bottin or Commercial Directory[1] which is to be found in almost every French café for the convenience of commercial travellers was available and this essential work was eventually procured through [the] US Embassy at Vichy. There was, moreover, a complete lack of the kind of material needed for Black Political Warfare: such things as letter headings of Government Departments, Banks, Chambers of Commerce, Gendarmerie, Prefectures, etc. All essential material which it would have been perfectly easy to lay in before the collapse of France was lacking.

Although large numbers of both French and British arrivals reached this country for several months after the collapse of France, there was no system organised for collecting political intelligence from them. Security measures were organised by MI5 and arrivals were detained at RPS for varying periods, but no system was organised through MI19 and MI6 by which political warfare intelligence was obtained from them until the beginning of 1942 – that is to say for eighteen months after the need for it was first urgently felt. This is not to say that no intelligence was obtained [from] them, since many, after release from the RPS, volunteered information when reporting to the Free French authorities, or sought interviews at the BBC in order to impart it.

SO2 Not Equipped for Work in France

While recording the lack of intelligence in this period it should be mentioned that SO2 was not in a position to provide any. France was an entirely new area and 'D' had made no [more] provision for the defeat of France than had any other Government organisation. SOE had indeed been called into existence in order to deal with the situation but time was needed before it could function. The position was described in these words:[2]

> It is no use attempting to introduce agents into the Continent until a number of properly trained, reliable men are available . . . to send out untrained men is obviously far worse than useless – it merely puts everything back and exposes our plans to the enemy. What therefore I should like to emphasise above all else is that for the moment and probably for some time to come, we are simply not in a position to effect any major sabotage operation in Western Europe . . . or even to do

1. A copy of the Bottin was obtained quite unofficially, through the American diplomatic bag.
2. Subversion, a memorandum by Gladwyn Jebb, 5.10.40.

> anything at all beyond sending an occasional man for the principal purpose of collecting our own type of intelligence.

Nor was 'C' in any better position to supply the type of intelligence in the quantities required. The first task of SO1 was therefore to obtain access to the required sources of intelligence and to build up an intelligence unit capable of supplying the needs of both Black and White propaganda.

Views on how the 'occasional man' should be sent in and the tasks he should fulfil were being put forward[1] at the same date by Nicholas Bodington, who was attached to the planning division of SOE under Brigadier van Cutsem. Mr Bodington pointed out the lack of intelligence owing to the absence of trained observers, the danger of thinking of the French in terms of De Gaullists, Monarchists and political intellectuals whereas the small labourer, craftsman, farmer and employee formed the mass of the population. It was necessary to plant agents among these classes competent to observe them scientifically and to spread propaganda whispers among them.

'Our work is for the most part psychological – that is to say that it is to prepare the minds of these people so that their physical reactions and efforts may later be to our advantage, and that they may be ready to take the later directives with regard to sabotage, etc.'

Mr Bodington proposed exploratory visits and surveys of about three weeks and favoured the more normal methods of getting into the country, with business or repatriation cover. He was in contact with a number of suitable Frenchmen who were being 'vetted' for this work.

Such views found acceptance in SO2 before they commanded assent in SO1. Thus in a discussion on the policy to be adopted in regard to training agents[2] Mr Jebb stated that our best hopes for arousing opposition to Germany lay among the industrial workers and our first efforts should be to train agents suitable for working among them, whereas Mr Leeper, supported by Mr Tower of PID, stated that we could not encourage a left-wing revolt as it would offend General Weygand. If there was to be a revolt it must be led by someone of position and most men of position, such as Weygand and Nogués, would not be associated with a left-wing movement. These arguments did not impress Dr Dalton who supported Mr Jebb and it was decided that the first agents should be men suitable for organising opposition among the working classes.

Secret Broadcasts to France during SO1 Period. Policy

From the first an important policy division was made between White and Black. On White it was considered injudicious to make personal attacks on

1. Note by N. Bodington of 7.10.40, minuted on by M. C. F. Warner and Mr Kingsbury.
2. Policy to France. Note of a meeting held 17.11.40, attended by Minister of Economic Warfare, Sir R. Vansittart, Mr Gladwyn Jebb, Mr Leeper, Mr V. Williams, Professor Brogan, etc.

Marshal Pétain for two reasons – the first that we were not anxious to underline the differences between the British and American attitude to Marshal Pétain, and the second was that we could never be perfectly sure that Marshal Pétain would not transfer himself to North Africa and inaugurate an anti-German policy from there. Though the emergence of Marshal Pétain as active leader of resistance was in the highest degree improbable, there was always a possibility that the feeble and aged statesman might be persuaded to board a plane and find himself in North Africa. Such a development would be politically embarrassing in any case, but it would be far more so if we had been openly attacking him as a renegade and traitor to France. A third reason, which was put forward, was that the majority of Frenchmen in 1940 felt personal respect for the Marshal, as a hero of the defence of Verdun in the last war. For these reasons then, there was a ban on direct personal attacks upon Marshal Pétain in the BBC French Service – a ban which did not extend, however to the spokesman of the Free French, M. Maurice Schuman.

In our secret broadcasts which purported to be inside France, there was no limit to the violence with which Marshal Pétain could be assailed.

The first problem confronting the SO1 French Region was to obtain speakers for Black who could compare with Duchesne, Bourdon, Oberle and Schuman on the BBC. SO2 were willing and eager not only to help in finding such men, but to share in their employment afterwards.

The French RUs were numbered F1, F2, F3, F4 and F5, but a complication is that F1 was first used to refer to Radio Inconnue, which was supposed to make right-wing appeal to the petit bourgeois, and F2 was used to refer to Radio Travail, which addressed itself to the industrial workers of the North. In practice Radio Inconnue specialised in violent attacks on Marshal Pétain and Vichy, whereas Radio Travail appealed more and more to the Conservative trade unionist elements. For this reason after August 1941 these two stations were re-numbered, Radio Travail becoming F1 and Radio Inconnue F2.

Radio Travail (F2 until August 1941, F1 after August 1941)

Radio Travail started in late November 1940, at the same time as Radio Inconnue. At all events according to Dr Beck both were in operation for some weeks before Christmas 1940, the house being TOR with Mr Kingsbury as housemaster.

Domestic Difficulties of F1 and F2

The need for maintaining an appearance of authenticity was not fully realised at first as Dr Beck discovered, just in time, that Radio Inconnue and Radio Travail were proposing to broadcast a joint programme on Christmas Eve as a method of celebrating the festivity. This lapse led to the introduction of far stricter security regulations. Unfortunately the above incident cannot be taken as evidence of perfect harmony between the two teams. The only speaker on Radio Travail until 29th July, 1941, was an ex-miner from the Lille area, who lived at TOR with his wife and children. As they belonged to the French working class, and the speakers on Radio Inconnue (Mr Kingsbury and Miss Mainwaring) were bourgeois, the miner and his family ate in the kitchen, and the bourgeois ate in the dining room and appropriated the drawing room for their leisure hours. This was endurable at first, but when a professional syndicalist organiser who was, unlike the miner, an educated man, was recruited as an additional speaker on Radio Travail, ill-feeling was aroused by his preferring the British bourgeois group in the dining room to the society of his humbler compatriots. The miner could not write his own scripts and friction arose between him and the housemaster who was the chief speaker on Radio Inconnue, in the course of their composition. The consequences of this ill-feeling were unfortunate. On 4th October, 1941, Radio Travail announced that the 'ouvrier' had been arrested in the neighbourhood of Lille[1] and he did not speak again.

The strain of living in one of the RU houses was great and it would appear inadvisable to have two teams, drawn from different social classes living in one house.

Character of Radio Travail

Radio Travail appealed from the first to the revolutionary traditions of Republican France and the greater part of its hate theme, as befitted a station in the occupied North, was reserved for the Germans. Specific attacks on Laval, Pétain, Darlan,* etc., were frequent.

In the early summer of 1941 the talks became more 'operational', advocating various forms of passive resistance and minor sabotage. By the autumn of 1941, considerable space was given to the subject of sabotage. The speakers dissociated themselves from both Communism and De Gaullism and always drew a distinction between the German working class and the Nazis. The example of Russian resistance and Russian readiness to adopt a scorched-earth policy were held up to admiration.

Radio Travail concentrated, however, almost entirely on internal affairs and put out detailed information on French internal politics. 'Darlan's private police are said to have informed him that there must be a Free Frenchman in the Vichy Cabinet as the information in "Travail" broadcasts

1. This announcement would scarcely have been made if he had really been arrested as his comrades would not have wished to inform the Gestapo of the fact. In actual fact, Mr Kingsbury had become convinced that the miner and his wife were extremely dangerous, and on his representations they were lodged in British gaols, from which, after considerable difficulties, they were liberated by the united exertions of Colonel Chambers and Dr Beck.

* [Admiral Jean Louis Xavier François Darlan (1881–1942), *capitaine de corvette* 1918; flag rank 1929; Minister of the Navy, Vice-President of the Council of Ministers, and Secretary of State for Foreign Affairs. In early days of the Vichy Government he was Minister for National Defence. Representing the Vichy regime in French North Africa, he co-operated with the Anglo-American forces in 1942 until his assassination by a young Gaullist in late December.]

could only be supplied by someone in the Cabinet itself. They say that it is not a question of leakage through careless talk by the Ministers – the information is too regular.'[1]

After the departure of the 'ouvrier', the 'syndicaliste' continued as the only speaker. The following spring it was decided to close Radio Travail[2] owing to the lack of intelligence on the subject of organised labour in France and the tendency of the speaker to express himself in pre-war formulas and language and Radio Travail was closed finally on 14th May, 1942. M. Henri Hauk, who had originally supplied the 'syndicaliste', agreed to apply for his full-time services and it was thus possible to close the RU without leaving him with the impression that he was being got rid of.

One incident[3] in connection with F1 deserves record as it illustrates one of the security difficulties of running several RUs from the same premises. The billiard room at Simpson's was used as a waiting room by speakers about to record. Owing to the walls not being sound proof, 'the syndicaliste' overheard the Gaulliste speakers recording for F4, of the existence of which he had been ignorant. He resigned on the spot and was only with difficulty persuaded to withdraw his resignation and continue his work.

F2 Radio Inconnue (Known as F1 prior to August 1941)

Dr Beck's statement that this station began broadcasting in November 1940 must be accepted in preference to the date of 2nd January, 1941, given elsewhere.[4]

The chief speakers on this station unlike all other French RUs were British – Mr Kingsbury and Miss Mainwaring – though there were at first two French assistants.

Radio Inconnue gave few indications of its location but it might have been supposed to be in the Paris area.

The speakers employed the language and ideas of petit bourgeois and addressed themselves almost entirely to the petit bourgeois class. The weight of the attack was usually directed at Vichy and in particular at Marshal Pétain personally. On 3rd July, 1941, the first reference was made to an imaginary organisation of Les chevaliers du coup de Balai, and from then on the station became increasingly 'operational' giving instructions in passive resistance, advocating slashing German tyres, etc. The murder of individual traitors was encouraged following the Colette attempt[5] and De Brinon and Darlan were particularly mentioned as high on the list.

---

1. Report No. 7 Research Units F1 and F2. 16th September–5th October, 1941.
2. Minute of Lt Colonel Sutton to Mr Leeper, 27.4.42.
3. Squadron Leader Halliday to Mr Bowes Lyon, 9.12.41.
4. Note on Two French Research Units Radio Inconnue and F3 La France Catholique, 24.11.41.
5. 'According to one report from CX sources, it was in listening to a secret radio station that Colette got the idea of shooting Laval and Deat.' Note on Two French Research Units, 24.11.41.

Success of F2 in Spreading Rumours

The authenticity of Radio Inconnue was not so carefully built up as that of Radio Travail, and the Chevaliers du coup de Balai sometimes taxed the credulity of [their] listeners severely. At a time when Darlan's police is said to have reported on a supposed leakage of Vichy Cabinet information to Radio Travail, the Vichy wireless denounced Radio Inconnue as an English station. The more thoughtful of its listeners might frequently have reflected, 'It is difficult in some cases to see how a Frenchman could have got the information broadcast from F2.'[1] This did not, however, detract from its usefulness in Political Warfare since it was our chief agency for spreading 'sibs' or rumours and it was mainly for this purpose that this station was kept going until early in 1944.

Its success in this direction can only be described as phenomenal and many of the rumours which it originated were taken up in the press in France and must be very widely believed at the present time.

Shortly before the shooting of the Nantes hostages, Radio Inconnue stated that Pétain would hand himself over to the Germans as a hostage. Not only had an American journalist cabled the 'news' home within forty-eight hours but ten days later the Marshal himself sought to gain credit by speaking of his attempt to do so.[2] The Marshal also made this claim in his defence during his trial. The object of the foregoing 'sib' was to discredit the Marshal. There was no hope of his offering himself as a hostage and being shot by the Germans, but there was a real hope of making many Frenchmen believe that he ought to do so, and Marshal Pétain showed considerable adroitness in immediately countering it with the story that he had attempted to do so.

In addition to spreading definite 'sibs' or rumours, some which had been approved by the UP Committee, Radio Inconnue specialised in fabricating myths some of which achieved great success, and some of which have been permanently accepted as historic facts.

Creation of Myths

The association of Pucheu, Bouthillier and many other Vichy office-holders with La Banque Worms was first launched as a 'sib' in July 1941, and within a month the same accusations were being made in the Paris press. The part played by La Banque Worms in the corrupt dealings of Vichy Ministers remained a feature to which F2 frequently returned and it is now firmly established as an article of faith in the minds of large numbers of Frenchmen. But the most extraordinary of Radio Inconnue's successes in the fabrication of a fantasy which has achieved an independent existence, and which is only to be compared with the theme of one of Pirandello's plays,

1. Report on F1 and F2 from 28.8.41–16.9.41.
2. Note on Two French Research Units F2 and F3, 24.11.41.

was on the subject of Synarchie, or 'Mouvement synarchique de l'Empire'. On 19th November, 1941, F2 broadcast the following revelations:

> Cette societe secrete a une existence reelle . . . le programme est resume en trois points, parfaitement clairs: 1. Orienter la politique du Gouvernement de Vichy de telle sorte que tout regime a caractere social soit banni du pays. 2. Supprimer tout mouvement social qui pourrait avoir pour effet d'affaiblir la position de certain groupes financiers. 3. Sauvegarder certains interets Franco-Allemands qui ont ete arranges avant l'ouverture des hostilites en 1939.
>
> Le chef du mouvement est le Sieur Leroy Ladurie . . . qui est un des directeurs de la banque Worms, son principal assistant est le Sieur Ives Bouthillier actuel ministre des finances at de l'economie nationale. Le Comite de direction comprend les membres suivants: Jacques Barnaud, Lehideux, Belin, Pucheu, du Moulin, de la Barthete, Bichelonne, et de Peyerimhoff.

It is perhaps necessary to state that the conception of a world ruled by expert technicians and financiers and the use of the word *Synarchie* to denote it, was not the invention of F2 and that a movement of the kind is said to have existed in Mexico. But F2 seized on the conception and applied it to the financial and economic exploitation of France by the Vichy collaborationists. The accusation spread rapidly in France, and one British agent, after devoting extraordinary efforts to unearthing the facts about the movement which he still regards as one of the most dangerous in the world, was finally able to procure a copy of 'Les treize fondamentaux et 598 propositions du pacte synarchiste revolutionnaire pour l'Empire français'.[1]

Many experienced men of the world are convinced that a secret synarchial society is still a potential danger to the peoples of Europe. Ninety per cent of evidence of synarchie originated from F2.

Denunciations

In regard to one of its frequent features, F2 showed more regard for truth: that was in the pilori, no candidates for which were denounced without good evidence, though a certain amount of licence was taken with regard to the moral character of these victims. Not infrequently the denunciation of a collaborator was useful in supporting one of F2's myths:

> Aujourd' hui nous signalons M. Million, le secretaire generale a la main d'oeuvre et aux Assurances Socials. . . . M. Million est le fameux

---

1. The present writer has accepted the risk of referring to this disappointing document in spite of the warning that: 'toute detention illicite du present document expose a des sanctions sans limite previsable.'

> Million des affaires Oustric et Stavisky . . . en 1938 M. Million etait un collegue de Ferdonnet . . . maintenant il est directeur de la Banque de France, actionnaire de la banque Worms . . . Chevalier de Vichy. Vous avez deja recu vos ordres. Million doit faire un petit tour a la campagne. Million a mort.[1]

Mere association with the enemy qualified for passing mention:

> Nous clouons aux pilori
> Le Prince et la princesse de Polignac,
> Le Comte et la Comtesse Jean de Castellane,
> M. Paul Morand, M. Serge Lifar.[2]

These denunciations undoubtedly added greatly to the scandalous attraction of F2, but they were unofficial and were therefore on a very different footing from those of F5 at a later date in the war.

F2, like all other French RUs, was jammed throughout its career and was also a special target for the Vichy secret broadcasting station Radio Révolution, which frequently held up the Chevaliers du coup de Balai to contempt and denounced them as Communists and de Gaullists and as provocateurs who sheltered safely in London while inciting weaker spirits to assassination.

F2 was continually referred to as an organ of the Gaullists:

> We now have the certainty, if not yet the mathematical proof that the murder of Paringaux, Pucheu's Chief of Cabinet, was conceived, decided on and organised in the Carlton Gardens office of Traitor de Gaulle. It is now quite obvious that all the appeals to murder are being drawn up in the office of the felon General who himself draws up the infamous scripts broadcast by the 'unknown radio', 'Honneur et Patrie', 'Chevaliers du Balai' and 'Radio Gaulle'.[3] Radio Révolution did not, however, accuse F2 of being actually Englishmen. Nor did General de Gaulle ever protest against this station, perhaps because he had no evidence that it was in fact British. Its existence has never been divulged to any ally, and it was finally closed on 10th January, 1944.

A French Report on F2

One report made on this station by a member of the French Resistance after his arrival in England[4] is worth quoting:

---

1. F2 Au Pilori, 11.1.42.
2. F2 Au Pilori, 7.8.41.
3. Radio Révolution, 29.1.42.
4. M. Renelière on 10.12.42.

> . . . ce poste portait étrangement, malgré l'outrance du ton et des informations, ou plutôt a cause d'elle.
>
> La plupart des grandes rumeurs (Worms, synarchie, retour des cendres et kidnapping du Maréchal, etc.) ont été crées.
>
> C'est ainsi que même des gens en place comme René Gillouin m'ont fait part de l'injustice que représentait leur mise en cause comme synarchistes.
>
> Worms (le bijoutier) et Bardy Worms (le publiciste) ont été écrouées à la prison politique de Val des Bains pour faire diversion en marge de la légende Worms, etc. Et tout le monde croit en France que le Marechal a failli être kidnappé a la faveur d'un complot Hitler-Laval en December 1940. Tout ceux qui m'ont entretenu de F2 m'ont assuré avoir entendu le poste secret des Communistes si bien informé. Il est certain que la violence du ton, la faiblesse de la syntaxe, la grossierté du vocabulaire donne l'impression qu'un camarade parle. Ce Poste est donc efficace.

The effectiveness of F2 can only be assessed when the subsidiary effects of rumours, appearing in the press, and widely believed by people, quite unaware of their origin, are taken into account in spreading confusion, mental suspicion and ill-will among collaborationist circles in France.

These effects are only comparable with the similar influence of GS1 in Germany, but that of F2 may well have been the greater since the men of Vichy were far more vulnerable than the Nazi leaders.

Mr Kingsbury's Extraordinary Feat

In conclusion, the extraordinary devotion to duty of Mr Kingsbury and Miss Mainwaring in running F2 must be emphasised. 'I can make no recommendations about leave for Mr Kingsbury or Miss Mainwaring . . . there is no alternative staff nor under present circumstances can they possibly be released from their work. . . . They write, type and speak 4,000 to 6,000 words a day, every day of the year and have done so for the past eighteen months. . . .'[1]

Mr Kingsbury's first and only leave would appear to have been from 14th to 31st July, 1943, when the station was kept going by Miss Mainwaring and Miss Kingsbury. The latter, Mr Kingsbury's daughter, although a penniless young girl had succeeded in making her way on foot from Dreux to Paris against the tide of refugees in June 1940 and after travelling all over France was finally able to reach England in the autumn of 1942. She joined the staff of F2 on 1st January, 1943, for some months.

1. Minute from Dr Beck to CAO, 28th May, 1942.

The Italian RUs during the SO1 Period

The first Italian RU known as W1 went on the air on 17.11.40. By January, two were in existence – Radio Italia and Radio Liberta.

The chief feature of Radio Italia was persistent attacks upon the Germans and frequent contrasting of British and Germans.

Radio Liberta made violent attacks on Mussolini's private life, alleging, for example, that he had married his half sister and compared badly with Nero and Caligula. For a time Radio Liberta broadcast only at weekends owing to lack of suitable speakers and occasionally, owing to 'a fit of temperament of the only artist' Signor Caltobiano, did not go on the air at all.

Six months after Radio Liberta or QC had enjoyed this desultory existence, 'discussion classified the distinction of the second Research Unit from the first,[1] as the mouthpiece of a group of young dissident Fascists disillusioned by Fascism in practice'. But uncertainty as to 'the objectives at which the RUs were aiming' continued until long after the SO1 period and the establishment of PWE. Thus for the first year of the war with Italy secret broadcasting was spasmodic, unplanned, and amateurish.

This judgement is confirmed rather than dispelled by a study of the most voluminous report of an RU ever made[2] extending to sixteen foolscap sheets in which the writer allows no doubts to assail him of the importance of his work as housemaster of Radio Italia.

> On 17 November the stenographers on the fourth floor in the Via Vittorio Veneto at Rome, tuning their sets through the 41 meter band, were startled by a new apparition in the ether. . . . It was a memorable day in Italian history. . . . Deafened by years of Fascist propoganda Italians were at last hearing the authentic voice of Italy.

A Breach of Security

Equally remarkable is the fact that this document, which is not marked Most Secret, Secret, or Confidential, gives the names of all employed and the exact locations of the RU house as well as referring to 'the Baker Street organisation' and quoting several Most Secret cipher telegrams verbatim.

Captain Ivor Thomas'* connection with W1 was abruptly terminated owing to representations by the Security Officer and, after being almost immediately returned to Parliament at a by-election, he became one of the most frequent critics of PWE methods of conducting British Political Warfare in the House of Commons.

---

1. Minutes of the Italian Region Station, 6.6.41.
2. Radio Italia. The First Year's Work by Capt. Ivor Thomas, 17.11.41.

* [Ivor Bulmer-Thomas (1905–93) was on the editorial staff of *The Times* 1930–7; chief leader writer, *News Chronicle*, 1937–9; served with Royal Fusiliers 1939–40 and Royal Norfolk Regiment 1940–2 and 1945; captain 1941; MP for Keighley (Labour 1942–8, Conservative 1949–50); acting deputy editor, *Daily Telegraph*, 1953–4. Churchman.]

During the first year the Italian RUs had carried certain 'operational' themes in the hopes of stimulating activities which were bound to arise spontaneously – such as to buy up radio valves, to hoard metals and the copper sulphate necessary for spraying vineyards, and to hoard wheat. The value of the RU as a medium for such themes was questioned by Mr John Barry who pointed out that less than 4% of the sets capable of hearing RU transmissions belonged to agricultural or industrial workers.

Mr John Barry Foreshadows Radio Livorno

A less partizan study of the Italian RUs had been made by Mr John Barry of the CHQ Planners group at the close of the SO1 period. The most valuable of his proposals[1] was that 'there is a strong case for the development of an RU appealing solely to the Fleet. The RU would be speaking to the officer class of the Navy, as they alone would be able to listen to us on short wave.[2] Our appeal would be to . . . their patriotism as the only weapon Italy has left against complete absorption by Germany.'

The Deception of Colonel Thornhill* by W1

One success of W1 should not go unrecorded for it provides a delightful element of comedy, though at the expense of Colonel Thornhill, then head of the SO1 Mission to the Middle East.

Colonel Thornhill's monitors listened in to W1 and assumed it was a Freedom Station in Italy. One day it was heard addressing a message congratulating the Cairo station on its Italian broadcasts.[3] Cairo duly replied and Colonel Thornhill reported home with obvious excitement[4] stating that proof that the station was genuine was afforded by the fact that it gave the winning numbers of lottery tickets drawn the same day.

A few days later Colonel Thornhill was able to announce[5] that Secret Wireless Station Radio Italia had been definitely located on 20th February in the neighbourhood of Brindisi.

The deception of Colonel Thornhill was a matter of self-congratulation at CHQ and his first telegram is marked by the Minister: 'Colonel Thornhill has been taken in. We should not undeceive him.'

1. Mr Barry to Mr Leeper, 14.8.41.
2. In this Mr Barry was misinformed. The chief audience of this station which was afterwards set up were the naval wireless telegraphists of petty officer rank.
3. Telegram GS1(K)41435 of 14.2.41.
4. Telegram GS1(K)41804 of 15.2.41.
5. Telegram GS1(K)43513 of 23.2.41.

* [Colonel Cudbert John Massy Thornhill (1883–1952) served in the Great War and became military attaché, Petrograd, 1916–18; North Russian expeditionary force 1918–19; served PID, India and Egypt, 1940–6.]

First Mission to Middle East. Propaganda to Russia

[March 1940]

The possibility of Russia coming into the war as an ally of Germany seemed a very real one in the early months of 1940, particularly in relation to the possibilities of the war extending to the Baltic, and Sir Campbell Stuart reported to the War Cabinet,[1] 'I have been making the necessary preparations for the task of introducing propaganda into Russia which the Government has committed to me.' In the event of war with Russia it was probable that Turkey would be involved and it was clear that Cairo and Istanbul would become far more effective centres for propaganda than England. There was also the possibility that Italy would come into the war, in which event an EH mission in Cairo would be essential, if the Department were to play any useful part in carrying on front-line propaganda with the Army in Egypt.

In late April 1940, Air Commodore Groves, who had become a member of the Staff of the EH Military Wing a few weeks before, was despatched to Cairo by air, to make the necessary arrangements for an EH mission so as to be prepared for either eventuality. Air Commodore Groves reported[2] on 6th May that Wavell had been informed that in the event of war with Russia he would be in command but that he thought that war with Italy would come first and that General Wavell recommended Lt Colonel J. H. Thornhill as head of the EH Mission which was *ostensibly* to be part of 'I' department HQRAF.

As a result of direct contact with the Commander in Chief, Air Commodore Groves was able to make all arrangements, and at the moment when Mussolini was broadcasting his declaration of war on 10th June, 1940, Lt Colonel Thornhill and his p.a. Lieutenant Christopher Sykes were in Cairo actually engaged in drafting the first leaflet for Italian troops and Air Commodore Groves had returned to England and was indeed in France trying to evacuate the EH Mission in Paris.

Thus, Sir Campbell Stuart, on his departure to Canada, was able to inform the Minister of Information that:[3] 'Colonel Thornhill and Lieutenant Sykes are in Cairo, and my staff here have worked out with the officials concerned at the Ministry of Information what appears to me an efficient plan of co-operation in respect of Italian propaganda.'

Overlapping Propaganda Authorities in ME [Middle East]

Before giving any estimate of Colonel Thornhill's work, it is important to underline that the same overlapping of function and duplication of authorities concerned with propaganda existed in the Middle East as existed in Britain.

1. WP(R)(40)105, 29th March, 1940.
2. In a letter to Colonel Brooks, 6.5.40.
3. Letter to Mr Duff Cooper, 23.6.40.

In addition to the MoI there were the following organisations concerned with propaganda activities at the end of 1940:[1]

The D/H organisation which dealt with sabotage and the distribution of propaganda.

The D/H organisation (under Mr Donald Mallett)[2] operating in Turkey.

The D/K organisation (under Colonel Longrigg) which handled subversive propaganda in the whole area with the exception of propaganda in Italy and the Free French propaganda in Syria.

Colonel Thornhill who represented SO1 and who handled all propaganda in Italy for distribution both in Africa and in Italy.

Certain independent agencies operated directly by the DDMI, Brigadier Clayton.[3]

In such conditions, complications were likely to arise. One instance is revealed by Colonel Thornhill's request[4] for authority to pay Captain Fellowes whom he proposed to appoint as assistant to Captain Steer,[5] who was not an officer of SO1, but had been attached to Haile Selassie as Propaganda Officer by Brigadier Clayton.[6] Captain Fellowes was to carry out subversive propaganda against the Italians in Abyssinia.

With goodwill and mutual understanding, such arrangements could work well and Colonel Thornhill was able to draw Colonel Brooks' attention[7] to the following extract from MEIC Daily Summary No. 529 of 11th June, 1941. 'Senior officers among Italian prisoners have blamed our propaganda for the wholesale desertions of native troops who are seldom reliable now' and comment 'The credit for this is due to Steer and Fellowes who have done excellent work throughout the campaign.'

Such goodwill and understanding was not, however, always present. Both in the field and at the base (Cairo), considerable jealousy prevailed between the rival agencies and not least between SO1 and SO2. It would be tedious to describe in detail each of the stages by which negotiations for the control of propaganda in the ME were carried on by the authorities concerned in

1. Memorandum to Mr Gladwyn Jebb from Colonel Taylor, dated 31.12.40, on Organisation Middle East.
2. [FOOTNOTE DELETED ON GROUNDS OF NATIONAL SECURITY]
3. Brigadier Clayton had been the head of the famous 'Arab Bureau' in Cairo (1914–18).
4. In early October 1940.
5. Captain Steer had revealed the Italian use of poison gas and the Italian attacks on the American Red Cross in the Italian conquest of Ethiopia.
6. Brigadier Clayton was responsible for propaganda to Italian native levies and tribes in I. East Africa and Eritrea.
7. Telegram No. 72515, C. in C. ME to War Office.

England – the Foreign Office, SO1 and SO2 and MoI with CHQ and the Embassy in Egypt. But the rivalry cannot unfortunately be ignored since it embittered the relationships of SO1 and SO2 – afterwards PWE and SOE. The distrust engendered by it did much to hinder the unity of purpose and the harmonious planning between covert propaganda and subversive action which were necessary in building up the resistance movements in Western Europe.

Colonel Thornhill Undertakes MoI Functions in ME

First, however, a few words must be said on Colonel Thornhill's work. Colonel Thornhill's main activity was to organise propaganda in Italian, both overt and covert. British overt propaganda to Italy, that is to say open broadcasting, was at that time under the MoI and, anxious to secure friendly co-operation, Colonel Thornhill enlisted the assistance of Mr Davies, the MoI representative, who was head of the Publicity Section at the Embassy, in drafting the first leaflets in Italian. Mr Davies, who found himself unable to cope with the MoI functions of propaganda to the Italian colony in Egypt, requested Colonel Thornhill to undertake this work. Colonel Thornhill did so. Thus in the early months of the war, the EH Mission was principally employed in acquiring an Italian newspaper which had been sequestrated by the Egyptian Government and reviving it as a Liberal and anti-Fascist organ. Considerable difficulty was experienced in ensuring that its contents were sufficiently moderate in tone for it to be read by ordinary Italians, and for it to be of any use in Italian prisoner-of-war camps. Colonel Thornhill had also to make sure that the newsvendors who sold it were protected from local Fascists.

At the end of August 1940 Colonel Thornhill reported a list of activities[1] all of which without exception were overt propaganda to the Italian Colony in Egypt and which were MoI functions. They included organising the display of a captured Italian bomber and a captured Italian tank. Colonel Thornhill was also concerned in the segregation and internment of local Italian Fascists and anti-Fascists after the Egyptian Government had agreed to the internment of Italians of military age.

Since overt propaganda to Italy was under the MoI, Colonel Thornhill at first obtained guidance from the MoI representative. On the entry of Italy into the war, British propaganda policy followed fairly closely the pattern which had been at first followed with regard to Germany. That is to say Mussolini's personal responsibility was stressed as Hitler's had been. But there was far more opportunity for stressing the friendship which united the British and Italian peoples and which had been sacrificed by the Duce. After November 1940, SO1 London telegraphed any alterations in propaganda directives to Italy to Colonel Thornhill and also telegraphed the texts

1. Memorandum of activities of Department EH Mission in Cairo, 31.8.40.

of leaflets disseminated from Malta. The chief points which developed in this way can be summarised as follows:

From the first, a stop in any jeers at the Italian armed forces. Examples of chivalry between the British and Italian forces were given prominence. This directive had to be repeated.[1]

After the first Italian reverses in Greece, a stop was placed on mentioning Italian need for German assistance.

From December 1940, the directive was to stress the German exploitation of Italy and to represent Hitler as having double-crossed Italy to obtain France.

On 25th April, 1941, British reverses and the entry of Italian forces into Egypt led to the British Government issuing a warning that we should bomb Rome[2] as a reprisal if Cairo or Athens were bombed.

The policy of the *Corriere* continued to give difficulty owing to the violence of the anti-Fascist leader Professor Calosso. Colonel Thornhill was forced on 29th May, 1941, to ask for a directive from London to curb his atheism and republicanism, and the Directive was duly sent.

But after the German attack on Russia the propaganda line towards the Vatican and the Italian throne, was modified: 'The Catholic Church has supported Fascism and would support it still further in a war with Russia. This applies also to the Monarchy, especially present King.'[3]

New tasks devolved upon the SO1 Mission as new fields of operation opened up. This with the presence of German troops on the Egyptian frontier led to directives for which the arrival of [Rudolph] Hess in England furnished material.

Political Warfare to the Balkans

Preparations were made for SO1 to take over propaganda to the Balkans. Directives were telegraphed to Colonel Thornhill[4] for propaganda to Bulgaria, Roumania and Yugoslavia, though as the experts were held up on the journey they could not be carried out in propaganda. The Roumanian directive contained the statement: 'It is contrary to Roumanian interests to be dragged into a vast Russo-German conflict.' This passage coming over a month before the German attack on Russia, but after Hess's arrival in Britain, would appear on the face of it to be an indiscretion. It was not till the end of July that Colonel Thornhill informed London that the Mission would start propaganda to the Balkans on 4th August, 1941. From early June, Colonel Thornhill was asked to undertake propaganda to the French forces in Syria and the French Fleet.

1. Directive of 31.12.40 (Groves ME to 4(1)).
2. Text of warning leaflet telegraphed 25.4.41.
3. Brooks to Thornhill No. 30.6.41 (Groves ME 4(1)).
4. 5.6.41. Telegram No. (Groves ME 4(1)).

Activities of SO1 Mission

The major activities of SO1 were:

1. A nightly broadcast in Italian from Cairo giving news and commentaries with a list of names of Italian Ps/W and messages to relatives in Italy or E. Africa.
2. Production of leaflets in Italian for dissemination by the RAF and FAA.
3. Publication of an anti-Fascist daily newspaper in Italian, *Il Corriere d'Italia*, for circulation among Italian Ps/W and the Italian local population. The circulation was over 9,000. This paper was printed by the Kasr-el-Nil printing press which formerly produced the Fascist newspaper *Il Giornale d'Oriente*. The building was leased by SO1 and the press used for all printing activities including work for GHQ, SO2 and the Embassy. Another newspaper was planned for publication in Asmara but had not been published by the time Colonel Thornhill left ME. In addition, Colonel Thornhill was actively engaged in covert political work among the Italian Colony in Egypt. This involved fostering an organisation known as the *Gruppe d'Azione Antifascista et Italiani Liberi*, the internment of dangerous Fascists and the replacement of Fascists by anti-Fascists in institutions where Italians were allowed to function.

Propaganda among Italian Ps/W on the lines of memoranda produced jointly by Miss Freya Stark* and Colonel Thornhill.

An Anglo-Yugoslav Recruiting Commission was working with SO1 in selecting Yugoslavs from among Italian Ps/W to enrol in the Yugoslav Army.

Propaganda to Italian Prisoners of War

From the first Colonel Thornhill had realised the great possibilities of propaganda among Italian prisoners of war and initiated it as soon as possible. On 22nd March, 1941, he was informed[1] that propaganda among Italian Ps/W in India had been officially recognised as an SO1 Middle East responsibility. On 18th July, 1941,[2] he was informed that [by] a decision of the JIC [Joint Intelligence Committee], propaganda to all Ps/W had been made an SO1 responsibility. In March 1941, in spite of the critical situation in the Middle East, Colonel Thornhill had visited India on the invitation of the C.

---

1. Telegram No. 57832 (Groves ME 4(1)).
2. Telegram No. 78928 (Groves ME 4(1)).

* [Dame Freya Madeline Stark (1893–1993) was an explorer, mountaineer and writer who published mainly travel books and autobiography between 1933 and 1982. Educated privately in Italy and at the School of Oriental Studies in London, she was 'engaged on government service in the Middle East and elsewhere' 1939–45.]

in. C. General Auchinleck[1]* in order to investigate the possibility of propaganda among Italian Ps/W.

Divergent Policies to Italian Ps/W

In view of this, it is somewhat surprising to find that Colonel Thornhill was informed on 16th July, 1941, that, without consulting with him, an SO1 mission was being dispatched from London to investigate the possibility of raising a Free Italian Force from among the Italian prisoners of war in India. In the same telegram he was informed that the FO had vetoed any propaganda among Italian prisoners of war in Egypt 'aimed at raising a Free Italian Force or enlisting Italians on our side'.

Thus the Foreign Office appears to have deliberately pursued contradictory policies to Italian Ps/W in different areas. Since the divergent policies could not in fact be kept from the knowledge of Italian prisoners of war, they largely stultified the efforts made and helped to produce the deepest disillusion among Italian prisoners of war everywhere.

On 27th June, 1941, SO1 in London suggested that personal messages from Italian Ps/W in Egypt should be broadcast to their families though it would appear that this had already been done. The first directive on the Political Education of Italian Ps/W in ME was telegraphed to Colonel Thornhill on 28th July, 1941, after he had been carrying on the work for almost a year. The directive was that the emphasis should be anti-German and the Fascists should be attacked for betraying Italy to the Germans. No political doctrine should be pushed. No instructions seem to have been sent regarding segregation, camp newspapers and literature, broadcasts, cinemas and lectures, or the teaching of English.

Estimates of Colonel Thornhill's Work

Colonel Thornhill won high encomiums on the quality of his work. After quoting a passage in General Wavell's Dispatch of 30th January, 1941, which ran: 'General impression our propaganda increasingly successful. Despite orders High Command for destruction of leaflets, some officers apparently took steps to ensure each of their men had copies. One officer prisoner volunteered opinion intensification similar propaganda in Italy

---

1. Colonel Thornhill telegraphed (No. GS1(K) of 19.3.41). Colonel Brooks on his return: 'On leaving C. in C. told me visit had been decidedly useful. Arranged printing in Delhi of *Corriere d'Italia* and discussed fully questions of segregation and propaganda.'

* [Field Marshal Sir Claude Auchinleck (1884–1981) saw action in Egypt and Mesopotamia 1914–18; colonel 1930; major-general and Deputy Chief of Staff, India, 1936; GOC-in-C Northern Norway 1940; Commander-in-Chief, India, 1941; Commander-in-Chief, Middle East, 1941–2, until replaced by Montgomery; Commander-in-Chief, India, 1943; Field Marshal 1946.]

would have an important effect.' The Minister of Economic Warfare[1] drew attention to the statement of a captured Italian Colonel commanding 158th Regiment: 'Your leaflets fell on Bardia. They have a very demoralising effect on the troops because they read them and come to the officers for explanation. We have no convincing arguments against the truth.' The Minister of Economic Warfare added: 'Credit for these leaflets goes primarily to Colonel Thornhill, one of my men attached to General Wavell.'

As late as mid-June 1941, the Minister of Economic Warfare dispatched the following telegram:[2] To Colonel Thornhill following from the Minister. 'I should like to congratulate you on success of your work during the past year. You may care to know that I am endeavouring to arrange for your promotion to Brigadier.'

But Colonel Thornhill had had to protest vigorously against misrepresentation and the withholding of a telegram vitally affecting his position, for several months.

SO1 and SO2 Friction

A co-ordinating committee of SO1 and SO2 had been set up in January 1941, and at Brigadier Clayton's suggestion, an officer of SO2, Mr Pollock, had taken the chair.

This officer on his return to England stated that Colonel Thornhill was willing to serve under him, and after consultations with Colonel Taylor of SO2[3] the Minister of Economic Warfare informed the C. in C. Middle East[4] that he intended to make important changes.

> Henceforth the distinction between SO1 and SO2 will only apply in this country and will consequently disappear in your area. There will henceforth be only one SO organisation in the Middle East under the general control of Pollock, who while remaining responsible to me, will operate under your direction. The functions of the SO Department will cover:
>
> 1. Subversive Propaganda.
> 2. Political subversion.
> 3. Raiding and sabotage.
>
> . . . I should like you to know that I have excellent reports of Thornhill's work and I hope he will play an even more important part under the new arrangements.

---

1. In a Minute to the Prime Minister, 7.2.41.
2. No. 72927 DMI, 19.6.41.
3. Colonel Pollock appears to have presented the memorandum agreed to by Brigadier Clayton, Colonel Thornhill and the C. in C. to Colonel Taylor of SO2 but not to have informed Colonel Brooks of its existence.
4. In a letter dated 5.1.41 (ref. IV b7).

Colonel Thornhill was notified of the changes.[1] On receiving this letter he immediately replied in a long personal and secret telegram:[2]

> I submit I should have been at least consulted before I Pollock was given control of my Department and I protest against decision in the interests of efficiency and harmonious working. I repeat I did not agree to serve under . . . except on co-ordinating committee, as clearly stated in memorandum taken home by him.

Three days later a telegram[3] was dispatched from SO2 to the officer in question which contained the following passages:

> If it is a fact that Thornhill does not wish to act under your direct control the Minister would not wish to insist on him doing so, provided only that he served under you on co-ordinating committee. . . . You should discuss this proposal with Colonel Thornhill and endeavour to affect common agreement without compelling Minister to take up question direct with General Wavell.*

Colonel Thornhill Not Informed of Dr Dalton's Decision

This telegram was withheld from all parties concerned by the officer in question and Colonel Thornhill, who learned of its existence in a letter from Brigadier Brooks received on 23rd February, finally obtained a copy of it on 4th May, 1941, which had been brought by hand from London by Lt Colonel K. Johnstone. The latter officer of the Welsh Guards, who had Foreign Office experience, was an expert on the Balkans with a particular knowledge of Bulgaria. Together with Captain Euan Butler, a German expert, and Second Lieutenant Trower, he left England on 8th April to undertake propaganda to the Balkans for SO1 under Colonel Thornhill. The reason for these reinforcements was the extension of the war to Greece and the landing of German troops, the Afrika Korps, to reinforce the Italians in North Africa. Unfortunately the party did not start until two days after the Germans had invaded Greece and Yugoslavia, and were sent off without proper papers and without having had the proper inoculations. In consequence, Lt Colonel Johnstone did not reach Cairo until after the evacuation of the Imperial Forces from Greece had been completed and his companions took even longer on the journey.

---

1. In a letter from Brigadier Brooks on 6.1.41.
2. Personal and Secret for Brigadier Brooks, 1.2.41.
3. CXG 584/5 of 5.2.41.

* [Field Marshal Archibald Percival Wavell, 1st Earl Wavell (1883–1950), served in India 1903–10; in France 1914–16; in Palestine 1917–20 and 1937–8; Southern Command 1938–9; formed Middle Eastern Command July 1939; defeated Italians at Sidi Barrani December 1940; Commander-in-Chief, India, July 1941; penultimate Viceroy of India 1943–7.]

Overlapping between SO1 and SO2

Although the extension of SO1 activities had been agreed by the Minister of Economic Warfare in consultation with General Wavell, the extension of new fields of activity for SO1 was not accompanied by restrictions on SO2. For this reason a conflict 'in the field', i.e. Egypt, Palestine and Turkey, with SO2 officers who were still carrying out propaganda as part of their function became inevitable. The conflict was not speedily resolved by an appeal for instructions. It was on the contrary drawn out for several months which ended in calling all SO2 activities into question and the closing down of SO1.

In June, Dr Dalton addressed a telegram to General Wavell, putting forward the SO2 case and suggesting that in view of the changed circumstances since the evacuation of Greece, propaganda to the Balkans should be a matter for SO2 rather than SO1. This telegram was referred to Colonel Thornhill, one of Dr Dalton's officers, for his comments, apparently for use in drafting a reply.[1] Nothing could illustrate more convincingly the failure to create a unified body to carry out the functions of preaching and organising subversion. Colonel Thornhill pointed out that the answer to the Minister of Economic Warfare's complaint that SO2 received inferior treatment in the Middle East compared with the free hand which it enjoyed elsewhere was that nowhere else was SO functioning within a theatre of war and under a military command: within such an area it must, like everything else, submit to military control and he added that at the back of the whole argument was the fact that SO2 was inefficient and unreliable and had to be kept under constant supervision if it was not to make havoc.

His other comments were that Jerusalem was unsuitable as a centre of Balkan propaganda and the Jerusalem W/T [wireless transmitting] station was barely audible in the Balkans.

General Wavell's reply[2] was substantially in agreement with Colonel Thornhill's memorandum which would appear to have been used in its drafting.

It is obvious from the above that although Colonel Thornhill was in fact an officer of SOE, the Commander in Chief was defending his position against the Minister of Economic Warfare who wished to restrict it. Though Colonel Thornhill held his position thanks to General Wavell, it is clearly improper that he should have drafted a reply to his own Minister, on his own functions.

Two of the passages in Colonel Thornhill's comments on Dr Dalton's telegram should be noted: 'Johnstone has come across and reported defects in SO2's Balkan organisation' [and] 'SO2 would welcome the removal of Johnstone.' Colonel Thornhill's anticipations with regard to Lt Colonel Johnstone were [widely rehearsed].

1. Most Secret Memorandum to Brigadier Clayton DDMI (O), 14.6.41.
2. Telegram to Troopers from Middle East, No. 1/73646 of 16.6.41.

On 18th June Brigadier Brooks telegraphed to Colonel Thornhill[1] that the Minister wished him to instruct Johnstone to return home as soon as possible.

Colonel Thornhill[2] adopted a policy of procrastination, urging in his reply that it would be difficult for him to spare Johnstone until reorganisation had been completed.

Brigadier Brooks rejoined:[3] 'The Minister directs me to draw attention to my 72926 18/6 and ask when Johnstone is leaving.'

Colonel Thornhill replied at leisure[4] that Johnstone would be leaving shortly. But Lt Colonel Johnstone did not leave and Colonel Thornhill stated[5] that 'in these circumstances it has been impossible for me to allow Johnstone to leave owing to continuous hard work required on the clandestine broadcasts to the Balkans, approved on 21st July'.

Colonel Johnstone's sojourn in the Middle East was regarded by SO2 officers as highly dangerous. A telegram was dispatched[6] accusing Lt Colonel Johnstone of indiscretion with regard to the Polish organisation Promethee[7] in Istanbul particularly in his dealings with Colonel Piatkowski.

On 7th August Colonel Bailey of SO2 in a private report accused Lt Colonel Johnstone of gross breaches of security in regard to a Bulgarian lady, Madame Karastoyanova. Sir Frank Nelson,* head of SOE in the Middle East, refused to accept two minutes from Lt Colonel Johnstone commenting upon these accusations. Colonel Thornhill addressed comments of his own to Sir Frank Nelson[8] in which the charges against his subordinate were vigorously rebutted and counter-charges were made against SO2. Colonel Thornhill had handed the reports on which they were based to the Minister of State.[9]

---

1. Telegram No. 72926 (DMI), 18th June, 1941.
2. Telegram No. 76347, 25th June, 1941.
3. Telegram No. 76768, 8th July, 1941.
4. Telegram No. 81791, 14th July, 1941.
5. Minute to Sir Frank Nelson from Colonel Thornhill, 10.8.41.
6. SO2 private code No. 4149, 6.8.41.
7. Promethee was an anti-Soviet secret society which theoretically had ramifications among all the subject peoples of the USSR. As British policy had been completely reversed after the German attack on Russia on 22.6.41, it is obvious that a different attitude had to be adopted after that date.
8. Letter with enclosures from Colonel Thornhill to Sir Frank Nelson, 10.8.41.
9. The reports were forwarded to the Minister of State on 28.7.41 and consisted of:
   (i) Letter and Memorandum from Sir Reginald Hoare.
   (ii) Memorandum by Mr Steven Runciman.
   (iii) Memorandum and report on Brittanova Agency by Mr Syme.
   (iv) Memorandum by 2/Lieutenant F. M. Sheldon. They form together a shattering disclosure of the inefficiency and corruption and waste of public money by the 'D' organisation and SO2 officers in the Balkans early in the war.

* [Sir Frank Nelson (1886–1966) was educated at Bedford Grammar School and Heidelberg; senior partner of a Bombay mercantile firm; served in Bombay Light Horse during the Great War; Conservative MP, Stroud, 1924–31; intelligence work in Basle 1939; appointed by Hugh Dalton to head SO2 1940; responsible for all SOE activities 1942, but resigned over ill-health later that year; air commodore in Washington and Germany.]

While these exchanges were taking place, the whole position of propaganda organisations in the ME had been examined by a committee[1] set up by the Minister of State.[2] The Committee reported on 24th July, 1941, after examining the work of nine separate organisations (including one of the Free French) engaged in parallel or overlapping propaganda activities in the Middle East.

Serious duplication and overlapping in which 'two or more bodies are carrying out propaganda to the same people or by the same media without knowing what the others are doing' were given, with the following examples:

(a) Underground whispering campaigns run by the Publicity Section and SO2.

(b) Work to influence religious Arab opinion by the Publicity Section and SO2.

(c) The existence of two British news agencies NEB [WORDS DELETED ON GROUNDS OF NATIONAL SECURITY] subsidised by the British Government and run in watertight compartments in competition.

(d) The distribution of pamphlets by almost every propaganda body without reference to the others.

(e) The rival claims of SO1 and SO2 to do Freedom broadcasts. The most disturbing example of this type of difficulty and confusion arising from lack of definition of spheres of activity is found in the work by SO1 and SO2.

The report recalled the agreement between the Minister of Economic Warfare and the Minister of Information of October 1940,[3] as to their spheres and pointed out that in the Middle East a position had arisen almost entirely at variance with that scheme. SO1 had taken over the whole of propaganda in the Italian language including the overt forms of it, while they were only authorised to a limited extent to make subversive and covert propaganda in the Balkans. SO2 had gone far outside their original sphere by disseminating rumours and pamphlets in ME countries not in enemy occupation where there can be no question of fomenting subversive political movements.

The Committee challenged the usefulness of the division of spheres between MEW and the MoI which had been founded on responsibility for answering Parliamentary questions and considered that there was no evidence that covert propaganda should be divorced from overt propaganda.

The Committee reported also on the inefficiency due to lack of communications. The MoI sent printed material round the Cape which was out of date when it arrived instead of sending proofs and negatives by air mail.

---

1. The Committee consisted of Mr A. N. Rucher, Mr T. A. Shaw, and Brigadier I. Clayton.
2. Mr Oliver Lyttleton appointed representative of the War Cabinet in ME, 1st July, 1941.
3. See p.37.

Reverting to SO1 and SO2 the report recommended that it would be desirable to leave SO propaganda to SO1 alone and that this was especially desirable in the Balkans.

The recommendations of the Committee were not, however, carried into effect and the representatives of SOE who had recently been sent out,[1] proceeded to carry out a reconstruction of their own.

Colonel Thornhill was no longer himself in an unassailable position and on 14th August, 1941, he was instructed by Sir Frank Nelson, on the authority of the Minister,[2] that he was relieved of all SO duties in the Middle East, and should leave Cairo as soon as possible but need not travel by air.

Colonel Thornhill had survived the departure of General Wavell from the Middle East for nearly six weeks. It is perhaps not impertinent to point out that in London, SOE was splitting up into its two constituents. What became known as 'the Charter of PWE' had been agreed between the three Ministers on 8th August and was signed by the Prime Minister on 19th August. If Colonel Thornhill had been allowed to remain only a week longer, PWE would have had its own mission in the Middle East and its abolition and the dismissal of its head could only have been effected by the joint action of the three Ministers. Moreover, the instruction that Colonel Thornhill was to return by the slow route, meant that the matter could not be raised immediately.

Efforts made by Colonel Brooks to intercept Colonel Thornhill on his slow journey, and to provide air transport which would bring him home quickly, were partially successful and Colonel Thornhill arrived in Britain on 25th September, 1941. The newly formed Political Warfare Executive had many urgent problems on its hands and there was no question of immediately reopening the question of representation in the Middle East. SO2 had triumphed but the price paid will later be shown to have been a high one.

SOE did not disclose to PWE evidence that Colonel Thornhill had proved himself unsuitable for his position. Thus the Colonel was thought to have been unjustly treated. Had SOE pointed out that Colonel Thornhill had shown grave lack of judgement in accepting sums subscribed for British propaganda by members of the Italian communists in Egypt and applying them to equip his mission with luxurious transport, it is unlikely that he would have been sent out to Egypt again.

1. Sir Frank Nelson and Mr Maxwell.
2. Letter 1 to Colonel Thornhill CMG, DSO, from Sir Frank Nelson, of 14.8.41.

PART II

PWE under the Triumvirates and PWE Missions

The Formation of PWE

The difficulties arising from the Ministry of Information's recognised authority for the direction of overt propaganda through the BBC European Services, on which no decision had been taken after the inquiry in December 1940, came to a head the following spring.

The Morton Committee

[March 1941]
The Committee on Foreign (Allied) Resistance (the Morton Committee) submitted a note on the subject of French propaganda asking that a standing committee should be set up to agree upon and formulate the strategy and tactics of our French propaganda.

Criticisms of MoI Policy to France

The Minister of Economic Warfare welcomed the proposal but the Minister of Information resisted it[1] as an example of that 'multiplication of Committees' which the Prime Minister had said was to be avoided. He pointed out that the Ministry was in day-to-day touch with the Foreign Office on the one hand and the BBC on the other on questions of French propaganda and that there was a weekly meeting at which 'the MoI, the PID and, more recently, the Ministry of Economic Warfare are represented', and which issued a weekly directive to the BBC. In resisting this demand the Minister of Information was on strong ground as for almost a

1. Letter from Mr Duff Cooper to Sir Alexander Cadogan, 19.3.41.

year the BBC French Services under his control had played an extremely important part in rallying Frenchmen to the support of Britain. It is no mere expression of opinion to say that the French Service of the BBC was conspicuously superior in quality and in influence to any propaganda service controlled at any time by Department EH or SO1 and it would have been disastrous had radical changes been made in it. But the critics persisted and on the matter being raised at a Cabinet level the Lord President of the Council (Sir John Anderson)* was directed to preside at a meeting attended by the Foreign Secretary, the Minister of Economic Warfare and the Minister of Information and to adjudicate on these 'frontier disputes'. This meeting was of importance, not only in regard to the French Services of the BBC. It resulted in the affirmation of the paramount position of the Foreign Office in regard to propaganda policy and in the setting up of an executive to carry it out. Although the responsibilities of the Minister of Information and the Minister of Economic Warfare were left precisely as they were, the authority of the Foreign Secretary in regard to the direction of policy was superimposed upon them both not simply in theory but in practical form.

A Ministerial Committee Set Up

To ensure that this direction was carried into effect the 'Anderson Award' set up a Standing Ministerial Committee of the three Ministers and a triumvirate of their deputies responsible for seeing that the work was properly co-ordinated and carried out. Progress in these matters was slow. A draft of the 'Anderson Award' was under amendment on 19th May. Nearly a month later, the Minister of Economic Warfare wrote to the Foreign Secretary welcoming the Prime Minister's approval of the Anderson Award, and on 6th July he wrote again: 'I agree that the sooner the new machinery is set up the better.' It was not, however, until after Mr Duff Cooper had ceased to be Minister of Information[1] that the Prime Minister finally initialled the document[2] setting up the Political Warfare Executive. In the meantime the recommendations made in the Anderson Award were being sensibly modified and made more concrete. The new Minister of Information, who was the fourth tenant of this office in two years, realised that his predecessors had been gravely handicapped by the distrust with which the Service Departments had regarded the Ministry and the consequent reluctance

1. On 20.7.41.
2. On 19.8.41.
* [Sir John Anderson, 1st Viscount Waverley (1882–1958), came first in Civil Service examination 1905; National Health Insurance Commission 1912; Ministry of Shipping 1917; Chairman, Inland Revenue, 1919–22; Governor of Bengal 1932–7; Independent Nationalist MP for the Scottish Universities 1938–50; Lord Privy Seal 1938; Home Secretary and Minister for Home Security 1939; Lord President of the Council 1940–3; Chancellor of the Exchequer 1943–5; OM 1957.]

with which they had disclosed secret information to an organisation which they identified with Fleet Street.

Mr Bracken* New Minister of Information

On taking up his office Mr Brendan Bracken was therefore receptive to the ideas of Brigadier Brooks whom he knew was persona grata with the Chiefs of Staff Committee. He was, moreover, willing to accept Brigadier Brooks as his deputy under the Anderson Award. On the one hand, Brigadier Brooks would be his 'man', and useful to him in forming accurate views with wide horizons; on the other, he would be ridding himself of a subject which had produced continued disputes in the Ministry in which the former Ministers had been involved. Mr Bracken's decision would have been tantamount to handing over the policy direction of the BBC European Services to SO1, if this had been all.

Draft Cabinet Paper

But Brigadier Brooks secured at the same time Mr Bracken's approval of a 'Draft Cabinet Paper' which was handed to Mr Bruce Lockhart[1] in order that he should secure the approval of the Foreign Secretary. This paper proposed the creation of a Department of Political Warfare under the control of one Executive Committee. The Executive Committee was to consist of Mr Bruce Lockhart (FO), Brigadier Brooks (MoI), Mr Kirkpatrick (BBC), Mr Leeper (MEW), and Major Morton.**

Though the principle underlying the paper expressed Mr Bruce Lockhart's views, the detailed working out of the principle was seen to be clumsy: the inclusion of a BBC representative as well as one for the MoI might be thought to give the Minister of Information an influence greater than that of the other two Ministers, and Major Morton was in the anomalous position of not being directly answerable to any of the three Ministers. Moreover, paragraph C allotted *personal responsibility* to the representatives of the Ministers for particular fields of work. No

1. Sent to Mr Bruce Lockhart at the FO by Lord Hood, 31.7.41.

* [Brendan Rendall Bracken, Viscount Bracken (1901–58), was born in Tipperary; sent to Australia 1916 after absconding from Jesuit college; returned 1919; spent two terms at Sedbergh; director of Eyre & Spottiswoode 1925; founded *Banker* and acquired *Financial News*, *Investors' Chronicle*, and jointly owned *The Economist*. Conservative MP, North Paddington, 1929–45, Bournemouth 1945–51; PPS to his lifelong hero Churchill 1939–41; successful Minister of Information 1941–5; founded *History Today*; Chairman, *Financial Times*.]

** [Sir Desmond John Falkiner Morton MC (1891–1971) survived a bullet wound in his heart serving with the Royal Horse Artillery in the Great War; as aide-de-camp to Field Marshal Haig came to the attention of Winston Churchill; entered FO intelligence department 1919; as head of the Committee of Imperial Defence's Industrial Intelligence Centre 1929–39 he kept Churchill briefed on German rearmament; Principal Assistant Secretary, MEW, 1939; personal assistant to Churchill 1940–5, with special duties regarding Enigma decrypts.]

Department can function smoothly unless the Executive is *jointly responsible* for all its work.

'The Charter of PWE'

A new document was accordingly drafted, which though more general in form, and therefore more acceptable to the Ministers, was in fact an immense advance upon Brigadier Brooks' paper. For in it, it is clearly laid down that the three officers shall be jointly responsible to the Standing Ministerial Committee which itself should exercise its powers of control jointly.

The document which afterwards became known as 'the Charter of PWE' was agreed on 8th August by the three Ministers, on which day the final form was communicated to Mr Bruce Lockhart by the Foreign Secretary with instructions to prepare a plan as indicated in paragraph 5. The document was initialled by the Prime Minister on 19th August the day after his return from signing the Atlantic Charter. Its text is as follows:

> 1. We (The Secretary of State for Foreign Affairs and the Ministers of Information and Economic Warfare) have given further consideration to the question of propaganda to enemy and enemy-occupied territories. We contemplate that we should continue to meet from time to time at the Foreign Office as a Standing Ministerial Committee to deal with major questions of propaganda policy requiring Ministerial decisions.
> 2. We desire that the Committee of Three, decided upon some time ago, on which each of us shall be represented by a senior official, should now be set up.
> 3. We have accordingly appointed Mr Bruce Lockhart, Brigadier Brooks and Mr Leeper respectively to represent us on this official Committee.
> 4. We propose that this Committee should now act as a General Staff for the conduct of political warfare, and that these three officers should be jointly responsible to the Standing Ministerial Committee, which itself will exercise its power of control jointly.
> 5. The three officers should now meet and work out a plan of organisation and operations. This plan need not, at this stage, go into great detail, since practical experience will suggest the best method of procedure. The function of this Official Committee of Three will be to co-ordinate and direct, in accordance with the policy of His Majesty's Government, as laid down by the Foreign Secretary, all propaganda to enemy and enemy-occupied territories.
> 6. It is of the greatest importance that the work of the Committee, and the various propaganda activities co-ordinated and directed by it, should remain secret. The names of the members should not be published, and there should be no widespread distribution of minutes or papers.
> 7. The Committee should be empowered to invite to its meetings, from time to time, other officials whose responsibilities are relevant to particular items which may appear on its agenda.

8. We ask the Prime Minister's approval of the scheme set out in this Minute and his authority for the attached statement to be made at a convenient moment in reply to a Parliamentary question.

This document was considered at a Standing Ministerial Committee but progress was slow. The Minister of Information delayed in giving up his powers over the BBC European Services and the Minister of Economic Warfare did not accept the proposal that SO1 should come directly under the joint authority of the three Ministers. The situation was disquieting and Mr Bruce Lockhart addressed a frank and pessimistic Minute to the Foreign Secretary.

Inter-departmental Strife Paralysing our Political Warfare

'It is the plain truth which will be denied by no honest person inside our various propaganda organisations that most of the energy which should have been directed against the enemy has been dissipated in inter-departmental strife and jealousies. If our war effort is not to suffer it is of paramount importance that our propaganda machine should be put in order at the earliest possible moment. I am not a pessimist by nature but I feel I must state frankly that in a fortnight's time, when the Executive Committee has to report, we are almost certain to come up against the same impasse between Mr Bracken and Dr Dalton as existed for ten months between Mr Duff Cooper and Dr Dalton. These are my private views but I feel sure they are shared by Brigadier Brooks and Mr Leeper.'[1]

The Minute the Foreign Secretary noted in red ink: 'If this is still the position I shall have to take the whole business to the Cabinet. I have done all I can do to bring warring departments together. A. E. [Anthony Eden]'

On 27th August the Minister of Information held a meeting in his room attended by Sir Walter Monckton, Mr Cyril Radcliffe,* Mr Bruce Lockhart, Brigadier Brooks, Mr R. A. Leeper and Mr David Stephens (Secretary of PWE). Mr Brendan Bracken stated that in his view the Committee had complete authority to act as they thought fit in regard to Political Warfare in the war zone. He was prepared to give them full powers:

(a) to execute propaganda to enemy and enemy-occupied territories through the BBC.

(b) to make such arrangements as they thought fit regarding personnel in the BBC and the MoI.

---

1. Extracts from a Minute to the Secretary of State for Foreign Affairs from Mr Bruce Lockhart, 22.8.41.

* [Cyril John Radcliffe, Viscount Radcliffe (1899–1977), was a fellow of All Souls 1922–37; called to Bar, where he excelled at the Chancery Bar 1924; Director-General, Ministry of Information, 1941–5; drew the frontier between India and Pakistan (in a manner helpful to the Viceroy) 1947; Lord of Appeal 1949; Chairman of the British Museum trustees 1963–8. Many other honours and posts made him the personification of the Establishment.]

After the meeting, the Executive Committee of PWE waited on Dr Dalton and asked him if he would give them the same powers in relation to SO1 as had been given to them in regard to the BBC and MoI. Dr Dalton demurred, but asked the three officials to put forward a plan for complete fusion and single Regional Heads for each area, to which request Mr Bracken also subscribed. Shortly before the next meeting of the Ministerial Committee, Dr Dalton put forward his own views:[1]

> The conception of three Ministers jointly controlling, through three officials jointly responsible to them, an important branch of our war effort, is a novel one. For the consideration of major questions only, and for co-ordination, as distinct from fusion, this arrangement would have been sensible enough. But I am far from happy about it now that we contemplate the formation of what will be virtually a single department.

Dr Dalton's Reservations

Dr Dalton made certain reservations that when any matter concerning MEW, SO2 or the Committee of Allied Resistance came up, representatives of these bodies should sit with the PWE Planning Committee and that wherever PWE wished to operate outside a British territory they should only do so through the medium of SO2.

> It will be the duty of the liaison section in Baker Street to ensure that the directives of the PWE are carried out by the SOE representatives abroad and the PWE will have the right, subject to the agreement of the SOE, to nominate expert propagandists to serve on the staff of any SO Mission in the field.

Other safeguards included that all Minutes must be available to each Minister who must have the right to summon any one of the PWE officials or to visit any PWE establishment.

The proposals were considered at a meeting of the Ministerial Committee on the same day and were in the main accepted. The reorganisation was announced in the House of Commons by the Prime Minister in answer to a Parliamentary question on 12th September, 1941, when he stated that the Secretary of State for Foreign Affairs, the Minister of Information, and the Minister of Economic Warfare had recommended, and he had approved, that a small special executive for the conduct of political warfare should be established, in lieu of the various agencies concerned to conduct such propaganda in all its forms. He explained in answer to supplementary questions that the executive would be responsible to the three

1. A letter from the Minister of Economic Warfare to the Secretary of State for Foreign Affairs, 6.9.41.

Ministers sitting together, but if the Ministers did not agree, then the matter would come to him as Minister of Defence.

Although PWE must be regarded as having officially come into existence on the date of the Prime Minister's initialling 'the charter', its effective existence can be regarded as dating from 12th September, 1941, since its separate existence and authority could not be challenged after the Prime Minister's announcement in Parliament.

The first document[1] announcing the establishment and functions of PWE was circulated with a covering letter from the secretary, Mr David Stephens, dated 20.9.41. It gave the names of the Executive Committee and, as the Department was a secret one, the cover to be employed, that of the Political Intelligence Department of the Foreign Office – and the address 2, Fitzmaurice Place, Berkeley Square, W1. Incidentally, the use of this cover frequently led to documents intended for members of the real PID organisation being delivered to PWE.

The Browett Report

On the formation of PWE it was hoped that economies would result as an opportunity apparently offered itself to abolish the overlapping and duplication in the organisation of CHQ and the BBC particularly with regard to Intelligence services. A small committee was therefore set up to recommend the best methods of bringing about such economies as would result from 'fusion' with the BBC European Services.

Mr David Bowes Lyon,* Mr Leeper's deputy at Country Headquarters, and Mr J. B. Clark were nominated as the PWE and BBC representatives respectively and a neutral chairman, Sir Leonard Browett, was nominated by the Treasury.

The Committee made its report on 7th November. Its chief recommendations were submitted to and approved by the Ministerial Committee by 6th December.

The main features of the report were that the work of PWE and ancillary services should be based on the principle of regionalisation. The PWE London headquarters should be in or near Bush House, that Country Headquarters must remain the centre for secret work and leaflets and that the BBC European Intelligence Section should be disbanded and the BBC European Records Unit amalgamated with the Library at CHQ, that the Secretary at CHQ should carry out the duties of Director of Intelligence and should have a small central Research Group and the Library and Records Unit under him. Regional Directors were to have two deputies, one in London and the other in the Country.

1. The document is undated and has no reference number.

* [Hon. Sir David Bowes-Lyon (1902–61), son of the 14th Earl of Strathmore and brother of the Queen Mother; lieutenant Hertfordshire Regiment 1939; MEW 1940–1; head of PWE mission to Washington 1942–4; various post-war directorships.]

The report helped to bring about the move from Fitzmaurice Place to Bush House, and PWE regional control of BBC output.

As the report was approved by the three Ministers it became a valuable weapon with which to overcome the opposition to the introduction of PWE Regional Directors into the BBC. The report recommended the abolition of the BBC European Intelligence section.

The arguments on Intelligence put forward jointly to the Browett Committee[1] by Mr Walter Adams, PWE and Mr John Salt, Director of the BBC European Services until the appointment of Mr Kirkpatrick, were that the first essential was that all sources should be studied within the same organisation. Secret sources could be available only to those working under Government establishment. There should therefore be a unified organisation under PWE covering Europe as a whole.

Mr Adams was thereupon asked to put forward a scheme for the reorganisation of Intelligence. This scheme, based upon the conclusions of the Browett Report, was acceptable as regards the abolition of the BBC Overseas Research Unit under Mr Abrams, and Mr Abrams was offered and accepted a post in PWE. His proposals[2] with regard to the BBC European Intelligence Section under Mr Griffin were not, however, accepted by the BBC.

Mr Kirkpatrick objected to Intelligence coming to the BBC via CHQ which led to the withholding of Intelligence.[3] This objection was one which cut at the root of PWE control, since it was essential that the PWE Regional Director should be able to decide that certain materials should be used exclusively on the RUs.

Mr Kirkpatrick also objected to the library being situated in the country. On this he was on stronger ground, and it is difficult to see how a library could serve both BBC and CHQ needs unless there was a branch in London and a certain amount of duplication of reference books.

Mr Kirkpatrick also suggested that members of the BBC staff would refuse to serve under Mr Adams, which appears irrelevant as anyone who refused to serve should have been got rid of and replaced. The reference appears to have been to Mr Griffin. The opposition with regard to the abolition of Mr Griffin's unit was maintained in the BBC. Mr Bruce Lockhart took the matter up with Mr Cyril Radcliffe, Director General of MoI[4] without result but the matter was not apparently taken up by the Minister of Information and Mr Griffin continued to produce the *BBC Studies of European Audiences* which were closely overlapped by PWE Intelligence

1. Notes on a PWE Intelligence Organisation submitted to the Browett Committee by Walter Adams and John Salt, 28.10.41.
2. PWE Intelligence organisation, 10.1.42.
3. Minutes of Staff Meeting, 2.2.42.
4. Minutes of Staff Meetings, 11.2.42.

documents dealing with the same subject. This overlap, which had no possible justification, continued until almost the end of the war.

PWE and the BBC European Services

The greatest and most immediate task before PWE on its formation was the reform and control of the BBC services. The deficiencies in these during the EH and SO1 periods were partly the inevitable result of the physical conditions in which the work was carried on, and no amount of policy control and guidance, or even the loan of specially qualified speakers, could be effective without increases in staff and accommodation.

The conditions under which the German Service [was] carried on in June 1941 had been that[1] eleven programmes a day were broadcast to Germany, starting with the first news and talks programme at 5 a.m. and ending with the Night Forces Programme at 2 a.m.

News

The news was written in English on one desk in the general European news room. At this desk worked the German Editor and his subs. Since they had to cover news for the full twenty-four hours of the day, producing eleven bulletins, in practice one sub-editor was often responsible for a whole bulletin. When, for instance, the story of Rudolph Hess broke, the German Editor was away on leave. Since he had no deputy this meant that the bulletins in the morning and early afternoon were composed by one sub-editor.

When the news had been written in English it was carried along a lengthy corridor to a very small room, where a shift of eight–nine translators translated the bulletins literally into German. Their work was supervised, not by the Editor, but by a language supervisor responsible to a different BBC department from the Editor. His job was not to edit the news in German, but to ensure that an accurate translation was provided of the English news written by the English News Editors.

Talks

The Talks Department was on the fourth floor of another block of Bush House. It took four and a half minutes on an average to reach either the News Room or the Rehearsal Studios, the translators, or the actual transmission studios from this Talks Room. In this one room were housed: the Talks Editor, his four assistants and their secretaries. Careful preparation and planning was out of the question.

Moreover, including the Talks editor, there were only five persons available to plan the programmes which were daily transmitted. Not much less work

---

1. The following facts are taken from existing conditions of German Broadcasting Memorandum by Mr R. H. S. Crossman, 6.6.41.

was required for the organisation of a quarter of an hour of talks programme than for preparing the feature page of a newspaper. Each Talks assistant had to be responsible for two whole programmes. They had to function physically remote from the News Editor, without a library or rehearsal studios, and had no leisure in which to plan, and think and have ideas.

Features

The Features Unit was at Bedford College, a mile and a half away from Bush House. It consisted of two full-time German assistants and three men on short-term contract. It was responsible for 'Vormarsch der Freiheit' and a few other small features. Owing to its separation from the rest of the unit it was unable to fulfil its proper function as a *production* staff for general use in the presentation of talks, features, etc.

Mr Crossman recommended that three shifts of News Editors were required and three subs on each bulletin. The editorial news staff, including two spare men for leave, required fourteen as against the four then employed. Similarly a talks assistant with a deputy was required for each main programme.

Mr Crossman also reported that all the staff should be housed in rooms adjoining one another. Propaganda could only be good when a genuine team spirit was created and when each section knew constantly what the other was doing. The minimum accommodation required was eleven in place of three and a half rooms.

Mr Crossman also pointed out that the BBC staff had only been able to carry on their programmes thanks to considerable assistance from outside, both from IP2 and from EH. These two departments not only directed policy, but provided a large proportion of the talks and features – as well as news items for the programmes. Moreover these departments lent the BBC assistants in the News Talks Department and provided star speakers like Sefton Delmer. EH also paid retainers to a number of Germans who rendered regular but informal assistance to the Service.

Mr Crossman also pointed out that the organisation was bound to result in a wooden translation of English into German and advocated that news and talks should be composed in German under British supervision.

PWE and BBC London Accommodation

The accommodation referred to by Mr Crossman in the above report was mainly in Bush House and, during the summer and autumn of 1941, the BBC European Services secured more space for expansion. PWE on its formation inherited the SO1 premises in Fitzmaurice Place, adjacent to those of the Ministry of Economic Warfare. They were obviously inadequate for housing all the Regional Directors, who would have to spend most of their time in London if PWE control of the European Service was to become a reality. Moreover, there was a security objection as the mezzanine floor, sandwiched between PWE Military Wing and PWE Secretariat, was occupied by the Ministry of War Transport which refused to surrender it. A search for new premises revealed a suitable building in Lowndes Square and negotiations were in progress for it [in October 1941] when a new proposal, based on the experience of attempts to control BBC policy, led to the abandonment of the plan.

Control of BBC Partly Due to Distance

When PWE had been based in Woburn, it had been assumed that the difficulties of the control of BBC policy – which in practice meant the frequent reference to PWE of items of news between their reception on the tape and their inclusion in news bulletins – were due to distance and that in London such reference would be an easy matter. But once the Regional Directors were based at Fitzmaurice Place, they soon discovered that for all practical purposes they were as far away as Woburn. The BBC Editors found it impossible to telephone to Fitzmaurice Place on every occasion; the Central News Desk was presided over on the spot by the dynamic figure of Mr Noel Newsome, who could not give the 'Regional slant' on which PWE set store, nor was he always sufficiently well-informed to know what news was politically dangerous and ought to be played down. The Regional Directors soon found therefore that their guidance was frequently too late. It took about twenty minutes to get from Bush House to Fitzmaurice Place and it would take still longer to reach Lowndes Square. Mr Kirkpatrick attended the daily Executive Committee meeting at Fitzmaurice Place, but Mr Newsome found it difficult to find the time to attend frequent *ad hoc* meetings which PWE considered necessary.

The Move to Bush House

The proposal was therefore made that PWE should seek accommodation in Centre Block, Bush House, and immediately the importance of being located in the same building as the BBC had been realised, the matter was taken up vigorously.[1] Initial objections to requisitioning the building, on the part of the Board of Works on the grounds that it was occupied by no less than thirty firms engaged in war production, were brushed aside and it was pointed out that Bush House merely provided accommodation addresses for these firms whose factories were located in the Midlands. Centre Block, Bush House, though not economically planned, offered ideal conditions for security and sufficient space for an expanding department and the BBC.

The whole building with very minor exceptions on the ground floor was requisitioned for PWE and the BBC European Services. Four floors were

1. The suggestion was embodied in the Browett Report on 7.11.41 and approved by the Ministerial Committee.

available for PWE, but this was thought to be more than was required and the BBC agreed to take the fifth floor as well. It was some months before the building could be equipped with the necessary telephone service with direct lines to Government Departments and to CHQ and the move did not take place until March 1942. When it came, however, Bush House was found to solve a large number of the difficulties between PWE and the BBC and to provide the space without which the European Services could never have developed efficiently.

But the control of the BBC was by no means only due to difficulties of space and time. There was indeed a fundamental clash of principle between the views which soon came to be identified with Mr Kirkpatrick and those of the PWE Regional Directors.

PWE Regional Directors and the BBC

The Regional Directors, some of whom had been working in that capacity under SO1, had their functions in regard to the BBC defined as follows:

> 1. Regional Directors are the officers appointed by the Executive Committee to direct and control, under the orders of the Executive Committee, all forms of Political Warfare to their respective regions.
> 2. In their BBC work they are responsible to the Executive Committee through the PWE Controller in the BBC.
> 3. Regional Directors will individually submit, for approval by the Executive Committee, weekly BBC directives which have previously been approved by the PWE Controller. . . .
> 6. The Regional Directors are responsible under the Controller, for ensuring that the Regional output conforms with policy and is adapted to the needs of the Region. They may supervise the work of News Editors in matters relating to presentation. They should keep in touch with one another and with the Editor in Chief in order to secure co-ordination of output.
> 7. Any differences between the Editor in Chief and the Regional Directors will be resolved by the Controller and in the last resort by the Executive Committee.[1]

Regional Directors Appointed

At the time of this instruction Regional Directors had been appointed for Germany (Mr R. H. S. Crossman), France (Colonel Sutton), Scandinavia (Mr Barman), the Low Countries (Mr Harman), the Balkans (Mr Murray). No suitable candidate had been found as Regional Director for Italy or Poland and Czechoslovakia.

1. Functions of Regional Heads in relation to their BBC work, 23.9.41.

Colonel H. R. G. Stevens, who had already won a great personal following for himself among the Italian audience of the BBC as a Commentator, was seconded from the BBC as Regional Director in November 1941 and was appointed as from 1st December.

Mr Moray McLaren, also a member of the BBC staff, who had had some experience of Poland, was appointed Regional Director for Poland and Czechoslovakia and joined the Department on 21st February, 1942.

Apart from these two, all those appointed had been working sufficiently long, either in Department EH or in SO1, to obtain considerable experience of the work of those departments, in regard to secret broadcasting, and leaflets, and it is unnecessary to say that all had very considerable pre-war experience of the countries for which they were appointed.

Mr Kirkpatrick's Dual Functions

Mr Kirkpatrick had taken up a Ministry of Information appointment of Foreign Adviser to the BBC, including the Home and Overseas Services, on 3rd February, 1941, and on the creation of PWE had been selected to fill the position of PWE 'manager in the BBC', a post which involved his appointment as Controller of the European Services of the BBC.

This was agreed to by the Governors of the BBC by the end of September, or early in October 1941, and carried with it a seat on the Control Board. It should be pointed out that Mr Kirkpatrick's responsibilities as Controller were not co-extensive with his responsibilities as PWE 'manager' since the BBC European Services included those to Spain, Portugal, Sweden and Iceland, for which the Ministry of Information was responsible.

Though this territorial overlap appears unimportant it was unfortunate as it emphasised a difference between the BBC European Services and PWE.

A memorandum on Mr Kirkpatrick's functions as defined by the Executive Committee[1] repeated what has already been quoted from the paper on the functions of Regional Directors issued on the same date. Both memoranda included the statement that Regional Editors who were responsible to the Editors in Chief should enjoy latitude in the selection and presentation of items for news bulletins within the general framework laid down by the Editor in Chief.

Mr Kirkpatrick had early put forward the view that Mr Newsome, the European News Editor, should be responsible for propaganda output as a whole though[2] he admitted that such a proposal would be resisted to the last ditch by the regular broadcasting staff.

1. Mr Kirkpatrick's functions, 23.9.41.
2. Scheme of BBC Co-ordination under PWE by Ivone Kirkpatrick, 22.8.41.

One of the main reasons for the formation of PWE was the admitted need to co-ordinate our propaganda through different media, and the instruments to achieve that end were the PWE Regional Directors. The introduction of the Regional Directors' authority into European Services of the BBC, as has been seen, was a cornerstone of the PWE policy and indeed was the reason for their being based in London, first at Fitzmaurice Place, and later for the move to Bush House.

Collisions between Mr Kirkpatrick and the PWE Regional Directors

As however, no modification had been made in the rigid BBC hierarchy on the appointment of Mr Kirkpatrick, to regularise their position and give them authority, it is not surprising that collisions soon took place between Mr Newsome and Mr Kirkpatrick on the one hand and Regional Directors on the other.

Mr Murray in a memorandum[1] protesting against an instruction issued by Mr Newsome to BBC Regional Editors that 'it was a waste of time to refer any of the matters in his Daily "General Directives" to the Regional Directors', stated:

> It is possible there exists a slight confusion as to the relative sphere of responsibility of Mr Newsome and the Regional Director; in conversation with me, Mr Kirkpatrick mentioned that Regional Directors were, according to the Charter, to conform to the general framework of the propaganda laid down by the Editor in Chief. I understand that the Editor in Chief's functions cover the treatment of news and that propaganda policy is the responsibility of the Regional Director.

Mr Kirkpatrick's Case against Regional Directors

Mr Kirkpatrick was invited to give his views by the Executive Committee and stated that the position of the Regional Directors had given dissatisfaction on three grounds:[2]

> 1. There is no functional chain of responsibility for the output.
> 2. The interference of Regional Directors in staff matters make[s] orderly staff administration impossible.
> 3. The requirements of our security authorities cannot be met. Before the appointment of Regional Directors the chain of responsibility was well defined. The policy of HMG was made known to me and I was

1. Memorandum to the Executive Committee, 10.11.41, from Ralph Murray.
2. Paper on position of Regional Directors submitted to Executive Committee of PWE by Ivone Kirkpatrick, 4.12.41.

> responsible for seeing that it was executed. The executor through whom I worked was the European News Editor and who in turn was responsible for the work of the various Regional Editors. The European News Editor solicited Government instructions through me and Regional Editors were compelled to accept his guidance. There was thus a complete chain of responsibility together with co-ordination. Now there is no co-ordination, nor a chain of responsibility. Regional Directors without consulting me, or even informing me, issue instructions to Regional Editors, of which I and the European News Editor are wholly unaware. It is open to the Regional Editors to accept instructions from the Regional Director which conflict with those of the European News Editor, or if they feel so disposed they may carry out the instructions I have given and disregard the instructions of the Regional Director. In both cases they are covered and in both cases there is chaos.

Need to Regionalise the BBC Overlooked

Mr Kirkpatrick had an unassailable case. Unfortunately he overlooked the fact that before the appointment of the Regional Directors the BBC output had been so unsatisfactory that reform and co-ordination had been decided upon by three Ministers as urgently necessary – and that the Regional Directors had been selected as instruments to carry out the regional co-ordination of British propaganda through various media. Mr Kirkpatrick, as he knew nothing of PWE printed or Black propaganda, was not in a position to do this. Nor were those who gave him 'HMG's instructions'. It is therefore obvious that both Mr Kirkpatrick and Mr Newsome and all the PWE Regional Directors had been put in a false position.

The demands for some final ruling on what the machinery of control should be were entirely on Mr Kirkpatrick's and Mr Newsome's side. The Regional Directors do not seem to have stated that they had been instructed to do a particular job without being given sufficient authority. No doubt this was because they felt confident of being able to do the work and believed, at that time, that they had the backing of the Executive Committee.

An Improvement in the BBC

During this period of stress the BBC European Services made a great stride forward and there was an all round improvement in the French, German and Italian Services. The credit for this cannot be given either to Mr Kirkpatrick on the one hand, or the PWE Regional Directors on the other. It can, however, be attributed to the intervention of PWE and indeed Regional Officers in the BBC European Service have informed the writer that the turning-point was when PWE 'took hold'.

'For the first time we had a real service, real direction, and real guidance with a close interest in supplying our needs especially as regards intelligence,' was the verdict of a BBC Regional Officer, Mr Ian Black.

The very conflict, upsetting to discipline as it was, meant that all were aware that the BBC European Services were being challenged to do better, and conditions of work were rapidly improving so that lasting improvement was possible.

Mr Kirkpatrick's Threat of Resignation

[Dec. 1941]

The precise position and authority of the Regional Directors in regard to the BBC hierarchy was never satisfactorily determined. Mr Kirkpatrick's paper, backed by a threat of resignation,[1] was considered by the Executive Committee and he was informed by its chairman:

> It was agreed that the Controller should have full executive power in relation to all matters affecting PWE work in Bush House[2] . . . further agreed that . . . the Regional Directors have no authority to give orders to Regional Editors, but should work with and through the Controller only or his nominated deputy.
>
> At the same time the Executive Committee expect you to exercise your authority in accordance with the broad lines of the Browett Report, the main principles of which have already been accepted by the Ministerial Committee. The Executive Committee therefore invite you to submit to them a plan of organisation providing for the closest possible co-operation with the Regional Directors in order to secure the co-ordination of all propaganda media controlled by the Executive Committee as recommended in the Browett Report. . . . The Executive Committee will also be grateful if, *for their information*, you would arrange to send them copies of all written directives issued by yourself or your subordinates.
>
> In order to ease a difficult situation, the Executive Committee recommend that you should hold a regular weekly meeting at Bush House at which the Regional Directors and such members of your own executive staff as you may care to nominate should be present.[3]

Mr Kirkpatrick drew up proposals, as requested, which can be summed up in a single sentence: Regional Directors were to submit Regional Directives to PWE for approval and when approved the controller was to be responsible for carrying them out through the existing BBC hierarchy.

---

1. Mr I. Kirkpatrick to Mr Bruce Lockhart, 4.12.41.
2. PWE had not moved into Bush House which is a synonym here for the BBC European Services.
3. Mr Bruce Lockhart to Mr Ivone Kirkpatrick, 6.12.41.

The Conflicting Policies Emerge

A meeting between Mr Kirkpatrick and the Regional Directors took place on 17th December in the course of which he advanced the thesis that 'the primary function of the BBC European Service is to give the European audiences pure news. By trying to assert regional control Regional Directors are interfering with this primary function of the BBC and are also causing serious hierarchical difficulties within the BBC.'[1]

'Pure' News

Mr Barman, then senior Regional Director, challenged the first of these propositions:

> Is the BBC a charitable organisation with no other function than to provide a free news service to occupied Europe? Is our success to be measured by the frequency of our scoops? Or is the BBC a powerful propaganda weapon? Is its primary aim to keep morale high so that conquered peoples may be ready to strike at the enemy on the day? If this is accepted then news becomes the handmaiden, not the mistress of broadcasting policy.[2]

The division of opinion on the primary importance of 'news' was somewhat unreal. The division was really between the importance of the news as supplied and treated by the Central News Desk, i.e. Mr Newsome and his deputy, Mr Douglas Ritchie, or between the news as treated by the Regional Editors. Behind these alternatives lay two different views on the proper approach to Europe which were elaborated in a document by Mr Douglas Ritchie (Colonel Britton) intended for purely internal circulation in the BBC which provides perhaps the best evidence, apart from an extensive examination of scripts, that the PWE had succeeded in doing its work by May of 1942 thanks to the Regional Directors.

A BBC Conception of the Function of the European Services

[May 1942]
The title of this paper 'Britain's Right to Speak'[3] indicated that Britain was being denied the right and it was Mr Ritchie's view that such a state of affairs was being caused by attention being focussed on the 'short-term aim of winning the war' instead of the 'long-term aim of bringing about an ordered civilisation in accordance with British ideas, British values, and

---

1. Memorandum on Regional Directors' meeting with Mr Kirkpatrick by Mr Barman, 22.12.41.
2. Memorandum on Regional Directors' meeting with Mr Barman, 22.12.41.
3. 'Britain's Right to Speak' by Douglas Ritchie, 10.5.42.

British needs', after the war was over. In Mr Ritchie's view the long-term aim should have taken precedence 'since the Allies will certainly win the war anyhow whether we continue to broadcast or not'. The vitally important task was to get the European audience accustomed to, and liking, British sense of humour and characteristics, otherwise we should fail 'to achieve our aim of imposing our will on the other peoples'.

Mr Ritchie referred to the programme 'Les Français parlent aux Français' which he admitted was brilliant, had a large audience and might be helping in the short-term aim of winning the war. Nevertheless he advocated that it should be brought to an end as the BBC broadcasts should be completely British.

The BBC, he said, had become over-regionalised partly because Regional Editors placed too much emphasis on regional differences, partly owing to the use of foreign nationals in broadcasting, and the use of British subjects of foreign origin in the preparation of scripts and partly owing to 'Foreign elements outside the BBC'. The remedy which he advocated was to strengthen the influence of Mr Kirkpatrick and Mr Newsome. Only so could his ideas be brought about.

The xenophobia revealed in this paper was diametrically opposed to the policy of PWE which, moreover, was solely concerned with the 'short-term' objective of helping to win a war which was to last another three years. Neither was PWE concerned in any way with the BBC post-war audiences.

This is not the place to argue whether Britain was not more likely to project British values by showing an understanding of the widely differing problems of her allies than by speaking to them through the mouths of the Man in the Street and of Colonel Britton, but it is clear that PWE, which was concerned solely with winning the war by means of Political Warfare, could not allow this short-term aim to be made a subsidiary one on the grounds that we had 'tanks, planes and ships enough' to win it anyhow. Mr Ritchie's paper reveals more clearly than anything else the need for PWE regional direction of the BBC European Services and provides satisfactory evidence that by the end of the first eight months of its existence PWE had done a large part of its job, in face of the opposition of Mr Kirkpatrick, Mr Newsome and Mr Ritchie.

BBC Regional Editors Support PWE

This was done largely by the Regional Directive and by the personal influence of PWE Regional Directors with BBC Regional Editors. The latter were BBC officials but it is noteworthy that Mr Kirkpatrick in making arrangements for a daily meeting with the PWE Regional Directors came to refer to the BBC Regional Editors as their deputies.[1]

1. Mr Kirkpatrick's letter to Regional Directors, 17.12.41.

PWE Executive Committee Fails to Solve the Problem

But though the problem of the hierarchical position of the Regional Directors remained anomalous, [the] PWE Executive Committee insisted on the principle of regionalisation being adopted:

> The Executive Committee consider that the news bulletins of the BBC should be selected and presented to suit the conditions and the mentality of the country to which they are addressed. The main responsibility therefore, for such selection and presentation must rest with the Regional Editor who has been appointed for his special knowledge of the country with which he deals. His function is to produce the best programme he can for his particular country.
>
> In carrying out this task the Executive Committee wish Mr Kirkpatrick to assist Regional Editors in the following ways:
>
> 1. Mr Newsome will provide them with the best service of general news from the Central News Room together with guidance in the handling of this news. For this purpose he will issue a Daily Directive, to be sent to the Executive Committee for approval, and will meet them each evening at 5.30 for a discussion of the latest news before the composition of the most important bulletins of the day. Both in his directive and in his meeting with Regional Editors he will convey to them any instruction[s] on policy which come to him from Mr Kirkpatrick.
> 2. The Regional Directors will draw up their weekly directives in close consultation with Regional Editors before submitting them to Mr Kirkpatrick and the Executive Committee. At this meeting the main lines of propaganda policy will be fully discussed. It stands to reason that the Regional Editors must have the right to apply to the Regional Directors at any time for advice in determining the way they will select and present the news in order to conform with the policy laid down in the weekly directive and that the Regional Directors must equally have the right to advise the Regional Editors as to how they think the selection and presentation of news should be made.
> 3. In order that Mr Kirkpatrick may be kept fully informed of the views of the Regional Directors on matters concerning their regions and may convey to them such instructions as he considers necessary, there will be a daily meeting between him and the Regional Directors at 5 p.m. at which Mr Newsome will be present.
>
> In this way the Executive Committee consider that the Regional Directors can best assist the aim of PWE to secure co-ordination of the different media on propaganda on a regional level, thus avoiding

discrepancies between the news contained in the BBC and in leaflets and ensuring a common policy throughout, and can also best assist the Regional Editors to produce the kind of programme best suited to their region.

The Executive Committee desire the closest co-operation between Mr Kirkpatrick and the Regional Directors on the one hand and between the Regional Directors and the Regional Editors on the other and invite them to come to a working arrangement on the lines indicated.[1]

Regional Directives

The character of the Regional Directives was largely determined by the needs of the Regional Editors of the BBC.

The French Region of the BBC had been in the habit of drawing up a long fortnightly directive for its own guidance. Soon after the formation of PWE, the Editor, Mr Gillie, realised that such a document would no longer be necessary, as the PWE Regional Directive was cast in much the same form. For this reason, while other PWE Regions issued a weekly Directive, the French Regional Director issued a fortnightly directive and a short supplementary directive every alternate week in which modifications in the directive were noted.

The method of drawing up directives was as follows:

Large meetings were held by the PWE Regional Director and attended by Regional Editors and important executives in the BBC region concerned, at which a draft directive was agreed. The Regional Director then visited the Foreign Office where the following officials were available at a fixed time once a week: Mr Speaight (France), Mr Roberts* (Germany), Mr Dixon** (Italy and the Balkans), Mr Grey (Low Countries), Mr C. F. A. Warner (Scandinavia).[2] After thus ensuring that their directives did not conflict with Foreign Office policy, Regional Directors submitted their directives for approval to the Executive Committee through Mr Kirkpatrick.

This procedure was modified on the appointment of the Director of Plans and the institution of a PWE Central Directive which became the master document, from which Regional directives only departed after

1. PW(D) (42 1st, conclusions. Meeting of Executive Committee, 1.1.42). (File PWD/42/65/BBC6.)
2. Instructions to Regional Heads, 13.9.41.

* [Sir Frank Kenyon Roberts (1907–98) entered FO 1930; Paris Embassy 1932–5 and Cairo 1935–7; German department, FO, 1937–45; chargé d'affaires to Czech Government 1943; British Minister in Moscow 1945–7; UK Deputy High Commissioner in India 1949–51; Ambassador to USSR 1960–2 and Germany 1963–8.]

** [Sir Pierson John Dixon (1904–65) took a double first from Pembroke College, Cambridge, and entered FO 1929, served in Madrid, Ankara and Rome, returning 1940. Staff of resident minister at Allied HQ, Mediterranean, 1943; Principal Private Secretary to the Foreign Secretary 1943–8; Ambassador to Czechoslovakia 1948–50; UK permanent representative to UN 1954–60; Ambassador to France 1960–4.]

consultation with the Director of Plans. Until the formation of the Directorate of Plans, PWE policy was embodied in a document 'PWE Instructions to Regional Heads for BBC News and Talks'. This document was supplemented and elaborated by meetings of the Propaganda Policy Committee at which Regional Directors were given political guidance by Mr Bruce Lockhart and strategic guidance by General Brooks.

Mr Newsome's Directives

Mr Newsome, the Director of European Broadcasts, had soon after his appointment in the BBC initiated a series of Daily Directives and Weekly Propaganda Background Notes. These documents, composed at great speed in forcible language, were of value to the less experienced and less confident of his subordinates, who were naturally anxious to know how their director saw the main news items of the day. Even if a Regional Editor saw the pattern of the news quite differently, it was most valuable for him to have on record the views of his superior. Mr Newsome was far too dynamic a journalist and forthright in his opinions ever to hesitate to commit himself. It was obviously inevitable that Mr Newsome should make mistakes, and, after the formation of PWE, it was the function of PWE to provide policy and strategical guidance which would so far as possible prevent mistakes. The need for a bold and colourful presentation of the news continually clashed with the need to wait upon events, and Mr Newsome sometimes either ignored the guidance he was given or followed his own reasoning in preference. Often he went elsewhere for inspiration. But apart from his interpretation of the news day by day, Mr Newsome had decided views of his own upon the conduct of Political Warfare.

Thus shortly after the formation of PWE, Mr Newsome produced a paper on Political Warfare,[1] the themes of which were that Germany could no longer even hope to win and that we must weaken the enemy's will to resist by defining our war aims and peace plans in which there was no place for revenge or territorial gains. The Executive Committee of PWE thanked him for the paper.

Mr Newsome's Attacks on PWE

Two months later, Mr Newsome circulated a paper of General Guidance in which he stated 'the best Political Warfare is that waged with the weapons of responsible journalism, not that carried out with the instruments of the clever advertiser'. As Mr Harman, Regional Director of the Low Countries, Mr John Barry of the CHQ Planners, then working in the BBC, and Mr Rae Smith and several other members of PWE had been employed in J. Walter Thompson and other advertising agencies, this comment could not

1. A turning-point on Broadcasting to Europe, 8.10.41.

fail to be taken by BBC Editors as a personal reflection on them. The chief interest of the paper was, however, the claim that only 'straight' news should be given over the BBC. 'We must give the truth as we see it, not from some bogus propaganda angle. News values are assessed by a professional estimate of what people are interested in and not by propaganda needs. If our case is genuine and honest the news will present it without being doctored. I cannot agree to give news entirely according to an estimate for what it would suit us for Europe to regard as the proper degree of importance.'

An analysis[1] made in PWE points out the confusion of thought in the paper. All were agreed that the BBC's reputation for absolute truthfulness was vitally important. It was not a question of 'doctoring' news but of its selection, and Mr Newsome had his own political criteria of news values. 'In brief, personal factors and the limits of time or space make any such thing as absolute or "straight" news a chimera. . . . It is obviously in the common interest to see that news which cannot be "straight" . . . is designed to further the ends of HMG in political warfare.'

Mr Newsome's Insubordination

At the beginning of 1942, Mr Crossman and the German Region drew up a plan in which a new and more friendly attitude to German Conservatives was proposed purely in order to help produce a political split between the German Army and the Nazi Party. The most serious objection to this ruse was that any such change would be misinterpreted in Britain if it were realised what was happening. A copy of Plan A was sent to Mr Newsome on 4.1.42 with a covering minute emphasising the secrecy of the proposals and that it was essential to avoid discussing them. On 11.1.42 Mr Newsome circulated a document[2] 'in lieu of the weekly Background Notes'. This was apparently because the Executive Committee, in order to muzzle Mr Newsome, had decided 'that the Weekly Directive produced by Newsome should cease'.[3] After laying down a political policy to Germany, based on the views of Thomas Mann and diametrically opposite to that proposed by the Regional Director for Germany, Mr Newsome went on: 'This precludes an apparent predilection for the Conservative elements in Germany. . . .' Mr Crossman saw in this paper 'a deliberate attempt by violation of all security precautions, to sabotage the scheme'.[4]

On the matter being discussed by PWE Executive Committee, Mr Kirkpatrick stated that Mr Newsome had written the offending passages before he had received Mr Crossman's paper,[5] but that he was prepared to apologise to Mr Crossman. But quite apart from the question of our policy

1. Comments on Mr Newsome's General Guidance paper of 9th December, 1941.
2. Propaganda to Europe during January, February, and March, 11.1.42.
3. Brigadier Brooks to Mr Bruce Lockhart, 24.12.41.
4. Mr Crossman to Mr Bruce Lockhart, 11.1.42.
5. Mr Newsome [may] have circulated his views after receiving Mr Crossman's minute of 4.1.42 asking him not to discuss the subject.

to Germany and of security, it was obviously improper for Mr Newsome to circulate a paper laying down British propaganda policy for three months ahead without consulting PWE. Apparently Mr Newsome did apologise and the paper was withdrawn.

Mr Newsome's Continued Attacks on PWE

But three months later, Mr Newsome was once more inciting the BBC editors to resist PWE policy and once again putting forward his almost mystical belief in 'straight' news, i.e. news selected by the Central Desk of the BBC European Services over which he had immediate control.

> Europe wants news above all else . . . straightforward news, good or bad, told simply, with a punch. They do not want parish pump politics, being far more interested in what we are doing or thinking . . . than in our views about what is happening to them. If that is properly understood this week will not be a constant struggle to secure for big news the space misguidedly allotted to piffling talks.[1]

This attack on the regional spirit which PWE was pledged to introduce, for it was nothing less, came when Mr Bruce Lockhart and Mr Leeper were making secret efforts to have Mr Newsome transferred from the European News Service to the BBC Home Service. The matter was delicate as Mr Bruce Lockhart warned Mr Bracken:[2] 'I should warn you that Mr Kirkpatrick regards Mr Newsome as his key-man . . . this matter will have to be treated with great tact otherwise Mr Kirkpatrick will think that this is a plot by the country to weaken his position.'

The proposal had to be abandoned as Mr Foot did not share Mr Lockhart's confidence that 'Mr Newsome would provide a healthy tonic to the Home News'.[3]

Meanwhile Mr Lockhart took up Mr Newsome's attack on the regional spirit with Mr Kirkpatrick and threatened disciplinary action by the Ministers if that kind of thing were not stopped once and for all.[4]

Mr Newsome. Some Further Indiscretions

[May 1942]
Just a month later there was a further indiscretion by Mr Newsome in which 'just to clarify our minds' he listed the BBC European audience in the categories of bad men, good men and the opportunists and wobblers and broadly

1. Weekly Propaganda Background Notes, 31.3.42.
2. Mr Bruce Lockhart to Minister of Information, 1.4.42.
3. Mr Bruce Lockhart to Minister of Information, 1.4.42.
4. Mr Bruce Lockhart to Mr I. Kirkpatrick, 3.4.42.

stated the ratio of the three categories in the different countries, picking out France, Yugoslavia and Czechoslovakia and Denmark as countries in which wobblers were a very large part of the populations and added 'instructions to BBC Regional Editors on how to vary their propaganda to them'.[1]

The Director General acted at once and Mr Kirkpatrick, expressing Mr Newsome's regrets,[2] agreed that: 'listing the Allies in order of merit in a document with such wide circulation to foreigners is indiscreet and undesirable'.

Mr Newsome. Some 'Howlers'

Apart altogether from Mr Newsome's far-reaching differences with PWE regarding policy, his daily directives were perhaps inevitably full of divergences from the political and strategic guidance which he had been given. No doubt PWE made mistakes and it was bad enough that the reputation of the BBC news should suffer from these. But Mr Newsome's energy led him continually to make 'howlers' of his own. When his views were either strategically incorrect, or clashed with a Service directive, Brigadier Brooks was naturally perturbed. A list of 'Some Howlers from Mr Newsome's Directives' dated 4.5.42 contains four major strategical blunders from the Daily Directive and one from the Weekly Background Notes in a period of two months.

Mr Kirkpatrick Withholds Mr Newsome's Directive from the Director General

As criticism of Mr Newsome's Daily Directive accumulated, Mr Kirkpatrick decided to withhold it from the critics.[3] In consequence the Director General of PWE had to ask that a copy might continue to be sent to him.[4] The request had to be repeated[5] a week later before copies of a Directive on Propaganda were forthcoming from the BBC for the Director General of PWE and the head of its Military Wing. As a result of cutting off the supply, criticism of Mr Newsome's directives declined but anxiety remained and Mr Scarlett inquired of Lt Colonel Metherell: 'Can you ascertain who reads the Newsome output, daily, weekly and ad hoc,'[6] and Mr Emmanuel replied:

> About 3 or 4 months ago both Air Commodore Groves and myself read Newsome's directives carefully and consistently, drawing to the Brigadier's attention any points worthy of mention. These points arose almost daily. For the last month I have only glanced through them, being somewhat discouraged by failing to find any improvement.

---

1. Mr Barman to Mr Bruce Lockhart, 8.5.42.
2. Mr Kirkpatrick to Mr Bruce Lockhart, 13.5.42.
3. Mr Kirkpatrick to Mr Bruce Lockhart, 18.5.42.
4. Mr David Garnett to Mr Kirkpatrick, 29.5.42.
5. Mr David Stephens to Mr Kirkpatrick, 6.6.42.
6. Mr Scarlett to Lt Colonel Metherell, 31.8.42.

The Director of Plans, Mr Ritchie Calder, then undertook the regular examination of these directives, but the following December had to ask that the Director General should request that a copy should be sent regularly to him.

The V Campaign and Colonel Britton's Broadcasts

The origin of the symbolic 'V' for a Victory of the Allied Powers would appear to be as follows:

On 14th January, 1941, M. de Lavelaye broadcast on Radio Belgique: 'I suggest that you should use the letter "V" as a rallying sign, because "V" stands for Victory in French and Vryheid in Flemish.' On 22nd January, 1941, a letter from a North Channel port stated: 'multitudes of little V's appear on all sides, for as La France Libre is listened to every evening, so Radio Belgique is followed with the same interest.' On 22nd March, *Les Français parlent aux Français* broadcast a special feature on the V sign. Through March and April reports showed that the V symbol was being chalked up everywhere. On 15th March, 1941, the BBC in French broadcast the instructions: 'Hide your sous' and within a few weeks reports were stating that stamps were being used for change in France and Belgium owing to the disappearance of sous.[1]

Mr Douglas Ritchie* was a young journalist who had followed Mr Noel Newsome from the *Daily Telegraph* to take up the post of Assistant European Editor of the BBC. The facts given above inspired him with the realisation of the immense possibilities of broadcasting in modern warfare.[2] Mr Ritchie's illumination, for it was no less, made for himself a niche in history and provided one more illustration of the difficulties which are produced by unco-ordinated excursions into Political Warfare.

The V Campaign Fulfilled a Psychological Need

The ideas put forward by Mr Ritchie were held by many others and were in fact the basis of much of the work being done by SO1. But at the time he put them forward the BBC was not controlled by SO1 and the persons to whom he circulated his paper were ignorant of the existence of many secret SO1 activities and for that matter equally ignorant of the existence of SO2.

---

1. The above facts are drawn from BBC Studies of European Audiences. The V Campaign, 8.10.41.
2. Broadcasting as a Weapon of War, by D. E. Ritchie, 4.5.41.

* [Douglas Ernest Ritchie (1905–67) was born in London but went out to farm in South Africa. Reporter and critic for *Rand Daily Mail* and *Johannesburg Sunday Times*, and then on editorial staff of *Daily Telegraph* 1935. Joined BBC European Service March 1939; Assistant Director, BBC European Broadcasts, 1941–4; Director, European News Department, BBC, 1944–6; General Overseas Service Organiser, BBC, 1949–50; Head of Publicity 1950–6.]

The spontaneous emergence of the V sign and of the ideas put forward by Mr Ritchie are a measure of the lack of direction exercised over the BBC by any British Government Department, and also of the psychological need for action felt all over Europe, both in enemy-occupied territory and in this country.

Mr Ritchie's paper was produced in answer to a psychological need which had not been recognised by any officials responsible for subversion. Ten days after producing his paper, Mr Ritchie called a meeting with himself in the chair, which was attended by the following BBC officials: the European News Editor, European Service Officer, European Intelligence Director, and the Regional News Editors for Holland, Scandinavia and the Balkans. The ideas in his paper were adopted and a Committee called the V Committee set up [in May 1941] on the grounds 'that the BBC, having proof that its European broadcasts are listened to with longing by a vast audience, is in a position to tell these people how they can help to procure a British victory . . . there is here, if it is properly used, an entirely new weapon of war, the importance of which can hardly be exaggerated. If the British Government were to work out a plan for the full and synchronised use of this weapon, the peoples of the occupied countries could greatly disturb the morale of the German troops, bring the whole European economy into a state of chaos, and finally destroy communications and cause disorders throughout the Continent on such a scale that, combined with the operations of Britain's fighting services, it might well prove decisive.'[1]

It was agreed that a representative of MEW should be invited to become a member of the Committee as well as the French, Czech and Polish News Editors and the Belgian programme organiser.

The 'Colonel Britton' Broadcasts

On 6th June, 1941, Mr Douglas Ritchie gave his first broadcast in the character of Colonel Britton which was promised as a regular feature of *London Calling Europe* in which Colonel Britton promised to deal with correspondence from the occupied countries.

On 9th June at the third meeting of the V Committee, Mr Rayner, the representative of the SO1 liaison section with MEW, rapped loudly on the table while discussion was general and pointed out he had used not only the morse code for V but the theme of famous passages in Beethoven's Fifth Symphony.

On 27th June, Colonel Britton broadcast on the V in sound: 'When you knock on the door there is your knock. If you call the waiter in a restaurant call him like this. . . .' His broadcast concluded with passages from the first bars and the scherzo of Beethoven's Fifth Symphony.

1. Minutes of meeting held in Bush House, 15.5.41. V Committee.

Reactions of Dutch Wireless

A response to this broadcast followed dramatically nine days later when the German-controlled Dutch Radio Station at Hilversum suddenly began broadcasting Beethoven's Fifth Symphony, broke off and explained the records had been broadcast 'in error'.

The results of the Colonel Britton broadcasts generally demonstrated that he was supplying a psychological need which was widespread throughout Europe. It might perhaps be defined as the listener's need to regain self-respect by some action which would identify him with the Allied forces.

'The broadcasts in the Colonel Britton period had a considerable effect on sabotage and other anti-German activities in Europe. The hiding of copper and nickel coins in France, Belgium and Holland, the wave of incendiaries in Belgium last autumn, and the cutting of cables in Belgium and Holland all followed on broadcasts of this type.'[1]

The annoyance of the Germans at the chalking up of V's was clearly proved by the somewhat clumsy attempt to annex it.

German Attempts to Appropriate the V Sign

On 20th June, the first attempt to do so was made by the Nazi-controlled newspaper *Faedrelandet*. On 15th July, the German Home News used a new interval signal based on the Fifth Symphony. The same signal was used by most of the radio stations in occupied Europe. On 16th July, Hilversum broadcast opened with the Morse V and explained that 'It is the V for victory which Germany is winning on all parts for the Freedom of Europe.'

The next day Fritsche, the German commentator, stated: 'What people are seeking is some small sign showing that they belong to the Community which was founded in this struggle. Lo! this sign exists. It is the sign V, the initial of the old call Viktoria.'

Following this, newspapers were ordered to publish V's on their front pages. The attempt, however, to annex the symbol was a failure and was rendered more difficult by the fact that Viktoria is not a German word. Moreover, the confusion produced by the attempt was sometimes to the advantage of the patriots, and the Germans actually acquitted a Pole who had been accused of pasting a V label on to somebody's attaché case.[2] The German attempt to annex the symbol could be easily defeated by chalking RAF after the V or in Norway H7 (for Haakon VII).

The Colonel Britton broadcasts were naturally extremely popular in Britain and received considerable publicity in British newspapers as, contrary to the usual custom, the Britton scripts were given to the British press as handouts.[3]

---

1. Memorandum on Mr Harriman's Broadcast by Mr Griffin, 31.3.42.
2. BBC Studies of European Audiences. The V Campaign, 8.10.41.
3. Minute of Lord Gage of 21.11.41, calling attention to a script in which Colonel Britton proposed to discuss spitting in beer before serving it to Germans and contaminating food.

SO1 was naturally keenly interested in these developments and on 15 July, 1941, Mr Leeper asked that SO1 responsibility for subversive propaganda of the kind[1] should be considered at the first meeting of the recently appointed Co-ordination Committee at which Sir Orme Sargent* and Mr Strang were informed that the V Committee was executing a foreign policy which it had itself devised and firm guidance should be given immediately.[2]

The V Committee was however active and the demonstrations first staged for 14th July and postponed till 20th July, were followed by a 'Go-Slow' week from 5th [to] 13th September.

Need to Provide Policy Guidance to V Committee

[July 1941] The spontaneous emergence of the V Committee was a cogent demonstration of the need for the formation of PWE. Until PWE had got into active operation, all that could be done was to impose a ban on direct incitement to sabotage or anything overstepping passive resistance.

Dangers of Colonel Britton Broadcasts

[Feb. 1942] An objection to instructions in sabotage being broadcast in English was conveyed from the Home Office through PWE Security Officer, Colonel Chambers, as disaffected elements working in Britain, such as Irish workers, might put such instructions into practice in this country. Weak-minded and easily suggestible persons existed in all industries who also might be influenced.[3] This objection really disposed of Mr Ritchie's plan that he should broadcast instructions each week in English which should be given in full in each of the languages of the occupied territories by a speaker who should be regarded as Colonel Britton's spokesman.[4] Moreover, since nobody in PWE or the BBC could form any estimate of the importance of this objection, and as PWE were not willing to take it up with Home Security, it had to be accepted.

PWE Control of 'Colonel Britton' a Cause of Friction with BBC

The dangers of the Colonel Britton broadcasts to Political Warfare in Europe were clearly realised in PWE but as all of them were not, or perhaps

1. Letter to Mr Bruce Lockhart, 15.7.41.
2. Minute to Sir Orme Sargent and Mr Strang from Mr Bruce Lockhart.
3. Minutes of Joint Sub-Committee on Operational Propaganda, 25.2.42 and 27.2.42.
4. Minutes of PWE V Committee, 10.11.41.

* [Sir (Harold) Orme Garton 'Moley' Sargent (1884–1962) was educated at Radley and in Switzerland; entered FO 1906; served in Berne 1917; Paris 1919–25; Counsellor, FO, 1926; Deputy Under-Secretary 1939; Permanent Under-Secretary 1946–9.]

could not, be clearly explained, Colonel Britton himself and his assistants in the BBC were frequently given the impression that he was being muzzled by a Political Warfare Department which had not realised the potentialities of Political Warfare as well as he had himself.

One obvious objection was that Colonel Britton's broadcasts might produce premature revolts which would be easily put down and which would set back the resistance movements all over Europe.

Lack of Regional Intelligence in 'Colonel Britton' Scripts

The other general objection to the Colonel Britton scripts was that they were not regionalised and that conditions were so widely different in different parts of Europe that they would not be universally applicable. As an example, Colonel Britton's broadcast urging farmers everywhere to employ an extra labourer so that each farmer would save one man from going to work in Germany was actually given in Dutch. As the number of labourers a Dutch farmer was allowed to employ by the Germans was proportional to the acreage of his farm, this instruction merely showed that the BBC had no knowledge of local conditions in Holland, which was damaging not only to the BBC but to British propaganda and claims to leadership.

More specific dangers arising as a result of the Britton broadcasts were the naming of Quislings and pillorying of collaborators, which was likely to result in compromising RUs which were running similar features. Apart from this, the naming of Quislings was disliked as it was widely felt that a British colonel had not the necessary authority to attack individual foreign nationals in this way. For these reasons Colonel Britton was eventually stopped from naming Quislings and the embarrassment ceased.[1]

On another occasion, Colonel Britton had to be stopped from putting forward the suggestion that members of the British public should send messages to the Continent by toy balloon. This would not only have led to a flood of private unco-ordinated propaganda reaching the Continent, but would have drawn attention to balloons which PWE were using for disseminating Black printed matter which purported to be of local origin.

Again, unless controlled, Colonel Britton was likely to direct attention to some place, or incident, to which it was of vital importance not to refer for fear of jeopardising the safety of SOE agents.[2]

---

1. A result of Colonel Britton's denunciation of Mlle Nicole Bordeaux, generally believed to be the mistress of Abetz, was that an indignant relative first threatened a libel action against the BBC for defamation, and then induced Lord Winterton to ask a question in the House of Commons. See folder PWE/42/185/14.
2. The only instance appears to have been that after the denunciation of the Quisling Chief of Police of Blankenberge, that individual purged his police force and surrounded himself with a bodyguard with grave inconvenience to SOE. Minutes of Sub-Committee on Operational Propaganda, 27.2.42.

On 21st October, 1941, PWE considered a request that SOE should be consulted on the texts[1] and on 18.12.41 an instruction was issued that a draft of Colonel Britton's script must be submitted to Mr Jebb of SOE.[2]

The first meeting of a PWE V Committee to deal with the question of providing guidance was held on 30th September, 1941, at Fitzmaurice Place. The minutes of these meetings reveal the difficult nature of the task of preserving the Colonel Britton broadcasts, as a possibly useful asset in the future, while preventing him from developing his instructions on sabotage. Week by week, various suggestions and makeshifts were adopted to keep 'Colonel Britton going' – Allied statesmen such as Dr Gerbrandy were pressed to speak after a brief introduction by Colonel Britton. Week by week, Mr Ritchie and Mr Kirkpatrick pressed for a forward policy – in vain. The fact was that if the Colonel Britton broadcasts were suitable for one part of Europe, they were unsuitable for another; that the Allied plans for a landing on the Continent would not be ready for years, that the Allied Governments preferred to give their own instructions to their own peoples and disliked a British spokesman doing so, and that PWE and SOE were carrying out their own methods of bringing 'Secret Armies' into being, and encouraging resistance by secret broadcasting.

Shortly before his suspension, Colonel Britton put out a talk which had no received clearance from PWE in which he said: 'Within six weeks from now, there will open what may prove to be the greatest battle in the history of the world. . . . The Nazi attack is likely, as I said, within the next six weeks. . . . But we, too shall attack . . . and the Russians will attack. And you in Europe will attack. . . .'

An immediate protest was made by Colonel Taylor of SOE to PWE but no disciplinary action was taken, though the incident no doubt influenced the decision to bring Colonel Britton's talks to an end.

The Director General informed Mr D. E. Ritchie of this decision and stated: 'I wish to congratulate you on a campaign which achieved remarkable success in capturing the imagination of the whole world and which I understand was mainly your own idea. You have done a remarkable piece of work which will have its place in the history of this war.'[3]

Proposals for Operational Propaganda in Opening Broadcasting

The dilemma in which the PWE V Committee found itself led directly to further exploration of other forms of 'operational propaganda' which could be carried out in BBC broadcasts, without, or even in conjunction with, the personality of Colonel Britton.

1. Minute of Executive Committee, 21.10.41.
2. Letter from Mr David Stephens to Mr Brenan.
3. Director General PWE to Mr D. E. Ritchie, 8.5.42.

As a result of this situation and of a meeting held at CHQ, and attended by Mr Calder, to consider the problem, the Executive Committee set up a joint sub-committee on operational propaganda of the Departments interested, to examine and report on the extent to which operational propaganda, with special reference to sabotage, could be used in open broadcasting.[1]

The members were:
Mr Ritchie Calder (Chairman)
Mr D. E. Ritchie, BBC
Colonel Sporborg, SOE
Mr O. L. Lawrence, MEW
Mr David Garnett, Secretary.

The Sub-Committee held meetings which showed that MEW and SOE were free from many of the doubts which affected PWE in connection with the subject.[2] Their attitude was based on a document[3] put forward by Colonel Sporborg. Mr Ritchie indicated that he would not object to withdrawing as Colonel Britton if a forward policy were pursued.[4]

The main points of the report were that the giving of instructions in subversive activity including sabotage by means of opening broadcasting was likely to result in a considerable increase in militant action in occupied Europe . . . The Committee recommended that the BBC should make use of operational propaganda provided that it was effectively controlled by a committee of the Departments concerned and that operational propaganda was undertaken with full realisation that the material suitable for one territory was unsuitable for another.

The Sub-Committee also recommended that it should be perpetuated in the form of a permanent co-ordination committee with representatives from PWE, MEW, SOE, the BBC and should be empowered to invite representatives from the Services.

Divergent Views on Instructions Being Given by the BBC

There is little doubt that the Sub-Committee would have reported less favourably on the possibilities of operational propaganda in open broadcasting had not the MEW and SOE representatives, and the Secretary of the meeting, taken a view substantially different from that of its Chairman, who put forward views associated with Mr Leeper and the Regional Directors.

Mr Bruce Lockhart and General Brooks agreed that Mr Leeper should be Chairman of the Directional Committee proposed, but the divergence of

1. Covering minute from Mr Ritchie Calder to the Executive PWE, 4.3.42, sent with a copy of the Sub-Committee's recommendations.
2. This was directly contrary to the view put forward by the majority of SO2 country sections on 16th August, 1941, V Campaign Operations Broadcasts. To CEO from ADA/1, but circumstances had changed.
3. Report of Sub-Committee on Operational Propaganda, 3.3.42.
4. Mr Ritchie Calder in a covering minute to PWE Executive, 4.3.42.

policy within PWE was such that Mr Leeper cancelled the first meeting and the Committee did not meet.

The subject was thereupon referred to the Director General's Propaganda Policy Committee and Mr Leeper stated[1] that the Regional Directors objected to the report, in particular Colonel Sutton was against giving instructions in sabotage to the French.

The Committee thereupon took the view that the proposals must be referred to higher authority, a course which was certain to delay the carrying out of the policy recommended and which might possibly reverse it.

The matter was thereupon referred to the Chiefs of Staff Committee by Brigadier Brooks and to the Foreign Secretary by the Director General.

Pending their decision the 'V' campaign and Colonel Britton's broadcasts came to an end and nothing better took their place.[2]

Kinds of Propaganda Proposed

The document put forward to the Chiefs of Staff Committee[3] sought approval for operational propaganda of the following types:

Labour recruitment. To stop labour going to Germany and to decrease the labour working for the Axis in German Europe.
Transportation. The rolling stock in Western Europe was being used to capacity. It followed that all damage to rolling stock and time lost by go-slow tactics, misdirection of trucks, etc., would result in a permanent decrease of supplies available to the enemy. Sabotage of transport by road and water were also valuable.
Fuel and Power. The shortage of fuel and power was such that any action by household consumers to intensify peak-load problems was likely to have adverse effects on industrial output. Efforts should be made to reduce the quantity and quality of the coal output.
Occupational Sabotage. Instructions should be given for simple sabotage in mining and quarrying, welding and rivetting, draughtsmanship, pattern making, tool making, foundry work.
Go Slow. The continuation of the campaign to go slow was particularly desirable. In N.W. France and Belgium it could be developed in the form of instructions to take cover during all RAF daylight sweeps. It was believed that the resulting decrease in industrial output would assist the primary object of these raids and make it imperative for the enemy to put up Fighter Demand.

---

1. 1st Meeting of PWE Propaganda Policy Committee, 17.3.42.
2. Mr Kirkpatrick reported that complaints had been received from C and from the Czechs with regard to the discontinuance of the V Campaign. Propaganda Policy Committee Minutes, 26.5.42.
3. PW(E)(42)48, 1.6.42. File Vb(L)40.

The Administration. Everything possible should be done to hamper the efficiency of Government machinery concerned with collaboration with the enemy.
Exportable Food and Raw Materials. Instructions should be given to peasants and farmers on how to hamper the requisitioning of their produce and how to spoil stocks which were requisitioned for Germany.

In considering these proposals the C. of S. [Chiefs of Staff] Committee drew a distinction between:

1. The formation of secret armies and general uprising of patriots.
2. Sabotage connected with actual operations.
3. The general sabotage and go-slow methods which went on all the time.

Chiefs of Staff Approve 'Operational Propaganda' Proposals

The C. of S. Committee considered that the PWE proposals belonged to the last category and were approved provided the third category did not endanger the first and second.

Approval having been given, the matter came up before [the] PWE Policy Committee on 2nd June and it was agreed that a committee should be set up under Mr Kirkpatrick to consider how the policy agreed to should be carried out.

At the first meeting of Mr Kirkpatrick's Committee Mr Lawrence of MEW suggested that the campaign should be initiated with a broadcast by Air Marshal Harris,* Chief of Bomber Command.[1] Mr Kirkpatrick undertook to invite Air Marshal Harris to do so. It was also agreed that operational propaganda should concentrate on transport and fuel and power.

Mr Kirkpatrick Seeks to Revive 'Colonel Britton'

At a second meeting at which the Regional Directors were represented by Mr Harman and Mr Crossman[2] instead of by Mr Barman, Mr Kirkpatrick stated that Air Marshal Harris would be introduced by Colonel Britton in the English programme, but that the Harris broadcast should be given in the different languages without any such introduction. Mr Harris and Mr

---

1. Minutes of Committee on Operational Propaganda held 4.6.42.
2. Minutes of Committee on Operational Propaganda, 17.6.42.
* [Sir Arthur Travers 'Bomber' Harris (1892–1984) joined 1st Rhodesian Regiment as a bugler 1914; joined Royal Flying Corps in England 1915; commanded No. 44 Squadron for training in night-fighting 1918; served in India and Iraq 1919–25; Air Vice-Marshal 1939; head of RAF delegation in Washington 1941; AOC-in-C Bomber Command 1942–6; Air Chief Marshal 1943; Marshal of the RAF 1946, but his great contribution to victory in the Second World War went shamefully under-acknowledged.]

Crossman expressed the view that 'The campaign in the long run[1] would be more effective if it avoided all "stunting" and concentrated rather on permeating BBC output with the idea of transport sabotage.' Mr Kirkpatrick, Colonel Sporborg and Mr Lawrence disagreed and took the view that direct instructions were also necessary.

There is no doubt that the Regional Director's objection to 'stunting' was a reference to Colonel Britton, and that it was a tactical blunder on the part of the Chairman to propose that Colonel Britton's broadcasts should be revived.[2]

In the effort to conciliate the rival parties, the Director General took over the Chairmanship of the Directional Committee on Operational Propaganda and invited Mr Leeper to serve on it.[3]

The Transport Campaign

Meanwhile, however, Mr Lawrence had supplied a script and Air Marshal Harris had agreed to initiate the transport campaign.

The purpose of this was to show the connection between RAF bombing and the European transport system, the most vulnerable point in the German economic system, and to prove that the enslaved populations of Europe could therefore best assist RAF bombing and shorten the period of their captivity by the sabotage of transport whether by road, rail or water. Even temporary delays helped materially, since time lost could not be made up.

The Harris Broadcast

The script, with very few alterations, was approved by Air Marshal Harris, translations were prepared and the date of the broadcast which would initiate the transport campaign was fixed.

Mr Crossman and the Harris Broadcast

Unfortunately, Mr Crossman, who, as described above, had attended one of the Operational Propaganda Committee's meetings, had seized upon the idea that Air Marshal Harris, Chief of Bomber Command and engaged in directing the bombing of Germany, should address the German people. The MEW script on transportation was clearly unsuitable. Mr Crossman therefore wrote a script of his own, largely concerned with political matters and putting forward its writer's personal views as to British policy to Germany. He convinced Brigadier Brooks that it was desirable that Air Marshal Harris should address Germany as well as the occupied countries

1. *Ibid.*
2. Colonel Britton's broadcasts had been suspended on 8.5.42. See *supra*.
3. Director General to Mr Leeper, 26.6.42.

and through General Brooks and Wing Commander Rose of the Air Ministry, obtained Air Marshal Harris's consent to father the second document as well as the first. Mr Crossman did not, however, seek policy approval for the script from Mr Lockhart, who remained in ignorance of its existence. Acting with great promptitude Mr Crossman gained Mr Kirkpatrick's consent to the second script being broadcast to Germany and then had it put out in the German programme twenty-four hours before any of the transport scripts were due to go on the air. The result was not only to stultify the transport campaign and delay it for several weeks but to cause grave concern in the Cabinet. Neither Mr Crossman, Brigadier Brooks,* nor Air Marshal Harris and his advisers, had realised that it was grossly improper for one of the Service Chiefs to discuss British policy to Germany without Cabinet sanction. During the inquiry which followed, Brigadier Brooks and Wing Commander Rose stated that they had not been aware that the script was for broadcasting purposes – though it would have been equally improper as a leaflet. Brigadier Brooks's memory had, however, betrayed him as he had previously informed the Secretary of the Operational Propaganda Committee that both broadcasts had been approved by high authority and that it was useless for the Operational Propaganda Committee to protest. The full weight of ministerial displeasure fell accordingly upon Mr Crossman alone.

The result of this incident was further to delay the initiation of the propaganda campaigns for which MEW and SOE were pressing but which were still objected to by certain, though not by all, PWE regional heads, and by Mr Leeper. As the British press had given Air Marshal Harris's controversial broadcast very wide publicity, it was impossible for that distinguished officer to give another broadcast – nor was his first experience such as to encourage him to do so.

After an interval for the Harris broadcast to be forgotten, another speaker was sought by the Operational Propaganda Committee and was found in Sir Archibald Sinclair,** Secretary of State for Air. The new PWE Director of Plans and Campaigns, Mr Ritchie Calder, wrote a new script which was approved by Sir Archibald Sinclair and was broadcast in his name in all languages except English to the peoples of occupied Europe. The theme was, of course, the same as that provided by MEW.

---

* [Sir (Reginald Alexander) Dallas Brooks (d. 1966) won the Croix de Guerre and DSO in 1918; was SOE's representative on PWE's standing Ministerial Committee after June 1941, and was Commandant-General, Royal Marines, 1946–9; Governor of Victoria, Australia, 1949–61 and 1961–3.]

** [Sir Archibald Henry Macdonald Sinclair, 1st Viscount Thurso (1890–1970), served as second-in-command to his friend Winston Churchill in France in 1916; Liberal MP, Caithness and Sutherland, 1922–45; Secretary of State for Scotland in National Government 1931; resigned 1932; Chairman, Parliamentary Liberal Party, 1935; condemned Munich Agreement 1938; refused office under Chamberlain 1939; Secretary of State for Air 1940–5; advocate of strategic bombing offensive; lost seat in 1945; viscount 1952.]

> The destruction of a locomotive in France means complications on the Russian front. The misdirection of a railway wagon in the South of France may throw a munition factory in the Ruhr out of gear. . . . You too can do your part. The bombs which the RAF carries are only the big brothers of the grains of sand or carborundum which can find their way into oil pipes and grease-boxes. If every one of you will do your bit the total effect will be such that the German transport system will crash. We will look after the big bombs; you will look after the grains of sand.[1]

Shortly before his appointment, the new Director of Plans had drafted a 'phase plan on Transport' on which the campaign developed during the following months. It included a script given by the Minister of Economic Warfare.

Mr Ritchie Calder's Phase Plan for the Transport Campaign

A summary of this plan shows how the subject was handled:[2]

> *First Phase*. Impregnation of news bulletins with items on Germany's transport difficulties.
> *Second Phase*. Air Marshal Harris to speak on relation of RAF to transport.
> *Third Phase*. Background talks. A pilot – why I attacked that train. How Russians destroyed or removed locomotives. How all routes lead to the Russian front. Description of movement of a train across Europe. Importance of routes from different countries to Germany.
> *Fourth Phase*. Education by suggestion. Examples of how the systems can be strained and break down.
> *Fifth Phase*. Direct destruction. *This phase depends upon simultaneous military action.* Material should be prepared, and the details including timing, agreed with SOE in advance, but *specific calls to sabotage, or detailed instructions in how to commit acts of sabotage must await the decision of the Chiefs of Staff and must synchronise with Allied intervention.*

The last paragraph was a reversion to the earlier PWE thesis sustained by Mr Leeper and Regional Directors and was contrary to the views of the majority of the Operational Propaganda Committee.

As a result of representations by these members of the Committee, Mr Calder sent a minute to the Director General saying:

1. Script of Sir Archibald Sinclair.
2. Phase plan for transport campaign.

> The only Directive from the Chiefs of Staff I have received is the one, unless there is a subsequent one, I intend to act on from now on . . . in these campaigns we are authorised to foment general sabotage and go slow methods by whatever in our opinion are the most effective means (not including direct instructions).[1]

The Director General thereupon referred the matter again to the Chiefs of Staff Committee, although their clear instructions of five months earlier had not yet been carried out. The opinion of Mr Bracken on the subject of instructions in sabotage is dealt with on p. 370.

International Transport Federation Participates in the Campaign

PWE Director of Plans also invited members of the International Transport Federation [ITF] to take part in discussions on the transport campaign and at this and subsequent meetings [the] ITF agreed to assist the BBC in the preparation of scripts, with speakers, and in the provision of intelligence.

A representative of the Directorate of Plans and a representative of the BBC attended the monthly meeting of [the] ITF when the ITF share in BBC broadcasts was reviewed, until about November 1944.

The transport campaign was the principal piece of operational propaganda carried out in open broadcasting during the years of '42 and '43 when instructions were general in character and could not be linked with military requirements. The methods followed have been indicated in Mr Ritchie Calder's 'Phase Plan', though the phases were not kept distinct. The servicing of this campaign was largely carried out within the BBC itself, chiefly by Mr John Palmer. Full advantage was taken of any facilities offered by the ITF though it must be confessed that scripts provided by the foreign members of the ITF were often unsuitable. Within the BBC itself there was a realisation of the fundamental importance of the transport campaign and all sources available were carefully scrutinised for material. Certain material however, which came to PWE through MEW, i.e. material from the Industrial Damage Report, was only passed on after reference to Mr O. L. Lawrence, or Mr Ingrams, to the BBC. The PWE representative on the Air Ministry Target Committee was also able to make occasional contributions of material. But the chief method of carrying out the campaign came to be the permeation of the news services with items which could only result in making BBC audiences aware of the importance of the sabotage of transport. Such items of news went on, week after week and month after month.

---

1. Minute to Director General from Ritchie Calder, 26.9.42.

The Agricultural Campaign

A small group of agricultural and economic experts in PWE and MEW who were familiar with the mentality of peasants of different parts of Europe were fully aware of the importance of the natural resistance of the peasants to the agricultural exploitation of Europe by Germany, and also of the difficulties of an approach to a class so suspicious of townspeople and official utterances.

A PWE committee on agricultural propaganda was set up by Mr Leeper at CHQ at a time when Major Baker White of the Military Wing, Mr Garnett and Mr Quentin Bell, were discussing the urgent need of defining PWE propaganda policy to peasants. As a result, Mr Garnett and Major Baker White were co-opted to the Agricultural Committee and Mr Garnett became its Secretary. Other members of the Committee were Mr Brinley Thomas, Mr Leonard Ingrams, Mr Lamartine Yates (MEW) and Miss Doreen Warriner.

The chief difficulty in policy was that the suspicion and hostility always latent between countrymen and townspeople had been enormously increased in almost every country by the food shortage. In no country were the peasantry going to starve if they could possibly circumvent the requisitioning orders. But requisitioning was not only or everywhere directly for export of food to Germany. It was also necessary for providing rations to townspeople and industrial workers.

Every exhortation to hoard food had therefore to be coupled with exhortations to sell it to the peasants' compatriots at reasonable prices. This involved a policy of encouraging the black market, or of advocating 'le marché rose'.

Many points were clear enough. Thus all over Europe Germany was forcing the agricultural communities to grow industrial crops – in particular the oil-bearing seeds, linseed and rape in the northern countries and sunflowers in the Balkans. It was fortunately easy to point out that these crops exhausted the soil and that the farmer was paid for them in inflated currency. Peasants and farmers were therefore urged to conserve the fertility of the soil.

The censuses of practically all domestic animals afforded excellent opportunities for peasant resistance and for propaganda.

In secret broadcasts there was little difficulty in executing PWE policy once it had been established in terms of the local conditions. But in open broadcasts on the BBC it was a very different matter. Few of the BBC Regional Editors were interested in agriculture and the occasional news items which were included were usually unsuitable and sometimes positively disastrous.

The BBC however had established a Dawn Peasants' Programme for every language and the PWE Agricultural Committee decided to supply suitable regionalised items for this programme. Mr Kirkpatrick agreed, although he subsequently stated[1] that he had not agreed that the scripts provided should be used.

1. Mr Kirkpatrick to Mr Garnett, 25.6.42.

BBC Refusal to Provide Copies of Scripts to PWE

One of the principal difficulties encountered in this 'servicing' of the BBC Dawn Peasants' Programme was to discover what material had actually been used, as the BBC failed to provide scripts and applications to Mr Kirkpatrick were made in vain.[1] The PWE Agricultural Sub-Committee finally only obtained them by discovering copies filed in the BBC Library. Exactly the same difficulty was met with by Headquarters Planning and Research Section at about the same date. Mr David Stephens minuted Mr Bruce Lockhart [on] 17.6.42, 'when scripts are asked for difficulties are almost always raised. The scripts either do not arrive or only arrive after considerable delay or in imperfect condition.' The failure to make use of the Dawn Peasants' items was sometimes due to the fact that they had not got further than Mr Newsome's office and sometimes to the Regional Editor, or the Dawn Editor, discarding them. Frequently material which the PWE Agricultural Committee regarded as disastrous was inserted. For example, tagged on to an item designed to encourage the sabotage of threshing machinery was the report of the death sentence being inflicted on a Poznan farmhand for agricultural sabotage.[2]

Ridiculous Blunders by the BBC

The following week an item which was calculated to make BBC news bulletins a laughing stock among all listeners with an elementary knowledge of agriculture was included: 'Germany's drive to get wool . . . is being defeated by peasants who are not shearing their sheep. A fleece on the sheep's back will help to protect the animal through the winter. . . .'

The system of servicing the BBC Dawn Peasants' Programme by supplying scripts did not work and attempts to improve it only led to collisions with Mr Newsome, who was invariably supported by Mr Kirkpatrick. In the period January to August 1942 the main result of such efforts was to embitter relations with the BBC. Nevertheless the small unit supplying the scripts did not give up and material 'slanted' for regional conditions in Western Europe, Scandinavia, Italy and the Balkans was supplied without a break until January 1944, that is for a period of two years. During that time much other agricultural propaganda was done, chiefly by Mr Klatt and Miss Warriner. A very great improvement was brought about in agricultural propaganda during this period as relations between PWE and the BBC slowly improved, and as the BBC Regional Editors slowly became imbued with the ideas underlying PWE policy.

1. Mr Garnett to Mr Kirkpatrick, 10.6.42, repeated on 18.6.42 and 24.6.42.
2. Mr Ritchie Calder to the Director General, 6.8.42

Radio Warfare and Aspidistra

[July 1940]
One result of the German occupation of Europe was that the broadcasting centres of the occupied countries came under the control of the German Propaganda Ministry. The numerical preponderance in transmitters so obtained could be used for jamming British broadcasts and for providing local services based on a German directive. Owing to the number of transmitters at their disposal, they controlled a large range of wavelengths.

The Germans did in fact use a large portion of their possible transmitter strength in jamming British foreign-language broadcasts though they never thought it worth while to interfere with the BBC Home Service. Owing to our inferiority in transmitter strength we did no jam any German or German-controlled broadcasts. The possibility of in some way overcoming the relative German superiority in the ether greatly exercised the minds of many in SO1 and [in May 1941] various proposals were discussed. It was natural in such circumstances to take counsel with [NAME DELETED ON GROUNDS OF NATIONAL SECURITY] who was responsible for the technical servicing and installation of all the RU secret broadcasts from Woburn. [NAME DELETED] apparently believed that it would be possible to offset the enemy numerical superiority by a single 'counter battery' which could overcome, or shout down any of the enemy's transmissions on medium wave by means of its very much greater power. A 500 k.w. transmitter which he believed would be capable of such interference with enemy programmes was in existence in the USA where it had not been licensed for use on account of its great power. [NAME DELETED] during a visit to the USA inspected this instrument and secured an option on it at a very reasonable figure, thus preventing its purchase by the Chinese Government. The transmitter in question was adapted to broadcast on a number of different frequencies making the changes with very great rapidity.

On his return to England, [NAME DELETED] prepared a plan for the purchase, erection and use of this transmitter. In this document he claimed that: 'This apparatus would create a raiding Dreadnought of the Ether firing broadsides at unpredictable times at unpredictable objectives of the enemy's radio propaganda machine,'[1] and he stated that:

> The weapon to perform this counter battery work must clearly have three principal qualities; it must be a complete surprise; it must be loud – as loud in the countries to which it is directed as the enemy-controlled transmitters themselves; and it must be flexible, to cope with the great variety of propaganda services controlled by the enemy.

1. A plan for Counter Battery work in Radio Propaganda.

In particular the plan was to interfere with reception on the Volkesempfangener or German peoples' radio set. [NAME DELETED] stated that the cost of the transmitter and its erection would be £165,000 and the running costs £28,000 per annum.

It is to be noted that from the inception the propagandists of SO1 and PWE were led to believe that the 'Grande Voce', or Aspidistra,[1] as it was soon afterwards called, would be able to overpower the German official wireless in Germany for short periods and plans were frequently put forward to use the transmitter for such purposes as interrupting the decennial celebrations of the Nazi Party in Berlin during daylight.[2]

Purchase of Aspidistra

[NAME DELETED]'s plan was submitted to the Prime Minister by the Minister of Economic Warfare[3] and the project was approved on 17.5.41. There can be no doubt that approval for the purchase was given in the belief that it could be used as a 'radio counter battery'. But from the SO1 point of view the authorisation meant that SO1 would control one of the most powerful broadcasting instruments in the world which could be used for broadcasting even if it were not able to shout the enemy down on his own wavelengths. At the time of the purchase SO1 had no control over the BBC.

The Prime Minister's decision was communicated to the Minister of Economic Warfare by Major Desmond Morton[4] who suggested that 'the Prime Minister's authority clearly allows you to purchase the instrument at once. Its cost in dollars is such a fragmentary portion of one day's war that should technical arguments prevent its being used in exactly the way you now propose little loss will in my opinion have been incurred.'

The purchase from the Radio Corporation of America was accordingly made and £111,801/4/10d. was accordingly remitted to HM Ambassador in Washington and work was immediately begun on preparing a site for its erection in Bedfordshire, without reference to any other authority.

On the Air Ministry being consulted[5] with regard to the height of mast proposed, serious objections were made with regard to the site and SO1 were informed that in any case the approval of the Wireless Telegraphy Board would be necessary.[6]

Work on the Bedfordshire site was therefore suspended; after the project had received the approval of the Wireless Telegraphy Board[7] in September

1. From the song 'The Biggest Aspidistra in the World'.
2. Plan for the use of Aspidistra, 21.1.43.
3. 16.5.41.
4. Major Desmond Morton to Minister of Economic Warfare, 19.5.41.
5. [The] Minister of Economic Warfare saw the Secretary of State for Air on 27.8.41.
6. Mr Gaitskill to Mr Leeper, XD/323/9, 29.8.41.
7. Meeting of Wireless Telegraphy Board with Services and GPO, 12.9.41.

1941, a site was eventually chosen near Crowborough on Ashdown Forest.[1] Financial responsibility for the project was transferred to PWE in November.[2] In December Treasury fears that Aspidistra was overlapping BBC plans for the installation of an 800 k.w. transmitter near the Humber were set at rest. The disclosure of the existence of Aspidistra had come as a surprise to the BBC technical staff. They gained the support of the Minister of Information to their being fully informed of the technical aspect of what was being planned.[3] [NAME DELETED] accordingly saw Sir Noel Ashbridge and reported verbally that Sir Noel was well disposed towards the scheme.[4] This view was unduly optimistic and the Minister of Information asked for a meeting which should be attended by Sir Noel Ashbridge and Sir Cyril Radcliffe to discuss the effect of the proposal upon existing policy and existing services, the circumstances in which Aspidistra would be used and the position with regard to other devices. A meeting was accordingly held, the BBC being represented by Mr Cecil Graves and Sir Noel Ashbridge, and a full discussion took place. The BBC objections were that the use of Aspidistra on enemy wavelengths constituted jamming and that a Cabinet decision directed that enemy broadcasts should not be jammed as we did not stand to gain in a radio war. If we jammed German Home broadcasts they would jam the BBC Home Service. Moreover, transmissions from Aspidistra would interfere with reception of the Home Service in Southern England. Italian attempts to butt in with a 'ghost voice' on the BBC Home Service had been a failure and Aspidistra might do no better. The BBC were carrying out research on transmissions from an aeroplane designed to butt-in on enemy broadcasts in the towns over which it flew.

Mr Bracken's Objections to Aspidistra

[Feb. 1942]

These objects and replies[5] by PWE were submitted to the Ministers[6] at a meeting at which the Minister of Information raised various other objections to the scheme:

1. that there had been no previous consultation with BBC engineers.
2. that the BBC would not be able to provide technical staff.
3. that the scheme had been carried out extravagantly.
4. that the project would interfere with the Home Services of the BBC.

The Minister of Economic Warfare contraverted these objections and recalled the history of the project in a letter to the Foreign Secretary.[7] A

---

1. Letter from Chairman of Wireless Telegraphy Board, 21.10.41.
2. Meeting of Standing Ministerial Committee, 25.11.41.
3. Sir Cyril Radcliffe to Mr Bruce Lockhart, 1.1.42.
4. Mr Bowes Lyon to Mr David Stephens, 17.1.42.
5. PW(M)(42)16.
6. Meeting of Ministerial Committee, 3.2.42.
7. Minister of Economic Warfare to Foreign Secretary, 11.2.42.

further meeting was held and an agreed statement of the PWE and BBC was drawn up by Sir Cyril Radcliffe.[1]

By this stage it had become apparent that the BBC was anxious to obtain control of Aspidistra which they now urged should be staffed by BBC engineers and used to supplement BBC services when it was not being employed as a 'secret weapon', or as 'a roving Dreadnought of the Ether'. PWE and the Minister of Economic Warfare considered it vital that it should be controlled by 'C''s engineers who were in charge of the technical operation of PWE's RU transmitters. The PWE case was strengthened by a letter from Colonel Lycett, Chairman of the Inter Services Wireless Telegraphy Board, to Brigadier S. M. Menzies[2] pointing out that the conditions on which the Board had agreed to the erection of Aspidistra would not be kept if it were to be used for ordinary broadcasting, and asking for another meeting.

Aspidistra Used to Reinforce BBC European Services

Meanwhile it had been proposed that if Aspidistra was used to reinforce the BBC Foreign Services, it would be included in Group E and the landline from the studios at Milton Bryant to Ashdown Forest should be routed through the BBC control room so that transmissions could be shut down on receiving orders to do so from the Director of Signals Air Ministry. These arrangements were confirmed.[3] Further negotiations were carried out by the Director General of PWE with the Directors General of the BBC and agreement was reached[4] that Aspidistra should be used to reinforce the BBC when not required for special purposes, [and] that Fighter Command control of the Crowborough station should remain with PWE.

The Minister minuted this: 'I agree. But I think point 3 should be reconsidered. The BBC should provide technicians to run the plant.' Mr Bruce Lockhart thereupon represented[5] the grave difficulties of dual control and the fact that the staff referred to as 'PWE staff' were in fact 'C''s engineers who would be required to operate the station.

The Minister, however, would not agree and further meetings betwen Mr Bruce Lockart, Sir Cecil Graves and Mr Foot at which a revised agreement was drawn up were necessary.

Mr Bracken Fails to Get Control of Aspidistra

Nevertheless in this agreement also Mr Bruce Lockhart managed to secure that [NAME DELETED ON GROUNDS OF NATIONAL SECURITY] and his assistant retained complete technical control. This agreement was

1. Aspidistra, 22.2.42.
2. 13.3.42.
3. Meeting in Director of Signals' Office, 24.5.42.
4. Mr Bruce Lockhart to Minister of Information, 22.5.42.
5. Mr Bruce Lockhart to Minister of Information, 25.5.42.
6. Mr Bruce Lockhart to the Minister of Information, 23.7.42.

finally signed by Mr Bracken.[6] The BBC had secured Aspidistra as an auxiliary transmitter when not otherwise employed and PWE plans for employing it otherwise showed little realisation of either its limitations or its possibilities. Nor had it been completed.

Relations with Colonel Donovan's* Organisation

Colonel Donovan's Organisation can be described as the American 'opposite number' of SOE in so far as SO functions were compatible with US neutrality.

Mr Robert Sherwood, a personal friend of President Roosevelt and a well-known dramatist, who was described at that time as 'head of Donovan's SO1', and Mr Cross, head of Broadcast Division Federal Communications Committee, visited England arriving early in September 1941.

SO2 New York announcing the impending visit stated:[1]

> Gross will report to Donovan on all British Radio Broadcasting, overt and convert as far as we may wish to inform him. . . . Both friends will be active and potentially useful opposite numbers to members of our organisation here and as such you will no doubt take them in hand and send them back duly impressed and improved in outlook.

The further objects of their visit were to:[2]

> Discuss the immediate erection and operation in England of a powerful medium-wave transmitter to cover the Continent with America calling. The reception in England of American short-wave transmission of news for rebroadcasting on medium wave. Co-ordination of monitoring. General close collaboration through SO New York.

Arrangements were made by SOE to meet them on arrival and carry them down for a visit to CHQ. This visit took place on 10/11.9.41. Mr Sherwood was a personal friend of Mr Bruce Lockhart and the visit to CHQ was arranged by him.

Although the USA was a neutral, PWE gave a very full account of the work which it was doing and supplied[3] Mr Sherwood with copies of recent leaflets and with a list of the whispers or 'sibs' which were being put into circulation in enemy countries.

---

1. In a telegram quoted by Major Neame to Mr Adams, 26.8.41.
2. Sir Charles Hambro to Mr R. A. Leeper, 3.9.41.
3. Mr Adams to Mr Sherwood, 22.9.41.

* [Major-General William J. 'Wild Bill' Donovan (1883–1959) was awarded the Congressional Medal of Honor in the Great War; Assistant Attorney-General of US 1924; Chairman, Boulder Dam Canyon Project Commission; special intelligence mission to UK 1940 and to Yugoslavia, Greece and Middle East 1940–1; Co-ordinator of Information 1941–2; Director of Strategic Services (OSS) 1942–5; Hon. KBE.]

Discussions during the visit ranged over the arrangements for liaison between FIS (Colonel Donovan's organisation) and PWE co-operation in planning and the exchange of plans, by American development of new media for propaganda, i.e. through the mails, by radio, new Black channels, news creation, etc., and by influencing of priorities in the supply of necessary equipment.

American Help for PWE

The most important field for co-operation was that of intelligence. Colonel Donovan could mobilise technical skill in 'Market Research' for PWE purposes, by training trade representatives and tourists going to Europe in methods of information gathering and could collect and tabulate information collected from persons arriving from Europe and could station intelligence officers at important points in Europe under suitable cover.

Specific requests made to Mr Sherwood[1] were for help in obtaining four seven-line and two twelve-line teletype Hellschreiber machines with their spare parts; for the names of Market Research specialists in [the] USA; for information regarding internal occupied territories given by US Consular officials who had recently left Europe; and for a copy of the new edition of *Le Bottin* which might be obtained by Admiral Leahy and sent back in the Embassy bag. Mr Sherwood paid a second visit to CHQ on 18.9.41.

A telegram[2] from New York discussing broadcasting arrangements stated that all short-wave stations in the USA had agreed to accept guidance and directives from Donovan and that he would directly control certain stations. In view of this, 'our position is one of retirement in favour of Donovan who is prepared to receive and make use of all material we can supply in the way of guidance directives and information'.

Mr Sherwood and Mr Gross were also told of the existence of many of the secret broadcasting stations or 'RUs' at CHQ.

Following Sherwood's visit, Major William Whitney set up an office in London early in November as Colonel Donovan's representative with Edmund Taylor, 'the best man we have in the strategy of Political Warfare'.[3] Whitney engaged Percy Winner and Maurice Gilbert as assistants.[4] Mr Sherwood's hope that 'Taylor should have plenty of opportunity to work with staff at CHQ'[5] was realised and Mr Taylor lived for some time at Crowholt working with Regional Directors and seeing all directives, plans, etc. Ed Taylor was at Crowholt when the news of Pearl Harbor came through and led the cheers which meant that from that moment the United States were in the war.[6]

1. Mr Adams to Mr Sherwood, 22.9.41.
2. No. 36613 dated 13.9.41.
3. No. 755331 of 31.10.41. Sherwood for Lockhart.
4. Telegram from SO New York, 16.10.41.
5. No. 75531, 31.10.41.
6. Information from Mr Adams.

Before Pearl Harbor, precautions had to be taken to prevent the extent of collaboration between OSS and PWE from becoming known. Major Whitney was warned:[5] 'Consider it dangerous for you to use such phrases as the British suggest or the British advise . . . you should say Taylor expressly advises . . . when you use the word expressly we will know the source is British.'

Americans Not Informed of Radio Inconnu

Although the policy at this period was to show the Americans all forms of our Political Warfare, Dr Beck, with whom Mr Ed Taylor was living, did not inform him of the existence of Radio Inconnu. The Americans were, however, told of the existence of Radio Gaulle by Colonel Sutton. The result later on was that during the period of tension before and for some time after the North African landings, it became necessary to shut down Radio Gaulle whereas Radio Inconnu could continue to attack Darlan and the other men of Vichy in the Algiers Government.

Foreign-Language Broadcasts from [the] USA

A report on American broadcasting received from Colonel Donovan dated 13.11.41[2] stated that short-wave broadcasting was carried on in seventeen languages but that some languages were not regularly used. There were daily news broadcasts in Czech, Swedish and Finnish. There were occasional French and German news broadcasts translated by Colonel Donovan's organisation from an English-language master script. Features in German, Italian, French, Spanish, Swedish and Finnish were distributed to the broadcasting companies by Colonel Donovan's organisation. This service was shortly being extended to broadcasts in Portuguese, Mandarin and Cantonese.

The news of Japan's attack on the US Fleet in Pearl Harbor was interpreted by Colonel Donovan's organisation as the entry of the USA into the European war. Colonel Donovan's directive[3] to short-wave stations began:

> United States of America war with Japan and Britain's war with Germany are one and the same war. Japan's attacks are same as Nazi attacks and declaration of war by Japan means that Germany will follow shortly under tripartite pact.

A later directive of the same date stated: 'War with Japan does not mean USA will stop sending supplies to Allies.'

---

1. No. 91816, 17.11.41, for G. 50,300 from G 50,100.
2. Forwarded to Mr Adams by Major Neame, 4.12.41.
3. No. 15307 New York, 7.12.41.

OSS immediately took over the functions of disseminating all war news[1] as an intermediary between the US Army and Navy and the United States public and OSS. The directives issued to radio companies which had been only advisory became mandatory.

Communications between PWE and Colonel Donovan's organisation were at first via SOE and [NAME DELETED ON GROUNDS OF NATIONAL SECURITY], the SOE representative in the USA but after the establishment of the Donovan liaison office were through Major Whitney and Mr Winner.

Status of American Political Warfare Organisations

Relations between PWE and Colonel Donovan's organisation, and indeed between PWE and all the US organisations with whom they worked during the war, were frequently influenced by British misgivings about the exact status of the American organisations. This uncertainty arose from the very nature of the American organisations, which can be described as non-hierarchic and drew their authority independently directly from the President. To us their credentials appeared often vague and sometimes mutually conflicting. Thus we were frequently afraid of collaborating too closely with an organisation which would be suddenly abolished or disowned. As a result of these doubts, we must have appeared to the Americans to blow now hot, now cold. There was obviously reason for caution. For example, Colonel Donovan proposed, before Pearl Harbor, that the RAF should drop leaflets in Germany which his organisation would supply and which would be clearly of American origin. As the texts of the leaflets would certainly be cabled back to the United States, PWE felt it necessary to cable inquiring whether Donovan had considered the effects on Isolationist opinion[2] and whether the scheme had the President's blessing. The proposal was not proceeded with.

The question of 'Channels' and procedure was also troublesome. Thus a suggestion was made direct to the RAF that postcards signed by US citizens and addressed to their friends should be dropped in Germany. PWE decided such a proposal could only be dealt with through Colonel Donovan after the position of his organisation had been cleared up.[3]

Broadcasts of American Programmes on the BBC

Even before Pearl Harbor, Colonel Donovan was proposing[4] that American short-wave transmissions should be rebroadcast on medium wave by the BBC in twelve 15-minute programmes in twelve languages.

---

1. No. 15908 New York, 8.12.41.
2. Telegram sent via SOE. Draft initialled R.H.B.L., 17.11.41.
3. Executive Committee Minutes, 30.12.41.
4. Cable received from Colonel Donovan via Embassy, 4.12.41.

On 13th December, 1941, the Secretary of PWE informed Major Whitney that there was not the slightest chance of such a programme being broadcast owing to the overloaded state of the transmitters, but that PWE agreed in principle to rebroadcasts in French, German and Italian.[1] On 6.1.42 Mr Winner was informed that the BBC could start rebroadcasts in a fortnight but he had to confess that he had no answer to the question of whether the programmes would represent the views of the US Government. The rebroadcasts were initiated on 6.2.42 in German, Italian and French,[2] exactly a month after the first American leaflet had been dropped over Europe by the RAF. BBC rebroadcasts of American programmes soon resulted in BBC editors cutting recorded scripts. Though this was done owing to their poor quality, rather than on policy grounds, it aroused considerable resentment and the protests were referred to the Ministerial Committee, which forbade such cuts without prior reference to American representatives.

PWE Uneasiness with Regard to Colonel Donovan's Status

The question of the status of Colonel Donovan's organisation in relation to the State Department was raised by PWE as it was manifestly unwise for an organisation, the policy of which was derived from the British Foreign Office, to collaborate fully with an American organisation the policy of which might be repudiated by the State Department. A draft telegram to Lord Halifax was accordingly prepared[3] but before its despatch a message was received from Colonel Donovan stating that a planning committee had been set up with representatives of the State Department and the US Army and Navy and PWE could rest assured American broadcasts adhered to plans so drawn up. The Ministerial Committee of PWE were nevertheless not completely satisfied[4] and after consideration it was decided to send a PWE representative to Washington to report on the best means of establishing co-operation. The name of Mr David Bowes Lyon was suggested, but his departure was delayed owing to doubts being raised by the Minister of Information as to the effect of a Bill dealing with Censorship of Foreign Propaganda from the USA which was awaiting President Roosevelt's signature. Mr Bruce Lockhart minuted: 'The American propaganda bill now awaiting the President's signature will not affect in any way our co-operation with Colonel Donovan's organisation.' This proved to be doubly the case as President Roosevelt did not sign the Bill.

The persistent doubts of PWE seemed justified when President Roosevelt transferred control of Colonel Donovan's organisation less the Foreign Information Services to the jurisdiction of the American Chiefs of

1. Minutes of Executive Committee, 13.12.41.
2. PWE Monthly Report on Propaganda for February 1942.
3. Minutes of Ministerial Committee, 20.1.42.
4. Minutes of Ministerial Committee, 20.1.42.

Staff. The FIS were transferred to the new Office of War Information [OWI] set up by the President under Mr Elmer Davis. PWE appears to have been apprised of these changes by Major Morton before Colonel Donovan, who was in London, had been made aware of them.

Reorganisation of PWE

The need for quick ministerial decisions was frequently felt in the first six months of the existence of PWE. Such decisions could not be obtained easily from three separate ministers, who might decide differently on points submitted to them and who would have good reasons to object if they were not consulted. Points requiring decision could not, however, always be left until the weekly meeting. In some ways the smallness of the Standing Ministerial Committee of three was an added difficulty since cleavages of opinion tended to occur on the same kinds of points of policy and to become habitual.

An opportunity for reorganisation of the department offered itself when Dr Dalton left the Ministry of Economic Warfare to become President of the Board of Trade in late February 1942, and the appointment of Lord Selborne* as Minister of Economic Warfare. Whereas Dr Dalton had been particularly concerned [that] our propaganda should address itself to the industrial workers of Europe and make a revolutionary appeal, Lord Selborne was only interested in safeguarding the interests of SOE.

An accommodation was soon reached. Mr Bruce Lockhart in a secret and personal minute to the Secretary of State for Foreign Affairs accompanying recommendations for reorganisation of the Executive Committee stated:[1]

> I have always said that the present organisation of PWE is unsound and that matters will never be properly righted until full authority is vested in one minister. I have always believed that PWE should be an outside department of the Foreign Office under the control of, say Mr Richard Law.

On 4th March, 1942, Mr Bruce Lockhart stated that the possible solutions were, the continuation of the Standing Ministerial Committee, a condominium of two ministers with the Foreign Secretary responsible for policy in the War Cabinet and the Minister of Information responsible for administration or full control by one minister. 'The Condominium of two

1. Aide-Mémoire for the Secretary of State for Foreign Affairs from Mr Bruce Lockhart, 4.3.42.

* [Roundell Cecil Palmer, 3rd Earl of Selborne (1887–1971), was Conservative MP for Newton in Lancashire 1910–18, Aldershot 1918–40; assistant director of War Trade Department 1916–18; Assistant Postmaster-General 1924–9; opposed India Act 1935; Ministry of Works 1940–2; Minister of Economic Warfare, responsible for SOE, 1942; son killed on active service 1942.]

ministers seems the best solution because it can be put through more easily than any other scheme.'

Mr Bracken refused to have any part in another committee of three ministers[1] and insisted that all propaganda should be brought under one control.

The proposal for a condominium of two ministers was therefore adopted. At the same time proposals for the reorganisation were put forward by the Executive Committee. They were as follows: abolition of the Executive Committee, full authority being vested in Mr Bruce Lockhart, who would be assisted by a policy committee which should consist of Mr Bruce Lockhart, Chairman, Mr Leeper, Brigadier Brooks, and Mr Kirkpatrick. Mr Leeper [was] to be deputy Chairman, and Mr Leeper and Mr Kirkpatrick to be responsible for the administration of CHQ and the BBC respectively. Brigadier Brooks [was] to be in charge of the Military Wing and the Secretariat which would be merged into headquarters staff at Bush House. Brigadier Brooks would also be responsible for relations with the Service Departments. The Regional Directors [were] to retain their existing functions under the direct control of Mr Bruce Lockhart.

On 10th March, 1942, the memorandum containing these proposals was minuted by Mr Eden: 'I agree, if Mr Bracken also agreed, so proceed.'

Mr Bruce Lockhart was thereupon appointed head of PWE with the title of Director General. These changes were formally announced on 20th March.[2] The need for further changes was felt and Brigadier Brooks stated[3] that the absence of an effective planning system was the reason 'for the creakings that still occur', and proposed the formation of a planning section, which was approved.

This body, consisting of Mr Peter Scarlett, Mr Ronald Emmanuel, Lord Birkenhead* and Mr Murphy, was divorced from the day-to-day problems of the Regional Directors and its deliberations and conclusions formed in vacuo cannot be said to have influenced propaganda output. Mr Emmanuel and Mr Murphy did however conduct investigations into the output of certain of the BBC regions, though they were gravely hampered by the withholding of scripts. (See pp. 112–13 Dawn Peasants.)

During the following months, the darkest of the war, after the summer of 1940, the need for new machinery to replace the weekly meeting of PWE Executive with Regional Heads made itself felt. The machinery had been for Mr Bruce Lockhart or, in his absence, Mr Leeper to take the chair and

---

1. Aide-Mémoire for the Secretary of State for Foreign Affairs from Mr Bruce Lockhart, 4.3.42.
2. In PW(E)(42)15.
3. Minute from Brigadier Brooks to Director General, 6.4.42.

* [Frederick Winston Furneaux Smith, 2nd Earl of Birkenhead (1907–75), Principal Private Secretary to Lord Halifax 1938–9; Lord-in-Waiting 1938–40 and 1951–2; captain, Staff College, 1940–1; major 1942; attached to PWE 1942; attached to British military mission to Yugoslav partisans 1944–5. Biographer of the Earl of Strafford, Prof. Lindemann, Lord Halifax, Walter Monckton and (posthumously) Rudyard Kipling.]

to run over the main political developments which had taken place, or which were impending, to outline Foreign Office policy and to answer questions. Brigadier Brooks then gave an appreciation of the strategical events of the week[1] and Mr Leeper occasionally discussed an outstanding economic problem.

The pressure of work upon the Director General and the increasing tempo of political events combined to render this method of personal guidance at a fixed time difficult to carry out. With increasing frequency the Director General was called away and no central document was issued or advice given by a fixed time except on purely military matters.

The Director General therefore decided to appoint a Director of Plans and Campaigns, one of whose responsibilities should be to issue a central directive to co-ordinate the Regional Directives.

Mr Ritchie Calder was accordingly appointed to this post on 17th August, 1942. At the same time a reorganisation of the Headquarters staff was decided upon. Mr Meikle was brought in as Chief Administrative Officer with Lt Colonel Metherell as his assistant and the former Secretariat which had dealt with both policy and administrative questions was abolished.

Directorate of Plans

As a result Mr David Stephens went to the German Region, Mr Garnett and Lord Birkenhead to assist Mr Calder in the Directorate of Plans.

Mr Ritchie Calder divided the work of the Directorate of Plans at first into *Plans* and *Campaigns*. In practice, however, it was found that a Campaigns section could not be divorced from the work of drawing up the Central Directive since a BBC campaign depended on servicing the BBC with the right material and the Central Directive and its annexes was one of the principal methods of 'servicing'. A campaign could be kept going so long as the supply of material could be assured, but no longer.

During the SO1 period, and for some time after the formation of PWE, attempts were made to initiate and carry out 'campaigns' on the BBC by means of plans, or phase plans drawn up in PWE and handed over to the BBC for execution. Such documents were admirable as far as they went, but they did not provide the BBC Regional Editor with the material he needed, and a campaign cannot be carried out without a flow of the news items, talks scripts, etc., of which it is built up.

> Plans, as conceived at the centre are meaningless and arid documents[2] . . . One of the conspicuous failures of the original Planning

1. Prepared by Air Commodore Groves.
2. Mr Ritchie to Brigadier Brooks, 24.8.42.

Group was the failure to grasp that stratospheric planning can have little reality to the groundlings of the BBC.

Attempts had been made in SO1 and the first years of PWE to overcome this difficulty. Mr John Barry of CHQ planners had 'gone into' the Italian region of the BBC rewriting scripts, 'angling' news, or arranging for its creation. Although this irruption had generated more heat than light, it had secured certain definite results. It was a far from ideal method as it exacerbated the BBC and could only be carried out successfully by men who were experienced sub-editors or broadcasters.

Another method had been attempted in the case of the agricultural campaign.[1] In this case the PWE Agricultural Sub-Committee had appointed a small unit which supplied scripts for the Dawn Peasants' Programme of all the BBC regions. The method continued for a very long period because there was a small and very patient body of enthusiasts in PWE who did the necessary intelligence and other work. But it was grossly inefficient since when the work had been done there was no method of seeing that the material was used, and the programmes might be entirely ruined by the insertion of some item which showed lack of agricultural or regional background knowledge.

The appointment of Mr Ritchie Calder as Director of Plans offered an opportunity not only for the development of a new means of carrying out 'campaigns' but for a 'new deal' with the BBC.

> I propose[2] to maintain contact between plans and the means of their execution. . . . What I want to do[3] is to remove any sense of the impracticable and that is best done by having experienced and imaginative BBC representatives working as closely as possible with us helping to shape campaigns . . . they should be representatives of the BBC and not persons seconded to the Department. . . .

Mr Ritchie Calder's suggested safeguard[4] against ignoring the contribution to be made by the Regional Directors was that Crossman and Sutton should assist him on the Central Directive Drafting Committee, together with Mr Noel Newsome of the BBC. The suggestion was approved as advisers to the Director General[5] on enemy and occupied territories respectively.

---

1. See *supra*.
2. Mr Ritchie Calder to Director General, 24.7.42.
3. Mr Ritchie Calder to Lt Col Metherell, 10.8.42.
4. Mr Ritchie Calder to Director General, 31.8.42.
5. PWD(GSN)9, 11.9.42.

Mr Noel Newsome accepted an invitation to become a member of the Drafting Committee.

Appointment of DPW (E & S) and DPW (O)

[Feb. 1943]
The appointment of these advisers was followed five months later by their elevation [as] Directors of Political Warfare for Enemy and Satellite [DPW (E & S)], and Occupied regions [DPW (O)] respectively.[1]

This was partly due to a growing tendency on the part of the Director General towards dealing by means of personal interview with fewer and fewer officers of the Department. The tendency was partly, but only partly, due to the increased pressure of work. The other equally powerful factor was physical and was to culminate in the series of recurrent illnesses which involved the absence of Sir Robert Bruce Lockhart on sick leave for an aggregate of nine months in the last two and a half years of war.

The effect of the appointments was different in each case. That of Mr Crossman was to last only an extremely short time before he went to North Africa. It served to make him familiar with the problems of Political Warfare to Italy which would occupy some of his time in North Africa, but its effect on our political warfare to Germany was bad and rendered worse by the appointment of a well-meaning[2] deputy, Mr Gudgeon, who was a not politically warfare-minded man, and who was not Mr Crossman's own choice.

The appointment of Colonel Sutton, who was replaced as head of the French Region by Lt Colonel Gielgud, did nothing to solve the growing strain within the French Region, between those who felt themselves forced to fall in with British Military Planning and those who felt it their duty to point out that these plans would have disastrous results in France.

Nor did the interposition of Colonel Sutton strengthen the position of the Regional Director for the smaller occupied countries.

The appointment of a DPW (E & S) can scarcely be judged as it was held only for so short a time; the appointment of a DPW (O) had little to recommend it. In any case the appointments were made chiefly to lighten the burden on an ill and nervously exhausted man. It can safely be inferred that in normal conditions there should be no grade of officer concerned with policy interposed between the Regional Director and the Director General.

Appointment of Mr Delmer as DPW (Special Operations)

[June 1944]
The appointment of Mr Delmer which was to follow[3] as Director of Special Operations (E & S) was on the other hand an extremely useful one and

1. 15.2.43.
2. Mr Walmsley's evidence.
3. 2.6.44.

might not have been made without the earlier precedent. For the appointment (only four days before D Day) merely confirmed the position which Mr Delmer had long in fact occupied in PWE. But it conferred upon him, at the moment when it would be urgently required, the authority to negotiate with outside bodies – with OSS and PWD/SHAEF on behalf of PWE.

Organisation of the Military Wing

A note on the organisation of the Military Wing will help to make its functions understood.

The head of the Military Wing was Brigadier Brooks; his deputy was Air Commodore Groves. Colonel Chambers was Security Officer.

Soon after the creation of PWE, the work of the Military Wing was divided into four sections:

1. Liaison with MI19 and other Military Intelligence: Captain Steege.
2. Bomb-damage assessment and material for leaflets: Captain Savage.
3. Leaflet liaison and dissemination: Captain Ryer.
4. Ps/W: Squadron Leader Hitch. Italians: Mr Hay
Germans: Mr Cyrus Brooks.
Capt. Steed.

Brigadier Brooks and Air Commodore Groves worked extremely closely together; Brigadier Brooks usually attending Service Committees and Air Commodore Groves drafting papers. In general, Air Commodore Groves dealt with material for leaflets, leaflet liaison and dissemination and Ps/W.

Organisation at CHQ

Mr Leeper was head of the Country establishment with Mr D. Bowes Lyon as his deputy and Mr Walter Adams as general secretary.

Finance

Finance and establishment was at first combined under Mr Stewart Roberts, who, after the move to Bush House, was in London on certain days in the week.

Finance and establishment were later split, Mr Kindersley becoming responsible for establishment in the Country.

Reorganisation of Intelligence

During 1942, the Director General grew dissatisfied with the organisation of intelligence in PWE. The practice was for intelligence material to be routed first to Woburn, where material was retained for the exclusive use of RUs and the balance sent to London to be made available for other forms of output to the BBC. As a result, PWE located in Bush House sometimes lacked the complete intelligence picture which was necessary for plans and campaigns. Owing to the local superiority of Woburn in this respect, the Saturday morning meeting of Regional Directors, etc., at Woburn tended to deal independently with matters which should have been raised at the meeting of Regional Directors with the Director at Bush House on Thursday.

Appointment of Director of Political Warfare Intelligence

On the recommendation of Lt Colonel Metherell, the Director General decided to appoint Lt Colonel Eric Sachs, KC, the Recorder of Dudley, then serving in the Adjutant General's Department War Office to be Director of Political Warfare Intelligence [DPWI] in Bush House.

The Director General informed the Minister of Information[1] of his proposal to appoint Lt Colonel Sachs and suggested that the latter should study the problem and make recommendations later and the Minister approved the proposal.

Lt Colonel Sachs's release and promotion to the rank of Brigadier was arranged with Major General Wallace, Director of Personal Services, and Lt Colonel Sachs took up his post as from 30.11.42 as a uniformed officer with the rank of Brigadier, and therefore equal in rank both with Brigadier Brooks and Air Commodore Groves and senior to Colonel Chambers, PWE Security Officer, who was responsible for the collection and distribution of Intelligence obtained from the Service Departments.

On his appointment, Brigadier Sachs proceeded to a careful study of all the problems involved and made a report in two parts – on functions and powers of the new Directorate and on the location of PWE intelligence.

The report stated[2] that wide scope existed for obtaining better means of getting 'I' material, distributing it to the Regions and servicing the Directorate of Plans and outside bodies and that such functions should be carried out centrally leaving the collation and evaluation of intelligence as a regional responsibility under a Central Intelligence Officer [CIO] for each Region. Since it was axiomatic that 'I' should be independent and give unbiased information, the CIOs should be free from executive propaganda functions.[3]

This statement seems convincing in theory but is in practice belied by the experience of the department. Intelligence officers were frequently able to

---

1. Mr R. H. Bruce Lockhart to Minister of Information, 18.10.42.
2. DPWI B/3 Directorate of PW Intelligence Recommendations as to functions and powers, 23.12.42.
3. See Mr Walmsley's remarks [p. 130].

combine their work with being first-rate propagandists. Their work gained enormously owing to their practical knowledge of what intelligence was likely to be available and of the kind of intelligence required to carry out a political warfare campaign. Thus, Mr Leonard Ingrams, head of PWE liaison with MEW, was a practised broadcaster and wrote large numbers of scripts. He was also a most valuable member of many planning committees and had an instinct for Political Warfare tactics. It would have been a great loss had his work been confined to that of providing PWE with intelligence from MEW.

Dr Beck for long periods combined the functions of CIO and housemaster of a French RU and was always concerned with output.

Mr Walmsley's opinion is:

> I am still not clear in my own mind whether intelligence ought to be independent of policy-makers in propaganda, and do not know whether what happened was for the best or not. On the one hand, it is very important to have an independent check in a man of powerful and brilliant though erratic mind like Crossman, while on the other a separate intelligence inevitably tended to become separated from policy-making.
>
> Perhaps one can only say that the problem should be considered in relation to the dominant personalities of the time and the nature of the operation. In Delmer's Black unit for instance, it was both unnecessary and unthinkable to have any intelligence independent of Delmer.

Moreover, partly owing to the separation between intelligence and output the Directorate of Plans could not rely on obtaining the kind of material needed for the annexes of the Central Directive which were almost purely intelligence documents. The writer of the annex had to know what lessons he was trying to drive home, what errors were likely to be made in the BBC, and what kind of intelligence the BBC editors wanted. The Directorate of Plans therefore contained a staff which tended to draw material from Chatham House and other outside sources instead of from DPWI. This practice led to frequent complaints both from Brigadier Sachs and from CIOs of the regions concerned.

In a schedule of his report dealing with his own functions, Brigadier Sachs agreed that the collection of intelligence from the Service Departments should remain the responsibility of Brigadier Brooks, 'who will for the purposes of the Intelligence Directorate be regarded as an outside Department'. In other words, Brigadier Sachs accepted the long-standing practice of the Military Wing to obtain Most Secret Intelligence from the Service Departments and to limit the distribution of it to a very few trusted officers. It was thus within Colonel Chambers' direction to inform Dr Beck or Mr Delmer of a piece of intelligence, the existence of which was unknown to Brigadier Sachs. Apart from this, even at a late date in 1943, after he had been Director of Political Warfare

Intelligence for almost a year, Brigadier Sachs was ignorant not only of the most important sources of intelligence on which Delmer was able to base the subversive portions of the Atlantiksender programme, but of the existence of Aspidstra[1] by means of which the programme was transmitted. Brigadier Sachs might with justice have complained that an officer of his rank and position in the Department should have been given an overall picture of all its functions and that his work was bound to suffer owing to his being left in ignorance of many activities of the Department.

Brigadier Sachs's Proposals for Reorganisation

Brigadier Sachs's proposals for reorganisation were simple and practical and involved the least possible disturbance to the existing practice and to the work of the Regions while providing for assistance by a central organisation in the shape of filing, distribution and servicing the Regions which was really needed.

Intelligence was to be moved to London. 'It is a basic fact that Regional Intelligence must serve both Black and White and cannot be divided in location.' The arguments for and against the move were impartially set out and Brigadier Sachs stated: 'I can see no serious effect on Black if "I" comes to London, though some initial difficulties in separating Black from "I" may be found in smaller regions . . . the number of genuine staff overlaps are relatively small and mostly arise through failure to separate "I" and Black executively.' The argument that Black would suffer from lack of 'hot' news was answered by the existence of six direct telephone lines and a teleprinter service between Bush House and Woburn.

Mr Leeper's Resignation from PWE

Brigadier Sachs's recommendations were accepted and 'Mr Leeper[2] expressed the view that in these circumstances his post of Director of PWE Country has ceased to exist and after a period of leave he will return to the diplomatic service.' Mr Barman deputised for Mr Leeper as Director PWE Country from 11.1.43.

A paper on the functions of the PWI Directorate[3] which was issued some time later contained in a last clause the statement that: 'Responsibility for or in relation to the collection and distribution of intelligence material from the Service Departments is not included in those set out.'

The layout of the PW Intelligence Directorate can be shown most simply in a diagram.

1. Personal knowledge.
2. Order signed by Director General circulated 7.1.43.
3. PWI 1A Director of PW Intelligence and relations with other PW Directorates.

D of PWI
PA

AD of PWI (Organisation)			AD of PWI (Servicing and Publications)
Sec. 1	Sec. 2	Sec. 3	Sec. 4
Distribution	Internal Organisation	Inter-Departmental relation	"I" Admin.
Intake	Fields	Output	Registry
Priorities	Filing	Distribution	
Releases	Classification	Lists	
Teleprinters & Tickers		Interviews	
Security			
Typing			

External
Liaison Officers

Sec. 5	Sec. 6	Sec. 7		
Library	Digest	Chief Servicing and Publications Officer		
General Information Bureau	Hot news			
Documents from Areas not covered by PWE Regions	Notes	SP 07	SP 02	SP 03
		Enemy	General	Enemy occupied

Brigadier Sachs added a recommendation in his report that in each Region the following appointments be made:

A Chief Intelligence Officer (CIO)
A Priority and Distribution Officer (P & DO)
A Chief Archivist (CA)
A Servicing and Publications Officer (SPO)

The Priority and Distribution Officer to be responsible for arranging the best and quickest flow of raw and other material to White, Black, Digest and Filing.

By leaving the collection and evaluation of intelligence on a regional basis, and by building up a numerically large central organisation, Brigadier Sachs was responsible for very greatly increasing the size of the Department. One result of this was a tendency to produce centrally and to circulate quantities of material of little or no value to those concerned in output – such as a yellow paper with the ordinary 'tape' news which was circulated by hand several times a day.

Brigadier Sachs relinquished his employment in the Department as from 15.5.45 when DPWI was broken up after the defeat of Germany.[1]

PWE Relinquishes Woburn Abbey

The decision to move intelligence to London and the resignation of Mr Leeper resulted in a great reduction of what was originally called Country Headquarters, a term which later became taboo in the London Office.

It was decided, therefore, to relinquish Woburn Abbey, retaining only the Riding School, Marylands, MB and the various houses scattered about the neighbourhood which housed not only the RU teams, but also Mr Stewart Roberts, Mr Kindersley and other administrative officers.

Woburn Abbey was then requisitioned by the Admiralty, and was not later available during the flying bomb and rocket period, when preparations had to be made to move the Department out of London if necessary.

One result of relinquishing the Abbey, which was to be felt increasingly, was lack of accommodation at Bush House. Premises were obtained in its neighbourhood, at Ingersoll House and in Carey Street.

After Woburn Abbey had been given up, work in 'the Country' was confined to Black and Grey broadcasting, and to the lay-out and setting up of White printed propaganda at Marylands.

Black printed material required all the sources of many different London commercial firms and could not be carried out in the Country.

Missions Abroad, PWE and SOE

We have seen how the claims of Sir Campbell Stuart to place agents in neutral countries conflicted with those of Section D to carry out all propaganda by means of agents and have traced how the rival claimants came under one minister for the space of a year only to separate again, with their conflicting claims unsettled.

Two separate problems were in fact involved though they were habitually confused, particularly in the SOE presentation of the case.

The first problem was that of agents in enemy territory. In this case the SOE case to control all agents engaged in subversive activities in enemy-occupied territory was unassailable, provided that SOE would include agents trained and briefed by PWE to carry out Political Warfare tasks. In this case PWE had no wish at any time to set up machinery of its own for sending agents in and bringing them out or for establishing communications of its own.

The question of sending missions abroad and of establishing bases outside this country from which to conduct propaganda was an entirely different matter.

1. Sir Robert Bruce Lockhart to Brigadier Sachs, 11.4.45.

There could be no operational objection to the dispatch of PWE personnel to the United States, India, etc., or to the setting up of a Political Warfare base in the Middle East, or anywhere else in territory controlled by Britain or her allies. The only reason which SOE could honestly bring forward against such action was that it wished to carry out Political Warfare from such bases itself – an ambition which in the opinion both of PWE and the Foreign Office was inadmissible.

PWE, as we shall see, fought SOE on these lines first to obtain a decision in principle in London and, after that had been won, to obtain control in the area in question. For after SOE had been defeated in principle in London, its officers continued to dispute the matter in each of the areas.

The establishment of its own missions, which might or might not be bases for Political Warfare, were important first in order to carry swift and direct negotiations in the United States, secondly in the Middle East in order to control and direct all political warfare to the Balkans, and thirdly in [the] Middle East, West Africa, and Gibraltar in order to carry out Political Warfare to the Italian and the Vichy French territories in North and North-West Africa.

The SO1 Representative in [the] USA

In June 1941, the Minister of Economic Warfare and Mr Leeper decided to make changes in the administration at Woburn, and invited Mr Valentine Williams, Mr Leeper's deputy at CHQ, to become SO1 representative in the USA.

Mr Williams' charter[1] was somewhat vague – he was to represent SO1 with [NAME DELETED ON GROUNDS OF NATIONAL SECURITY], the SO2 representative, to as to ensure the views and aims of the country house were properly appreciated and he was to keep CHQ informed of the views and background of [NAME DELETED ON GROUNDS OF NATIONAL SECURITY] organisation.

He was paid a salary of £3,000 p.a. tax free, together with travelling and entertainment expenses. The appointment was for six months with three months' notice on either side. Mr Williams' departure was regarded as an urgent matter, and travelling by clipper, he reached New York on 28th July, 1941. The importance and urgency of Mr Williams' mission evaporated immediately he left British shores[2] and from the moment of his landing he received no communication whatever either from the Minister or from Mr Leeper, his immediate chief.

It is therefore difficult to resist the conclusion that the Minister and Mr Leeper wished Mr Valentine Williams to be out of this country during the time when the fate of SO1 was uncertain and when PWE was coming into existence.

1. Mr Valentine Williams to Mr Brendan Bracken, 12.4.42.
2. Mr Valentine Williams to Mr Brendan Bracken, 12.4.42.

SO1 was not only in touch with [NAME DELETED] through SO2, but was also in direct contact with the leading members of Colonel Donovan's organisation. Requests were made direct to Mr Sherwood and after the formation of PWE, Colonel Donovan appointed Major Whitney as his representative and he was given a room in PWE premises.

Exactly six months from Mr Williams' landing in New York, he was given three months' notice by SOE on the grounds that SO1 had become a separate organisation and that his services were no longer required, Mr Valentine Williams protested that he was not, and never had been, an SOE body, but employed by PWE. He was informed that all SO1 representatives abroad had been taken over by SOE on the creation of PWE and that 'whatever the merits of the case[1] he had never, in fact, been employed by PWE'. It is difficult to accept this statement in view of the fact that Mr Williams' princely salary was paid out of PWE funds until his employment was terminated.[2]

It seems clear that in this case PWE had been able to invoke the SOE claim that PWE could have no missions abroad in order to wash its hands of an unpleasant predicament although at the time of doing so it had already dispatched two representatives on an exploratory mission to the United States.

PWE Mission to Washington

The first PWE Mission to Washington was despatched in March 1942, and consisted of Mr Bowes Lyon and Mr Ritchie Calder. Its terms of reference[3] were to examine and report on collateral organisations for co-operation. The Mission left [the] USA on 12.5.42 and reported on 18.5.42 that the position was confused and that changes in responsibility were impending and forecast the changes which took place one month later.

This admirably lucid report gives a complete picture of the competing agencies, which had developed as a result of the war, which were concerned with information and propaganda. The Office of Facts and Figures (afterwards OWI) under Mr McLeish, the Co-ordinator of Information (Colonel Donovan), the Rockefeller Warfare Bureau, and the Board of Economic Warfare, with the State Department critical and hostile.

The report also pointed out that FIS suffered from lack of direct contacts with the US Army and Navy by whom they were regarded as a publicity organisation. This handicap was certainly not decreased after FIS was taken over by OWI.

After pointing out that Political Warfare activities were divided into those to the Far East and those to Europe, the report recommended the

---

1. Telegram No. 2685 Lockhart to Valentine Williams, 25.4.42.
2. Telegram No. 970 Viscount Halifax. For Leeper from Valentine Williams, 20.2.42.
3. Signed by Mr Bruce Lockhart, 12.3.42.

appointment of a Political Warfare Mission to the USA, the head of which should be in Washington, with Sir George Samsom as his adviser on Far Eastern matters and two officers, one responsible for Far Eastern output, based in San Francisco, and one responsible for output to Europe, based in New York.

The recommendations were in the main accepted and Mr Bowes Lyon was appointed head of the PWE Mission, with Mr Walter Adams as his deputy, and left by separate planes during the latter half of July 1942, when the transfer of FIS to the new Office of War Information, which Mr Bowes Lyon had forecast, had taken place.

A Supplementary Report[1] on the First PWE Mission by Mr Ritchie Calder deals with conversations in which many suggested forms of co-operation between Britain and America were discussed.

Mr Calder was particularly interested in committing America in regard to post-war reconstruction in Europe and defeating the isolationist swing to be anticipated after the war.

An immediate result of the setting up of a PWE Mission was that SOE ceased to have responsibility for Political Warfare work. Certain of the SOE staff who had been engaged on it were transferred to the PWE Mission.

An interesting account of the activities of SOE and of what FIS and, in particular, Mr Sherwood owed to SOE, is contained in a report which was brought to the attention of the Minister of Information by Lord Selborne.[2] The document describes the organisation of short-wave radio programmes over the Christian Science Station WRUL. The fact that these programmes were British inspired had been carefully kept secret. It is claimed that during the occupation of Syria, WRUL broadcasts played a part in influencing Syrians in favour of Britain and that the WRUL broadcasts to Yugoslavia (as many as five daily transmissions) produced 'diplomatic and public pressure which was the deciding factor in swinging Yugoslavia to the side of the Allies'. SOE also bought up a news agency which devoted itself to catering for the foreign-language newspapers of the racial minorities in the USA. By the summer of 1941, this news agency had a virtual monopoly of the foreign-language press. Only the paid Nazi organisations remained outside its orbit.

SOE established personal contact with Mr Sherwood as soon as he was appointed by Colonel Donovan, and

> only thanks to SOE help, was Mr Sherwood able to survive his early difficulties. . . . Difficulties which occurred almost daily would have killed Mr Sherwood's organisation but for the assistance given by British Security Co-ordination [BSC] . . . the latter acted as the sole channel of communications . . . vetted his recruits, trained them,

---

1. Dated 5.6.42.
2. Minister of Economic Warfare to Minister of Information, 25.9.42.

> transported them to the field where it placed them in contact with British officials . . . in the broadcasting field it gave Mr Sherwood directives which he could not obtain from his own State Department.

The report goes on to point out the dangerous consequences to be anticipated from setting up a PWE Mission in Washington under Mr Bowes Lyon.

> BSC must renounce all responsibility for PWE activities in the Western hemisphere. This would mean that the proposed PWE Mission would be cut off from the sources of secret information . . . and that Great Britain stood in danger of losing control over the rapidly expanding American Political Warfare effort . . . as a result of the change Great Britain stands in grave danger of losing the peace. . . .

These warnings came too late as the question of PWE having its own missions abroad had already been settled. SOE was soon to fight a similar battle and to lose it over the PWE Mission to the Middle East.

Incidentally it is difficult to see how the threat that sources of secret intelligence must be withheld from the head of a Mission of a secret Department, who had been administratively responsible for all activities at Woburn, many of them closely linked with SOE, could be justified. Claims and threats of this kind did much to impair the relations of PWE and SOE.

The Mazzini Society Welfare Mission to India

In March 1941, Colonel Thornhill, head of the SO1 Mission to [the] Middle East, visited India on the invitation of the C. in C. General Auchinleck in order to investigate the possibilities of propaganda among Italian Ps/W. Colonel Thornhill was informed that propaganda to Italian Ps/W in India was the responsibility of SO1 Middle East.[1]

Nevertheless, the Mission, sponsored by SO1, was dispatched to India to carry out Political Warfare to Ps/W, four months later without Colonel Thornhill being consulted or informed.

The SO2 organisation [NAME DELETED ON GROUNDS OF NATIONAL SECURITY] had contacted the Mazzini Society in the USA and made arrangements that a party of ten members of the Society should be sent, first to Britain, and then to India. Before leaving America[2] they were told they were being sent to do propaganda work for the Mazzini Society and that they should work under its orders and not those of any British officers. They were to carry out work under the cover of being an Italian-American Welfare Mission. They were all extreme republicans and were only ready to work for an Italian republic after the war.

1. Telegram No. 57832 (Groves ME 4(i)).
2. Telegram No. 1918/G from C. in C. India, 29.11.41.

The son of a leading member of the Mazzini Society, Dr Tarchiani, fortunately joined the party en route. He was the only educated man in it, the others being a lift-attendant, a bricklayer, a trousers-presser, etc. Five of the party were of American nationality. They left the United States and were brought to Britain without passports or papers of any kind.

Misbehaviour of the Members of the Mission

Mr George Martelli of the Italian Region SO1 expressed doubts about the suitability of the party and advised that the activities of the Mission should be limited to the distribution of comforts until its members had been tested. But on balance it was decided to let the Mission proceed rather than cause unfavourable repercussions with the Mazzini Society of America by sending the party back. Furthermore the Mission was regarded as 'a lever by which we could open the door to India'.[1] Apparently the Italian Region was either unaware of Colonel Thornhill's visit or had no confidence in him. The 'Welfare Mission' travelled in charge of a British officer via the Cape, where the party insisted on being allowed to go on shore. One of its members attempted to post letters to the United States and the party aroused interest in South Africa, which was heightened, after its departure, by an article in the *Natal Daily News* referring to an enthusiastic move in America to turn 300,000 Italian Ps/W into an anti-Fascist spearhead.[2] The reproduction of the article was stopped in India.

Shortly after the formation of PWE it was decided to dispatch another Mission which could report on conditions in India. This was always referred to as 'The Martelli Mission' though Mr Martelli did not accompany it. It consisted of Major Stevens (brother of Colonel Harold Stevens, the famous broadcaster), and Major Munro.

On their arrival these officers reported on the Welfare Mission. They found that Dr Tarchiani was anxious to dismiss six of the party. All were ignorant and useless but six were suspicious and undisciplined troublemakers. Had they been allowed in Ps/W camps they would probably have been lynched.

A Cause of Friction between Ministers

The problem of the disposal of these men occupied the attention of the PWE Ministerial Committee for months. None of them had papers, no one wanted them in Britain and Japan's entry into the war made their direct return to the USA impossible. The problem was frequently referred to by the Minister of Information at meetings of the PWE Ministerial Committee in terms uncomplimentary to SOE. The 'six undesirable Italians' thus

1. Mr Martelli to Mr Leeper, 2.12.41.
2. 17211/G from C. in C. India, 8.11.41.

became more of a nuisance in London by increasing friction between PWE Ministers in London than they can have been in India.

Eventually Tarchiani was given a commission as an interpreter officer, three of the Americans volunteered as non-commissioned interpreters, four of the party were interned as enemy aliens and one, formerly a garage hand, took a job as a fitter. The American waiter, who denounced Dr Tarchiani to United States consular officials in 'a misguided effort to improve his own status', vanished from PWE records between April and August 1942. He was sixty-two years old and it is possible that he may have died in the hot weather.

PWE Mission to India

After a visit to India, and shortly before the closing of the SO1 Mission to [the] Middle East,[1] Colonel Thornhill had recommended that the Department should be represented in India in order to carry out propaganda to Italian Ps/W in India. As we have seen, SO1 and, after its formation, PWE decided to dispatch ten members of the Mazzini Society and then a Mission under Commander Martelli. His duties were to look after the members of the Mazzini Society then on the high seas, ascertain the possibilities of raising a Free Italian Force and carry out propaganda to Italian Ps/W.

Difficulties in obtaining air travel priority for Commander Martelli held up his departure until after Colonel Thornhill's return to this country. It was then first proposed that Colonel Thornhill should accompany the Mission, the absurd suggestion being made that he should act as technical adviser on front-line propaganda.[2] Japan was not at that time in the war and there was no front-line propaganda to be done.

The matter was considered by the Standing Ministerial Committee and it was agreed that Colonel Thornhill should lead the Mission himself. Delay, however, ensued though the need for a directive was urgent as there were fifty-five Italian generals in India, some of whom with careful nursing might form the spearhead of an anti-Fascist movement[3] and the only propagandists who had arrived in India were the Italian-American Mazzini Society pants-pressers. Majors Munro and Stevens were dispatched but Colonel Thornhill's departure was delayed and he did not reach India until February 1942.

Within a few weeks of his arrival, Colonel Thornhill reported that if segregation of Fascists and anti-Fascists could be effected, volunteers could be found for a Free Italian Force provided HMG did not abandon the project once it had been launched. He was informed that the project had the full

1. C. in C. India to War Office. No. 31651, 30.7.41.
2. PW(M)(41)12. Note by D. Stephens on Mission to India.
3. C. in C. India to War Office. No. 18084, 17.11.41.

support of the Foreign Office, but that there was a possibility that it might be dropped if the Indian Government demanded it.

Progress seems to have rapidly been made in the segregation of Fascist and anti-Fascist Ps/W, and by the summer of 1942, Colonel Thornhill had obtained authorisation for the formation of a special camp for anti-Fascists at Jaipur, and a Treasury grant of £10,000 for its construction. Considerable delay resulted owing to the great shortage of building materials in India.

Propaganda was carried out through the medium of an illustrated newspaper with a strong love and sex interest, *La Diana*, which appealed strongly to the sex-starved Italian prisoners of war, and by the teaching of English. Professor Adolph Myers, Director of the Indian section of the Orthological Institute, was attached to the Mission to organise classes in basic English. The Mission had the full approval of the C. in C. India, of the DMI and the DPW but it incurred the hostility of the Joint Secretary of the Defence Department India, Mr Mackworth Young, who reported unfavourably upon it.[1]

Progress was made at this period and numbers of 'whites' volunteered to join a Free Italian Force, at some risk to themselves and to their families. They were concentrated at the Jaipur Camp, pending a decision on their employment, and after a War Cabinet decision,[2] five hundred were eventually incorporated in two Pioneer Labour battalions[3] and there were good prospects of thousands more joining the movement – Italia Redenta. It was obviously essential that an Italian anti-Fascist force would have to be part of a world-wide movement and could not be confined to India. It would be necessary to carry out similar propaganda in South and East Africa where the conditions in Italian Ps/W camps were, in one case at least, extremely bad. While these matters were under consideration, the India Office asked for information as to PWE policy, as following the Dieppe raid it had apparently put forward suggestions with regard to the possible manacling of Italian generals in India.[4]

After Colonel Thornhill's repeated requests to return home to report on the need of extending PWE work to Ps/W, and owing to his severe illness and prolonged ill-health, Colonel Johnston, DSO, MC, who had been appointed Head of the Ps/W Section of PWE Military Wing, was sent out to relieve him. One of the objects of the Mission, as laid down in Colonel Johnston's instructions, was 'the organisation of self-declared anti-Fascist Ps/W into Pioneer battalions and labour units, bearing in mind the possible conversion of these labour units, at a later stage, into an anti-Fascist combatant force'.

1. Minute by Major Baker White, 10.9.42.
2. WP(43)73, 18.2.43.
3. 1.6.43.
4. Mr A. F. Morely to Mr P. Scarlett, 16.11.42.

Colonel Johnston reached India in the spring of 1943, and two months later reported that a proposal had been made through the High Commissioner of Australia in London for the transfer of 10,000 Italian Ps/W from India to Australia owing to the labour shortage there.

Colonel Johnston informed PWE[1] that the Ps/W asked for had to be physically fit and not Fascists and stated that 'these conditions precisely those required Pioneer Corps Italia Redenta. Suggested transfers to Australia would therefore prejudice if not preclude formation Corps. Is intention to have two competing schemes.'

Brigadier Brooks accepted Colonel Johnston's views of the incompatibility of anti-Fascist labour battalions and of a labour force for Australia without question and asked the Ministers for instructions as 'if the Australian proposal should go through as it stands, the logical result can only be the recall of our Mission from India'.

The Foreign Secretary after discussion with the Minister of Information accordingly informed the C. in C. India that they had decided to withdraw the PWE Mission. Field Marshal Lord Wavell concurred with regret.

The decision to withdraw the Mission at the moment when it had begun to achieve positive results caused surprise in India and at the War Office and it seems to have been arrived at owing to a misapprehension of the position.

Field Marshal Wavell was not consulted before he left, nor was his successor, Lord Auchinleck, asked for his views. There were 67,000 Italian Ps/W in India and Australia had not asked for anti-Fascists, but only that known or suspected Fascists and troublesome types should be excluded. In other words, they had asked for 'Greys'. The DPW War Office pointed out these facts, but PWE accepted the Ministerial decision. Colonel Johnston, who is unlikely to have realised the probable results of his somewhat misleading telegram, returned by air at the request of the DMI India, and believed he would return there, not realising that he had destroyed his own mission by his unco-operative attitude. Colonel Johnston, though he had held the appointment of Director of Army Education in India and had been a most gallant officer in the field, later proved himself a tactless and unsuitable commandant of the PWE School Brondesbury and had to be replaced. He knew nothing of Political Warfare and should never have been employed in the Department.

But though Colonel Johnston was chiefly responsible, Brigadier Brooks must bear some of the blame for the decision to run away from a commitment which the Department had freely accepted, on which very large sums had been spent and which should have been carried through to completion.

The object of PWE's efforts was to make the Italian Ps/W an additional strength to the British war effort. That they signally failed to do in India.

The Mission was wound up and its principal officers transferred to PWB AFHQ.

1. Colonel Johnston for PWE, 22.5.43. No. 0323/SG.

Colonel Thornhill was appointed Head of the Ps/W section of the Military Wing after his return to London though he was by no means a fit man.

Lt Colonel Gauld, a member of the Mission, continued to run re-educational activities under GHQ and PWE continued to finance the Ps/W camp newspaper *Il Corriere*.

PWE Outpost at Berne. Miss Wiskemann

Miss Elizabeth Wiskemann had worked as a newspaper correspondent in Germany and had numerous contacts with varying classes of anti-Nazis, particularly with persons belonging to the liberal and Social Democratic groups. She had written one or two books.

It was realised that the kind of gossip and rumours circulating among Germans hostile to the Hitler regime would be of considerable value to our Black propaganda. Though not 'intelligence' in the ordinary sense of the work, it would be from that of the Department. It was thought that Miss Wiskemann would be particularly well fitted to tap such kinds of gossip not only from Germany but also from Italy, Austria and France. She was accordingly sent out to Berne as SO1 representative with the cover of Assistant Press Attaché, but responsible only to the Minister.

Miss Wiskemann was unaware of the extent and nature of PWE Black propaganda and of the way in which much of her material was used.

Communications

Miss Wiskemann's information was seldom urgent; she communicated at first in letters through the FO bag until November 1942, after which British communications were entirely by telegram until August 1944.

Miss Wiskemann's Contacts

Miss Wiskemann's material was chiefly gathered from the following sources:

1. Very old personal friends such as Albrecht Bernstorff, Guglielmo Alberti, Mestrovic.

2. The Oprecht family, through whom she met the German theatrical director, Hilpert, to whom Goebbels had handed the Max Rheinhardt theatres in Berlin and Vienna. She also obtained clandestine German trade union material through Hans Oprecht.

3. Swiss journalists. She was able to meet the Berlin correspondent of the *Neue Zurchner Zeitung* whenever the latter was in Switzerland. She was also in touch with a German journalist, F. Kramer, attached to the German Press Attaché in Berne. Kramer, Q3, was extremely useful to her [PASSAGE DELETED ON GROUNDS OF NATIONAL SECURITY].

4. The Counseil Oecumenique des Eglises at Geneva. This body was in touch with oppositional elements in Germany owing to its Ps/W work.

Through it Miss Wiskemann met Adam Trott (executed in Berlin, August 1944).

5. J. Kopechy (subsequently Czechoslovak Minister in Berne).

6. OWI. Through G. Mayer of OWI Miss Wiskemann re-established contact with Antinori, Italian Press Attaché in Berne, who provided her with material.

7. René Janin introduced her to M. Vaidie, the French Financial Attaché in 1940 and the director of Hoffman Laroche through whom Q2 German material was obtained.

8. A young Croat official who had been at school with Q1, supplied her with Q1 material which Miss Wiskemann regarded as the best intelligence from N. Italy for a considerable time.

Relations with SOE

Miss Wiskemann's relations in the field with the SOE representative in Switzerland and with the Press Attaché were extremely bad and she has many complaints of their hostility, non-cooperation, and intrigues against her. She was on the best of terms [with NAMES DELETED] and with Mr Kelly and Mr Norton.

SOE at first objected to the employment of Miss Wiskemann, but PWE refused to give way on the matter and received FO support.

PWE and the Gibraltar Transmitter

[Summer 1941]

The importance of propaganda to French North Africa had been obvious ever since the fall of France and the abortive visit to French North Africa by Lord Gort and Mr Duff Cooper in July 1940. The proximity of Gibraltar made it the obvious centre for SO2 activities, with an outpost in Tangier. Propaganda activities were also centred at Gibraltar, and the MoI had ordered a 5 k.w. transmitter which it was proposed to instal in Gibraltar in order to supplement MoI broadcasts to North Africa, and to Spain through the agencies of the BBC and WRUL. The Ministry of Information was opposed to the formation of a centre which should initiate propaganda at Gibraltar[1] and proposed to establish a relay station. The task of drawing up a plan for propaganda from Gibraltar was allotted to Mr Bruce Lockhart's Committee for Co-ordination of Propaganda.[2] On 1st September, 1941, Lord Gort, who had arrived in this country to obtain a decision on propaganda, had a private conference with Mr Bracken, no one else being present. A meeting was arranged for the following day at the War Office with Mr Bracken in the chair. At this meeting, Lord Gort's proposal[3] that Captain

---

1. Z6753/663/G minutes of a meeting held at FO, 9.8.41.
2. *Ibid.*
3. Letter from Mr Bruce Lockhart to Lord Gort, 3.9.41.

Holland RN should be PWE representative on his staff, responsible for ensuring that propaganda carried out from Gibraltar to French North Africa was in accordance with PWE directives, was accepted. PWE agreed to provide Captain Holland with a trained propaganda staff including French and Arabic-speaking announcers and leaflet writers. Sir Noel Ashbridge would supply the necessary technical staff from the BBC.

The naval representative stated that the transmitter would be installed and working within a few weeks.

SOE Opposition to PWE Gibraltar Mission

These agreements were unwelcome to SOE which maintained the SO2 thesis that PWE or SO1 should have no agents 'in the field'. SOE therefore proposed that 'all[1] new machinery which it is proposed to establish at Gibraltar could suitably be run by the SOE representative, Mr Hugh Quennell, under the supervision of Captain Holland RN who could represent Lord Gort'.

Mr Jebb informed Mr Bruce Lockhart[2] that the Minister of Economic Warfare adhered to this view since if there were two organisations in the field, one responsible to the PWE and the other to the SOE, there was bound to be friction and confusion however strictly their terms of reference might be laid down in London. For example, a local representative of PWE might wish to bring to the microphone some North African who would be objected to by Quennell and leaflets had better be run by those responsible for the actual dissemination and who would be more likely to know the technical requirements. Gibraltar was moreover too small a place to contain a third secret organisation in addition to the two already established there.

SOE did not object to particular persons being sent out by PWE to form part of the SOE Mission and clearly recognised that policy should be determined by the PWE if execution outside Britain was left to SOE.

The Executive Committee considered Mr Jebb's letter the following day but decided that as they considered themselves bound by the agreement reached with Lord Gort they were unable to entertain the SOE proposal. The suggestion that SOE should control open broadcasting anywhere involved a departure from first principles. They therefore decided to proceed on the lines of their agreement with Lord Gort 'unless and until they receive instructions to the contrary from the Ministerial Committee'.

Fortunately an agreement was reached on a basis proposed by Mr Jebb without the matter having to be referred to the Ministers. By this it was agreed[3] that Captain Holland should be the joint SOE/PWE representative and that PWE should nominate an officer to control the BBC broadcasting

1. Secret and personal letter from Mr Gaitskill to Mr David Stephens, 9.9.41.
2. Letter to Bruce Lockhart from Gladwyn Jebb, 22.9.41, SCC/2796/55/13.
3. Mr Bruce Lockhart to Mr Jebb, 29.9.41, and Mr Jebb to Mr Lockhart of the same date.

team. The PWE agreed to let SOE have copies of their correspondence with this representative and SOE agreed to let PWE liaison officers see their correspondence with Quennell. In the event of covert propagandists being sent out they would be selected and trained by PWE but paid by SOE, and would receive all their directives via Holland and Quennell. While these arrangements were being made, Mr Donnelly, a Marconi Company engineer, had been put in charge of erecting the transmitter by the MoI.

Technical Errors and Delays in Erecting Transmitter

The technical difficulties of erecting an additional wireless station in the confined area of a fortress, close to the existing naval and military stations, had not been realised and were to prove almost overwhelming. On the 24th April the following year, preliminary tests showed[1] the station had a day range of 100 miles over Spain and the African coast, but it could not be heard over the Atlas Mountains, French North Africa was out of range. A 20 k.w. transmitter would be required to reach it and it was recommended that new equipment be ordered. The expenditure up till 31st March of £23,000 had exceeded the original estimate by nearly £10,000.

PWE Mission Dispatched

PWE appointed Mr Gordon Vereker, late British Minister in Finland, as their representative in Gibraltar with Mr G. Brereton of the BBC as head of the broadcasting staff. In August 1942, Mr Anderson, a BBC engineering expert, was sent out to take charge when Mr Donnelly handed over. On 4th May, 1942, Mr Grubb[2] had asked whether the PWE Mission would proceed to Gibraltar in view of the fact that its transmissions could not be heard in PWE territory. Anticipating, however, that the station would soon be functioning better, PWE dispatched its Mission in mid-May. After a week in Lisbon, the Mission proceeded to Madrid as HM Ambassador was closely concerned with the policy to be followed in broadcasts in Spanish.

Failure of Installation

On 2nd June, 1942, Mr Vereker and his staff arrived at Gibraltar. Mr Bruce Lockhart was informed of the decisions in regard to the North African landing early in August and must have congratulated himself on having the Gibraltar transmitter ready in time to play a useful part in the operations. These hopes were quickly disappointed. On 11th August, Mr Vereker reported[3] that eight months after the work of installation had begun, the

1. Telegram 13642 cipher 24/4. C. in C. Gib. to WO, 24.4.42.
2. Letter from Mr Grubb to Mr Vereker, 4.5.42.
3. Secret and Personal letter from Mr Vereker to Director General.

Gibraltar station was by no means ready; the main studios were not wired; the landline connecting the studios to the transmitter was not functioning; the emergency studio which might have been used as a makeshift was not completed; the main aerial was not erected; the feeder cable connecting the transmitter to the main aerial was not laid. Only the last of these specific facts had been reported to London. The effectiveness for reaching French North Africa of the installation of a new 20 k.w. transmitter on the north front of the Rock to which Mr Donnelly had committed PWE was problematical. Tests showed that the 5 k.w. transmitter was only capable of reaching a small area within 80–100 miles in Southern Spain. Mr Anderson, the BBC engineer, however suggested a new site on the south of the Rock which was approved by the military authorities. On 17th August, the Governor[1] telegraphed to the Chiefs of Staff that he was sending Anderson to London at the first opportunity.

On Mr Anderson's arrival, a conference was held on 20th August at Broadcasting House with Sir Noel Ashbridge of the BBC* and Miss Benzie of MoI Broadcasting Division to consider the position.[2] It was agreed to utilise the southern site on Europa point, to install a 50 k.w. transmitter for broadcasts to French North Africa and to continue with the plans for installing a 20 k.w. transmitter in place of the 5 k.w. on the north face, the studios being connected with each by landline. In view of the pending North African operations which would, if successful, make a propaganda centre at Gibraltar unnecessary, but of which the majority of those present at the Conference were unaware, these plans were not proceeded with. During July the Governor and C. in C. Gibraltar[3] had suggested that the PWE teams should be recalled but had reason to complain in his telegram on 17th August that he 'could not get a decision out of PWE'. The reason for this was that the Governor was not at that date aware of the plans for a North African landing, and PWE was making desperate efforts to discover a transmitter which could function in time to be of use in connection with it.[4]

PWE Mission Recalled

It was soon realised that during the operations there would be objections to the use of Gibraltar as a broadcasting centre and that in any case a sufficiently powerful transmitter could not possibly be installed in time. Accordingly the recall of the Mission was sanctioned on 5th September,

1. Telegram 16302 C. in C. Gibraltar to Chiefs of Staff, 17.8.42.
2. Minutes of Conference held at Broadcasting House, 20.8.42 (Stewart Robert's file).
3. General Mason MacFarlane.
4. Minute to Secretary of State for Foreign Affairs from Director General PWE, 19.8.42 (DGS Files '42).

* [Sir Noel Ashbridge (1889–1975) was a pioneer of broadcasting who served with the Royal Fusiliers 1914; among the first operators of wireless equipment on Western Front; joined Marconi; chief engineer, BBC, 1929; forefront of TV technology 1935; Deputy Director-General, BBC, 1943; Marconi board 1952–9.]

1942. On 15th October, the Director General PWE agreed to the MoI taking over the 5 k.w. transmitter and equipment as the Governor regarded broadcasts to Southern Spain as useful. On 25th October, the 20 k.w. transmitter was released to the MoI as no longer required by PWE. Both Mr Anderson and Mr Brereton put forward reports. If the former is accepted it should have been recognised when they were made that the proposals both for 5 k.w. and later for a 20 k.w. transmitter to be installed on *the north face of the Rock* were doomed to failure. The responsibility both for these proposals, and for the actual delays in erecting the 5 k.w. transmitter, must be borne by Mr Donnelly. Had he reported at any time during the first six months of his stay in Gibraltar that broadcasting to French North Africa could never be carried out, the PWE Mission would not have been sent out.

Propaganda in West Africa

Propaganda from West African bases both to the French and native populations of French possessions in West and Equatorial Africa falls into two periods.

The first, dating from the days of SO1 and SO2, was carried out by SO2 through the medium of the Franck Mission, etc., on behalf of SO1 and PWE. This worked well and there were no divergences in policy or other causes of serious friction. SO1 and PWE sent out a weekly directive telegram, after consultation with M. Bourdillon of the Colonial Office, through the Colonial Office. This telegram went to the Chairman of the West African Governors' Conference and served the double purpose of keeping the Governors informed and of a PWE directive.[1]

The second period, beginning in the summer of 1942, and originating as a preparation for the Anglo-American landings in North Africa with their attendant deception plan of a landing at Dakar, developed into a demand on the part of PWE to have its own Mission in the field and when this had been achieved, involved such long delays in the recruitment and dispatch of personnel for the Mission as to render it useless.

Period November 1940–June 1942

During this period the position can be summarised as follows:

> The local situation was that the Colonial French were becoming increasingly pro-Vichy and anti-British. The chief reason for this was the abortive attempt to seize Dakar, the attack on the French Fleet at Mers el Kebir, British failures in Greece and the Mediterranean and more important, that practically every Frenchman in AOF was there because he held a post directly or indirectly dependent on the Vichy Government which he did not wish to lose.

1. Minute from Colonel Sutton to David Stephens, 5.11.41.

The port of Dakar was also packed with shipping.

The natives did not distinguish between Vichy French and Gaullistes. They were generally rather pro-French and were not anti-British but were generally anti-German owing to memories of the German administration of the Cameroons.

In September 1941, a decay of morale among the French in French Equatorial Africa (which had joined the Fighting French) was reported.[1] The French Vichy authorities were active in preventing the spread of any printed propaganda of British or Free French origin. In Togoland[2] all British newspapers were barred and all native Africans entering the territory searched at frontier ports. Anyone found carrying propaganda was given a long term of imprisonment.

Propaganda during the First Period

During the period in question, the responsible authority for propaganda emanating from the West African Colonies was the Colonial Office, acting through the Chairman of the West African Governors' Conference, Sir Bernard Bourdillon.

Mr Louis Franck, who had gone out on the expedition to Dakar on an economic mission, returned much struck with the need for propaganda, and was accordingly chosen by CD to organise the machinery for SO1 and SO2 work in West Africa. He visited CHQ on 11.11.40 and discussed the policy to be pursued. His headquarters were to be Bathurst.

In February 1941, Mr Franck asked for tendentious articles which he had arranged to have inserted in the Dakar press and for large quantities of matchboxes bearing suitable slogans. He was able to collect and send home quantities of intelligence material. He also proposed developing the French broadcasting station at Accra which was agreed by the Governor of the Gold Coast. Since it was an open broadcasting station, SO1 regarded such development as outside its responsibilities.[3]

By April, he was producing 10,000 copies of a weekly news pamphlet in French as well as leaflets in the vernacular. By August 1941, he was producing propaganda in eight different languages at Lagos.

Mr Franck was continually pressing for further propaganda material, and as a result received letters, directives and texts, etc.

It is perhaps permissible to surmise that this activity was partly responsible for a recommendation by the West African Governors for a more active line of propaganda.[4] The suggestion aroused fears that such a policy

---

1. Appreciation of Free French attitude in West Africa, 18.9.41, to Colonel Sutton from Charles.
2. Letter from District Agent Accra to Mr Rawlings, 20.6.41.
3. Reply to minute from Captain Sheridan to Mr C. F. A. Warner.
4. W/97 from Sir B. Bourdillon to S. of S. for Colonies.

would provide Vichy with a *casus belli*, and native discontent in Vichy areas might spread from being anti-French to an anti-White movement throughout Africa.[1] These fears were successfully dispelled,[2] provided that covert methods were employed.

The same fear of the results of stirring up discontent with the Vichy administration prevailed a year later when the death occurred, in mysterious circumstances, of Moranaba, the chief of two million Moshis with another million and a half affiliated tribesmen. SOE West African section reported:[3]

> A most potent weapon has been put into our hands. A whispering campaign indicating murder by Vichy might produce the nearest thing to active revolt possible in the circumstances to an unarmed people . . . the Moshis are in a most dissatisfied state.

Mr H. Bourdillon of the Colonial Office informed Colonel Sutton that:

> As there is no immediate chance of English or American activity . . . it would be very dangerous to encourage by propaganda any unrest which starting by being anti-French might out of disappointment become anti-everybody.

Proposals for the strengthening of the Accra transmitter were taken up again and were being pressed with the MoI and PWE during the autumn and winter of 1941 and other proposals for expansion were under consideration.

The SOE authority responsible was by that time PERO under Colonel Wingate.* The Franck Mission had been transferred to deal with neutral territories.

Early in 1942, the following programme was being carried out in West Africa:[4]

1. *Written*

From Lagos (Nigeria). A weekly bulletin and occasional leaflets in French. Stickers in French and Arabic. Leaflets in vernacular languages. Propaganda on cigarettes, etc. This material was sent by air to the four local centres at Kano, Accra, Freetown and Bathurst from which it was distributed to Vichy territories by native agents (Niger, Dahomey and Togoland).

---

1. No. 123 from S. of S. for Colonies to Sir Bernard Bourdillon, 23.4.41.
2. W/113 Sir B. Bourdillon to S. of S. for Colonies, 27.4.41.
3. Major Neame to Colonel Sutton, 26.3.42.
4. External Propaganda from British W. Africa to Vichy Territories, 27.2.42 (W. Africa, 1027/17).

* [Major-General Orde Charles Wingate (1903–44) was born in India of Plymouth Brethren parentage; Royal Artillery 1923; Sudan Defence Force 1928–33; intelligence staff, Palestine, 1936–9; Middle East 1940; crossed Abyssinian frontier with Emperor Haile Selassie 1941; entered Addis Ababa May 1941; sent to India to command long-range penetration group; fought behind Japanese lines 1943; killed in air crash over North Assam 24 March 1944.]

From Freetown (Sierra Leone). Fortnightly bulletins in English. Monthly edition of same in French and three native languages for French Guinea.

From Bathurst (Gambia). Leaflets and special devices in French for Senegal.

2. *Spoken Propaganda*

Radio Gambia. 5½ hours a day with talks in French, Arabic and Wallof. Radio Gold Coast (Accra) 1¼ hours per day organised by Free French. No French broadcasts by SOE owing to lack of personnel.

3. *Films*

Gambia. A showboat on the Gambia River with films commented on by an African, controlled by a European officer.

Proposals for strengthening such propaganda were designed to take effect after the installation of the new transmitters at Accra and Brazzaville, when it was proposed that Accra should become purely British and Brazzaville purely French and that Radio Gambia should cease to transmit propaganda to Vichy territories which would be better covered by Accra. It was proposed that the new team under Captain Lamond should remain SOE bodies under Colonel Wingate, and that Captain Lamond should recruit his team from Canadian French speakers.[1] Lamond (then promoted Major) accordingly departed to New York where a conference was held with Colonel Donovan, Mr Sherwood, Mr Ritchie Calder and Mr Bowes Lyon at which Colonel Donovan confirmed an offer of immediate help in the way of material and personnel.[2]

A divergence of opinion as to the responsibility then arose as the Ministry of Information demanded that all broadcasting personnel everywhere, engaged on open broadcasting, should be under the Broadcasting Division MoI. PWE considered it vital that they should be employed by SOE[3] in order to carry out West Africa Plan 2903 which had been drawn up by PWE and SOE jointly.

Further difficulties in agreement on the terms of reference of the Head of the Mission (Major Lamond) soon afterwards arose with SOE.

The first period of harmonious co-operation as regards propaganda based in West Africa ended with an acrimonious inter-departmental squabble between MoI, PWE and SOE on responsibilities.

SOE had stipulated that the propaganda officer for PWE work was to be appointed by the Head of the PERO Mission and that communications from PWE should be through him.

> I am quite certain neither Mr Bracken nor the Ministry of Information will agree to the terms. . . . How on earth can we operate with speed and

1. External Propaganda from British W. Africa to Vichy territories, 27.2.42 (W. Africa 1027/17).
2. Telegram 68006–68406, Major Lamond to CD.
3. Mr Mangeot to Mr Bruce Lockhart, 27.6.42.

> efficiency if we have to send all communications to the Head of the Mission who may be hundreds of miles away from Lamond. . . . You yourself have always said to me that, in matters of propaganda, SOE act solely as the agents of PWE. I am bound to say quite frankly that this principle has rarely, if ever, been honoured by any observance on the part of your officers in the Field.
>
> Literally months of time have been wasted on SOE PWE negotiations in relation to propaganda. I leave it to you to judge what has been the effect on the war work of both organisations.[1]

Agreement with SOE on PWE Missions

In the following month SOE was forced to abandon the veto which it had sought to maintain on PWE Missions abroad and a new agreement was arrived at to provide the closest measure of co-operation between SOE and PWE in the Middle East, West Africa and any other centres to which it might later be agreed to apply the same principle.

By this agreement[2] SOE recognised PWE's desire to establish independent missions to conduct all forms of propaganda to the areas covered by their charter. SOE agreed to hand over to PWE all broadcasting stations which they owned or controlled in the areas concerned and not to establish other stations of their own. PWE undertook to provide SOE with clandestine broadcasting facilities on the following terms:

> The broadcasts to be made on the transferred stations by SOE teams whose identity SOE was not bound to disclose. SOE would submit scripts in advance so both parties could be satisfied the broadcasts did not conflict with HMG policy.
>
> PWE recognised that operational policy did not necessarily form part of PWE propaganda policy.
>
> PWE agreed not to put agents into the field for dissemination of written propaganda or whispers or to obtain intelligence on the effect of propaganda. All such work to be done as in the past by SOE as agents for PWE.

Local opposition to this agreement as regards West Africa was not, however, overcome:

> I should be grateful if it could be made clear to PWE that any personnel coming to British West Africa must come under the control of local propaganda Committee and be directed by those with knowledge of local affairs.[3]

1. Mr Bruce Lockhart to CD, 15.7.42.
2. PWE/SOE Agreement, 2.9.42.
3. Telegram 152098 cipher 7.9.42 from GOC in C West Africa to WO.

Attempt to Control PWE Mission by SOE Locally

This attempt to reverse ministerial decisions in London by the local SOE officers was not to be accepted tamely and the S. of S. for Foreign Affairs informed the Minister Resident in West Africa[1] that 'The SOE representative is Chairman of the local propaganda Committee. As the new agreement which had been approved by the Minister of Information, the Minister of Economic Warfare and myself, leaves PWE master of propaganda in its own territories, it would seem highly anomalous to make the PWE Mission responsible to this local Committee.'

The MoI claims were compromised by MoI agreeing to the MWE Mission being dispatched and to PWE having its own announcers and broadcasting team as well as being responsible for policy.[2]

PWE proceeded to appoint Colonel R. T. Somerville who resigned on 7th October, 1942, so an advance party under Major Altherr was dispatched. The material necessary for the Mission was eventually shipped on 1.12.42.

Preparations Not Made by MoI

Owing to the time wasted in arriving at a decision as to the Department responsible, little had been done in Africa and Major Altherr reported that Ministry of Information studios, offices and living quarters had not even been built.

Meanwhile the landings in North Africa had taken place and a month afterwards the Resident Minister in West Africa pointed out[3] that PWE existed for the purpose of conducting propaganda into enemy and enemy-occupied territory but there would shortly be no such territory within the range of the new Accra transmitter.

The Resident Minister was informed that a new head of the Mission, Colonel F. W. C. Morgans, had been appointed and would shortly be proceeding to Accra, and the view that propaganda to French territories should cease to be a PWE responsibility immediately upon their liberation was not accepted. The suggestion that the Mission should be called the West African Broadcasting Unit was agreed.

Charter of PWE Mission

Colonel Morgans, the head of the PWE Mission, reached Accra on 11.1.43. His 'charter'[4] was to conduct propaganda through all available media into

1. Telegram No. 42 from S. of S. for Foreign Affairs to Minister Resident West Africa, 14.9.42.
2. Note recording meeting of Mr Bruce Lockhart and Mr Cyril Radcliffe, 8.9.42.
3. Telegram No. 479. Resident Minister to S. of S. for Colonies, 30.11.42.
4. Mission to W. Africa. To Col. Morgans signed by S. of S. for Foreign Affairs and Minister of Information, 8.12.42.

enemy and enemy-occupied countries and any adjoining French African territories, excluding Chad, in accordance with regular directives furnished by PWE headquarters London. He was also to maintain constant liaison with the office of the Resident Minister* in order to obtain day-to-day political guidance.

Opposition of Resident Minister to Propaganda from West Africa

Colonel Morgans, however, was unable to carry out his mission as[1] the Resident Minister was quite convinced that he did not want any propaganda to French territories conducted from Accra. The dilatoriness in equipping and sending out the Mission had resulted in its finding the situation entirely changed. While Colonel Morgans was at sea the AOF territories adhered to the Allied cause. The Resident Minister agreed with the French representative M. Boisson not to conduct propaganda to the AOF. This agreement was apparently not known in London. As Colonel Morgans himself pointed out, the Mission should have been recalled immediately upon his arrival. As it was, he put up to the Resident Minister various proposals for incorporating French broadcasts from Accra into a programme of straight news and entertainment for all West Africa from the new Accra transmitter but the Resident Minister remained adamant on his veto of any emissions in French and maintained that 'a war of propaganda was not wanted in West Africa'.

Not only had the political situation changed so by the time Colonel Morgans had arrived that the Resident Minister had decided that the Mission would not be required, but the staff had been ill-chosen and the administrative officer was untrained. Team work was not understood, the team was never brought to strength for full-time work, and in any case, the studios and accommodation at Broadcasting House were not ready till the end of May. Colonel Morgans had, at least, the satisfaction of seeing the completed studios for he did not leave Accra by air until the 10th of June.

No evidence has come to light of any attempt by PWE either to overrule the Resident Minister's veto or, failing that, to withdraw the Mission without delay. PWE can hardly have been unaware that no French-language broadcasts went out on Radio Accra for the six months during which the head of its Mission was at Accra.

---

1. To DG PID London from Col. Morgans. PWE Mission (WABU) at Accra. Winding up, 30.6.43.

* [(Maurice) Harold Macmillan, 1st Earl of Stockton (1894–1986), was thrice wounded with the Grenadier Guards Special Reserve in the Great War; Unionist MP, Stockton, 1924–9 and 1931–45; Parliamentary Secretary, Ministry of Supply, 1940–2; Minister Resident at Allied HQ in North-West Africa 1942–5; Secretary for Air 1945; Minister of Housing 1951–4; Foreign Secretary 1955; Chancellor of the Exchequer 1955–7; Prime Minister 1957–63.]

Thus during the early period when SOE acted as PWE agents considerable initiative was shown and propaganda from West Africa was carried out extremely well considering the resources available.

When propaganda became important owing to impending Anglo-American operations in North Africa, PWE decided to send out its own Mission. The opposition to this both in London and in West Africa itself effectually prevented any propaganda being carried out at all at the time when it was most needed.

PWE Mission to Middle East

When the PWE SOE Agreement of 2.9.42 had been concluded PWE proceeded to send out two Missions. The fate of that sent out to West Africa under Colonel Morgans has been described. That sent to Cairo was a very different matter, if only because the propaganda from Cairo was directed to enemy-occupied Europe and the work was correspondingly more important.

Mr P. C. Vellacott DSO, MA, was appointed Director of Political Warfare Middle East with effect from 5.10.42. Mr Vellacott's terms of reference were:[1]

> To conduct Political Warfare through all available media with enemy and enemy-occupied countries in accordance with regular directive furnished by PWE headquarters, London.
>
> To maintain constant liaison with the Minister of State's office HM Embassy, in order to obtain day-to-day political guidance.
>
> To maintain constant liaison with the Commanders in Chief of Naval, Military and Air Forces.
>
> To sit as representative of the Political Warfare Executive on any coordinating board.
>
> To be responsible for and sole British representative for the policy of the Political Warfare Executive and for the collection of propaganda intelligence material.

The Agreement with SOE had provided, with safeguards for SOE interests, to hand over to PWE all broadcasting stations which they at that time owned or controlled and not to establish any other stations in their stead.

SOE Local Opposition to Transfer of Transmitters to PWE

Before the arrival of Mr Vellacott in Cairo, Lord Glenconner* put a considered statement of his interpretation of the agreement through Sir Arthur

1. Mission to the Middle East. To Mr P. C. Vellacott, 12.10.42.

* [Christopher Grey Tennant, 2nd Baron Glenconner (1899–1983), was head of SOE in Cairo.]

Rucker,* to the Minister of State, Cairo.[1] In it he maintained that the Agreement admitted and confirmed SOE's right to disseminate operational propaganda and that though the actual station was to be transferred to PWE, SOE were entitled to time so that all broadcasts which SOE needed could be transmitted by its own teams. Nor did the agreement say that SOE broadcasts should be controlled by PWE in any way. SOE broadcasts could not be vested in some other department, if SOE were to remain responsible for subversive warfare as a whole. In view of these considerations, Lord Glenconner stated that 'with the best will in the world' he could not hand over his technical staff to PWE since it would be very difficult to replace them and he needed them for the SOE transmitter to the Arab world. He suggested therefore that the best solution would be for SOE to continue to service and maintain both the transmitters. Similarly, SOE would continue to require the services of many of the teams of scriptwriters, speakers and monitors at present employed though there were Italian and German-speaking teams which could be transferred. All the others, however, he would continue to need for SOE broadcasts. Lord Glenconner then remarked: 'You may ask where does Mr Vellacott come in?'

Soon after his arrival, this letter was handed to Mr Vellacott who stated his case with some tact.[2] He began by paying tribute to all which had been and was being achieved by SOE but thought that 'a measure of relief given to SOE from the burden of control in one activity will not necessarily detract from the cogency of their effort in another and, as I understand, their chief activity'.

He pointed out that his charter entrusted him with the responsibility of conducting Political Warfare through all available media into enemy and enemy-occupied countries and that he was therefore bound to take over all broadcasting stations at that time owned or controlled by SOE and he could not therefore agree with the suggestion made by Lord Glenconner that SOE should continue to service and maintain the transmitter for the Balkans. He fully recognised SOE's need of special clandestine broadcasting facilities for operational purposes, and therefore desired to be in full consultation and alliance with Lord Glenconner so that he could make the arrangements serve an agreed purpose. He asked for a meeting to discuss the principle through which the Agreement could be put into effect.

The desired meeting, however, only confirmed differences in interpretation of the PWE/SOE Agreement and a telegram was accordingly sent to the S. of S. for Foreign Affairs asking for further elucidation,[3] and stating both sides of the case.

---

1. Lord Glenconner to Sir Arthur Rucker, 14.10.42. G/PR/98.
2. Mr Vellacott to Lord Moyne, 9.11.42.
3. No. 1938 cipher to S. of S. Foreign Affairs from Deputy Minister of State, 14.11.42.

* [Sir Arthur Nevil Rucker (1895–1991) served in the 12th Suffolk regiment in 1915–18; entered Civil Service 1920; Private Secretary to successive Ministers of Health 1928–36; Principal Private Secretary to Prime Minister 1939–40; seconded for special duties 1941–3; returned to Ministry of Health as Deputy Secretary 1943.]

The Secretary of State replied[1] that no arguments could be admitted regarding the transfer of control of broadcasting stations to PWE and that PWE and SOE were instructing their representatives to work out plans for covert propaganda country by country and to try to weld them into one combined plan. Any points of difference should be referred by them to Lockhart and Sir C. Hambro* respectively for consideration by the co-ordinating Committee in London.

Continued Opposition of SOE to Instructions from London

At a meeting held on 22nd November, 1942, it was agreed that Mr Vellacott and Mr Ralph Murray should visit the SOE broadcasting station in Palestine with Lord Glenconner and Colonel Butler to see what was being done there and should draw up working plans. Lord Glenconner at this meeting[2] showed that he did not intend to allow his organisation to be anything other than the senior and indeed the predominating partner in policy as well as in planning but apparently thought that 'PWE might be grafted onto SOE'.

Mr Ralph Murray's Report on SOE RUs in [the] Middle East

Mr Vellacott reported on the SOE broadcasts from Palestine which consisted of two 7½ k.w. transmitters at Beit Jala connected by landline to studios in Jerusalem which provided five hours transmitting time per day and ran one station to Greece, two to Yugoslavia, two to Roumania, two to Bulgaria, two to Hungary, one to Italy, one to Germany and one to Austria. Before Mr Vellacott left London he had been informed by SOE that they had no operational interests in the Hungarian, Italian, German or Austrian station. It was thus clear that at least five of the RUs run by SOE from Palestine had no operational value. After a meeting with the SOE experts on 2.12.42 Mr Murray reported on the state of affairs which revealed the degree of overlapping and lack of co-ordination which might have been expected and which were, indeed, a reason why PWE had wished to establish a mission in the Middle East:[3]

> *Italy*. Having had a look at the Jerusalem RU and talked to the man who runs it, I had come to the conclusion, with which he and Butler agreed,

1. No. 2882 S. of S. Foreign Affairs to Deputy Minister of State, 21.11.42.
2. Secret and Personal letter from Vellacott to Lockhart.
3. Ralph Murray to Mr Vellacott, n.d. (*circa* 2.12.42).

* [Sir Charles Jocelyn Hambro (1897–1963) won MC serving with Coldstream Guards in France 1916–18; company secretary, C. J. Hambro & Son; director, Bank of England, 1928; joined MEW 1939; worked in SOE, visited Sweden 1940; deputy head, SOE, 1941–2; executive chief 1942–3; head of British raw materials mission to Washington 1943–5; Chairman, Hambro's Bank, 1961–3.]

that there was not much point in carrying it on. The Italian Region in London had also told me before I left that they did not see very much point in it . . .
Germany and Austria. The report on these stations shows that the RUs are only semi-clandestine. We all agreed that there was no case at all for keeping them in Jerusalem and that we had better transfer the teams, making allowances for their personal arrangements and the use of their voices, to Cairo. The idea is to start a service of medium (and short) wave here in German designed for occupying troops in Greece and in the Balkans as far as we can reach them . . .
Hungary. The Jerusalem RUs have no information on which to work and were cutting across what we were doing in London. SOE were not really interested, so I suggested suppressing the Jerusalem show immediately and using the personnel made available for other things.
Serbia. I suggested that Sumadija[1] might be closed down. I did this for several reasons:

(i) The present Sumadija speaker Teodorovic wants to go to Canada for six months' special trainin . . .
(ii) I wanted to make a co-operative gesture in this matter of relationship.
(iii) Karageorge[2] and Sumadija *are* duplicating each other . . .

Croatia. Just as in the case of Serbia (for this is what Karageorge really speaks to) my idea was to prevent one station striking at the authority of another. In the case of Croatia therefore, I thought that SOE should not set up a Croat station such as they had till recently in Jerusalem, because it would strike at the authority of Zrinski, on which I lay considerable importance. They of course said that they might 'become operational' in Croatia and would therefore require a Croat station in the Middle East. I pointed out that if they did 'become operational' then by communication through us to England of their requirements they could utilise the well-established Zrinski instead of starting up a new show which would strike at Zrinski's authority and need three or four months to establish itself. This seemed rather to surprise them as an idea, but I think can probably be made effective through the Planning Committee which is now being set up by our Agreement of yesterday . . .
Slovenia. Again my aim was to prevent the establishment of a not very well thought-out station here, enjoying no intelligence, in preference to the possibility of a station in the UK . . .
Roumania. We agreed not to alter anything for the moment. The SOE operational man, with whom I had separate talks, had been extremely

1. The PWE RU to Serbia.
2. The SOE RU to Serbia.

enthusiastic about our RU which he says is first-class and very important. I had been perfectly prepared to offer to eliminate ours in preference to Jerusalem, because intelligence this end is better than that which is got in England, but after hearing his opinion, I sheared off . . .
Greece. As we have no RU at all in the UK I think we can settle the matter here. I hope also that the Anglo-Greek Committee may come in useful for the supply of ideas and material and guidance for composing directives for the BBC.
Bulgaria. The Bulgarian 'B' team . . . is of no significance to either SOE or PWE. The personnel, however, are fairly intelligent. The best thing to do seemed to be to bring them down to Cairo and employ them on monitoring and strengthening the Bulgarian output on Cairo radio, which is very feeble. This was unanimously agreed.

I had originally been prepared to suggest that our Levski Bulgarian RU should be suppressed as duplicating the Bulgarian 'A' (Agrarian) from Jerusalem. Again I wished to do this as a sign of real will towards co-operation, and because I think, other things being equal, it would have been the proper thing to do. However, I had had a talk with Dimitrov before, and he had earnestly begged me not to remove our RU because its reception in Istanbul, where he had been, was brilliant and far superior to that of the Jerusalem station. I was rather reinforced in that opinion by a report (sent by telegram) of the formation of a Levski organisation in Bulgaria. The report does not appear to be particularly well authenticated but the mere suggestion of such an organisation does make me think that our RU may be doing some good. In spite of the duplication therefore, we decided that the two stations should carry on.

It is clear that even a visit of a few days was bearing fruit and likely to result in greatly improved services.

On 3.12.42 Mr Vellacott was invited by the Minister of State to become a member of the SOE Sub-Committee of the Defence Committee. Nevertheless, Lord Glenconner was not ready to relinquish SOE control[1] of the following broadcasts:

Yugoslavia. The station known as 'Karageorge', which purported to be the voice of General Mihailovic.*

Roumania. The station known as 'The Struggle for Freedom' (Vlaicu).

---

1. Lord Glenconner to Mr Vellacott, 4.12.42

* [General Dragoljub Mihailovic (1893–1946), a Serbian army officer in the Great War who rose to the rank of colonel in the Yugoslav army. In 1941 he organised mountain-based 'Chetnik' guerrilla resistance to the German occupation. Fought against Tito's Communists and was executed by the Tito Government for alleged collaboration.]

Greece. A new station, possibly to be called 'The Third Brigade', to represent the policy of the Anglo-Greek Committee.

Bulgaria. The station known as 'The Station of Freedom' supervised by Dimitrov.

He also stated that SOE might require time for a new station for Croatia and another for Slovenia. SOE would require to retain in their employ the teams of writers, speakers and censors who were engaged on these broadcasts.

Nevertheless, an agreement did not seem impossible and Lord Glenconner and Mr Vellacott accordingly signed an agreement[1] which provided for the transfer of office, transmitters and building from SOE to PWE and of administrative and technical staff. PWE agreed to give SOE time for Karageorge, Bulgarian A, Roumanian B, a new Greek station and the broadcasting teams operating them. The administration at St Pierre was not, however, transferred to PWE though it would have been an obvious economy to do so. The PWE Mission regarded this, however, as only a first step towards what they would obtain by negotiations proceeded in London. The following spring, Sir Robert Bruce Lockhart informed Mr Vellacott[2] that it had been agreed that PWE was responsible for direction and control of propaganda instruments in the Middle East, and asked if he was satisfied with the arrangements with SOE.

Mr Vellacott accordingly raised the question of the transfer of the administration at St Pierre to PWE but Lord Glenconner resisted the proposal[3] as relations between SOE and PWE had not been finalised.

On 4th March Mr Vellacott was informed that the S. of S. for Foreign Affairs had written to Lord Selborne[4] that the claim of SOE agents in the Middle East to maintain their own special teams of broadcasters and technicians in order to carry out 'operational propaganda' had not been found necessary in Britain and that he could not understand why it should be necessary in the Middle East.

SOE Claims to Carry out Propaganda

Mr Vellacott commented that SOE[5] Middle East claimed the right to persistent and continuous 'operational propaganda' and that the right implied a policy so linked with their operations that it and its propaganda was in practice independent of any control other than their own. In the same

1. Heads of Agreement between SOE and PWE in Middle East covert broadcasting from Jerusalem station, 6.12.42.
2. 656 Pilot, 1.3.43.
3. G/PR/324/P.3. Lord Glenconner to Mr Vellacott, 3.3.43.
4. 696 Pilot FO to Minister of State, 4.3.43.
5. Pilot 511 for Lockhart from Vellacott, 5.3.43.

telegram he pointed out that though in practice PWE had been able to influence SOE policy and output it was absurd that there should be two organisations charged with propaganda to the same countries. Moreover, as Mr Vellacott informed Lord Glenconner,[1] that until these matters were brought to a conclusion the energies of both organisations tended to be misdirected and the work of both hampered.

PWE Finally Gains Control of Political Warfare in Middle East

Discussions had, however, been proceeding between Sir Robert Bruce Lockhart and Sir Charles Hambro and an agreement was reached[2] by which SOE reaffirmed their acceptance of the principle that propaganda control in ME was vested solely in PWE and agreed that such control could only be effectively exercised by physical control of instruments of propaganda. PWE should be responsible for dissemination of subversive propaganda except where such dissemination was carried on inside enemy or enemy-occupied territory it should be done by SOE acting as agents for PWE. All scripts should be approved by PWE and all broadcasting personnel paid by them.

The new agreement was satisfactory to PWE Middle East[3] in all respects save the physical possession of the Kasr printing press which was originally taken over from the Egyptian custodian of enemy property by Colonel Thornhill for SO1 and had reverted to SO2 and hence to SOE.

Following the new agreement the PWE/SOE Co-ordination Committee was brought to an end and was replaced by a Planning Committee.[4]

PWE policy was meanwhile greatly strengthened vis-à-vis policy with regard to Greece by the appointment of Mr R. A. Leeper as Ambassador to the Greek Government.

Mr Leeper had been charged by the Foreign Secretary with an enquiry into the SOE machinery for subversive warfare in Greece and the policy which had in fact been pursued.[5] This, however, does not come into the history of PWE.

Development and Organisation of PWE Mission ME

Mr Vellacott soon raised the status of the PWE Mission owing to his excellent personal relations both with the Resident Minister Cairo and the C. in C. and his staff.

By the summer of 1943, the Mission was organised on the lines of the parent Department. Brigadier Jeffries was appointed Deputy Head, and

1. Mr Vellacott to Lord Glenconner, 11.3.43.
2. FO to Minister of State, Cairo.
3. Pilot 793 to Lockhart from Vellacott.
4. P. C. Vellacott to Rt Hon. Lord Moyne, 27.4.43.
5. Lord Glenconner to R. A. Leeper, 12.4.43.

Head of the Military Wing. Mr Murray was appointed Psychological Warfare Adviser with responsibilities for propaganda policy and method and general planning of Political Warfare. Lt Colonel Street became Head of Propaganda Output, responsible for the control and mechanism of output, an Intelligence section was set up under Major Robinson and Lt Colonel Norman Smith became Finance and Administrative Officer.

Following the model of the parent Department, work was organised regionally into country sections for Greece, Bulgaria and Roumania, Yugoslavia, Albania, Italy and Germany. In addition, there was a Visual Propaganda Division and a Radio Division. The latter was divided into Cairo FTD radio and a Palbase Radio Division operating from Palestine. A training school was set up under Lt Colonel Kenneth Johnstone and front-line units were later developed as required.

PW in ME Changed by Military Plans

British Political Warfare to the Balkans from PWE Mission was at first based on a military plan for a large-scale Balkan campaign. This plan was whittled away owing to shortage of manpower and by the decision to invade Italy.

The original plan was thus first reduced to a plan to contain a large German Air Force in the Aegean by a diversionary attack. With the failure of the Dodecanese operations in October 1943, these plans were considerably modified.

Thus early in 1943, PWE ME were making all the preparations necessary for a post-invasion period, in Balkan countries – stockpiling supplies of literature, receiver sets, films, projectors, etc. It was during this period that PWE ME opened its own school for training officers in PW functions.

But though the plan for immediate occupation was cancelled, plans continued for the eventual dispatch of sub-missions to all the Balkan countries, including Turkey. The school therefore continued in being until the subject of the waste of manpower involved was raised by Mr Vellacott at the end of April 1944.[1] After that date, some of its instructors became available as instructors at PWE School, Brondesbury.

PWE Units in the Dodecanese Campaign

One front-line unit (known as 363 Unit) took part. Owing to lack of shipping only five officers were able to go in the first wave and equipment was limited to what they could carry. Although the circumstances were most unfavourable and ended in defeat, the PWE Unit successfully carried out liaison duty and Italian propaganda in all the islands. They had begun the organisation of newspapers in Cos and Kalinos when the islands were seized by the enemy. They controlled newspapers in Samos, where they carried out

1. Mr Vellacott to Sir Orme Sargent, 22.4.44.

negotiations in most tricky and difficult circumstances with the Italians and Greeks. They carried out interrogations and collected most valuable intelligence. Their advice was sought and taken by the staff on political questions. Several of them distinguished themselves in fighting. Captain Paul Lieven, who had distinguished himself during the landing at Algiers, organised the defences of the Brigadier's HQ on Leros with a mixed body of signallers, clerks, etc., and was awarded a bar to his MC for his part in the fighting.

Practical Lessons of Dodecanese

Apart from the oldest lesson – that in emergencies every man must be equipped and trained to fight – several essential lessons were pointed out by the PWE commanding officer.[1] The first was that the OC of the PW unit taking part should be informed of all plans at an early stage and should be introduced to the brigade or divisional staff on a high level.

An Intelligence Officer is an essential member of every unit. A typist clerk is also essential as reports should be sent back in duplicate early, and frequently.

The language of the country must be spoken really well by one or two officers, and a German-speaking expert is essential to interrogate prisoners. Officers should report back at the earliest possible moment. Equipment should include monitoring sets, a Gestettner, portable typewriters, motor bicycles and one or two dubbed films.

PWE Sub-Mission to Bari

PWE Mission ME dispatched a sub-Mission to Bari at the end of 1943, but it was merged in PWB Bari in February 1944, and the PWE ME Mission itself was merged with OWI Cairo to form PWB Cairo the following May [15.5.44].

Mr Vellacott had by that time resigned owing to ill-health and other causes and Brigadier Jeffries left Cairo for Algiers, being appointed British Military Director PWB AFHQ shortly afterwards [7.7.44].

Colonel Lethbridge became 'Chief of the Centre' of PWB Cairo on Brigadier Jeffries' departure. PWB Cairo was finally closed the following year [15.5.45].

---

1. Lecture by Major Sir John Makgill at PWE School, Brondesbury.

PART III

Regional Problems and Media of Political Warfare

The Regional Aims and Problems of Political Warfare

The narrative of events will now be interrupted in order to take a rapid review of the main regional aims of Political Warfare, of the media by which it is carried out, of a number of RUs and of the basic PWE intelligence document, the News Digest.

Political Warfare to Germany

Overt or 'White' Political Warfare to the German Home Front and the German Forces can be divided into four phases.

September 1939 to June 1941 (Germany attacks Russia).
July 1941 to July 1943 (fall of Mussolini).
July 1943 to May 1945 (end of German resistance).

The themes employed in White Political Warfare to Germany were more or less identical in both broadcasting and in leaflets. From June 1940 until August 1942, leaflet disseminations were comparatively small; after that date leaflet dissemination increased enormously,[1] but broadcasting always remained the most important medium to the German Home Front, as leaflets were to the German Armed Forces.

[June 1940–June 1941] While Britain stood alone, our Political Warfare objectives were:

1. Dissemination of leaflets by the RAF increased from 47 million in 1940 to 253 million in 1943 and dropped to 180 million in 1944 owing to the development of leafleting by the USAAF. Total RAF disseminations to Germany amounted to 757 million leaflets.

1. To attract an audience by providing a reliable news service. The failure of the German Air Force during the Battle of Britain and its concealment by the German Propaganda Ministry, led many Germans to listen to the BBC. One of the few slips made by the BBC: that the Potsdamer Bahnhof had been hit in one of the early raids, was still being quoted against it in 1944. The fact that this single instance was always quoted and no other could be found was a tribute to the accuracy of the BBC.

2. To persuade the Germans that Britain could not be defeated. After the failure during the Battle of Britain we could argue that what they had failed to achieve then, could never be done later.

3. To persuade the German people that the Nazis were set on world domination. Most Germans would have liked peace after the victories of 1940.

It was PWE's constant object to fasten responsibility for war upon Hitler in particular and upon Germans in general for supporting him, and to point out that Hitler's record made it impossible for us to make peace with him.

The boastings of German leaders during victory, and particular recordings of Hitler's speeches with his promises of wiping out British cities and annihilating Russian armies, proved to be useful weapons.

During the second period [July 1941–July 1943] the following additional themes became important:

1. To convince Germans that their defeat was inevitable. Hitler had attacked Russia and declared war on the United States. His assumption of the command of the Army, and the failure of German arms after October 1942 showed that the tide had turned. British Political Warfare constantly referred to the inexhaustible resources of the USA, the recovery of Russia, the German shortage of manpower and the RAF raids. In particular it stressed that the importation of millions of foreign workers ('The Trojan Horse') would become increasingly dangerous as Germany's fortunes waned.

2. To persuade the Germans that defeat would not necessarily be disastrous to them. This was in its nature a difficult task, and was rendered harder not only by German fears of Russian vengeance, the Propaganda Ministry's 'Strength through Fear' campaign, and German scepticism of Allied good intentions, largely based on the Nazi version of the part played by President Wilson's Fourteen Points in the last war, but also by lack of material in the shape of Allied official announcements by Mr Churchill, Marshal Stalin and President Roosevelt. The main emphasis had therefore to be put on the punishment of certain classes of Germans, the Nazi leaders and war criminals, and on showing that there was room for a reconstituted Germany in a peaceful Europe.

In spite of the difficulties due to insufficient definition and insufficient authority, the two golden rules were to keep our short-term and our long-term war aims absolutely distinct and to present both in terms of our own interest.

[July 1943–May 1945] With the fall of Mussolini, the failure of the last

German offensive in Russia, the bombing of German cities, and the landing of British and American armies in France, German hopes were reduced to the possibility of Allied disunity.

The changes of emphasis in our Political Warfare were to stress:

1. Certainty of German defeat. We stressed the military rather than the political side of the war, particularly the mathematics of war expressed in terms of manpower and production.

2. 'Five past twelve'. Hitler's promise that unlike the Kaiser he would not capitulate until five minutes after the last possible moment, was used constantly to show that Hitler knew Germany was defeated and was involving her in appalling and useless sufferings.

3. It can only get worse. The increasing British and American air raids and the destruction of German Fighter production were used to illustrate the hopelessness of Germany's position.

4. Allied unity and British strength. The effect of Goebbels' propaganda was to make the Germans doubt whether Russia would allow Britain and the USA to behave with moderation to a defeated Germany. It was therefore important to convince the Germans of British strength and of Britain as a strong but just enemy. The projection of British strength and of the British way of life became therefore more important during this period.

After D-Day, the importance of propaganda to the German forces increased enormously and the importance of propaganda addressed to the civilian population correspondingly decreased.

Overt Political Warfare to the German Armed Forces

Apart from front-line propaganda, carried out chiefly by leaflets and by Black and Grey transmissions, the distinction is somewhat unreal.

The BBC ran special programmes for the German Army, Navy and Air Force, but these were less popular than the Grey Atlantik-sender and Calais-sender transmissions which were widely listened to because owing to their 'hot' music, and the up-to-date inside information on the German service conditions, they provided a better entertainment than the German forces could get elsewhere. The chief attraction offered by the BBC was in programmes written and broadcast by German Ps/W themselves.

The BBC Forces Programmes were on the following lines:

1. Technical appeal to the soldier, sailor and airman on such subjects as: tactical detail of current operations, particularly on the Eastern Front, about which the Germans were reticent. Details [of] units involved in heavy fighting were given.

2. Details of Allied superiority in armaments particularly in new aircraft types.

3. Failure of German strategy. Hitler's incapacity as a Commander in Chief and readiness to sacrifice strategy to political expedience as at Stalingrad.

Weakness of Germany's allies. Difficulties of German production.

Appeal to the German soldiers' interest in conditions in Germany. News of air raids, food and housing conditions in Germany and the possible activities of foreign workers. It was important, however, that we should not appear hypocritical by showing concern on these subjects. Treatment of German prisoners of war. The broadcasting of the names of German Ps/W was always an important bait for German listeners and increased steadily. Messages from Ps/W camps showed the consequences of surrender were not unpleasant, and carried the implication that Germany should also surrender. After Overlord the broadcasting of scripts written by German and Austrian Ps/W became an important feature. (See Brondesbury-Ascot scheme pp. 419–20.)

In addition to the main effort of trying to convince the Germans of certain facts, White propaganda to a limited extent tried to get the Germans to do things. Thus the Typhus campaign which was carried out in conjunction with 'Black' was aimed at increasing malingering, wasting medicines and doctors' time with imaginary illnesses and avoidance by the civil population of soldiers coming from the Eastern Front.

Similarly the Trojan Horse campaign was partly designed to get Germans to treat foreign workers well in order to propitiate them, partly as a form of nerve warfare to lower morale.

On the whole, however, White propaganda was designed to spread defeatist ideas; Black propaganda was to induce defeatist action, and to corrupt discipline.

Political Warfare against Italy

British propaganda to Italy began at the time of the Munich crisis and during the interval before Italy entered the war in June 1940, the BBC built up a reputation for truthfulness. Colonel Harold Stevens, formerly Military Attaché in Rome, became a first-class radio personality enjoying considerable prestige with a wide following among the Italian public. Although Italians distrusted all propaganda, they turned to the British radio because they believed it to be more credible than their own.

PWE started in the autumn of 1941 with the immense advantages that the war was unpopular with the great majority of Italians and that they were sick of the Fascist regime and heartily disliked the Germans.

The themes employed in British propaganda during the SO1 period were:

1. The war would be long.
2. Britain recognised an absolute distinction between the Fascist regime and the Italian people.
3. Every misfortune of the Italian people had been due to Mussolini personally.
4. The Germans were hated by the Italian people.

During the opening phase of the war – until the autumn of 1941, the early Italian disasters were set off by the victorious German campaigns in

Greece, Yugoslavia and Cyrenaica. British propaganda during this period dwelt on the certainty of ultimate British victory owing to the material support of the USA, the subservience of the Fascist Government to Germany, and the odious behaviour of Germans to Italians. If Germany won the war, the Italians would become a subject people.

By the spring of 1942, the Italian Empire in East Africa had been conquered and large numbers of Italians were prisoners of war. A new plan for Political Warfare was drawn up with the object of reducing Italian help to Germany to a minimum and to prepare for a crisis which would make Italy a liability to Germany.

PWE carried out propaganda to prevent Italian troops being sent to Russia and the Balkans, to emphasise the sea crossing to Libya as the 'death-run' to Libya; to discourage Italian workers from going to Germany; to stress the inferiority of Italian equipment and the failure of the Germans to give support to Italian troops. We also carried on a campaign to Italian peasants advocating the hoarding of food, and of copper, giving instructions for making copper sulphate necessary for spraying vineyards, of which there was a shortage.

After the Battle of Alamein, PWE took a more positive line as Italy became more vulnerable. The vulnerability of Italian shipping to air attack from North African bases was continually stressed, and the desertion and surrender of Italian troops was represented as due to the absence of German support and solidarity.

Our Political Warfare to Italy met with the following difficulties:

1. The hatred and contempt felt by our allies, the Greeks and the French, Abyssinians and Arabs for the Italians. It is always dangerous to speak with two voices to adjacent countries, and while our line was too 'hard' for the Italians, we were regarded as dangerously 'soft' by our allies.

2. The tendency of British commanders and the British press to ridicule the Italian forces and to outrage the Italian sense of military honour.

3. Our failure to adopt a definite policy with regard to anti-Fascist prisoners of war and the formation of an Italian anti-Fascist legion.

4. The impossibility of taking a universally satisfactory line with regard to the House of Savoy. As we wanted high Army officers to surrender and they were bound by the oath of allegiance to the King, we did not commit ourselves to support any of the popular movements, all of which were Republican.

On 21st March, 1943, PWE issued a working plan based on the following points:

1. That since defeat was inevitable Italian resistance merely prolonged the war.

2. That it was in the power of the Italians to get out of the war and to shorten it.

3. That it was in the interests of the Italians to stop the war.

4. That it was not dishonourable for them to stop the war.

After the Allied invasion of Sicily a war of nerves on Italy was maintained at full blast as this was consistent with our deception plans and proved, indeed, most effective. It was by this time also necessary to cover the protracted negotiations with General Badoglio.* By attacking Badoglio's avowed policy of continuing the war with Germany, we helped to force his hand. On 8th September, 1943, Italy's capitulation was announced.

It is impossible to estimate the part played by PWE in bringing about the capitulation of Italy, but though it would be unwise to make any claims that Political Warfare did more than keep driving the remorseless logic of events into the ears of the Italian people, the success of our invasion of Sicily and the reactions of the Sicilians showed that the effect of our Political Warfare was greater than had been expected.[1]

Political Warfare to the Occupied Countries

Political Warfare to occupied countries proved in its nature both far easier and far more effective than to Germany and her satellites, since the majority in every occupied country hated the Germans and respected us for continuing the fight.

Nevertheless there were certain handicaps from which propaganda to the enemy was free. Hasty agreements had been made with the refugee Governments as a result of which they were entitled to carry out their own propaganda to their own peoples. The Norwegian Government had exclusive claims to broadcast, but all the Governments had 'free time'.

Leaflet Dissemination

The Political Warfare media to occupied countries were rather more restricted than those available to enemy countries. In the early years disseminations of printed material were neither large nor regular as for long periods Bomber Command raids on Belgium, Holland and Norway were exceptional and there were very few on Czechoslovakia, Poland, and Denmark. Although leaflets were dropped in France and Belgium by aircraft undergoing training, such disseminations were at first inadequate. Great improvements in disseminations took place in the six months before Overlord.

The Clandestine Press

The clandestine press in every occupied country was largely dependent on PWE and monitoring the BBC or RUs for material. It thus became an

---

1. See p. 293.

* [Marshal Pietro Badoglio (1871–1956) completed the conquest of Abyssinia 1935–6; Commander-in-Chief of Italian forces when Mussolini entered the war June 1940; resigned in December 1940 after Italian defeats at Greek hands in Albania; formed a non-Fascist government on Mussolini's fall in 1943; declared war on Germany; resigned 1944.]

important medium for PWE propaganda. In many cases blocks and microfilm material was sent out by agents to service the clandestine press.

Political Warfare Agents

Owing to the claims of SOE, only a very limited number of agents were available for Political Warfare work in any occupied country except Belgium. Political Warfare was therefore chiefly a matter of broadcasting by means of Black secret broadcasts and the BBC.

The Black broadcasts would have been more effective if there had been more agents able to organise monitoring and to report on the needs of resistance organisation, and those of the clandestine press.

BBC broadcasts were not always under effective PWE control and for periods the BBC disregarded or disputed PWE policy. BBC editors of the smaller regions were more influenced by Mr Newsome's directives than the French and German editors.

The V Campaign

In the early years, the BBC by itself, largely by means of the V campaign, had done much to kindle resistance and bring about a feeling of solidarity against the Germans. But the countries of Europe differed so much in conditions and outlook that widely different methods were essential. The conception of a BBC spokesman directing the regimented resistance movements of Europe by open broadcasts was illusory.

Tasks of Political Warfare

The main tasks of Political Warfare to the occupied countries were, however, the same. They were:

To prevent the economic exploitation of the countries by Germany and in particular to prevent the recruiting and deportation of labour to Germany.

To build up resistance movements and to service the clandestine press.

To educate the population in sabotage.

To organise attacks on the moral[e] of the German occupying forces.

To discredit and terrorise quislings and collaborators.

To maintain control of opinion in moments of crisis and to educate the various sections of the population on the parts they should play during liberation.

These themes were carried out in many ways on Black and in the form of special campaigns on the BBC.

France

In 1940, France offered the greatest field for Political Warfare in Europe, but the results were less brilliant than they might have been owing to differences of opinion between Britain and America in regard to Pétain and the Vichy administration and the undecided attitude of the British and hostility of the American Government to De Gaulle and to the personality of the General himself.

Whereas in our White propaganda we did not attack Pétain personally lest he should at some time break with the Germans and remove himself to North Africa, we consistently attacked him in secret broadcasts.

The situation in France soon after June 1940 was as follows: We were dealing with a former ally which had signed an armistice with the enemy. France itself was split in two, one half occupied by Germans, the other under an apparently independent Government, recognised almost universally as the legitimate Government of France. The French people stunned by the speed of the German victory were either apathetic, or definitely hostile towards Great Britain, and the British people revealed a comparable hostility to the French. The Germans, acting under instructions, were behaving in an exemplary and conciliating manner to the French people. This enabled the Germans and anti-British factions to inflame bad feeling against Britain on the following lines:

The British had left the French in the lurch at Dunkirk.
Britain had refused air support to the French Army during the German advance.
Britain was starving France by her blockade.
Britain had acted with typical treachery against the French Fleet at Oran and Dakar.

The picture presented to those responsible for propaganda to France in the early summer of 1940 was of an apathetic, if not hostile country governed by, or under the influence of, an openly anti-British Government. This unduly pessimistic assessment was, it must be admitted, partly the result of ignorance of the French people and partly to the shock of the French collapse on those directing policy in EH and SO1. It was not accepted by the team of French broadcasters at the BBC who felt confident of addressing an immense audience of French patriots. The comparative optimism of the French broadcasting team influenced the British experts of the Ministry of Information. In so far as the pessimistic assessment was correct, it was largely due to the belief of the French people that the war was over, that France was finally defeated and that Britain would soon be occupied.

[June 1940–June 1941] The first aim of propaganda to the French was to convince them that Germany had not yet won the war. Our next step, after the Battle of Britain, was to show that Germany had lost her first battle.

Subsidiary themes were that French shortages were due to German requisitioning and not to the British blockade, and insistence on the sufferings of the British people during the winter Blitz of 1940–41 which proved a useful emotional bond between us and the occupied French.

[June 1941–Nov. 1941] Halfway through 1941 we were able to drop counter propaganda on the blockade after the Germans had requisitioned French wine. The resulting shortage proved that shortages were due to the Germans and not to us. German propaganda also abandoned the 'blockade theme'. The split between the occupied and unoccupied zones became very marked. Organised resistance, the clandestine press and sabotage were beginning, partly as a result of the volte-face of the Communists following Germany's attack on Russia. The failure of the Germans to take Moscow enabled us to develop our propaganda on the theme 'Germany cannot win the war'.

During the first six months of 1942, the encouragement of resistance became a large element of our campaign. This was followed on Black, and on the BBC by the theme of passive resistance, and by General de Gaulle's detailed instructions to his followers.

[Nov. 1942–June 1944] The occupation of North Africa, without serious bloodshed, gave promising appearances of the opening of a second front in the West, and of the re-entry of a French Army into the war. But the recognition of Darlan was a disquieting setback and difficult for Frenchmen to understand and the disagreements which followed Darlan's death left us in a weak position as we could not take sides openly against the policy of our American ally. Resistance in France had definitely sided with De Gaulle as opposed to General Giraud. Our equivocal attitude laid us open to considerable suspicion. It was not till after the setting up of the French Committee of National Liberation that we could speak again with assurance to the French resistance movement in terms of the union of all Frenchmen against the German invader.

Three themes from this period dominated our propaganda to France:

Germany has lost the war.
France is back in the war again.
The Allies are resolved to restore France to her full sovereignty.

The months preceding the landing in Normandy were devoted on the one hand to an internal struggle to bring home a realisation of the unity of France and the military value of the resistance movement to our political and military leaders, and to secure equipment and recognition for the FFI and on the other to servicing all elements of the resistance movement so as to enable it to play the fullest part in the liberation of France. An important side of our work was in bringing about a fuller comprehension of French resistance and of the French people by our American allies. The Brondesbury Training School proved an essential means for opening the eyes of American members of PWD.

The Low Countries

Political Warfare to the Low Countries had the following five basic aims:

1. To maintain the morale of the Belgian and Dutch patriots at a steady level and to demoralise the German garrison and administrative personnel.
2. To deny the use of Belgian and Dutch manpower to the German war machine.
3. To disorganise the enemy's transport system in Belgium and Holland.
4. To force the enemy either greatly to increase the personnel in his administrative services or to lose control of the administrative machinery of the two countries.
5. To neutralise the services of Belgian and Dutch Quislings to Germany.

A sixth aim was added in the autumn of 1943:

6. To train the Belgian and Dutch people to render maximum assistance to the armies of liberation, after D-Day.

Morale was extremely low in both countries after Dunkirk, but it recovered more quickly in Holland than in Belgium. This was because the Belgians were more shaken by the collapse of France and the defeat of the French armies than the Dutch, who, on their part, had greater understanding of British sea power. Moreover the Queen of Holland had immediately taken up her residence in London, whereas the King of the Belgians had remained a prisoner and M. Pierlot did not reach London till October.

The recovery of morale in both countries was due to the realisation that Britain was continuing the struggle and to the hatred of the Germans, of German exploitation and of the German encouragement of the Quisling parties. This hatred increased steadily as the population got to know the Germans better.

The BBC services made these themes the basis of its output. In January 1941 the Belgian service of the BBC launched the V campaign which had two far-reaching results. It created a feeling of unity between all the occupied countries which made them eager to learn the technique of resistance from each other, and it brought home to the Germans that the occupied peoples were not ready to accept their rule and swallow the New Order. The V campaign therefore kindled the spirit of resistance throughout occupied Europe and shook the confidence of the enemy in his ultimate success. (See pp. 99–104.)

Demoralisation of the Enemy. Holland

The Dutch and Belgian attitudes to occupying troops were different. The Dutch boycotted the invaders and produced an effect of freezing and hostile silence. No suggestions were therefore made to the Dutch for demoralisation of German troops by association with them and defeatist talk. After the failure of the general strike in Holland in 1943, PWE began to urge them to take a more active role.

Belgium

The Belgian sense of humour found full scope in associating with the Germans and in rubbing home the parallel with the occupation of Belgium which ended with German defeat in 1918. Defeatist literature in German printed in Belgium was widely circulated and reached German troops in a variety of ways. (See p. 222 on the work of the agents Mandrill and Porcupine.)

Manpower

One of the chief German aims was to exploit Dutch and Belgian manpower for the benefit of the German war machine. The struggle to deny it to them followed the following course.

[Spring 1941–spring 1942] This was the period of voluntary recruitment of Dutch and Belgian labour for Germany, which was supported by reducing rations to a bare subsistence level and offering much better wages and conditions of living in Germany. Our Political Warfare adopted every available means of discouraging volunteering for Germany but with limited success. About 300,000 Belgians and 200,000 Dutchmen left for Germany.

[Spring 1942–autumn 1942] Belgian and Dutch manpower was mobilised for war work in Belgium and sterner measures were employed to assist recruiting for Germany. Our counter-measures were more successful. The attempt to persuade Dutch farmers and technicians to colonise territory in the east of Europe by the formation of the Netherlands East Company proved a complete failure, partly because of a warning from London that this was the prelude to the complete transfer of the Dutch population from Holland. Recruiting dropped in Belgium and less than 50,000 volunteered.

[Autumn 1942–liberation] German impatience with recruiting led them to adopt a policy of round-ups and forcible deportation. Resistance flared up and was particularly fierce in Belgium. All media of Political Warfare were used by us to encourage this resistance. Thanks to the resistance of the patriots, the deportation dropped to under 100,000 in 1943 and the Germans realised they had not the manpower to keep the country under control.

Rather than obey deportation orders, Belgian students and workmen went underground and formed bands in the Ardennes which raided food centres and liquidated local Quislings. Thus a 'Maquis' was formed.

Deportations in Holland. Trojan Horse Campaign

Voluntary recruiting in Holland was never so effective as in Belgium as food conditions were always better. Those Dutchmen who did go to Germany proved the most difficult, surly and non-cooperative of all foreign workers. Yet after the Germans began deportations from Holland, active resistance never developed on a widespread scale. We therefore started a Trojan Horse campaign for Holland, urging those Dutch workers who were deported to undermine the enemy's fortress from within. This campaign met with success, and of 450,000 workers who went to Germany, 150,000 had been returned, or allowed to return, by 1944.

In May 1943, the Germans ordered the re-internment of all ranks of the Dutch armed forces. The Dutch replied with a general strike. The Germans suppressed it ruthlessly. Our propaganda had to concentrate on preventing a general armed rising and directing the resistance to hide men who would otherwise have been interned or deported to Germany.

The Black Market and Manpower

Until the autumn of 1942, we did not attack the black market because it prevented the Germans from controlling the Belgian and Dutch food supply and provided a means by which those who had 'gone underground' to avoid going to Germany could obtain food. When we learned, however, that the Germans were buying all they could on the black market at enhanced prices so that it had become almost impossible for patriots to obtain supplies, we changed our policy and started a campaign to force farmers to sell at reasonable prices. This had some effect and the Dutch rural population played a prominent part during the general strike in the spring of 1943. Numbers of farmers continued to make large profits by supplying the black market buying on German account.

Oil Seeds

The Germans were encouraging the growing of rape and colza. A campaign against the cultivation of oil-bearing seeds was started and those farmers who persisted in cultivating these crops had their crops and sometimes their farms set on fire.[1] As a result rape and colza cultivation was abandoned in many areas, and where grown, the farmers would propitiate patriots by selling their other produce cheap.

Transport

It took a long time for British Political Warfare to convince the peoples of the Low Countries of the primary importance of transport to the German

1. See p. 223, activities of the agent Othello.

war machine. From the spring of 1942, a steady stream of indoctrination was carried on by means of leaflets and radio.[1] The results were more successful in Belgium than in Holland, which was partly because far more vital enemy communications passed through Belgium than through Holland. A private report stated in 1943 that 800 sabotage attacks on enemy transport had taken place in one month. Some complaints were received of RAF attacks on Dutch trains and barges.

Administration

In Holland the Germans introduced their own civil administration large enough to supervise the work of the Dutch administration. All legislation was initiated by Seyss-Inquart*, the Reichs Kommissar.

In Belgium, the Germans introduced a small military administration and left much more to the Belgian authorities, headed by the Secretaries-General, who had been left in charge of the respective Ministries by the former Ministers.

In Holland, our policy was by provoking small acts of sabotage in the administration, to prevent the withdrawal of German administrative personnel for use elsewhere.

In Belgium, our task was to undermine the authority of the Secretaries-General.

PWE therefore did everything possible to get the Belgian and Dutch Governments in England to issue orders to their Civil Services to shield the populations against German oppression. The Dutch Prime Minister made a speech on these lines in January 1943 but the Belgian Prime Minister did not follow suit until August 1943. In both cases administrative resistance increased.

In Belgium, the judges were encouraged to deny the right of the Secretaries-General to initiate legislation. As a result the Germans found themselves in a violent dispute with the judges and were eventually forced to take repressive measures against them, which undermined the legal basis of the regime in Belgium.

Violent attacks and threats of punishment after the war were made on official services which were directly assisting the enemy's war effort; e.g. the labour offices, recruiting workers for Germany. This campaign, which was supported by the work of our agents, was most successful. It is no exaggeration to say that the whole Sauckel scheme of mobilising Belgian and Dutch manpower was frustrated by the lower ranks of the Dutch and Belgian Civil Service.

---

1. See Transport campaign, pp. 108–11.

* [Artur von Seyss-Inquart (1892–1946) was born in the Sudetenland; practised in Vienna as a lawyer; spied on Austrian Chancellor Schuschnigg for Hitler; ruthless Reichs Kommissar for the Netherlands 1940; hanged at Nuremberg.]

Traitors

The problem was to offer an inducement to Quislings to cease working for Germany without giving the patriots the impression that traitors could escape punishment at the last moment. We therefore urged the Belgian and Dutch Governments to revise their penal codes for treason. The Belgian Government did so but the Dutch did not. Following the revision of the Belgian code a number of collaborators abandoned their posts and sought refuge in obscurity. We exploited the rivalry between different groups of Quislings, e.g. Walloon and Flemish groups in Belgium and old-fashioned Dutch Nazis and SS groups in Holland. Our principal media for this were various forms of Black – including secret broadcasts. The most fruitful theme proved to be to create a sense of grievance against Germany in the minds of Quislings. This was developed with great intensity in the spring of 1943 and was followed by large-scale desertions from both Dutch and Belgian Quisling parties.

Preparations for D-Day

For preparations for D-Day see p. 342 on Joint PWE/SOE Plan.

In White propaganda special emphasis was laid on the necessity for the mass of the population to stay put and keep off the roads, on the need to construct shelters against air bombing and artillery fire, on the value of noting German defences – particularly the laying of road mines and booby traps, on methods of imparting such military information, and on the need to shelter [key] personnel who would be going into hiding to avoid deportation to Germany.

Denmark

From 9th April, 1940, until 29th August, 1943, the Germans in Denmark took refuge behind the fact that the country continued to be governed by Danes in accordance with the Danish constitution. It was true that the Coalition Government of Stauning and Buhl was replaced by that led by Scavenius, who reverted to the policy of appeasement of Germany he had so successfully followed in the war of 1914–18, and that various prominent political personages who held views hostile to the Germans were thrust into the background; but there was all the outward appearance of the continuance of Danish sovereignty. The Danes were not deceived and at the general election of March 1943 they exposed the pitiful weakness of the Danish Nazis and demonstrated their faith in their own institutions. The rising tide of sabotage, strikes, and popular opinion against the Germans reached such a height during 1943 that the latter were driven to presenting an ultimatum for summary powers against saboteurs which the Danish Government rejected on 28th August, 1943. Thereafter the King was virtually a prisoner and neither the Government nor Parliament met. The day-to-day affairs of the country were conducted by the Civil Service and the Germans proved unable to break this deadlock. Meanwhile sabotage continued on an increasing scale, until the final collapse of Germany and the arrival of the first Allied forces.

Political Warfare Objectives

Our objectives in political warfare were as follows:

To encourage the Danish people to maintain the attitude which found expression in their revolt against German demands on 29th August, 1943.
To support the active sabotage front without estranging Danes who were doing equally effective work along other lines.
To persuade the Danes that even nations as small as Denmark could render an important contribution to Allied victory.
To make our audience conscious of the unity of Danish resistance with that of other occupied countries.
To stimulate Danes to demoralise the Wehrmacht and other Germans in their midst.
To place obstacles in the way of exploitation of Denmark for the German war effort.
To prepare the minds of the Danish people for the tasks involved in liberation.
To project the inevitability of an Allied victory.
To destroy the illusions of all those who sought refuge in appeasement or neutrality.

Political Warfare Methods

The lack of German control over the wireless in Denmark and the omission to confiscate wireless sets enabled us to maintain close contract with the Danish people through the means of the BBC which was our main Political Warfare medium. German control of the Danish press led to the appearance of clandestine newspapers, which were fed with news and comment from the British press, leaflets, and the news magazine *Vi Vil Vinde* (*We Will Win*). The stupid brutalities of the Danish Nazis' Schalburg Korps and the manifest discipline of the Danish resistance movement, organised through a Council of Freedom, which had the secret sympathy of the organised political parties, and the absence of an exiled Government in London, simplified PWE's task. All we had to do was to provide an accurate news service and maintain the spirit of the people with BBC broadcasts and service the resistance movement with Black. The principal failure of PWE was to obtain regular disseminations of leaflets over Denmark. This was due to a large extent to the strength of German Fighter and anti-aircraft defences which made the RAF unwilling to risk aircraft over Denmark. There were no adequate disseminations until shortly before D-Day.

Norway

The surprise descent of the Germans on Norway on 9th April, 1940, achieved with the connivance of Quisling and his party, Nasjonal Samling, resulted in the defeat of the Norwegian armed forces and the British forces sent to assist them, and the flight to this country of the King and his Government on 7th June, 1940. Norway was at once subjected to intense attempts at Nazification carried out by Quisling and his adherents under the watchful eye of the German Commissioner Terboven and the protection of the Wehrmacht. As a consequence there evolved a Home Front resistance, which in the initial phase took the form of sabotage, strikes and direct action against the Germans, but which after savage retaliatory measures of the Nazis was directed into passive and intellectual resistance.

Political Warfare Objectives

British Political Warfare objectives were to support the Home Front and the exiled Norwegian Government in all phases of their struggle against the Nazis and the Quislings. Initially, our purpose was to stimulate direct action in all its forms as the reaction of the Norwegian people to their betrayal. As soon as it became clear that such direct action inevitably resulted in arbitrary executions and similar reprisals calculated to endanger Norwegian morale and capacity to resist, our objectives were to support the Home Front in its revised policy of passive and intellectual resistance, non-cooperation, coupled with controlled direct action, and to sustain the morale of the Norwegian people. From 1943 onwards, our main object was to prepare the people of Norway for the coming of the Allied forces.

Political Warfare Methods

The Norwegian press and radio were subjected to control of the Quisling party at an early stage, political meetings were banned and wireless sets were ordered to be surrendered in the autumn of 1941. Political Warfare methods were largely dictated by the necessity to relieve this intellectual blackout, and took the form of the dissemination of clandestine newspapers, serviced with news by the BBC and the Norwegian RU, aircraft-borne leaflets, and the miniature news magazine *Det Frie Norge*, printed in London and smuggled into Norway in all kinds of disguise. Through all these different channels the Norwegian people were provided with accurate news of the course of events in their own country and in the larger world outside as well as of the progress of ideas in Britain. The true stories of Quisling's behaviour were much more damaging to the collaborationists than any which could have been invented, so that the dissemination of rumours and similar methods of subversive propaganda were unnecessary except against the Wehrmacht.

Finland

Finland received considerable material and moral support from Britain and the United States during her war with Russia in 1939–40. After signing the peace treaty with Russia in March 1940, Finland gravitated to the German camp and after admitting German troops in September 1940, joined with Germany in the attack on Russia in June 1941, without concluding any military or other pacts with Germany. Great Britain declared war on Finland on 7.12.41. The United States and Finland remained at peace throughout the war.

Political Warfare Aims

The aims of British Political Warfare were to convince the Finns that they had made a wrong choice, to persuade them that they had been ostracised by the northern democracies, to expose German brutality in Norway, Denmark and other occupied territories, to warn them of the consequences of German defeat, to dispel the illusion that Britain and the United States would mediate on their behalf, to convince them that the longer they remained in the war, the worse terms they would get after it, and to expose the activities of Finnish Fascists.

Methods

Owing to the distance involved it was not possible to drop leaflets in Finland and PWE relied upon the Finnish service of the BBC as a propaganda medium. In the time available for broadcasts to Finland, we concentrated upon giving news which had been withheld by the Finnish censorship. We also vigorously attacked various personalities, such as Tanner, the anti-Russian Finance Minister, and Antoni, the Chief of Police, who was eventually removed in January 1944.

On the announcement of Russia's moderate armistice terms in February 1944, we declared that Finland must choose between this settlement and suicide.

The Balkans

The Balkans and Hungary formed one Region in PWE. This was, at all events in the early years, an advantage in that the Regional Director could plan complementary propaganda campaigns notably those designed to exacerbate Roumanian and Hungarian jealousies and suspicions which served to diminish the usefulness of each country to Germany.

PWE policy to the Balkans as a whole was to unite the Balkan peoples against our enemy and in doing so to lay the foundations for closer co-operation between them after the war.[1] Such an attempt has been proved like

1. Plan of Political Warfare for the Balkans, PW(M)(42)3.

most PWE Political Warfare to Eastern Europe to be unrealistic by events. PWE, however, could not foresee decisions by higher authority not to proceed with plans for military intervention in the Middle East under a British commander. Had Turkey entered the war on the side of the Allies, an entirely different situation would have arisen; it was for such contingencies and plans that PWE had to prepare. The task of PWE was incomparably harder than that of German propagandists who sought to foment hatred. In general, the task of promoting hatred was easy and PWE was most successful when increasing the hatred between Roumanians and Hungarians and ineffective when preaching unity.

The other main object of our Political Warfare was to increase resistance to the German and Italian troops of occupation everywhere.

Jugoslavia

Our Political Warfare policy to Jugoslavia was rendered extremely difficult owing to our desire to promote unity in an area in which a German conquest had been followed by the release of long-standing hatreds between the Croats, Serbs and Slovenes and between differing ideologies.

It was moreover greatly influenced by our obligations to the young King of Jugoslavia who had rallied to our side and had carried out the coup d'état in Jugoslavia, and who was in Britain with his government.

Thus the policy of Britain was, for a great part of the war, identified with the restoration of King Peter II* and the voice of Britain was ineffectually devoted to urging a unity between irreconcilable elements.

The more immediate British aims were to make the occupation of Jugoslavia a drain on enemy resources, to demoralise the occupying troops and maintain the maximum threat to German communications along the Morava and Vardar valleys.

PWE attacked Pavelic, the leader of the Croat Ustashis, so as to avoid indicting the Croats as a whole for atrocities practised on the Serbs, and attacked Nedic, the Serbian Quisling, for collaboration. But PWE refrained from attacking Mihailovitch for political reasons even after it became known that he had collaborated with the Germans against the Partisans.

The astonishing rise of the Partisan movement headed by Tito, which amounted to a popular revolution, involved a change of policy as it became clear that [the] Partisan movement was inflicting severe casualties on the Germans.

A feature of our propaganda to Croatia was to spread rumours in Italy, via the Croat population of Istria, and to make the Italian military authorities regard Croat troops as unreliable. We were successful in these efforts.

---

* [King Peter II, King of Yugoslavia (1923–70), was a grandson of Peter I who succeeded his father Alexander I, who was assassinated in 1934. He assumed sovereignty from his uncle, the Regent Prince Paul, in 1941 but lost his throne in 1945 when Yugoslavia became a republic.]

After the establishment of the PWE Mission Middle East our Political Warfare to Jugoslavia was carried out principally from Cairo and Bari.

Greece

The crucial problem in our early propaganda to Greece was how to treat the evacuation of our forces. German propaganda was to the effect that the German Army was irresistible; that it was insane to trust the British who were cowards who had run away after forcing the Greeks to fight for them and had seized the occasion to steal their ships. This purely materialistic argument was countered with[1] the arguments that the Germany Army had been irresistible because it had fifteen tank divisions to our one. With American help we should one day have 150. We accepted the reproach of being cowards; we were as much cowards as the French, the Poles, the Norwegians, etc. We did not answer accusations of treachery or counter them except by broadcasts given by the King of Jugoslavia and Greek statesmen.

The King of Greece and the Greek Government were at first in London and later in Cairo, but were however regarded with some suspicion in Greece. British policy was to give full support to the King and his Government and to do everything to increase Greek resistance against the Italian and German forces of occupation.

The latter task was chiefly an SOE responsibility. Short-term military requirements were at variance with the long-term Foreign Office requirements and the latter were subordinated to the former. Thus EAM received arms and support because of the geographical position of its guerrillas astride an important railway.

British overt Political Warfare to Greece was to a great extent that of providing a news service and avoiding dangerous subjects. Owing to widespread famine, the subject of food was a difficult one until we raised the blockade in respect of foodstuffs.

The value of broadcasting was greatly limited by the lack of wireless sets outside the principal towns and the lack of power within them. Black propaganda was carried out by SOE ME alone. There was no Greek RU operated by PWE.

Bulgaria

The political object of our propaganda was to increase the suspicion and hatred of the Bulgarian peasants and agrarian intellectuals for the Germanophile upper class and the King. A second political object was to reconcile the Bulgarian people and troops with the Jugoslavs and Greeks. PWE had considerable success in the first task, but was quite ineffective in promoting good relations between the Bulgarians and Greeks.

---

1. Propaganda Plan to cover the Evacuation of Greece, 18.4.41.

The main strategic object was to create such resistance in the Bulgarian Army and population as to make a German advance upon Turkey difficult and the use of Bulgarian troops for an attack upon Turkey impossible.

Leaders of the agrarian party were brought out from Bulgaria and were given facilities for both Black and White propaganda to Bulgaria. A feature of our White propaganda was the campaign to peasants against growing industrial crops for Germany.

Roumania

The chief objects of Political Warfare were to create resistance and non-cooperation with the Germans and Hungarians, to reduce the German oil supplies from Roumania.

PWE sought to increase disgust with the war and unwillingness to allow Roumanian troops against Russia. By keeping alive the Transylvanian issue PWE sought to complicate German difficulties with her two satellites and to divert Roumanian attention from the acquisition of Bessarabia at the expense of Russia.

The value of our Political Warfare rapidly decreased as it became evident that Roumania would become a Russian-occupied zone. Nevertheless quite unrealistic plans for Political Warfare to Roumania and Bulgaria continued to be made to a late date leaving Russian influence out of account.

Hungary

The aims of our Political Warfare to Hungary were to reduce Hungarian military and economic help to Germany and to impede German communications through Hungary and to compel the Germans to occupy Hungary as a safeguard against sabotage.

PWE was greatly assisted by Hungarian dislike of the Germans and by prevailing discontent. The chief difficulty was Hungarian fear of Soviet Russia.

Our principal themes were to convince Hungarians that Germany would be defeated and to induce such nervousness about the future that they were unwilling to allow Hungarian troops to be used outside their frontiers.

Our chief difficulties were to disprove German propaganda that we had sold Eastern Europe to Soviet Russia and to make an effective appeal to the landless and discontented classes which would not alienate the Catholics, Liberals and more progressive aristocrats.

In covert propaganda our aim was to build up an opposition party which would become an instrument against the Germans. In the later stages of the war, considerable operational propaganda was carried out to Hungary from PWB AFHQ. Thus the effect of time bombs was supplemented by leaflet warnings which went down with the bombs.

Poland

British propaganda in Polish had to be designed not only for Poland but for the two and a half million Poles in France and the Polish troops in Britain, the Middle East and Italy. Whereas the Polish miners round Lille were left-wing, the Polish Army was right-wing. This divergence had to be taken into account in our broadcasts.

Mr Moray McLaren was appointed Regional Director for Poland and Czechoslovakia early in 1942 and held the former position for just over three years, resigning after a mental breakdown in April 1945. A separate Regional Director for Czechoslovakia was appointed in September 1943.

Our listeners in Poland consisted of specialised groups who listened in secret places far away from the cities in order to overcome the enemy jamming, and supplied the secret press and the organised body which disseminated propaganda against the enemy. PWE broadcasts occupied a large share of the secret press. PWE also supplied material for nerve warfare on German occupying troops.

The Polish Government in London was given free time on the BBC which was devoted to Radio Polskie and represented the views of the Polish Government subject to BBC and FO censorship. PWE organised the RU known as P1 or Swit, which serviced the Underground Movement in Poland which recognised the Polish government. Later the Polish Women's RU was started.

Difficulties on Account of Russia

The signing of the Anglo-Russian Treaty of Alliance in June 1942 led to Polish suspicions, which proved to be well-founded, that Britain would agree to Poland sacrificing territory in the East and to Russia having a preponderant influence in Poland.

The Polish Government in London was not willing to agree to the transfer of any territory to the USSR. Britain realised that this was unrealistic and that Poland's claim to territory beyond the Curzon line could not be defended from a strictly impartial standpoint. Nor was Britain willing, at that time, to concede Poland's claim to the German-speaking territories west of the Oder. Thus the advance of the Soviet Armies into Poland made the question of Poland's future frontiers a subject on which we could give no satisfactory assurances in our propaganda to Poland. The widespread belief that the Russian Armies had encouraged the rising of the Polish Underground in Warsaw, and had deliberately refrained from going to its relief, made the situation even worse.

[Feb. 1944] The British Government finally announced that, in its view, Poland should accept the Curzon line as its eastern frontier.

It was clear that if we were compelled to throw the Polish Government in London overboard, and if the Polish troops which had fought so gallantly with our armies against Germany were unable to return home, we should have suffered a political defeat. The intransigence of the Polish Government in London on the one hand, and of the Polish Communists supported by Russia on the other, for a long time made a compromise virtually impossible.

PWE not only found itself in an extremely difficult position with the Poles, but also found that the RU Swit was making Anglo-Russian relations worse.

During the summer of 1944, the situation was such that Swit frequently had to close down either because the situation in Poland was obscure or because it had become too delicate for the Polish staff to broadcast.

The Polish Women's RU was closed at the end of May and [on 25.11.44] Swit was finally closed on the resignation of Mr Micolajczyk and the formation of a Polish Government committed to an avowedly anti-Russian policy.

Some sensation was caused by a broadcast [on 31.1.45] in Polish monitored at the beginning of 1945 on the PWB AFHQ Cairo frequency, in which the British and American Governments were accused of the betrayal of Poland.

No broadcast in Polish had been authorised from PWB AFHQ that night and the staff of the Cairo station denied that one had been transmitted. One result of the inquiry which followed was that broadcasts in Polish from PWB AFHQ were stopped on 31.1.45.

But the mysterious broadcast provides a fitting epitaph to British Political Warfare to Poland:

> Rejected by the Bolsheviks, the Atlantic Charter is cast off. Britain's guarantee to Poland means nothing. All agreements at Allied Conferences become nothing before the advancing Totalitarian Soviet might which aims at world conquest.

Czechoslovakia

In 1938, Czechoslovakia was ready and determined to oppose the Nazis with arms and the agreement arrived at by the Western Powers at Munich and subsequent occupation by the Germans was regarded as an act of treachery and betrayal by the people of the Protectorate. The so-called 'Quisling' Government in the Protectorate was formed before there was any hope of assistance from any quarter. Czechoslovakia was the most inaccessible occupied country in Europe and this fact greatly limited British Political Warfare. For various reasons, PWE was willing to let the Czechs carry out their own Political Warfare from London with a minimum of interference.

Nevertheless about 70% of the time reserved for Czechoslovak broadcasts from London was in the hands of the BBC editorial staff, and consisted mostly of news bulletins, with occasional talks; the remaining 30% was completely in the hands of the Broadcasting Department of the Czechoslovak Foreign Office in London, and consisted of commentaries and talks on current events. In both services Czech and Slovak bulletins and talks were given alternately, Czech being given a larger share.

Czechoslovakia was included in the Polish Directorate PWE from the spring of 1942 until September 1943 when Mr Godfrey Lias was appointed Regional Director.

One aspect of the BBC relations with the Czech Foreign Office should be noted. Czech Government officials wrote their scripts and broadcast them in BBC time and were then well paid for doing so. Payments to twelve officials of the Czech Foreign Office averaged over £30 each during March 1942, the highest sum paid to an individual being £59.

The Czech Government was criticised for using the free time allotted to it on the BBC for propaganda *about* rather than *to* Czechoslovakia.

Leaflets were widely disseminated in March 1940 but owing to the infrequency of RAF raids, only seven leaflets were produced between November 1942 and February 1944.

In spite of constant severe punishments including death sentences, broadcasts from London were widely listened to and circulated. Early in the war London sent orders for a demonstration by a few days' boycott of all daily papers in the Protectorate which were completely controlled by Nazi authorities. The order was promptly obeyed as a sign of co-operation with the exiled Government. Nazi wireless and papers both in the Protectorate and in Slovakia often reacted promptly to broadcasts from London. The decision to desert to the Russians on the part of a Slovak Brigade was the result of a call sent out by the BBC.

It should perhaps be recorded that the Czech authorities were able to provide the Director General, an old personal friend of Dr Benes,* with invaluable intelligence material.

Leaflets. Leaflet Writers

PWE leaflets were written in the respective regions and must be regarded as being to a considerable extent the joint work of a number of regional experts. Leaflets can be classified into periodicals, such as *Luftpost* and *Courier de l'Air*, which gave news and information and were profusely illustrated; occasional leaflets devoted, for example, to speeches by the Prime Minister or the President on particularly important occasions such as the Torch landings; miniature magazines which had articles on a wide variety of subjects and attempted to dispel the intellectual and cultural black-out resulting from German occupation; Warnings or *Avis* – which

* [Dr Eduard Beneš (1884–1948) worked with Thomas Masaryk for the creation of Czechoslovakia and was Foreign Minister of the new state 1918–35; President 1935–8; set up government-in-exile 1939; returned in 1945; elected President 1946; resigned after Communist coup 1948.]

were operational leaflets giving instructions to the civil populations in the name of the Inter-Allied High Command, such as Admiralty warnings to the French fishing fleet; and 'Black' leaflets and printed material of various kinds. The latter are dealt with separately.

Printing

PWE printing of leaflets, with the notable exception of the miniature magazines which were a responsibility of the Editorial Unit, and of Black leaflets, etc., which were printed by the Howe Unit, were the responsibility of Mr Harold Keeble, Head of the PWE Production Unit.

Marylands

The work of the Production Unit was laid out, set up, read in proof by language experts, in the well-equipped printing shops at Marylands, near Woburn. It was then usually delivered to contractors who were equipped to machine very large numbers at high speed. The work was at one time done by the Stationery Office, but from 1941 until the autumn of 1943 PWE made all the arrangements and paid for leaflet printing out of secret funds. The cost of leaflets printed for the Americans was also defrayed by PWE.

Layout

Mr Harold Keeble who was a printing expert formerly employed in the *Daily Express*, had a flair for reinforcing sensational news by striking devices in lay-out. He habitually employed all the methods used in such newspapers as the *Daily Express* in the lay-out of all PWE newspapers and leaflets with the exception of those for Holland, as the Dutch Government disliked a Fleet Street lay-out and imposed printing standards of its own which Mr Keeble regarded as dreary and old-fashioned.

The proposal that PWE leaflets should be produced as nearly as possible in the style of printing and lay-out current in the countries in which they were to be dropped so that they would meet with the minimum psychological sales-resistance had been urged on the department in vain.[1]

Rotogravure

Mr Keeble strongly favoured printing by the more expensive rotogravure methods whenever possible, partly because it was possible to reproduce photographs of much better quality, partly because, from the point of view of the printer, it was 'a better job'.

---

1. By the present writer in 1941, and, independently, by Mr Neville Lytton after his return from France shortly afterwards.

An argument which carried weight was that leaflets technically well printed on paper of good quality would impress the inhabitants of Europe with the lavish resources at our command. This was particularly the case in Germany. Mr Keeble's predilection for rotogravure printing was particularly strong in the case of newspapers, in which there were many photographs, but it was to cause difficulties later on owing to the shortage of rotogravure paper.

Thanks largely to Mr Keeble the standard of PWE production of leaflets and publications steadily improved by commercial standards. The value of this in the case of photographs is incontestable.

The Editorial Unit

The Editorial Unit under Mr McMillan was instituted in order to produce PWE miniature magazines and some occasional booklets. The objects of these publications were to relieve the intellectual and cultural black-out, to provide serious information on a wide variety of topics, and to 'project Britain' in occupied countries.

As many such articles were suitable for all, or for more than one, country it was an obvious economy to have articles commissioned centrally.

In addition to making arrangements, in conjunction with the Regions, with regard to the contents of the magazines, Mr McMillan was responsible for their layout and printing. By setting up in large type and photographic reduction, and by printing on thin paper, the magazines were able to contain a large amount of reading matter very clearly printed.

Air Ministry Approval

Before PWE leaflets were printed, they were submitted for approval to the Air Ministry by Captain Ryder, PWE Military Wing, who was in liaison with PR7, Wing Commander (afterwards Group Captain) Rose being the usual link. Air Commodore Groves handled matters which needed reference to Air Vice Marshal Sir Richard Peck. The Air Ministry claim to a veto was supported by arguments that RAF pilots might be punished if they were found to have disseminated material containing incitement to certain acts such as sabotage, murder, etc., etc.

The Air Ministry was also concerned with the accuracy of material relating to the RAF or the Luftwaffe, or with anything which would affect either the prestige of the RAF or the morale of RAF pilots and aircrews.

Delivery to Bomber Stations

All arrangements with regard to numbers of leaflets required, their delivery by a certain time, and the collection and pulping of unused out-of-date leaflets were made by Captain Ryder and Flight Lieutenant Taylor of PWE Military Wing.

The patience and efficiency of Captain Ryder and Flight Lieutenant Taylor should be mentioned in passing, as should the repeated but vain efforts which they made to alter the cumbrous wasteful and inefficient methods of dissemination.

Dissemination by the RAF

Except in special cases, such as the leaflets dropped to inform the French population of the reasons underlying the landings in North Africa, leaflets were disseminated only by aircraft employed on operational missions planned solely on other considerations. Leaflet dropping was therefore entirely incidental to operational requirements.[1]

PWE deliberately did everything to encourage the RAF to disseminate leaflets whenever possible, and its policy proved so successful that the unpopularity of leaflets in the RAF was so far overcome that leafleting came to be accepted as inevitable.

The PWE attitude in regard to this, held by Major General Brooks, was clearly stated by Mr Harold Keeble in the words: 'The greatest care must be taken not to break the automatic rhythm by which the RAF now load leaflets as though they were as essential as petrol. It is essential not to rekindle the old hostility to leaflets.'[2]

In order that bombers should be able to take leaflets on every possible occasion it was essential that there should be large stocks of leaflets at the bomber stations, so that they could be loaded in sufficient quantities for whatever operational mission was decided on.

This policy inevitably influenced the contents of the leaflets themselves as PWE was averse to recalling leaflets and pulping them. Thus the methods of dissemination encouraged 'timeless' leaflets, and discouraged leaflets dealing with topical events, or aimed at particular targets.

An account of the activities of the Naval Intelligence Operational Propaganda Section NID 17Z, written by a member of the section describes how White leaflets were suggested to PWE on the war at sea and photographs of U-boat 'kills' were provided.

> But the flaw in this type of propaganda was the slow and sometimes faulty collaboration between Admiralty, PWE and the Air Ministry with the result that leaflets were sometimes dropped when they were out of date or on to non-naval targets.

Similarly a leaflet directed at Bavarian Catholics was useless if the RAF policy, of which PWE leaflet writers were unaware, was to concentrate on Berlin, Hamburg and the Ruhr.

---

1. See paper put forward to Major General Brooks by PWE Leaflet Committee, 16.7.44, *inter alia*.
2. Minutes of 8th Meeting of the Leaflet Committee, 8.1.44.

The methods of dissemination did result, however, in very large quantities of leaflets being dropped. Indeed, it finally broke down as paper stocks in Britain proved insufficient to keep pace with the scale of British and American bombing. But though the statistics were impressive, the results were unsatisfactory to PWE as well as extraordinarily wasteful, both from the point of PWE of airlift and paper. The majority of leaflets were dropped in the neighbourhood of RAF targets, but owing to drift, and the pilots' natural desire to get rid of the leaflets before serious work began, immense quantities were dropped over desolate country. After the practice of loading parcelled leaflets into the bomb bays had been adopted leaflets were dropped when the pilot decided to test whether his bomb doors opened. Many pilots are said to have made a practice of doing this over the North Sea.

No requests for a scientific study of the rate of drift and rate of fall of leaflets of different sizes from varying heights under varying wind conditions seem to have been made by PWE, or its predecessors, after the first experiments made in 1939 since PWE was anxious not to call the system into question, lest the Air Ministry should give worse facilities. But the outstanding failure was, in the words of the Director General:[1] 'Leaflets can only be disseminated when and where operational missions have been planned which are by no means necessarily when and where they are most likely to be effective.'

The Director General did not make this appeal for the system to be changed until the summer of 1944. Nevertheless the faults of the system had been apparent for years to all regional experts in PWE, and both Major Ryder and Squadron Leader Taylor had repeatedly put up proposals for reform.

The Leaflet Bomb

The first information with regard to a leaflet bomb was supplied to Wing Commander Blackford by Colonel Brooks[2] with regard to a bomb by Commandant Naud, of the French Air Force. The bomb cases were of cardboard with wooden tops. Commandant Naud offered to supply drawings to suit British requirements.

No answer to this communication has been found either in PWE or Air Ministry records and no experiments were carried out either with the type of bomb described by Commandant Naud or with an adaptation of the principle. The Air Ministry were not interested and no one in EH or PWE realised the advantages which would result from its use. The leaflet bomb, like the leaflet shell,[3] had to be invented a second time.

1. Sir Robert Bruce Lockhart to Air Chief Marshal Sir Arthur Tedder, Deputy Supreme Commander, 19.7.44.
2. Colonel Brooks to Wing Commander Blackford, 3.12.39.
3. Major General Brooks informed the present writer that the leaflet shell had been invented in 1939. It was reinvented by Capt. Con O'Neill during the Tunisian campaign.

Major Mitchel Innes, who was one of the few PWE officers to take part in a leaflet raid, reported[1] on the deficiencies of the old method – slowness of loading and of disposing of leaflets package by package through the flare shoots when over the target – and also announced that a precision leaflet bomb was being experimented with at Kairouan. It had been invented by Squadron Leader Morrison of the RAF. It could be loaded, attached and released in exactly the same way as an ordinary bomb and was detonated by a time fuse so as to open at any desired height.

Specifications of the Morrison bomb were sent to the Air Ministry but no one appears to have realised that it would solve the problems of dissemination. Indeed both in PWE Military Wing and in the Air Ministry arguments[2] were brought forward against the bomb. For example, it was said that there was a high wastage in a city compared with open country as so many leaflets fell on roofs, and that city dwellers were unwilling to pick up leaflets for fear of being seen doing so, but dwellers in lonely places could do so without fear.

A reason why the leaflet bomb did not interest RAF experts may possibly have been that it was a precision weapon, and for that reason of less value for bombing at night at a period when British bombers were unable to pin-point their targets accurately. But this no longer applied when the bomb was reinvented in 1943.

Fortunately the Morrison bomb attracted great interest among the mechanically-minded Americans, and in particular was taken up with enthusiasm by Mr Kaufman of OWI. As a result the Americans were able to evolve an improved version, the Munroe bomb, which became the standard means of leaflet dissemination by the special squadron of leafleting Fortresses allocated for leaflet dissemination. The dissemination of the newspaper for the German troops, *Nachrichten für die Truppe*, was entirely by Munroe bomb. But it was not until the end of September 1944[3] that the Air Ministry admitted the superiority of the leaflet bomb and arranged for a supply of Munroe bombs from America.

Black Printing

The early attempt[s] at Black printing in the EH period, by the 'D' unit have been mentioned. The work done then and in the SO1 period which followed consisted of forged typewritten circulars, etc., etc., and of matter purporting to be produced by oppositional groups in Germany. There was, however, little chance of any of this material deceiving the enemy for long, as the work was technically not well enough done.

---

1. Report of Col Thornhill's Mission on Political Warfare in General Eisenhower's Command.
2. Arguments used in discussions with the writer by Major General Brooks and Air Commodore Groves.
3. Air Marshal Sir Norman Bottomley to Major General Brooks, 28.9.44

The production of forged printed and other documents of a quality which would defy expert examination only became possible after November 1941 when Mr Ellic Howe joined PWE.

Mr Howe, a professional typographical expert and student of the history of printing, first wrote a paper on Black printing in the summer of 1940, when he was a sergeant at HQ Anti-Aircraft Command, but his proposal was turned down. A year later he wrote another paper, 'The documentary weapon'. This was forwarded to MI5 by the I branch at HQ AA Command and sent to PWE, which took immediate action to interview the writer and get him transferred to the Department.

On Howe's joining the Department the only activity was a small postal operations unit under Mr Leonard Ingrams. Howe assisted by providing forged stamps and suitable envelopes, overprinted with French commercial headings.

Howe continued to work under Leonard Ingrams until June 1942. There was a weekly meeting at CHQ but there was no systematic method of planning operations, producing material and supplying SOE. Nor were there adequate facilities. Nevertheless, there were always excellent relations with SOE.

With the approval of Colonel Chambers, Howe proceeded to build up an independent unit, the most important member of which was Miss Elizabeth Friedlander, a typographical artist and a consummate forger. She joined in August 1942. Howe's method was to consult the best technical brains in the London printing trade for each kind of job, i.e. paper-makers, typefounders, compositors, etc. An immense quantity of equipment had to be specially made. All German printing is done with type on the Didot Continental body. It was necessary therefore to use only types on this body, and all composing equipment had therefore to be made to fit it. A simple example of the technical accuracy needed is the perforations of forged stamps.

All continental perforating machines are made with the pitch measured by millimetres, whereas British and American machines are measured by thirty seconds of an inch. Perforating machines had therefore to be made specially.

Mr Howe was able to make use of the Launier and Boulton laboratory for all investigations into the analysis and combinations of different ink. Howe owed much to the Monotype Corporation from which he borrowed a vast range of printing matrices originally designed for French and German markets.

Projects at first filtered through the 'Black' Committee, but the Committee dissolved by the autumn of 1942 and was replaced by a triangular relationship of Delmer, Howe and Wintle (SOE). The procedure established by Wintle and Howe for ordering and delivering material functioned perfectly, thanks to which relations between the Howe Unit and SOE were uniformly good throughout three years of collaboration.

After Delmer had taken over the provision of Black texts, the Howe Unit began to operate on a large scale. Delmer sent project after project for execution and SOE would independently re-order reprints of items successfully disseminated. Although Howe worked for both the French and Low Countries Regions, the main output came from Delmer. By 1943, Howe had become a production organiser rather than a designer. Miss Friedlander was responsible for detailed work. Howe was busy in enlisting experts throughout the London printing and paper-making trade. Most of the composition work was done at the Fanfare Press. At peak periods, as many as seventeen firms, with night-shifts at two of them, might be working for the Unit. Thus with a total establishment of three or four, the Unit handled close on 2,000 separate orders during its existence, orders ranging from batches of five million German ration cards to a single forged letter.

About 10% of the different jobs were 'straight' forgeries, i.e. of stamps, ration-cards, etc., the remainder being material purporting to have been printed clandestinely.

The output by countries was roughly 75% Germany, 10% France, 10% Belgium, and 5% rest of Europe.

The most important piece of work was the malingering booklet which was produced in many different editions bound up in fifteen or more different forms such as books on physical culture, etc. The booklet was produced in batches of 16,000 at a time for dissemination by balloon. The text was continually improved upon. Altogether upwards of a million of the booklet were produced.

The most difficult job in connection with it was its production on tissue paper inside a packet of cigarette papers. Other jobs which require mention were the production of the Himmler and Franck stamps which served as supporting evidence of an earlier 'sib'.

A number of jobs were done for the Free French by the Howe Unit between 1942 and the end of the war. The printing jobs were authorised by Dr Beck. But in addition, Mr Howe used to supply M. Briac with any type, paper and ink which the Free French might require without reference to anyone. Co-operation of this sort at the technical level, did much to overcome the troublesome relations at higher levels.

Mr Howe, with Colonel Chambers' authority, also did a number of jobs for OSS. Their ideas were, in Mr Howe's opinion, never up to Delmer's standards, but they were highly satisfied with the result.

Mr Howe also did five Black leaflets for OWI in the summer of 1942. In addition, the Howe Unit reprinted the OSS yellow book on the French Armistice in a more convincing format. One project of Mr Rayner's, which aroused question in various quarters, were forgeries of the Communist newsheet *The Week* produced before the war in this country. Only twenty copies of each issue were produced and not more than six numbers altogether. They were circulated in Eire as a vehicle for 'sib' dissemination, but the project was regarded as dangerous and was brought to an end.

The Unit's contribution owed much to the fact that Mr Delmer used it to the very limit of its capabilities and he was not dissatisfied with the result.

Methods Adopted for Operating RUs

The teams of scriptwriters and speakers for PWE RUs were as a rule housed separately and kept apart from each other. Exceptions were made in some cases, e.g. the young Gaulliste soldiers (F4) lived in the same house as the French priest (F5) who was also a member of the Fighting French, and who ministered to their spiritual needs.

The impression which it was sought to convey to the teams was that each RU was unique and alone in enjoying the facilities offered by the British Government to state its case.

Secondly it was realised that segregation would prevent conscious or unconscious copying of technique and ideas.

The development of a uniform method would have defeated the whole purpose of the RUs.

Recording was carried out in three studios at a common centre – Simpson's. The times at which the separate RU teams visited the studios had therefore to be very carefully regulated. In coming and going no two teams were ever allowed to meet or see each other, and as much as possible antagonistic teams were not allowed in the building at the same time. On one occasion F2, after recording, had to return to re-make their record owing to news which had just broken. While waiting they overheard, through the fireplace of a supposedly sound-proof wall, a team of F5 recording and immediately resigned.

Each team was accompanied to Simpson's by a censor, who in most cases lived with the team, collected its intelligence and edited scripts. He had to see that the recordings tallied with the agreed scripts and sign the final lay-out sheet as censor. This duty was sometimes delegated to secretaries or assistants.

Reasons for Recorded Transmission

Censorship of recorded transmissions could be done by play-backs of the records, usually immediately after they were made.

Switch censoring, whereby the censor controls a switch between the speaker and the transmitter, would have destroyed the illusion of a Freedom Station and is ineffective in preventing two or three objectionable words from getting out before the censor can take action.

Recording also allowed for trial and error and for a speaker to improve a broadcast which he had 'fluffed'.

There were not the studio facilities available for all broadcasts to be made live. Recordings allowed for 'repeats' as often as wished, for extra records to be made in advance to cover leave, and for the sessions at Simpson's to be spread out.

Records Used

The records which, like the recording and transmitting equipment, were American were 16" glass based and played at 33⅓ revolutions per minute. They were capable of taking a 15-minutes' programme but the last portion was of poorer quality and was seldom used. 12½ minutes was the normal length for a record.

Disadvantages of Recording

In order to keep up the illusion of genuineness it was essential to prevent the fact that a broadcast was recorded from appearing, as a genuine 'Freedom Station' would not have had recording equipment.

Sometimes owing to carelessness, the tone arm would jump or a groove would repeat. Occasionally, in warm weather, 'ghosting' would occur when, owing to the softness of the base, the speech on one groove would appear faintly on its neighbour's. But on the whole the system worked admirably.

At one period there were twenty-three RUs operating at the same time, their broadcasts being radiated from only four transmitters in most cases with 'repeats' or more than one broadcast a day. This would have been impossible but for records.

Exception to Use of Records

In the summer of 1941, there was a sudden shortage of records, and all RU transmissions had for a time to be made live.

When the news demanded it, an RU team could instead of recording material broadcast 'live'. Permission had to be obtained, from the Director CHQ and from [NAME DELETED ON GROUNDS OF NATIONAL SECURITY] who was responsible for the security of the landlines involved. The Regional Director concerned had in theory to be present but this rule was not usually observed.

The Grey stations Kurzwellensender Atlantik (G9) and Soldatensender Calais/West were all transmitted 'live' except for the musical items.

The experimental 'intruder' programme to Italy (W6) was also transmitted 'live'. These stations broadcast from MB and not from Simpson's.

Changes of Frequency

It was obviously necessary that RU transmissions should be on different frequencies. Moreover the aerial beam had to be altered. A 2½ minute gap was therefore necessary in radiation between each RU transmission. Before this rule was instituted one of the engineers was electrocuted while changing a frequency.

The normal length of the transmission, 15 minutes, was therefore curtailed to 12½ minutes.

Too strict an adherence to the length of 12½ minutes was deprecated as tending to destroy the illusion of a Freedom Station. GS1 and the Roumanian Oil (R2) were content with short broadcasts but there was a tendency to use every available minute.

Transport of Teams and Records

RU teams were taken to Simpson's by car, the cars being driven by drivers chosen for their integrity. These drivers also transported the records to the transmitters. Each programme was accompanied by a lay-out sheet with full instructions as to time of transmission and frequency to be used, which was initiated by the engineer after each transmission.

Car runs were scheduled to reach the transmitters 30 minutes before the time of transmission.

In bad weather, in snow or fog, or if a team were late in finishing the recording, this margin almost vanished, but in five years not a single transmission was missed at the correct time through failure of transport.

Types of Secret Broadcasting

Very varied methods were adopted. The principal were:

Freedom Stations, purporting to be secret stations operating in an enemy-occupied or satellite country.

Co-operational Stations, working in direct contact with Resistance organisations and supplying their needs.

Black Stations, purporting to be of enemy origin with the object of discrediting him and producing action of different kinds.

Nomenclature

The PWE secret stations were known as RUs, i.e. Research Units. Each RU had a name by which it was known to its audience and a letter and number by which it was usually known in the Department. These were originally given by the Signals Officers for their own convenience which explains why the Italian RUs were numbered W1, W2, etc., W standing for Wop.

The houses in which RU teams lived were known by their initials, e.g. LF, FOR, etc.

Germany

The aim of our Black transmissions to Germany was to corrupt the discipline of the enemy. This could be done in various ways. GS1 (see pp. 41–6) denounced corruption in order to show it was safe, profitable and widely prevalent, and appealed indirectly to the 'inner swine hound' in the German.

The German Catholic priest corrupted the discipline of the Catholic soldier by showing that he could not combine allegiance to Hitler with allegiance to his faith.

Fuller accounts of G1, G2 and G3 are given on pages 33, 41–6.

G9 (Kurzwellensender Atlantik) is dealt with in the section under Grey broadcasting on pp. 207–10.

G7 German Priest

The object was to widen the breach between the forty million German Catholics and their Nazi rulers and to stimulate separatist aspirations in South Germany and Austria.

One of the main lines was the antithesis between Christ the King and Hitler the Fuehrer.

The RU was run by a German Catholic priest who spoke five or six days a week with two transmissions on the 49 metre band.

The priest wrote and spoke his own scripts; had a S. German voice and purported to be inside Germany. He kept his views closely in line with the pronouncements of the German Catholic bishops. Some of his scripts were used as leaflets.

The station was clearly heard in Sweden where it was believed to be in Germany. On 26th May, 1943, the priest solemnly condemned a talk given over the Paris radio by Dr Friedrich, the leading German propagandist in Paris, in which the Pope was attacked as responsible for the war. Dr Friedrich repudiated his talk the following Sunday, saying it had not been delivered by him but by one of his French colleagues using his name without authority.

Italy

Fuller accounts of W1 and W6 are given on pages 60 and 61.

Radio Livorno. W3

[Started 25.7.43] The station purported to be run by an Italian naval officer and a naval wireless operator situated somewhere in the Leghorn area who posed as the spokesman of a secret and patriotic association within the Italian Navy.

Some difficulty was experienced with the personnel. The first speaker, an Italian ex-naval officer, refused to continue after the first transmission and had to be replaced; his substitute proved extremely touchy.

The station was under the direct control of Mr Mossbacher of NID 17Z and received its directives and intelligence direct from the Admiralty.

A secret account of the activities of NID 17Z prepared for the DNI defines the work of Radio Livorno as ‘to build up solidarity in the Italian Navy, to convey the impression that the Germans were the real enemy, and to suggest that attempts to scuttle would be made only in accordance with

German wishes'. At the same time White propaganda was encouraged to speak sympathetically of the difficulties under which the Italian Navy laboured and to hint that the British Naval Authorities were not really hostile to it. Throughout the war NID 17Z had, sometimes with difficulty, restrained the BBC Italian region from making capital out of the inefficiency and ineptitude of the Italian Navy.

[1944] Finally a signal was drafted for promulgation by the C. in C. Mediterranean at the appropriate moment, inviting the Italian Navy to surrender and indicating how it might effectively do so. 'The draft of this signal was submitted . . . and finally approved. It achieved remarkable success.'

Radio Livorno transmissions were extremely convincing and the station was the most widely quoted of our Italian RUs. The writer has reason to believe from hearsay information[1] that Radio Livorno was believed by Italian naval officers and that it played a considerable part in preparing the surrender. It has not been possible however to obtain documentary proof of this from the records of the Department or from NID 17Z.

W4 Italia Risorgi

[Started 16.2.43, closed 15.9.43] The RU purported to be the mouthpiece of a group of well-informed anti-Fascists with the entrée into diplomatic circles in neutral countries. The policy advocated was the return to power of the House of Savoy and the placing of Badoglio in power. Contact with Badoglio and the Court was implied. The object was to encourage dissatisfaction with the Fascist regime and action against it.

The transmitter purported to be in the north of Italy. The broadcasts were 80% fact and 20% fiction. Rumours were created by distorting facts and giving diverse significance to actual events, as well as by completely fictitious stories.

The speakers were chosen from anti-Fascist Ps/W who had volunteered to do propaganda work. They were not good speakers, and became depressed owing to the security restrictions on their liberty. The employment of Ps/W was ill-advised. Security restrictions also limited the supply of intelligence and made it impossible to give the impression sought.

Nevertheless the RU took a very definite line particularly after the Fall of Fascism, calling upon the Italian people to rise and strike. By a fortunate coincidence the RU chose the same date (the evacuation of Sicily) to call for the general strike as the Socialist Party in Italy.

W6 Giustizia et Libertà

[Started 11.7.43, closed 26.6.44] The RU not only purported to be the mouthpiece of a group of anti-Fascists belonging to the Giustizia et Libertà

1. From Mr Ritchie Calder.

group, in contact with all active anti-Fascist organisations in Italy but having no connection with the Allies or anti-Fascists outside Italy, but it actually was so. The only deception practised was that it purported to be in Italy when it was actually at Woburn.

The aim was to convince the Italian people to accept no compromise with the King or Badoglio until the surrender and to co-operate with the Allies.

The personnel originally consisted of five prominent members of the Society of whom three were speakers. Two of the speakers later left for Italy. The fact that it was genuinely staffed by members of the movement gave it a special value. Its members had great political and psychological understanding of the position in Italy and association with them greatly helped the housemaster (Captain Skeaping) who was also housemaster for W4 and W3. Captain Skeaping was able to profit from this to make W4 more convincing.

Balkans. Roumania. R2 Porunca Maresalului. (The Marshal's Orde[r])

[Started 21.7.42, closed 26.6.44] The object of the RU was to reduce Roumanian aid to Germany and lower Roumanian morale.

The station was taken over from the old R1 (started in 1940) by 'ghost-voicing' with an overlap of one month and then closing R1.

The audience aimed at was the Roumanian middle and upper class. Whereas R1 was anti-German, making a direct approach, R2 was impossibly pro-German and pro-Antonescu,* feigning an exaggerated loyalty and complete subservience to Germany.

Rumours, stories and operational propaganda were put out by slips, exaggeration, denials, misconstructions and patently weak German or Antonescu propaganda.

A 'campaign' technique was used, i.e. a progressive campaign on inflation was carried out in order to prepare the audience for a final 'operational' rumour, or a series of talks on a promised revision of the Vienna Award in order to produce a drop in morale when it was announced this would not be fulfilled.

There was one speaker who was part-author of the scripts; transmission was twice daily one of which was a repeat.

The technique of jamming R1 with R2, successfully deceived both SOE ME and the Istanbul monitoring units who described it as an activity of the Roumanian radio.

The Russian Freedom Station described the RUs campaign on the Vienna Award as 'propaganda inspired by Antonescu'. There was a protest from Budapest against the anti-Hungarian material put out 'in the name of Antonescu'.

---

* [Ion Antonescu (1882–1946) was Romanian Chief of Staff in 1937; suspended from army after failed coup 1938; Prime Minister 1940; assumed dictatorial powers; deposed King Carol; executed 1946.]

R3 Prahova

[18.10.43–30.4.44] The object of the RU was to reduce supplies of Roumanian oil to Germany by go-slow methods, in order to conserve Roumanian oil-supplies. Sabotage was not instigated as to do so would have destroyed the RU's cover. The RU implied that it had the support of the Roumanian Government and the Roumanian oil companies.

The co-operation of MEW and the Ministry of Fuel and Power in running this RU was essential.

R3 was run on the above lines until January 1944 when a new policy of greater violence was introduced, including suggestions of sabotage not only in regard to oil but also in regard to oil-seeds, transport, cereals, etc.

Bulgaria. X1 Vasil Levsky

[6.11.41–11.1.44] The object of the RU was, until his death, to undermine the influence of the King and of the Bulgarian Government and expose their subservience to Germany.

Two voices were used, male and female, and the station broadcasted every evening. In a series of special transmissions lasting twenty-four hours a day for six days the RU reconstructed the circumstances of King Boris's death at the hands of the Germans.

Every effort was made to conceal the use of records. Four of the names listed in the RU's 'gallery of national traitors' were eliminated in a year.

There is evidence that the station had a large audience in Bulgaria.

X2 Voice of Europe

[2.7.43–15.7.44] Like H3 Blauwvoet and C1 Nova Europa, X2 followed the indirect method of undermining faith in Germany, purporting to be a station of German origin.

It gave a bulletin news and comment, playing in with the opening bars of the Bulgarian and German anthems. The bulletin consisted of extracts from the German High Command Communiqué and six to eight news items, some false, some falsified and some specifically chosen for the audience.

The technique was that of over-emphasis, falsification, tactlessness, juxtaposition of genuine contradictory German items.

The RU was attacked by the Bulgarian RU in the ME and reported as a German station by the Americans from Istanbul.

Hungary. M1 Magyar Nemzet

[6.9.42–7.1.45] The object was to increase opposition to Germany and to diminish the Hungarian aid to Germany. It was addressed to the middle class. The station identified itself with the leading opposition paper *Magyar Nemzet* and purported to be connected with it.

Eight transmissions were given on Sundays only; two of the transmissions were repeats and all were recorded. There was only one writer for all scripts and one speaker. A special feature was a transmission period devoted entirely to rumours. The rumours were co-ordinated with Balkan and German stations by denial, variation, reporting, etc.

Reception was confirmed from Hungary, Istanbul, the Middle East and [the] USA. There were indirect advertisements of the station in the paper *Magyar Nemzet*, and other results were believed to be the sudden dropping of a pro-Nazi speaker from Budapest Radio immediately after an attack made on him in M1 and also the stopping of a broadcast prayer for troops at the front. An inflation campaign was followed by reports of economic hysteria. SOE Middle East reported that the location of the station inside Hungary had been proved by its quotation of morning papers.

F3 La France Catholique

This station began broadcasting on 1st July, 1941, and closed on 14th May, 1942, as the speaker Capitaine Lagrave felt, as a matter of conscience, that he should engage in active service. He accordingly joined the Free French Air Force and underwent training as a pilot. Some months later the Air Ministry agreed to put Capitaine Lagrave at the disposal of PWE for two or three days a week, and the RU reopened on 3rd June, 1943, with Capitaine Lagrave and Capitaine Florent, another French priest, as his assistant, to record when Capitaine Lagrave was not available.

Some weeks after the reopening of F3, Capitaine Lagrave fell ill and as he was unfit for further flying service, he was seconded from the Free French Air Force to PWE. The following January, Capitaine Lagrave underwent an operation but returned to work for the Department in March 1944. F3 was finally closed on 14th May, 1944. The station therefore ran for two periods, each being of rather under a year, with an interval of slightly over a year between them.

Purpose of F3

The purpose of F3 was to encourage and maintain a spirit of resistance among Catholics in France, to enable French priests to preach unhampered by the enemy, and to assist priests in France by providing material for their sermons.

In his opening remarks, the priest stated that he was speaking with the sanction of his bishop. Two days a week were devoted to prayers of a strongly propagandist character; 'for our children who are starving', 'for our prisoners in captivity in Germany', etc., and these prayers were said to be offered in response to a request from the Pope.

Attitude of the Vatican to F3

Although enemy broadcasts on occasion suggested that F3 was broadcast from the Vatican in order to provoke an official denial, the Vatican never denounced F3, though it was fully aware of the station's existence.

On 15th August[1] Mr Osborne* was requested to enquire whether the Vatican could supply us with 'any information about a short-wave station calling itself "La France Catholique" which has been heard occasionally in Great Britain'.

Mr Osborne replied:[2]

> On indications supplied by the Jesuits and checked by myself I find that 'La France Catholique' is the title used for broadcasts in French of a station of unknown origin. . . . The Vatican knows nothing of it, but I am inviting their attention to the above particulars. The Jesuits do not know where the station is but think that it may be in Hungary. . . . It is quite clearly audible in Rome.

The attitude of the Vatican to F3 was undoubtedly influenced by the genuinely Catholic nature of the broadcasts and may not have been unaffected by the fact that the station gave many talks on such subjects as Catholic missionary work and religious instruction which were untinged by propaganda.

In the second series, when two priests were available, there was a daily morning transmission which was purely religious instruction, the intention being that parents who listened to the talks should have facilities for the instruction of their children.

Character of F3 Propaganda

Talks were given at first on such themes as a comparison of the methods of Hitler and of Satan. Priests were exhorted to encourage their parishioners in resistance. Employers working for the Germans were told to keep their factories open for the sake of their workers but to see that their products were of poor quality. Great stress was laid on the Russian war being one of defence by the Russian people and that the Russian church was no longer persecuted.

At first, the speaker avoided direct attacks on Vichy, but after the first months collaborationists were repeatedly attacked.

'Hitler a trouvé parmi nous la poignée de traîtres qui lui étaient nécessaire.'

---

1. FO Telegram No. 1125, 15th August, 1941.
2. FO Telegram No. 2039, 15th September, 1941.

* [(Francis) D'Arcy Godolphin Osborne, 12th Duke of Leeds (1884–1964), was British Minister at Washington 1931–5 and Minister to the Vatican 1936–47. He died unmarried the year after succeeding his cousin to the dukedom.]

Nor did the priest scruple to threaten collaborationists, including collaborating priests, with the fate awaiting them after victory had been won, as they would be tried as traitors.

F4 and F5

Full accounts of these important RUs will be found on pages 264 and 266 as they played an important part in relations with the Gaulliste organisation.

Belgium

The case for an RU broadcasting to Belgium was first put by the Regional Director towards the close of the SO1 period,[1] in these words:

> Subversion, education in passive resistance and in sabotage, preparation for, and appeals to action must be the essential task of our propaganda . . . because only finally by getting *action* can our propaganda help in winning the war. . . . Nothing can inspire hope and confidence more fully . . . than the feeling of being able to take an active part in the defeat of the enemy.

Lack of intelligence from Belgium was not regarded as a serious obstacle as the RU would not go out of its way to persuade its audience that it was in Belgium – the object of the RU was not to deal with current news but to preach and educate its audience in subversion. In the event of the Belgian Government protesting, we should deny knowledge of the RU while applauding its work. The RU should not be associated with any party or minor political issues but have only one purpose: to recruit, instruct and organise Belgian patriots for the task of driving the Germans out of their country.

B1 Vrijschutter (Flemish)

[9.5.42–8.6.44] This was an operational RU run in connection with the activities of agents in the field who were asked to make recommendations.

There was one 12½-minute transmission a day six days a week at an hour late enough not to clash with the BBC. Recordings were made twice a week; two of the three speakers worked in London.

B2 Sambre et Meuse (French)

[9.5.42–29.12.42; reopened 31.1.43, closed 4.6.44] Directed to Walloon industrial workers to prevent deportation of workers to Germany and to

---

1. Proposal for a Belgian RU, 6.5.41.

maintain discipline and control by socialists rather than by communists. A socialist leader was a chief contributor. Carried out recommendations of our agents.

Two transmissions six days a week, one at lunch hour and one after work. Lunchtime transmission was a repeat of the previous night. Two speakers, all scripts being recorded, one speaker being in London.

Programmes trailed in the clandestine press. The RU had a large audience, most arrivals from Belgium had listened to it.

H3 Blauwvoet

[28.3.43–4.5.44] This programme appears to have been started as a result of a suggestion made in the Directorate of Plans by the present writer, that RUs to occupied countries might try to influence their audience indirectly, following Delmer's method with GS1.

'The Quislings in Belgium and Holland would lend themselves to such an attack . . . particularly with regard to bringing into contempt the recruitment of SS troops and Legions for the Russian Front.'

H3 was set up shortly afterwards professing to emanate from a dissatisfied group of Quislings in order to stir up suspicion between rival groups and the Germans.

There were three or four transmissions a week, all being recorded. Repeats were never used. There were two speakers. Constant feuds developed within the Flemish Quisling party soon after the RU began.

Denmark D1

The first Danish RU was started in February 1941 and closed in April 1942.

An investigation into whether the Danish RU (D1) was reaching its mark was made 21.10.41 through a questionnaire addressed to Agent 4351.

He reported that the material was right and voices excellent, that breaks should be introduced in order to give the impression of a genuine Freedom Station in Denmark, but that the ineffectiveness of the RU was due to the fact that the Danish people did not feel they were in the war. He strongly advocated the bombing of Copenhagen and forcing the Germans to take over.

The most popular broadcast in Denmark where the German language is widely understood, in the summer of 1941, was the highly scandalous programme of GS1 which seemed to give evidence of German corruption and internal dissension in the Nazi Party.

D2 Danish Freedom

[1.7.42–25.9.43] This RU was started to inflame feeling when Denmark was a 'model protectorate' and took a strong line on personalities, the King, sabotage, etc.

Two voices were used, sometimes in a dialogue form, three transmissions being given a day from records.

The RU Was attacked on the Danish radio, and a series of strikes for better ARP in Denmark followed the repeated demands for this on the RU.

Norway. N1 Norwegian Freedom

[Started 5.2.41, closed 16.12.42] The original task of the RU was to increase opposition to the Germans by revealing German methods.

The need for an RU was strongly felt as the Norwegian Government had complete control over talks and the BBC bulletin was entirely given up to news. There was therefore no method of educating the Norwegians in the part they might have to play in liberation.

The most striking reaction to the RU was the '1918' campaign which was carried in September and October 1942 and produced widespread action in painting up '1918'.

The RU was widely listened to in Sweden and believed to be in Norway.

The RU was closed as the Norwegian Government refused to allow the Norwegian Staff to continue working unless it assumed control of the station.

Yugoslavia. Y1 Radio Zrinski

[31.5.41–1.12.43] The object was to destroy the authority of the Quisling Government in Croatia, particular in Zagreb.

The audience aimed at was the town bourgeoisie which alone was able to listen to short-wave radio.

The RU adopted a policy of Croat nationalism based on that of the Croat Peasant Party and agreed with responsible Croat politicians in Britain. This was designed to fill a gap in White propaganda owing to the failure of the émigré Jugoslav Government to appeal to Croats.

The transmissions took the form of connected talks and made use of stories, rumours, jokes, threats and reasoned arguments.

The RU transmitted for 12½ minutes every evening; two writer/speakers were employed and talks were recorded the same day, or a day in advance.

Y1 was reported as clearly audible over a wide area of the Balkans and in France, Russia, the USA and the ME.

The RU was at first generally accepted as a secret local transmitter, and a search for it by the Ustashi in Zagreb Cemetery was reported by three separate sources.

Later Zagreb politicians referred to it as connected with the Jugoslav Government in London.

Y2 Shumadia

The aim of this RU was to destroy the authority of the Nedic Government in Serbia and hinder Serb collaboration with the Germans, and to expose German exploitation of Serbia.

It addressed itself particularly to the Serb bourgeoisie in Belgrade. The RU transmitted every evening for periods of from 12½ to 27 minutes. Each transmission opened with a Serbian pipe tune and closed with the Yugoslav national anthem and the words 'Long live King Peter II!'

Each transmission included a talk of about 10 minutes. Four days a week the programme included Serbian national songs from a stock of records.

Y2 was kept going entirely by a single Serbian writer and speaker, as it was impossible to find him a genuine Serb assistant who was reliable on both the Mihailovitch/Partisan and Serb/Croat issues.

Campaigns were run on the RU to bring about disobedience among provincial officials, to expose conditions of work in the Bor mines and 'nerve warfare' campaigns against German and Bulgarian troops in Yugoslavia.

Many listeners continued to believe the station was within Yugoslavia even after Nedic denounced it by name and stated that it was in Cairo.

The station was attacked both by supporters of Mihailovitch and of the Partisans.

Y4 Staro Pravdo

[23.1.43–19.12.43] The main objective originally was to undermine Italian morale by stories and rumours spread by Slovenes in their contacts with the Italian population. After the surrender of Italy the station switched to trying to obtain maximum collaboration between Slovenes and Italians against the Germans.

A secondary objective was to unite Slovenes.

The RU's attack on the Fascist regime and appeal for collaboration with Italians against Germany was made under cover of extreme Slovene nationalism, thus providing the listener with what he wanted to hear.

The RU transmitted for one period every evening with an additional early period on Saturdays and Sundays.

Two writer-speakers were used. The use of records was concealed by new recordings in an altered form when repeats were wanted. Great care was taken to maintain the appearance of [a] genuine clandestine station. The RU 'played in' for several months with a fictitious calling and testing sequence.

The RU may have achieved an important operational success.

During the Tunisian campaign the RU made great efforts to compromise the Slovenes in the Italian Army in the eyes of the Italian military authorities in order to make them withdraw 20,000 Slovenes from the line regiments and draft them to Slovene labour battalions in Italy. As a result, the Italian authorities diverted all Slovene recruits called up from the Army to labour battalions.

Czechoslovakia RD

A Czech RU was started in March 1941 but was closed in September that year on the formation of PWE.

C1

[26.3.43–30.6.44] A second Czech RU Stania Cesko was started at the end of March 1943 as a pseudo-collaborationist station and stimulated passive resistance and industrial sabotage by indirect means appealing to the Czech spirit of ridicule.

Owing to the lack of SOE contacts with Czechoslovakia the RU was an important channel of communication and was the only medium for spreading rumours, giving indirect advice on resistance and stultifying German propaganda.

It was closed in June 1944, after running a year.

S1

[4.9.43–19.7.44] The Slovak RU was started in October 1943. Its object was to increase the unpopularity of the Collaborationist Government and increase German difficulties by increasing Slovak hatred of the Hungarians, and to undermine the allegiance of Slovak troops in the German Army.

Poland

[2.11.42–25.11.44] It is remarkable that the first PWE Polish RU was not started until the war had lasted for three years and two months.

P1 Rozglosnia Polska Swit

The chief function of the RU, which purported to be in Poland, was to service the Polish Underground with news and with orders from the Polish Government in London.

A Polish RU 'Kociuszko' had been organised in Moscow and it was not long before Swit was denounced as speaking for an aristocracy fighting for its own interests. Russian policy in Poland, as everywhere else, was to bring about immediate armed risings at whatever cost to later resistance, and Swit issued warnings against this.

Thus Swit reported that posters had been put up in Polish technical schools warning young people threatened with deportation to Germany to leave their homes, but not to join the Communist partizans 'since the time is still not yet'.

[19.3.43] Kosciuszko abused Swit for 'Repeating the old fairytale of Goebbels that our partizans are not Poles but soldiers of the Red Army dropped on our territory by parachute, they then add that our partizans do not fight at all but adopt a waiting policy. . . . Swit is not camouflaged very well, it is a station of Hitler.'

In addition to news and to broadcasts on policy questions, Swit sent out code messages passed to it by the Polish Government which stated that the messages were at the request of the staff of the Directorate of Underground Warfare in Poland, who provided current news from the field of battle in return and consented to the station operating in the name of KWP.

PWE were not informed of the meanings of these code messages.

Full translations of the Swit broadcasts have not been available, but it is clear that even if Swit had never taken an anti-Russian line, it would have been regarded with hostility by Russia.

After the failure of the Warsaw rising, and during the prolonged Polish Government's negotiations with Russia, it became difficult to keep Swit running, and it closed temporarily on several occasions. It was finally closed after the fall of Mr Micolajezyk with a provision to revive it should he return to office while it was still credible for P1 to be operating in Poland.

P2

[26.10.43–30.5.44] The Polish Women's RU was devoted chiefly to servicing the clandestine press.

'Grey' Broadcasting

Whereas the 'cover' of Black stations had to be sufficiently convincing to deceive listeners with regard to location and origin, all that was required for Grey transmissions was a plausible cover that they were not under British control. A 'Grey' station depended on the attractiveness of its programme to obtain an audience. The cover merely provided the audience with a psychological excuse, or an alibi, and at the same time ensured that the programme was presented in the manner which did not offend its prejudices.

G9 Deutscher Kurzwellensender Atlantik

The possibility of a 'Grey' programme had been conceived by Mr Delmer in 1941, but it was not opened until 22.3.43. Its inception was largely owing to the desire of NID 17Z and of the Admiralty to do everything possible to undermine the morale and subvert the discipline of U-Boat crews.

The Admiralty therefore guaranteed extensive daily information, both accurate and deliberately misleading, which enabled PWE to expand the specifically naval programme into a full size news service and entertainment programme which spoke as though from inside Germany.

The Air Ministry soon followed the example of the Admiralty and was able to supply more detailed information, partly from Ps/W material, partly from the interpretation of photographs of bomb damage. The accurate news was largely military and professional of a kind which the serviceman could check. Impressed by this he was willing to transfer his belief to the invented and half-true items about economic, domestic and political happenings in Germany. Frequently Delmer's guesses as to the stories underlying our intelligence proved correct and the verisimilitude, local colour, and detail were such that the Gestapo was led to believe that we had numerous sources inside Germany.

Object of Atlantik Programme

The primary object of Atlantik was to subvert the discipline of U-Boat crews. This was rapidly extended to include that of all German armed forces in Western Europe, by creating alarm in their minds about conditions in Germany, by unsettling their faith in their equipment and leadership, by rationalising bad discipline and performance of military duty in their minds and by encouraging surrender and desertion.

Method

Atlantik was on the air without intermission from 18.30 to 08.00 hours BST. It played recorded dance music continuously, with short intervals for features and news flashes and longer ones lasting 15 minutes for news bulletins. The music in many cases was specially recorded for the programme by dance bands, and German singers in the USA, and was very carefully chosen to attract the German serviceman. New words were specially written for any new songs being brought out in the USA and were sung by such artists as Marlene Dietrich.

Atlantik therefore provided a first-class entertainment programme, which all those who were not exceptionally serious-minded preferred both to the BBC and to genuine programmes from Germany. The success of Atlantik in this respect forced the German Propaganda Ministry to provide an imitation entertainment programme, but it was not able to compete successfully and Atlantik remained the favourite entertainment of the German forces.

News

Bulletins consisted of reports from the Front and from inside Germany and Germany's allies and included material taken straight from the official news agencies beside slightly 'doctored' material, and invented items of a plausible nature.

A feature of the news were expertly written sports bulletins and a number of human-interest stories. Cover was also obtained by pretending to 'hook-up' with Soldatensender Mittelmeer, a German official station broadcasting for German troops from the Balkans.

Every item used was given as a plain statement of fact without comment and no viewpoint was expressed except in the special naval talks in which the attitude was that of defending the interests of the ordinary seaman. Regular features included talks warning U-Boat crews against reckless and incompetent commanders, naval greetings, and reports of air-raid damage street by street in German towns after Allied bombing raids. The latter were always followed by reference to the German High Command order entitling members of the armed forces to compassionate leave if their homes had been bombed.

Except for the recorded music the programme was broadcast 'live' from MB, all through the night. This enabled the station to provide an up-to-minute news service which was frequently in advance of the official Reich Radio. A large number of announcer voices and compères broadcast the programme.

Co-ordination with Rumours and Leaflets

There was close co-ordination between rumours put out by Atlantik and by other Black stations. Stories carried by Atlantik were picked up by the Balkan and Italian stations and vice versa, and Atlantik was used to launch a theme afterwards developed by the RUs – e.g. that the Nazis planned to educate the young King of Bulgaria in Germany and thereby keep control of Bulgaria. Reports put out by Atlantik were afterwards used in leaflets, particularly on themes of malingering and desertion. Similarly, Atlantik quoted material from leaflets once their circulation in Germany had been established.

Effect

The station could be heard well in Central and Northern Europe, in the Mediterranean and North and South Atlantic. It could even be heard in South America.

It rapidly acquired, and kept, a very large audience in the German services, greatly exceeding that of the BBC German service.

The German press continually denied the truth of various rumours on Atlantik. German Ps/W frequently paid tribute to the popularity of the musical items and to the cleverness of the cover, which had enabled them to listen to the news bulletins openly.

Mr Delmer had to overcome a tendency on the part of the news-editors to 'bury' news items which they knew to be invented, instead of treating all the items, true and false, equally on their inherent news-value.

Operational Use of Grey

Besides being a medium for political warfare the Grey programmes were used for operational purposes. So much accurate technical material was put out that the enemy intelligence had to monitor and analyse the output.

This was used to mislead them. Thus Atlantik carried false information about German torpedoes, which confirmed their hopes and which they believed.

The blockade runners at Bordeaux were also a target for operational broadcasts from Atlantik.

The development of this programme on medium wave and as a daily newspaper for German front-line troops is dealt with on p. 387.

Appendix

No.	RU	Name	Country & Language	Start	Finish
+ 1	G1		German	26.5.40	15.3.41
+ 2	G2	Sender der Europaeischen Revolution	German	7.10.40	22.6.42
+ 3	R1	Frats Romun	Roumanian	10.11.40	20.7.43
+ 4	F2	Radio Inconnue	French	15.11.40	10.1.44
+ 5	W1	Radio Italia, Stazione Clandestina	Italian	16.11.40	15.5.42
+ 6	F1	Radio Travail	French	17.11.40	21.5.42
+ 7	N1		Norwegian	8.1.41	16.12.42
8	It. Soc.	–	Italian	1.2.41	6.3.41
+ 9	D1	Radio Denmark	Danish	16.2.41	27.4.42
10	RD	Radio Nazdar	Czech	13.3.41	28.9.41
+ 11	G3	Gustav Siegfried Eins	German	23.5.41	18.11.43
+ 12	Y1	Zrinski	Yugoslav Croat	31.5.41	1.12.43
13	W2	Radio Libertà	Italian	8.6.41	27.11.41
+ 14	F3	La France Catholique	French	2.7.41	14.5.44
+ 15	B1	Radio Heraus, Vrjschutter	Belgium, Flemish	4.7.41	8.6.44
16	H1	Flitspuit	Dutch	17.7.41	19.8.42
+ 17	Y2	Radio Shumadia	Yugoslav. Serb	7.8.41	19.11.43
+ 18	Y3	Radio Triglav	Yugoslav. Slovene	23.8.41	9.4.42
+ 19	F4	Radio Gaulle	French	25.8.41	15.11.42
20	A1	Radio Rotes Wien	Austrian	3.10.41	27.12.41
+ 21	X1	Levski	Bulgarian	6.11.41	11.1.44
+ 22	W3	Andrea Viaghiello, Livorno	Italian		
23	G6	Astrologie und Okkultismus	German	28.3.42	19.4.42
+ 24	B2	Sambre et Meuse	Belgium in French	9.5.42	4.6.44
25	G5	Wehrmachtsender Nord	German	9.5.42	7.2.43
+ 26	D2	Danish Freedom	Danish	1.7.42	24.9.43

27	G8	Workers' Station	German	17.7.42	23.3.43
+ 28	M1	Magyar Nemset Radioja	Hungarian	6.9.42	7.1.45
+ 29	G7	Deutsche Priester	German	15.9.42	28.4.45
+ 30	P1	Rozglosnia Polska Swit	Polish	2.11.42	25.11.44
+ 31	F5	Honneur et Patrie	French	11.10.42	2.4.44
+ 32	Y4	Za Staro Pravdo	Yugoslav. Slovene	23.1.43	19.12.43
33	D3	Radio Skagerak	Danish	6.2.43	5.5.43
34	H2	Fluistergids	Dutch	6.2.43	28.3.43
+ 35	W4	Italia Risorgi	Italian	16.2.43	15.9.43
+ 36	G9	Deutscher Kurzwellensender Atlantik (short wave) Soldatensender West (medium wave)	German	22.3.43	1.5.45
+ 37	H3	Blauwvoet	Flemish	24.3.43	4.5.44
38	C1	Stanice Cesko, Nemecke Spoluprace. Nova Europa	Czech	23.6.43	30.6.44
39	X2	Slushayte Glas'tna Noua Europa	Bulgarian	2.7.43	15.7.44
+ 40	W5	Giustizia e Libertà	Italian	11.7.43	26.6.44
+ 41	R2	Porunca Maresulului	Roumanian	21.7.43	26.6.44
+ 42	S1	Bradlo	Slovak	4.9.43	19.7.44
+ 43	W6	Intruder into Italian Republican Fascist Radio	Italian	18.9.43	27.10.43
+ 44	R3	Prahova	Roumanian	18.10.43	30.4.44
+ 45	P2	Glos Polskich Kobiet	Poland	26.10.43	30.5.44
46	D4	Hjemmefronte Radio	Danish	6.12.43	28.10.44
47	G10	Kampfgruppe York, Waffen SS	German	11.12.43	18.4.45
48	U1	Hagedorn	German	26.1.45	27.4.45

+ Mentioned in text

Rumours or Sibs

Rumour-mongering was a medium of Political Warfare the possibilities of which were realised in the early days of Department EH particularly as a means of attacking the morale of the enemy's armed forces.

[28.12.39] Thus Air Commodore Groves, then DDI4 at the Air Ministry, suggested a rumour on the poor quality of German aviation spirit to Department EH. The subject of particular rumours took up some of the time of the EH Services Consultative Committee.

Sib procedure was first recorded in the records of the Underground Propaganda Committee at CHQ. Sibs of a military nature only were submitted by Colonel Brooks for approval to the Inter-Services Security Board and the Joint Intelligence Committee.

A meeting held on 13.11.40 considered that the existing machinery was unsatisfactory. The Services wanted information about the fate of sibs they had proposed. Captain Sheridan of SO2 put forward a claim that SO2 should be responsible for the dissemination of all rumours through all channels, [PASSAGE DELETED ON GROUNDS OF NATIONAL SECURITY]. Mr Cavendish-Bentinck* pointed out that Legations had not been used to spread rumours but could do so and Mr Valentine Williams suggested that sibs could be inserted in our scientific and technical journals which the Germans studied.

It was agreed dissemination should be the sole responsibility of SO2 and that all channels should be put at the disposal of 'CD', head of SO2. Captain Sheridan was accordingly nominated to the JIC and attended the weekly meetings of the UP Committee as CD's representative. He undertook to circulate a list of sibs and of channels by which they were disseminated, and any come-backs, and to stop the censorship of sibs disseminated by post.

Sibs of a military nature were submitted to the ISSB and then to the JIC by the UP Committee, then redrafted and passed to Captain Sheridan for dissemination. Non-military rumours were not submitted to any authority.

[7.1.41] The system established was not satisfactory to SO1 and Mr Rayner was appointed rapporteur for sibs. He collected them from regional heads, invented them and they were considered by the UP Committee, then consisting of Ralph Murray, Rayner, CD's representative and Sir Hanns Vischer.

The sibs were then passed for approval not only to [the] ISSB and [the] JIC but also to the Foreign Office for approval.

[16.1.41] Mr Crossman had to complain that rumours for Germany were fabricated without his knowledge.

Early in 1941[1] the channels employed by SO2 are listed as SO2 agents: agents at ports and airports, agents in touch with clubs and hostels for neutral seamen, agents in touch with Communists and others suspected of communicating with the enemy, agents in touch with neutral journalists and diplomatic missions in London, agents working in night-clubs and hotels. Reports introduced into the British and American press [PASSAGE DELETED ON GROUNDS OF NATIONAL SECURITY]. Letters written to people abroad and passed by special arrangements with the censorship; OSS: RUs. Members of British embassies and legations. SO2 decided which channels were most suitable for any particular rumour.

---

1. Memorandum of 6.2.41.

* [Victor Frederick William 'Bill' Cavendish-Bentinck, 9th and last Duke of Portland (1897–1990), was educated, to his chagrin, at Wellington College, Berkshire; 2nd lieutenant in the Grenadier Guards 1918; HM Legation, Warsaw, 1919; FO 1922; attended Lausanne and Locarno conferences; Assistant Under-Secretary of State 1944; Chairman of the Joint Intelligence Committee of the Chiefs of Staff 1939–45; also FO adviser to Director of Plans 1942–5; Ambassador to Poland 1945–7.]

The need for agents to report on the channels they had employed, and to provide any come-backs was stressed apparently in order to prove that SO2 was more efficient than Section D had been.

Lack of a Scientific Approach to Sibbing

The need for consumer research was not realised, and all attempts to improve the quality of sibs were by greater attention to the objectives of the Services, MEW and FO and never by analysis of what kinds of rumours and forms of presentation supplied a psychological need and therefore were most acceptable, spread the fastest and were most firmly believed.

Throughout the history of PWE, sibbing suffered owing to its not having the attention of a wholetime specialist gifted with the rare combination of a scientific approach and a brilliant imagination. As a result it was a case of 'too many cooks spoiling the broth'.

Channels were listed again in the spring of 1941 [18.3.41], in greater detail and included material communicated to Ps/W or inserted in their letters home. The ports of Avonmouth, Glasgow, Liverpool and Fleetwood and the airports of Poole and Whitchurch were mentioned, particular attention being paid to Dutch pilots of the Whitchurch to Lisbon line who were suspected of communicating with their families in Holland. Arrangements were being started in Eire. Shortly afterwards the question of using the MoI censorship as a channel was raised. The first hint of the need for consumer research is contained in a questionnaire by Mr Peterson of SO2 to agents [25.3.41]. But the first attempt to attack the subject scientifically is contained in a paper by Mr John Barry of the CHQ planners, written shortly before the formation of PWE [2.8.41]. Mr Barry proposed that sibbing should be linked with the propaganda plan for each Region and that a whole-time specialist should study the medium. He stated that 95% of sibs were propaganda and only 5% designed to produce a precise result. He stressed that sibs should not be merely oral, but the technique should include news creation for the American and world press, e.g. in planting interviews. He stressed also that radio was by far the quickest means of dissemination and suggested that RUs and [the] BBC should use quotations from a neutral or other source furnished to them.

Mr Barry's suggestions were, however, unwelcome in SO2.[1] The suggested use of the BBC was deplored and in any case SO2 claimed a veto in order to safeguard their agents. As a result no more was heard of his admirable suggestions.

After the formation of PWE, the UP Committee became a sub-committee of the Executive Committee. The question of co-operation with the Americans came up after the US entry into the war [25.2.42], and it was agreed that Britain should leave sibbing in the USA to Colonel Donovan (OSS) as this would prevent repercussions if British sibbing leaked out.

1. Sir Charles Hambro to Mr David Bowes-Lyon, 17.8.41.

Nerve Warfare

During the latter part of 1942, a special sib campaign 'Antelope' was run in connection with British Commando raids as part of our nerve warfare on German troops manning coastal defences. A typical sib was that 3,000 'ghost-killers' armed with absolutely silent automatics and daggers were at large in France.

A new 'direction Committee' for sibs was formed in the spring of 1943, its members being Mr Ritchie Calder, PWE Director of Plans, Colonel Sutton, DPW (O), Mr Crossman, DPW (E & S), Mr Scarlett, Colonel Chambers, with Mr Rayner as the central sib officer.

The functions of the Committee were to lay down policy, define targets and plan campaigns. No radical improvement in the quality of sibs appears to have resulted from its formation.

Good and Bad Sibs

The really good sib is a poisoned sweetmeat – it is sugarcoated and the deadly dose is not immediately evident. It will be remembered that early in the war, the *Ark Royal* was bombed and a GAF pilot was later decorated for sinking the ship which had, however, only been damaged. Considerably later the *Ark Royal* was actually sunk. This placed the German Propaganda Ministry in the dilemma of having to repeat its claim or ignore a success. A perfect example of the ideal poisoned sweetmeat sib was then put out by PWE to the effect that both the first and second claims to have sunk the *Ark Royal* were true, the explanation being that Britain had broken the Anglo-German Naval convention by building a duplicate of the *Ark Royal* before the war.

The chocolate offered to the enemy was that he had won two victories and that all his claims were trustworthy in spite of appearances. The poison was the reflection that if there were two *Ark Royals* there might be two of each of Britain's other capital ships still afloat.

What was probably the most widely reported sib of the whole war was suggested by Major Baker White[1] at the time when a German invasion of Britain appeared imminent. 'That the British have a new weapon which spread an inflammable surface over the sea for an enormous area and sets fire to it.' This sib spread like wildfire over the Continent and reports of train-loads of incinerated German corpses, of hospitals filled with German soldiers suffering from terrible burns and of the failure of an attempted invasion, soon followed its dissemination.

It was successful because it satisfied the longing of conquered peoples of Europe.

But it [is] not unfair to say that the vast majority of sibs were feeble and often childish. For example a sib, which was attacked in the *Daily Mail*, that

1. UP Committee, 27.9.40.

the British Government had imported 200 man-eating sharks from Australia and had let them loose in the Channel, can only have made Britain appear ridiculous.

By far the most successful agencies in putting out rumours proved, as Mr John Barry had forecast, to be radio. Radio Inconnue was particularly successful in blackening the characters of Vichy personalities and in embroiling them with each other by certain rumour campaigns. (See pp. 56–9)

The development of 'news-creation' strongly recommended by Mr John Barry in order to spread worldwide rumours was never undertaken as a definite organised function of the department.

The 'Hackett School' or STP

This training school had been set up in August 1940 by the old section D, about the time of its fusion into SOE. The original idea was to train political organisers of underground resistance: agitators rather than guerilla leaders.

The idea of a school for training émigrés – the first since the days of Pitt – arose before the unfortunate division line between SO1 and SO2 had been drawn. By the summer of 1941, it had become clear that any fruitful training must be done in conjunction with current propaganda production and political direction. Exploration of the possibilities of co-operation with PWE was authorised by the SOE Director of Training and carried out by John Hackett who was re-employed in the school in July 1941, and an experimental syllabus worked out for a course at Beaulieu. This syllabus remained the basic syllabus employed.

Discussions were held between SOE and PWE on the policy of employing propaganda agents and a decision taken in September 1941 to set up a joint scheme for propaganda training.[1]

A new school incorporating the old No. 17, known as STP, was set up on 13.10.41.[2] Premises were opened at Pertenhall twenty-five miles from CHQ of PWE. This distance proved too great for fruitful co-operation and was reduced by a series of moves. The school was run by Major John Hackett on a civilian basis, the first residents being two Belgians. Both these men carried out successful missions later on, one making the first effective contacts with the clandestine press.

For reasons explained elsewhere[3] Belgium was the country in which PWE was able to plan political and propaganda work carried out by agents in the field. PWE French section was eager to send agents into the field, but its efforts were not very effective though a number of students were passed through STP. Some Norwegians and many Poles received training at the school. Least attention was paid to Holland and Czechoslovakia.

---

1. Memorandum by Major General Gubbins, 3.9.41, and of Sir Charles Hambro, 10.9.41.
2. SOS Circular from Director of Training to Regional Heads and Country Sections, 13.10.41.
3. See p. 217.

In March 1942, an additional instructor, Captain Waddicor, was employed, chiefly owing to the School not receiving the continuous help from PWE which had been looked for. Major Hackett, with only the assistance of a non-resident secretary, had been responsible for household management, transport, and obtaining rations, as well as tuition.

In May 1942, the School moved for a second time – to within six miles of CHQ. A printing shop and a desk room were set up and assistance provided by a PWE compositor from Marylands. Training in photographic work for communication purposes was given by Captain Waddicor.

The numbers of agents trained varied between four and ten at one time and each was trained individually. The preliminary tuition was always given separately to each, and no problems were dealt with in open session.

Outdoor exercises were concerned with: political reconnaissance (in conjunction with Home Intelligence Section MoI); practical training in broadcasting (in conjunction with [the] BBC); co-operation with the printing trade.

The first of these subjects was to improve the reporting of political intelligence and was justified by results, particularly in Norway. The second was to enable the agent to meet criticisms of the BBC and to take advantage of opportunities which might arise after liberation. The third was to enable agents to utilise sympathisers in printing works, a useful method of supplementing clandestine 'cellar printing'.

In the autumn of 1942, a third instructor, Major Gallie, joined the School, a full-time secretary was supplied by SOE and a secretary was supplied by PWE and a part-time research worker by PWE and a move was made to a house in the vicinity of CHQ. A system of visiting instructors from PID and PWE and, in certain cases from Allied Governments, was developed, and the training in printing was greatly improved by help from PWE production department.

In the spring of 1943, owing to the move of PWE from CHQ to London, new premises were found for the School at Wall Hall near Watford and it passed fully under SOE administration. It reopened on 26th July with military personnel on normal STS lines. The methods of instruction and the participation of PWE remained unaltered.

In October 1943, Major Gallie became Commandant as Major Hackett had been transferred to SOE HQ.

Apart from the training of agents, the School had helped PWE in the training of officers for Torch and undertook an entire PWE course for training liaison officers in connection with Overlord. The personnel of the school assisted in the training courses given at Brondesbury on 'Fact and Opinion Research'.

In May 1944, the School closed down.

Records are not complete but the total number of attendances for courses (some students returning for a revision course), amounts to about 200, during the existence of the School.

The achievements of the School were:

1. To produce a handful of extremely good agents.
2. A collection of instructional material and methods on propaganda principles, statistical method, improvised printing, photography and radio.
3. A system of individual coaching which influenced the outlook of the students.
4. Effective practical training with outside organisations.
5. A study of motivation in agents.
6. Contributions to other training courses: OWI and OSS in America and PWE and PWD in this country.

Failures arose chiefly from the arrangement made for the execution of propaganda and political work in the field and the consequent divorce between the facilities of SOE and the responsibility of PWE.

The chief failure was:

1. The unambitious planning of political projects owing to the failure to provide for the no-man's land between the extreme of propaganda on one hand and the physical sabotage on the other. For example, there was a failure to provide for organisation and direction of civilian effort in the event of counter-attack. Thus had the German offensive in the Ardennes proved more successful, we should have benefited little by the period of liberation.
2. The final decision against building links between the Resistance movements and PWE's activities in the field from D-Day onwards.

PWE Agents. Belgium

It will be remembered that SO2, later SOE, had always sought to prevent SO1, and then PWE, employing its own agents in the field. This limitation had been accepted and the work of secret and subversive Political Warfare had suffered as a result. The subject of the employment of Political Warfare agents in the field is sufficiently important to excuse a fairly detailed record of the activities of PWE agents in the one theatre in which they were officially able to operate – namely in Belgium.

The subject is treated as a whole here out of its chronological order. The entire work of these agents was to carry out the kind of task later called for in the PWE/SOE plan, and should be referred to in studying the preparations for Overlord.

SOE had been handicapped in its work in Belgium by bad relations with the Belgian Government and Sûreté, and by difficult relations with SIS during 1941 and 1942. The Belgian Army authorities concerned, the 2e Direction, were suspicious of the security of the Belgian Government and would not co-operate with M. Lepage of the Sûreté; M. Pierlot, the Prime Minister, on the other hand stated that 'M. Lepage c'est moi.' It was essential to work with the 2e Direction in regard to the Secret Army; but on the other hand, it was difficult to send agents into Belgium without the help of the Sûreté. On the other hand SIS [PASSAGE DELETED ON

GROUNDS OF NATIONAL SECURITY] was most anxious not to compromise the security of its agents by contacts with those of SOE and thus SOE found itself almost unable to organise either a Secret Army or sabotage in Belgium. M. Pierlot indeed at that time was opposed to sabotage as he believed it would result in reprisals on the Belgian people.

As a result PWE was able to play the part of the honest broker for which Mr Harman, head of the Low Countries section, was particularly well-fitted as he commanded the confidence of all parties. PWE was therefore able to arrange with the Sûreté for the dispatch of propaganda missions to the field, through SOE at a time when relations between SOE and the Belgian Sûreté had actually been broken off. In these missions 'PID were responsible[1] for the creation of missions of propaganda organisers, but SOE were responsible for the W/T operations in the field.'

The following tribute to the usefulness of PWE occurs in the SOE War Diary:

> During the 4th quarter of 1942,[2] all missions but one were arranged by PID in conjunction with the Sûreté. This agreed with the general atmosphere which was that SOE had no relations with Sûreté on sabotage matters. There was constant triangular contact SOE–PID–Sûreté Propaganda Department under Captain Aronstein. Tribute must be paid to the Belgian section of PID for keeping the Resistance flag flying.

Although relations between SOE and the Belgian Sûreté afterwards became more co-operative PWE retained a position in regard to Belgium with SOE quite unlike that in any other country, and the whole job of organising resistance by propaganda agents on the spot, of carrying out sabotage, often of a Political Warfare character, and of equipping the Resistance and Secret Army organisations was undertaken in a spirit of partnership between SOE and PWE. As a result of this experience it remains the firm conviction of the successive Low Countries Regional Heads that SOE and PWE would function better as one department under one Minister and that in any future war it will be most important to see that Political Warfare is not prevented from sending its own agents into the field, nor divorced from sabotage and the equipping of Secret Armies.

The subject of the employment of agents in the field for Political Warfare purposes is sufficiently important for a detailed examination to be made of how many agents were sent and what they achieved.

It should be emphasised that PWE did not merely act as 'cover' for SOE in this matter. These agents were carrying out PWE tasks and were the

1. War History of T Section, SOE, p. 37.
2. *Ibid.*

kind of agents which PWE ought, in the opinion of many leading members of the department, to have had in other countries.

PWE Agents Sent to Belgium

[1941] Absil P. J. (silk merchant), returned 20.7.42. Mission to create an organisation of the liberal and Socialist parties concentrating on passive resistance.

[1942] Catharine O. (Man Friday), arrested 17.1.43. Propaganda Mission to send back political information, to contact existing organisations; work for the clandestine press and passive resistance; to organise reception committees for subsequent agents.

Aarens G. M. C. (Intersection), W/T to Catharine, arrested 27.3.42.

De Liederkerke (Collie), returned 17.7.42, went out again in third quarter of 1943, returned 4.10.43, went out again in third quarter 1944. Mission to contact the Belgian paramilitary clandestine organisation known as the 'Chemise Khaki'.[1] In view of the doubtful political colour of this organisation, PWE had a good deal to do with the drafting of the Mission which must be considered as drawn up jointly in the names of SOE and PWE.

Cerf R. (Tiger), W/T to De Liederkerke, arrested early and shot.

Van Horen (Terrier), W/T to Absil.

Passelecq V. M. (Incomparable), arrested 9.8.42. Propaganda Missions for PWE and to contact sabotage groups.

The period in question was almost disastrous as there were many arrests and two W/T sets fell into German [hands] without SOE's knowledge.

Coyette J. E. M. G. (Porcupine). Mission to demoralise the German Army of Occupation. Sûreté/PWE Mission.

Osterreith R. R. (Platypus), arrested on landing 27.6.42. Mission to influence industrialists to go slow. The strained relations between SOE and the 2e Direction of the Belgian Army on the one hand, and the Belgian Sûreté under M. Lepage on the other, grew worse until by September 1942 all relations between SOE and the Sûreté ceased.

During this period the following PWE agents were dispatched:

Harmesfeger (Dinigo), returned 1.2.44. Mission: the reorganisation of various trades union syndicates.

Van Dorpe (Baboon), returned 16.11.43. Propaganda for 'go slow' in industry.

Stroobants (Borzoi), returned early September 1943. Mission: liaison with the Flemish clandestine press.

Ceyesseus (Gibbon), arrested 17.1.43.

Heffinch (Shrew), returned 22.8.44. Sabotage of ONT (the Belgian Labour office recruiting workers for Germany).

---

1. War Diary of SOE 'T' Section.

Durieux (Caracal), returned 3.3.44. Mission: destruction of certain records of the ONT.

Shrew and Caracal successfully destroyed all ONT records at Tubize, Charleroi, and the Maison du Peuple, Brussels, and also blew up a waterworks at St Ghizain station.

[1943 first quarter] Weldekers (Samoyede), returned 16.11.43. Mission: to establish contacts to carry on propaganda. (The results of Samoyede's Mission will be treated later.)

Bar L. (Dormouse), arrested, wounded and tortured in autumn of 1943. W/T for Samoyede.

Coyette (Porcupine), to demoralise German Army.

Fillob (Mandrill), returned 7.1.44. Assistant to Porcupine.

Lorreau (Othello), returned 25.12.43. To contact people with influence in the distribution of food.

PWE not only 'kept the flag of resistance flying' but played a considerable part in bringing SOE and the Sûreté together for the work of maintaining the 'Front de l'Indépendance', the largest left-wing and partly Communist organisation which had sprung up spontaneously.

As a result of a conference, two agents were dispatched for PWE:

De Liederkerke (Claudius, previously Collie), returned 12.10.43.

Wenderlen (Tybalt, previously Mandamus), returned 6.12.43.

The mission of both these agents was to obtain information with regard to the *Front de l'Indépendance et Libération*. They came back with excellent news. Claudius had had satisfactory negotiations with the FIL and put forward the Claudius plan which he had agreed with their leaders, by which the activities of all Resistance groups other than the Secret Army were grouped under one direction, and divided into: sabotage, propaganda, financing resistance, supporting the families of those who were in hiding to avoid deportation to Germany and communications by W/T. As a result of this organisation, the Secret Army and the FIL received almost identical directives based on that received by SOE from COSSAC which stressed the great importance of the sabotage of communications on D-Day.

During the first quarter of 1944, the following PWE agents were sent out:

Newman (Montano), arrested 11.3.44. Mission: recruiting PWE agents to carry out SOE/PWE Plan.

Dendoncker (Yapock). Mission: Assistant to Hector II who had been commissioned to take on a Political Warfare task with the FI by the SOE agent Hector I.

Van Dyck (Volumnia), returned 25.5.44. To develop distribution of propaganda.

Thanks partly to PWE Low Countries Region, partly to the good sense of SOE and partly to a changing attitude on [the part of] the Belgian Government to its responsibilities, the relations of SOE with the Belgian

Sûreté underwent a great change. It is true that M. Pierlot refused to appoint a co-ordinating officer for the 2e Direction and the Sûreté. Thus on D-Day, SOE had to deal separately, through separate channels, with the Secret Army and with civilian resistance. As a result, on D-Day , the preservation of the port of Antwerp was first entrusted to the Secret Army, then Claudius was sent out to arrange, at the request of the Admiralty, that the preservation of the port should be entrusted to dockers and others connected with the FIL. He reported, however, that the Secret Army arrangements were so good that he had decided not to change them.

As D-Day drew nearer and then passed, agents naturally became more concerned with SOE functions and less with Political Warfare. The contribution made by both [the] Secret Army and civilian resistance was considerable. Thus the Claudius organisation by concerted attacks on electricity distribution centres caused a loss to the Germans of 15,000,000 working man hours during the first quarter of 1944, chiefly in heavy industry.

During the second quarter of 1944, two PWE agents were sent out.

De Winter (Enorbarbus). Mission: to financial head of resistance in Belgium, the banker known as 'Socrate', with wireless.

Chabart (Menas). Mission: to contact Samoyede organisation and hasten preparations for action.

In the third quarter of 1944, the following agents were sent out for PWE.

Lepoivre C. L. E. D. (Cato-Celest). Mission: to be PWE representative with the Communist FI. To replace Hector II in his dealings with the FI and to find him a successor.

Plissart (Cimber/Yonne). Mission: to re-establish communications between Othello and Mandrill organisation.

Gardiner S. H. (Diomedes/Kelling), W/T operator to Lepoivre.

Jackson Mrs O. (Emilia/Babette). Mission: demoralisation of certain high German officials in Belgium.

Corbisier G. F. J. (Mardian/Mathilde). Mission: assistant to Lepoivre (Cato).

In all, thirty PWE, or joint PWE/Sûreté agents, have been here listed. In order to realise the strictly Political Warfare functions which these men carried out the records of some of them have been examined and one or two examples will be given, since the question of employing agents for Political Warfare is a crucial one.

Work of Samoyede

Samoyede reported on 6.12.43, after his return, that he had been successfully dropped on the night of 12/13.3.43. He took trams into Brussels and made his contacts. He was introduced to a policeman who secured him a lodging and did not have him registered. He had all his meals in Black

Market restaurants without trouble. He recruited Samoyede II, a high-grade civil servant, employed in the Ministère des Affaires Economiques, and was able to carry out the following tasks:

1. He located the registers of wireless owners and their addresses and made plans for the cupboards in which they were stored to be blown up. The attempt was made after his departure and the result was not known at the time of his report.
2. His 'No. 6' was employed in locating the transmitters used for wireless broadcasts in French and Flemish, which was accomplished.
3. He discovered that the wireless material commandeered and stored by the Germans had been practically all used by them so it was not worth raiding the stores.
4. He made arrangements for setting up six transmitters in different provinces in Belgium and to have men listening on a certain wavelength at certain hours.
5. He studied the possibility of protecting radio studios from destruction in the event of a German retreat.
6. He approached the Cardinal and the Rector of the University to make records for use on D-Day but they refused.
7. He forgot to make arrangements for recordings of speeches by notorious traitors for subsequent use in Britain.
8. He made a list of eight jamming stations used to jam the BBC with their exact locations and the number of men working in each.
9. He saw the President of the Association des Radios distributeurs and made arrangements that on D-Day all radio distribution stations would cut off German broadcasts and switch to the BBC.
10. He made a rough inventory of printing firms and concealed stocks of ink and paper which would be available immediately after liberation.
11. He set on foot plans for the protection of cinema material and the concealment of German films illustrating traitors' activities.
12. He undertook some recruiting reception committees, etc. He himself was recognised by many people and after he had been followed by Gestapo agents, he left Belgium on 27.5.43.

Work of Mandrill and Porcupine

Mandrill landed 13.4.43 and went first to Liège where conditions were extremely dangerous owing to German wholesale arrests and checking of papers, then to Brussels. His first task was to arrange for landing grounds, reception committees and safe dumps of stores. He then helped Porcupine in propaganda to demoralise the German Army. They arranged distribution of PWE Black leaflets which purported to emanate from Germany and were believed to do so by the German troops. This distribution was effected by mailing to Germans billeted in Belgian houses, they were introduced in barracks by Belgian workmen carrying out repairs, put on seats of cinemas used by German troops by charwomen, distributed through empty troop trains by lemonade sellers, before German troops entered, etc., etc. All material sent by PWE was distributed in such ways. Mandrill was in contact with the clandestine press and arranged for printing of Black leaflets for Germans in Belgium. All his contacts were with Socialists; none with Communists. He appointed Mandrill II, who handed over to Mandrill III, and leaving Belgium on 7.11.43 returned over the Pyrenees reaching London on 7.1.44.

Work of Othello

Othello was successfully parachuted into Belgium on 14.6.43. His mission was 'to contact people with influence on the distribution of food' and to do everything possible to prevent Germany receiving food from Belgium. His mission was partly economic, partly carrying out PWE agricultural propaganda in the field.

Othello was able to adopt an identity not unlike his actual one. He became, owing to influence of friends, an inspector in the SNCFB; as such he could circulate freely in SNCFB cars, having two cars with drivers at his disposal and obtaining extra petrol from the German police authorities. He took three flats, one of them as an eventual hide-out, one of them to meet his helpers in underground work and one in which he lived openly. He bought replica cars with replica numbers – one with a false 'gas chamber' on the roof, fitted to carry pigeons. One of his drivers and an engineer in the SNCFB knew of his illegal work: he used these men for night work. He kept on good terms with the German police having drinks with Secret Service men four or five times a week. He was careful to dress correctly, always to have clothing in his flat, and official papers in his briefcase. He never carried a weapon but had a revolver concealed in each flat and in his car. He made contact with farmers all over Belgium and carried out propaganda against the cultivation of oil seeds. He found himself the chief means by which the Germans obtained deliveries was by buying them up at high prices on the black market – and that there was also a black market by which individual Germans obtained supplies. It was impossible to compete by forming a patriotic black market as our financial resources were not big enough. He therefore decided to make an agreement with committees of farmers to increase legal deliveries on condition that the legal rations were raised and no stocks allowed to accumulate. He therefore approached the Secretary General of the CNAA (Corporation Nationale Agriculture et Alimentation) and, laying his cards on the table, put forward the agreed programme for an increase in the bread ration, and an improvement in flour, and equitable distribution of the potato ration, a reduction in the acreage of flax and colza planted and the forbidding of sending food parcels to Germany. The programme was accepted, except with regard to flax and colza. The increased deliveries and increased rations were carried out with the result of diminishing the amount of food which the Germans were able to obtain, either for the Reich or privately.

Othello had a number of articles printed in clandestine newspapers, and on one occasion was able to get forged copies of *Terre et Nation* sent out from Britain by PWE inserted in the official envelopes to officials in the CNAA by the simple expedient of sending the man who was putting genuine copies of *Terre et Nation* into envelopes out of the room and putting a packet of forgeries on his desk with which he carried on with his work when he came back into the room.

Othello also organised the sabotage of flax and colza crops on a large scale. He appointed his assistant Van Dorpe as Othello II before he left, giving out that he was being sent on a mission to buy seeds. He returned successfully to Britain on 25.12.43 having accomplished one of the most skilful pieces of economic and political warfare. (See note on Othello II.)

Worker of Cimber

Successfully dropped on 4/5.8.44 at the same time as Mrs Jackson but could not find her or the packages. Eventually went to Brussels to contact who procured lodging for him. Samoyede III came to see him and reported and on 9.8.44 he first met Mandrill III. Found that Mandrill III was printing very great numbers of tracts, chiefly for demoralisation of Germans and distributing them to occupying troops. Met Othello IV some days later Othello II (Van Dorpe) and gave him 2,000 American dollars. Othello II was carrying on agricultural propaganda on lines of London directives, and was still sending out subversive tracts when the Allied Armies unexpectedly arrived on 3.9.44. On their arrival, Othello II immediately placarded all thirty-two buildings of the CNAA commandering them in the name of Service Othello, Section Civil Affairs. As a result none of the buildings were sacked or interfered with and Othello II handed over his completed mission to the Commission des Affaires Civiles, headed by General Tschoffen, on 17.9.44.

Emilia Babette (Mrs Olga Jackson)

Was dropped 4/5.8.44 but jumped a few seconds too soon and was separated from her companion and packages. She reached Brussels and stayed, as arranged, with a brigadier of Belgian police, making contact with other persons, including the Chef Huissier at the Palais de Justice, who had already placed two domestics in the house of Herr Jungclaus, and who proposed to set up a bureau to collect information on the private lives of German personalities, whom Mrs Jackson had been instructed to influence. Mrs Jackson's mission was making rapid progress when the liberation of Belgium brought it to an end.

News Digest

The following material was supplied by Mr Ireland who edited the News Digest for duration of the war.

The News Digest began publication in the first week of the war (4th September, 1939) with a staff of four (including typist). It consisted of a few foolscap sheets of roneoed material taken from the German press and radio, and was first intended for internal circulation only within Department EH but it was shortly afterwards circulated to the I branches of the Services. During 1940, the scope was extended to cover the occupied countries in Europe (especially after the events of April/May 1940 and the Fall of France). Czechoslovakia (in two sections, 'Protectorate' and 'Slovakia'), Norway, Denmark, Holland, Belgium, Luxembourg, France, and Italy were all appearing (though irregularly) in the Digest by November 1940. The German Balkan campaign in April 1941 brought in Roumania (No. 491), Hungary (No. 493), Yugoslavia (No. 495) and Bulgaria (No. 501). These appeared irregularly until the supply of material was arranged about August 1941. Albania and Greece were added later. Finland first appeared in August 1941 (No. 586) and the special section 'Swedish Comment' (later: 'Sweden: Comment and Axis Activities') was added in March 1942 (? No. 777) to deal with German activities in Scandinavia as a whole.

The system of arrangement and prefix-lettering of sections was stabilised early in 1942 and was not altered when certain sections became 'liberated' in 1944.

It had been decided that each country should drop out of the Digest as it was liberated, but before this actually happened to any country it was arranged, by agreement with the Ministry of Information, to include 'liberated' material in 'liberated sub-sections' for these countries. These sub-sections preceded such 'enemy-controlled' propaganda or factual material as was still available. The first issue containing 'liberated' material (from Belgium, Holland, France and Italy) appeared on 24th October, 1944 (No. 1586). Some of the Balkan countries soon followed, and then the northern countries. Germany and Austria were dropped entirely after the capitulation of Germany. 'Liberated' material was for special reasons limited to four printed columns per issue per country, and the whole scheme was on a temporary basis.

The Digest Printed by Stationery Office

Owing to the increase of circulation, the problem of roneoing had become acute by the beginning of 1942, but it was not found possible to print. A special night staff of about six young girls, with an experienced supervisor, was engaged to roneo and staple the Digest. This work, which had hitherto been done by three Digest secretaries who also did the shorthand work and typed the stencils, started at 9 p.m. and was finished at any time between midnight and 3 a.m. The Digest kept expanding (it was at that time between forty and fifty foolscap pages) and its circulation (about 300) was having to be deliberately curtailed. In October 1942, the possibility of printing was again investigated. The printing office of a local paper offered to print the

Digest in newspaper form, but fortunately this was rejected in favour of the Stationery Office (Harrow printing works) offer to produce a side-stapled booklet. After a trial (which failed to produce more than eight copies in the scheduled time) at the end of October 1942, the lay out was slightly modified to meet the printers' requirements and, on 26th November, 1942, a second trial was made. The Digest copy was typed in duplicate; one copy was roneoed for limited issue, and the second successfully printed. The first printed issue (No. 990) was circulated on 28th November, 1942.

The layout, with four main divisions (Germany, Dominated and Occupied territories (after 'liberation': 'South Eastern, Northern and Western Europe'), France, Italy), each starting on a fresh page, and with the various sections under single column headings, was planned in conjunction with the printers to assure the maximum speed and simplicity in making up the forms. The SO set the Digest in monotype (7 pt) and printed on one flat-bed machine. The copy was sent by car in two consignments (leaving at 4 p.m. and 7 p.m., arriving at 5 p.m. and 8 p.m.). In June 1943, after the Department had moved to London, the SO transferred the printing by sub-contract to St Clements Press. This made contact with the printers much easier and also made it possible to provide the printers with copy in driblets as required, whereas at Harrow they often finished the first consignment before the second arrived so that the operators were 'on the slate'. This meant a saving in costs of wages. St Clements Press set the Digest in linotype, with seven operators, four readers and four compositors.

Printing meant that the circulation could be unlimited (apart from policy considerations) and no limit was ever fixed either upwards or downwards for the size of any particular issue. The original SO contract provided for an *average* issue of thirty-two pages. This was changed to forty-two when St Clements Press took over, but the situation in Europe made (fifty–fifty-five (maximum ever: sixty-four) the more usual size until the 'liberation' reduced it again.

Sources

The earliest sources were the German press and radio broadcasts monitored by the BBC. Some material from the DNB Hellschreiber service for Europe was monitored by Reuter and passed on to the Digest in very incomplete, inaccurate and half-illegible carbon copies. By early 1940, the Stockholm PRB was providing a service of cabled extracts (in English) from the press of Germany and several occupied countries (Holland, Belgium, Norway, Denmark, Czechoslovakia, Poland). This service (Empax) soon became the mainstay of Digest material, and in 1941, it was extended to cover the S.E. European countries – which it did much more efficiently than the Balkan PRB in Istanbul. (Where the two bureaux duplicated material, the Stockholm version was preferred even in spite of the longer delay). The Berne PRB provided French (? and Italian) press material, which was supplemented by Reuter monitorings of *Havas* and *Stefani* (these were in French, and *verbatim*, and so better than the Reuter DNB translations).

Other sources were the press of the various countries (read and translated in the Digest sections), Stockholm Savinggrams, *Transocean* (in English Morse, monitored at that time by the Foreign Office), and the BBC monitorings of voice broadcasts. The use of these last in the Digest was severely restricted to avoid duplication. But as the BBC expanded its own Digest to include agency monitorings (which were the province of the News Digest) the restrictions were relaxed (they were indeed never observed at all in the French Section).[1] The BBC gradually took over the monitoring of *Transocean*, DNB for Europe, *Havas*, *Stefani*, and were constantly picking up new *Transocean* and DNB services as well as other Axis agency transmissions (the Hungarian *MTI*, Roumanian *Rador*, etc., etc.). The most valuable service of all was the DNB Hellschrieber transmission for the home press. The acquisition of this made the basic material of the German press available before it appeared in the press, and one result was a great saving in time spent on reading the German press itself.

Importance of Enemy Local Newspapers

The monitored agency material was important because it eliminated the delay in the arrival of the press (which was often subject to disturbances due to transport bombing, etc.) and, by shifting the emphasis on to the search for odd items of purely local news, revealed the enormous importance of local papers. Press reading in the German section at any rate was eventually concentrated almost exclusively on local papers, in which the more individual expression of views and the insignificant items of local interest threw valuable light on morale, conditions, the effects of air attacks, etc. Once the full importance of these local papers was realised (both here and in Stockholm) the system of banning the mention of their names in all output (especially the BBC and Allied press) was devised to avoid losing the material by a German ban on its export. In two or three cases the Germans did ban the export of local papers in circumstances which suggested that inconvenient extracts from them had been 'quoted back' from this side. The embargo (imposed in the Digest by marking the papers 'do not quote') was based on lists of newspapers agreed jointly by PWE, MoI, and the Stockholm PRB. (The lists were never entirely satisfactory as PWE worked on the principle of what papers were most important for intelligence and propaganda work, while PRB worked on that of which papers were most difficult to procure in Stockholm. But every effort was made to get the BBC and British press to conform to the rule, and the *Times* itself received more than one warning letter for infringing it.)

1. For details of directive to Digest editors, see Memorandum on News Digest Policy and Practice (Appendix C). File PWI 110, May 1945.

The term 'private report' was used in the Digest with a variety of meanings. It originally meant that the report came from a secret source (censorship [PASSAGE DELETED ON GROUNDS OF NATIONAL SECURITY], etc.) but as the extension of the circulation made it necessary to curtail the use of such material, it came to be used as a cover for any report of which the substance was not secret but the use of which in output (BBC, press, etc.,) it was desired to keep under strict supervision, or the source of which could not be disclosed [PASSAGE DELETED ON GROUNDS OF NATIONAL SECURITY]. In the Norwegian section 'private report' meant material received from the Norwegian Legation in Stockholm.

For a short time before printing started, such 'private reports' as were still secret were typed at the end of the relevant section and blocked out on the stencil before rolling off the copies intended for certain outsider consumers.

Circulation

From internal Department EH consumption, the circulation was intended first to the BBC, then progressively to other Government Departments, Allied Governments, the British and Allied press, the editors émigré bulletins, etc. (including enemy aliens), and certain private individuals (including three or four MPs by special dispensation); a daily copy also went to the House of Commons Museum, National Library of Scotland, Harvard, California University and the Universities of Zagreb and Ljubljana (through the Yugoslav Government in London). The Allied Governments were most assiduous in asking for back numbers to keep their files complete.

Until late in 1942, a subsidiary distribution was undertaken by MoI. No check was kept on this, and, apart from many duplications which came to light when the MoI list was taken over by PID, a number of private individuals were found to be getting the Digest whose credentials, in the absence of any record, it was not possible to check, and whose presence on the list made it difficult to enforce the qualification requirements later introduced.

In fact the Digest itself (though its source was theoretically secret) never had any 'security' ranking (unlike the BBC Digest which was 'Confidential'). Circulation was deliberately kept down for other reasons. Staff difficulties were eliminated by going over to printing, and between November 1942, when printing started, and June 1943, when St Clements Press took over, the circulation rose from about 400 to 870 (6.6.45). Thereafter it continued to rise, and in May 1944 in deference to the Treasury (which did not realise that compared with the total cost of editing and printing, the cost of running off extra copies is infinitesimally small), all readers were circularised with a request to justify their receiving the Digest. The results were small; circulation remained in the 1,300s. A similar circular in April 1945 produced a slightly bigger reduction, but circulation remained in the 1,400s, and increasing demands from the Control Commission staffs then being built up brought it up to 1,500 (1,522 on 29.4.45), from which peak it began to descend as wartime activities ceased (1,493 on 20.5.45, after which no increases were made).

After May 1944, new applicants for the Digest were strictly required to show that they needed it for purposes connected with the war effort (which included the editing of a bona-fide newspaper or periodical). In April 1945 new subscribers were limited to Government Departments, but, shortly afterwards, requests from newspaper editors were referred to the MoI which at once began to authorise many additions to the list.

The Digest was always issued free of charge, and was distributed partly by hand and partly by post. As it was not confidential, open wrappers were used (though not at first) to save postage.

For a fuller analysis of consumers, see Memorandum on News Digest Policy and Practice, etc.

Editorial Staff

The editorial organisation was influenced by the fact that the Digest began as a purely German document. At the end of 1940, the Digest section was still only a part of the German Region, and the other countries were done by one or two persons inside that section. As regional intelligence sections were built up for the various occupied countries, they formed Digest sections of their own to take over the work of preparing and editing the material, and only the final responsibilities for ensuring adherence to rules and directives remained with the central editorial section. But until the Directorate of Political Warfare Intelligence was set up late in 1942, this central editorial section was identical with the German Digest section, and prepared and edited the German material. When DPWI was set up, the German part was transferred to the German Region, but the 'A' section (German comment) was still kept in the central editorial section (under DPWI) as forming a kind of general 'editorial' to the Digest as a whole. This continued until the German sections A and B were dropped after the capitulation.

Thus the ultimate set-up was a central editorial section, closely attached in spirit to the German part of the Digest, controlling and supervising the material prepared in the various regions, and responsible for its final shape, its appearance on time, etc., and adherence to policy directives, as well as for circulation and correspondence with consumers, dealing with the printers, etc.

The regional editorial staffs were immediately responsible to their own regional editor (who had a deputy), who was responsible to the central editor. The regional staffs worked very closely with their own intelligence sections, which provided essential help in the form of language experts (for translation, spelling of names, etc.), and background material from files, secret reports, etc. This meant that it was possible to use expert and detailed knowledge in selecting and evaluating Digest material without requiring the regional editors themselves to be experts.

It was not found practicable to make a general index to the Digest and there was no central Digest file. Apart from the regional intelligence files, most regional editors kept their own quick reference systems of back references. There is evidence that readers were helped by this system of back references and also by the system of cross referencing items from section to section in a single issue of the Digest.

Part IV
PWE and the Campaigns in N. Africa, Sicily and Italy

Political Warfare and the Commando Raids

The policy of carrying out raids by Combined Operations on the coast of Europe presented both the enemy and ourselves with opportunities for Political Warfare. Those offered to the enemy were the presentation of the raid in the news, and reprisals on any of the population who gave us assistance in order to act as deterrent in future. PWE was concerned to counter the enemy's propaganda in regard to the raids. In addition, they offered opportunities to collect intelligence, to bring back volunteers, and to carry out propaganda locally during the raid itself.

For these reasons close liaison between PWE and Combined Ops was required and Mr Murphy was selected as a liaison officer. His appointment was delayed for some weeks by ill-health and he was only able to take up his duties after the raids on Bruneval [16.3.42] and shortly before that on St Nazaire [27.3.42].

St Nazaire

At St Nazaire the French population received no warnings and took the British landing to be an invasion. Numbers of Frenchmen therefore came out and co-operated with the commandos. After the Germans had returned these men were arrested and shot. Thus an extremely successful raid, which amounted almost to a military victory, was transformed into a Political Warfare defeat.

Dieppe

Plans were therefore carefully laid to minimize the exploitation of the Dieppe raid by enemy propaganda [19.8.42].

From the Political Warfare angle the Dieppe raid was ill-timed. There was in the summer of 1942 a loud clamour in Britain, inspired partly by Russia, partly by mere ignorance, for a Second Front. The news of an interview between Mr Churchill and Stalin had broken the day before the raid and there was the danger that the raid would be linked with the visit. The scale of the raid, the landing of tanks and the use of Canadian and of US troops, made it easier for the enemy to treat the raid as an attempt at invasion. The protagonists of the Second Front were exasperated that if we could do so much we had not attempted more.

The intangible results achieved which in the public mind boiled down to the 'valuable experience' of undergoing heavy losses of men and of equipment, made the presentation of the news a difficult matter. Nevertheless the short-term PWE plan achieved a temporary propaganda success, but as the plan had only been drawn up for the initial period we soon lost the initiative.

Newspaper Correspondents and Dieppe

Facilities had been provided for British, American and Canadian war correspondents to take part in the Dieppe raid, but nothing of the sort had been provided for the representatives of the Fighting French Information services. As a result no mention of the presence of Fighting French Commandos appeared in the American press and the Gaullistes were left with another unnecessary grievance.

Nothing however, could have neutralised the effect of the German Propaganda Ministry's documentary film showing the hundreds of corpses, wrecked landing craft and shattered tanks on the beaches and the large numbers of prisoners. The Dieppe raid was kept alive by the shackling of commando prisoners in reprisal. An effective German Political Warfare move following the Dieppe raid was the release of all French prisoners from the Dieppe area held in Germany as a mark of Hitler's appreciation of the behaviour of the Dieppe population in the raid.

Commando Raids in Undefended Areas

As commando raids frequently took place in remote and undefended places, it became necessary to prove that demolitions had not been carried out by the local population.

PWE therefore designed posters, with the Royal Arms in colours, for the commandos to put up as proof that it was the British who were responsible. The propaganda slogan accompanying these posters was the promise to return.

Mr Murphy's appointment with PWE was terminated by his transfer to SOE as from 1.1.44; he later proceeded to the SEAC area.

Madagascar and Operations Bonus and Ironclad and Stream-Line Jane

After the fall of France propaganda to Madagascar had been carried out by radio from Mauritius where there were three transmitters.

P.1. Radio Meurice, was a privately owned transmitter controlled by the Information Officer (and therefore ultimately by the MoI) which broadcast for 4 hours in French per week.
P.2. Radiophonique de l'Ile Meurice, directed to Réunion. It was also controlled by the Information Officer. It broadcast on 41.98 m. and was a 50 k.w. instrument. One hour daily was broadcast in French and reception was good in Madagascar though it was severely jammed.
P.3. France Libre d'Outre Mer a 1½ k.w. transmitter broadcasting on 41 m. was an RU purporting to be a secret station operating inside Madagascar. It was controlled by SOE and ultimately, through directives, by PWE. In November 1941, it was reported to be 'not very effective'.

All the stations above mentioned received the same slanted information telegram which PWE sent to the Franck (SOE) Mission in West Africa.

In addition to these broadcasts it was planned to instal a more powerful amplifier at Mogadishu which would enable the Nairobi broadcasts to be heard in Madagascar on 15.3 and 27.96. m. The Governor of Mauritius had also put forward plans for strengthening the broadcasts from the Island.

Plans for the landing of a British Force and for the capture and occupation of the port of Diego Suarez (Operation Bonus) were drawn up by the Chief of Combined Operations, Admiral Lord Louis Mountbatten, and were communicated to Brigadier Brooks, who informed the French Regional Director, Lt Colonel Sutton, on or about 23.12.41 and a meeting was held at which GCO, Brigadier Brooks, and Lt Colonel Sutton were present.

PWE Opposes Participation by Fighting French Forces in Madagascar

The original plan included participation by Free French forces but the French Regional Director insisted that this would be undesirable since it was known that the Governor of Madagascar and many of the functionaries were strong supporters of the Vichy Government. Other reasons for not wishing to employ Free French forces with the expedition were founded upon British experience at Dakar and in Syria where they had been used. On those occasions Vichy propaganda had been able to accuse the British of wishing to involve Frenchmen in fratricidal strife, and to accuse the Free French of treachery. The French population looked with horror at the spectacle of Frenchmen fighting each other over the ruins of their country and were ready to blame the attacking side. PWE was anxious not to give Vichy propaganda arguments to prove that the Free French were puppets of the British Government. Moreover, PWE was not convinced that the Free French movement represented a majority of the French people or even of the Resistance movement in France, or that it would eventually do so. In general, PWE was extremely sensitive to public opinion in France and somewhat indifferent to French opinion in London. The result of not only excluding the Free French but of not even informing General de Gaulle that the attack was going to take place was to wound the susceptibilities of the Free French and to produce an uneasy feeling that relations between General de Gaulle and the British Government was not good.

PWE Opposition to Participation by S. African Troops

The French Regional Director made it clear that in his opinion it would be most injudicious for South African troops to take part in the operation on account of their attitude to coloured peoples who in Madagascar regarded themselves, and enjoyed the status, of French citizens. He also stressed the position of the powerful and important Jesuit Missions on the island. The PWE representatives found that CCO had already had leaflets drafted by his adviser Mr Murphy. The texts of these, which were intended as impact leaflets to be dropped at the time of the initial assault on the Vichy Air, Land, and Naval Forces began: 'Les Japonais se préparent à vous attaquer. Vous ne voudriez pas que ces misérables chacals de l'axe fasciste vous soumettent à un esclavage honteux,' and concluded with the exhortation: 'aidez-vous à soustraire ce beau coin de votre patrie au joug fasciste'.

PWE Opposition to CCO's Draft Leaflets

The French Regional Director pointed out that the language was hyperbolic, that a reference to Free French forces participating in the attack should be omitted and that no Free French forces should take part, that the term *fasciste* was only used either for Italians, or in French party politics, but would not be understood in reference to the Japanese.

The PWE view was not accepted until the French Regional Director had stated that he declined any responsibility for an operation in which these leaflets were used. He therefore submitted alternative texts – based on the opinion that there should be no apologies or threats but that the operation should be explained as the direct result of Japanese aggression in the Pacific. The French Regional Director also noted that it was 'essential to have one or two experienced and active people to employ all propaganda media immediately after the attack'.[1]

The views of the French Regional Director on the participation by Free

1. MS. Note by French Regional Director, 16.1.42.

French or South African troops and his criticisms of the leaflets drawn up by CCO were finally accepted.

French Regional Director Informed of the Operation Too Late

On 13th January, 1942, however, he was informed that the whole operation had been cancelled. Owing either to inadequate liaison between CCO and the Military Wing of PWE, or else to a false view of security requirements, the French Regional Director was not informed that the operation was once more impending until 17th March, 1942. It was not until 29th April that the French Regional Director learned that the original plan 'Bonus' had been limited to the capture of Diego Suarez, and that it had been expanded into operation 'Ironclad' which provided for the subsequent capture of Tamarive and Majunga and finally the whole island.

On 17th March, the impact leaflets to which PWE had taken objection were put forward again. The same arguments which had been used in January were repeated with the same results and leaflets written in the PWE French Region were printed and delivered to WO on 20th March and were used during the attack.

Lt Colby Given Forty-eight Hours' Training

On 17th March a meeting was held at the War Office attended by GOC Force Major General Sturges and his staff, and by Brigadier Brooks and Lt Colonel Sutton representing PWE. At this meeting, Lt Colonel Sutton learned for the first time that GOC's staff included one officer, Lt Colby, GSO3 i/c Force, part of whose duty would be to conduct Political Warfare in the island under GOC's orders. This officer was completely untrained in Political Warfare methods. The French Regional Director raised the subject of the issue and nature of the communiqué announcing the assault and discussed the probable effects of leaflets. He also handed in intelligence material prepared after the meeting in January. He learned that no plans had been made for Political Warfare after the assault. He was able to arrange that Lt Colby should spend forty-eight hours immediately following the meeting, at CHQ (18th and 19th March), to obtain intelligence and theoretical plans. During this short stay Lt Colby was indoctrinated as fully as possible in Political Warfare methods and was particularly impressed with the fact that he should prepare 'cock-shy' plans for every possible alternative. He was told to consider the operation from three points of view: (1) The Attack. (2) The propaganda effort on the port of Diego Suarez. (3) The rest of the island.

He was impressed with the necessity of travelling in the same ship as G2, and of getting to know the Air Force officers and staff. He was warned that the pilots would not be expert leaflet droppers and would probably not be keen on the leaflet side of their work. It was arranged that the PWE packages of leaflets should be labelled with the targets 'Army', 'Navy', and 'Air Force', for which they were designed. He was asked to check all possible media of propaganda taken by the Force, such as field wireless sets, field printing presses. He was urged to prepare a plan asking that immediately on landing an armed party should be detached to take possession of any printing press known to exist, and to hold it. PWE agreed to provide directives for the three transmitters on Mauritius which would be timed so that suitable background propaganda should be turned on at the right time to support the operation. Lt Colby showed himself to be eager and anxious to learn, though quite ignorant and inexperienced.

Dr Beck was strongly of the opinion that a French-speaking Catholic priest should accompany the expedition to act as envoy to the missionaries and Roman Catholic authorities in Madagascar. This proposal[1] was submitted to EPS Admiralty (Captain Hughes-Hallett) on 20th March, 1942. The proposal was agreed by Colonel Jefferies (M11 A) and Chaplain Squadron Leader R. V. Butler OBE was selected. He proved, however, to be medically unfit and never reached the island.

PWE responsibilities thereafter consisted firstly in supplying Captain Colby with directives and background intelligence, and with suitable propaganda material. Secondly, in supplying Mauritius with the same. Thirdly, in furnishing an explanation of the operation to Metropolitan France which would forestall and defeat the violent Vichy propaganda reactions.

Presentation of News of Madagascar Operation to France

On 29th April the French Regional Director drafted a plan with regard to the explanation to be provided to France when the news of the attack broke. This draft proposed the publication of British and American communiqués and the dropping of 5,000,000 leaflets on unoccupied France and 2,000,000 leaflets on occupied France on defined urban targets, the preparation of a special directive to the French BBC service and a general directive to all other BBC services and for telegraphing directives to Cairo for General Spears' Mission and to West Africa and to Mauritius.

On 30th April, the French Regional Director proposed to the Director General that 1,000,000 leaflets containing extracts from President Roosevelt's speech broadcast on 29th April and printed as coming from the US Government should be dropped on named urban targets in unoccupied France in order to provide the necessary strategical background for the impending news. In this speech, President Roosevelt had warned the French people: 'Les Nations unies en cas de besoin prendront les mesures nécessaires pour empêcher l'utilisation, à des fins militaires, par les puissances de l'Axe, du territoire Français dans quelque partie du monde que ce soit.'

1. Minute from Lt Colonel Sutton to Brigadier Brooks, 20.3.42.

The proposal was at once referred to the S. of S. for Foreign Affairs who not only warmly approved but urged immediate action. Mr Keeble had already been warned by Lt Colonel Sutton to be ready to carry out a rush printing order. The dropping was planned to take place on the night of the 3/4 May. The special arrangements for the dropping were negotiated by Air Commodore Groves and Air Marshal Peck on 1st May. Further arrangements were made to drop special leaflets over the same areas explaining the operation.

Brigadier Brooks informed Mr. Leeper[1]: 'The aim will be to disseminate during the 48 hours following the raid 5,000,000 of the leaflets over the targets put forward by Colonel Sutton.'

The leaflets in question were the official British leaflet with the Royal Arms and the words *Au Peuple Français* on one side, and an American leaflet with the Arms of the United States and the words *Communication Officielle du Gouvernement des Etats Unis au sujet de Madagascar*. The statement ended with the words: 'Imprimé pour le Gouvernement des Etats Unis et distribué par la RAF.'

The signal 'Ironclad has begun' was received from the Admiralty on 5th May, 1942, and 2,484,000 leaflets were dropped on urban targets in unoccupied France that night.

As a result, particularly of the statement issued by the United States, the violent anti-British outburst of Admiral Darlan fell flat and opinion even in Vichy circles tended to be resigned.

On 14th May, 1942, the Director General informed Lt Colonel Sutton that he was instructed to convey to him the congratulations of the S. of S. for Foreign Affairs and the Minister of Information.

The Operation in Madagascar

In the opinion of the PWE French Regional Director and of Dr Beck the operation was surprisingly satisfactory and in their opinion great credit is due to Captain Colby's intelligence and initiative and to his anxiety to obtain and conform to PWE directives. This view is borne out by those nearer at hand and less likely to overestimate the effects of Political Warfare.

On 14th May, 1942, the GOC in Madagascar reported:[2]

> 'Broadcasting has had a marked effect on security, modus vivendi and general relations with the French . . . French are in a receptive mood and there are infinite possibilities for propaganda to which I attach importance second only to operations. Directives most useful.

---

1. Brigadier Brooks to Mr Leeper, 3.5.42.
2. No. 50045/G cipher 12/6, 121 Force to WO for PWE.

The Government of Mauritius[1] reported on the Diego Suarez broadcasts:

> Speakers' voices much admired. Calm dignified friendly tone with attractive English accent. Radio has large listening audience in Quite and Réunion owing to tactic of establishing friendly relations by giving family news before embarking on propaganda . . . I have offered military authorities a half k.w. transmitter to increase audibility.

This transmitter afterwards reached Diego Suarez and proved a useful supplement to the 5 k.w. military transmitter which was not always available.

PWE had provided £500 for propaganda expenses. Captain Colby spent £75 of this on luxury goods such as toothpaste, soap and scent which he distributed on arrival.

After the initial attack, and the capture of Diego Suarez, operations were suspended for two months and this interval afforded a golden opportunity for propaganda to make the French Forces 'think again'.

There was no broadcasting station at Diego Suarez. Lieutenant Colby therefore created one using a Force Signals No. 5 set and broadcast on the Tananarive wavelength directly after Tananarive closed down, announcing himself as a British officer and reading out personal messages from citizens in Diego Suarez. The first broadcasts were made from M. V. Winchester Castle. After the transmitter was put on shore the programmes were frequently interrupted by livestock as the studio was in a farmyard. Other radio features in the form of a discussion called 'Les Entretiens de Freddy' were popular and military music was provided by various regiments in 121 Force.

A local weekly paper in Diego Suarez was taken over. At first one page in English was devoted to news for British troops but the two papers were later divided.

Before operations were resumed, Captain Colby's resources had been reinforced by the Mauritius transmitter, and many other propaganda influences had been brought to bear on the population and garrison, ranging from the provision of goods which had vanished from the island for some time, for profitable trade, and social exchanges between officers of the occupying forces and the principal inhabitants. In addition, Germans and Italians had been rounded up, and rabid Vichy sympathisers deported to the mainland.

Operations began again, on 11th September, 1942 (Operation Streamline Jane). After the capture of Tananarive, Captain Colby took over the broadcasting station there leaving Radio Diego Suarez in the hands of Lieutenant Wormald RN until it closed on 11th October, 1942.

---

1. No. 387 to S. of S. for Colonies, 12.6.42.

After the capture of Tananarive M. Annet, the Vichy Governor, was without any means of carrying out wireless propaganda and could only counter British propaganda from Réunion, or from Vichy. M. Annet had recently been given an honour and it was rumoured that Colonel Moranges, the mainspring of resistance, had been made a general. This was exploited in a feature with a chorus 'Félicitations'. Madagascar was immensely amused and M. Annet's furious rejoinders from Réunion added to the French appreciation of our humour.

In November, the British took over the Information and Propaganda Office in Tananarive and Captain Colby became Chief Information Officer with a Franco-British staff. The propaganda media at his disposal were:

1. Two daily broadcasts.
2. The official daily 'Informations de Presse', extracts from which were telegraphed to towns in Madagascar and put up in local post offices.
3. Distribution through a mailing service to individuals and to local newspapers of propaganda material received from London, S. Africa, Nairobi and US Consul.
4. The sale in Tananarive and other towns of 1,200 copies of *L'Eclaireur* which was flown in from Diego Suarez.
5. Personal contacts between the Information Office and the population by setting up a reading room and an exhibition of war photographs. The Information Office thus became a rendezvous for the Fighting French and pro-Allied elements of the population and was always crowded in the afternoons. There were many volunteer helpers.

On 31st January the Information Office was handed over to the Fighting French Information Officer, M. Siriex. The policy towards the Fighting French had always been to treat them as allies but not to carry out propaganda in favour of General de Gaulle. This policy won over many waverers and helped to unite all Frenchmen in the island against the common foe.

The Madagascar episode shows the high military value of Political Warfare when dealing with an indeterminate situation where neither the opposing garrison or the population has yet decided on its actions and mental attitude. PWE propaganda from England both via leaflets and BBC broadcasts showed how dangerous political results can be averted by getting the facts presented in the right light without any delay at all. Had the leaflet disseminations taken place a week or two weeks later they would have had little result. The harm done or the good achieved depends on the right presentation of the facts as the news breaks.

In conclusion, it must be recorded that the estrangement caused between the British and the Fighting French was to some extent offset by the subsequent handing over of Madagascar to a Fighting French administration under General LeGentilhomme, and was also forgotten in the great British propaganda exploitation of the heroic French defence at Bir Hakeim. The handing over of Madagascar to a Fighting French administration also provided very valuable propaganda material since it was an implementation of the promise made in our leaflets explaining the operation and it came earlier than could have been anticipated. No better argument exists for the propagandist, or for the borrower, in obtaining further credit, than to be able to point to a promise which he has fulfilled.

Handbooks

[6.9.42] The JIC requested PWE and MEW to assume responsibility for the production of handbooks to the different countries of Europe which would be required after our armies had returned to the Continent.

The handbooks were designed to provide the latest information on the administration, police, social services, social life, political conditions, national characteristics, economic resources in the detail required by Civil Affairs and Political Warfare officers, by those planning operations, by the Military Sub-Committee at Richmond Terrace, the Post-War Commodity and Relief Department, etc.

[18.9.42] A draft syllabus was worked out by Dr Beck and Mr Tower, MEW, for a basic French handbook and the need for zonal handbooks dealing with the separate administrative regions of France was foreshadowed. Mr Leeper was entrusted with responsibility for the handbooks and became chairman of the handbook Committee.

Brigadier Cavendish Bentinck informed PWE that absolute priority should be given to the handbook for Italy with special reference to Sicily and Sardinia.

After the resignation of Mr Leeper, responsibility for handbooks was entrusted to Brigadier Sachs. Although much preliminary work in collecting material, and co-ordination with ISTD, MI11 and NI handbooks was begun, the work did not make rapid progress until after the appointment of Mr Pitt, whose sole responsibility was the production of the handbooks. Mr Pitt was responsible for co-ordinating the work undertaken by the handbook teams of specialists in PWE regions, and in MEW for fixing time-tables, for co-ordinating PWE handbooks with handbooks produced by other Government Departments.

Later liaison was established between Mr Pitt and OSS so as to make the handbook material immediately available for the Charlottesville handbooks prepared for US Army Civil Affairs.

The system of producing the handbooks in loose-leaf sections enabled parts of a handbook to go to press without reference to the completion of other parts. Thus, large parts of a handbook might be available even if the whole were incomplete. It also enabled sections to be re-written as necessary and the whole handbook kept up to date with the minimum of waste.

A handbook group was formed within each region of PWE with editors, assistant editors, etc. Thus in the Low Countries Region there was a general editor, with a staff of sixteen persons under him.

A certain flexibility in the syllabus and particularly in the degree of detail attempted was necessary in the treatment of different countries. Thus it was unnecessary to give so much detail with regard to friendly countries where information would be immediately forthcoming as for enemy countries.

The handbooks may be criticised for the over-ambitious scope on which they were planned. But in the absence of direct instructions that handbooks would not be required for certain areas, PWE had to undertake the work for all areas. Moreover, when the work was undertaken, it was impossible to tell that British officers would not be carrying out civil affairs or similar functions in any area as part of a joint United Nations administration.

By the summer of 1943, PWE had completed basic handbooks for France, Italy and Greece, and those for Yugoslavia, Albania, Belgium and Norway were in proof. Eight zone handbooks for Italy were in an advanced state of preparation.

The handbooks were a very notable achievement and served a wide variety of uses. Thus they were invaluable in the different training schools and as there were no American publications comparable to them, they became the basis of teaching in American schools over which PWE had no control – such as the PWD Training School at Rushton, Northants – and thereby served to disseminate PWE regional policy.

The present writer was able to secure inclusion in certain handbooks of lists of notable cultural monuments of which special care should be taken, at the request of Colonel Webb, Chief Monuments Officer, PWD SHAEF. This is an example of how the handbooks were able to serve as a useful medium for a variety of purposes.

Disclosure to Allied Governments

It was originally planned that the handbooks should be written without reference to Allied Governments. Matter was therefore included which was bound to offend national susceptibilities and the production of the handbooks would have aroused, or helped to confirm suspicions in certain quarters.

In other cases, the exiled Government was not considered sufficiently impartial for its collaboration to be of value. Thus policy was to keep the existence of the handbooks secret for certain countries. On the other hand, the PWE Regional Director pressed for disclosure of the handbooks to the Dutch and Belgian Governments.

Moreover, disclosure to a certain number of Allied officers became inevitable when they attended courses at which the handbooks were used – as at Wimbledon (Civil Affairs).

The decision was therefore to disclose the existence of the handbooks to some Allies but not to others.

Revision

Continual revision of the handbooks was carried out, fresh leaves being issued to replace those containing erroneous or out-of-date material.

In conclusion, it should be said that the smooth production and high qualities of the handbooks was largely owing to Mr Pitt who carried out his work with a minimum staff and complete absence of red tape.

Pocket Guides

The importance of the briefing of soldiers on their relations with the civilian inhabitants of the countries in which they operated seems to have arisen partly in imitation of the admirable booklet issued to US troops, before their arrival in England, partly from the initiative of PWE.

The first such briefing appears to have been with regard to the troops taking part in the Dieppe Raid.[1] This was followed by the preparation of a booklet on Sicily written by Colonel Harari of PWE Plans which was submitted to the military and sent to Algiers. AFHQ prepared and printed its own version. Later, PWE was asked to provide 55,000 copies of the Harari booklet for Canadian troops being shipped direct from Britain. The booklet therefore came to be known as the Maple-leaf booklet. 25% of the copies were in French for French Canadian soldiers.

These beginnings were followed by the JIC commissioning PWE to produce pocket guides for use of troops of all three services, covering all the enemy and enemy-occupied countries in which they would operate. The guides dealt with national character and civilian life and the way in which soldiers should behave to the civilian population – also a short phrase book.

Simultaneous orders for printing pocket guides for all Western countries were given for security purposes. The preliminary British order was for France 300,000; Belgium 100,000; Holland 70,000; Germany, Denmark and Norway 60,000 each to be delivered by 30.4.44.

The preliminary US Army order appears to have been 1,000,000 copies for France and 8,000 for Belgium, Holland and Norway. If the orders were broken up among different firms, it was impossible for the printers making copies to know the total numbers.

There were French editions of the pocket guides for French Canadian troops.

The pocket guides won high praise from the Military Authorities.

Completion and Control of Aspidistra

The progress of the erection of Aspidistra was being impatiently watched by the Prime Minister who asked for a report on the station. On its receipt the Prime Minister minuted: 'First explain what advantages it gives us (8 lines) secondly, report every three days the day it is expected to be ready to function. W.S.C. 6.9.42.'

The Director General did not refer this enquiry either to Mr Leeper but

1. Mr Peter Murphy to Brigadier Brooks, 12.6.42.

to Sir Noel Ashbridge, how, it will be remembered, had consistently opposed the uses for which Aspidistra had been designed and who had been anxious to obtain control of Aspidistra by providing the technical staff, in order to harness it to the BBC.

The report agreed with Sir Noel Ashbridge[1] was as follows:

The Advantages of Aspidistra (for transmission on medium wavelength only).

1. It has a higher power than any station known to be in the use of the enemy.
2. It will strengthen the BBC by making reception possible up to 1,100 miles during darkness where there is no local jamming.
3. It will overcome jamming in North and Western France unless the Germans take very rapid counter measures and can therefore be used for operations.
4. If necessary, it could create confusion in enemy broadcasts in Western Europe. This might provoke a jamming war on a large scale in which at present we should come off worst.

Reasons for the Prime Minister's Interest in Aspidistra

Three days later, the Director General reported to the Prime Minister that one part which would be flown from America and was expected any day was required to complete the instrument but that there was no reserve equipment. This report was not completely accurate as in fact only one of three masts had been erected. No doubt the Prime Minister's eager interest was to make certain that we could neutralise enemy propaganda to France and give our own explanations of the landings in North Africa which were in preparation.

[PASSAGE DELETED ON GROUNDS OF NATIONAL SECURITY], however, found reporting every three days that there was nothing further to report somewhat irksome. He therefore got in touch with Major Desmond Morton. In the light of these conversations Major Morton drafted recommendations with regard to the nature of the reports to be submitted to the Prime Minister.[2] These re-stated the importance of Aspidistra as an offensive propaganda weapon broadcasting on enemy wavelengths. The full text of Major Morton's letter was not, however, communicated either to Squadron Leader Halliday,[3] [NAME DELETED], and the next report to the Prime Minister[4] did not even give the technical information as to direction masts which had been asked for. The Prime Minister minuted: 'When will it be able to work? W.S.C. 21.9.42.' Luckily

1. Mr Bruce Lockhart to Capt. A. M. Galsworthy (Prime Minister's Private Secretary), 7.9.42.
2. Major Morton to Brigadier Brooks, 16.9.42.
3. Mr Scarlett to Squadron Leader Halliday.
4. Lt Colonel Metherell to Mr Peck (one of the PM's Secretaries).

an answer to this was not to be long in coming and on 23.9.42 the Director General was able to reply that Aspidistra was complete, that the second mast was one-third up, and that the third mast was on the way to the site from the docks. The Prime Minister was not however satisfied and demanded: 'When will it work full blast? W.S.C. 24.9.42.'

Mr Bruce Lockhart replied[1] that [NAME DELETED] (now named for the first time) informed him that Aspidistra should be able to operate full blast by 13th October. The Prime Minister realised that pressure could be relaxed and minuted: 'Good. Report any adverse change only. W.S.C. 27.9.42.'

The Prime Minister had, however, to be invoked to assist in obtaining spare parts. A telegram from the Prime Minister to Mr Harry Hopkins* asking for tubes or valves brought, however, the unfortunate reply that the valves asked for were 'obsolescent'.[2] This provoked the enquiry: 'Have we really built this gigantic machine dependent on valves which are obsolete with no provision for replacement?'[3]

Mr Hopkins was however, able to provide three new and three used valves by 13.10.42, which in itself provided part of the answer to the Prime Minister's question and Mr Bruce Lockhart minuted[4] that for technical arrangements . . . PWE was in the hands of [NAME DELETED] but that in spite of bottlenecks and the sinking of ships he had probably performed a remarkable feat in getting Aspidistra ready in two months. Because of Torch he had had to put on extra speed.

Director General's Lack of Confidence [WORDS DELETED]

The Director General had already informed the Secretary of State[5] that Aspidistra had been tested at full power and that the tests were satisfactory. The fact that the Director General should have put forward Sir Noel Ashbridge's views in reply to the Prime Minister's question as to the advantages that Aspidistra would give us is an indication that he did not feel full confidence in the technical advice [PASSAGE DELETED ON GROUNDS OF NATIONAL SECURITY]. Further evidence of this lack of confidence is to be found in an earlier minute forwarding a PWE paper on Aspidistra to the Foreign Secretary,[6] in which he quoted Sir Noel

1. Mr Bruce Lockhart to Mr Peck, 26.9.42.
2. Serial T. 1319/2. Personal and Secret to PM from Harry Hopkins, 9.10.42.
3. Prime Minister's personal minute D. 173/2, 16.10.42.
4. Mr Bruce Lockhart to Brig. Jacob, 16.10.42.
5. Air Commodore Nutting to Mr Bruce Lockhart, 20.8.42.
6. Mr Bruce Lockhart to Foreign Secretary, 22.8.42.

* [Harry Lloyd Hopkins (1890–1946), born at Sioux City, was Federal emergency relief administrator in the depression of 1933; US Secretary of Commerce 1938–40; supervised lend-lease programme 1941; a close friend of President Roosevelt, he undertook several important missions during the Second World War, primarily those to Churchill and Stalin.]

Ashbridge as the source from which he concluded that the claims made in the paper were somewhat exaggerated. He added that he would welcome any vetting of the instrument through the Inter Services Wireless Board. The Foreign Secretary endorsed the suggestion. This led to an inspection of the Crowborough installation by members of the Wireless Telegraphy Board.

Meanwhile the problem of control and of the security of Aspidistra so as to conform with Air Ministry requirements led the Director General to seek the advice of Air Commodore Nutting, Director of Signals, Air Ministry, who suggested[1] the appointment of Air Commodore Blandy to PWE.

Air Commodore Blandy's Appointment

The appointment of Air Commodore Blandy received the approval of the Ministers and Mr Leeper and [NAME DELETED] were informed[2] that Air Commodore Blandy had been seconded to PWE for special duties in connection with 79/80 (Aspidistra).

Air Commodore Blandy was not, however, introduced personally [NAME DELETED] nor was he authorised to visit either CHQ, or Crowborough. Air Commodore Blandy was to suffer continual difficulties in the following months owing to Air Ministry complaints of Aspidistra transmissions for testing purposes being carried out without notification. Air Commodore Blandy had been appointed to control such transmissions, but he was given no evidence of their existence by the Department and received no support [PASSAGE DELETED]. One must conclude that this appointment completely failed to achieve its purpose and was a mistake as [PASSAGE DELETED] was, owing to his position, perfectly competent to deal on security questions with the services direct. Air Commodore Blandy did, however, become a most valuable wireless adviser to PWE. He was of particular value as a source of wireless intelligence to the PWE Department of Plans.

Discussions of the best uses of Aspidistra had continued at CHQ since the spring of 1942 when a committee had been appointed by Mr Leeper. Many of the plans suggested were based on false estimates of the capabilities of the instrument. Its limitations were summed up in the phrase: 'kilowatts cannot overcome kilometres' by its critics.

The distance at which a medium-wave wireless signal is audible is proportional to the square root of the power by which it is transmitted. As distance increases an enormous increase in power is therefore required, and the power necessary to make a medium-wave wireless signal audible *during* daylight at a distance of several thousand miles is not in fact available. The question of how far [NAME DELETED] would be able to increase the

1. Air Commodore Nutting to Mr Bruce Lockhart, 20.8.42.
2. Mr Bruce Lockhart to Mr Leeper, 25.9.42.

signal of Aspidistra by directional methods was unknown. Aspidistra could be used in overt competition with the enemy whenever its signal was comparable in strength with that of an enemy station in the following variations of what is known as 'white intruder' operation.

1. By transmitting on exactly the enemy wavelength during intervals in the enemy programme or when the programme closed down.
2. By transmitting on exactly the wavelength of an enemy station when it went off the air owing to the approach of an RAF raid.
3. By transmitting on a wavelength very close to the enemy's 'coming in alongside', so that many listeners would be likely to tune in to it. Such a programme might be the genuine enemy programme with added material.

Later experience showed that Aspidistra was indeed a unique instrument of Political Warfare. On medium wave it was able to transmit alongside and drown most enemy transmissions except in the immediate neighbourhood of the enemy transmitter, owing to its power, or to switch at short notice into a vacant frequency owing to its special equipment, or to intrude into an enemy programme at the moment it was taken off, owing to RAF activity, by relaying into the channel, with only a minute interruption, the same programme taken from another German station still on air. In the latter case the enemy audience remained unaware that the programme to which it was listening had closed down. It was then possible to insert special announcements, etc., into the enemy programme which bore all the marks of being genuine and which would completely deceive the audience.

Political Warfare and the North African Landings. Political and Strategic Background. The Second Front Agitation

Throughout 1942, taking its cue from official Soviet propaganda, a popular demand for the opening of a Second Front in Western Europe in order to relieve German pressure on the Eastern Front, grew in intensity. Those responsible for this agitation which was conducted by public meetings, by speeches, and questions in Parliament, and in the press, stated that British strategy was in the hands of timid and incompetent soldiers whose policy of caution was the result partly of the wish to put off an exposure of their own incapacity and partly by malevolence towards Russia. The extreme partizans of the Second Front continuously declared that Britain's honour was at stake and large numbers of the public, which was necessarily ignorant, became perturbed. The agitation for a Second Front was damaging to our propaganda to Western Europe, since it was difficult to reconcile the delay with British and American propaganda on the vast output of munitions, and the excellence of the armies in training.

All through the summer of 1942, the agitation for a Second Front increased and it was not allayed by the large losses at Dieppe, where our

Sir Stephen Tallents, Controller of the overseas broadcasts of the BBC, 1940–41.

Sir Campbell Stuart, whose Crewe House organisation of the First World War provided the model for PWE in the Second.

Sir Reginald 'Rex' Leeper: a senior PWE figure in the early days.

'Let Nation Speak Unto Nation': the BBC's Bush House in 1949.

The University of London's Senate House in Malet Street, the imposing headquarters of the wartime Ministry of Information.

Richard Crossman: journalist, politician, intellectual and diarist, a master of the art of psychological warfare.

Sefton Delmer: Britain's most fertile 'Black' propagandist, the hero of this book.

Hugh Dalton as Minister of Economic Warfare in June 1940, only weeks after Churchill ordered him to 'Set Europe Ablaze!'

Alfred Duff Cooper in June 1940: in the hot seat as Minister of Information.

Woburn Abbey, ancestral home of the Dukes of Bedford used by PWE during the Second World War.

Sir Stafford Cripps, Ambassador in Moscow 1940–42, leaving Downing Street during a visit to London in June 1941.

Brenden Bracken having just been appointed Minister of Information in July 1941.

Colonel William 'Wild Bill' Donovan, American spy-chief and a founder of the CIA.

The intense gaze of a young David Garnett:
novelist, intellectual, journalist and Bloomsberry.

troops had landed and successfully maintained themselves for nine hours only to be withdrawn.

In the early summer of 1942, the proposal for landings in French North Africa with a simultaneous landing in the South of France was under examination by the advisers of the President and the Prime Minister; the adoption of such a plan would obviously go far to meet the Soviet requests and might allay the agitation for a Second Front. The United States diplomatic representatives had made extensive preparations for such landings.

Such landings could not be considered strategically apart from the military situation in Egypt and were timed to occur after a decisive battle for the defence of the Nile valley had been fought. The battle of Alamein was fought on 23rd October, and the Axis forces were in full retreat across Cyrenaica when the landings in French North Africa showed that before long they would have to fight on two fronts in Africa, if not in Europe.

Mr Robert Murphy, the representative of the State Department in North Africa, had twice made tentative proposals to General Weygand and had each time been repulsed, after which he was finally forced to look elsewhere for a leader. Mr Murphy was firmly of the opinion, expressed two years before by Mr Leeper, that 'if there was to be a revolt it must be led by someone of position and most men of position such as General Weygand and General Nogués would not be associated with a left-wing movement'.

Reasons Against Fighting French Participation

Mr Murphy was undoubtedly right in thinking that General de Gaulle would be positively harmful for the purpose they had in mind. In 1941 and 1942, Gaullisme was not only a negligible political force in French North Africa, but the participation of General de Gaulle in the landings would have violently antagonised all the men who held positions under the Vichy Government, whose support the Americans rightly regarded as essential if bloodshed on a considerable scale was to be averted.

For the same reason though British troops were to take part in the landings, their presence was not announced and the British paratroops who captured the Algerian aerodrome wore armlets with the letters 'US' upon them. The landing was planned throughout as an American operation. The instructions given from the Prime Minister to PWE was to act as a 'handmaid to the Americans'.

The Pro-Allied Conspiracy in Algiers

Mr Murphy was in close touch with a group of conspirators in Algiers which included M. Henri d'Astier, M. Rigault, M. Lemaigre-Dubreuil, Dr Aboulker and others. Although drawn from varying political groups, a number of these men were not only ardent monarchists but held positions of importance in the Vichy Administration of Algiers. General Mark Clark* landed from a British submarine to make final plans in concert with these conspirators for the landing. General Giraud, who had been approached again had finally agreed to come to North Africa and shortly before the landings was picked up by a British submarine off Bandol and taken to Gibraltar. He was, however, under the misapprehension, first, that he was to be Commander in Chief of all forces in North Africa including the American and the British, and secondly, that a landing in the South of France would be made which he thought was likely to force the Vichy Government to take up arms against Germany in the mountain redoubt of the South of France. General Giraud had made preparations for this eventuality with General de Lattre de Tassigny, whose subsequent attempt at a rising led to his arrest.

Mr Robert Murphy was at the last moment faced with an embarassing wealth of 'men of position' with whom to negotiate, as Admiral Darlan, who, apparently aware that something was in the wind, mysteriously returned to Algiers, ten days after having completed a formal inspection of the North African defences.

The explanation of Admiral Darlan's presence in Algeria at the time of the landing may have been due to some arrangement with Mr Murphy and the State Department, or may only have been due to the fact that the Admiral's son was in hospital and was only just off the danger list after an attack of infantile paralysis.

The North African landings were astonishingly successful as regards the deception of the enemy. The concentration of Allied ships and transports was known, but both the Germans and Vichy French were at first convinced that a second assault on Dakar was intended and on the eve of the landings, reinforcements were sent from Algeria to the AFO territories. Even after the Allied Fleet and transports had passed through the straits of Gibraltar, both the German and Vichy authorities were convinced that it was destined for Malta to build up a force for an attack on Sicily. In Algeria, however, a conviction that American landings were about to take place was widespread.

PWE Preparations for the Landings in North Africa

There is some difficulty in tracing the exact developments of PWE preparations for the landings in North Africa. PWE was ordered to render all possible assistance to this American operation but arrangements with the

* [General Mark Wayne Clark (1896–1984) came from a military family and graduated from West Point in 1917; wounded on active service in Europe; commander US ground forces in Europe 1942; narrowly escaped capture by Vichy security police when he landed secretly in Algeria prior to the Operation Torch Allied invasion of North Africa 1942; commanded 5th Army in Italy, US forces in Austria and then US forces in Far East.]

Americans were largely verbal and there are few formal requests from the Americans in PWE files.

Delay in Ticketing French Regional Specialists for Torch

The Director General was aware before 18th August, 1942, that preparations were in progress for landings in French North Africa.[1] But the French Regional Director was not informed of the impending operation by Brigadier Brooks until 3rd September when he and his secretary were ticketed for 'Torch',[2] but for some weeks he was unable to carry out any extensive preparations as his subordinates were not ticketed and he was forbidden to inform them. Throughout the period of preparation, security precautions rendered the work difficult owing to the exaggerated fears of the Security Officer who, at that time, regarded some of the most senior members of the Department as insecure.

Lt Colonel Sutton, who had the lessons of the Madagascar landings to guide him, requested that a certain number of British officers should be immediately trained in order that they should accompany the landing parties. Brigadier Brooks thereupon saw the DDMI(O) at the War Office who agreed to his request. The conditions governing their release were that they should be transferred to PWE pay-roll and that no requests for the commissioning of o.r.s. would be agreed.[3] Twenty-four officers and eleven o.r.s. were chosen for a knowledge of French and were sent to CHQ for a training period of about three weeks. The arrangements for the course were made by the PWE Security Officer, Colonel Chambers. The training was under the direction of Major Sedgwick, assisted by Major Hackett of the SOE/PWE Training School, and the principal lecturer was Dr Beck. The training was hampered by the stringency of the security rules which forbade that they should be informed of where they were to be employed.[4] The object of the course was to impart detailed local knowledge of what they would find in North Africa with merely a background knowledge of conditions in France.

Other PWE responsibilities assumed by the French Regional Director, or asked for by the American representatives, Mr Percy Winner and Mr Warburg, were the arrangements necessary for presenting the news of the landings to the French people by leaflets and broadcasts, providing printing

1. Minute from the Director General to S. of S. for Foreign Affairs, 18.8.42, on the subject of the withdrawal of the PWE Mission in Gibraltar.
2. Inquiry into N. Africa (conducted by D. Jenkins), 14–22.2.43. Torch was the code name for this operation and will be used here.
3. Brigadier C. S. Vale (DDMI(O)) to Brigadier R. A. D. Brooks, 6.10.42.
4. The 'Cover Plan' which had the merit of being true was that these officers had been transferred to the strength of PWE and that they were being given a general course of training in PWE before taking up their duties. Lt Col Ken Johnstone, who was to be head of the British party for N. Africa and who had previously been a member of PWE, was 'put in the picture' shortly after 7.10.42.

facilities including the printing of certain Black documents of American origin, purporting to have been printed in France; transmitting certain operational code messages through the BBC to inform OSS agents in North Africa of the time of the operation; and drafting texts of communiqués and statements by General Eisenhower.

Joint PWE/OWI Plan for French Empire

Representatives of PWE and OWI drew up a Joint American British plan for Psychological Warfare within the French Empire.[1] The chief interest of this plan, which had slight influence upon events, or upon the policy pursued in North Africa, lies in the amendments made to it by the Secretary of State for Foreign Affairs. Thus the sentence 'to create a representative French authority in French North Africa acceptable as such to Frenchmen everywhere' was amended by the insertion of the words 'free of Axis influence', and the object 'to cause all French territories to rally to the United Nations' was amended to read 'to sever their connection with Vichy and to rally to the United Nations'.

These corrigenda indicate that the Foreign Secretary was alive to the dangers ahead and wished to have on record provision against collaboration with Vichy. The French Regional Director was, as might be expected, less well-informed about American intentions.

In addition to the American British plan the French Regional Director drew up a draft contingency naval plan to cover procedure in case of opposition by the French fleet and a plan for propaganda to the French Merchant Marine in North African harbours.

A time plan 'of arrangements necessary to initiate broadcasts, leaflets and other notifications that the Torch operation was in progress'[2] dealt with arrangements at Gibraltar and in London, Washington, and in North Africa itself after the capture of the Algiers transmitter.

Apart from the practical arrangements in which PWE was responsible for the release of the President's and General Eisenhower's broadcasts from its high-powered station (Aspidistra) and for initiating leaflet disseminations over unoccupied France,[3] or, if the landings were postponed, notifying SOE agents by a short-wave message in code, the plan included a statement of the organisation of the Psychological Warfare Section.

---

1. Dated 15.10.42.
2. Memorandum for Chief of Staff signed by Brigadier General Lemnitzer, US Army, 24.10.42. Brig. Gen. Lemnitzer was one of the officers who had landed in N. Africa with General Mark Clark from a British submarine to discuss plans with leaders of the local resistance movements headed by M. Henri d'Astier and Dr Aboulker.
3. The plan refers to dissemination by US aircraft in the UK but actually all the leaflets in connection with Torch dropped in France were disseminated by the RAF and all the leaflets for French N. Africa by the Fleet Air Arm and RAF aircraft of Coastal Command. No disseminations were made by US aircraft.

Organisation of Psychological Warfare Section

Chief of the Political Section on Staff of C. in C. (General Eisenhower):	Mr W. H. B. Mack (British)
Senior Supervisor:	Mr Percy Winner (American)
Associate Supervisor:	Mr Edmond L. Taylor (American)
	Lt Col K. Johnstone (British)

Under the direction of Mr Mack, Mr Winner will be responsible for co-ordinating the activities of the four teams: HQ, Oran, Algiers and Casablanca, of which the section is composed. He will be assisted by Mr Taylor and Lt Colonel Johnstone in questions affecting American and British personnel.[1]

The organisation set out in this plan was not final. It would appear that during the early days of Torch OWI personnel were seconded to the staff of the C. in C. and that some weeks later PWB [Psychological Warfare Branch] took over in the person of Colonel Hazeltine. The exact status of such civilians as Mr Winner and Mr Taylor at different times is rather obscure and in some cases Americans have acted in dual capacities as members of OWI and officers of PWB.

PWB[2] was a branch of the US War Department and functioned as part of Military Intelligence, under the US Chiefs of Staff to whom its executive chief was directly responsible. Its work was based on the assumption that Psychological Warfare was an integral part of the Armed Service, and not a new Service in itself, and that therefore Psychological Warfare must be based on the plans of the Chiefs of Staff.

Colonel Hazeltine Head of PWB

Colonel Hazeltine's power in Algiers was due to his being part of the American Army.[3] As such he was able to obtain such necessities as billets, uniforms, transport, typewriters, etc., which are the sinews of psychological war, but which were not as easily obtained by American civilians, or British handmaids.

The British members of the teams were: nineteen officers and o.r.s. for AFHQ at Gibraltar, afterwards transferred to Algiers. This team was under the command of Major Macfarlane who had had printing experience in France, and included three experts from PWE staff, namely Captain Greenless from the Italian Region, Mr Lambert, a Moroccan expert, and Mr Brereton, a wireless expert formerly on the PWE Gibraltar Mission.

1. From Memorandum dated 12.10.42.
2. Political Warfare Operations in the Americas.
3. He was an American cavalry colonel, twenty-six years in the service.

There were two parties for the Oran landings, the first of three officers and one sergeant, the second of three officers and three o.r.s. There were two parties for the Algiers landings, the first consisted of Lt Colonel Johnstone, Major Sturt and Captain Lieven, with one o.r. clerk, and the second Algiers party, of three British officers. Independently attached to the navy, there were two officers. The Casablanca party was entirely American.

The Policy Problems of the Landings

While PWE was actively engaged in furnishing the American Psychological Warfare Branch and OWI with the practical assistance they were likely to require, many of the policy problems raised by the landings were foreseen and were causing grave concern. It was realised that the universal disappointment that the landings had not been in Western Europe would be accompanied in France, by suspicions of our motives for launching attacks in the Torch area. There was also the question of how far our appeal should be based on a straight Nationalist anti-Boche issue and 'at what point we should introduce the "class" element and introduce "anti-Fascism"'.[1]

The ignorance of American plans which were to govern the course of events is strikingly evident in the above. Its writers were far from suspecting that Mr Murphy was contemplating installing le Comte de Paris in power as a Bourbon Regent or of coming to an agreement with the Vichy authorities.

An appreciation of the Political Warfare Situation in Western Europe in the Light of Torch was drawn up on the orders of the Foreign Office and the Chiefs of Staff and is dated 15.10.42. Among the conclusions were:

> In general, between now and zero hour, PWE's policy towards France should be changed as little as possible. This recommendation also applies to PWE's present policy of discrediting Vichy.
> In the event of a naval clash with the French fleet, either before or after the landings the responsibility must be pinned on Hitler, Laval and Darlan.

The above paper was approved by the Foreign Office and the Chiefs of Staff on 20.10.42 and the French Region was requested to revise the French Working Plan where necessary.

A final version of a General Directive for the Torch Operation was drawn up on 30.10.42. Beyond stressing that Torch was an American operation, and that no reference to British participation should be anticipated until announced, that it must not be represented as a Second Front, or as a

---

1. PWE Memorandum entitled Military Communiqués in their relationship to Political Warfare, 11.10.42, put forward as a basis for discussion [of] problems connected with Torch by the Director General, 12.10.42.

signal for revolt in Europe, and that no direct instructions must be given except by subversive agencies, the directive added little. But it committed PWE to fixing the blame for a possible naval clash on Hitler and 'his French agents' Laval and Darlan.

General Directive for Torch Reveals Lack of Contingency Planning

It is inconceivable that this would have appeared in a directive dated twelve days before the landings had there been a full and frank discussion of policy to be adopted in all possible contingencies, between the State Department and the Foreign Office, or even between OWI and PWE. No joint Anglo-American contingency planning on policy matters for Torch apparently took place. It does not seem to have occurred to anyone that the policy underlying the training of officers who were to serve in the Prime Minister's phrase, as 'handmaids to the Americans', should have been jointly agreed with OWI. The need for such planning was revealed when a 'Black' publication of American (OSS) origin was shown to PWE. This was a yellow book, purporting to be produced by anti-German elements in the Vichy Administration. It was entitled 'Les Violations de l'Armistice Franco-Allemand'.

PWE policy objections to this publication[1] were that no moral indignation was shown against those who had favoured the Armistice and that it made no moral or emotional appeal to resume the fight. PWE also made the practical objection that the format given it by OSS would reveal its origin. Should this happen, it would cause indignation among patriotic Frenchmen. An edition was therefore printed in a more plausible Vichy format and produced by PWE[2] by about 15th October for OSS.

By serving as a 'handmaid', PWE was, however, able to exert some influence on American policy, particularly in regard to details. Thus Mr Panaguian drafted a booklet entitled 'North Africa', a copy of which was handed to all members of the United Nations forces participating in the Operation. Although it was considerably amended by Mr Winner, PWE views on many fundamental points found expression in it.

> Millions of Frenchmen are going to see the point no matter what their Nazified Government tries to tell them. . . . In France itself, especially in the Occupied Zone, the people have been putting up a better fight against the Nazis than their leaders succeeded in putting up . . . ever since 1940, many Frenchmen have continued to fight openly on our side, in the armed ranks of the United Nations.

---

1. Memorandum from Mr Paniguian to Brigadier Brooks, 25.9.42.
2. By the Howe Unit.

PWE Propaganda to France in Connection with Torch

PWE was able to plan propaganda to France for Torch on the model of propaganda in connection with the landing on Madagascar, but was able to command greater facilities.

Leaflets

The leaflets dropped in France were:

1. The texts of President Roosevelt's message to the French people.
2. The *Avis* issued in the name of the Governments of the United States and of Great Britain.

Eisenhower's appeal to the French forces in North Africa.
Eisenhower's general appeal to the French in North Africa.
An illustrated booklet recalling American and French co-operation in the First World War.

A detailed analysis of the numbers of leaflets dropped over unoccupied and occupied France[1] during the forty-eight hours of D and D+1 shows that a total of 16,102,400 were dropped out of 17,051,200 supplied. All the targets were well covered except Toulon, a priority target which was of the first importance on account of the presence of the French Fleet. But of a total of 1,020,800 leaflets supplied for dissemination there, 486,400 or rather less than half were dropped.

The grand total dropped in France during the four days that the operation lasted amounted to 22,388,200 leaflets out of a total of 25,568,000 supplied by PWE.

The priority targets for unoccupied France were Vichy, Lyons, Marseilles and Toulon; those for occupied France were Paris, Lille, Roubaix and Tourcoing. The operation was extremely satisfactory.

Broadcasts

The special broadcasts by the BBC in connection with Torch consisted of:

1. A broadcast message to the French people by President Roosevelt in French which had been recorded and brought over.
2. A general warning *Avis* in the name of the United States and the British Governments.
3. A broadcast by General Eisenhower's spokesman.
4. A British supporting statement.

With the exception of the supporting statement, leaflets and broadcasts were identical.

---

1. Supplied to Brigadier Brooks by Major Ryder, 13.11.42.

Aspidistra

At a meeting of technical experts under the chairmanship of General Ismay and attended by Mr Bruce Lockhart[1] it was agreed that Aspidistra could only operate effectively from one hour after sunset to one hour before dawn, and that for a special operation the instrument could be safely used for longer than ten minutes in spite of the danger of its serving as a navigational guide to hostile aircraft.

The principal object during Torch was to make known the official proclamations by President Roosevelt and the Prime Minister to the populations of France and French North Africa. The counterfeiting of enemy-controlled programmes was a purely subsidiary object. For the first purpose it was wisely decided to use Aspidistra to reinforce the BBC[2] French Services on one wavelength and not to broadcast President Roosevelt's and Mr Churchill's proclamations either alongside a Vichy wavelength or on a new wavelength of its own. It takes time to build up an audience.

The Chiefs of Staffs Committee[3] agreed that any risk in using Aspidistra during the forty-eight hours after Torch would have to be accepted, but that if it were required to use Aspidistra after that period on other than BBC wavelengths, authority must be sought from the Chief of Air Staff.

Aspidistra was accordingly used[4] from 12.21 hours on 8.11.42 for forty-eight hours to reinforce the BBC Foreign News Service, except for two periods of a quarter of an hour each from 04.45 to 05.00 and from 05.45 to 06.00 hours on 8.11.42, when Aspidistra broadcast independently on the Rabat Vichy-controlled Moroccan wavelength. Following these broadcasts at 10.30 a.m. Vichy radio warned listeners that 'so-called official broadcasts from Rabat' emanated from an unknown clandestine station. One of the results of the transmissions on Rabat wavelength was to cause a temporary impression in the Admiralty OIC[5] that Rabat had been captured by our forces, owing to our communiqués being heard coming from Rabat.

This was an early example of the difficulty of carrying out counterfeit operations without informing all on our side who might be misled by them. This difficulty dogged the Aspidistra plans till the end.

Aspidistra continued linked with the BBC European Services after the first forty-eight hours and continued to give them 40% extra power. Thus thanks to Aspidistra, PWE was able to overcome the jamming of the BBC French Services at a most crucial moment in the formation of French opinion.

---

1. Mr Bruce Lockhart to S. of S., 1.10.42.
2. Use of Aspidistra in Torch, 25.10.42.
3. COS(42)369(0) 305 meeting, 2.11.42.
4. Mr Bruce Lockhart to Lt Gen. Ismay, 13.11.42.
5. Air Commodore Blandy to Brigadier Brooks, 13.11.42.

The value of Aspidistra can be gauged by the following: Aspidistra radiated 650 kilowatts. The total power of the BBC Foreign Services was 200 kilowatts. The range of a medium-wave radio transmitter in daylight increases as the square root of the increase in power of the transmitter.

The use of Aspidistra is stated to have increased the effective range by 175%, and must have made an enormous difference to the reception through jamming in Metropolitan France. The frequency changes to Rabat wavelength were made by a team of inexperienced men, and completed in from 7½ to 9 minutes. These times were considerably reduced later.

Aspidistra had done all that it had been allowed to do with triumphant success on its first trial. [NAME DELETED ON GROUNDS OF NATIONAL SECURITY] was promoted to Brigadier early in 1943.

Leaflet Disseminations on North Africa

Leaflets were disemminated partly by RAF Coastal Command Catalina Flying Boat and Hudson Aircraft based on Gibraltar and partly by Fleet Air Arm aircraft belonging to three aircraft carriers of the Royal Navy.

The quantities were as follows:[1]

By Catalina aircraft on Algiers	
By Hudson on Oran	A total of 1,296,000 copies.
By Hudson on Casablanca	

Dissemination by Fleet Air Arm aircraft over Algiers and Oran was planned as follows:[2]

HMS *Furious*:	444,000 single leaflets.
HMS *Formidable*:	600,000 single leaflets.
HMS *Victorious*:	672,000 single leaflets.

A total of 1,716,000 copies.

In addition, 1,260,000 of General Eisenhower's leaflet No. 2 and 756,000 of a Special Naval leaflet were available at Gibraltar for dropping on the Torch area, the decision resting with General Eisenhower. It is believed that these plans were carried out.

Political Events in Algiers during and Immediately after the Landings

The exact time of the landings was communicated to OSS agents by code signals transmitted by the BBC on orders from PWE acting for the Chiefs

1. Brigadier Brooks to Colonel Sutton, 8.10.42.
2. Brigadier Brooks to Colonel Sutton, 7.10.42.

of Staff at Allied Force HQ. On receipt of this signal the group of conspirators headed by Dr Aboulker and Mr Henri d'Astier seized power for twelve hours in Algiers and were waiting for the American landing parties to enter the town. They captured Admiral Darlan and all the leading Vichy officials and Mr Murphy had an interview with Darlan while the latter was under arrest. But the Rangers under General Ryder hesitated and delayed with the result that the conspirators had lost control before their arrival.

General Giraud who had discovered that he was not to fill the position of General Eisenhower refused to proceed to Algiers and remained at Gibraltar, with General Eisenhower and his British political adviser, Mr Mack.

In the desperate situation caused by General Giraud's delay, Dr José Aboulker made a broadcast pronouncement in which he impersonated the General. But within a few hours the conspirators lost control of the position.

In the precarious situation which developed, Mr Murphy had a second interview with Admiral Darlan, after the latter had regained his freedom, and secured his support in return for recognition as the High Commissioner and legitimate head of the French administration.

The results of this recognition were to secure an immediate ceasefire order which enabled the Allied troops to land in full security. General Giraud and General Eisenhower arrived shortly afterwards, but the former went into retirement for three days. Later on he was appointed by Admiral Darlan to be Commander in Chief of French Forces.

The Landings in North Africa

Although the majority of the Psychological Warfare Branch officers who did much to make the landings possible were British and members of PWE, no reports were received by the French Region of PWE of the operation in which they took part. All communications had to be made by them through official military channels that is to say through Colonel Hazeltine, the American head of the Psychological Warfare Section who took over from Lt Colonel Johnstone on 18th November, and if any reports were made, they were not forwarded. PWE French Region was for some weeks without any information as to what the officers which it had trained were doing or had done, and without any of the intelligence material which was urgently needed for Political Warfare to France and other parts of Europe.

It was not until PWE officers returned to Britain, or felt impelled to send back reports on their own initiative and found means to have such reports smuggled out of North Africa, that PWE obtained detailed information of what had taken place.

Story of the Landings

Later on the sequence of events was made clear in an Inquiry into the Events in North Africa conducted by Mr Jenkins for the Director of Plans.

Lt Colonel Johnstone stated that the Algiers party was to go in two waves, six with Johnstone with the first wave of troops, the remaining ten with the second wave.

Johnstone and the leading six 'by mere chance' went in the same boat as the 6th Commando to Algiers. There was no prearranged plan for contacting the French, and on the way out Johnstone volunteered the chance suggestion that he should contact the French if possible. OC 6th Commando agreed.

The landing on 8.11.42 was at 4 to 4.30 a.m. instead of at 1 a.m. as planned. Lt Colonel Johnstone, Major Lieven and Lieutenant Donegan US Army landed with 6th Commando.

> During the morning [8th Nov., 1942] a French Colonel came to 6th Commando (by chance, not previous arrangement) and said that orders had been given not to resist but that these orders had been countermanded by the local French General (Juin's) Chief of Staff. Owing to delay the situation was becoming strained and there would be serious consequences unless we got 3 battalions into the town at once. We had not this force, but ultimately during the afternoon the Americans attacked against resistance (getting into the town on 9th) the show having by this time developed into a full military operation.

Captain Lieven, who was with the party detailed to take Fort Duparre, was able to reduce resistance by shouting through a megaphone and also to help in smoothing matters down as negotiator after cease fire.[1]

Johnstone did not get much chance during the battle stage (though he did what he could with his megaphone) as the force he was with were operating at long range. That night they lay in a wood outside the town, and next morning received news of the armistice (concluded about 5.30–6.30 p.m. on the 8th).

In the morning [9th Nov., 1942], the armistice having been arranged, Johnstone went in a US truck on a cleaning-up expedition, ending at the German Consulate in Algiers. Johnstone carried out the arrest of the German Consul and his staff, and sent them off to the fort appointed for their reception. Later the same day, Johnstone made contact with the Americans, reported to Colonel Holmes (who was with Murphy at Allied force HQ) and put himself at his disposal.

The remaining three of Johnstone's advance six turned up [10th Nov., 1942].

Radio contact with US via London on short wave was established [14th Nov., 1942] for McVane (NBC) and Collingwood (US News representatives) and Dunnett of [the] BBC. Algiers Radio was equipped with both medium and short wave, the medium designed for internal use, with relays

1. Captain Lieven was awarded the MC.

at Bone and Oran, was taken over by Johnstone but was handed back to the French on Murphy's instructions.

Colonel Hazeltine (US Army) arrived from Gibraltar [17th Nov., 1942] with Winner (OWI) and Taylor (OSS), Hazeltine said he had come to take over control of psychological warfare. Johnstone (as 'handmaid to US') agreed and thereafter operated under him.

Johnstone left to visit Constantine, Suk Akras and Bone [28th Nov.–6th Dec., 1942] – contacted local officials. At Suk Akras he found Lieven in hospital (wounded in foot). He had been at Bone and in Tunisia with 6th Commando and had done very well.

Brigadier McClure (US Army) was sent out from London [in December] to deal with Allied Force HQ in all matters concerning Political Warfare, Censorship, Public Relations. Holmes thenceforth acted under McClure and was relieved of censorship.

On 24th December Darlan was assassinated.

The Effects of Mr Murphy's Policy

The first event after the cease-fire order which appeared to justify Mr Murphy's policy politically was that M. Boisson declared that French West African territories accepted Darlan's authority. General Nogués, the Resident in Morocco, also recognised Darlan's authority, but did all he could to serve Vichy and Axis interests by dispatching military intelligence to Vichy and getting officers loyal to Vichy out of Morocco, via Tangier and Spain.

The immediate military gains of Darlan's recognition were obvious. The political disadvantages have been well summed up by a Frenchwoman[1] whose assessment is accepted by Colonel Sutton, Mr Paniguian and M. Mangeot who was sent out to North Africa by PWE.

> As to the normal result of the State Department's policy, I think purely and simply that it was disastrous in this particular instance. The whole of Europe was shaken by the cynical use made of Darlan. For Belgium, Norway, Holland, Yugoslavia, Greece, Denmark, Poland, Czechoslovakia, all had their renegades of tomorrow, ready to be made use of by the United States.

The evil effects of the policy in Algiers itself was reported to PWE in a letter[2] signed by three British officers which was smuggled out of North Africa. It gives a clear picture of the plight of PWE officers serving as 'handmaids'.

---

1. 'Algiers 1941–1943' by Renée Pierre-Gosset.
2. Letter to Major Baker White PWE from Captain Robertson, Lt Skeaping and Lt Vernon, 22.1.43.

> Radio Alger is completely in French hands and does not permit the Allies to use it in any way for propaganda. They also jam all incoming French stations so that monitoring is rendered useless as far as French is concerned. . . . Leaflets are not being considered as yet. . . . We are powerless to do anything to improve the situation or even to communicate through the proper channels with you. . . . In conclusion, we implore you to give this report your most urgent attention as the situation, from our point of view, is deplorable.

Fortunately the British officers were not the only members of the Psychological Warfare Branch to realise the dangers. Their American opposite numbers, though officially in agreement with State Department policy, soon diverged from it.

> How could the American diplomats possibly have heard the ditties sung by little girls in the courtyards of council houses:[1]
>
> Y a pu d'feu
> Vive Pucheu
> Y a pu d'pain
> Vive Pétain
> Y a pu d'argent
> Vive Darlan.[3]

OWI Opposition to the Murphy Policy

On the other hand, the members of the Psychological Warfare Section were recruited from newspaper reporters and Gallup Poll experts, accustomed to pry into everything. They questioned everybody. As their eyes opened to the truth, the policy of the Psychological Warfare Section deviated more and more from that of the diplomats, still frequenting only a limited circle of friends.

> Very soon[4] the Office of War Information found itself in total opposition to the representative of the State Department. . . . And Mr Robert Murphy, in his violent self-defence, soon became the instrument that merged the Gaullist cause with that of all patriots fighting with all their might to rid themselves of Vichy. Without intending to do so, he associated himself in his fight against the Gaullists with everything in Algiers which represented the survival of a dishonoured régime. The

1. 'Algiers 1941–1943' by Renée Pierre-Gosset.
2. Letter to Major Baker White PWE from Captain Robertson, Lt Skeaping and Lt Vernon, 22.1.43.
3. One of the songs originated by the BBC 'Les Trois Amis'.
4. 'Algiers 1941–1943' by Renée Pierre-Gosset.

> more the systematic opposition of the State Department towards Gaullism grew, the more did the Gaullist movement itself gain power. Mr Robert Murphy was not erecting a wall in front of de Gaulle supporters, he was placing a spring-board under [their] feet. . . . Admiral Darlan, put into power and maintained there by American bayonets, did more for Gaullism than the most devoted propagandist of the movement.

Effects of the Darlan Agreement on PWE Propaganda

The embarrassment [in] which the American recognition of Admiral Darlan placed PWE was not confined to the effects on our friends in all the countries of occupied Europe. On receipt of the news almost the whole British staff of the French region of the BBC stated that they would resign, in which they were supported by the Director of European Broadcasts, Mr Newsome.

A meeting was held which lasted for several hours and the resignations were only finally withdrawn on the impassioned pleading of M. Jacques Duchesne as well as of the PWE French Regional Director.

The period before Admiral Darlan's assassination was a time of acute strain and depression for all members of PWE. The assassination which was apparently the culmination of a Royalist plot (Mr Murphy would apparently have supported the recognition of the Comte de Paris as High Commissioner) removed an odious personality and an embittered enemy of Britain, but it did little else. For after General Giraud had become High Commissioner almost all those who had conspired and collaborated with the Americans before the landings, such as the Aboulkers, were arrested on the fantastic charge of conspiring to assassinate Mr Murphy.

The realisation of the grotesque discrepancy between President Roosevelt's words: 'Je salue encore et acclame encore et encore ma foi dans la liberté, dans l'egalité, dans la fraternité,' and the policy of the American representatives of the State Department grew steadily, and as we have seen, Mr Murphy himself unconsciously helped to bring about union with General de Gaulle. But as Britain had never decided on a joint Anglo-American policy in North Africa, and as we did not attempt to justify the recognition of Darlan, or the installation of the nominees of Vichy except as a temporary expedient, we were able to profit from American mistakes and British prestige began to rise.

The need for a joint Anglo-American policy was first felt by OWI representatives, who for reasons which have been explained above were more in sympathy with the British attitude than with that of the State Department.

As a result of a visit to Algiers of high OWI officers, Milton Eisenhower and Brophy, it was decided[1] that North Africa should be an Allied and not

1. Telegram No. 59 HM Consul General, 22.12.42. To Bruce Lockhart from Colonel Johnstone.

exclusively American propaganda base and that PWE should be asked to participate on equal terms under agreed joint directives, the American participants being OWI and OSS.

Recognition of PWE Services in Connection with Torch

Before the landings had taken place, Brigadier General Bedell Smith, General Eisenhower's Chief of Staff at Allied Force Headquarters (Norfolk House), wrote to the Secretary of State for Foreign Affairs to express his gratitude for the help PWE had provided during the planning for Torch,[1] and stressing PWE's work in acting as translators and printers to the expedition, a service which only PWE could have performed under the necessary conditions of secrecy.

The Secretary of State for Foreign Affairs brought this letter, nonetheless gratifying because written before the landings had taken place, to the attention of the Prime Minister and conveyed the thanks and congratulations of His Majesty's Government to the Director General and his staff.[2]

The recognition of PWE's work expressed in this letter was reinforced by the inclusion of the Director General in the New Year's Honours List as KCMG and the promotion of Brigadier Brooks to the rank of Major General and of Lt Colonel Sutton as Colonel.

The Director General passed on the congratulations he had received in personal letters to Mr Leeper, Mr Kirkpatrick, Brigadier Brooks, Mr Meikle, [NAME DELETED ON GROUNDS OF NATIONAL SECURITY], Mr H. K. Robin, Mr Calder, Colonel Sutton, Mr Crossman, Mr Melson Smith and Mr Scarlett.

The PWE Inquiry on Torch

Though locally successful, the policy adopted in North Africa was a setback to Political Warfare in Europe. As we have seen it brought about violent protests in the shape of threatened resignations in the BBC staff and protests from such bodies as the ITF and hostile comment in the Liberal and Labour British press and in Parliament. What was more important was that it produced a mood of abrupt disillusionment among resistance groups and the BBC audience in occupied Europe.

For these reasons the Director General agreed to an Inquiry[4] in[to] the North African Operation being made by Mr David Jenkins, KC, assistant to the PWE Director of Plans.

This inquiry showed how completely subordinate the position allotted to

1. To the Rt Hon. Anthony Eden MC, MP, from Brigadier General W. Bedell Smith, Chief of Staff US Army, 2.11.42.
2. Letter from the Rt Hon. Anthony Eden MC, MP, to the Director General, 9.11.42.
4. Inquiry on North Africa, 22.2.42 (Director of Plans files).

PWE had been – that of handmaid to an American body which had itself been unable to influence American policy.

After establishing the course of events, the paper set out certain recommendations[1] as regards future policy.

> It will be well to consider what course PWE is to take if similar situations arise in the future. The line of least resistance is obviously to interpret 'handmaid' instructions as justifying PWE in ministering without question to US policy wheresoever it may lead, and disclaiming all responsibility for the result. If this is the line to be taken then *cadit quaestio*. If, on the other hand, it is felt that in such circumstances PWE notwithstanding the strict letter of the terms of reference should endeavour to exert an effective influence in the right direction on US policy, when it seems to be going wrong, the following suggestions are made:
>
> 1. PWE should prepare its own appreciation and plan, which should be practical and constructive documents, founded on the most complete and up-to-date intelligence which PWE can command, and dealing with the actual facts, personalities (acceptable or otherwise), political parties, etc., in relation to the particular country concerned in sufficient detail to form a basis for positive action in accordance with British policy. Such appreciations and plans should so far as possible be prepared in advance as 'Contingency Plans', and approved in the contingency stage by the Foreign Office. If left until the country concerned actually becomes the object of a joint British-American operation, the time factor is likely to refer PWE back to the Americans when guidance on policy is sought.
> 2. Armed with an appreciation and plan of the order contemplated in 1 above, PWE will have something constructive to set against America's ideas in so far as these differ from PWE's and will have far more prospect of arriving at a joint plan acceptable to both than if (as in the North African case) they embark on discussion with the US without any appreciation or plan of their own.

Mr Jenkins recommended also that planning should be done centrally, that if a difference on policy arose with the Americans, PWE should state its case in writing. Mr Jenkins also recommended in regard to practicable details that longer should be devoted to training PWE personnel and that they should be given more instructions and the details of the plan they are expected to carry out. Major Jenkins also stressed the need for communications with PWE and for the supplies of British propaganda material.

---

1. Inquiry on North Africa, 22.2.43 (Director of Plans files).

Secret Broadcasting and Torch. F4 Radio Gaulle

F4 began broadcasting on 25th August, 1941, and closed down owing to difficulties arising from the divergence in policy with the De Gaulle organisation after the landing in North Africa and the Anglo-American attitude to General Giraud and Admiral Darlan.

The speakers on F4 were serving officers of the Fighting French forces, provided by it, and owing allegiance to it, and for the greater period of its existence, the policy of the station was worked out at a weekly meeting between PWE and Fighting French representatives at Hill Street, presided over by M. André Philip, Commissaire for the Interior.

Policy

The chief propaganda themes of Radio Gaulle were that French misfortunes were due to the Compiègne Armistice for which Marshal Pétain was responsible; that General de Gaulle had rejected the Armistice from the beginning and had become the symbol of French resistance; that French interests and honour alike, made it imperative for France to re-enter the war on the side of the Allies.

All forms of sabotage and underground activity were persistently applauded and encouraged. Active campaigns were carried out on the need for French labour to resist going to Germany. Radio Gaulle also attacked the anti-Semitic policy of the Vichy Government.

Radio Gaulle was conceived of as a medium through which to train certain types of Resistance groups. But neither PWE nor the Fighting French evolved any concrete plan in this direction and little was done to direct activity into such channels as gathering information about enemy troops, supply dumps, aerodomes, etc., listing local collaborators, forming contacts with personnel holding key positions such as telephone operators, railway workers, police chiefs, etc.

The speakers did not explicitly state that the station was in France but they frequently implied it. Nevertheless, after the station had been running for a year, a member of the Resistance movement stated that the BBC was not the only successful medium of propaganda – there was Radio Gaulle which was much listened to and which was universally believed to be in France. He was much impressed by the cleverness of its organisers in avoiding the police.

The first difficulty encountered was that none of the team supplied by the Fighting French, Messieurs Hattu, Vourc'h and Faul, were experienced speakers with a command of microphone technique, nor were any of them instinctive orators. The first task of those in charge of the station was to make the speakers study elocution and the oratory of the French revolution and learn their scripts by heart. But no study of this kind could make them the equal of naturally talented broadcasters.

The weekly meetings with the Fighting French at Hill Street were attended by Mr Cunard for PWE who was at this time Housemaster for both F3 and F4. If any doubtful point involving a divergence of policy between PWE and the Fighting French arose, it was Mr Cunard's duty to refer it to Dr Beck, who in turn might refer it to Colonel Sutton, the Regional Director.

There was therefore from the beginning far more attention paid to the policy of F4 than to the policy of any other RU and this close supervision to some extent defeated its own ends, by destroying the illusion of complete independence which is one of the attractions of a secret broadcast and one of the proofs of its authenticity.

F2, for example, enjoyed freedom and consistently attacked Admiral Darlan, both before and after his arrival in North Africa. It was therefore generally believed to be a Communist station. When violent differences arose between the De Gaulle organisation and the British and Americans, it was incredible that a Gaullist station, inside France, should be trimming its sails and supporting the latter. Yet it was difficult to give Radio Gaulle as much freedom as F2 since several American visitors had been let into the secret of its existence before the landings in North Africa. The Foreign Office had quite enough on hand without the complication of defending a policy of allowing General de Gaulle to use his own Freedom Station in England to denigrate Anglo-American policy in North Africa.

The difficulties continually arising owing to the increasing strain between De Gaulle and HMG led to the proposal that Radio Gaulle should be closed at once. Mr Paniguian pointed out[1] that PWE's constant efforts to tone down Gaulliste directives would do more to cause bad feeling on the part of the Fighting French than closing the station altogether. On the other hand if the National Committee became more representative, a voice would be needed to explain the changes. The silencing of Radio Gaulle, after closing Radio Catholique, at a time when aircraft disseminations had decreased was a serious matter. Mr Paniguian therefore suggested an agreement with the Fighting French to avoid controversial points. Such an agreement however would cut at the authenticity of the RU.

PWE was determined in any case not to put out any line in the General's name which he could regard as objectionable. 'I can just imagine[2] what the feelings of ardent resisters in France must be when they hear the author[3] of the phrase "les Allemands généreux" shouting "Vive le Maréchal" under the protection of the Stars and Stripes and the Union Jack.'

The attitude of PWE to the question of closing F4 was influenced not only by the political difficulties involved in keeping it going, but by the relatively poor quality of the broadcasts, the failure of F4 to develop into an operational station directing resistance, and by the fact that F5, which

1. Mr Paniguian to Mr Leeper, 3.10.42.
2. Mr Paniguian to Colonel Sutton, 14.11.42.
3. Admiral Darlan.

suffered from none of these drawbacks, had been opened in the last days of September 1942.

Matters came to a head early in December and on 9th December, 1942, M. Boris was informed that F4 had been suspended at short notice.

It would appear that the Fighting French authorities attached considerable importance to Radio Gaulle as a potential instrument for directing resistance in France, since M. André Philip made two approaches to PWE, one on 3rd January, 1943, and one on 4th February, 1943, to reopen this station. But, as it will be seen, the question of reopening it was linked with the maintenance of F5 not less closely than had been its suspension.

F5 Radio Patrie

Early in 1942, Nicholas Boddington returned from an exploratory visit to the South of France having made contact with a resistance organisation the leader of which was known as Carte. The information as given by Carte to Boddington, and brought back by him to SOE, was that this organisation had many links with the relics of the French Army, that it was widely spread and had great potentialities as the nucleus of a 'secret army'. This news was welcome in SOE which under Brigadier Gubbins was becoming militarised and thinking in terms of 'secret armies' of trained men.

The Carte organisation, as originally described, made an immediate appeal to the trained military mind.

As Carte had expressed himself anxious to have a transmitter in Britain for the purpose of directing his organisation, Dr Beck was instructed to run a new resistance radio for SOE, the personnel of which would be provided by SOE and paid by that body.

Major Boddington was accordingly sent back to France in the summer of 1942 to collect suitable personnel and returned after an agreeable and prosperous voyage from the S. of France to Gibraltar in a sailing felucca, with Messieurs Gillois and 'Massidou' who were both experienced broadcasters.[1]

F5 or Radio Patrie was started immediately after their arrival in the last days of September 1942. About a month later M. Massidou returned to France to report on reception, leaving sufficient recordings of his own voice to give the Gestapo the impression that he was still broadcasting from Britain. He was, however, arrested and, after many misadventures, was imprisoned in Buchenwald concentration camp from which he was liberated in the spring of 1945. To take his place Claude Dauphin[2] and his sister were brought over, arriving in England about mid-November 1942.

It is not surprising that the Fighting French National Committee in England should have been extremely critical of these developments at a

1. Gillois had been programme director of Radio Cité and 'Massidou' editor of the Radio Journal de France.
2. The famous French actor.

time when acute strain had developed between General de Gaulle and the British Government over Anglo-American policy in North Africa,[1] and the Gaullist RU had been closed.

On the one hand, General de Gaulle had reason to suppose himself supplanted outside France by General Giraud and even by Admiral Darlan as personalities more acceptable in American eyes; on the other, he saw [the] Gaulliste movement inside France supplanted by the resistance organisations led by Carte, Radio Gaulle suppressed and Radio Patrie started. Nor was this all, since Radio Patrie frequently referred to General de Gaulle himself as 'a symbol of resistance', and the General, whatever his faults, had no wish to become a mere symbol.

While the Carte organisation was probably even more of an unknown quantity to the Fighting French than to SOE and PWE, certain features of the broadcasts of Radio Patrie aroused profound misgivings among Fighting French experts. The first step taken in this matter would seem to have been warnings by Radio Brazzaville to the French people against broadcasts by non-qualified organisations.[2] General de Gaulle expressed his indignation at the use of his name by Radio Patrie with the implication that he and the National Committee approved of the instructions which it gave in a letter to the Secretary of State for Foreign Affairs, and demanded that the station should be closed immediately.[3]

More serious criticisms were raised in the course of December by M. André Philip, who not only protested against the political attitude of Radio Patrie to the Gaulliste groups inside France but drew attention to the dangers which were likely to befall those who followed the instructions given by the station.

Ill-Conceived Instructions Broadcast by F5

One of Radio Patrie's functions was to broadcast instructions that registers written on small pieces of paper should be made of loyal Frenchmen and that a chain of members affiliated to the organisation should be built up, without any two members knowing the identity of a third. Officers of the organisation were to present themselves and be identified by the members by giving a pass word on their first visit which should be included in the broadcast of F5 before their second. The methods suggested, which had been approved by SOE, were seriously criticised by M. Philip on the grounds that broadcast instructions of this sort would lead to the

1. Neither the French National Committee nor those responsible for daily negotiation with them on the subject of F4, were told of the existence of F5. The discovery came as a shock which led General de Gaulle to believe he was being doubly 'double-crossed' by us.
2. Colonel Sutton drew the attention of the FO to these warnings in a letter of 25.12.42, surmising that they were directed against our own secret broadcasts. The warning was coupled with an instruction that Free Frenchmen were not to broadcast over the BBC.
3. Letter from Gen. de Gaulle to Foreign Secretary, 30.12.42.

recruitment of well-intentioned and stupid people who were the predestined victims of the Gestapo which would be able to use the organisation to obtain lists of French patriots. After an impartial study of the correspondence it is difficult not to believe that M. André Philip was right.

The objections raised were countered by three general lines of argument, first that the plan had been drawn up by experts, secondly that it was a matter for SOE and thirdly that it was controlled by a Resistance organisation in France. Dr Beck, however, admitted M. Philip's criticism but attempted to belittle it.

> Some people in France may give themselves away by foolishly acting in such a way as to betray that they are attempting to form a link in the general organisation. Such people exist in all countries, and it is better that they should be eliminated, or eliminate themselves at the very beginning.[1]

Such an admission bears out M. Philip's accusation that 'le plan est exécuté, sinon conçu avec une légèreté singulière'.[2] For no underground movement can afford to throw away the enthusiastic raw material of resistance for lack of instruction, nor can any underground movement show itself indifferent to the damaging effect of presenting the enemy Gestapo with a number of easy victories and of gaining a reputation for leading its innocent and inexperienced supporters to disaster.

M. Philip coupled his criticism of the instructions issued by F5 with a strong protest at the way in which the station had referred to the Gaulliste groups in France which F5 had declared were: 'Trop connues par la police et reperées par l'ennemi.' He was therefore on strong ground in declaring: 'Nos amis ont vue dans les propos de Radio Patrie une intention délibérée de saboter nos organisations et d'en débaucher les membres.'[3]

F5 Exacerbating Relations with General de Gaulle

SOE and PWE were naturally unwilling to concede that F5 and the Carte organisation was not what they had been led to believe and the dispute dragged on, seriously endangering the British efforts to bring about a working agreement and a meeting between General de Gaulle and General Giraud.

Mr Peake indeed asked that instructions should be given to Radio Patrie, 'a particularly stinging thorn in De Gaulle's flesh at the moment', to keep to the general directive of the BBC French Services.[4]

General de Gaulle's letter of protest on the subject of Radio Patrie was

1. Memorandum from Dr Beck to Mr Leeper, 20.12.42, commenting on M. Philip's letter of 18.12.42.
2. Letter of M. Philip to Colonel Sutton, 31.12.42.
3. *Ibid.*
4. Mr Peake, British Representative to the Fighting French National Committee to Foreign Office, 16.1.43.

left unanswered for three weeks. When given, the answer was evasive stating that Radio Patrie was the mouthpiece of a resistance organisation in France which was responsible for the instructions given.[1]

Five days later, General de Gaulle unwillingly attended the Casablanca Conference and his attitude was not uninfluenced by the thorn of Radio Patrie rankling in his flesh.

Disillusionment with Carte

Matters had reached this state when Carte himself was brought over to this country and the PWE and SOE representatives were profoundly disquieted by the conferences which followed.[2] Carte had quarrelled with his principal lieutenant and both the 'secret army' and the Carte organisation were to all intents and purposes imaginary. It was moreover clear that the policy of carrying on Radio Patrie in the face of warnings given against it by the Fighting French could only result in splitting up and weakening resistance in France. Once this had been realised, the problem became not merely how to save what was possible from the wreck, or how to save face, but how to effect a real understanding which would prevent such divisions occurring in future. In this PWE played a notable and remarkably adroit part by insisting on bringing all the warring elements together in a weekly meeting, which it was foreseen, would have a great influence on matters far outside the direction of Radio Patrie.

PWE Reconciles Warring Elements

After a conversation with Dr Beck on 10th February, 1943, M. Philip agreed to the creation of a single station for all resistance movements, combining the activities of Radio Patrie with those of Radio Gaulle.[3]

The proposal in this letter was immediately accepted and the reply[4] underlined the necessity for any station devoted to French resistance to work in collaboration and complete harmony with the important resistance groups inside France such as *Combat* and *Libération* which had already rallied to General de Gaulle. The full details which followed[5] accepted all the proposals in M. Philip's letter but stated that a weekly meeting on which all the interested parties would be represented would be required to control the programmes. The right to exercise censorship was explicitly reserved and technical differences of opinion on resistance matters would be decided by the British representative of SOE, Mr Robin Brook. In spite of the two last

1. Letter to Gen. de Gaulle from Foreign Secretary, 21.1.43.
2. Major Boddington states that Carte was mad. Dr Beck qualified this by the words 'not actually certifiable'.
3. Letter from M. André Philip to Dr Beck, 15.2.43.
4. Letter of Dr Beck to M. André Philip, 16.2.43.
5. Letter of Dr Beck to M. André Philip, 20.2.43.

reservations, the letter expressed a wholehearted wish that Radio Patrie should serve the needs of the Gaulliste organisation as well as those of SOE and M. Philip had every reason to be satisfied.

Just as the agreement was being concluded the assistance of Major Desmond Morton was invoked by the Fighting French to stop the Carte instructions regarding the formation of a register of patriots.[1]

F5 reconstituted

But the controversy regarding these registers was already closed in favour of the Gaullistes. A month's delay ensued while the views of the Gaulliste resistance leaders inside France was being obtained, but, by the end of March, the only outstanding point was to be the name of the station. This was satisfactorily settled by the suggestion of *Honneur et Patrie Poste de la Résistance Française*. There was a further delay in working out the directive. The station began functioning under its new name on 17th May, 1943.

The wavelengths of Radio Patrie were kept for these transmissions and two further transmissions a day were added at 22.30 and 23.00 hours.

The chief points of the reconstructed programme were:

Personnel: M. Gillois, M. Claude Dauphin (accepted by France Combattante as their representative), M. Schmoll (representing France Combattante).

Control of F5: PWE were the responsible managers with a right of censorship particularly with regard to military security and international policy or relations of France and her allies. PWE was also responsible for seeing that the Control Committee's directives were carried out. SOE, both D/RF and F sections,[2] were responsible for co-ordinating instructions given with the policy of the General Staff in regard to underground resistance movements. The directives were worked out at a weekly meeting attended by representatives of PWE, SOE F and D/RF sections, France Combattante, the personnelof Honneur et Patrie and any representative of resistance groups when present in England, with Dr Beck in the chair.

By the end of the year, Radio Patrie was the recognised official voice of French resistance and was widely known in France, though it did not have a large and regular audience as it was very heavily jammed and could not be easily heard in the north and coastal regions of France. The efforts made to improve the service were to increase the supply of intelligence by a reorganisation of the French intelligence section [of] PWE, by strengthening the already good broadcasting team and by cutting down the time between

1. Letter from Major Desmond Morton to Colonel Sutton, 10.2.43.
2. That is to say the Head of the Free French Liaison Section and the Head of the British section working independently in France.

recording and transmission to a minimum. The most obvious need for F5 and other RUs, that of increasing the power of the transmitters used, was not proposed as it was known to be impossible to obtain more powerful transmitters at that period in the war.

On 23rd April, 1944, the French National Committee proposed that F5 and F3 should be closed down in the near future as M. Gillois was required to broadcast as the official voice of the De Gaulle organisation for giving instructions to resistance movements over the BBC. PWE accepted this view and Honneur et Patrie accordingly closed down on 14th May, 1944. After an interval of a fortnight, when the audience might suppose he had reached England, M. Gillois began broadcasting instructions on the BBC.

F5 in the form of Honneur et Patrie, had done a magnificent piece of work, not the least important of which was to bring together in weekly session the competing elements directing French resistance from Britain.

Co-operation with the Americans in London and [the] USA. Mr Crossman's Visit to [the] USA

Mr Crossman had made a visit of sixteen days to Washington and New York in October 1942 and submitted a report on his return. In it he pointed out that the fundamental weakness of OWI was lack of Intelligence, whereas the strength of OSS was Intelligence of which no use was made. OWI was therefore ready to rely, for its Intelligence and Planning as regards Europe, on London, but was building up its own organisation for the Far East. There were bound to be reactions against such dependence on the British and Mr Crossman advised that an OWI representative should be seconded to the Directorate of Plans London and that a British representative should attend OWI directive meetings in New York. He also pointed out the need for a BBC European Services transmitter beamed to America and the setting up of an 'American desk' in London to service the PWE Mission in America with the necessary guidance in advance on news before it became public. He also stressed the need to keep the Mission in touch with regional problems.

Although these recommendations were made in the middle of October, those concerning the servicing of the Political Warfare Mission in America with weekly letters and full guidance did not become effective until most of them had been made again, a month after Mr Miall's* return at the end of the year, when he was appointed American Relations Officer.

* [(Rowland) Leonard Miall (b. 1914) was President of the Cambridge Union 1936; joined BBC and inaugurated talks broadcast to Europe 1939; BBC German talks features editor 1940–2; member of the PWE Mission to US 1942–4; director of news, San Francisco, 1943; head, NY office, 1944; personal assistant to Deputy Director-General PWE London 1944; attached to Psychological Warfare Division of SHAEF 1945; rejoined BBC 1945; chief correspondent in US 1945–53; controller, overseas and foreign relations, BBC, 1971–4.]

Mr Miall's Report. OWI Broadcasting to Europe

Mr Leonard Miall was seconded to the British Political Warfare Mission with orders to co-operate with OWI Radio Division New York. He found that OWI had built up its own radio organisation. This meant that it was not staffed by experienced broadcasters and there was ignorance of technical facilities.

Limitations of OWI Broadcasting from [the] USA

It was therefore technically far behind the BBC. Mr Miall stated that the private stations had continued to broadcast up till the day before the landing in North Africa without being given any direction. They were then taken over.[1] There was an absence of any intelligence material except that received from PWE and BBC owing to the hostility of OSS. OWI had no proper monitoring organisation and were not allowed to do monitoring themselves. The monitoring reports they got gave insufficient data. It was also almost impossible to listen to any BBC European Service. Mr Miall recommended that the main BBC language bulletins should be beamed so as to be audible in [the] USA. It was particularly necessary that OWI should know the line the BBC was taking on any story as it broke and for checking details of news items such as figures of aircraft shot down, etc., for demonstrating British standards of presentation and finally it could be useful for the foreign minorities in the USA.

A weakness was that OWI, by insisting on all programmes being written in the languages and not translated, had been forced to employ émigré staff.

PWE Influence on OWI

British PWE representatives in New York influenced OWI output by attending the daily editorial conference, the daily policy guidance meeting, central and regional directive meetings, and by helping to draft regional directives. Finally the British representatives were continually appealed to for every kind of information.

British influence was instrumental in making OWI realise such elementary points as the influence of jamming and of the time of day when the audience could listen. It was also exerted to secure the appointment of Americans as heads of the German and Italian sections instead of émigrés, to persuade them that intelligence was the basis of output, and to arrange for regional directive meetings in which writers and sub-editors could meet intelligence officers and those in control of policy. OWE were also persuaded to introduce personality broadcasters and to aim at making the broadcasts a projection of America rather than a belated and frequently inaccurate version of the BBC.

1. It is not clear whether they were still working on a Donovan directive.

Mr Miall reported on the extremely high standing of the British Political Warfare Missions. His reports ended with the words: 'It is a great personal pleasure to co-operate with such friendly colleagues British, American and Canadian in work in which British supremacy is so generally recognised.'

Mr Miall after working for three months in the PWE Directorate of Plans returned to America on 4.3.43. During his period working as American Relations Officer he inaugurated a series of regional background letters from one officer in each of the Regions to Mr Bowes Lyon which form a particularly valuable record of how PWE was dealing with the day-to-day regional problems. Interesting as they are they suffer from the fact that no hint of the internal struggles which at that time were rending the French Region was allowed to appear.

The day-to-day work of the British Political Warfare Mission was naturally largely concerned with attempting to get OWI to conform with PWE regional policy and to act on PWE regional intelligence. One such example is the objection to the use of Yankee Doodle as a signature tune to American rebroadcasts in Holland, Norway and Italy in which there were heavy penalties for listening to the Allied Radio which could be immediately identified if Yankee Doodle were to be overheard. Another was the proposal made in [the] USA by the mother-in-law of the owner of the *Petit Parisien* and *Le Dimanche Illustrée* to publish a pro-Allied weekly in North Africa. PWE French Region pointed out that the *Petit Parisien* was one of the first French newspapers to collaborate whole-heartedly with the Germans and that *Le Dimanche Illustrée* drew a large subsidy from Vichy and consistently attacked the British and Americans.

OWI Co-operation with PWE

The proposals which had been made by Mr Crossman with regard to the attendance of an OWI representative in planning and at regional directive meetings in London and of the British representative in New York at OWI central and regional directive meetings were put into effect and by the beginning of the following year Bowes Lyon reported that Sherwood recognised the importance of joint action everywhere: i.e. in North Africa where[1] PWE should not be dependent on OWI. Sherwood was about to visit North Africa himself. Soon afterwards the BPW Mission warned the Director General[2] that there was danger in accepting North Africa as a precedent unless OWI and OSS were willing to accept British direction in British theatres, and the Director General was also warned to obtain at least Mr Elmer Davis' endorsement for all agreements made by Mr Sherwood and if possible the approval of the State Department and the Chiefs of Staff should be sought. The reason for this warning was that Sherwood's position was

1. Bowes Lyon to Lockhart, 3.1.43.
2. Bowes Lyon to Lockhart, 28.2.43.

thought to be precarious owing to complaints that OWI were sabotaging the State Department. These complaints undoubtedly referred to the fact that OWI men in Algiers had become aware of the disastrous effect of Mr Murphy's policy in North Africa on French opinion everywhere. The fears of Sherwood's losing power proved groundless.[1] Not only did President Roosevelt issue an order making OWI responsible for all phases of foreign propaganda activities involving the dissemination of information which should be subject to the approval of the Joint Chiefs of Staff in areas of projected military operation but the OWI budget was passed after hearings by the Congressional Appropriations Committee, without any of the charges made against OWI having been substantiated.

PWB North Africa

The chain of authority and organisation of PWB North Africa had been established by a charter of 3.12.42[2] issued from AFHQ. This document stated that 'the Psychological Warfare Section is part of the Civil Affairs Section co-ordinated by G1' and was organised into five sub-sections or groups. The organisation is made plain by a diagram.

Psychological Warfare Section
Group A
Executive

Group D Collection and Evaluation		Group B		Group E Preparation and Distribution	
Group F Monitoring	Group G Collection	Group H Evaluation	Group I Preparation	Group J Dissemination	Group K Selection

Group G
Special Missions

The Psychological Warfare Section did not long remain part of Civil Affairs.[3] On 1.2.43 Brigadier General McClure was appointed head of a newly formed Information and Censorship Section on General Eisenhower's staff. Colonel Hazeltine remained head of PW Branch under Brigadier General McClure for nearly a year.

The staff memorandum[4] of 1.7.43 under *Organisation* stated the PWB 'amalgamated the activities performed by Office of War Information,

1. Mr Sherwood actually lost most of his power in February 1944.
2. AG 321.9.
3. Psychological Warfare in the Mediterranean, 31.8.45.
4. Staff Memorandum 56, AFHQ, 1.7.43.

Psychological Warfare Executive, Ministry of Information, and part of the Office [of] Strategic Services'.

> The Psychological Warfare Branch will co-ordinate the Office of War Information – Psychological Warfare Executive joint propaganda directives with the plans of the theatre as directed by the C. in C. On the tactical level all Psychological Warfare Branch detachments in the field or on special missions will be attached to the HQ of the unit in whose area they are serving and will be for the support of the area commander.

Colonel Hazeltine visited London in February 1943 and made known his requirements both from British and American sources. The American side of PWB was being heavily reinforced[1] and OWI had established a 'school of indoctrination' at which fourteen men had been trained and for which a future forty were being recruited.

Colonel Hazeltine's requirements from British sources were impressive and bore out the views of M. Mangeot as to his intention of making N. Africa the base of all PW teams for liberated Europe.

They were formulated in discussions with Lt Colonel Fairlie of PWE and amounted to seventy officers (some of whom might be civilians) and forty-three o.r.s. including a certain number of technicians and sergeants. In all, his requests were for over 110 British personnel. Colonel Hazeltine was anxious to have Major MacFarlane appointed as his second in command and head of the British team, but PWE did not favour the choice of an officer with no experience of the Department.[2] It was therefore proposed to appoint Colonel Jefferies – who was equally without experience – and to give him training.[3] Whatever the advantages of such an appointment it necessarily delayed what was urgent.

While these discussions were proceeding, PWE was taking steps to secure better representation in North Africa and obtain the information which was sorely needed both for policy decisions and output.

M. Mangeot's Report on PW in N. Africa

Mr Barman was sent out temporarily, attached to the staff of the Resident Minister. In addition, an experienced officer of the Department was needed to carry out some of the urgent work of pro-British propaganda which Lt Colonel Johnstone had reported as necessary. Mr Sylvain Mangeot was temporarily seconded to the MoI to carry it out, making use of *Panorama*, a lavishly illustrated periodical edited and produced by PWE for the MoI as the chief propaganda medium.

---

1. Mr Walter Adams British PW Mission Washington to Director General, 6.2.43.
2. Lt Colonel Gielgud to Director General, 15.2.43.
3. Lt Colonel Gielgud to Director General, 10.2.43.
4. Mr Sylvain Mangeot to French Section, 4.3.43.

Mr Mangeot reported on the conditions[4] stressing that the press and local wireless operated under and extremely oppressive French censorship and that British newspapers, weeklies, monthlies, illustrated magazines, etc., were desperately needed as background and ammunition for the local press. He suggested also that Duchesne should go out for a very limited time to see things for himself.

Colonel Hazeltine's Ambitions and Character

Mr Mangeot reported that Colonel Hazeltine quite openly regarded North Africa as the coming centre of PW operations for all liberated territories and himself as the man at the wheel. 'Hence his voracious cries for bodies and still more bodies.'

Mr Mangeot's estimate of the dangers of PWE was one of the factors in PWE's decision to send out a representative powerful enough to influence events.[1] For Colonel Hazeltine was not only an ignoramus but was quite prepared and, in fact, determined to carry on all propaganda in the name of his C. in C. from Algeria to Tunis and thence to Italy, France, Germany and Scandinavia.

Mr Mangeot reported:

> the more I see of things here, the more imperative I feel is the need for policy to be framed and enforced from London. If we repeat the tragic mistake of letting things slide and awaiting events, there is no telling what ghastly muddles we shall not be involved in – wading across Europe in tow of incredible American ignorance, and even more incredible American personalities. All the good work that PWE has done from London will be wasted and we shall appear as first-class hypocrites or plain fools, or both.

Mr Mangeot's letter though addressed personally to Mr Paniguian was read by the senior members of the Department and, reinforced by Mr Barman's report, did much to bring about the decision that Mr R. H. S. Crossman should go out.

Mr Mangeot warned PWE that[2] Bergeret was particularly dangerous because of his control of the military intelligence bureaux and his pretensions to contacts with resistance inside France. Bergeret believed that the only salvation for France was a coalition between the remnants of the Army there and the military set up in North Africa – an authoritarian government which would restore order from N. Africa.

1. Most Secret and Personal letter from Mr Sylvain Mangeot to Mr Paniguian, 15.3.43.
2. Most Secret Personal letter from Mr Sylvain Mangeot to Mr Paniguian, 15.3.43.

The Relative Importance of French Military Bodies and of Civilian Resistance

Mr Mangeot could not have written more appositely. The view that the important element in French resistance was to be found in the relics of the Army rather than among the civilian resistance movements was one which had always been prevalent in SOE. It was the existence of this view which had led to the foundation of F5, Radio Patrie, devoted to the interests of the Carte organisation after the closing of F4 Radio Gaulle at the time of the North African landings and PWE/SOE policy in respect of these stations had done much to increase the difficulties of bringing about a modus vivendi between Generals Giraud and de Gaulle which PWE on other grounds was most anxious to secure. Although Mr Mangeot was unaware of the situation in regard to Radio Patrie, he had reached exactly the same conclusions as were forced on those responsible for it in PWE after the arrival of Carte for discussions. During the spring of 1943 PWE became convinced not only that the Carte organisation was itself dangerous and not what had been claimed, but that the SOE view that small secret bodies of trained soldiers, or ex-soldiers, was the most important factor in French resistance was a major blunder. From this estimate PWE never receded and the work of the Department in securing the acceptance of its views of French resistance as a widespread popular movement was one of its major contributions to the speedy liberation of Western Europe.

Reorganisation in North Africa

During his visit to North Africa, Mr Sherwood planned a reorganisation[1] which should ensure greater authority to OWI by making it responsible both for supervision of domestic information to North Africa and foreign propaganda from North Africa. As regards the latter PWE/OWI were to carry out the joint PWE/OWI directive.

On Mr Sherwood's return to [the] USA, Mr C. D. Jackson was appointed head of PWE/OWI integrated set-up in North Africa under General McClure, head of PWB. An ambiguous telegram from Major General Brooks announcing this reorganisation alarmed Mr Vellacott, head of PWE Mission Cairo, who pointed out that this might mean that he would be responsible to Jackson. However, a definition of spheres which followed dispelled these fears.

After his return to America, Sherwood cabled to Lockhart on the need for two good men – one OWI and one PWE – to work under Jackson. Mr Sherwood had agreed that Major MacFarlan (British) should be in charge of front-line propaganda and that 'Hazeltine would consequently be eliminated from the picture'.[2] It was some time before this was in fact brought about.

1. Sherwood to Lockhart, 13.4.43.
2. Sherwood to Lockhart, 27.4.43.

PWE and OWI Co-operation in Broadcasts

Divergent British and American policy to France, following the Torch landings, had offered an obvious opportunity to German propaganda and both PWE and OWI were concerned in countering this. One method which was to prove effective was Radio 'Reciprocity'. That is to say OWI transmissions agreed to stress points connected with the British war effort in exchange for the BBC doing the same in regard to the American. Thus OWI would put the emphasis on the 8th Army and the BBC on the American Army in Tunisia. Moreover, in the spring of 1943, considerable extension of the BBC European Services owing to more transmitter time being available enabled the BBC to increase the time allotted to OWI rebroadcasts on medium wave.

Miall returned to America specially in order to be on the spot when these services were inaugurated and was immediately concerned to improve their quality[1] as their feebleness had caused concern in the BBC and PWE.

During June 1943,[2] OWI was anxious to attack such prominent Fascists as Grandi,* Ciano,** etc., and consulted PWE, which however opposed[3] such attacks on the grounds that to single out certain Fascist leaders for attack implied there were others who were better and that 'we could not treat with any Fascists or crypto-Fascists'.

Shortly afterwards the resignation and arrest of Mussolini forced the policy issue to the forefront, and military needs called for its modification.

OWI and Mussolini's Resignation

The OWI treatment of Mussolini's resignation produced a major crisis within that organisation, as the first new commentary was that 'Fascism in Italy had merely put on a new face and rouged its lips . . . the moronic little king, who has stood behind Mussolini's shoulder for twenty-one years has moved forward one pace.' This treatment of the news appeared to OSS and the State Department to provide the opportunity for the overthrow of OWI and a violent press campaign was launched charging OWI with being dominated by Communists. After a week of crisis the violence of these attacks

1. Mr Miall to Mrs O'Neill, 6.5.43.
2. No. 2865. Washington to FO, 22.5.43.
3. No. 4195 of 24.6.43.

* [Count Dino Grandi (1895–1988) was a Fascist quadrumvir after the March on Rome 1922; Italian Foreign Minister 1929–32; Ambassador to London; warned Mussolini of opposition to Abyssinian invasion; count 1937; proposed the motion in the Fascist Grand Council which brought about Mussolini's resignation 1943.]

** [Count Galeazzo Ciano (1903–44) was Italy's Propaganda Minister 1935 and Foreign Minister 1936–43; initially supported his father-in-law Mussolini's war policy but by 1943 he voted for his overthrow; the following year he was dragged from hiding by the Fascists and shot after a brief trial.]

defeated themselves and OWI was able to show that in the absence of further guidance it had in reality only adhered to the directive of unconditional surrender.

Perhaps the most illuminating feature of the episode was the readiness of practically the whole radio staff of OWI to resign if Warburg were made a scapegoat and Warburg's intention to resign[1] 'If American policy was to support another Darlan'. A result of this incident was the proposal that Washington should become the centre for the co-ordination of propaganda policy of London, Washington and Algiers. This danger was averted by the prompt action of Mr Bowes Lyon,[2] the Director General[3] and the Secretary of State for Foreign Affairs.[4]

A note on Combined Control of Propaganda by Washington, drafted by the Director General of PWE, points out that London, not Washington was the base for the vast bulk of propaganda:[5] 'We built up the listener audience: we relay all American medium-wave broadcasts, we fly 90% of the leaflets. Is it seriously proposed to put this smoothly running machine under the control of four amateurs sitting thousands of miles away in Washington?' The same paper pointed out that decisions would be influenced by the Presidential election campaign and would surrender the conduct of political warfare to soldiers.

The Reverse in Tunisia

The Political Warfare problems of Torch, the recognition of Admiral Darlan, his assassination, and the summary execution of his young assassin, and the arrests of our friends, the continued detention of other friends of democracy in concentration camps, were concurrent with the inauspicious opening of the Tunisian campaign.

Military historians may say that with skilful planning and greater initiative and daring, the Tunisian campaign could have been avoided. Had it been possible for preparations to have been made on a sufficient scale, Tunis might have been seized shortly after Algiers. Lack of contingency planning and the relegation of Political Warfare to a subsidiary role made this impossible.

The opening of the Tunisian campaign offered a field for Political Warfare which was not exploited. From the point of view of Political Warfare the confused and heroic early campaign is only memorable for an outstanding piece of uncoordinated front-line propaganda carried out almost single handed by a British intelligence officer with Foreign Office

1. Mr Miall to Mr Bowes Lyon, 30.7.43.
2. No. 3652 and 3653 for Lockhart from Bowes Lyon.
3. Memorandum for Secretary of State from Sir Robert Bruce Lockhart.
4. Telegram from Secretary of State to Prime Minister, 13.8.43.
5. Combined Control of Propaganda by Washington.

experience who had previously been a member of the German Region of SO1, Captain Con O'Neill.*

The American troops had made an almost universally bad impression in Algiers owing to their lack of discipline, their drunkenness and their pursuit of women, an impression which was to lower American prestige throughout the length and breadth of Europe.

Bad First Impressions of US Troops

In their first battles in Tunisia, the Americans confirmed the bad impressions they had created, by being defeated and had it not been for British and French troops, the defeat might well have had far-reaching consequences. From the Political Warfare point of view the contrast between these defeats and the rapid advance of the Eighth Army under General Alexander and General Montgomery was an awkward problem since the invincible strength of the Americans was one of the main themes of our propaganda. Luckily General LeClerc, the Fighting French Commander, by executing a magnificent march across the desert from the Chad territories in time to assist in turning the defeat into victory in Tunisia, provided some material to counterbalance the initial failure of the American troops.

In April 1943, while a joint Anglo-American team for PWB was being built up in Algiers, Captain Con O'Neill had carried out a 'one-man show' of front-line Political Warfare with the 1st Army which is in many ways the most remarkable effort of its kind during the war.

> I managed to fix myself up with the head of the 'I' branch at this HQ that I should get myself transferred to do propaganda to German troops on this front. Only after the transfer had gone through did it transpire that I was trespassing on 'Psychological Warfare' but I managed to overcome their objections and am now attached to them. The fact that Psychological Warfare had made no preparations of any kind for German propaganda made it easier for me to come in as I did, and since then I have in effect had the German field completely to myself.[1]
>
> I have had to settle my own policy, to compose my own leaflets and to get them printed. I have had to provide my own intelligence chiefly by

1. Letter to R.H.S. Crossman from Captain Con O'Neill I Corps, circa 4.4.43.

* [Hon. Sir Con Douglas Walter O'Neill (1912–88) was a fellow of All Souls 1935–46; called to Bar 1936; entered FO 1936; third secretary, Berlin, resigned over appeasement 1939; served in Army Intelligence Corps 1940–3; FO 1943–6; leader-writer, *The Times*, 1946–7; returned FO 1947; head of News Department, FO, 1954–5; Ambassador to Finland 1961–3, the EC at Brussels 1963–5 (where he contracted chronic europhilia); Deputy Under-Secretary of State, FO, 1965–8; leader at official level of British delegation to negotiate entry into EEC 1969–72; director, Britain in Europe Campaign, 1974–5.]

interrogating prisoners of war – and to fix up means of distribution including, till latterly, the actual hand filling of 25 Pdr shells by myself.[1]

Captain O'Neill's Reinvention of the Leaflet Shell

Captain O'Neill stated that the dissemination of his leaflets by air was very unsatisfactory, that dissemination by patrols worked well because the patrols found it good fun; that he provided with leaflets various French and British organisations and individuals who were said to have the means of getting them across, but that he didn't know whether they did. He regarded shells as by far the best and most important method of distribution. He could dispose of about 35,000 leaflets a week by shell and thought 1,000 leaflets by shell were worth 50,000 by aircraft.

> German troops, though plentiful enough are after all fairly thin on the ground. An aircraft may drop its leaflets 25 miles behind the line, where unless they fall near a road no German will ever see them; it may drop them in forests, in swamps, in lakes, in the sea or in inaccessible mountains. But a shell can put them down accurately on an actual German position, on the few square yards out of many square miles where Germans are to be found. The only limiting factors are range, wind-drift during a fall of about 300 feet and the imperfections of the shell itself – which is far from perfect as a vehicle for leaflets as a fair number of them always get scorched or torn.[2]

Captain O'Neill suggested using signal lamps for sending propaganda messages in morse to German troops by night. On the Tunisian front of high hills and wide valleys it would be feasible for such messages to be read at a distance of ten miles or more – the further (compatible with visibility) the better, as the base line over which the signals could be seen would be longer. His idea was to send very slowly, and to repeat several times a slogan such as 'Die Toten kommen nicht nach Haus' or a news flash such as 'Smolensk has fallen'. The object would be to spread rumours and gossip.

In a postscript dated 4th April Captain O'Neill was able to report that firing over 10,000 of a special Austrian leaflet at an Austrian regiment, seven deserters had come over in the course of five days. All knew about the leaflets, and five brought copies with them which they presented on arrival. By the end of April, 85% of the prisoners said they had read leaflets and 15% carried copies on them.

Captain O'Neill rejoined PWE temporarily at the request of the Director of Plans, but no steps were taken by the Department to have experiments on leaflet shells carried out, or the invention improved. His ideas on front-line

1. Letter from Capt. O'Neill I Corps to R.H.S. Crossman, circa 4.4.43.
2. *Ibid.*

propaganda met indeed with active opposition in the Department, particularly in the Military Wing, and an article which he wrote for the Army quarterly on his experiences was suppressed[1] though there was no security objection. Captain O'Neill shortly afterwards rejoined the Central Department, Foreign Office.

The Tunisian Campaign

While the British Eighth Army was steadily advancing across Tripoli and Tunisia to the Mareth Line, and Captain O'Neill was carrying out his own Political Warfare campaign with the British First Army, PWE Directorate of Plans was drawing up documents to guide Political Warfare policy and service propaganda output during the operations that were to ensue.

The first of these was a paper on *Italians in Tunisia* which dealt with the historical, political and economic position of the Italian population, Italian grievances, and the principal French and Italian personalities of the colony. Dr Beck, Chief Intelligence Officer French Region, criticised as exaggerated a statement that Admiral Esteva was directly responsible for the German occupation of Tunisia[2] and for bringing about fratricidal strife among Frenchmen.[3]

Lack of Co-operation between PWE Specialists

The paper had been prepared entirely by the Directorate of Plans since it was quicker and easier to produce the material needed from sources available outside the Department than for it to obtain it from all the relevant branches of the Directorate of Intelligence. At this period it was easier for a member of the Directorate of Plans to go to Balliol College and do the work himself at the Institute of International Affairs than to enlist the whole-hearted co-operation of all the PWE specialists.

This instance is mentioned as it was typical of a grave fault in PWE organisation over a long period of its existence. The paper in question was written in twenty-four hours by the present writer but the practice of producing what were principally intelligence documents in the Directorate of Plans as 'Annexes to the Central Directive' was one which persisted. These annexes provided the material essential to the BBC and all concerned with propaganda output and they were a means of by-passing the restrictions on circulation of PWE intelligence documents enforced by the PWE Security Officer. The necessity for producing such annexes is an indictment not so

1. The article was published later after Captain O'Neill had left the Department.
2. Dr Beck to Lt Col Gielgud, 29.3.43.
3. Admiral Esteva was sentenced to life imprisonment on 13.3.45 on charges of having 'aided the establishment of German and Italian troops on N. African coast and having recruited soldiers for the enemy'.

much of the Directorate of Political Warfare Intelligence, as of the division of the whole British Political Warfare machine into almost watertight compartments and of the use of security rules by different branches of the organisation to maintain their own position at the expense of the efficiency of the whole.

There is no obvious remedy for such a state of affairs, but it was undoubtedly accentuated by the fact that so large a proportion of those concerned with output were not Government servants but members of the BBC.

The New Kind of Planning in PWE

A Political Warfare aide-mémoire on the Tunisian campaign was drawn up in the Directorate of Plans after discussions with Mr Sherwood of OWI and Service representatives. Section 1 dealt with *Immediate Requirements as regards Equipment of Personnel*. This covered communications, interrogation of prisoners of war, photography, radio transmission of photographs, censorship, loud hailers and leaflet shells, and language broadcasters and reporters available for broadcasting reports of the operation to Europe. Section 2 dealt with policy desiderata, Section 3 with definition of periods, Section 4 dealt with themes for each period, Section 5 dealt with proclamations, Section 6 with channels and Section 7 with targets. This aide-mémoire was developed at Policy and Plans Committee meetings which were attended by Mr Wallace Carrol and Mr Hottelet for OWI and DPW (O) (Colonel Sutton) into a Political Warfare Plan. But it was not a paper plan so much as a record of the preparations necessary and the steps taken to make them available in time. As each point was discussed concrete decisions were taken and many of the proposals were as a result put into effect. Thus Mr Lindley Fraser was released from the BBC and sent out to broadcast first-hand reports of the enemy débâcle.

Though in some cases the aide-mémoire did not affect events, it provided useful experience for the Director of Plans and his staff. The chief positive achievement as compared with Torch was to foresee the probable political complications and to commit OWI and PWB to an agreed policy.

PWE Contingency Plans

PWE Directorate of Plans at this period produced two contingency plans which marked an advance in Political Warfare planning.

The first was the contingency plan for the Iberian Peninsula. This document was prepared with the assistance of two Spanish experts, Mrs Pickering of PWE and Mr McCann of OWI, and after conversations with SOE experts on Spain and Portugal. The most searching analysis of all political parties and of their behaviour in face of almost every possible military contingency was embodied in the plan. Thus, had the enemy attempted to cut our lines of communication for the invasion of Sicily,

PWE could have supplied ready-made directives agreed by the FO for the very complicated political situation which would have arisen. The planners had to take into account in all countries violent popular reactions which were the legacy of the Spanish Civil War and which were certain to be aroused when Spain became involved.

The second Iberian plan was prepared in case conditions made it imperative for the UN to forestall a German descent on Spain or to seize the Balearic Islands.

A contingency plan was simultaneously prepared for Turkey. This, however, was not carried out in such detail.

The Surrender of Pantellaria

One month before the attack on Sicily (Husky) an extremely powerful air attack (Corkscrew) was launched on the islands of Pantellaria and Lampedusa. These bombardments were partly with a view to seeing what could be done by bombing unsupported by landing parties, and partly in order to reduce these formidable positions which stood directly in the path of Husky. PWE and OWI were asked[1] to secure necessary control of press and radio so as to prevent any special prominence being given to the bombing of the objectives which should be presented as routine operations to complete Torch. If successful the operation was to be represented as liquidating an Italian Gibraltar and putting the final touch to our command of North Africa; if unsuccessful it should be represented as a large-scale commando raid.

The air bombardment was accompanied by leaflets and letters to Admiral Pavesi calling on the garrison to surrender. On 9th June, 1943, the refusal of the garrison to surrender in answer to these demands was mentioned in the Italian communiqués and the MoI asked[2] for information regarding the bombardment so as to be able to handle the matter. The difficulty proved a short one as Pantellaria surrendered two days afterwards to the first officer of suitable rank who landed on the island.

Lt Commander Martelli, of the PWE Italian Section, who had been seconded to PWB, AFHQ, was responsible for the PW arrangements[3] in regard to Pantellaria, writing the letters calling on the commander to surrender and the leaflets, and accompanied the first landing parties.

The personal letters from General Spaatz to Admiral Pavesi, dropped with large streamers attached, had not reached him as the garrison and population remained underground owing to the intensity of air bombardment, and Admiral Pavesi only knew of the summons to surrender from the leaflets.

1. NAF 233 from Eisenhower to Combined Chiefs of Staff, 5.6.43, and No. 7675 from Eisenhower to War Office, 4.6.43.
2. No. 88069, War Office to Freedom Algiers, 9.6.43.
3. Letter from Lt Com. Martelli to Mr Victor Cunard, 22.6.43.

Lt Commander Martelli reported that he did not find one man who was not anti-war, anti-German and anti-Fascist. Most had seen our other leaflets and produced copies.

Admiral Pavesi's decision to surrender was taken and was communicated by wireless signal to Malta before he was aware that a convoy with landing parties was approaching the island. It would appear that the Admiral justified his decision to surrender on the grounds of a lack of water; it was however considerably influenced by the appeals made to him to surrender through our leaflets.

Husky and the Conquest of Sicily

The operations which ended in the complete clearance of the enemy in North Africa were followed by the invasion of Sicily – which appeared a most formidable undertaking before it had been embarked upon. It was the first full-scale landing upon open beaches of a sea-borne expeditionary force during the war. Moreover Sicily was so obviously the next move strategically that it was difficult to hope that the enemy would not concentrate his forces for its defence; indeed the task of strategic deception with regard to 'Husky' appeared at first sight virtually an impossibility. Actually strategic deception of the enemy was most successful. The method of achieving it was 'the double bluff' – that is to say so much discussion and news in the press and on the wireless about military operations directed against Sicily was permitted that the enemy came to the conclusion that we were going to land either on the Greek islands or in the South of France.

PWE and OWI were invited to prepare plans for propaganda and psychological warfare to assist in Husky,[1] both before and after the invasion had begun. In reply[2] the following policy was laid down:

> Up to the moment of invasion a firm line should be followed without any promises, emphasising 1. The hopelessness of Italy's position. 2. The attack will be pursued with all possible force on all possible occasions. 3. Passive resistance and sabotage of the Italian war effort should be encouraged. 4. Appeals to premature revolt and ridicule of the Italian armed forces should be avoided.
> Immediately after the invasion hope should be held out for the future of Italy and the Allies should be presented not as conquerors but as liberators.
> Assurances that Italy will survive as a nation after the defeat of the Fascist Government should be given with no territorial commitments.

1. NAF 163 Eisenhower to Combined Chiefs of Staff, 4.3.43.
2. FAN 117 for Eisenhower from Combined Chiefs of Staff, 16.4.43.

The expectation that Italian troops would fight more stubbornly in defence of Italian soil than they had done in North Africa was strongly held[1] and the policy directive was considered insufficient to weaken Italian resistance to the uttermost.[2] It was pointed out that threats would merely make the Italian people rally round their leaders, that encouragement of passive resistance and sabotage was unlikely to produce real assistance to Husky and the assurances about Italy's future were insufficiently explicit.

It was urged therefore from Algiers that we should emphasise that a continuation of the war or its cessation rested with the Italians themselves. That if they stop the war they would be entitled to a peace with honour, and that the Allied Governments pledged full nationhood for Italy with the benefits of the Atlantic Charter, the only obstacle being the Fascist Government.

The telegram called for an official Allied Statement on the above lines.

The proposed modification, which was certainly that advocated by Mr R. H. S. Crossman, was referred to President Roosevelt and Mr Churchill who replied:[3]

> Most certainly we cannot tell the Italians that if they cease hostilities they will have peace with honour. We cannot get away from Unconditional Surrender . . . accordingly the existing approved statement of policy . . . of April 16th . . . will be adhered to.

Helga. A Proposal for a Black Political Warfare Operation in Support of Husky

On 26th April, General Alexander[4]* telegraphed to the Chiefs of Staff giving his views regarding the propaganda warfare angle of Husky and stating that in his opinion the Italians would fight much better in the defence of Italy than they had in North Africa. The telegram contained the statement:

> During Husky itself the spreading of false rumours, etc., by agents, freedom stations, etc., may have important results and we suggest if not

---

1. CC from C. in C. ME to Chiefs of Staff, 26.4.43, and NAF 221 Eisenhower to Combined Chiefs of Staff, 17.5.43.
2. *Ibid.*
3. FAN 127 from Combined Chiefs of Staff to Algiers, 24.5.43.
4. Telegram I Z 1535, C. in C. ME to Chiefs of Staff (C. 221 cipher).

* [Field Marshal Harold Rupert Leofric Alexander, 1st Earl Alexander of Tunis (1891–1969), served in the Irish Guards in France 1914–19; MC 1915, DSO 1916; acting brigadier-general 1918; member Allied Relief Commission to Poland under Sir Stephen Tallents 1919–20; Imperial Defence College 1930; North-West Frontier 1934; youngest general in the British Army 1937; commanded 1st division in France and supervised Dunkirk evacuation 1939–40; commanded army in Burma 1942; Commander-in-Chief Middle East 1942; Commander-in-Chief 15th Army Group in invasion of Sicily; last British Governor-General of Canada 1946–52; Minister of Defence 1952–4.]

already arranged, a comprehensive and carefully timed plan should be prepared now as an essential part of the operation.

General Eisenhower concurred in the recommendation to use Black radio in order to spread a false rumour that Italy had asked for and had been granted an armistice and requested a favourable ruling from the Combined Chiefs of Staff.[1]

The matter had apparently been referred to the authorities on strategic deception and Colonel Bevan had proposed that Black leaflets should be circulated and Aspidistra employed to put out the rumour.

General McClure[2] informed General Brooks that the Black leaflets were regarded as highly undesirable.

Proposals for Black Radio Put Forward by Major General Brooks without Consulting Mr Delmer

The project was meanwhile being urgently examined in London and Major General Ismay after a meeting with Major General Brooks, PWE recommended that the Chiefs of Staff should agree with General Eisenhower and General Alexander and the US Chiefs of Staff and that the project of using Black radio to spread the rumour of an armistice should go forward. The method recommended was by short-wave Black radio from the United Kingdom supplemented by rumours and Black leaflets disseminated by Black methods from North Africa. The use of Aspidistra was not recommended as the use of a medium-wave transmitter would make it much more difficult to prevent publicity.

Mr Delmer, however, had not endorsed these hurried recommendations and when he was consulted he strongly disagreed with the methods suggested by Major General Brooks and Major General Ismay.

Mr Sefton Delmer's counter proposals were so ingenious that they deserve particular attention since the method was technically novel and the basis of a Black operational medium far more effective than the old Freedom Station. It was in essence the counterfeiting of the official enemy wireless news broadcasts. Such a medium would command attention of a kind very different from a vague rumour picked up from a dubious transmission.

Proposals to Insert Items on the Enemy's News-Tape

The basis of the method suggested was the use by the enemy for all his news services of Hellschreiber transmissions which were picked up by Hellschreiber receivers which issued the news on a single line of tape. There

1. Telegram W 3723/5734 Fantox, 29.6.43.
2. 34818 5733 cipher McClure to Brooks, 29th June, 1946.

are normally interruptions in the transmissions of news items, when the enemy Hellschreiber machines are idling and at certain times the services close down. Mr Delmer's proposal was that we should either transmit a special announcement at a time when the enemy transmitters were idling, or carry on when they had closed down with the item of counterfeit news which it was desired to circulate.

These items, appearing on the tape of the official news agencies, could not possibly be distinguished from the genuine parts of the bulletin.

Mr Delmer had given the name Helga to this technique.[1] His proposal was that the actual news of the armistice itself should be put out only by Helga and on as many different transmissions as we could counterfeit – if possible on DNB Stefani and Transocean. Black radio should contribute only by carrying on with its two-months-old campaign to suggest that there was a strong and active peace party anxious to come to terms. If the enemy tried to denounce the report put out on his own DNB Stefani and Transocean as an enemy report, he would meet with very little public belief. Such a denunciation would be treated as a ridiculous lie invented by the Germans to cover up an internal German–Italian crisis.

Mr Delmer pointed out that the Admiralty could help by transmitting on their Cleethorpes long-wave frequency which interfered with DNB long wave which would drive the monitor to listen in on short wave. He added that it would be valuable if Aspidistra were also used. The original proposals were thereupon modified.[2] Colonel Bevan's text of a bogus declaration was not to be used.

The Prime Minister Vetoes the Plan

PWE had been given a free hand to draft their own declaration for the announcement.[3] Other forces were, however, at work. The Prime Minister did not hear of the plan until late and immediately took the strongest exception to a proposal which 'would not materially influence the battle, but would rob victory of its fame'.[4] HMG could not approve and if necessary he would discuss it directly with the President.

In a further telegram to General Eisenhower he expressed a more tactful hope that the scheme would not be pressed as he believed it would do far more harm than good.[5]

The Prime Minister's telegram to General Alexander expressed his real sentiments and it is improbable that the Helga technique had been explained to him.

1. Mr Sefton Delmer to Major General Brooks, 3.7.43.
2. Draft telegram from PWE from Brooks to McClure and Crossman, 4.7.43.
3. Brigadier Hollis to Sir Robert Bruce Lockhart, 3.7.43.
4. OZ 1885 Personal Most Private Most Secret from Prime Minister to General Alexander.
5. No. 3706 telegram for the eyes of General Eisenhower only from the Prime Minister, 4.7.43.

The origin and development of this proposal and the procedure adopted in regard to it had been extremely unsatisfactory.

PWE had every reason to complain[1] of procedure by which Colonel Bevan, without full consultation with PWE experts, initiated a purely Political Warfare plan. The Director of Plans pointed out that Delmer should have been fully in the picture on Husky from the earliest discussions. He was not, and Mr Ritchie Calder protested that it was invidious that the Director of E and S Black should not have been brought into an operation against enemy territory, when obviously Black had a role to play.

An Untried Black Medium

Mr Ritchie Calder's complaints were well founded but his hope was disappointed. The Helga technique was never put into operation as when the proposals were re-examined in 1944–5 it was found there would be difficulties in ensuring its success, which the Admiralty[2] wireless telegraph experts were not able to solve. The method remains untried and is a matter on which experiments should be carried out.

Husky

In view of the belief held by Generals Alexander and Eisenhower that the Italians would put up desperate resistance on Italian soil, PWE Directorate of Plans prepared a contingency plan for the failure of Husky[3] and laying down the policy lines to be followed. PWE recommended that the real impact of Husky as a large-scale invasion should be concealed until success was assured. The Foreign Secretary was not however willing[4] to 'explore these unpleasant possibilities, particularly if it involves discussing them with the Americans'. This natural reluctance is perhaps an indication that contingency planning for all eventualities should be carried out on a low level by Allied planning staffs as a matter of routine without continued reference to Ministers.

General Eisenhower's Proclamation

A proclamation from General Eisenhower to the Italian people to be broadcast after a successful invasion of Sicily was drafted by PWB Algiers and the text submitted for approval.[5] It bears strong evidence of Mr Crossman's determination to ensure that the invasion of Italy should not be accompanied

1. Mr Ritchie Calder to Air Commodore Groves, 5.7.43.
2. Information from Lt Commander McLachlan.
3. Husky, 27.6.43.
4. Note on minute to S. of S. from Major General R. A. D. Brooks, 29.6.43.
5. NAF 235, 7.6.43.

by any temporising with Fascism such as had made Political Warfare so difficult after Torch.

In the first draft the following sentences occur:

> . . . The Allied Forces . . . will take all necessary measures to eliminate the doctrines of Fascism. Accordingly the Fascist Party will be dissolved, and its appendages the Fascist Militia and so-called Youth Organisation will be abolished. Fascist doctrines in any form will be prohibited.

Small changes in the text[1] were made, but the proclamation was sufficient to ensure that the experiences of Torch would not be repeated on a plea of military necessity.

It is perhaps worth remarking that the original: 'Political prisoners will be promptly released' was altered to 'Measures will be taken for the prompt release of political prisoners', with the reason given: 'From North African experience immediate release of all political prisoners is not necessarily desirable.' This was the reverse of the view held in PWE: that the continued imprisonment of enemies of the Axis powers had been most damaging to our Political Warfare.

Meanwhile PWE was seeking other measures to assist Husky by suggesting that:[2] 'the switch from hard to soft' which it had been agreed should take place immediately before Husky should be carried out by means of a Declaration by the Prime Minister and the President. PWE asked whether General Eisenhower could provide aircraft for the dissemination and printing facilities and paper for the production of 10,000,000 leaflet copies of the Declaration during the three days following such a declaration which should be made six days before Husky.

These proposals were considered by the PWE Ministers[3] and it was decided that no such joint declaration was called for, and that PWE must use the 'means at their disposal for introducing the soft line at the moment suggested'.

A War of Nerves

In view of this decision, PWE put up a paper[4] stating that the 'PWE view is that pre-Husky softening would not aid the operation and would prejudice the usefulness of Political Warfare in precipitating the collapse of Italy after the attainment of the Husky objective'. In point of fact no sudden 'switch from hard to soft' can be traced on the suggested dates. Any alteration in tone was so gradual as to be almost imperceptible and overwhelmed

1. FAN 140. For Eisenhower from Combined Chiefs of Staff.
2. Husky Political Warfare, to S. of S. Foreign Affairs, 7.6.43.
3. Memo of PWE Ministerial Meeting in S. of S.'s room, 10.6.43.
4. Husky Political Warfare n.d.

in a war of nerves which was combined with an absolute ban on strategic speculation including the reports of enemy speculation on the subject of our intentions. For several weeks the Central directive line had been: 'All services must concentrate attention on Italy . . . the line laid down by Roosevelt at the Press Conference[1] . . . had modified the tough line to the Italian people. It has underlined the distinction between the people and the regime.'[2] There must be no relaxing of the theme: 'Relentless force against Italy so long as the Fascist regime continues and Italy remains part of the German war machine . . . we must underline within the limits Roosevelt gave us the distinction between the people and the regime.'[3]

'We must continue to concentrate our war of nerves on Italy. We must show that the fate of Italy will not, as Mussolini suggested, be the fate of Fascism.'[4]

The effect of Allied propaganda which conformed to these directives in softening Italian morale before Husky was probably not very great – certainly it produced no sudden revolution in what was already extremely weak. There is every reason however to believe that, combined with the raids on Crete carried out early in July, it completely succeeded in blinding the enemy to our strategic intention of attacking Sicily. If these views are correct, Political Warfare help to Husky was considerable though not in the field of weakening enemy morale, for which help had been asked.

The arrangement for the release of the communiqué announcing the invasion of Sicily[5] and General Eisenhower's proclamation to the people of Sicily was by broadcasts from Algiers in English and Italian which were to be maintained alternately throughout the day. A request that alternations of English- and Foreign-language broadcasts should be carried out in the BBC European Services was successfully resisted by Mr Kirkpatrick[6] as the repetition of English texts would be a waste of time. Mr Kirkpatrick proposed to 'plug the thing' in Italian and French, and 'do an English transmission or two for the sake of not appearing to run counter to the wishes of the Commander in Chief'.

Sicilian Booklets for Troops

A large number of the troops employed in the Husky operation were Canadians shipped direct from the UK. This fact enabled PWE to produce a booklet on Sicily, a copy of which was handed to each of the Canadian soldiers before the landing. It was written at short notice by Colonel Harrari of PWE Directorate of Plans.

1. On the occasion of the surrender of Pantellaria.
2. PWE Central Directive, 24.6.43.
3. Central Directive, 1.7.43.
4. Central Directive, 8.7.43.
5. NAF 277. To Combined Chiefs of Staff from Eisenhower.
6. Mr Kirkpatrick to Sir Robert Bruce Lockhart, 7.7.43.

PWE Successfully Opposed a Presidential Broadcast

Although the PWE proposal of a declaration by the President and the Prime Minister six days before the operation had been rejected, President Roosevelt made known his intention to broadcast to Italy 'at the opening of Husky'. PWE pointed out[1] that this committed us to the success of the operation about which considerable misgivings were felt, and that it would have a minimal effect at that moment. PWE also pointed out that fresh substance would be required in an official pronouncement and asked that it should be postponed until success had been assured. The Foreign Secretary accordingly took the matter up with the Prime Minister and a draft declaration, to be made only after the success of the operation, was approved.

The declaration, which did not appear to add very much new substance to previous pronouncements, repeated Mr Churchill's indictment of Mussolini.

Indictment of Mussolini Effective

This repetition of Mr Churchill's personal indictment undoubtedly had considerable influence in the vote against Mussolini in the Fascist Grand Council which preceded his arrest. For it made clear that if Mussolini could be sacrificed as a scapegoat, some negotiations might be set on foot, but that on the other hand, the United Nations would never treat with him.

The effect of the declaration which was taken as the PWE directive[2] was considerably increased by propaganda which was based on it.

The landings in Sicily took place on 10.7.43 and had been preceded by airborne landings. The first day was marked by heavy air engagements, but the landings were immediately successful. In ten days a third of Sicily was in Allied hands. The whole of Sicily was in Allied hands after a campaign of thirty-nine days.

Appreciation of Italian Morale Falsified

The operations therefore showed that the appreciation of Italian morale when Husky was being planned was completely wrong. The effect of Political Warfare had been much greater than had been expected.

> The success of our political warfare[3] was discernible in Sicily after our landing on July 10th when resistance by Italian troops was practically nil, especially on the part of soldiers of Sicilian origin . . . the state of mind created in Sicily must largely be attributed to the propaganda of

---

1. Minute to Secretary of State from Brigadier Brooks, 24.6.43.
2. PWE Central Directive, 22.7.43.
3. Political Warfare to Italy Aims and Results March 18th–September 3rd 1943, 16.10.43.

the last three years (as is shown by the chalking up of 'Viva Stevens' on village walls) . . .

PWB Teams in Sicily

On 13th July, 1943,[1] three days after the first landings in Sicily, two PWB teams disembarked, one with each army. Each team consisted of three men, their task being to act as a reconnaissance party and to report back to Algiers on the state of morale of the civil population and enemy troops.

On the Eighth Army Front, the first team commanded by Lieut Colonel Macfarlane landed at 0900 hours on 13th July near the village of Portopalo on the south-east corner of the island. It was not possible to land a truck with them and so they were dependent on the 8th Army for transport.

The team proceeded to Bachine (pop. 17,715) where it was found that an AMG official had already arrived.

AMGOT had issued an order confiscating all wireless sets, but this was later cancelled. Visits were also paid to Rosoloni and Noto and posters were distributed.

Work of PWB Teams in Sicily

On 14th July the team arrived in Syracuse. Temporary HQs were set up in a hotel. Arrangements had already been made for the publication of an English and Italian newspaper edited by an 8th Army officer, with a page in Italian entitled 'Corriere di Siracusa', under the supervision of PWB. No power was available in the town and a hand press was requisitioned. Paper stocks were sufficient for immediate needs.

The lack of an amplifier unit to supplement the few copies of the 'Corriere di Siracusa' which it was possible to produce, and of a mobile printing press were felt as severe handicaps in our propaganda to the population.

On 15th July Lieut Colonel Macfarlane left Syracuse for a visit to the 7th Army. On the way Modica and Ragusa were visited and posters handed to the podesta and AMG officials respectively. In Comiso and Vittoria the civil affairs officers reported that they had overcome a tendency among the population to hoard food by informing them that when Allied supplies arrived the prices would drop and their stocks become valueless. This announcement had an unfortunate reaction with the result that people began to use up their reserves and even killed off livestock.

By this time three more officers, one sergeant and two civilians had arrived in Syracuse, and on 20th July Lieut Colonel Macfarlane set out with one of the civilians to visit the Catania front. Stiff opposition was being encountered and the divisional staff agreed to a suggestion that enemy

1. The following material is taken from the Thornhill report on Political Warfare in General Eisenhower's Command.

morale might be softened with a few propaganda shells. The idea was abandoned owing to delay in obtaining the shells.

On 22nd July, a team consisting of Lieut Colonel Macfarlane and two other officers pushed forward to be ready to enter Catania. Three officers were left in Syracuse to produce the 'Corriere di Siracusa'. In the meantime, a further unsuccessful attempt was made to fire shell leaflets, which was frustrated by the rapid withdrawal of the Germans. With the entry of the 8th Army into Catania this rapid withdrawal continued and there was little opportunity during the remainder of the campaign for propaganda by the front-line team, which was turned on to occupational work.

The withdrawal of the enemy on the 7th Army front was even more rapid than on the 8th Army front, and as soon as sufficient information had been gathered by the PWB team a report was sent to Algiers. Apart from a statement of the complete collapse of the Italian Army morale, it included a request that news should be given out on the radio stating that German prisoners of war would be well treated.

Interrogation of the civil population on the subject of leaflets revealed the following figures:

5% had them in their pockets
15% had them in their houses
50% had read them
15% had heard of them

A listening circle, organised to listen to the BBC, had been reported on the 8th Army front.

In Ragusa contact was made with an anti-Fascist group, who offered assistance in the distribution and preparation of propaganda material.

Before leaving arrangements were made with the senior civil affairs officer to issue passes to several of the group to allow them through the lines to Catania and Palermo and back. The head of the group urged that an educated Italian should assist in the production of 'Corriere di Siracusa', which was already appearing. It was found, however, that Sicilians were inclined to use facilities given them for this type of work for their own separatist propaganda.

In the initial stages of the campaign the enemy was withdrawing so rapidly that front-line propaganda was impossible. The team, therefore, turned its activities to occupational propaganda. Posters, which had not been brought ashore with the first team, were urgently needed. It was recommended to Algiers that they should be included in the equipment of every team, as they take little time to distribute by PWB transport vehicles.

Tactical Leaflets

Once, however, the second detachment had been disembarked it was possible to extend the scope of the teams' activities. A special leaflet entitled

'Capitulation with Honour' directed at Italian officers was prepared. A fighter flew it to Tunis where one million copies were printed and distributed by the Tactical Bomber Force prior to the drives on Marsala and Palermo. Another leaflet was written and printed in Sicily to counteract the belief among German prisoners of war that they would be badly treated. At the request of G2 1st Division and G2 II Corps, leaflets were also prepared calling on podestas and civilians to save their towns by coming out on the main road under a white flag.

The Podesta leaflet was carried in a jeep to the Trapani area and used in support of the 82nd Airborne Division. Four hours before the surrender of the town by the Italian Admiral, a PWB officer flew over Trapani, distributing the Podesta leaflet on the city and the 'Capitulation with Honour' leaflet over the Italian lines. As this method of distribution always drew heavy anti-aircraft fire, the II American Corps obtained two British 25 pdr guns, the only weapon then adapted for shell leaflets. They were only actually used once. A further 40,000 leaflets were later distributed over a surrounded German Division by Cub plane, at the request of the II Corps.

Palermo fell on 22nd July and a few days later a PWB team was pushed forward to reconnoitre the town.

15th Army Group

Up to the end of September the HQ 15th Army Group was located in Sicily near Syracuse. The attached PWB team was a leaflet and monitoring team. Lt Commander Martelli was OC. Under him were a leaflet team of three and a monitoring team of six. Liaison between the PWB team and the Army group HQ was provided by a special section of the General Staff called 'G (Special Operations)'. This section was originally created to bring under staff supervision the activities of several organisations such as SOE and PWB. Propaganda operations were planned in conjunction with it and the necessary orders issued through Staff channels.

Tactical leaflets were written by the leaflet team at Syracuse and printed on a captured press at Catania, operated by Italians. Up to the end of September, when the whole PWB team moved with the HQ 15th Army Group to Italy, they were still using captured stocks of paper; 1,300,000 leaflets had been produced since they arrived in Sicily during the first week of September, including 300,000 copies of a special leaflet at the time of the Italian armistice. They were distributed by the Tactical Bomber Force in five sorties.

Liaison with the Tactical Bomber Force was provided by the G (Air Staff) who had direct communication with Air Liaison Officers in the field.

The team at Syracuse also included a detachment for Liaison with PRO. It was equipped with a 1 k.w. static transmitter for sending back war correspondents' despatches to Algiers. It was operated by a lieutenant and two other ranks. Transport consisted of a 5 cwt truck and a trailer.

Occupational Propaganda. Press

In addition to two daily papers, the *Sicilia Liberata*, in Palermo, with a circulation of 40,000 copies per day, and the *Corriere di Sicilia*, with a circulation of 20,000 copies per day, there were two bi-weekly productions at Caltanissetta and two weekly papers at Enna, all with very small circulations. The American troops' paper *Stars and Stripes* and the British army paper *Union Jack* were both printed and distributed on the island.

The news compiled by the monitoring teams at Palermo and Catania was distributed through PWB and through AMG at Caltanissetta and Enna and editorial material was supplied by PWB. The papers were obliged to carry all AMG proclamations but were allowed to express their opinions very freely in regard to AMG decisions.

Radio

The only transmitter in operation on the island was Radio-Palermo, broadcasting on a wavelength of 530 metres, i.e. 565 kcs with actual power of 2½ k.w.s and a coverage of the whole of Sicily.

The station operated from 1930 hours to 0130 hours. The estimated number of receiving sets in the island was eighty-three thousand but their coverage was reduced by a shortage of power. In Palermo and Enna, power was only available from 7 p.m. to 8 p.m. In Messina there was no power at all.

Posters

Not much was done with posters after the initial use on landing. AMG requirements for printing proclamations were met by PWB.

Films

Much damage was done to the forty cinemas which existed on the island before the war. Ten houses were reopened in the Palermo and Catania districts. The supply of films distributed through the normal commercial channels consisted principally of documentary material from London which was very much appreciated. To these were added a number of old re-censored Italian films. The supply of American feature films was inadequate.

Books

There was a serious shortage of all types of literature on the island. Existing stocks of Fascist books were seized and the distribution of the publications which were received from London and Washington proceeded through the normal commercial channels. A stock of the following literature existed in Palermo:

Italia di Domani
Col. Stevens al Microfono
Vieni Garibaldi
Il Mondo Libero

Of these the most popular were *Italia di Domani* and *Col. Stevens al Microfono*.

AMGOT

The success of Husky involved a problem for Political Warfare, which was, in spite of all precautions taken in drawing up General Eisenhower's proclamation, comparable with that produced by Mr Murphy's policy following the success of Torch.

The Allied Military Government Occupied Territories, which was a military administration for hostile countries, did not carry out the terms of the proclamation as that document was interpreted by the Sicilians. Although the Fascist party was dissolved, the police force, which was its instrument of repression, was retained and very large numbers of Fascist officials were retained in key administrative posts.

> In the Catania area[1] people had begun to clamour for a radical reorganisation as early as August. They regarded the Fascist functionaries including the police as responsible for food shortages.
>
> It is not recorded what measures were taken by AMGOT except to disperse the crowds through the agency of the Carabinieri.

There is a volume of evidence that the ex-Fascist officials retained by AMGOT were very largely responsible for maldistribution of food.[2]

> All the evils noted[3] . . . were aggravated by the presence of an army of occupation whose clubs, messes, and other institutions were open and regular customers of the black market . . . it was the regular practice of the Allied officials, agents, or citizens, to live on the black market.

AMGOT's failure to purge Fascist officials was due to serious shortage of manpower, to lack of knowledge of Italian and the local political situation and to a shortage of educated men in Sicily capable of replacing the Fascist officials.

---

1. Report on the activities of AMGOT by Mr Richmond, Italian Section, PID, 29.2.44.
2. *Ibid.*
3. Report on the activities of AMGOT by Mr Richmond, Italian Section, PID, 29.2.44.

Failure to act was a political error of some magnitude for it affected every side of AMGOT's activities.[1]

It was also most damaging to Anglo-American Political and Psychological Warfare. General Eisenhower had proclaimed the Allied 'aim to deliver the people of Italy from the Fascist regime'. In Sicily that regime appeared embodied in the Fascist functionaries who continued their malpractices under AMGOT and police which was called in by AMGOT to disperse the population when it protested.

It was fortunate for our Political Warfare that the defects of AMGOT rule in Sicily were such as to enable a new policy to be followed upon the mainland.

The title of AMGOT itself was changed to AMG in deference to the status of Italy as a co-belligerent. The great difference between AMGOT and AMG was that the latter was able to receive assistance from the local committees of liberation and that [a] serious purge of Fascist officials was carried out without delay. As a result there were none of the disturbances directed against ex-Fascists that had led to trouble in Sicily.

Efforts were made to check the black market and by the following January troops were forbidden to have meals in restaurants.

Relief funds were organised for those entitled to Italian war allowances. AMG in Naples won golden opinions by its efforts to get essential services going. Benedetto Croce* stated:[2]

> I have seen Englishmen in Naples spending their energy for the sake of our city . . . constantly showing their friendly and cordial feelings and find it hard to remember that they are the victors and we the vanquished.

The Bombing of Rome

The main object of Allied strategy before the invasion of Sicily and during the campaign which followed it, was to hamper the movement of German reinforcements and supplies. The Italian railways which are extremely vulnerable owing to the numbers of tunnels, cuttings and viaducts in mountainous country consequently became an important target for attacks by strategic bombing based either in Britain, or in North Africa, by naval bombardment, or raiding parties, and later by the Italian partisans.

The British and American Air Staffs therefore put forward plans for strategic bombing in support of Husky which included attacks upon the marshalling yards in Rome.

---

1. *Ibid.*
2. Speaking to the Bari Congress, 23.1.44.

* [Benedetto Croce (1866–1952), the Italian philosopher, historian, critic and senator, was buried and lost his parents and sister in an earthquake on the island of Ischia in 1883; studied in Rome and Naples; founded *La Critica* in 1903; developed a theory of aesthetics; Minister of Education 1920–1; resigned professorship at Naples when Mussolini came to power; after 1943 he helped resurrect liberal institutions in Italy.]

The special position of Rome owing to its containing the Vatican City, and the importance of the historic monuments of Rome, made any bombing of the city a matter of great importance in Political Warfare.

On the one hand there was a great danger of outraging Roman Catholic sentiment by dropping bombs on the Vatican itself, or of giving the enemy an opportunity of carrying out a 'Black bombing' of the Vatican using captured British or American bombs; on the other hand, nothing could more impress the Italian people with our ruthless determination. General Eisenhower's staff examined the proposal to bomb the marshalling yards at Rome[1] and concluded[2] that the material effect on supplies to Sicily would be slight but the psychological effect of such bombing would be very great if undertaken after a successful landing and that we would communicate the date chosen for such an attack.

The proposal made in the original plan contained the statement that our objectives were on the outskirts of Rome. The Chiefs of Staff considered[3] this statement[4] in the light of a letter from Sir Alexander Cadogan* which put forward several justifications for the bombing of Rome 'as the centre of the Fascist government and in view of the participation of Italian planes in the bombing of London' and concluded that we should not tie our hands unnecessarily with regard to later attacks since 'there is no reason why Rome should be immune for all time because it happens to contain a number of religious and cultural monuments'. The attitude of the Chiefs of Staff was that of wholehearted advocates of Total Warfare and contrasts strikingly with General Alexander's policy of restraint in regard to the bombing or bombardment of Florence.

The Political Warfare aspect of the bombing of Rome was considered and the justification suggested by Sir Alexander Cadogan was strongly opposed by PWE and the PWE directive on the subject[5] forbade mention of Mussolini's personal request to Hitler to be allowed to take part in the bombing of London, or that religious and cultural monuments in Britain had been damaged or destroyed in the type of raiding begun by the Germans and condoned and assisted by the Fascists. In other words, PWE would not tolerate any justification of the bombing of Rome on the grounds of exacting an eye for an eye.

The same instructions had been the subject of a previous telegram to the Resident Minister Algiers. The directive stressed that our objectives were strictly military being a focal point in a railway system and that the specially

---

1. Made in Telegram Fortune 398 FAN 144, 26.6.43.
2. NAF 251, 30.7.43.
3. OZ 1829, 29.6.43.
4. Sir Alexander Cadogan to Brigadier Hollis, 25.6.43.
5. Special Directive on the Bombing of Rome, 19.7.43.

* [Sir Alexander George Montagu 'Alec' Cadogan (1884–1968) entered FO 1908; head of League of Nations section 1921–33; minister, Peking, 1934–5; Permanent Under-Secretary, FO, 1938–46; Chairman, BBC, 1952–7. Diaries published posthumously in 1971.]

trained crews had been briefed to insure that no damage should be done to sacred and cultural monuments.

The first bombing of Rome took place in a daylight raid on 19.7.43 and considerable accuracy was achieved, only one church being damaged. Warning leaflets were dropped during the raid. The psychological effect on the Italian people was as great as had been anticipated by the PWB experts and the bombing of Rome was in all probability one of the factors which led to Mussolini being outvoted in the Fascist Grand Council on 25.7.43.

The Fall of Mussolini and the Badoglio Government

On 19th July, the day on which the Rome marshalling yards were first bombed, Mussolini met Hitler at Verona. Five days later the Fascist Grand Council which had not met since 7th December, 1939, was called together and a discussion lasting ten hours followed a motion hostile to Mussolini calling upon him to invite the King to take over the actual command of all the armed forces. This motion presented by Count Grandi received seventeen votes to nine and next day Mussolini waited upon the King with his resignation and was arrested as he left the building.

The resignation of Mussolini and the fact that Marshal Badoglio had been entrusted with the formation of a Government were broadcast on the evening of 25.7.43. Marshal Badoglio's first pronouncement was: 'The war will continue.'

The Prime Minister informed the House of Commons: 'We shall let Italy stew in her own juice and hot up the fire to accelerate the process,' and PWE had already taken the same 'tough' line: 'Nothing that they have done so far[1] warrants a modification of our attitude to the Italian Government. . . . Treat Marshal Badoglio as the self-proclaimed instrument of the Germans.'

It was in any case necessary to adopt a hostile and suspicious attitude to Badoglio if he was to be able to play a useful part. But the resignation of Mussolini and his arrest had been a surprise to PWE experts, one of whom had recently predicted that Mussolini would attempt to lead Italy out of the war on the grounds that Germany had failed to keep her promises in the Alliance.

But although maintaining a tough line on Italy, PWE did not discount the enormous propaganda value of the fall of Mussolini since the revolution against Fascism in Italy would promote the revolution against Fascism in other countries.[2]

Considerable division existed at this time within PWE regarding the right attitude to the resurgent anti-Fascist groups in the north of Italy on the one hand and to the House of Savoy on the other.

This division of opinion led to PWE maintaining a policy of silence

---

1. Special Directive on Resignation of Mussolini, 26.7.43.
2. Central Directive, 29.7.43.

with regard to King Victor Emmanuel[1] in contrast to OWI which attacked 'the moronic little King'.

Badoglio was at first attacked, but the attitude changed to neither attacking nor supporting him.[2]

Immediately after the fall of Mussolini, Mr Osborne at the Vatican asked that a further bombardment of the city should not take place.

From Cairo the situation was exploited in propaganda to the population of Crete and Greece. 'The Germans are seeking to disarm and imprison the Italians. If the Italians resist, do not impede them; they will not bother you, they have their hands full. The Germans are the real enemy.'

These broadcasts were the result of information received after the Chief of Deuxième Bureau Siena Division had contacted a British officer and asked for British assistance and a British landing.

The Italian Surrender

The Badoglio Government was in the strange position of being unable to discuss terms with the Allies without giving the Germans an opportunity to take action against them. In these circumstances, the Italian General Castellano made a hazardous journey to Portugal to arrange the terms of an armistice which should include immediate Allied help against the German forces in Italy. The detailed story of these negotiations does not belong to PWE but the part played in them by PWB requires mention.[3]

The Italian Armistice

General McClure informed Colonel Hazeltine, Mr Crossman and Mr Jackson of armistice negotiations in detail on 1.9.43. They immediately set to work to draft plan Cyclone which was designed to carry out the PWB tasks of authenticating the news of the Armistice and exploiting [it] after it had been announced by telling the Italians what to do, spreading the news among Germans in Italy, and convincing British and American public opinion that Allied policy to Italy was justified. This working plan was modified after Mr Crossman and Mr Jackson had proceeded to Advanced Headquarters and met the Deputy Chief of Staff and the Italian representatives. Mr Crossman recorded that:

> I shall never forget[4] the negotiations in the tent in the Olive yard under a crescent moon, with the Italian General in civilian clothes.

---

1. *Ibid.*
2. Central Directive, 5.8.43.
3. Authority had been given to General Eisenhower to prepare a plan for dealing with the surrender (Chiefs of Staff Minutes 207 meeting item 7).
4. Mr Crossman to Sir Robert Bruce Lockhart, 14.9.43.

> Throughout the negotiations a dragonfly kept nestling on his shoulder and every now and then fluttering on to his nose. . . .

To authenticate the news to the Italians it was at first considered necessary for the King of Italy to broadcast the first announcement on an Italian station and for a leading member of the Italian Government to broadcast from Palermo with orders to the Italian Army not to resist the Allies.

Plan Cyclone

The plan envisaged an order from the King to the Army, Navy and Air Force, a general appeal to Italian workers by an Italian labour leader. These orders and appeals were to be agreed by PWB and put out on Palermo, Tunis and an Italian station.

Special leaflet droppings by Tactical Air Force and shoots of leaflets by units in the line to German troops were to be the subject of special directives.

London and Washington were to be asked to monitor carefully and follow the Algiers line precisely.

The Commander in Chief was to give the first press conference so as to guard against the news being reported as a second Darlan episode.

Cyclone also dealt with the need to get Italian spokesmen to Palermo and for Italian orders to be given to stop all jamming of Allied radio. As the original plans for the Armistice included the dropping of an Allied Airborne Division on the Rome Airport, Cyclone included instructions that the Airborne Division should seize and protect Rome Radio including the transmitter studios and power.

It was later decided that Mr Jackson and Lt Colonel Munro should go with the first wave of the Division and they left on Tuesday, 7.9.43, to join the Division. On 8.9.43 General McClure informed PWB of Marshal Badoglio's message 'that he was very sorry[1] that he could do nothing; that he was very sorry that the sending of the Airborne Division to support the Italian troops near Rome had to be cancelled and that he was very sorry that he could not even announce the Armistice from Rome as arranged'.

Mr Crossman Successfully Urges Restraint

A proposal was then made that the Allies should put out a faked proclamation by General Castellano, Marshal Badoglio's representative. This proposal was strongly opposed by Mr R. H. S. Crossman who warned[2] the Generals off Black propaganda faking, and advised them to tell the truth and give Badoglio a chance. His advice was followed and there is little that

1. Mr Crossman to Sir Robert Bruce Lockhart, 14.9.43.
2. *Ibid.*

the understanding which our restraint showed of Badoglio's difficulties that compelled him to go on the air an hour and a quarter late.

The propagandist had got his way in face of military opposition[1] and as a result the whole release was re-shaped in order to include a statement on the background of the negotiations.

At 6.30 the United Nations radio went on the air with its four-language broadcast. At 7.30 the appeal to the Italian Fleet and Merchant Marine was given and repeated every hour. At 7.45 Marshal Badoglio spoke in Rome and was recorded in Algiers and the record used throughout the night in transmissions to Italy. Meanwhile the Press and Information Bureau was making available to the French press the translations into French of the various releases. This had the excellent result that the French press on the next day carried the story as we wished to have it carried.

Although the original version of Cyclone had stated that it would be impossible to cable directives for security reasons, draft directives were in fact drawn up on the instructions of the combined Chiefs of Staff[2] by 6.9.43 and forwarded to them for transmission to OWI Washington and PWE London.

The directive was to drop all discussion of the surrender; to avoid discussion of the character and motives of the Italian King and Government; to avoid discussion of the Armistice terms; to ban all Italian émigré appeal. Mr Crossman has since stated that:

> For a few weeks in that summer of 1943, the back door of Europe was wide open. The Churchill strategy might have won the war outright. . . . Mr Churchill's monarchism proved the undoing of his strategy.[3]

Mr Crossman Responsible for a Policy He Has since Attacked

This indictment is peculiar since he was himself the author of the directive which ended with the order 'to say nothing which could suggest to the Italian or military leaders that we are fomenting working-class movements against them'. In view of this it is plain nonsense to attack Mr Churchill for a decision taken on the grounds of military expediency in N. Africa and imposed on British Political Warfare by Mr Crossman himself.

The directive drawn up by Mr Crossman in Algiers and adhering strictly to the spirit of the Armistice and carrying on Mr Crossman's policy of trusting Badoglio to keep his word, was adhered to by PWE and PWE Central Directive was cancelled for the week beginning 9.9.43. The following week

1. Record of PWB activity with regard to the Italian Armistice, by R. H. S. Crossman for Gen. McClure, 9.9.43.
2. FAN 212.
3. *New Statesman*, 6.10.43.

the PWB directive line of 'avoid all discussions of the Italian Government and King', was maintained.[1]

The announcement of the Armistice was immediately followed by the military operations covered in Baytown and Avalanche.

It was some days before an Allied Mission in personal contact with Marshal Badoglio was established. The situation was then described as unpromising but there was tremendous scope and a fruitful field for both PWE/OWI and SOE/OSS activities.

Allied Policy to Italy after the Surrender

Allied policy towards the Badoglio Government presented an immediate problem in view of the weariness and lack of enthusiasm of the Badoglio Government, the inclusion of war criminals such as General Roatta among its members, and Italian popular antipathy to the King.

The views prevailing at AFHQ were set out in two telegrams[2] which set out the alternatives of accepting the Government of the King and of Badoglio as the legal Government of Italy and regarding it and the Italian people as co-belligerents and of sweeping this government aside and setting up an Allied Military Government of occupied Italy. The first alternative was strongly recommended on military grounds.

The benefits already obtained from the Armistice were tremendous[3] and the need for further benefits was urgent. For example, Middle East was asking[4] that AFHQ should arrange for the King and Badoglio to issue a proclamation to all Italians in British-occupied islands in the Dodecanese and Aegean instructing them to co-operate with us.

Nevertheless the British Foreign Office was unconvinced by General Eisenhower's request that Italy should be given the status of a quasi-ally owing to complications[5] with the French, Greek and Yugoslav Governments, the discouraging effect on the populations of those countries and every sort of suspicion among the Russians.

The matter was discussed in the War Cabinet and it was decided that[6] the essential thing was to build up the authority of the King and the Brindisi administration as a Government. The first essential was that the King should go to the microphone at Bari.

While these discussions were proceeding, AFHQ submitted a directive on propaganda to Italians[7] and reported that Bari on 714 k.w. was serviced

---

1. Central Directive, 16.9.43.
2. NAF 409, 18.9.43, and NAF 410, General Eisenhower to Combined Chiefs of Staff, 20.9.43.
3. NAF 409, 18.9.43.
4. CC 309, 19.9.43.
5. Italian Policy. Mr Macmillan's telegram No. 1812 and NAF 409. Draft Foreign Office minute of 20.9.43.
6. Mr Macmillan Algiers from Prime Minister, -.9.43.
7. NAF 412, 20.9.43.

by PWB technical staff and transmitting daily as Radio Italiano, the official station of the Italian Government. The draft directives from AFHQ stressed the importance of propaganda to Italy on sabotage and General Eisenhower paid a tribute to the work of PWB shortly after the capture of Naples,[1] both as an integral part of the Fighting Forces and for its contributing towards the friendly and co-operative attitude of the local population.

Italy Admitted as Co-belligerent

Meanwhile the status of the Italian Government had been raised with the Russians, and agreement had been reached with regard to its admission as a co-belligerent. This enabled a proclamation to be made by the Badoglio Government declaring war with Germany and calling upon all Italians to resist and fight the German invader, and announcing that Italy was no longer at war with Russia or any of the United Nations. The proclamation on 12.10.43 was followed by a tripartite declaration published in Washington, Moscow and London.

The broadening of the Badoglio Government was not, however, to prove any easy matter. Professor Croce, the great historian, had been liberated by action of Allied Commandos on the capture of Naples. But he and other politicians in Naples made the abdication of King Victor Emmanuel a condition of joining the 'Provisional Government of Technicians'.

The Foreign Office attitude[2] was that this deadlock was one which only the Italian people could resolve and the Prime Minister and the War Cabinet endorsed this view.[3]

AFHQ thereafter asked that the OWI/PWE Directive should show that the Badoglio Government was only a temporary one and that we should refrain from stating that it was representative or democratic.

Aspidistra Reinforces the BBC European Service

The question of the use of Aspidistra for offensive radio warfare was raised soon after the transmitter had been so successfully employed in the Torch operation.

Various proposals were mooted. Mr Delmer had been engaged in training a German announcer[4] 'to listen through earphones to the German news bulletin repeating it to himself and intruding into the middle his own particular news. Repeated tests have proved that this can be done.' It was thought that items could be added to current German news bulletins by use of the relay technique.

1. NAF 441, Eisenhower to Combined Chiefs of Staff.
2. PM/43/388 Sir Alexander Cadogan to Prime Minister, 5.11.43.
3. Item 4 Minutes of War Cabinet Meeting, 8.11.43.
4. Aspidistra used for Black purposes. R. A. Leeper, 22.12.42.

Mr. Leeper's proposal was that by this method 'PWE should broadcast a counterfeit German official news bulletin containing news of such a nature as to give the German listener the utmost satisfaction but which would involve Goebbels in issuing an official démenti. Morale would have risen as sharply as it would then fall.'

The Director General forwarded this proposal to the two Ministers with a covering minute[1] stating that Mr Delmer had perfected a method of coming in near a German programme, and inserting in an undetectable manner items of news likely to cause the maximum confusion among the enemy and inviting the two Ministers to attend a demonstration.

A meeting was held attended by Sir Orme Sargent and Mr Strang for the Foreign Office and by Mr Delmer, Mr Barman and [NAME DELETED ON GROUNDS OF NATIONAL SECURITY]. While no objections were raised to the proposal a caveat was raised against the dangers of German retaliation[2] and it was also argued that such use might be premature.

The Director General accordingly invited Sir Noel Ashbridge to submit answers to a questionnaire on enemy retaliation. Sir Noel replied[3] that German jamming on the BBC Home Service could be started immediately from their existing transmitters and would be effective over the whole country though the effect would be negligible within 10 miles of a BBC 50 k.w. transmitter, [of] high nuisance value between 10 and 20 miles from one, [and] would make the Home Service practically unintelligible in areas at a distance of over 20 miles from one. He also stated that 'with a 100 k.w. transmitter in France or Holland the Germans would be as well placed to interfere with our bulletins as is the PWE transmitter with transmitters in the west of Germany. The slight modifications for quick wave change should only be a matter of a few days work.'

In view of this evidence, and without submitting it to other experts, Major General Brooks, in the absence of the Director General, recommended to the Ministers[4] that 'no black use of this instrument should be made until reasonable evidence is available of a major political crisis either inside Germany or Italy, and that the instrument should be used regularly to strengthen the signal of the BBC medium-wave transmissions to Europe'. The Foreign Secretary endorsed these recommendations.

Thus a proposal of a combined RAF raid to force one of the German transmitter networks – either Berlin, Cologne, or Bremen – off the air and of a transmission by Aspidistra on the vacant enemy wavelength in order to interrupt Hitler's speech at the Sportspalaast on 30th January, the tenth anniversary of National Socialism, was almost automatically negative.

---

1. Sir Robert Bruce Lockhart to the Foreign Secretary, 25.1.43.
2. Sir Robert Bruce Lockhart to the Foreign Secretary, 18.1.43.
3. Sir Noel Ashbridge to Sir Robert Bruce Lockhart, 22.1.43.
4. Major General Brooks to Foreign Secretary, 26.1.43.

The proposal of the combination of the use of Aspidistra on the enemy wavelength and of an RAF raid to shut down enemy transmissions was the most practical that had yet been made, and was later to be carried out. It is doubtful, however, whether a sufficiently strong signal could have been transmitted to the Berlin area[1] during daylight.

Hitler's speech was anticipated between noon and 4 p.m. Nor was it probable that Bomber Command would have been willing to have reversed the policy of only raiding Germany at night merely to enable PWE to attempt a Political Warfare exploit.

An agreement[2] to link Aspidistra with the BBC, except from the hours of 01.30 to 04.40 and 14.30 to 16.15, and that Brigadier Gambier Parry* should give forty-eight hours notice if he required extra time for experimental purposes, was arrived at. Two results followed the regular use of Aspidistra as a reinforcement of the BBC European Services network. In the first place, PWE was able to obtain evidence of the strength of Aspidistra's signal. 'At Rabat reception during daylight was definitely poor. At night fair to good.'[3] The result was in many ways better than had been anticipated by the critics. Rabat is approximately 1,250 miles from Crowborough – about the same distance as Bucharest. But it was at right angles to the directional beam in which Aspidistra radiated. A 'definitely poor' reception at Rabat would have meant a very fair signal anywhere within Germany during daylight.

The second result of the employment of Aspidistra in this way was to produce 'impenetrable interference with the BBC Home Service' in the neighbourhood of Crowborough. Within a few weeks the inhabitants were organising public petitions of protest. Such interference had been one of the arguments produced against independent use of Aspidistra by Sir Noel Ashbridge but it was regarded with complete indifference by the BBC now they were using the transmitter for their own purposes.

PWE had already arranged for a D stop notice to prevent discussion of the subject in the newspapers and the Clerks of the House of Commons were warned to prevent questions appearing in the Order paper. The BBC however decided to close down Aspidistra when important public announcements were being made on the Home Service, so as to avoid unnecessary impediments in speeches by His Majesty the King, and the same care was extended to speeches by the Prime Minister.

The value to Political Warfare of reinforcing the BBC transmitters with Aspidistra was naturally very great. It was most valuable in enabling the BBC programmes to overcome jamming, particularly in the western sea-board

1. Mr Garnett to Mr Ritchie Calder. Report on Aspidistra.
2. Notes of a meeting held 10.2.43.
3. No. 53 from Mr Stonehewer Bird to FO, 17.3.43.
* [Brigadier Sir Richard Gambier-Perry (1894–1965) served with the Royal Welch Fusiliers and RFC in France and Belgium 1914–18; public relations, BBC, 1926–31; attached to FO 1938; colonel 1939; brigadier 1942.]

countries. But it must be regarded as a purely temporary measure, until the Department had produced its own programmes which appeared likely to be more important media of Political Warfare than those of the BBC European Services.

W6 National Fascist Radio

This RU unlike all others was carried out by 'intruder' technique on medium wave by Aspidistra, under the direction of Mr Delmer.

[18.9.43–27.10.43] The object was to produce a counterfeit of the National Fascist Government Radio which would discredit Germany and the National Fascist Government in the eyes of Italians, and cause them to act favourably for us.

The programme starting at 20.20 BST was continuous until midnight. It relayed the genuine National Fascist radio programme, either direct, or from records, picked up from medium-wave German transmitters and inserted subversive news items and talks. Apart from these it was identical with the genuine programme.

Most of the insertions were recorded in advance, but some of them were inserted 'live'. Operational items such as reports that an area of Central Italy had been declared a neutral zone, or that the German authorities had arranged for a free distribution of food for the population at Fascist HQ in certain towns were included in order to cause movement along roads on enemy lines of communication at certain times.

Other features were an attack on the Vatican in the name of Fascism, talks announcing that Italian women were to assume the same war burdens as German women, and that a new Fascist lire would be issued at a new rate under German auspices.

The success of the technique was such that all trained monitors were duped. It had an immediate crop of come-backs from monitors in Sweden, Switzerland, the USA and also the BBC.

The difficulties attending the operation of W6 were that if most of the material were relayed and counterfeit items inserted there would be a noticeable difference in quality between relayed and counterfeit material when reception was bad.

There would also be a discrepancy between the programme announcement and the actual programme (unless the programme announcement was counterfeited – but this does not seem to have been tried).

If the entire programme were counterfeit the transmission quality would be uniform. But there were actually insufficient skilled operators for this to be possible. In fact the programme though successful was abandoned owing to the lack of speakers and the requirements of another RU [27.10.43].

The dangers represented by the ambitions of Colonel Hazeltine and other American military officers who wished to make PWB the centre for all Political Warfare had been fully realised by PWE and by OWI who saw themselves in Mr Sylvain Mangeot's words:[1] 'involved in ghastly muddles, wading across Europe in tow of incredible American ignorance and even more incredible American personalities', unless a drastic reorganisation could be carried out.

The situation had been rendered urgent owing to an accident to Mr Crossman which was followed by a severe illness, and later after his return to England, by a dangerous relapse.

By the end of 1943, OWI and PWE had succeeded in replacing military control of PWB by Civilian Control, and on 23.9.43 Colonel Hazeltine 'was summarily relieved of his assignment with PWB'.[2]

The appointment of General Eisenhower to SHAEF and of General Sir Maitland Wilson to succeed him at AFHQ brought about a complete reorganisation in the Mediterranean theatre and much greater British participation in PWB. General Eisenhower's departure was soon followed by that of Brigadier General McClure who was replaced as head of INC [Information News Censorship] by Brigadier General McChrystal.

Mr Harman, formerly head of PWE Low Countries Section, had been sent to replace Mr Crossman, but his authority was not sufficient to prevent American blunders. In these circumstances, early in January 1944, proposals were initiated for the reorganisation of PWB in the Mediterranean theatre in view of the political and strategical adjustments of the campaign in Italy.

PWE proposed[3] the appointment of a Political Warfare Officer to co-ordinate the policy and activities of the PW organisation at Algiers, Cairo and Bari.

> The proper integration of political warfare with policy and strategy throughout the Mediterranean Theatre is a matter of considerable importance. . . . We believe this course would in practice be more satisfactory than the extension of the responsibilities of INC. . . . We propose to offer the appointment of Vellacott. . . . OWI accept this proposal if you approve it. They wish to add it was they who first suggested Vellacott for the headship of an overall Mediterranean organisation.

Mr Vellacott arrive[d] in England on 19.1.44 but like Mr Crossman he was a sick man and though discussions with Sir Robert Bruce Lockhart and Mr Sherwood were most satisfactory, he was not able to leave England until 22nd May, 1944. The delay was disastrous. A reorganisation which might have been carried through without great difficulty in January was opposed by vested interests of four months' growth.

---

1. For fuller quotations of this Most Secret letter from Mr Mangeot to Mr Paniguian, 15.3.43, see above p. 276.
2. Psychological Warfare in the Mediterranean Theatre, 31.8.45, Part I, p. 8.
3. To SAC Mediterranean from PWE, 26.1.44.

On 21st February, 1944, the Supreme Army Commander had created the post of Psychological Warfare Officer[1] whose duties were to act as 'Adviser to the C. in C. to senior US Diplomatic representatives and British Resident Minister. Co-ordinator for Psychological Warfare Policy, plans and activities. Director of Psychological Warfare Branch (PWB) which included . . . agencies of Office of War Information (OWI), Political Warfare Executive (PWE) and Ministry of Information (MoI). . . . A deputy Psychological Warfare Officer will be designated by this Headquarters for each zone. . . .'

After his arrival at Algiers, Mr Vellacott spent a week with General Alexander and inspected PWB centres in Naples and Bari.

> On my return here question arose whether or not I carry executive responsibility for PWB or am only advisory to SAC [Supreme Army Command]. General Gammell at first suggested that the right solution was to separate PWB from Information News Censorship (INC) and invest me with executive responsibility for the former. Subsequently this view was revised and it was decided to refer the question to General Devers and Mr Murphy. The wish of these latter is that the existing arrangement under which executive responsibility rests with Brigadier General MacChrystal as head of INC should not be disturbed. For the preservation of good Anglo-American feeling SAC and Mr Macmillan concur with this. They also agree with my view that as an adviser without executive responsibility my post is reduced and its duties unreal. As instructed by SAC I am returning to United Kingdom, after a visit to Cairo.[2]

On the receipt of this telegram, Sir Robert Bruce Lockhart minuted the Minister of Information:[3]

> I am perturbed by this development which will have the following serious consequences:
> 1. Although the Mediterranean is a British Command and British interests are paramount in this area control of PWB activities will be vested entirely in American hands.
> 2. The Balkans in which the Foreign Secretary has a special interest and towards which American policy is one of indifference, are in this area.
> 3. We have known for some time that confusion and a sense of frustration prevail and both American and British personnel have been waiting eagerly for Mr Vellacott's arrival. Brigadier General MacChrystal, an American . . . has no knowledge of Political Warfare or

1. AG 321-1 (PWB) INC-AGM. Allied Force HQ APO 512, 21.2.44.
2. No. 770 Personal for Lockhart from Vellacott, 11.6.44.
3. Sir Robert Bruce Lockhart to Minister of Information, 14.6.44.

> Mediterranean problems. Mr Russell Barnes is an American . . . and in Mr Sherwood's opinion is unfit for a job of this magnitude. Mr Sherwood wished to remove him some time ago. . . . I may mention the complaints from General Mason MacFarlane* and Sir Noel Charles** regarding the irresponsibility and subversive activities of American members of PWB in Italy. . . . I am afraid that Mr Vellacott's departure will have a deplorable effect on the morale of the large PWE representation in the Mediterranean. . . . I also fear that his withdrawal will . . . be regarded by PWB SHAEF as a triumph over the civilians and our difficulties with this organisation are already great owing to its scarcely concealed ambition to take policy control into its own hands. . . . Mr Vellacott has not resigned.

Although the Foreign Secretary and the Minister of Information asked that the matter be reconsidered their efforts were unavailing as on his arrival in Cairo, Mr Vellacott had again fallen ill with general poisoning. But apart from the illness which was serious Mr Vellacott informed Sir Robert that he would not in any case have been willing to take up the post after the incident at Algiers. Mr Vellacott stated that it was not so much Mr Macmillan's and SAC's view that PWB should continue to be run by the Americans as 'the timing of its communication to me' that made it impossible for him to contemplate any renewal of association with PWB.[1] But it is impossible to resist the inference that Mr Macmillan, as Resident Minister, did not wish for a British head of Mr Vellacott's standing.

In view of Mr Vellacott's health, Brigadier Jeffries was appointed Chief Military Officer of PWB [7.7.44] but in Sir Robert Bruce Lockhart's view:[2]

> . . . arrangements for Political Warfare in the Mediterranean theatre are most unsatisfactory. American military control of propaganda is incompetent, and the civilian propagandists, both American and British, welcomed the arrival of Mr Vellacott in the hope that it would put an end to an intolerable situation. Morale already low is now likely to sink. The Americans are determined not only to maintain Brigadier General

1. No. 1607. Personal for Lockhart from Vellacott, 8.7.44.
2. Minute from Sir Robert Bruce Lockhart to the Foreign Secretary, 12.7.44.

* [Lieutenant-General Sir (Frank) Noel Mason-Macfarlane (1889–1953) was gazetted to Royal Artillery 1909; served in 1914–18 and Afghan (1919) wars; military attaché, Berlin, 1937–9; Director of Military Intelligence, BEF, 1939–40; improvised 'MacForce' 1940; Deputy Governor, Gibraltar, 1940; head British military mission Moscow 1941–2; Governor, Gibraltar, 1942–4; Chief Commissioner, Allied Control Commission, Italy 1944; Labour MP, North Paddington, 1945–6.]

** [Sir Noel Hughes Havelock Charles, 3rd baronet (1891–1975), won MC serving in France 1915–18; entered FO 1919; Counsellor and Minister, Rome, 1937–40; Minister, Lisbon, 1940–1; Ambassador to Brazil 1941–4; High Commissioner in Italy with ambassadorial rank 1944–7.]

> McChrystal as the overall head of PWB Algiers, but also to appoint another American, Mr Russell Barnes, as his chief executive Political Warfare officer. Mr Barnes is persona ingrata to both the British and American members of PWB and Mr Sherwood, the head of the foreign side of OWI, has long wanted to remove him, but postponed his decision until Mr Vellacott had reported. It is a matter for Ministerial consideration whether a radical solution should be enforced immediately by splitting the Mediterranean theatre into two for Political Warfare purposes. . . . If Anglo-American integration is considered essential, the Western Mediterranean should be reorganised as predominantly an American interest and PWB Western Mediterranean should have an American head. Similarly, the Eastern Mediterranean should be reorganised as predominantly a British interest and have a British head.

This minute was endorsed by the Foreign Secretary with the words: 'I agree with the above.'

Mr Robert Sherwood visited Algiers, Naples and Rome and reported on his tour:[1]

> It is too late in the war to be making drastic changes, particularly in the midst of a highly important campaign and with further campaigns in prospect it would be unwise. The line of command established by Brigadier General McChrystal is clear and direct. Mr Russell Barnes is chief of PWB and Mr Terence Harman is his deputy. Brigadier Jeffries is in command of all British military personnel and Colonel Hall of all US military personnel. Mr William Tyler is Chief of the Western Mediterranean Division pointing towards France; Mr John Rayner is Chief of the Central Mediterranean Division, conducting operational propaganda against the enemy in Italy and Austria; Mr Ralph Murray is Chief of the Eastern Mediterranean Division pointing towards the Balkans. . . . Plans for the Anvil Operation[2] appear to have been thorough and well conceived.

Mr Macmillan accordingly stated that Sherwood had rather switched round while he was in North Africa[3] and put forward his own opinion that the important thing was to seize control of the actual operating theatres of which there were four. The Western, which would pass out of the Mediterranean command as soon as Anvil forces passed under General Eisenhower's authority; the Italian, the Dalmatian theatre operating from Bari; and Greece, Roumania, etc., operating from Cairo. Of these the British

1. Report on PWB/AFHQ, 23.7.44, from Robert E. Sherwood, Dir. Overseas Ops, OWI.
2. Anvil was the code name for the American landing in the Riviera and South of France.
3. Mr Harold Macmillan to Sir Robert Bruce Lockhart, 25.7.44.

had the complete control under excellent officers of three. The fourth area, Southern France, was under an American but would in any case pass out of the Mediterranean area in a few weeks. To obtain this we had had to concede American headship of the whole.

On his return to England, Mr Sherwood did not disclose the existence, or the nature, of his report to Sir Robert Bruce Lockhart.

Meanwhile the Foreign Secretary and the Minister of Information had dissented strongly from Mr Macmillan's view that weak and inefficient leadership at the centre was of no importance and they were confirmed in their opinion by Mr Sherwood whom they consulted on his return, who stated that his hand had been forced by the American and political authorities who had told him that military urgency made it impossible to carry out any reorganisation of PWB.[1] Actually his original views about the unsatisfactory state of affairs in PWB had only been strengthened by his visit. He declared that McChrystal and Barnes were totally unfit for their posts, and that a reorganisation was essential as soon as circumstances permitted.

Mr Macmillan found this somewhat bewildering and referred to Sherwood's report, after which the PWE Ministers could only ask the Resident Minister to re-examine the problem since they found it hard to believe that the outposts could do their work if the centre was rotten.[2]

Colonel Sutton who had been appointed Head of Mediterranean Desk in PWE was sent out to report, and possibly some major reorganisation might have been pushed through. But Sir Robert Bruce Lockhart was again taken ill and in his absence the question of imposing a reform lapsed.

In practice, it will be seen that Mr Macmillan proved to be substantially right. The outposts, all PWE men of proved competence and experience, became the heads of largely autonomous units which were serviced to a great extent direct from London, and the centre was often short circuited.

The 'Vellacott incident' can thus be seen to have arisen owing to a divergence of views between the united PWE and OWI authorities in London on the one hand, and the British Resident Minister and the Supreme Army Commander, General Sir Maitland Wilson, who were ready to sacrifice Political Warfare interests for the sake of appeasing officers of the US Army, on the other. General Wilson had appointed British officers to posts on his staff coveted by US officers and Mr Macmillan agreed to the appointment of Brigadier General McChrystal partly as a quid pro quo.

It would be more correct to attribute the incident to friction between the British Foreign Office and the British Resident Minister than to Anglo-American rivalry. Many officers of OWI and American members of PWB were greatly disappointed by the decision. Finally it must be remembered that by 1944 the participants were all very tired men and Mr Vellacott's illness and his relapse must be borne in mind.

---

1. Foreign Secretary to Resident Minister, Caserta, 31.7.44.
2. No. 313 FO to Resident Minister, Caserta 17.8.44.

Abundant justification for the statements regarding the incompetence of Brigadier General McChrystal and Mr Russell Barnes is provided in letters not only from experienced PWE officers to the Director General PWE, but also in a letter from Mr Harman to Brigadier General McChrystal himself.

PWB AFHQ Becomes a Special Staff Section

PWB at AFHQ was not functioning under their direction and by the early autumn a system of devolution and reform had to be adopted by which PWB (Italy) was merged with PWB. AFHQ Combat propaganda in Italy was carried out by a DPWO (John Rayner) from General Alexander's HQ instead of from PWB AFHQ. Control of PWB by INC was brought to an end [23.10.44] and PWB dealt direct with the Chief of Staff AFHQ. This really meant that General McChrystal disappeared and that Barnes and Harman remained as head and deputy of PWB, AFHQ. Rayner controlled forward Italy; Edmond (American), occupied Italy, and there was an English head at Bari and at Cairo. It was agreed that Political Warfare in the Balkans should in practice be carried out under Harman's control.[1] A Psychological Warfare Sub-Committee of the Supreme Commander's Political Committee was formed at this time.

Partly owing to this scheme of devolution, much brilliantly successful Political Warfare was carried out in Italy.

PWB AFHQ Moves to Naples

The stages which have been passed over can be recapitulated as follows:

> Following the capture of Rome [27.7.44] AFHQ moved to Naples–Caserta and this involved the move of PWB to Naples. In the autumn of 1944 the PWB machine in Italy was reorganised in three areas. Eastern Mediterranean including Balkans, Central Mediterranean (Italy and Sicily) and Western Mediterranean (Southern France).

The Invasion of Italy

Two PWB 'Combat teams' originally took part, one with the Fifth and one with the Eighth Army, control still being maintained from Algiers, but considerable autonomy later developed at Naples and Bari respectively. As the invasion of Italy progressed the employment of civilians increased very greatly and the same tendency grew for civilian to replace military control as had occurred in North Africa.

1. No. 239. Resident Minister, Caserta, to FO, 2.9.44.

The 1st PWB Combat team with the Eighth Army was headed first by Mr John Whittaker of OSS, later by Lt Colonel Weaver, both Americans.

The PWB team working with the Eighth Army 'was at first hampered by the rather cool reception given it by the members of the Military staff'.

The personnel of the 2nd Broadcasting station Radio Detachment, however, captured the radio transmitter at Bari and members of the 1st Mobile Radio Broadcasting Company assisted in staffing the studio.

Studio Bari later became the principal Allied radio transmitter directed to the Balkans. Later on Bari became the production centre for PWB AFHQ.

Combat Propaganda in Italy

The direction of propaganda in the field of Italy was largely British and to a great extent carried out by former members of PWE.

Anzio

The landing at Anzio took place on 24th March. Mr John Rayner reached the beachhead on 28.3.44 taking with him a 1½ k.w. portable medium-wave transmitter, in a torpedo boat, travelling at high speed to find fires blazing, the port shattered, a cruiser turned turtle and streams of wounded coming off. The enemy had just started using radio-controlled glider bombs to attack Allied shipping.

Mr Rayner suffered at first from lack of status. He had no insignia to show what he was, uniform had not been provided and for some time he had difficulties with the American Army authorities. At one time he wore an American GI uniform as no other was available. At first General Mark Clark's staff refused to allow him to use the transmitter for fear it should draw fire. Eventually he got permission to use it. The aerial was camouflaged by being taken up by a balloon similar to the barrage balloons round the port, the transmitter and studio were in a cave. The transmissions which were clearly audible in Rome were a 'great success'.

As the campaign in Italy progressed, Mr John Rayner was appointed officer i/c PWB 15th AG, i.e. responsible for all propaganda activities in the army area. The army area was defined by the demarcation line between AMG territory and territory which was under the jurisdiction of the Allied Control Commission. The headquarters of PWB 15th AG was established in Rome. From there it moved to Milan until 15th June when PWB officially ceased to exist.

Mr Rayner, who had an American deputy John Minnifie, was responsible for:

(a) Combat propaganda (i.e. co-ordination of tactical and news leaflets to the enemy and news and instructional leaflets to Italian partisans).

(b) Front-line broadcasting by way of loudspeakers or radio transmitters.

(c) Leaflet dissemination (by shells, subs and aircraft)
(d) Propaganda in the rear of the battle area (i.e. control of radio, press, films and information centres).

The Officer i/c PWB 15th AG was responsible to PWB AFHQ for matters of policy. He could only communicate with London and Washington through AFHQ; this proved to be a serious handicap to PWB activities as on many occasions speedy decisions were required and the views of PID or of OWI in Washington only became known long after a decision had been taken on the spot. Communications between Florence and Naples were extremely bad; when visits were imperative the journey alone often took two days in each direction. It was repeatedly felt that PWB AFHQ were not in the picture and showed no understanding of the conditions in the battle area.

Rome

Rome was captured at dusk on 4th June. Mr Rayner with the advanced unit S Force entered twelve hours later at dawn on 9.6.44. On the night of 5/6 June they produced the first newspaper for the civilian population, but scrapped it in the early morning in order to put in the news of the landings in Normandy which Mr Rayner had picked up on the monitoring set. This enabled them to omit a proclamation by General Bencibenza which had unfortunately been accepted by Colonel Munro.

That morning, twenty-four hours after Rayner's arrival, they had got the Rome radio working. The value of radio and newspaper in preventing rumours and panicmongering by Fascist elements was very great.

Florence

In September 1944, Florence was reached. No plans had been made for Germans holding it – but fighting went on for three weeks, and Alexander regarded the preservation of Florence as more important than rapidly overwhelming the enemy. The Germans blew up all the bridges except Ponte Vecchio, of which they destroyed the ends. SOE and the partisans, however, ran a telephone through the German line and over the ruined bridge.

Rayner produced a daily paper on the s[outh] bank of the Arno using a Jeep engine as the power supply for his printing press and the paper was taken over to the n[orth] bank, through the German lines and circulated among the Italians on the n[orth] bank. They lived under continual mortar and sniper fire.

Subsequent Operations

On several occasions, partisans sent messages that enemy troops were on the move along certain roads in the Appenines. A few hours later these troops were not only bombed but showered with leaflets advising them to quit the fight before it was too late, and not get killed five minutes before the end. On many occasions concentrations of troops in the Bologna Cento and Medicina areas were showered with news leaflets a few hours after the news had become known.

On one occasion in February 1945, the 92nd US Negro Division was to deliver a large-scale attack on the Italian Fascist [WORDS MISSING] the front in an area between Lucca and the west coast. [WORDS MISSING] were shelled with leaflets headed 'Surrender or Death' just before the Allied barrage went into action. As a result hundreds deserted. Front-line broadcasters were sent to the front at certain specific points where it was known that the enemy morale was low. At first the broadcasts, in German and Polish, were met with an intense artillery barrage. Later, after February 1945, there was complete silence during the broadcasts and the barrage started only when that had finished. This was intended to prevent would-be deserters from coming over to our lines. It is, however, known that the words of front-line broadcasts were always passed on from mouth to mouth. On one occasion, Dr Frend, who gave a broadcast in the 5th Army area, was credited with having brought over to our lines no less than forty-seven deserters through a single broadcast. Poles in the Wehrmacht were induced to join their comrades in the Polish Corps in Italy. During the early months of 1945 each broadcast contained the latest news of Russian or Allied advances in Germany. This news was at one time disseminated every twenty-four hours by Cubs over the battle area in the form of latest news slips. The regular Frontpost dissemination missions generally took place twice a week. The leaflets were prepared in Florence and flown to bases in Corsica. Each edition of Frontpost was contained in over 200 bombs. They were flown in twelve Mitchells and the bombs were released in the army concentration area behind the lines, generally in the Bologna, Medicina, Cento, Imola areas and along the main road leading from Bologna to the front towards Rimini. These aircraft only dropped along the front itself on two occasions. They never penetrated beyond the River Po. On many occasions they came back holed and several aircraft were lost in these nickling missions.

An example of co-ordination between Psychological Warfare and the Army was that of the surrender of Marshal Graziani.* He was captured in Milan and flown to Florence; after being interrogated by CSDIC he was taken to Florence Radio where he was made to broadcast an order to surrender to his Ligurian Army. With him was his Chief of Staff Lt General Premzel, who confirmed his surrender order. A recording of this broadcast was flown by the PWB officer of HQ 15th AG to Milan which had only just

* [Marshal Rodolfo Graziani (1882–1955) conducted the Italian conquest of Abyssinia from the south 1935–6 and was its Viceroy 1936–7; ejected by Wavell from Egypt 1940–1 and resigned; after fall of Mussolini in 1943 emerged as head of Fascist resistance; captured 1945.]

been occupied by leading troops; this message was immediately broadcast on Milan['s] powerful transmitters. This aircraft was one of the first to land on the Milan airfield. A few hours later the Germans and Italians of the Ligurian Army began to surrender.

The PWB officer at HQ 15th AG was in constant touch with PWB teams in [the] Fifth and Eighth Armies. Any news of importance or requests were immediately passed on to Mr Rayner, who then consulted his leaflet experts, Mr Tosca Fyvel and Mr Norman Cameron, who decided on the wording of the leaflet which was then produced and printed on the large printing presses in the Nazione building in Florence.

During the closing stages of the offensive the instructions to the partisans had to be changed every day and sometimes several times during the day. All these messages were duly approved each time by the proper authority at HQ 15th AG. After the surrender of the Germans the partisans in the north continued to harass the enemy and prevent German emissaries from getting in touch with the Allies. A complaint to this effect was received by General von Vietinghoff, the Commander-in-Chief. General Mark Clark immediately approved a stern warning to the partisans, telling them to continue to be as obedient and helpful as they had been before and during the campaign, and not to rob themselves of the fruits of victory. Next day partisan activities ceased, and three days later the German surrender team arrived at HQ 15th AG.

PWB also concerned itself with the handling of civilians in the army area. In the Appenines particularly, where large districts were laid waste, the problem of refugees was a serious one. In this respect, PWB was in liaison with G5 (Civil Affairs) and produced at their request a number of posters in Italian. The text of these posters was also broadcast from Florence and over the Eighth Army Radio. The press officer of PWB 15th AG organised the dissemination of news to newspapers in Tuscany. In many instances telephonic and telegraphic communications did not exist, and the latest news was broadcast daily from Florence at dictation speed for the benefit of local newspapers. The shortage of paper was also acute and on certain occasions it was released by the Army authorities so that civilians could be kept informed of the development of the battle in order to contradict the numerous rumours which were cunningly spread by Fascist[s] all over the countryside. In this way PWB prevented states of alarm and despondency which spread so easily among the stunned population.

On several occasions the civilian population which was about to fall under Allied occupation was told exactly what to do, e.g. keep off the roads and harass the Germans whenever possible. As a result of leaflets of this kind Italian partisans were able to give front-line troops valuable information on German positions. One of the difficulties was the handing in of arms by Italian partisans. Two days after the capture of Bologna a mass demonstration was organised by AMG and PWB at which thousands of partisans handed in their arms to American troops in the most orderly fashion.

Effective liaison at HQ 15th AG showed that whenever secret missions were sent to the partisans the plans contained thousands of Italian leaflets which were later disseminated by partisans behind the lines. The best evidence of the effect of Allied propaganda is contained in the bi-weekly propaganda reports which were produced at HQ 15th AG and which were contained in the weekly overall report of PWB activities. Towards the end of the campaign from 80 to 90% of all German soldiers had seen or heard of Frontpost at one time or another. Even a greater proportion carried safe-conduct passes hidden in their pockets, shoes or watches 'just in case'.

In the early spring of 1945 when MATAF increased their bombing effort on bridges and railway stations in N. Italy, MATAF, whose HQ was also in [the] Florence area, were concerned with the number of casualties which Italians had to suffer. Italian population [was warned] to keep away from these objectives.

Relations with SOE

Relations with SOE (Cdr Holdsworth) could not have been better and PWE and SOE directives were complementary. Rayner's directives would back up SOE needs for the patriots and SOE in turn would back him in his requests for leaflet distribution, etc. When a new situation developed Rayner would often spend a night with SOE and discuss what line should be taken. He would then formulate a new directive and would go with it to Alexander's Chief of Staff, Hardinge, and explain his proposals in the light of military plans and obtain approval and amendments. Rayner decided all political policy questions himself, without reference but kept in close touch with the Embassy.

Each propaganda campaign started by Rayner writing a proclamation for Alexander to sign. Once written, it was usually passed and signed with only minor corrections, if any, within four hours. The C. in C. was thus responsible for the propaganda campaigns and Rayner did not have to secure approval from Brigadier Jeffries and Colonel Metherell at AFHQ.

A propaganda D day for handbills, leaflets and broadcasts disseminating each proclamation would be chosen. This would be followed up with interpretations, variations, etc., for four or five weeks, being modified in the light of patriot reactions and needs.

His relations with 'C' (called ISLD in this theatre) were equally good and on the same unofficial basis as with SOE.

Service from PWE London

Rayner stated that this was good. The weekly directive the usefulness of which he had often questioned in the past turned out to be invaluable – it showed him how people were thinking in London and it gave the background information not otherwise available. Rayner always read it carefully and gave a lot of thought to it.

Captain Alexander, a former member of PWE and at one time instructor at Brondesbury School, who was Mr Rayner's liaison officer at 15th Army HQ, concludes his evidence on Combat Propaganda in Italy with the words: 'I have seen the use of Political Warfare at its best and carried out almost to perfection. I know from my own contacts at HQ 15th Army Group that the military authorities, both British and American looked upon us as being the Fourth Fighting Army.'

German Intelligence Section PWB Forward Teams

On the fall of Rome, Mr Hartshorne, Lieutenant Joachim and Dr Frend were ordered to investigate the morale of German civilians in Rome. They had interviews with an assistant to the German Air Attaché in Vatican City, proving that political dissensions existed in the German Command. Their reports to PWB/AFHQ were not forwarded to London.

[23.7.44–2.8.44] Three days after the failure of the plot against Hitler, Hartshorne and Frend began meetings with the German Ambassador to Vatican City, who revealed the entire political plans and background of the plot against Hitler. Their reports were not forwarded to PWE. As a result PWE Black and Grey and the BBC were deprived of vitally important intelligence on the plot. The discussions were interrupted by a peremptory order from PWB/AFHQ. Three days later they were instructed to introduce [NAME DELETED ON GROUNDS OF NATIONAL SECURITY] whose object it was to let out that we intended to attack at Genoa so as to divert German attention from the Anvil operation. The interview failed in its object.

By September, the section had been offered full information about anti-Hitler officers and officials in N. Italy, but PWB/AFHQ again ordered them to cease contact on the grounds that the war would be over in October 1944 and that contacts with the German Embassy would rouse Russian suspicions, and the German Intelligence Section was closed down at twenty-four hours' notice [13.9.44].

Dr Frend's Further Discoveries

At the end of September, Dr Frend discovered the diary and engagement book of the German Consul in Florence. PWB/AFHQ again failed to forward Dr Frend's reports to London, made no use of the information and did not even acknowledge it.

These details appear to prove that PWB/AFHQ persistently suppressed information and obstructed researches which might have hastened victory.

Colonel Metherell's Responsibility

The person responsible appears to have been Colonel (later Brigadier) Metherell who, moreover, made himself inaccessible to members of PWB Forward Teams visiting Naples. The civilians in PWB Forward Teams suffered in many ways from lack of support from AFHQ. Again, this was Colonel Metherell's responsibility.

Organisation of PWB AFHQ on Move to Naples

The organisation of PWB AFHQ after the move to Naples was as follows:

[13.7.44]	Mr Russell Barnes	Head of PWB AFHQ
	Mr Harman	Deputy Head
	Brigadier Jeffries	Military Director (British)
	Colonel Hall	Military Director (US)
[Appointed 10.8.44]	Colonel Metherell	Principal Finance and Administrative Officer (British)
	Mr Schneider	Policy Head (US)
	Mr Ralph Murray	Balkan Policy Adviser (British)
	Mr Bessie	Head of News (US)
	Mr Radford	CIO

Mr Harman relinquished his appointment at the end of January 1945, returning home in order to go out on a mission to [the] USA. He was succeeded by Brigadier Jeffries as Deputy Director PWB and appointed Mr Radford as his deputy.

Brigadier Jeffries relinquished his appointment at the end of July soon after the end of the war with Germany.

Colonel Metherell was appointed Deputy Director and Temporary Brigadier in place of Brigadier Jeffries [30.7.45] and a few days later, Mr Russell Barnes, the American Head of PWB, resigned and nominated Brigadier Metherell as his successor as Director PWB AFHQ.

PWB Gives Up N. African Responsibilities

After the success of the southern French landings, Lt General Devers of the US Army, pressed for all American soldiers to be removed from N. Africa. This affected PWB uniformed personnel. The US Army was reinforced in its demands by the State Department. As a result, by the autumn of 1944, PWB functions in North Africa had been passed back to the MoI and OWI respectively. It is interesting to note that following this transfer, certain US Army leaders and State Department officials complained that British subject matter was more prominent in propaganda display shops formerly operated by PWB.

PWE/PWB Bari. Political Warfare from Bari

By October 1943, Bari had been captured and the radio station and the excellent printing facilities were in the hands of PWB.

It was clear that Bari offered advantages over Cairo as a base, and negotiations between PWB Algiers and PWE Mission Cairo, resulted in an arrangement to share the Bari facilities.

PWE Middle East formed a sub-mission to carry out political warfare to the Balkan area from Bari. Time was allotted for the Balkans on the Bari transmitter and facilities were made available.

The PWE Mid-East sub-mission arrived at Bari on 9.12.43 and produced its first Balkan broadcasts within a week and its first leaflets within three weeks.

It almost at once became clear that it was absurd to maintain two separate Political Warfare units in the same place making use of the same transmitter and the same printing press, etc., with separate control from Cairo and Algiers. PWE Mid-East sub-mission therefore fused into PWB Bari and in February 1944, Lt Colonel P. C. Anderson was appointed to preside over the fused bodies.

Bari for many reasons tended to become largely British. The PWE/Mid-East sub-mission had imported teams with Balkan experience. Moreover, the progress of Allied forces in Italy led to Naples becoming the centre for Italian affairs and when the following summer AFHQ moved from Algiers to Caserta, PWB AFHQ moved to Naples. Most PWB personnel engaged in PW to Italy were therefore moved from Bari to Naples.

In March 1944, Bari took over responsibility for PW to Hungary, Yugoslavia, Albania and Cairo remained responsible only for Greece, Rumania and Bulgaria.

By March 1944, Bari radio was transmitting six hours a day to the Balkans and ten hours a day to Italy, the Italian programmes being largely carried by landline from Naples.

With the transfer of aircraft from N. Africa to Brindisi and Foggia, Bari [became] responsible for printing not only its own leaflets for Yugoslavia, Hungary and Albania, but also most of the Cairo output for Greece, Rumania and Bulgaria, and a large part of Naples (later Rome) output for Italy. Bari also printed and disseminated leaflets addressed to German troops produced by all three centres. Later Bari printed a large part of the leaflets for the invasion of southern France. Bari indeed became the chief leaflet printing centre for the whole of the Mediterranean and Middle East, printing being carried out largely on a large rotary printing press by the directorate of British Military Printing Presses which had taken the machines over from the Italian owners.

This system is severely criticised[1] where the absence of any commercial relationship is stated to have restricted PWB control of type and to have 'clouded incentive and initiative on the part of the printers'.

---

1. Survey of No. 9 Unit Bari by Mr J. D. Stewart, 9.12.44.

Nevertheless in nine months Bari produced almost one billion leaflets – a production greater than that of PWE London during the same time.

Owing to leaflets being loaded at fifteen different airfields and the lack of advance information as to targets, many of the same problems arose as had attended PWE and RAF relationships in Britain.[1] Thus each airfield had to be supplied with leaflet stocks for all targets and an extensive and uneconomic system for transport, stock-keeping, briefing and loading had to be built up. Moreover, there was inevitable wastage as stocks went out of date. On the other hand, there were none of the difficulties attending the introduction of new methods of dissemination.

The following methods were employed as well as that of package or 'snowstorm' droppings.

1. By US parachute flare, which held 16,000 leaflets. A block and cordite pad was placed above the nose-fuse to eject the leaflets at a predetermined height.
2. By RAF parachute flare, a smaller version of the above, 8,000 leaflets occupying the space of the parachute.
3. Delayed action parcels – four packets with a time fuse breaking the string at a predetermined height.
4. Kitbags of leaflets for agents or resistance groups.

The figures given by Mr J. D. Stewart show dissemination of 982 million leaflets and a total wastage of 392 million printed, but not disseminated in nine months, or roughly 40%. Only part of this wastage can be attributed to the methods of dissemination. Nevertheless, these figures explain Colonel Barbrook's view[2] that 'the system by which bombing aircraft carry leaflets is essentially amateurish and exhausting to the crews and also produces that state of mind in PWE of "I never miss 1 lb of lift" which means that the operation is planned statistically. Moreover, every operation is arranged on an "old boy" basis with the Air Force.'

No RUs operated from Bari at any time.

'SOE were highly efficient under Brigadier Miles and were extraordinarily helpful', nevertheless, 'a main lesson is that it is essential for PWE to have its own agents in the field.[3] SOE agents are too busy with their work and not specialists.'

Major Lord Birkenhead's visit to Yugoslavia was invaluable. Some excellent native agents did both PWE and SOE work, but the chief lack which Bari felt was intelligence regarding the effect of its propaganda.

A very brief account of some of the operations carried out from Bari can be given here.

---

1. Survey of No. 9 Unit Bari, by Mr J. D. Stewart.
2. Notes of a conversation with Col Barbrook and David Garnett. Col Barbrook succeeded M. Stewart at Bari.
3. *Ibid.*

Bulgaria

In May 1944, it was decided in Cairo to saturate the principal Bulgarian towns with leaflets owing to the political crisis in that country. Mats were flown from Cairo and 26 million leaflets were printed in Bari and dropped on four consecutive nights.

Yugoslavia

A leaflet, poster and radio campaign was organised against the German forces in order to support a drive by Tito's forces and Allied Air Forces.

Hungary

Special leaflets warning workmen to keep away from areas attacked by the USAAF with delayed action bombs.

France

Large numbers of leaflets were printed at Bari to cover the landings in the South of France, most of them being packed in Munro bombs.

Front-Line Propaganda

In June 1944, a Special Liaison Section was formed which went forward to the island of Vis. The members of the Section took part in attacks on [the] German-held Dalmatian islands. Special leaflets were disseminated by aircraft and by shell, also by hand. Loudspeaker teams addressed German troops from small naval craft and a number of surrenders occurred. A further unit accompanied British operations in S. Albania when the town of Sarande was freed. Following this [Sept. 1944], the island of Corfu was saturated with leaflets demanding its surrender, which took place within eighteen hours. A German vessel surrendered in reply to a loudspeaker appeal.

A unit of four officers accompanied British forces in Montenegro.

Major Randolph Churchill's* Attachment with Brigadier Maclean's Mission to Tito

The decision, forced upon the British Government, to withdraw support from General Mihailovitch and to supply Marshal Tito led to the dispatch

---

* [Hon. Randolph Frederick Edward Spencer Churchill (1911–68) was, after three attempts to enter Parliament, Conservative MP for Preston 1940–5; GSO on general staff (Intelligence) at GHQ Middle East 1941; served in Western Desert, North Africa, Italy and Yugoslavia. Fought and lost three more general elections in 1945, 1950 and 1951. He wrote much journalism and several books. Being the son of Winston Churchill was both his making and his undoing.]

of a military mission under Brigadier Fitzroy Maclean.* On 20.1.44 Major Randolph Churchill was sent to Yugoslavia (taking with him Captain Evelyn Waugh**) having been charged with responsibility for all propaganda matters that affected the Maclean Mission.

This appointment was not made by PWE, but 'by higher personages'.[1] It was in its nature one which overlapped PWE Mid-East functions and it seems clear that Major Churchill should have been attached to PWE before taking up his appointment. This, however, was not done. Three months after the appointment, the Minister of Information informed Major Churchill that: 'I shall have to talk to PWE about your position'.[2] As a result of this, Sir Robert Bruce Lockhart replied to a Cairo[3] telegram which had remained unanswered for over two months during Sir Robert's absence on sick leave. In his telegram, the Director General asked Cairo[4] to do everything to assist Major Churchill in his work and send him all possible material.

Cairo promptly informed Bari which by that time was responsible for propaganda to Yugoslavia, and as Mr Ralph Murray shortly afterwards went out to Bari, a meeting was arranged between him and Colonel Anderson of PWB Bari, with Major Churchill.

Major Churchill had, however, been moved to anger by a telegram sent from PWE Mission Cairo to Brigadier Maclean in January stating that they had no objection to Major Churchill's distributing material supplied by them and would consider any suggestions he made, but they could not consider him as a source of PWE Guidance, nor could his presence be taken to meet PWE needs in Yugoslavia. He should therefore not represent himself as connected with PWE or as introduced into Yugoslavia for the purpose of making propaganda.

At the meeting between Ralph Murray, Colonel Anderson and Major Churchill, the latter accused Mr Murray, whom he at first mistook for one of Colonel Anderson's subordinates, with the authorship of this telegram and abused him roundly. After this scene, Major Churchill wrote to Mr

1. Bari Telegram No. 1213 Pilot, 13.12.43.
2. No. 200, 30.3.44. To Brigadier Maclean for Captain Randolph Churchill.
3. No. 211 Pilot, 28.1.44.
4. Telegram No. 1194.

* [Sir Fitzroy Hew Maclean of Dunconnel, 1st Baronet (1911–96); FO 1933; Moscow 1937; resigned from FO and enlisted as private in Cameron Highlanders 1939; 2nd lieutenant 1941; joined SAS 1942; lieutenant-colonel 1943; commanded British military mission to Yugoslav partisans 1943–5; Conservative MP, Lancaster, 1941–59, Bute and North Ayrshire 1959–74; Parliamentary Under-Secretary for War 1954–7. Author, especially *Eastern Approaches* (1949).]

** [Evelyn Arthur St John Waugh (1903–66) was educated at Lancing and Hertford College, Oxford; assistant master in several schools 1924–7; wrote *Decline and Fall* 1928, the first of many novels; war correspondent for the *Daily Mail* in Abyssinia; present at the fall of Crete 1941; served with military mission to Yugoslavia 1944; published *Brideshead Revisited* 1945; published *Sword of Honour* trilogy on wartime experiences 1952–61. Perhaps the greatest British novelist of the 20th century.]

Vellacott[1] in order that 'an obviously scandalous piece of sabotage against the war effort might forthwith be terminated and punished'. Mr Murray also wrote a letter giving his version of the facts.

Mr Vellacott,[2] who did not receive the letters for several weeks, replied to Major Churchill that both were bad letters that revealed that the passages which had occurred were out of relation to good sense. Mr Vellacott explained that the delay in clearing up Major Churchill's position was due to the fact that both he and Sir Robert Bruce Lockhart had been away ill. There was no more sabotage or ill-will on Murray's part than on that of Brigadier Maclean who had refused a joint proposal of PWE and PIC endorsed by the Ambassador to Yugoslavia and SOE Mid-East, that Mr Clissold should join his staff.

Major Churchill visited London a month later which provided an opportunity for a programme of his propaganda requirements in the way of literature, newspapers, films, etc., to be agreed with PWE.

The situation remained unsatisfactory from PWE's point of view and the Director General decided that the proper course would be to send out a PWE representative Major Lord Birkenhead, who was able to exercise personal influence on Major Churchill, [who] accordingly returned to Yugoslavia with him. During his stay Lord Birkenhead was able to supply Bari with invaluable information and his two reports to the Director General gave the most complete picture of the popular revolution accomplished by the Communists which the Department had received.

A divergence in Anglo-American policy occurred in September, 1944, when an operation in Greece was being planned, as the State Department ordered the withdrawal of American participation and this included PWB.

The British side of PWB AFHQ based at Bari continued to carry out Political Warfare activities to the Balkans without American participation.

1. Major Churchill to Mr Vellacott, 8.5.44.
2. Mr Vellacott to Major Churchill, 12.6.44.

Part V
Political Warfare Preparations for the Invasion of Western Europe

Planning for the Liberation of Europe

The plans, stockpiling and other preparations for the Liberation of Europe can be most readily understood if a short outline is first given of the various agencies with which PWE had to work and the factors governing PWE ideas at this time.

In the first period – from January till September 1943 – PWE was chiefly concerned with MoI, the Civil Affairs Directorate at the War Office, and the Administration Territories (Europe) Committee usually referred to as the Bovenschen Committee from the name of its chairman. At first it was believed that the liberation of north-western France, Belgium and Holland would be a British responsibility carried out by British Armies under a British Commander in Chief and that southern and eastern France would be the responsibility of General Eisenhower operating from a North African base. But as plans progressed, the importance of complete co-ordination in planning with OWI, amounting almost to 'integration', became evident. OWI alone could supply the men and the machines necessary for propaganda in the field and in the liberated areas; PWE hoped to supply the political experience and political doctrine necessary, by taking the Americans into complete partnership.

COSSAC Period

At the end of August or in early September 1943, Lieutenant General Morgan, who had been nominated Chief of Staff to the Supreme Allied Commander designate, communicated the Overlord plan to PWE and a number of PWE officers were 'ticketed'. The immediate result was that PWE was called upon to provide the relevant plans. Much of this work had fortunately been done beforehand, and only slight changes were needed in their presentation. But the delay in nominating the Supreme Allied Commander had led to uncertainties with regard to the forms which Political Warfare activities would take both in the field and after liberation. Moreover the absence of the Director General for several months upon sick leave combined with the views of the Minister of Information in regard to OWI, held up the process of Anglo-American integration and irretrievably damaged PWE's position with the Americans concerned.

SHAEF Period

The nomination of General Eisenhower as Supreme Allied Commander resulted in Psychological Warfare becoming a responsibility of Supreme Headquarters and the Psychological Warfare Branch (later Division) was created as PWD SHAEF as it will be called in this history in preference to the military designation G6. This branch could only be formed by calling upon PWE and OWI ('the civilian agencies') for men and materials.

PWE was being steadily weakened at this period by the need to nominate its best men to posts in PWD SHAEF. Nor was PWD–SHAEF always willing to accept those offered. Thus the PWE nominations of Colonel Thornhill and Colonel Sutton were refused and Mr Crossman, who had the advantage of having had experience as senior British representative in PWB North Africa, was personally asked for by Brigadier General McClure. Unfortunately, however, Mr Crossman had returned to Britain seriously ill, and he was not able to return to work for some months.[1]

The winter of 1943–4 can be described as a turning point in the history of PWE from the effects of which the Department never fully recovered.

Illness in the Department

The work of the Department suffered from the illnesses and long absences from work of many of its leading members. These illnesses particularly affected its work in the autumn and early winter of 1943–4, when the preparations for Overlord and co-operation with OWI and OSS were critically important and in the early months of 1945, when the Department was making its utmost efforts to assist in breaking the German will to resist.

During the illness of the Director General in these earlier months, co-operation with the Americans was held up by a ruling of the Minister of Information. His illness the following year came when Major General Brooks, his deputy, had just left the Department and it was three months before Major General Bishop was appointed as General Brooks's successor.

Absences on sick leave of several members of the Department are shown

---

1. Sir Robert Bruce Lockhart agreed to lend Mr Crossman as Deputy Director co-equal with Mr C. D. Jackson at the request of General McClure as from 7.3.44. Minutes of DG's meeting, 11.3.44.

for the period from the beginning of 1943 to the surrender of Germany in graphic form. The records are from the personnel files of the Finance Department.[1]

In addition to the period covered by the chart, Colonel Sutton was absent from May till the end of July 1942 and Mr Leonard Ingrams for the month of February 1942. Mr Wheeler-Bennett* was ill from September 1945, until he left the Department owing to ill-health on 15th October, 1945.

Deaths in the Department

The following deaths must be noted:

Mr H. O. Lucas, Deputy Director of Plans, died in January 1945, after leaving the Department owing to ill-health, Sir Hanns Vischer, PWE [WORDS DELETED ON GROUNDS OF NATIONAL SECURITY] died suddenly on 19th February, 1945. Colonel Chambers died suddenly in April 1945, almost certainly as the result of prolonged overwork.

Mr Bracken's Authority Increased by Director General's Absence

One practical result of the Director General's absence in the autumn and winter of 1943–4 was to increase the number of matters which were referred to the Minister of Information alone. This would appear to have been partly owing to the fact that Major General Brooks had originally been the representative of the Minister, and when in need of Ministerial authority, asked for a ruling from that Minister, whereas Sir Robert Bruce Lockhart usually sought the guidance of the Foreign Secretary. Though in theory the Minister of Information was responsible only for administration and the Foreign Secretary for policy, practically all matters involved both policy and administration.

Mr Bracken's views accordingly governed many of the arrangements made in preparation for Overlord, and as will become only too apparent in detailed consideration of these plans, they were frequently opposed to the views of the Department represented by the Director of Plans, and Mr Delmer.

---

1. Not reproduced.

* [Sir John Wheeler Wheeler-Bennett (1902–75) was assistant publicity secretary to the League of Nations 1923–4; founder of the Information Service on International Affairs 1924–30; assistant director of the British Press Service, NY, 1940–1; special assistant to the Director-General of British Information Services in US 1942–4; European Adviser to PID 1944; assistant to British Political Adviser to SHAEF 1944–5; attached to prosecution team, Nuremberg, 1946; British editor-in-chief captured German Foreign Ministry archives 1946–8. Many publications, including *Nemesis of Power: The German Army in Politics 1918–1945* (1953) and *King George VI* (1958).]

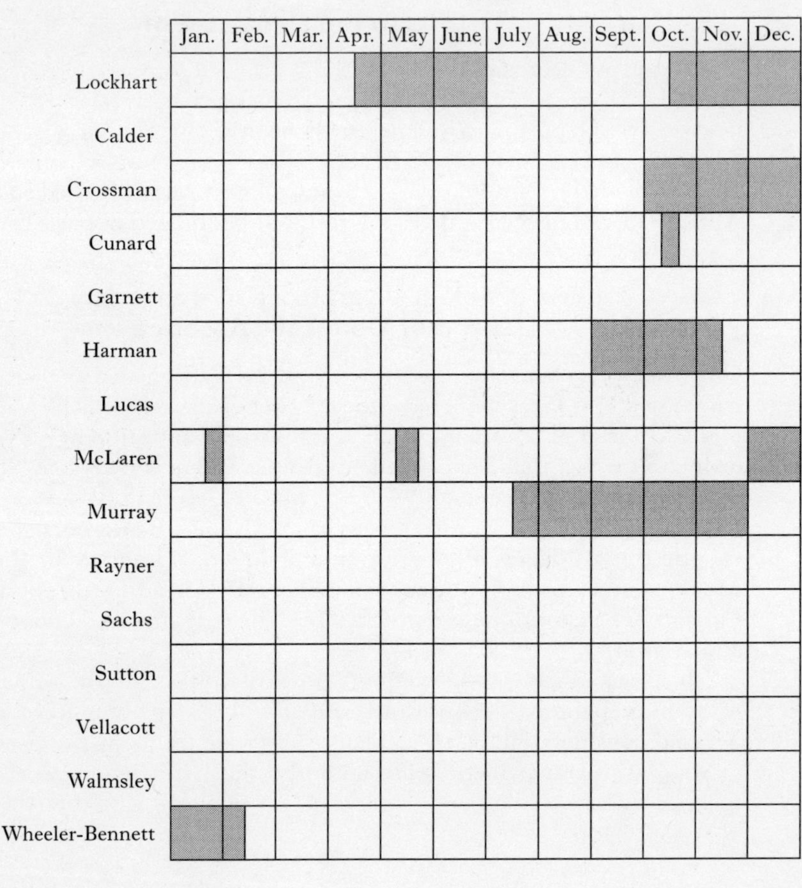
1943
Jan.
Feb.
Mar.
Apr.
May
June
July
Aug.
Sept.
Oct.
Nov.
Dec.
Lockhart
Calder
Crossman
Cunard
Garnett
Harman
Lucas
McLaren
Murray
Rayner
Sachs
Sutton
Vellacott
Walmsley
Wheeler-Bennett

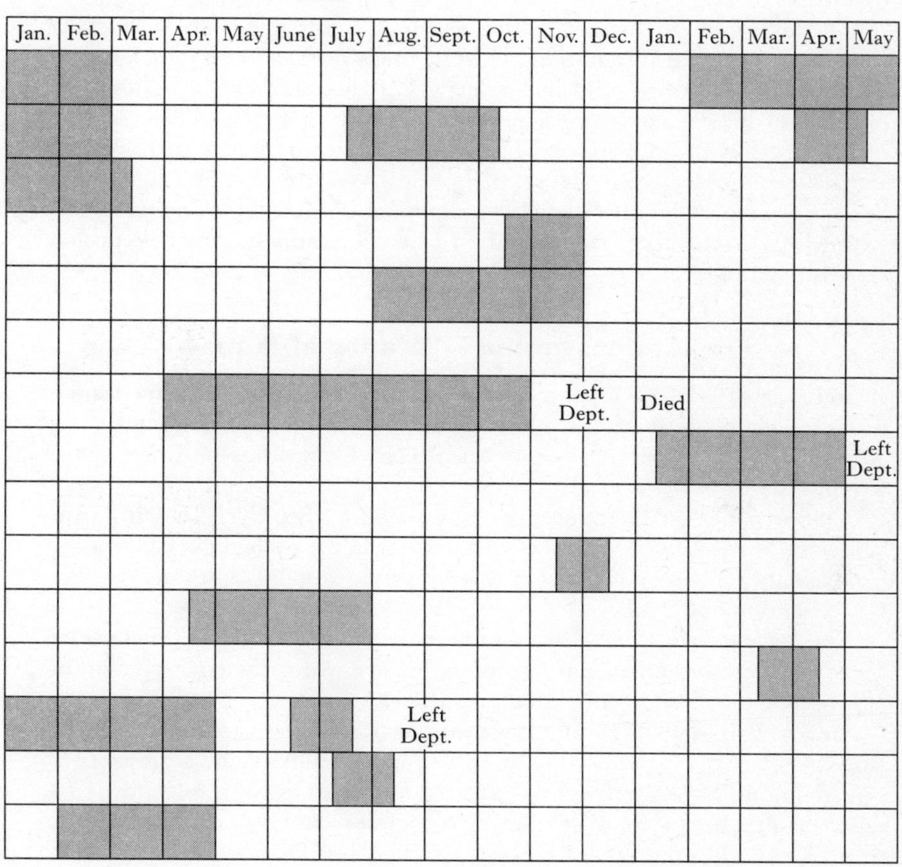
1944
Jan.
Feb.
Mar.
Apr.
May
June
July
Aug.
Sept.
Oct.
Nov.
Dec.
Jan.
Feb.
Mar.
Apr.
May
Left Dept.
Died
Left Dept.
Left Dept.

Mr Bracken's Opposition to Political Warfare Project

Mr Bracken remained hostile to the independent use of Aspidistra by PWE and indeed, on one occasion, refused a request from SHAEF for its use. The Minister also led Major General Brooks to hold up 'integration' with OWI owing to political considerations which were irrelevant to the work which had jointly to be carried out. The Minister also revealed a failure to understand our operational propaganda, and the servicing of French Resistance by PWE and SOE.

The failure of the Minister to understand the nature of the Transport campaign, the vital importance of SOE messages, and the reluctance of Major General Brooks and Mr Scarlett to enlighten him, provide powerful evidence of the dangerous consequences for a Department of the magnitude of PWE of having no Minister of its own. A Minister of Information must inevitably approach the problems of Political Warfare with preconceptions derived from his own officials. Unless Political Warfare has its own responsible Minister, it is therefore bound to suffer from amateur interference on the Ministerial level.

Preparations for the Liberation of Europe

In February 1943, the Director Generals of MoI and PWE agreed in an interchange of letters[1] to put forward a joint memorandum to the Administration Territories (Europe), AT(E) Committee or Bovenschen Committee.

A draft paper on their functions suggested by Sir Cyril Radcliffe was agreed by Sir Robert Bruce Lockhart subject to the exclusion of front-line propaganda on the grounds that this was: 'the responsibility of the War Office' and not of PWE.

The Bovenschen Committee had been set up in June 1942 'to consider the steps necessary on military grounds . . . to ensure efficient civil administration of the territory liberated in Europe'.

Sir Cyril Radcliffe communicated[2] the joint views to Sir Frederick Bovenschen,* who replied[3] that he agreed that a study of the regions mentioned should be made from the propagandist's point of view and that a report should be drawn up containing recommendations of the measures to be adopted. He asked that DPR War Office and Brigadier Lee, Deputy Chief of Civil Affairs, should be brought into the joint study.

---

1. Sir Cyril Radcliffe to Sir Robert Bruce Lockhart, 18.2.43, and Sir Robert Bruce Lockhart to Sir Cyril Radcliffe, 19.2.43.
2. 24.2.43.
3. *Ibid.*

* [Sir Frederick Carl Bovenschen (1884–1977) was Private Secretary to Lord Haldane, Secretary of State for War 1908–12; Assistant Secretary, War Office, 1921; director of army contracts 1932; Deputy Under-Secretary of State for War 1936–42; Joint Permanent Under-Secretary of State for War 1942–5.]

The result of these exchanges was the setting up of a joint PWE/MoI/BBC Committee – the Reoccupation Committee, as a sub-committee of the Bovenschen Committee with the following terms of reference:

> On the assumption that a successful invasion of North-West France has taken place, you are required to submit as a matter of urgency, a joint PWE/MoI plan showing the nature of the requirements in personnel and material (i) for the conduct of propaganda and publicity inside the 'released area' (ii) for the use of the released area as a base for the conduct of political warfare.

The composition of the Reoccupation Committee was:

Chairman: Mr Ritchie Calder
Colonel Sutton, PWE
Mr Scott, MoI
Mr MacGregor (Broadcasting Division MoI) BBC
Mr Routh, MoI
David Jenkins, PWE Joint Secretaries

In spite of the terms of reference, the Committee considered that it was not concerned with Political Warfare to the enemy or to Allied nationals on the other side of the line, but only with Political Warfare and Information Services to the inhabitants of the liberated regions, but it included the needs of Germany within its scope. Sub-committees were set up to deal with Germany, North-West France, printed matter, supply and distribution of news, paper stocks, books, joint publications, finance, films, radio equipment, civil intelligence, personnel and communications.

The work of these committees was thorough and painstaking and involved studies of all equipment which might be needed and which might be available, but owing to its being carried out on the false assumption[1] that British officers would be responsible to a British Commander in Chief for the civil administration of liberated territories, a very large part of the work was unreal and bore no relation to the responsibilities which had to be assumed when the time came.

Much preliminary work of value was however done in regard to the location, and earmarking of necessary equipment which afterwards became available to the very different authorities which carried out Political Warfare and information services.

The Reoccupation Committee was also important since it drew attention to the needs in regard to personnel and to the training of personnel, and because it immediately raised a policy point of the first magnitude – the

1. Information from Major David Jenkins, KC, secretary to the Committee.

participation of the Allied nationals, Resistance movements and Governments, in the liberation and administration of their own territories.

At the first meeting of the Reoccupation Committee[1] Colonel Sutton pointed out that Section 16 of the Provisional Military Manual of Civil Affairs had not been agreed to by the Director General with the Chairman of the AT(E) Committee. The Committee asked that the War Office be asked to withdraw this section which dealt with a detailed definition of information and propaganda services and that no new section to replace it should be approved until the Committee had reported.

The Committee thereupon drafted two documents R.C. 7 and R.C. 8 in the later of which PWE views were expressed on the participation by Allied nationals in the civil administration of Belgium and Holland.

> . . . a de jure Government exists and it will certainly insist on resuming its local authority with the minimum of delay . . . the main and most obvious point is the unreality of the policy apparently followed so far by DCCAO of making our own preparations for recruiting and training British personnel without consulting, or even informing the Governments for whose benefits these officers will, in fact, largely be working.

War Office Refusal To Consult Allied Governments

This criticism drew the following rejoinder from Brigadier Lee,[2] the DCCAO.

> I cannot accept the statement that personnel working under the CCAO will in fact be working for the benefit of Allied Governments. . . .
>
> I would not for one moment consider consulting the Allied Governments until I had made up my mind on the general methods to be employed to meet emergency requirements. Having made up my mind I would be quite willing to discuss my intentions with the Governments. It is on these lines that I think Section 16 must now be rewritten. Having written it we shall know exactly what we want and then tell the Allies what we intend to do . . . executive officers working under the CCAO during the military emergency period must be British and in fact, section 9 of the Manual is a sine qua non. It follows therefore that personnel provided by the nationals will have to come under the heading of 'Advisers'. I agree that the Governments concerned will recommend these advisers . . . but I must stand out against any suggestion that the Government nominees will be acceptable just because of the nomination. . . . We are glad to accept co-operation from the recognised Governments with the all-important conditions

1. Minute of 1st Meeting Reoccupation Committee, 29.3.43.
2. Brigadier Lee to Mr Ritchie Calder, 15.4.43.

> That the C. in C. is the decider.
> That British officers are the Chiefs.
> That the nationals are the advisers working under the Chiefs.
>
> The last thing we can agree to is to give Belgian and Dutch officers an equal status to British officers during the military period.

Brigadier Lee continued:

> It seems to me the paper indicates a great fear of offending the nationals' susceptibilities. . . . I go on an entirely different line. . . . I do not think we shall hand over completely entire administration in rear areas . . . it will in fact be done piecemeal . . . the C. in C. retaining control . . . of certain services . . . this will apply in particular to broadcasting . . . for obvious reasons and for a fairly long time. . . .

The attitude of the DCCAO in regard to co-operation with the recognised Allied governments of Belgium and Holland and to the employment of Allied nationals in them seems to have deterred the Joint Reoccupation Committee from putting forward a separate paper on France. We may, however, safely assume that proposals to employ Frenchmen in the administration of France, or for British officers to work on equal terms with French maquisards, would have been 'hit for six'.

Brigadier Lee's letter, though indicating intentions which were politically disastrous, was not directly combatted by the Reoccupation Committee, which indeed accepted his dictum that 'executive officers must be British'.[1] Colonel Sutton and Lt Colonel Gielgud in particular devoted their energies to the recruitment and equipment of officers whom they hoped could be taught to cause the minimum offence to the susceptibilities of our Allies by PWE training.

The more Brigadier Lee's intentions were examined by PWE experts, the more dangerous and the more unrealistic did they appear. To what lengths was the ruling that 'executive officers must be British' to be carried? Executive officers were not all British in the BBC, or in PWE itself. Would it be impossible to send Mr de Lavelaye to Belgium to organise broadcasting, or to send M. Duchesne to France although we had already sent him to North Africa? These questions were being asked by PWE experts while the Reoccupation Committee proceeded to take steps for the recruiting of necessary bodies and their training.

1. Information from Major David Jenkins, KC.

War Office Ruling on Allied Nationals Causes Split in PWE

Brigadier Lee, by laying down conditions within which the Reoccupation Committee felt it necessary to work, but which the experts of the French Region of PWE regarded as inacceptable, was the cause of a policy split on the Regional level within PWE which reinforced the division of opinion on the subject of the Cockade *Avis* and leaflets.[1]

The French Regional view is stated by Lt Colonel Fairlie who replaced Lt Colonel Gielgud as French Regional Director in August 1943:

> The Commander-in-Chief will require a civilian population ready and willing to help him in any way he tells them and a willing maintenance of order and obedience to his edicts.
>
> It is therefore up to us to plan for France in such a way that he will have most chance of obtaining these two conditions. Our thinking must be based on the assumption of complete co-operation with the Comité Français de la Libérational Nationale and also the Conseil de la Résistance within France. In no other way can we honestly advise him.
>
> We have got to face the fact that Frenchmen, while gladly accepting the full responsibilities which they would have to shoulder if admitted as fully-fledged fighting Allies, have no intention of tolerating interference with their future. Anything which looks like occupation (except in a limited military first phase, which they all gladly admit as necessary) will be resisted by them to a degree which, if they deem it necessary, will find them actively resisting us just as they are now resisting the Germans. Needless to say, this would be a very severe handicap indeed to the Commander-in-Chief and his troops in France; and although it may sound rather a tall story, it is the considered opinion of the French Region of this Department that it is merely a plain statement of fact.
>
> To avoid such a situation, we must have French liaison officers in plenty. . . . By previous arrangement with the London representatives of the Conseil de la Résistance, and the Comité, we can have these men provided for us from within France, men who will meet our troops when they arrive and make contact with out own appointed officers. . . .
>
> The French are already deeply suspicious of our activities. This suspicion will assume dangerous proportions if we do not take the normal course of opening up and asking for their co-operation. . . .
>
> If we train our students to do various jobs *only for the* initial military stages, all the emphasis of our teaching being that just as soon as possible they change places with the French liaison officers, who will be with them, and become merely rather special liaison officers themselves, then we have nothing to fear and everything to gain from co-operation with the French at the earliest possible moment.[2]

---

1. See p. 342.
2. Lt Col Fairlie to Lt Col Lethbridge, 11.10.43. Col Lethbridge was CCAO's representative on the Joint Selection Board.

Lt Colonel Fairlie had previously addressed a minute in similar terms[1] to Air Commodore Groves, who as ADC had been put in charge of training.

A somewhat peculiar situation resulted. While Colonel Sutton and Lt Colonel Gielgud were preparing to make the best of what was being planned for a British Military Government in France, other members of the French Region, in lectures at the Civil Affairs School at Wimbledon, were stating that any attempt to set up a British Military Government in France would be a disaster. No hint of any plans for such an administration were allowed to appear in British propaganda to France or other occupied countries.

An amendment to section 16 of the British Manual of Civil Affairs dealing with information, news and press censorship was considered at a meeting of the AT(E) Committee[2] on 17.8.43 which was attended by the Directors General of PWE and the MoI but although various points were discussed the amendments were neither adopted nor rejected.

A complication which tended to make the plans of the Reoccupation Committee doubly unreal was that while Brigadier Lee was insisting on the *sine qua non* that all executive officers must be British, requests to the War Office for the seconding of British officers for Political Warfare work were being met by refusals and delays pending the approval of a War Establishment which was never approved. The internal difficulties within PWE were thus rendered easier of solution owing to the Adjutant General's Department being unwilling, or unable, to supply the officers necessary to carry out Political Warfare work on the lines insisted upon by Brigadier Lee of Civil Affairs.

Attempt to Make Washington Central Authority for PW

The Prime Minister and the Minister of Information visited Washington at the end of August 1943 and among the subjects discussed was the emergency co-ordination of Political Warfare[3] – a matter which had been raised earlier in the year[4] with the proposal that Political Warfare should be planned in Washington.

General Eisenhower had sent a telegram[5] which, after stating the major Political Warfare policy points in connection with the impending landings in Italy, had criticised existent machinery for disseminating instructions in regard to military and political events of major importance which were likely to arise as a result of the invasion. General Eisenhower therefore suggested that 'for the period of these operations and as a test for future operations that the responsibility for the co-ordination and dissemination be with the Combined

1. Dated 30.9.43.
2. Minutes of 34th Meeting AT(E)M(43)17, 21.8.43.
3. JSM 1149, 2.9.43.
4. See p. 135.
5. NAF 343, 29.8.43.

Chiefs of Staff' in Washington. As this proposal was made only four days before the Italian Armistice the Director General had no option but to accept the proposal in regard to the Italian Armistice and the landings in Italy.

But seeing that if this were to become a precedent, it would mean that the direction of Political Warfare during operations would be in the hands of Mr Crossman and Mr C. D. Jackson in the field, and the Combined Chiefs of Staff in Washington, and that PWE London would have no voice in policy with regard to 'political events . . . of major importance' the Director General minuted the Foreign Secretary recapitulating the objections[1] he had put up to the previous proposal and added that he saw in these proposals the thin end of the American wedge for the control of the political conduct of the war.

The Foreign Secretary agreed and asked that telegrams to the Prime Minister and to Mr Bracken should be drafted.

The Prime Minister was therefore briefed to deal with the proposals, which one suspects had originally been inspired by Mr Crossman. The Washington discussions resulted in an agreement to set up three Political Warfare Committees, one in London for the European theatre, one in Washington to deal with the Pacific theatre and one in New Delhi to deal with the S.E. Asian Command. The decision of each of these committees should be mandatory in all theatres.

The agreement was followed by a visit to London of Mr Warburg, who was accompanied by Mr Adams of the British PW Mission, with the object of[2] agreeing to the machinery of this committee and to discuss changes in approach to Germany, and the possibility of achieving a Unified Central Directive organisation in London and to inquire into general relations between PWE and OWI London. Mr Bowes Lyon's telegram stated that Warburg was eager to set up a Unified Anglo-American Central Directive in London, but that Mr Bowes Lyon believed that it would be an error as it would incur the hostility of the State Department. Mr Bowes Lyon also stated that Mr Sherwood and Mr Elmer Davis were concerned that Mr Wallis Carroll no longer enjoyed the full confidence of PWE. The latter point evoked the reply[3] that Mr Carroll had the complete confidence of PWE but that OWI had not the confidence of the military authorities.

Mr Warburg's visit coincided with a request from COSSAC for a joint PWE/OWI plan for Overlord (the Normandy landings) and Rankin C (the evacuation of France by Germany in order to shorten their line, before the landings in Western Europe).

The London Political Warfare Co-ordinating Committee

In considering the work of this Committee, it must be remembered that its formation was agreed to by the Prime Minister and the Minister of

1. No. 4074, 11.9.43.
2. No. 4074, 11.9.43.
3. No. 6203, 16.9.43.

Information in order[1] that emergency decisions on policy matters regarding Political Warfare should be made in London as had up till then usually been the case, and not by the Combined Chiefs of Staff in Washington as proposed[2] by General Eisenhower and his Political Warfare advisers in North Africa. The need for such a Committee had never presented itself to PWE and the amount of work done by it is a measure not so much of its usefulness, but of how far PWE had previously failed to carry out its functions in providing the required directives in time.

The Chairman of the Committee was Sir Orme Sargent and its members representatives of the British Chiefs of Staff, of ETOUSA, of the American Embassy, of US Chiefs of Staff and of PWE, MoI and OWI.

The Committee during thirteen meetings was more occupied with contingencies for which agreements on policy would be required than with giving directives at short notice with regard to sudden emergencies. In other words, although it had been set up to make decisions, it continually sought policy direction with regard to hypothetical situations. For example, the Agenda of the fifth meeting of the Committee[3] consisted of considerations of three Political Warfare problems:

(a) A proposal that a Russian request for participation in the Committee should be anticipated by an invitation to a more limited form of co-operation. PWE and OWI were instructed to take the matter up with their respective Governments.
(b) The discussion of a broad directive in case we were accused of supporting the Italian King against the wishes of his people. In this case, the Committee decided to telegraph to General Eisenhower that the Allies did not propose to concern themselves with this controversy but this did not mean that they had departed in the least from their declaration that the Italian Government should be more democratic.
(c) Counter propaganda against a German secret weapon. The Committee suggested that there was no reason to regard this as an emergency matter and that it should be handled by PWE and OWI through the ordinary channels.

The above agenda is a good example of the Committee's work and it is fair to say that the only real function of the London Co-ordination Committee was to prevent a similar Committee controlling Political Warfare policy from Washington. The decisions which were required in real emergencies continued to be made sometimes by PWE Director of Plans or by the Regional directorate of PWE, often indeed in the BBC by the Regional Editor or the

1. See Concrete No. 670. To Prime Minister from Foreign Secretary, 1.9.43. 'I am forced to agree to this experiment but am strongly opposed to propaganda control for Europe being exercised from Washington.'
2. In NAF 343, 29.8.43.
3. Held 11.11.43.

programme editor on duty. For speed is the essence of propaganda and when news of real importance which has not been foreseen 'breaks', the man at the microphone can only refer to an authority who is close at hand. If he cannot find him, the man at the microphone makes policy himself.

Alacrity. The Occupation of the Azores Islands

The possibility of a German occupation of the Azores, as an air base from which to threaten the Atlantic Communications of Britain and the United States was a danger which had to be averted before operations were undertaken to Western Europe. Moreover, the Azores would provide a base for Allied flying boats which could protect British convoys and do much to guard against enemy submarines and to hamper enemy blockade runners.

The occupation of the Azores was accordingly decided on and negotiated with the Portuguese.

On 16.9.43 the Joint Staff Mission in Washington[1] telegraphed stating that a request had been received for the US for information as to the propaganda line which PWE would follow so that the State Department and OWI might be in accord with it. A directive was thereupon drafted in PWE, and received approval by those concerned and communicated[2] to the Joint Staff Mission. The directive was that the operation was an implementation of the 600-years-old alliance between Britain and Portugal and had been freely negotiated and HMG hoped that Portugal would continue its policy of neutrality. There should be no suggestion that Portugal was climbing on the bandwagon, or slapping Germany in the face, or that Portugal had abandoned neutrality or succumbed to pressure. The temporary nature of the facilities and Portuguese sovereign rights should be stressed. British and Portuguese relations with Spain were unaffected. Finally the large Anglo-American convoy should not be mentioned as it was an operational matter. This directive which had been agreed with the MoI was carried out in the British press and Home Services of the BBC and in the BBC Foreign Service and in PWE leaflets. The operation calls for no comment and is only mentioned as an example of the kind of routine co-ordination between all the interested parties which had been achieved at this date.

Strategic Deceptions Operations Starkey, Wadham and Tindall

It had for long been clear to the Combined Chiefs of Staff that no important operations outside the Mediterranean area could be undertaken in 1943. It was therefore highly desirable, in order to help the Russians and our own forces in Sicily and Italy, to keep as many German Divisions in the

1. JSM 1182, 16.9.43.
2. COS(W)847, 30.9.43.

West as possible. There were obvious drawbacks to Commando raids: the very heavy losses at Dieppe; the fact that such raids provided experience at least as valuable to the defenders as to the attackers and might result in the enemy building an even more impregnable West Wall at the points where we should have later to land an army in real earnest. It was, however, militarily desirable to give the enemy the impression that we were going to attempt an invasion of France six or nine months before we actually planned to do so. The methods employed in this strategic deception were by a rehearsal of some of the actual methods which would inevitably later be employed during invasion – such measures as concentration of troops, of ships, landing craft, transport and dumps of military materials. Naturally no hint of the secret devices which were later made use of was given, nor was it possible to use battleships owing to the objection of Sir Dudley Pound to risking them in the Channel. One of the chief objects of British air strategy was to weaken German fighter strength before the date of invasion. This was the reason for the policy of precision bombing carried out by Mosquitos on German factories of aircraft and aircraft components and it was highly desirable to supplement this by the maximum wastage of German fighter pilots and aircraft in the actual service. Fighter Command therefore sought every opportunity to make the GAF fighters give combat, and it was GAF policy to refuse combat until D-Day unless they had local tactical superiority.

A secondary object of the deception plans was therefore to bring about an air battle in order to inflict losses on German fighters.

The strategic deception plans drawn up were as follows:

Tindall: preparations for an attack on the Stavanger area of Norway by forces based in Scotland.

Starkey: preparations for a British and Canadian expeditionary force to establish a bridgehead astride Boulogne.

Wadham: preparations for an American airborne landing resulting in the seizure of capture of Brest.

The preparations for Tindall Phase I were arranged to culminate on 25th August, 1943, after which the Germans were to be led to believe that it was a feint.

Operations Starkey and Wadham would be completed on 8th September, 1943, after which date the Germans would be aware that they were only feints.

Tindall Phase III would then be remounted to give the appearance of an invasion of Norway being carried out in mid-November.

The entire series of deception plans were known to PWE as Operation Cockade. The plan for Cockade, submitted by Lt General Morgan, was approved by the Chiefs of Staff and PWE and SOE were invited to draw up detailed plans to offset the political disadvantages likely to attend it.[1]

1. COS(43) 131st meeting item 9, Para. k, 21.6.43.

Cockade

PWE and SOE accordingly drew up a joint plan[1] which was personally discussed with General Morgan and submitted to the Chiefs of Staff Committee.[2]

The Political Warfare problem raised by Cockade was that the operations would be taking place on the eve of the most desperate winter of the war and their effect would be to heighten to flash-point expectations of relief before the winter and then, at the very onset of the winter, to disappoint them.

The Joint Planners' paper[3] proposed to counter the effects heightened, as they would be, by the enemy propaganda presented of Cockade as a failure to invade, by dropping leaflets addressed to the population telling them that the operations were only a rehearsal, for a week before Cockade. The argument in favour of this proposal was that it would have the double advantage of misleading the enemy and of maintaining the confidence of the patriots in the accuracy of our instructions.

The PWE/SOE Plan for Cockade agreed and added that the BBC should be used as an unconscious agent by being allowed to react in a normal and uninformed manner to the news and to leakages in the press.

It was agreed[4] that the French Region should work out the text of the leaflets, the numbers required and targets on which they should be dropped.

Objections to Cockade *Avis* in French Region PWE

The only member of the French Region concerned in the PWE/SOE plan for Cockade was Lt Colonel Gielgud, the Regional Director, who had taken up a new appointment before the final stage of Cockade came into operation without discussing it with his successor Lt Colonel Fairlie. Dr Beck and other members of the French Region were not ticketed for Cockade until 20th August.

Meanwhile a time-table of operational talks and *Avis*, which would assist in the deception of the enemy, had been drawn up by Colonel Sutton DPW (O) and Lt Colonel Gielgud. It was planned to begin with a talk on Resistance preparations and physical fitness on 14th August, to be followed by *Avis* No. 14 on 18th August, a talk on local topography by Lt Colonel Gielgud on the 19th, one on resistance and security by Colonel Sutton on 21st August which was to be followed on the 24th and 26th by talks on recognising Allied troops and enemy dispositions and plans by Lt Colonel Gielgud.

---

1. PWP/C1 'Cockade', 8.7.43.
2. COS(43) 169th meeting, 386(O), 22.7.43.
3. JP(43)209 (Final).
4. PWP/C1, minutes of meeting held 2.7.43.

The early talks and *Avis* No. 14 were duly broadcast – the *Avis* being repeated for several days in succession. The reactions from France are stated to have been extremely bad,[1] but they can hardly have been more violent than those within the French Region of PWE. The result of the operational broadcasts connected with Cockade brought to a head growing dissatisfaction with the chain of authority resulting from the creation of DPW (O) and they resulted in a change of Regional Director, Lt Colonel Gielgud being replaced by Lt Colonel Fairlie.

Further Objections to Cockade *Avis*

Avis No. 14, and the talks, had produced equally violent repercussions within the BBC which led to last-minute alterations in the drafts made by Lt Colonel Gielgud. By a curious mischance, the fact that these alterations had been made resulted in protests from Mr C. D. Jackson from PWB. Mr C. D. Jackson's complaint was that Radio France Algiers had been forced to broadcast the text cabled to them, before the corrections had reached Algiers. As a result the BBC gave a version[2] in much better French than that of Radio France. Since PWB had broadcast from French North Africa, Mr Jackson had found the fact distressing.

The *Avis* itself would certainly seem to indicate that action on the Continent was imminent:

> Une nouvelle étape vers la libération des Pays occupés de l'Europe commence. Il va sans dire que nous ne révêlons pas d'avance dans quelle direction le prochain coup sera porté. . . . Il faut vous préparer jour par jour, semaine par semaine, au rôle que vous aurez à jouer, dans un avenir qui pourrait être proche.

Lt Colonel Fairlie and Dr Beck believed that the cumulative effects of these *Avis* would be most unfortunate and Lt Colonel Fairlie sought to modify the leaflets still to be dropped. *Avis* No. 15 recalled that 'for the last ten days we have invited the French to bring their preparations to perfection in order to be ready for every eventuality on the day when we will be able to announce the direction of the next Allied operation. This day has not yet come.' But having said this, the *Avis* added nothing except to counsel extreme prudence, 'all the more necessary as we approach the moment when the plans of the Allied High Command will be put into execution'.

There is little doubt that such an *Avis* laid British propaganda open to ridicule, and that it would depress and mystify our friends. It was a case of our crying wolf without an obvious excuse.

---

1. Information from Dr Beck.
2. Minute from M. Georges Picard, Chief French Radio Section PWB, to Major MacDonald.

It was agreed[1] therefore that *Avis* No. 15 should be cancelled and *Avis* No. 16 was amended. This *Avis* stated that exercises were being carried out on a large scale but that 'it must not be assumed that this is a prelude to the disembarkation of the Armies of Liberation. . . . Present operations constitute only a rehearsal on a large scale. . . . Today we say: The invasion is not yet.' Dr Beck, however, remained convinced that that leaflet also would have a most unfortunate effect, and Lt Colonel Fairlie was able to have the leaflet cancelled[2] and *Avis* No. 17 substituted. This was in effect a denial of German rumours 'that we are concentrating armies on our coasts with intentions of invading the Continent . . . these provocations are intended to create among you manifestations and disorders which the Germans will use as an excuse for repressive measures.'

The proposal was to drop this *Avis* from 1st September until 8th September but its dissemination was postponed[3] as the possibility of cancelling Starkey altogether was being debated by Chiefs of Staff on 2nd September. This postponement allowed time for the question of its dissemination to be re-examined.

By 1.8.43 the position with regard to Starkey was that all troop concentrations were complete, actual embarkation of troops and mine-sweepers had begun, telephone censorship was in force in various areas and most of the landing craft were at their stations.

Lt Colonel Fairlie and Dr Beck had by that time become convinced that it would be wiser to suppress all warnings and their advice was accordingly agreed to. Thus PWE played no part in trying to offset the damaging results of these exercises.

Failure of Deception Plan

It only remains to add that on the scheduled D-day, the ships sailed at the appointed time and after approaching the French coast turned back. The hoped for air battle did not materialise as the enemy took no notice whatever of the operation.

Starkey, though no doubt valuable as a rehearsal for Overlord, was in other respects a failure. It had been a period of great difficulty for the French Regional experts of PWE, but it had resulted in the replacement of a weak Regional Director[4] who was not willing to oppose the military authorities by a stronger man who would oppose them whenever their plans conflicted with political realities. The change saved PWE from acquiescence in disastrous blunders and enabled it to play a useful part in regard to France.

1. Notes of a meeting held at Norfolk House, 20.7.43.
2. Notes of a meeting held at Norfolk House, 27.8.43.
3. Minute from General Brooks to Director General, 30.8.43.
4. See p. 343.

Plan Jitler

Nor were the deception plan experts more successful in what may be called a frontier excursion into Political Warfare with Plan Jitler, put forward at the end of October or early in November 1943 by LCS.

The plan, which need not be considered in detail, was to induce mutual distrust and suspicion among the high personnages of the Nazi Party and the German High Command by means of rumours circulated through 'high grade channels'.

It was immediately apparent in PWE that Plan Jitler had been drawn up by persons with a very superficial knowledge of what had been done in the field of 'sibs'.

The Director of Plans, PWE, while agreeing with the plan in principle pointed out that:[1]

> The examples of suggested stories in Plan Jitler are, for the most part, the type of stories from which multiple variations have already been wrung by PWE/SOE. It is felt that a different calibre of rumour is necessary for the channels suggested by LCS. PWE therefore propose that LCS should take part in the weekly rumour discussions of PWE and SOE.

Deception Plans in Connection with Overlord. Zeppelin

Many of the security precautions taken by PWE were in the nature of deception, for example the printing of guide-books for troops for Holland, Denmark and Norway simultaneously as for France and Belgium and the drafting of routine leaflets for Germany and France which were never printed while the special leaflets for Overlord were in production. But the chief assistance PWE and PWB were able to give was in connection with Plan Zeppelin which was designed to suggest that we were preparing to attack 'the soft under belly of the Axis' in the South of France and in the neighbourhood of Istria.

During Stage 4, beginning on 10.5.44, PWE was asked to reveal in its propaganda output:

1. Increased Allied interest in the French Resistance movement between Toulouse and the Mediterranean.
2. Special interest in conserving facilities in the regions of Pola and Trieste by appealing to sympathisers in those places not to carry out wanton sabotage.
3. Dropping of leaflets aimed at the morale of German forces should be concentrated on the S.W. of France and Istria.

---

1. Plan Jitler, 15.11.43.

4. Propaganda to resistance groups in Istria and not in the Balkans generally.
5. Appeals to Bulgaria to show a noticeable decline.

Communications on this subject were between Colonel R. E. L. Wingate for LCS and Air Commodore Groves for PWE.

PWE/SOE Plan

The problem which had stultified much of the work of the PWE/MoI Reoccupation Committee owing to the acceptance of Brigadier Lee's ruling, was dealt with far more realistically in the PWE/SOE plan for the period up to and during the invasion which was drawn up in the summer of 1943, in accordance with a decision of the PWE/SOE Coordinating Committee.[1] The underlying need for such a plan had been stated[2] by Major Gallie who had succeeded Hackett as head of the Hackett School. After pointing out that civilian reaction after liberation might well be surprising, and putting such questions as: 'Will there be a civil war in France, a constitutional crisis in Belgium, a refusal to co-operate with us on the part of the Dutch?', he pointed out that: 'One factor will exercise a determining influence . . . the degree to which the at present suppressed peoples feel that they have been partners with the invading armies in obtaining and accelerating victory.' It was vital to restore to the oppressed peoples their [n]ational self-respect, 'For lack of self-respect is not a moral zero, it is an active virus.' That virus would find expression in criticism, non-cooperation and internal conflicts unless it were removed; the antidote to it 'was a sense of active contribution towards the defeat of the enemy and the revival of European freedom'.

Moreover German resistance was likely to be extremely bitter to our first attempts at invasion and it was 'vital to mobilise fully the marginal forces in our support and this means not just activist groups but whole populations'. The paper pointed out that the necessary work had not been done 'because there are at least two Government Departments whose charters make them, ostensibly, responsible for the field under review and that those . . . responsible for preparation of military offensives would suppose the task was being done by those within whose charter it falls'.

Mr Hackett was nominated as the SOE representative on the Joint Planning Sub-committee. PWE was represented by Mr Harman (Regional Director for the Low Countries), Mr Garnett (Directorate of Plans), and Mr Parker (Low Countries Region).

The introduction to the plan states:

1. Meeting of 21.6.43.
2. The Civilian Component in the coming Battle of Europe.

The problem is one of harvesting and should yield such results as Deterioration of German troop morale, Co-operation of civilian population in accordance with the needs of Allied forces, Availability of reliable local leaders, Facilitation of the tasks of Allied occupying authorities.

The table of objectives of the plan includes, under three headings:

A. Immobilisation of enemy transport.
Destruction of records useful to the enemy.
Stirring up troubles and strikes among workers in German-occupied territory.
Arming prisoners of war, political prisoners, etc.
Depriving the enemy of the services of Quislings and collaborators.
Depriving the enemy of stocks of food, fuel and ammunition.
Undermining the enemy troop morale.
Confusion and deception of enemy.
General guerilla activities.
Organisation of attacks on grounded aircraft.
Organisation of attacks on enemy headquarters.

B. Utilisation of population's local knowledge of topography, enemy disposition, dumps, etc.
Utilisation of local labour resources.
Utilisation of local personnel for social services, firefighting, ARP relief, etc.
Preservation of records useful to Allies.
Utilisation of loyal local administration and police.
Utilisation of local intelligence for Allied security services.

C. Propagation of an understanding of how the civilian population can protect themselves, injure the enemy and aid the Allies.
Securing information necessary for direction of propaganda to civil population.
Distribution of news and instructions to civilian populations.
Establishment and maintenance of contact.

Value of PWE/SOE Plan

The plan covered a vast field and after it had been drawn up and accepted by both departments an officer, Major Ingram Fraser, was appointed in order to follow up the work necessary for carrying out the plan in the different regions. The value of the overall plan was great. It formed the basis, with practically no alteration, for the PWE/OWI and SOE/OSS plan called for by COSSAC and accepted by SHAEF. It required the drawing up of [a] regional working plan, to implement it. Much of the work had already been done, but the PWE and SOE regional experts were made to see what would be required of them, and how far their work fell short.

Apart from the degree to which this overall plan influenced the course of events, it is a document of interest as showing what advantages a commander in the field can hope to receive from a resistance movement and a co-operative population under ideal conditions.

Certain amendments were in fact made to the plan. The project of arming Allied prisoners of war in Germany was vetoed on account of the fear of a general massacre of Allied prisoners of war. The project of encouraging 'displaced persons' to trek home and German civilians to evacuate their homes in front of our advance, in order to cause the uttermost confusion on the enemy's lines of communications, was struck out of the plan as being militarily undesirable, though much the same operation was actually carried out, as regards the German population, during the Allied crossing of the Rhine,[1] and once our troops had over-run an area in Germany nothing could stop displaced persons from trekking home so that we suffered from the disadvantages without enjoying the advantages proposed.

The plan was approved first by COSSAC and then by the Chiefs of Staff.[2] Thus SHAEF was 'committed' to co-operation with the Resistance movements as partners in the work of liberating their countries.

The Overlord Plans

Detailed plans for the landings in the West of Europe were drawn up by General Morgan, Chief of Staff to the Supreme Army Commander who was at the head of the COSSAC organisation at Norfolk House and these detailed plans became available to ticketed officers of PWE in and after September 1943.[3] It is worth remarking that these plans were subsequently carried out the following June unaltered as to place and scarcely altered with regard to a large number of details.

PWE was intimately concerned with planning in connection with a large number of military plans which had been drawn up in connection with Overlord. The following contingencies had been studied:

Rankin A

Such a weakening of the German armed forces as would enable us to attack in the West with available Anglo-American forces – (that is *before* the date fixed for Overlord).

Rankin B

The Germans in order to shorten their lines [of] communications withdraw from the Western Occupied Countries.

1. See p. 440.
2. Item COS(44)108(O), 8.12.43, and item 5 COS, 10.2.44.
3. The present writer's ticket no. 14 was dated 12.9.43.

Rankin C

German unconditional surrender with the cessation of organised German opposition in the West.

Whereas Rankin A and B speeded up the anticipated timetable, Rankin C would present PWE with an entirely new series of urgent problems in all theatres simultaneously. It involved the control of populations, resistance movements and of workers in Todt organisations in friendly countries, and of all the elements within Germany itself.

PWE informed[1] that 'COSSAC would require an outline propaganda plan which would cover Rankin and Overlord'.

The assumption for Rankin was that plans were in existence for a rapid return to the Continent in the event of a German collapse. That for Overlord was that an invasion would be made in maximum strength in May 1944 in order to give Germany the knock-out blow. It was suggested that 'the interim propaganda plan for Rankin must be capable of developing into the full plan for Overlord', a statement which seems to show a failure to grasp the problems involved which were entirely different.

In answer to questions raised at the meeting which followed between COSSAC, Sir Robert Bruce Lockhart, Major General Brooks and Mr Wallace Carroll, General Morgan said that for Overlord he required a plan to cover both the period between October 1943 and D-Day and the period after D-Day. The question of whether separate plans were prepared was for PWE and OWI.

PWE/OWI Outline Plan

PWE Director of Plans prepared a plan in conjunction with OWI securing SOE approval for the passages relevant to their work.

Underlying the plan was the statement that to render maximum assistance to Overlord and Rankin, Political Warfare must 'exploit and canalise[2] the political ferments behind the enemy lines', but that Political Warfare can only do so effectively 'if the highest authorities gave their support to such movements'.

The plan included in its aims such hardy annuals as: 'So to affect the will of the German people and the German armed forces as to make them refuse to continue the war' and 'to cause satellites to abandon Germany in circumstances which will assist Overlord'. But its main purpose was to complete the process of enlisting, preparing and mobilising the peoples of occupied countries for action within the framework of United Nations plans in such a way as to render maximum assistance to Overlord and Rankin.

OWI had added an aim of its own with which PWE was not concerned: 'to create maximum goodwill . . . towards the United Nations cause among the peoples of neutral countries'.

---

1. Item COS(44)108(O), 8.12.43, and item 5 COS, 10.2.44.
2. PWE/OWI outline plan, para. III.

The plan was submitted to the two PWE Ministers for approval before being sent to COSSAC. Sir Alexander Cadogan minuted: 'Serious comment cannot be made on this without the annexes.'

It is fair to say that the greater portion of the Annexes in question were, with the alterations already noted, the PWE/SOE plan which had been prepared that summer and put forward as a separate document.

Thus the preparatory work done in the Directorate of Plans was not lost or superseded. It was merely 'geared to the requirements of Overlord and the contingency of Rankin'.

Appendix III was, however, new material and dealt with the complex subject of 'Propagation of a Realistic Understanding of what is involved to the Civilian Population in an Allied invasion and the need for machinery for opinion sampling in occupied territories'.

The plan concluded with an extremely detailed estimate[1] of the Provisional Aircraft lift required for leaflet dissemination on D-Day.

The plan was approved[2] by Major General Bedell Smith (for General Eisenhower) on 4.12.43 and submitted to the British Chiefs of Staff. The London Co-ordination Committee made certain amendments and on 24.1.44 the plan with an outline plan for Rankin C was again forwarded to the British Chiefs of Staff for transmission to the Combined Chiefs of Staff in Washington.

Joint PWE/OWI/OSS Plan for Covert Attack on the Morale of German Forces

[17.12.43] This plan was complementary to the larger plan. The objects listed were to spread the view among the German forces in the West that the German High Command regarded the defence of the Atlantic coast as a sideshow and intended to make their real stand on the frontiers of Germany, particularly on the East and that outlying garrisons would be abandoned.

The other main object was to stimulate fear of being posted to the Eastern front. Special attacks should be made on the allegiance of foreign soldiers in the German forces – Poles, Slovaks, Czechs and Croats.

Formation of Psychological Warfare Branch for Overlord

Mr Warburg's arrival in Great Britain[3] coincided[4] with the invitation from COSSAC to prepare a joint PWE/OWI plan of Political Warfare for Overlord and Rankin. The plan described in the foregoing pages was taken to the USA by Mr Warburg on his return. During Mr Warburg's visit a decision was

1. Annexe II, Appendices i, ii, iii.
2. Brigadier General McClure to Director General PWE, 7.2.44.
3. See p. 338.
4. Major General Brooks to Mr Bowes Lyon, 7.10.43.

taken to 'integrate' PWE and OWI so that the two organisations should pool resources and each should concentrate on the work it did best.

The Supreme Army Commander himself had not been chosen and his nationality, British or American, was not to be known for several months. The relationship of PWE and OWI and an integrated Anglo-American Psychological Warfare Branch had to be worked out without delay as Psychological Warfare in connection with Overlord had to be tied in with the Supreme Commander's plans as early as possible. In any case, as the BBC and the new American Radio ABSIE which had been built in Britain by OWI would for a long while dominate all radio output to Western Europe, it was obvious that PWE and OWI (the 'civilian agencies' as they were called) would play a far larger part in the liberation of Western Europe than they had done in North Africa and Italy.

After discussions with the Public Relations Officers of the three Services, the Minister of Information, and General Devas of the US Army, Lieutenant General Morgan submitted proposals[1] for the formation of a branch for Publicity and Psychological Warfare at the Headquarters of the Supreme Allied Commander.

A feature of the organisation proposed was that Psychological Warfare should be placed under a colonel who would have advisers without executive authority, from the appropriate agencies.

> It is suggested that the civil agencies concerned with Psychological Warfare should be invited to attach to the branch one or more technical advisers on propaganda addressed to enemy, enemy-occupied, and liberated peoples. It should be emphasised that these advisers have no executive authority this being the function of the Major General (Publicity and Psychological Warfare's staff).

The proposals were submitted to the Chiefs of Staff Committee[2] which approved the formation of such a branch and instructed the secretary to submit the proposals to the US Chiefs of Staffs. The US Chiefs of Staff[3] put forward counter proposals at a meeting of the combined Chiefs of Staff. The US Chiefs of Staff were convinced[4] that two heads were essential (one British and one US) in view of the problem of public relations and the reactions of the press, since both US and British would be more confident in the organisations 'if they knew their interests were being looked after by their own representative'. The proposal would seem to have been only concerned with the needs of war correspondents. The British Chiefs of Staff Committee dissented from this proposal. 'So far from such an

1. COSSAC(43)45, 7.9.43.
2. COS 217 meeting item 7, 16.9.43.
3. CCS 124 meeting item 4, 22.10.43.
4. JSM 1277, 23.10.43.

arrangement[1] satisfying the correspondents we think it would separate them further each feeling they had an advocate and each head being in danger of finding himself played off against the other.'

The US Chiefs of Staff finally agreed to leave the question of the appointment of one or of two heads to the discretion of the Supreme Commander[2] and this proposal was agreed to by the British Chiefs of Staff.

Most elaborate organisational charts were drawn up in this initial period and much time was spent on discussing the rank and functions of the Political Warfare Advisers who were to be without executive authority.

The organisation proposed bore a curious similarity to that which had been created by the introduction of PWE Regional Directors into the BBC. It will be remembered that they had been inserted, without executive authority, into a hierarchic organisation to control its policy. It is unlikely that such a system would have worked with less friction in [the] Anglo-American military hierarchy of SHAEF than in the BBC. Fortunately the plans were substantially modified.

After his appointment, General Eisenhower appointed General Robert McClure head of the Publicity and Psychological Warfare Division. No proposal for separating Psychological Warfare and Publicity each under its own head seems to have been suggested or considered.

In the end, the pattern evolved was substantially that which had been reached by PWB AFHQ. Four civilian deputies were appointed for Psychological Warfare, one drawn from each of the 'civilian agencies' PWE, MoI, OWI and OSS.

Brigadier General McClure

Psychological Warfare		Press	
Mr Jackson	Mr Crossman	Mr Oechsner	Mr Routh
OWI	PWE	OSS	MoI

Responsibility for Black and Grey

In theory, Mr Oechsner should have been Deputy for all 'Black Operations', but in practice, this would not have worked well as Mr Oechsner lacked that harmonious understanding of Mr Delmer's ideas which was the first requisite for success.

The difficulty was overcome by attaching Lt Commander McLachlan of NID 17Z to the staff of Admiral Ramsay, the Supreme Naval Commander for Overlord. Lt Commander McLachlan had been voluntarily assisting Mr Delmer on Special Operations from January 1943. In March 1944, he was made responsible for the co-ordination of PWE Black and Grey operations with SHAEF. The following October Brigadier General McClure appointed him Chief of Special Operations Section PWD. He

1. OZ 3517, 2.11.43.
2. JSM 1437, 20.1.44.

thus became Mr Crossman's opposite number. Squadron Leader Hodgkin became his assistant.

The danger of such an organisation was that the Departments might be devoured by their own children. Nor, in the case of PWE, was Mr Crossman the Department's favourite child, though he was certainly one of the most brilliant. In other words, there was a tendency for the civilian deputy to make his own policy and to demand the seconding of the best men from his parent department in order to usurp its functions with improvised services which it might have carried out better. In some instances this gave rise to duplication. The danger was augmented in the case of PWE, by the absence of the Director General on sick leave, and by the distrust and antagonism which subsisted between Mr Crossman and certain officers of the Department. This distrust had led to an attempt to nominate Colonel Thornhill and Colonel Sutton for the key positions in SHAEF. Mr Crossman obtained his position only by a request for his services from Brigadier General McClure to the Director General.

It was perfectly proper for PWD SHAEF to make the fullest possible use of the resources of the Department, and it mattered little what label or shoulder-flash was affixed to what individual, so long as the work was done. The danger was, with Mr Crossman in charge of Psychological Warfare plans, of uncontrolled policy-making. This danger was, however, later on corrected by the formation of the Tripartite Committee with Sir Robert Bruce Lockhart in the chair.

Policy Dangers

The chief danger which was foreseen in PWE was the divergence of British and American policy to France and the Western Allies and the possibility that the Americans might repeat the political mistakes of the North African landings, without the justification of short-term military advantage. A comparable danger was threatened by the unrealistic nature of the War Office preparations for an Allied Military Government, with British officers only in charge of civil affairs.

It was clearly the function of PWE, and especially of its French and Low Countries Regional experts, to open the eyes of the American and British Army authorities to the nature of French, Belgium and Dutch resistance and of the part which they would play in the liberation of their countries. This was carried in various ways in which PWE staff acted as missionaries anxious to make converts to the PWE views.

Dr Beck's Visit to the USA

One of the most useful of these appears to have been the visit of Dr Beck to the USA in November 1943. Mr Bowes Lyon reported:[1]

1. No. 2694. Mr Bowes Lyon to Major General Books, 13.11.43.

> Besides successfully conducting negotiations on particular matters (like the adoption by OSS for the War Department of PWE European Handbooks, and the approval by OWI Overseas Branch for the French Plan for the winter 1943/4 he had had a variety of contacts. . . .
>
> Field Marshal Dill, for example, had Beck to lunch privately and I am sure was able to clarify his picture in France by questioning Beck closely about the strength and organisation of resistance, etc. Dill was clearly impressed because shortly afterwards General Macready asked to see Beck and spent an hour and a half in listening to his analysis of the French underground. General Donovan had Beck to dinner alone – a rare honour. The Charlottesville School of Military Government invited Beck to lecture there and to address their special Seminar on France. . . . Chancery arranged for Beck to meet the head of the French desk in the State Department at lunch; next day another member of the State Department asked to see him, obviously because the first one had reported what good value Beck was. He had lunch with Walter Lippmann and breakfast with Edgar Mowrer and got them both a bit straighter on France. He did not confine himself to the illustrious; he got right down to the working desk in OWI and OSS. . . . Galantière, head of the French desk in OWI, has spoken to me enthusiastically about the benefit to his section's work of Beck's visit. . . .
>
> I think I am not exaggerating when I say that Beck's influence over here may have significant political results.

Later Dr Beck was to supplement his lecture at Charlottesville by a number of lectures on conditions in France given to the American Training School for Civil Affairs personnel at Shrivenham, Wilts. The head of the Training School, Colonel Dillard, informed the PWE Director of Training that these lectures had made a very great impression and asked for other PWE lecturers to visit Shrivenham and this was done in due course with regard to Germany by Mr Duncan Wilson and other lecturers from PWE.[1]

Proposals for 'Integration' with OWI

One of the results of the proposals for 'integration' with OWI was the formation of the Leaflet Committee set up under the Chairmanship of Sir Percy Loraine in order that 'PWE should get its own plans cleared[2] and leaflet output co-ordinated with the Central Directive before we tackled the problems of co-ordination with the Americans which would arise partly owing to the US setting aside aircraft entirely for leaflet distribution and partly owing to the intensification we expected in leaflet propaganda.'

1. See p. 400.
2. Minutes of 1st Meeting of Leaflet Committee, 25.11.43.

Difficulty of Separating Leaflet Writers from Regions

One of the first problems which arose was the proposal to move all PWE persons connected with writing and producing leaflets to new premises leased by OWI in Grosvenor Square. Some forty persons were involved. The offer to provide premises had been made by OWI owing to shortage of accommodation which was anticipated owing to the demands for Overlord even after moving several of the PWE Regions to Ingersoll House and others to Carey Street. But 'leaflet writer' was not a category with strictly defined limits. 'Black' leaflet writers were not to be moved for security reasons, but the same experts in many cases wrote Black and White leaflets. At the second meeting of the Committee, protests were made by Regional representatives and the Committee decided that it would be detrimental that leaflet-writing staffs should be separated from the other personnel of the Regions. Pressure was, however, put on the Regional Heads to agree to the move as CAO stated that the space asked for could only be obtained by moving the leaflet writers.[1] The wider policy of integration was also involved. Sir Percy Loraine* stated[2] that the whole tendency was towards integration of English and American effort wherever it was useful to do so. On a high level OWI were dissatisfied with their leaflets and were anxious to benefit from PWE experience and the psychological effects of securing this American ground would be great. An interesting by-product of the dispute over accommodation was a destructive analysis of the papers produced by DPWI's Department (which occupied the whole of the sixth floor) and their usefulness.

A compromise was arranged[3] by which the Keeble and McMillan Units which were non-regional and concerned with printing and production of leaflets and newspapers and booklets and magazines respectively should be moved to Grosvenor Square. As a result, the Keeble Unit was entirely integrated with its OWI opposite number and occupied three floors. The McMillan Unit had a floor entirely to itself. It was decided, however, that the leaflet writers should not be separated from the Regions.[4]

If the proposals for integration, as originally put up, had been hurriedly agreed to, PWE leaflets would have suffered in quality owing to the destruction of the authority of the Regional Director and the break-up of Regional team-work. On the other hand the value of complete integration in any department of effort with the Americans would have been very great.

With the problem of accommodation out of the way, the Committee was able to devote itself to the immediate problems of Overlord. Several

---

1. Minutes of 3rd Meeting of Leaflet Committee.
2. *Ibid.*
3. Minutes of the 4th Meeting of Leaflet Committee.
4. *Ibid.*

* [Sir Percy Lyham Loraine, 12th baronet (1880–1961), served in Boer War 1899; entered FO 1904; attached to peace conference delagation 1918–19; Minister, Teheran, 1921; High Commissioner, Egypt and Sudan, 1929–33; Ambassador, Italy 1939–40]

Regional experts pointed out that there had been 'a disastrous failure in the case of North Africa owing to lack of guidance of the political side'. It had been by pure luck that PWE French Region had secured the deletion of a reference to 'mon vieil ami Philippe Pétain' by President Roosevelt.[1]

Meanwhile, although a political policy had not been defined, Mr Backer of OWI was planning twenty publications for use in France after the bridgehead had been established. Occupational publications would have to [be] put in hand early as operational leaflets would have priority later on. But a political directive in regard to their contents was lacking.

Detailed demands for increases of staff were put forward to the Committee and approval secured by the Chairman. The Committee acted therefore as a clearing house by which all problems and needs in connection with leaflets could be focussed and approval obtained from Major General Brooks by the Chairman.

A paper on Problems of Anglo-American Co-operation was drafted by the Secretary (Mr Garnett) with the assistance of Major Ryder and the Regional experts. The proposals contained in this paper were incorporated into a paper covering other matters on Anglo-American Co-operation which was submitted by Major General Brooks to the Minister of Information. It is obvious that Major General Brooks and PWE had been working wholeheartedly for the greatest degree of Anglo-American integration which was compatible with efficiency (i.e. Britain and America would do better to make separate approaches to the occupied peoples). But it was contemplated that these should be planned jointly.

The proposals in the paper put up to the Minister of Information[2] contemplated integration with regard to planning, training, printing and dissemination of leaflets and the first paragraphs dealt with the reorientation of OWI.

Proposals for Integration Sent to Mr Bracken

> I have been told privately by OWI that Mr Robert Sherwood has cancelled his projected visit to Australia and intends to come to London about January 18th. The reason for this change of plan is, I am told, that he has reached the conclusion that since the London Co-ordinating Committee's directives are mandatory for the European theatre of operations, it will make for efficiency if all political warfare activities in this theatre are co-ordinated here. He proposed accordingly to transfer the majority of OWI's European experts to London en bloc, where they will work under Mr Jackson.

1. Minutes of 6th Meeting of Leaflet committee, 10.1.44.
2. Major General Brooks to Minister of Information, 9.1.44.

> From our point of view I regard this as the best possible arrangement. I am confident that as a result, PWE's control of output will be simplified and improved. It will mean, of course, that with Mr Sherwood's arrival PWE will be asked to make arrangements for the maximum co-ordination of effort with OWI. I am therefore summarising below the activities which we should agree to undertake jointly and would ask your general authority to negotiate with OWI on the basis of these proposals.

The joint activities listed were planning by a joint planning staff; production by a joint team under Mr Keeble at 43, Grosvenor Square; training at Brondesbury and leaflets. The proposals in connection with leaflets were that the PWE Leaflet Committee should become a joint PWE/OWI Committee; that British and American leaflet quotas should be based on the respective USAAF and RAF disseminations by all leaflet-carrying aircraft based on Britain, which was estimated as approximately one to two; that the RAF and USAAF should be asked to agree to disseminate leaflets as a reciprocal service, and that the allocation of the estimated USAAF potential of 50 million single-sheet leaflets monthly should be 30% each for Holland, Belgium and Norway, 10% for France.

Dissemination of leaflets by the USAAF was rapidly increasing. (By establishing a quota on the 2 to 1 ratio PWE would have secured most advantageous disseminations of its own leaflets as compared with those of OWI until figures were revised.)

Advantages of Integration for PWE

By an agreement that dissemination was to be a reciprocal service PWE would have secured a 2 to 1 regular dissemination of its leaflets compared with those of OWI in areas in which the RAF were not disseminating any leaflets at all, and had not disseminated leaflets regularly at any period during the war: that is to say in Belgium, Holland and Denmark with a possibility of regular dissemination in Norway. But apart from these advantages PWE had everything to gain by taking the lead in a policy of wholehearted co-operation in a field in which its predominance up till that time was assured, but in which the Americans were to make immense strides which soon outstripped the arrangements which subsisted between PWE and the RAF.

Mr Bracken Reverses Plans for 'Integration' with OWI

The Minister was, however, less impressed by these advantages than by the news of impending difficulties within OWI itself which had recently reached his ears and to which he appears to have attached too great an importance. He therefore replied in a letter in his own hand which was little less than a polemic on the internal politics of American institutions:

General Brooks. *Your paper dated (Jan. 9th) on OWI*
I am not persuaded of the benefits of any closer association with OWI. Here are my reasons:

1. The people who control this organisation are incompetent, shifty, and hare-brained.
2. They will issue a great deal of silly stuff which they miscall propaganda and when they are attacked in America (as they surely will be) an attempt will be made to make PWE the whipping boy.
3. They have no consistent policy. The content of their hectic output depends on American electoral considerations. The Polish vote, the Balts vote, the Jewish vote and above all the German vote will slant what politeness forces me to call their thought.
4. Their absurd actions followed by their gibbering explanations have earned them the contempt of most of the American newspapers, broadcasts and indeed all who understand the elements of publicity.
5. OWI may be wound up at any time. Or what is left of their functions may be collared by General Donovan. Why therefore should we waste valuable time on this decaying and despised organisation?

My advice to you is to show great politeness in any dealings you must have with them. Do not take any responsibility for their actions. For if you do they will surely try to make you wallow with them in the squalid mess they created in America and wish to reproduce here.

We shall have a talk about this business when I return to work.

B.B.[1]

In the absence of the Director General, who was still seriously ill in a Nursing Home in Scotland, Major General Brooks, who was, in a peculiar degree, the representative of the Minister of Information, did not refer the policy matters contained in this letter to the Foreign Secretary, or to the Foreign Office. As a result, he found himself having initiated policies which he was not authorised to implement but from which he could not diplomatically withdraw.

Results of Mr Bracken's Letter

As a result a temporising policy was adopted which became increasingly difficult to maintain. Sir Percy Loraine reported to the Committee that no decision was possible[2] as we did not know who was going to carry leaflets or where they were going to be carried. The entire question of the authority under which aircraft would operate was involved.

---

1. Letter from Minister of Information to General Brooks, 10.1.44.
2. Minutes of the 9th Meeting of the Leaflet Committee, 31.1.44.
3. *Ibid.*

At the same meeting, Mr Keeble stated that 'he was attending[3] a meeting that afternoon with the Americans who were offering us a proportion of their dissemination over Belgium and Holland . . . if later on we said we did not want such facilities the impression would be deplorable'.

A month later, Mr Keeble, who, as he had previously reminded the Committee, was 'in the happy position of being fully integrated', said that the Americans were baffled at not being invited to attend the meetings of the Leaflet Committee.[1] With regard to the Low Countries they had offered us generous facilities for disseminations but were not consulted. He himself had taken evasive action to avoid having to answer their questions. The Americans were unable to understand our reluctance to plan the use of our joint facilities in dissemination.

The Chairman suggested that a case should be stated on paper, but as Squadron Leader Hodgkin pointed out the case had already been stated but no decision could be obtained.

By the time authority to go ahead with discussions with the Americans had been obtained[2] (after the return to work of Sir Robert Bruce Lockhart) the Committee was informed that such rapid developments had taken place in American daylight disseminations that we could no longer put forward the figures contained in the original paper. Three months had been wasted, the Americans were estranged and PWE never regained the leadership which it had held within its grasp.

OWI Crisis

During January 1944, an internal crisis arose within OWI[3] owing to a dispute between Mr Robert Sherwood, who until then had been left in unrestricted control of the OWI Overseas Branch, and Mr Elmer Davis, who had decided to exercise personal supervision of it. Mr Davis wished to shift authority from New York, the centre of broadcasting, to Washington and decided that Warburg, Barnes and Johnson should be sacked.

As a result, Mr Sherwood appealed to President Roosevelt, but the quarrel was one of those dilemmas which the President preferred to leave unsolved.[4] Mr Sherwood was the President's personal friend. Mr Davis was popular and a political force, and Mr Joe Barnes might, if he resigned, become an unwelcome reinforcement to Mr Wendell Wilkie's resources.

But although President Roosevelt rebuked both men[5] and refused to allow resignations, Mr Elmer Davis proceeded on 6th February to demand the resignation of Mr Barnes, Mr Warburg and Mr Johnson. Personal loy-

---

1. Minutes of the 13th Meeting of the Leaflet Committee, 28.2.44.
2. Minutes of the 15th Meeting of the Leaflet Committee, 13.3.44.
3. No. 431 Washington to FO, 30.1.44.
4. Letter from Mr Miall, 3.4.43.
5. No. 546 from Bowes Lyon to Major General Brooks, 3.2.44.
6. No. 616 Bowes Lyon to Major General Brooks, 7.2.44.

alty[6] to President Roosevelt, who refused to accept his resignation, led Mr Sherwood to remain at his post, but he decided to leave immediately for London in order 'to save what he could from the wreck'.

The loss of these experienced men who had been concerned with Psychological Warfare since its beginning in America was not only a severe blow to OWI but to PWE/OWI co-operation. In an analysis of events after his return from London, Mr Miall reported[1] that there was a new attitude towards collaboration with the British and for a time he had been excluded from the Editorial Board.

Results of Changes in OWI

Mr Adams had already warned PWE[2] that the abrupt disappearance of Barnes, Warburg and Johnson would lead to confusion and that there was 'a far greater chance of bloomers occurring than three weeks ago'.

An example of the new spirit in OWI was the development of a habit of building up a broadcast programme out of large numbers of quotations in order to avoid committing the American Government by the 'Voice of America'. Such quotations were sometimes embarrassing to PWE – for example OWI French programmes[3] were very fond of using quotations from F5 Honneur et Patrie and asking for them to be rebroadcast on the BBC.

With Mr Sherwood's departure to Britain as OWI representative in London a complete change came about in the former close relationship between the British Political Warfare Mission and OWI in the United States.

Mr Bowes Lyon reported[4] that OWI had become almost exclusively an informational service and news agency and had almost ceased to be an agency of Political Warfare. The efforts of Elmer Davis, Barrett, and Wallace Carroll to prevent the institution of a joint directive in London, and their desire to preserve a greater measure of directive formulation in Washington, were definitely injurious to the war effort.

The deterioration in the relations between OWI and the British PW Mission with regard to the European field was to grow steadily throughout the summer of 1944, until[5] OWI was ignoring the PWE Mission as much as it could without being openly hostile, it never of its own initiative discussed any problems with it. OWI was issuing all its directives (except the Central Directive) without consultation and had in fact adopted an attitude of studious evasiveness to every approach. Ever since the departure of Sherwood and the appearance of his successors the intention of OWI had been plainly to steer clear of PWE.

---

1. Letter from Mr Miall, 3.4.43.
2. Mr Adams to Mrs O'Neill, 14.2.44.
3. Letter from Mr Adams to Dr Beck, 4.4.44.
4. Letter from Mr Bowes Lyon to Director General, 24.7.44.
5. Secret and Personal Letter from Bowes Lyon to Lockhart, 5.9.44.

A memorandum by Mr Elmer Davis on projects undertaken for other agencies dated 6.7.44 illustrates the shift of interest from Political Warfare to informational work:[1]

> Projects which merely increase the health and happiness of foreign peoples, without directly and clearly tending to increase their effective good will towards the United States lie outside our field of activity . . . we are under no obligation to conduct propaganda for United Nations agencies (such as UNRRA). Unless such an agency has a clear propaganda value for the United States, as distinguished from the United States information offices.

It is only reasonable, however, to surmise that the American attitude was influenced by the temporising and baffling policy adopted by PWE after the Minister of Information had refused to allow integration between PWE and OWI to proceed as planned.

ABSIE and Relations with OWI in Regard to Broadcasting in 1944

A policy of complete integration between PWE and OWI in view of Overlord would have been particularly welcome to the Americans in respect of broadcasting. For whereas the allocation of a leafleting squadron of Fortresses and the technical developments of the leaflet bomb were to make the USAAF a more valuable disseminating agency for printed propaganda than the RAF there was no hope of American broadcast programmes to Europe seriously competing with the BBC which was not only technically far superior to any possible American radio service to Europe, both in strength of signal and in quality, but also acquired immense prestige among all the peoples of Europe.

Mr William S. Paley, the OWI director of broadcasts to Europe, accordingly addressed a long letter to the Minister of Information[2] in which he put before the Minister 'a problem which is giving us increasing concern' namely that the BBC re-broadcasts of American programmes and OWI broadcasts from medium- and short-wave transmitters in Britain were inadequate. The signal from the short-wave transmitters was weak and the medium-wave transmitters were not powerful enough to defeat jamming.

Of 1,100 BBC programmes only 107 were allocated to the 'Voice of America'.

Mr Paley suggested, as a remedy, either that a larger number of periods of the BBC service be allocated to the Voice of America or the amalgamation of British and American radio activities so that all broadcasts designed

1. Communicated by Mr Bowes Lyon, 17.7.44.
2. Mr William S. Paley to the Minister of Information, 11.2.44.

for occupied and enemy countries in Europe would be identified as representing both Great Britain and the United States.

Mr Paley admitted that informal discussions had shown him that neither of these proposals was acceptable to the BBC but he concluded with a moving appeal for British help in one of the few fields in which United States equipment was inferior to British.

> Radio broadcasting is an arm of warfare just as are guns and bullets. When it comes to guns, bullets and the like, we have shared with each other all our resources. . . . In radio, here in Europe, we suffer a serious lack of facilities. You, with your admirable foresight, have in operation very full means for carrying on radio warfare. Were it possible for us at this time to make up part of our deficiency through some satisfactory sharing arrangement with you, we should not only be doing a more efficient job, but PWB would, at the same time, be in a much better position to carry on very important work which we must do once the Continent has been invaded.

PWE was consulted and recalled that the proposals went back to 1942 when US radio operations from European bases were first discussed when they decided to build six 50 k.w. transmitters in Britain so as to have their own independent transmissions. The BBC at the time pointed out these would be inadequate. Only three out of the six medium-wave transmitters had in fact been built.

The Americans had provided six short-wave transmitters for the BBC which provided 1/20 of BBC transmitter strength. In return they had been given 1/10 of the BBC European programme and the BBC was also making four short-wave transmitters available to reinforce the American independent programme.

PWE added that the underlying reason for Mr Paley's approach was that he knew an independent American transmission had no prospect of establishing an audience or a goodwill remotely comparable with that of the BBC. His proposals were therefore designed to appropriate BBC experience, personnel and goodwill.

The PWE Memorandum opposed amalgamation on the grounds that Anglo-American direction would involve continual reference to Washington whereas 'the essence of propaganda is speed'; that there was a constitutional difficulty as the Minister of Information would have to answer questions in Parliament about an integrated service; that Canada had been refused similar facilities; that the BBC could no longer keep its agreements with European allies for free time; and that there was no reason why OWI should not ask for joint control of the Home and Empire services since they had large audiences in Britain and the Empire and that the Soviet would probably also ask for similar facilities.

The conclusion was that a joint output would reduce efficiency owing to inexpert American output, delays and the blurring produced by compromise.

There can be little doubt, in view of his letter to Major General Brooks[1] of 10.1.44 that the Minister of Information would have refused Mr Paley's requests in any circumstances. Armed with Mr Kirkpatrick's arguments he was able to follow his own precept of showing great politeness to the Americans and taking no responsibility for their actions. He concluded:

> Two years ago it might have been possible to make arrangements on the lines you have in mind. But a different plan was agreed on then and we feel there is really no alternative now to carrying it through. If you decide to do so you can count on PWE and the BBC to give you all the help they can.

There can be no doubt that the British refusal was justified on the grounds that the BBC output would suffer in quality had amalgamation taken place. Yet it is to be regretted on wider grounds that Mr Paley's request to us to share our radio facilities just as the United States had shared other munitions of war with us should have been refused.

Mr Paley and OWI were thus forced to make the best of the facilities at their disposal and initiated the American service of ABSIE (also referred to as Y1 and Y2. The output of these transmitters is no part of the history of PWE).

Progress of PWE/OWI/SOE/OSS Plan

The task called for in the PWE/SOE plan could only be completely carried out by the work of agents.

Although the shortage of suitable agents and training facilities for them held up all SOE work on these lines, a certain number of PWE agents were dispatched to Belgium. Apart from this, a 'production plan' to implement the purely PWE role of the plan was worked out.[2] It included a white manual to educate the general populations on the tasks until D-Day and after it, a Black counterpart of 'Action booklet' to be distributed by Resistance groups, and a transport booklet.

All were written by Mr Parker, a part-author of the PWE/SOE plan and an original member of 'D''s Black propaganda section. A White booklet on the ways and means of damaging enemy morale was produced by Mr Delmer's unit. Working Plans for France, Belgium and Holland were drafted.[3]

1. Quoted on p. 358.
2. Minute of meeting, 3.1.44 and 6.1.44.
3. Minutes of 1st Meeting of Working Committee of the Joint PWE/OWI and SOE/OSS Political Warfare Plan, 2.11.43.

France

SOE work in France had been inevitably adversely affected by the long continued uncertainty with regard to General de Gaulle which resulted from the different attitude of the British and the American Governments with regard to Vichy.

These difficulties had resulted in SOE organising its work in France in two divisions. The F section which worked as far as possible without consultation or co-ordination with De Gaulle and was staffed with officers of British nationality, and the RF section which worked with the Gaullistes and the Conseil de la Résistance and adopted the Gaulliste point of view. A third, but minor division of SOE worked through Giraudist officers in Algiers. One lasting dispute between SOE and the French Resistance groups in France was due to SOE's demand for decentralisation in the field on security grounds, all integration being carried out in London. (This was the result of SOE's disastrous experience in Holland.) The lower levels of French Resistance were particularly insistent on unification of resistance in France itself.

Colonel Hutchinson, head of SOE RF section, made detailed comments on the PWE/SOE plan[1] which showed that the greater part of the activities called for were being carried out, either by agents in the field or on the RU Honneur et Patrie. He stressed also the shortage of trained agents and of training facilities.

A progress report on the plan was called for by Colonel Sutton from the Regional Directors.[2] Dr Beck, PWE French Regional Director,[3] stated[4] that the two factors which conditioned the development of the plan had not been fully realised. These were co-operation with the (a) Conseil de la Résistance, (b) a clear distinction between professional SOE/SO tasks and activities organised by PWE/OWI. The last sentence shows a failure to understand the plan. For the majority of the activities could not be properly carried out either by SOE or by PWE acting alone.

Dr Beck stated that it had been impossible to take the plan to the French and asked for their collaboration. In consequence of this political holdup, PWE lacked agents.

A steady supply of material produced by the German Region had been sent to the field to undermine German troop morale and one agent had undertaken as a part-time job organising the distribution of this literature.

Guerilla Activities

This had been the major theme on the RU.

---

1. 10309/JRHH Colonel Hutchinson to Dr Beck, 15.10.43.
2. 28.3.44.
3. Dr Beck succeeded Lt Col Fairlie as Regional Director on the appointment of the latter to PWD-SHAEF.
4. Joint PWE/OWI and SOE/OSS Political Warfare Plan French Regional Progress Report, 11.4.44.

Stirring Up Strikes

On this a great deal of progress was reported. Regular consultations had taken place with Resistance groups especially with the CGT and the Communist Party representative. A fundamental directive on this point had been drawn up with the approval of SOE and sent to the corresponding authorities in France by special mission. The campaign for this organisation of a general and regional strike had been carried out by the radio on this side with the appropriate speakers from Resistance groups in France itself by syndical and other clandestine newspapers, so that part of the PWE/SOE plan was almost complete.

Other points on which progress was reported in collaboration with the Conseil de Résistance were destruction of records, chiefly of the requisitioning of labour for Germany, the concealment of food stocks and instructions to sow larger crops for 1944. The Conseil de la Résistance had issued a directive on the treatment of collaborators on the lines of that in the plan.

Directives for Political Warfare agents and in the field and the clandestine press were called for shortly before D-Day.[1] Dr Beck replied that the clandestine press in France would only take directives from CFLN or the Conseil de Résistance[2] but that he proposed the following directive to agents as regards propaganda:

> The function of a PW agent was defined as to act as liaison officer to contact any groups of Frenchmen able to influence opinion in the way which will help our objectives, to contact editors of clandestine newspapers and to service them, particularly by establishing an elementary news service based on monitoring PWD and BBC. He should work in close contact with SOE agents and he should report on opinion and morale, reactions to Allied propaganda, BBC, ABSIE, etc., and make suggestions.

Dr Beck's reports show that PWE French Region had adopted a negative attitude to the PWE/SOE plan. This was undoubtedly due to political difficulties which still existed with the French and was partly a legacy from the policy before Lt Colonel Fairlie had replaced Lt Colonel Gielgud as Regional Director.

The war records of F and RF sections of SOE continued by Colonel Buckmaster and Major Thackthwaite respectively show that SOE activities in France had been largely concerned for some time in preparations for the activities listed in the PWE/SOE plan. The usefulness of the plan for France was not, however, as a directive in the field and in any case the FFI was not prepared to act on British directives. The value of the plan was that

1. Mr Scarlett to RDs for France, Low Countries, and Northern Countries, 2.6.44.
2. Dr Beck to Mr Scarlett, 3.6.44.

it committed SHAEF and could be used to obtain authority for the necessary training of agents, airlift, and supplies of arms. The need for the SOE/PWE plan for France had been recognised in SOE.

'It will be necessary to co-ordinate the efforts of Western European regions[1] and PWE who are engaged on plans which in some respects will supplement the SOE plans.'

'With regard to PWE[2] F used to attend regularly the weekly meeting under the presidency of Colonel Sutton or Dr Beck, and discussions as to the future policy of PWE were reviewed from the SOE angle and the policy for the clandestine radio station, Radio Patrie, was settled.'

SHAEF Views on French Resistance in April 1944

A French Military Mission with SHAEF was agreed to in April. The functions of this mission under General Koenig were laid down in a SHAEF study[3] which is noticed here because of the erroneous estimate it contains of the part likely to be played by the FFI.

The writer was alarmed by the dangers of overhasty arming of liberated Frenchmen unaccustomed to military discipline and suggested holding back supplies of ammunition. A second SHAEF study on Resistance by the General Public[4] showed greater sense of the realities of resistance but stated 'no serious damage to the German effort against our forces will be inflicted by active resistance in the occupied countries during the critical stages of the battle from the lodgement area. It must be counted on only as a bonus and not form part of a military plan.' Fortunately, however, the writer realised that the matter was largely out of our hands and that the political results of declining civilian co-operation would be worse than those of accepting it.

The results of operations by the FFI involving the liberation of Paris and of very large parts of France itself, showed that the PWE estimate of the part which our Allies could play was far more accurate.

Belgium. 'C''s Objections to PWE Agents

The PWE/SOE plan, which required the employment of increased numbers of agents, had alarmed 'C' who directly accused[5] PWE agents of endangering those of the SIS and stated that in many cases PWE agents had turned to those of the SIS when in dire need with results 'which have been almost uniformly disastrous'.

1. Directive to French Country Sections for future planning and Operations, (n.d. issued in autumn of 1943 by Colonel Buckmaster).
2. History of F section by Colonel Buckmaster.
3. SHAEF/17245/6/1/Ops.
4. SHAEF/17253/1/Ops.
5. 'C' to Major General Brooks, 2.2.44.

Major General Brooks replied that as PWE requirements arose from the Overlord Plan approved by the Supreme Commander he could not discuss the matter unilaterally.

A meeting was held[1] with General Eisenhower's political adviser in which it emerged that PWE policy was in accordance with the SIS wishes and it was agreed that prior consultation would take place between PWE and SIS with regard to PWE plans.

Documents prepared in PWE Low Countries Region rebut 'C''s charges and state that in no known instance did the field activities of PWE agents compromise or result in casualties to the SIS. Moreover, PWE had counter-charges to bring particularly in regard to instructions given to SIS agents regarding Othello[2] that he was extremely dangerous and 'if he annoys you betray him'. The words used were 'le livrez' which Mr de Sausmarez could only suppose was a mis-reading for 'le laissez' 'abandon him'. Fortunately the instructions from London were ignored by the SIS agents in the field.

It seems probable that 'C''s major objection was that which took first place in his letter – that PWE would compete with SIS in recruiting agents as there was a great scarcity of qualified persons.

Numbers of PWE Agents Required for Belgium

The PWE/SOE plan had been communicated[3] to Captain Aronstein of the Belgian Sûreté and a request made for seventeen organisers and thirteen W/T operators to carry it out. Only nine organisers and one W/T operator were forthcoming.

SOE Claims Priority over PWE in Belgium

Still more disturbing was SOE's failure to deliver bodies and containers to the field. PWE asked for the delivery of sixty-nine containers in the March moon, but SOE replied they could only deliver nineteen in March and nineteen in April and that unpacking containers and repacking with more up-to-date material was impossible 'owing to the strain on the SOE packing station'. SOE, however, increased the delivery of PWE containers to sixty after PWE had protested.

Further trouble arose when it became known that SOE had telegraphed their agent Virgilia that: 'For your private information High Command allot low priority to all PWE activity.' Commander Johns had to admit that the telegram had been dispatched[4] without any SHAEF ruling as to priorities having been received. The only SHAEF directive on priorities

1. Meeting under 'C''s chairmanship, 8.2.44.
2. Mr de Sausmarez to Major General Brooks, 7.2.44.
3. Letters from Mr Dadson to Capt. Aronstein of 14.12.43 and 20.12.43.
4. Commander Johns to Mr Dadson, 4.4.44.

afterwards dispatched stated that 'SOE/SO should on demand continue to distribute propaganda to an extent which does not unduly interfere with the security, the work and the preparation of resistance groups'.

It is scarcely necessary to point out that since there were definite PWE resistance[1] groups the directive could not apply. The telegram had been sent by SOE without justification.

Implementing PWE/SOE Plan in Belgium

In spite of the difficulties with SIS and SOE, a memorandum on the PWE/SOE plan reveals that considerable work had been done.

Immobilisation of Enemy Communications

'Samoyede's mission would ensure necessary action.'

Undermining Enemy Morale

Action ensured by Mandrill organisation complemented by Gibbon and Samoyede.

Confusion and Deception of Enemy

Action ensured by Samoyede organisation.

Destruction of Records

Action ensured by Caracal.

Depriving Enemy of Services of Collaborators

Result likely from other activities.

Only on *Stirring up Strikes* had no action been taken. *Guerilla Activities* and *Depriving enemy of stocks of food* had been listed as SOE commitments.

Holland. Black Propaganda in the Field

SOE attempts to build up a secret army and sabotage organisation in Holland had been attended by a series of disasters. The first agents and wireless sets sent out fell into the hands of the Gestapo, without the knowledge of SOE, and a large number of further agents, wireless operators and wireless sets were dropped in places indicated by the Germans. Needless to say they were all arrested on landing. This experience greatly influenced SOE policy in favour of decentralisation in the field, all co-ordination being carried out in London, a policy which later involved SOE with many disputes with the Gaullistes and the FFI in France.

1. Mr Dadson to Mr Garnett, 3.7.44.

The disasters in Holland did not enable the Germans to penetrate Dutch resistance but deprived it of assistance from this country. The SOE failure involved a failure of PWE to carry out Black propaganda in the field. Nevertheless an attempt to undertake this work was made, though on a very limited scale.

PWE Agents with Missions to Dutch Clandestine Press

On 18.10.43 Brutus and another agent were dispatched to make contact with the Dutch clandestine press. Although the aircraft in which he was making the trip was shot down, Brutus made his way through Belgium into Holland by 29.10.43. During the following month, SOE discovered that the W/T channel which they had allotted to Brutus was being operated by the Gestapo.[1]

In the PWE/SOE working plan[2] it was proposed to send out an agent with matrices of a booklet of which he was to arrange the printing and distribution. 'The target should be one booklet per household, i.e. approximately two million booklets.' This distribution was to be supplemented by dissemination by air.

'Draughts was accordingly sent out with a wireless operator, Bezique, both being dropped 31.3.44. The wireless set was buried, but was dug up and stolen before they could retrieve it. Draughts made contact with the editor of the clandestine paper *Je maintiendrai*, to whom he gave the name Draughts II and instructions before he returned successfully via Spain, reaching Gibraltar 8.7.44.'[3] Before the dispatch of Draughts, SOE was able to inform PWE that some twenty students had completed training as agents and that it might be possible to allocate two organisers and two W/T operators to PWE.[4] A month later, SOE informed PWE of the position with regard to Draughts and offered a brother and sister who had both done their jumps as PWE agents.[5] On his return in August, Draughts reported that the clandestine press covered the whole of Holland and that every patriot was able to obtain a copy of one of the underground papers, the most important of which were:

Trouw. A circulation of 70,000 in the autumn of 1943. Trouw had organised raids on food offices and the liquidation of traitors.

Het Parool. Circulation of 25,000.

Christorphoor. A big Catholic paper in S. Holland.

In August, the brother and sister, known as Tiddleywinks and Rowing, were dispatched and Draughts II reported that they had arrived safely but that Rowing had broken her leg in landing and had to be taken to hospital, She had therefore destroyed her codes.

---

1. SOE War Diary for Holland.
2. PWE/OWI and SOE/OSS Political Warfare Plan – Revised Working Plan Holland, 16.11.43.
3. SOE War Diary for Holland.
4. Cmdr Johns to Eric Dadson, 6.3.44.
5. Cmdr Johns to Eric Dadson, 26.4.4.

Requests followed on 28.8.44 for PWE propaganda material – Vrie Nederland and Wervelwind. Rowing was recovering, but she afterwards broke her leg again. Draughts II was then giving PWE/SOE instructions to the Dutch resistance groups.

On 17.9.44 Draughts II reported the exact position of a V2 rocket site and on 21.12.44 sent a request for a regular delivery of the *Times* newspaper for servicing the clandestine press which was provided.

The scale of PWE field activity in Holland did not, for reasons we have seen, compare with that in Belgium. Nevertheless it was sufficient to show the importance of having its own agents to carry out purely Political Warfare missions in the field. There can be little doubt that the Dutch resistance movements would have been more formidable to the Germans if they had received more assistance from PWE and SOE.

Denmark

As Denmark was the only occupied country without a Government in exile, far greater freedom existed for PWE and SOE to carry out Political Warfare and sabotage.

An immediate result of the PWE/SOE plan was that all SOE agents were given Political Warfare training and that SOE at once made efforts to recruit suitable agents amongst Danes who had taken refuge in Sweden and to train at least some of them there, owing to difficulties of transport to Britain and back. A total of six agents and four replacements was aimed at for Political Warfare purposes. In addition, greatly increased airlift for PWE/OWI containers and dissemination of White leaflets was asked for before D-Day.

Norway

Owing to the jealousy of any 'interference from outside' on the part of the Norwegian Government, PWE and SOE activities were limited in scope. The Norwegian Government maintained effective control of the BBC. The only RU had been forced to close down by the Norwegian Government and SOE were bound by agreement not to undertake activities without Norwegian Government approval.

The operations in the PWE/OWI and SOE/SO plan could only have been carried out if collaboration between PWE/OWI and the Norwegian authorities could have been established.

The Transport Campaign and the Minister of Information

An article in the *Sunday Times* about the beginning of January, 1944, entitled 'Propaganda for Invasion' attracted the attention of the Minister of Information. He called Major General Brooks's attention verbally to a statement in it that the BBC had been broadcasting appeals to French railwaymen telling them how to disrupt the enemy's communication lines. The Minister, who had formed the opinion that any broadcasts on such subjects would assist the enemy, asked Major General Brooks for an explanation. In reply he was informed[1] that transport had been a main target of our operational campaigns for over a year, but that only generalised instructions stressing the importance of railways to the enemy were given and that localised and technical instructions were avoided. 'They are strategical talks . . . the tactics are left to the men on the spot who receive their operational instructions by channels other than open radio.'

The explanation did not, however, satisfy the Minister who wrote on the margin of the letter in his own hand, in red ink, as follows:

> If Railway Workers in France wish to wreck installations they will be handicapped by 'Strategic' talks. And Germans will put more Gestapo thugs on the job of watching them if the BBC give any more of these talks. B.B.

On the receipt of this Ministerial dictum a somewhat belated attempt[2] was made by Mr Scarlett to enlighten the Minister with regard to operational propaganda in general and the transport campaign in particular, and he was asked to consider certain matters before instructions were issued to bring the transport campaign to an end.

The fact that the only real German counter would be to guard all French rail, road and water means of communication was pointed out and the Minister was also told that the French resistance groups were parties to the talks and supplied the speakers; that these men had organised transport sabotage in France themselves and were strongly in favour of such broadcasts. The minute concluded with: 'In the light of Overlord, I hope you will agree that it is of cardinal importance that we do nothing to undermine the confidence of these people and for this reason alone these talks should continue.'

Mr Bracken remained, however, convinced that he knew more about the dangers of such talks than the leaders of the French Resistance. The Minister, however, confined himself to verbal comments 'in the light of which' the Director of Plans was asked[3] to supply a report on the transport campaign. A full and informative report was accordingly prepared but was not submitted for some three weeks and then sent with a covering note[4] suggesting that perhaps Major General Brooks might prefer to deal with the matter verbally, rather than to submit the full report. Major General Brooks passed the letter to Mr Scarlett with the note. 'So far as the Minister is concerned I think we should NOT re-raise the issue. 11.2.44.'

1. Major General Brooks to the Minister of Information, 11.1.44.
2. Mr Scarlett to Minister of Information, 15.1.44.
3. Mr Scarlett to Mr Ritchie Calder, 20.1.44.
4. Mr H. O. Lucas to the DDG, 10.2.44.

Mr Scarlett noted: 'I agree. Let this particular dog sleep.'

Thus Mr Bracken was able to continue to hold his own personal beliefs and the transport campaign was able to continue to play its part as partner of the RAF in reducing enemy means of transport before the Overlord landing.

We owe a debt of gratitude, however, to Mr Bracken for the report which would not have been made without his intervention.

The report[1] stated that the transport campaign had continued since September 1942 both on Black and White media and that the themes employed were:

1. The vulnerability of the German-controlled transport system.
2. Talks to railway and other transport workers on how they could help to wreck the German war machine.
3. Talks relating the campaign to current events.

The report stated that the campaign had been successful. Sabotage of railways, locomotives and transport targets far outnumbered all other forms of sabotage. The number of sabotage incidents on French railways was believed to have been 4 to 500 a month and was increasing. In the month September/October 1943, the number was known for certain to have been 1,421. There had been forty major instances of sabotage on waterways each involving serious interruption of traffic.

The report also pointed out that practically all variations on the transport theme had been used and that PWE proposed to enlarge it.

The French Region with the French Resistance movements, the CGT and Communist Party and SOE had been discussing a Black campaign which had already been launched in certain clandestine newspapers on the theme of a general strike. The object of the strike would be to immobilise the enemy's back areas. It was to be planned to include sit down strikes and active participation in the fight. The word of command would be given by the Supreme Allied Command. The major preparation was to get the workers to co-ordinate their activity through their trade unions. The clandestine illegal CGT had a fairly good organisation with close links inside the legal trade unions.

When D-Day arrived, instructions were given for the plans, of which the transport campaign was a part, contained in the PWE/SOE plan and the plans subsequently based upon it to be implemented in the Special Directive[2] issued soon after D-Day, at the request of SHAEF. This was the launching of a special campaign by radio and supported by leaflet, calling upon French and Belgian railway workers to dislocate and paralyse the enemy's lines of communication in the rear.

The Directive was addressed to three Zones: *In the Battle Zone*, the railwaymen's first duty was to survive and remain hidden until the arrival of

1. Transport campaign, 8.2.44.
2. Special Directive on instructions to be given to railway workers in France and Belgium.

the Allies. They should not commit sabotage. *In the Action Zone*, north of the SHAEF line from the mouth of the Loire to Orléans through Chaumont to Strasbourg, the railwaymen should paralyse communications by 'non-specialist' sabotage. Specialists will receive instructions direct. Specific instructions will be issued to various categories of workers. Certain categories of workers are to disappear and take with them or hide essential parts. *Back Zone* (France south of SHAEF line). Railwaymen to stay where they are. To continue sabotage against present targets but not to extend it except to trains carrying Germans. The only exceptions are railwaymen working under direct instructions from the local Resistance group.

A military assessment of the effect of the destruction of rolling stock was included as an annexe to the Central Directive next day.[1]

'Impressions of Railway sabotage in France gained in December 1944'[2] is a tribute to the transport campaign organised by PWE and carried out largely on the BBC. It shows in detail how completely the French railway workers were organised, first in order to carry out undetectable sabotage, and, after D-Day, how exactly they carried out PWE/SOE plans and the PWD directive on transport.[3] On D-Day railwaymen held up German communications by direct wrecking – for example by running locomotives into turntable pits, and also by switching as many trains as possible into lines on which trains had been derailed, or bridges blown up. 'Virtually all the French railwaymen helped to carry out the SHAEF requirements.'

SOE Messages on the BBC

With the increase of SOE activity in the field in preparation for Overlord, the number of code messages carried by the BBC French Service increased greatly. These messages were regarded as a nuisance by Mr Kirkpatrick and Mr Bracken, and the latter gave instructions that it should be abated. As a result SOE agreed to the messages being transferred from the news period to the evening programme. SOE also succeeded in cutting down the number of messages from 1,051 in November to 869 in December.[4]

The chief purposes for which these BBC code messages were required were as follows:

1. Information to an agent that a message was coming to him.
2. Information that droppings would take place, or were cancelled.
3. Information that money would be included in parcels dropped.
4. Verification of 'blackmailing' agents' bona fides. SOE agents had developed a fruitful technique of blackmailing the managers of French firms working on German account. The manager was informed at a personal

1. Annexe 1 to Guidance for Output Military Effects of Destruction of Rolling Stock, 15.6.44.
2. R3332 Appendix C to SOE History of RF Section.
3. Annexe I to SHAEF Directive, 15.6.44.
4. Major General Brooks to Minister of Information, 11.1.44.

> interview that unless he brought about stoppage of output for a certain period by means of an 'accident', his factory would be bombed by the RAF. At the same interview the manager was informed by the agent that a certain phrase would be broadcast by the BBC at a particular time and date. The agents' advance knowledge of this was proof of his message being true.

It is clear that most of these messages were of an 'alerting' kind. Their value lay precisely in the fact that an agent was able to listen to the BBC and not tie himself down to monitoring with his own short-wave set.

SOE therefore resisted a proposal from Mr Kirkpatrick that the messages could be put out on short wave. That of course was already being done to selected agents. SOE replied that most of their agents had no short-wave receivers.[1]

The Minister of Information seems, however, to have been doubtful whether the messages were necessary at all, for he marked Major General Brooks's minute:[2] 'The bustling SOE may think all these messages are necessary. Why not ask "C" for his opinion?'

This suggestion was not adopted. A month later SOE informed Mr Kirkpatrick that the flow of messages would be very greatly increased.[3] After consulting Mr Bracken, SOE was informed that the BBC could not increase the time already allotted.[4] The question of the time allotted to these messages came up at [the] PWE/SOE Co-ordination Committee and it was decided that SHAEF should be asked to pronounce on the relative value which they attached to these code messages as compared with propaganda broadcasts.[5] This decision was challenged by Mr Kirkpatrick as being likely to be unwelcome to Mr Bracken, at the next meeting. Mr Kirkpatrick suggested that the messages might be carried by Aspidistra during daylight hours.

These objections were brought to an end two days later by SHAEF support in a letter which concluded: 'An increase of your present time allotment on the BBC . . . is considered operationally desirable by this Headquarters and you are therefore requested to ensure that the full-time allotment is made available to you.'

Threat to SOE Messages from Home Defence Executive

SOE messages on the BBC had also been threatened in the interests of Overlord security. The Chairman of the Home Defence Executive circulated a message [4.4.44] proposing the suspension of all BBC personal messages because he had never been told of their real purpose.

---

1. Mr Kirkpatrick to General Brooks, 10.1.44.
2. Major General Brooks to Minister of Information, 11.1.44.
3. Mr Kirkpatrick to General Brooks, 8.2.44.
4. Mr Kirkpatrick to Colonel Nicholls, 10.2.44.
5. Minutes of PWE/SOE Co-ordinating Committee, 31.3.44.

Major General Brooks consulted Mr Kirkpatrick and instructions were issued to suspend all messages forthwith. SOE and MI6, which had not been consulted, protested effectively and explained the nature of their messages and their importance.

The Voice of SHAEF

PWE and OWI planners decided to revive the principle of the *Avis* which had been issued earlier in the war, by an official Voice of SHAEF to each of the Western sea-board allies; the procedure was later extended to the German people and to foreign workers in Germany.

In order to prevent counterfeiting, it was agreed that there should be a 'set rubric' by a master-voice in English, introducing each of the language speakers.[1]

The project was discussed at meetings with OWI and PWD SHAEF and at PWE central directive meetings and occupied territories meetings attended by Dr Beck or a deputy. Dr Beck apparently failed to inform the French authorities, for the first Voice of SHAEF in French evoked a letter of protest from M. George Boris of the CFLN[2] with which Dr Beck associated himself. M. Boris, however, was unaware of the imminence of D-Day. Three weeks after it had been established, it was decide to reserve Voice of SHAEF announcements to instructions of real military significance.[3]

The Voice of SHAEF on the BBC and ABSIE became the recognised medium for giving instructions to the civilian populations of Western Europe and later of Germany.

Mr Newsome's Broadcasts

Mr Newsome in addition to his work as Director of European Broadcasts was in the habit of broadcasting regularly himself as 'The Man in the Street', in the European News in English 'London Calling Europe'.

PWE regarded this service as unimportant as the numbers of European listeners to English-language broadcasts was small and there was evidence that they preferred the BBC Home Service or Empire Service which were not jammed to 'London Calling Europe' which was. Moreover, the Continental listener in English regarded the BBC Home Service as more authentic since it was not designed for abroad. No effort had therefore been made to stop Mr Newsome's broadcasts as it was recognised that the BBC editors could be relied on, in most cases, either to ignore them altogether or

1. Special Directive on the Voice of SHAEF. The Speaker selected to broadcast the 'Rubric' was Mr Douglas Ritchie of the BBC, formerly 'Colonel Britton'. This did much to remove the bitterness of past disputes, 19.5.44. PWD/AH/44/2/37.
2. M. G. Boris to Dr Beck, 23.5.44.
3. Voice of SHAEF Revised Procedure, 16.6.44.

to temper the insularity of the tone of any quotations given in translation from them.

In Mr Newsome's view the war was far more than a war of defence by countries which had been the victims of German aggression, or a war to re-establish the rule of law as a guiding principle in Government – it was a war of the common people against their privileged oppressors. As the Man in the Street, his broadcasts were designed therefore to express the fervour of one of the Cromwellian Levellers. It was in this spirit that as The Man in the Street he broadcast the following:[1]

> . . . Supposing the Germans – as might indeed happen – become genuine fighters for freedom and tolerance while those to whom we have become allied displayed themselves as the last bulwark of privilege and intolerance, what would the British citizen do then? What is this war about? Presumably about the fundamental struggle between the people and the privileged.

This script was read by Mr Bracken who was filled with indignation at the suggestion that Britain might join to fight in alliance with Germany against fellow members of the United Nations.

In a three-page letter in his own hand[2] the Minister of Information demanded 'the name and departmental record of the Gentleman who composed this maudlin and mischievous script'.

Major General Brooks was at some pains to defend Mr Newsome: 'He is a man of strong and virile personality, friction is now a thing of the past and Mr Newsome has become one of us. I hope you will agree not to take the matter further.'[3]

Mr Bracken replied with Churchillian force and wit: 'I am not in the least interested in news of his virility or of his domestication, I am anxious to know the precautions you have taken to stop broadcasts which insult our Allies, laud the Germans and air political and economic prejudices.'

Major General Brooks replied that the imposition of special precautions with regard to the Director of European Broadcasts would undermine morale in the BBC.[4]

The Minister was not to be put off and threatened that 'if members of your staff disregard the warnings given by you and Kirkpatrick,[5] they will be removed without notice'.

On 28.3.44 Lord Selborne wrote to the Foreign Secretary alleging that a broadcast by the 'Man in the Street'[6] was continuous left-wing propaganda

1. Man in the Street, 14.12.43.
2. Secret and Personal note. Mr Bracken to Major General Brooks, 10.1.44.
3. Major General Brooks to the Minister of Information, 6.1.44.
4. Major General Brooks to the Minister of Information, 11.1.44.
5. To Major General Brooks from Mr Brendan Bracken, 12.1.44.
6. Major General Brooks to Minister of Information, 6.1.44.

to all Europe, frequently not in line with HMG policy. It had celebrated the Yugoslav accession to the United Nations for ten minutes without once mentioning King Peter's name and praising Tito who had nothing to do with the coup d'état. 'It struck me as particularly monstrous that the King should not receive one word of praise from the BBC for the part that he played in the Yugoslav revolution.'

The Foreign Secretary called for the Man in the Street script and minuted that it deserved all the harsh things Lord Selborne had said. Historically it was disgracefully inaccurate and the BBC should tell the truth.[1]

As a result, the Director General informed Sir Orme Sargent that[2] in future Mr Newsome would submit any talk dealing with Central or South-Eastern Europe to Mr Kirkpatrick for approval.

Mr Kirkpatrick informed the Director General that Mr Newsome would speak less often and submit scripts[3] but that he had said that the view taken by the Minister showed such lack of confidence in him that he must consider his own position. Mr Paley was anxious to secure his services for broadcasts on Continental stations.

Mr Newsome's Journalistic Activity

The displeasure of the Minister of Information with Mr Newsome had also been aroused by the receipt of the prospectus for a publication called Europe to be edited by Mr Newsome which was to treat of such subjects as 'Making a Peace', 'The Clandestine Press', 'Gaullism', etc. He drew the attention of the Director General[4] to the proposed publication, who agreed that PWE provided the BBC European Service with a large part of its information, some of which was secret. All experience had shown that without control Mr Newsome was liable to go off at his own political tangent. The whole concept seemed entirely wrong in wartime and the Director General could see no reason for it except self-boosting. No more was heard of this project.

The last occasion on which Mr Newsome aroused the criticism of the Minister of Information appears to have been in connection with May Day celebrations in 1944. Mr Newsome's directive contained the following:

> Official deeds and utterances which seem to indicate a reactionary tendency cannot be suppressed or glossed over, but in news and comment we should overshadow them thoroughly with any material to hand which gives the opposite impression and contains the reassurance that the progressive tide is running too strongly to be stemmed.

---

1. Note initialed 'A.E.', 6.4.44.
2. Director General to Sir Orme Sargent, 8.4.44.
3. Mr Kirkpatrick to Sir Robert Bruce Lockhart, 11.4.44.
4. Director General to the Minister of Information and Sir Cyril Radcliffe.

This document fell into the hands of the watchful Minister of Information who minuted the Director General[1] that the directive provided all the evidence the Foreign Office or Tory MPs could wish that PWE planned a left autocracy for Europe after the war.

On this occasion, however, the Director General was able to put up a vigorous defence[2] and countered with the complaint that 'at the present moment we are hardly allowed to mention Poles, Yugoslavs and Greeks except in terms which bear little or no resemblance to reality'.

Mr Newsome remained at his post as Director of European Broadcasts until the liberation of France, Belgium and Luxembourg, when he became assistant to the Chief of the Radio Section PWD/SHAEF. In April 1945, he was appointed Chief of the Radio Section PWD/SHAEF and Chief of Broadcasts Radio Luxembourg.

Transfer of Cost of PWE Leaflets from Secret to Open Vote

The cost of PWE leaflets rose during 1943 to roughly £900,000 or double the production costs in 1942. Only one tenth of this was in respect of Black or clandestine printed matter.

The Treasury had from the first been opposed to any expenditure upon the secret vote which could by any arrangement be borne on the open vote. Accordingly Mr Brittain enquired in August 1943 whether the Director General PWE would agree to either the production costs of PWE White leaflets and/or that of the News Digest, being borne on the open vote for the Stationery Office. The Director General agreed at once to the cost of the News Digest being so borne but asked that the question of leaflets be examined further. Meetings of PWE Director of Finance, Mr Keeble, Mr Brittain and the representatives of the Stationery Office took place during October.

The Stationery Office reassured certain doubts expressed by PWE by stating that contracts would not be disturbed, direct access to printers would remain, etc.

'But they would normally want to choose[3] the contractor, settle the conditions of contract, agree the price, and of course, examine the final bills.'

The proposed transfer was opposed by Mr Keeble in spite of the cooperative attitude of the Stationery Office. 'If at any time their views[4] on the general urgency and importance of our work do not coincide with ours they have the power to put all kinds of grit into the machine.'

He therefore asked that a definite agreement should be made in writing.

The Minister of Information expressed uneasiness at the proposed

1. Mr Brendan Bracken to Sir Robert Bruce Lockhart, 2.5.42.
2. From the Director General to the Minister of Information, 4.5.44.
3. Memorandum from Director of Finance on proposed transfer to open vote, 10.10.43.
4. Mr Keeble to Major General Brooks, 10.10.43.

transfer.[1] But the Chancellor wrote expressing his wish that the transfer should be made.[2]

Mr Bracken accepted the proposal.[3]

The change led to none of the parliamentary difficulties which the Minister of Information had feared and thanks to the co-operative spirit of the Stationery Office there was no failure to produce such orders in time.

On one occasion, however, a Stationery Office complaint of waste of paper was made and it shows such a divergent outlook from that of the PWE production unit that it is worth recalling.

The Courier de l'Air was printed as a miniature newspaper by photogravure by Odhams at Watford. Its size had been originally fixed as that of the aircraft parachute flare hole, through which it was disseminated. This became the standard size for other miniature newspapers. In order to print it on the available presses considerable waste of paper was involved, which by April 1944 amounted to some 500 tons of paper a year. This paper was pulped and made into paper again. The Stationery Office were concerned to avoid this wastage and pointed out that it could be avoided by either of two methods – printing half of the paper upside down, or by increasing the size of the paper an inch all round. Printing every alternate page upside down would 'give the paper an almost lunatic appearance'[4] but increasing the size, a proposal the Stationery Office was quite willing to accept, would not have saved a penny in cost or an ounce of paper in weight – but it would have decreased the circulation.

It is indeed obvious on reflection that if the weight disseminated and the numbers of the magazines printed had remained constant, 500 tons of printed matter would have to be pulped instead of 500 tons of trimmings. The Stationery Office proposal meant either a smaller circulation or greater demands on the RAF to maintain the existing one.

Dartboard

Almost throughout the war the British Air Staff had struggled to overcome German defences against our bombers. During the summer of 1943, the Germans had developed an increasingly successful technique of intercepting our bombers with night fighters which were given directions by wireless of British bomber approach as detected by Radar. [Just] in time these instructions on short wave were jammed so successfully by us that the enemy was forced to employ medium wave, but he endeavoured to conceal that he was doing so.

---

1. Draft Memorandum from Minister of Information to Chancellor of Exchequer, 25.10.43, which was not sent.
2. Sir John Anderson to Mr Bracken, 19.11.43.
3. Mr Bracken to Sir John Anderson, 26.11.43.
4. Mr Keeble to Director General, 6.4.44.

For some time PWE technical experts had been convinced that certain medium-wave musical transmissions concealed a code of instructions for German night fighters. When this had been proved, Bomber Command sought for means to jam these programmes while our bombers were over Germany. Squadron Leader Halliday pointed out that the ideal instrument for the purposes was Aspidistra for which he was programme manager. Permission was accordingly sought and readily obtained from the Minister[1] of Information for the use of Aspidistra to jam the German Anna Marie programmes on the night of 5/6 December 1943. An agreement was accordingly made for the use of the transmitter by Bomber Command[2] at Kingsdown, giving Bomber Command priority for the operational use of the transmitter. Moorside Edge 3 (a transmitter of the BBC Network) was used for the same purpose. The use of Aspidistra for this purpose proved invaluable and was the means of frustrating enemy fighter interceptions. Some months later [NAME DELETED ON GROUNDS OF NATIONAL SECURITY] suggested[3] that the Calais-sender programme would be just as effective in jamming the German medium-wave programme as records of jamming noises. There would be the additional advantages that the enemy would then either have to jam his own direction signals or put up with our programme.

This suggestion was agreed to by all concerned and was put into effect. Thus on receiving a request for the use of Aspidistra for Dartboard all that was necessary was to change the frequency on which the Calais programme was going out to that of the enemy wavelength which it was wished to jam. The Calais programme then continued on that wavelength. Sir Noel Ashbridge raised no technical objection on such occasions to our jamming German wavelengths with our own transmissions. Incidentally a 'radio war' and jamming of the BBC Home Service did not follow the employment of Aspidistra for Dartboard purposes. All the predictions of disastrous consequences following from the use of Aspidistra which had been made by those associated with the BBC were falsified in the event.

The value of Aspidistra alone in Dartboard operations was estimated by the Chief of Bomber Command and the Chief of Air Staff at six or seven bombers a night.[4] The aggregate effect of Dartboard for the last nineteen months of the war during which the bombing of Germany took place on the largest scale must have saved many hundreds of aircrews and aircraft to the value of millions of pounds, and by enabling our bombing programme to be carried out, must have greatly shortened the war.

---

1. Air Vice Marshal Tait to Major General Brooks, 6.12.43.
2. Dartboard CMS 79 with covering letter from Air Commodore Warton, 29.12.43.
3. A.V.M. Tait to Major General Brooks, 2.3.44.
4. Major General Bishop to Brigadier General McClure, 17.3.45.

Aspidistra Used to Transmit the PWE Grey Programme

On 21st July, 1943, Mr Delmer put forward a proposal for the use of Aspidistra to transmit the Kurzwellensender Atlantik programme on medium wave. He listed all the objections and demolished them seriatim. The proposal was renewed in a paper of 12.8.43,[1] on the grounds that six months would be required to build up a German forces audience. The object was that G9 should meet the special requirements of the Overlord plan by adding to the special programmes for the German Air Force and German Navy, a programme specially directed at the German land forces in the West. This proposal was approved by the Minister of Information in general terms. After this decision, however, the Director General appears to have been influenced by the arguments so frequently put forward by those associated with the BBC. He therefore minuted the Minister[2] that there were many serious objections. With a powerful transmitter there could be no secrecy about this news service which would be monitored everywhere. Thus the Allies would be as easily deceived as the Germans. The whole value of British propaganda lay essentially in its reputation for veracity. Once that was gone, no one would believe us or obey our instructions when the time came. If the Atlantik programme was put out, the Combined Chiefs of Staff would probably demand control of all propaganda media. It is difficult to follow these arguments, since the proposal was only to transmit on medium wave what was already going out on short wave.

Mr Bracken indicated agreement and that day left Britain with the Foreign Secretary for the Quebec Conference. The Director General informed Mr Delmer[3] [PASSAGE DELETED ON GROUNDS OF NATIONAL SECURITY] of the changed decision stressing that Aspidistra should not be used for putting out news which might deceive our friends. Mr Delmer replied[4] that if these instructions were to be taken literally, the only course was to close down all the units he was directing and added that if we were to deceive the enemy we had to be prepared to deceive all listeners, including friends. 'I am entirely unable to share the view – which I know has been put forward to you very forcibly this weekend in my absence by some of my colleagues that there is something in itself dishonourable and damaging about deceptions.'

The Director General and the Minister had apparently accepted the fantastic standpoint that to deceive our friends on short wave was perfectly admissible but to do so on medium wave would be criminal and dangerous.

Mr Delmer continued to press his views on the Director General who vacillated and, in the continued absence of the Ministers, submitted a paper

---

1. Mr Sefton Delmer to Sir Robert Bruce Lockhart, 21.7.43 and 12.8.43.
2. Mr Bruce Lockhart, 16.8.43.
3. Director General to Mr Delmer, 16.8.43.
4. Teleprinted message from Mr Delmer to Director General, 17.8.43.

to Sir Orme Sargent[1] and Mr Strang,* who opposed it. After the Foreign Secretary's return he wrote to the Secretary of State for Air[2] asking that the rule that Aspidistra should not broadcast for more than ten minutes be relaxed. 'What PWE wish to do is to broadcast . . . between the hours of 20.00 and 23.00 BST. . . . I regard the proposal to use Aspidistra in this way as of particular importance and urgency.'

Sir Archibald Sinclair replied that there was no longer any objection to the independent use of Aspidistra. The actual decision to take the plunge and use Aspidistra was not however taken until November after Sir Robert Bruce Lockhart had gone on sick leave.

A minute informing Sir Orme Sargent of the reasons in favour of using Aspidistra in order to provide medium-wave coverage for Atlantiksender was put up[3] with the assurance that it would in no way jeopardise the value of Aspidistra for intrusion operations. Sir Orme Sargent agreed to the proposal. The Minister of Information and the BBC were informed and Colonel Chambers prepared a D stop notice to prevent comments on the programme from appearing in the press.

No evidence of damage to HMG's reputation for veracity in propaganda, or confusion of our Allies after the decision to put out a Grey programme on medium wave had been taken, has come to hand, though a certain amount of bewilderment was caused among inhabitants of Sussex with a fluent knowledge of German.[4]

The first transmission was on the night of 14.11.43 between the hours of 8 and 11 p.m.[5] and was called Soldatensender Calais. These three hours were announced as: 'Here is Soldatensender Calais linked with the short-wave transmitter Atlantik.'

At other times the programme continued to go out on short wave under the name of Atlantik only. When it appeared probable that our forces would occupy the Channel ports, Calais was re-named Soldatensender West.

A final effort was, however, made by the BBC to modify the decision to use Aspidistra for PWE transmissions. Mr Kirkpatrick's objections were formulated five days after the programme had first gone on the air on medium wave.[6] He submitted that within a short period listeners would realise that it was not a German station and would therefore assume it was

---

1. Sir Robert Bruce Lockhart to Sir Orme Sargent, 25.8.43.
2. Mr Eden to Sir Archibald Sinclair, 29.9.43.
3. Mr Scarlett to Sir Orme Sargent, 6.11.43.
4. Private information.
5. Major General Brooks to Secretary of State for Foreign Affairs, 15.11.43.
6. Minute of meeting held on 18.11.43.

* [William Strang, 1st Baron Strang (1893–1978), served in the army 1914–18; joined FO 1919; Moscow 1930–3; head of League of Nations section, FO, 1933–7; Central Department 1937–9; Assistant Under-Secretary for Europe 1939–43; British representative on European Advisory Commission and Ambassador, 1943–5; political advisor to Commander-in-Chief, Germany, 1945–7; Permanent Under-Secretary, FO, 1949–53; peerage on retirement 1954.]

of British origin and that British propaganda would stand convicted of acting a lie and the whole currency of British propaganda would be depreciated. He therefore proposed that G9 should continue in its present form but 'under a British name and with its British origin openly admitted, thus disposing of the major falsehood'.

Sir Noel Ashbridge supported Mr Kirkpatrick but their arguments were found unconvincing. Colonel Chambers pointed out that the intelligence supply on which the programme depended could not be continued to an avowedly British station, and Mr Ritchie Calder pointed out that the programme gave the listener intellectual and psychological alibis and that even if they did think the programme was of British origin its form and its contents would give the feeling that it was being done by their own people.

Mr Kirkpatrick's proposal was accordingly dismissed. No doubt the BBC case was weakened by the fact that the arguments used applied very nearly as strongly to Atlantiksender transmissions on short wave as they did after it had entered the medium-wave field in direct competition with the BBC German service.

It is worth pointing out that had the BBC proposal been accepted the reputation of all our Black stations must have been infallibly damaged by such an admission as to a 'Grey' station. Such damage would have had very serious consequences to our covert propaganda in connection with the resistance movements in all the occupied countries in Europe at the very time when such operational propaganda was becoming a matter of paramount importance for Overlord.

Enemy Reactions to Calais-sender Transmissions

Major General Brooks reported three months after[1] the inauguration of Soldatensender Calais that as soon as the service started German COs called their men together and informed them it was British and must not be listened to under pain of arrest. Heavy jamming was immediately started, transmitters being taken off ordinary German programmes for this purpose. To overcome this we added to the frequencies employed and were able to change frequencies in mid programmes.[2] The enemy reaction to this had been to jam frequencies which [they] were not using even though by so doing they prevented the transmission of their own programmes. Evidence from German Air Force, Navy and Mercantile Marine prisoners had shown that Calais/Atlantik was being heard by Germans over a wide area; that airmen, sailors and U-Boat men listened while on operations; that it was not unusual for German officers to listen to the programme in their messes.

Prisoners generally showed themselves impressed by the accuracy, detail and interest of the information provided. The music was appreciated. They

1. Major General Brooks to Minister of Information, 17.2.44.
2. The rapid change of frequencies was one of the unique features of Aspidistra.

attributed the starting-up of Soldatensender Anna-Marie to a desire to compete with Calais. The captain and wireless operator from the sunk blockade-runner *AlsterUfer* had listened to Atlantik Calais all the way from the Cape and had been depressed by what they thought was our complete knowledge of the movements of blockade-runners. A German Air Force officer who had been sent under conditions of the utmost secrecy to interview blockade-runner captains waiting in the Gironde had been amazed to hear Soldatensender Calais address a message to the hush-hush ships on their forthcoming operations. These ships had not yet dared to set out.

The military, diplomatic and 'inside Germany' news of the programme was soon being repeated in the form of rumours and 'traveller's tales' all over Europe, to the confusion and embarrassment of the neutral press.

The report concluded with the request that Calais-sender time should be extended by one hour from 8 p.m. till midnight. The request was approved by the Secretary of State and Minister of Information.

A Tribute to Calais-sender

Perhaps as good a description of Calais-sender programmes as could be given is contained in a letter from an OWI officer which was intercepted by the Postal Censorship.[1] The writer was unaware that Calais-sender was of British origin.

> . . . there is a German station on the air, comes through as strong as the BBC and it calls itself Calais. It is the best piece of propaganda I have ever listened to – the station pretends to be a Nazi station speaking about the Allies as the enemy, giving lots of personal messages to German soldiers and sailors outside Germany. . . . It gives reports of the bombings of German cities by the enemy and goes into detail about the addresses naming numbers and streets in the cities bombed. It tells as if it is straight news – that (for instance) gas and water in such and such a section of Berlin have not yet been repaired after such and such a night. Then it mentions soldiers by name and rank bringing to one of the greetings of his wife in Hamburg, to the following a reminder not to forget his fifth wedding anniversary next week Thursday, to another the admonition not to share his package of delicatessen from home with the officers 'they have enough' and the music . . . ah . . . there again you have the master touch. It is American jazz with a German flavour . . . even the music sounds authentic German . . . you have never heard Ted Lewis' 'Me and My Shadow' with a German singing in German in the

1. Jan Houbolt OWI American Embassy London to Barbara Levèque 329E. 58th St New York.

> Lewis manner. The American music changes with pure German music, German choirs and soldiers' songs by what sound like a mass singing of large numbers of people. In the same sentence which gives a back-handed slap to the Nazis, you will hear how many enemy (viz Allied) ships were sunk giving the names of the captains of the subs and who got wounded on the sub in the encounter. That thing is so cleverly done that friend and foe have just got to listen to it. It is as refreshing, commanding and appealing as anything I have listened to.

Atlantik and Calais-sender were designed particularly for German troops on the Western Seaboard. A voluntary poll[1] of 180,000 German Ps/W in Italy carried out by PWB after the cessation of hostilities showed that of those answering the questionnaire who listened to Allied broadcasts, Atlantik-sender was the most listened to station after the 8th Army PWB transmission which had the strongest signal locally.

The percentages of listeners was: 8th Army 30.1%, Atlantik-sender 24.4%, BBC German programme 14.2%. The listeners to Moscow formed 1.7% of the total. Thus the Atlantik-sender programme was considerably more popular than the BBC with the German forces in an area for which it was not designed.

Gestapo Investigations in Regard to Atlantik Broadcasts

Documents captured after the defeat of Germany[2] show that the Gestapo were so impressed with the accuracy of Atlantik-sender reports that they investigated them individually. A letter from R.F. SS und Chef der Deutschen Polizei to the Reichsicherheitshauptamtt dated 17.8.43 stated that Atlantik military reports were so accurate as to suggest that the station had close contacts in the German Armed Forces. The officer in question believed that Atlantik-sender was located in Switzerland. A letter from the Reichsicherheitshauptamtt dated 11.3.44 to Geheim Staatspolizei in Vienna asked for an investigation of an Atlantik report that two Vienna doctors had killed twenty infants in medical experiments. The answer admitted the deaths of the infants and traced the Atlantik report to a research on Vitamin A reserves of infants which had been published in No. 18 of the Munich Medical Weekly for 1942 and exonerated the doctors one of whom had been connected with the Hitler Youth and was a party member. The investigation is also of interest as revealing a source used by Delmer in collecting material for Atlantik broadcasts.

A request followed from the Gestapo that details of experiments of this type should not be published in future.

1. Propaganda Reaction Survey covering period 9.9.43 to 2.5.45 Italian campaigns, 1.8.45.
2. Gestapo and SD investigations of Reports Broadcast by Sender Atlantik. Np. DE 453/D is 202. Information Control Div. 6.9.45.

An Atlantik report that a woman had been acquitted for not attending war work on the plea that the streets of Breslau were unsafe for women was similarly investigated from the same office on 13.4.44. In reply the Breslau Staatspolizeistelle denied the truth of the Atlantik report.

A questionnaire of a random sample of German civilians between eighteen and fifty-five in three small towns in Prussia[1] showed that 51% of the population listened to Allied Radio. The stations most listened to were Radio Luxembourg 48%, BBC 31%, Soldatensender-West 23%. One of the main objections encountered was to the use of swing music which some Germans found distasteful and contrary to the German spirit.

The investigation showed that the stations were listened to in the order of their signal strength. Occasional references show that Atlantik and Calaissender programmes were believed. A thirty-four-year-old[2] locomotive engineer with eight years of schooling who listened to Soldatensender West (Calais) and the BBC German programme explained that he did so because they brought the truth clearly and bluntly.

Delmer's Conversations with Fritsche

In the autumn of 1946, Mr Delmer induced Fritsche of the Propaganda Ministry to discuss the Calais/West programmes. Mr Delmer was informed that the feature which was found most disturbing was that they proved that the British had a source of information inside the Fuehrer's headquarters. All the items about the Fuehrer's headquarters were correct. Greater and greater inaccuracy appeared as the subjects dealt with distant parts of Germany. He added that several arrests were made but they had never got the right man. This evidence shows that Calais/West programmes were a means of carrying out nerve warfare on Hitler, his personal staff and the Nazi leaders.

There was undoubtedly an unconscious psychological compulsion to believe in a traitor close to the leader – a Judas among the Apostles.

Nachrichten für die Truppen

Approval for the 'Grey' transmissions of Soldatensender Calais (on medium wave), which had been added to Atlantiksender in order to support Overlord, was followed by a proposal[2] for a 'Grey' newspaper for the German forces in the West, the material of which should be substantially that of Soldatensender Calais programme. As it would be disseminated by Allied aircraft, German soldiers would realise that it was of enemy origin, but it was proposed to lessen the effect of being of enemy origin by careful slanting in the language, e.g. referring to Germany as Die Heimat.

It was to be as 'newsy' as possible and was to take up an objective reporting attitude, avowing neither enemy nor German origin and none of

1. Listening to Allied Radio Broadcasts, by German civilians under the Nazis, PWD, 3.5.45.
2. Mr Delmer to Major General Brooks, 15.2.44.

the news was to be of a kind which could be disproved by the experience of the ordinary soldier. It was hoped to disseminate 1,000,000 copies a night.

To have produced such a newspaper independently would have needed a quality and number of writers beyond what was available. By combining the wireless and newspaper operations, great economies were secured. But Mr Delmer's proposal was based on the knowledge that the German soldier was not an intellectual being and that if certain irrational prejudices were observed his hunger for news and his habits of obedience and gullibility could lead him to read and to believe what he read.

Moreover, the actual military news provided from SHAEF was not only later than that of any other news medium but was kept strictly accurate. The propaganda and the lies were to be found in the news from inside Germany.

The project for the 'Grey Daily Newspaper for the German Forces' did not materialise until after the return of the Director General from sick leave. He was informed on 6.4.44 that the arrangements were[1] that the paper would be written at MB in the early morning, laid out, set up and dispatched to press from Marylands by 11 a.m., printed at Luton and delivered from there – ready packed into the Munroe bomb – to the 42nd Squadron USAAF (stationed at Cheddington), reaching the airfield in time for the bombs to be loaded into the aircraft in daylight.

The supply of information for the paper was already aroused by the arrangements made for the use of Soldatensender West to support Overlord. Information was supplied direct, together with guidance on its use, from SHAEF operations room and was exempt from every censorship save that recommended by Lt Commander McLachlan after consultation with G2. As SHAEF moved forward, a liaison officer for Mr Delmer moved with it. This duty was performed by Lt Commander McLachlan and Squadron Leader Hodgkin and in the final stage by Captain J. P. Dickson of the US Marine Corps, who had been attached to Lt Commander McLachlan by the US Navy.

Although Nachrichten für die Truppe was in all respects a PWE publication being conceived, written, printed and largely paid for by PWE, a 'first report' on a 'Newspaper for the German Forces' was sent to Sir Robert Bruce Lockhart with a covering letter[2] from Brigadier General McClure which stated that 'copies of this newsheet should have reached you. Any comments or criticism by members of your staff would be welcomed here.' In fact, Brigadier General McClure was responsible to SHAEF for its use, distribution and security. Without the anomalous authority of PWD it would never have been dropped.

---

1. Mr Keeble to the Director General, 6.4.44.
2. Brigadier General McClure to Sir Robert Bruce Lockhart, 2.5.44.

The distribution of Nachrichten für die Truppe began on the night of 25th April. 300,000 copies were dropped over selected areas in Northern France, in leaflet bombs aimed at billets and headquarters. The operation was repeated on 26th April and following days.

The first issue was numbered No. 11 in order to increase the difficulties of the Gestapo in assessing the start of the operation.

Target areas were prepared for three weeks ahead with the assistance of G2, SHAEF. They ranged from western France through northern France, across Belgium, Holland and Denmark to Norway. Droppings were in the following proportions: 11 a month over France, 4 over Belgium, 4 over Holland, 1 over Denmark, 2 over Norway making a total of 22 droppings a month, or about 6½ million copies. American and British personnel were co-operating at every stage of this operation, and OWI and OSS had given Mr Delmer valuable assistance over the provision of staff and facilities. Dropping was done entirely by the only squadron of night-flying Fortresses.

The choice of widely separated targets for Nachrichten before D-Day was dictated by the need for strategical deception of the enemy. Directly the Normandy landings had taken place, Nachrichten was dropped on and behind the enemy's front line, particularly at places where his troops were held in reserve.

War Criminals

In addition to the longer-term intelligence material included in the zone and regional handbooks, PWE undertook to make copies of the Personality Cards of traitors and dangerous or suspect persons available to SHAEF region by region. They included lists of personnel in Quisling formations such as the NSB. An indication of the quantity of information is given by the fact that there were about 9,000 cards for Belgium, 2,400 for Holland and 500 for Luxembourg. The material was supplementary to the zonal handbooks.

The PWE view on making joint lists with the Allied Governments varied according to its relations with the authority concerned. Thus Dr Beck welcomed the visit of a Free French security officer to check and supplement the PWE card index, and Mr de Sauzmarez was equally willing to disclose the Belgian list to the Belgian Sûreté. He firmly opposed any disclosure to the Dutch Government as it would jeopardise PWE unofficial relations with individuals in the Dutch service.

The value of the PWE lists to SHAEF in making arrests and for purposes of military security is obvious and it should be stressed that no other department had anything like such complete personality files as PWE. The records of C and SOE were far more specialised or confined to enemy intelligence services.

Flying Bombs, Incendiaries and Rockets in Propaganda and in Fact

From early in the war, German propaganda had made considerable use of open references to rumours about secret weapons which were being perfected and which would win the war – particularly the war against England and against British ships. The theme can be considered as an intelligent counter to the theme of the overwhelming war potential of the United States which was a constant feature of British and American propaganda.

During 1943, we became possessed of information which tended to bear out the German propaganda claim that various secret weapons were in existence and were being perfected. A pilotless aircraft, possibly remotely controlled by wireless, like the 'Queen Bee' from an accompanying aircraft, a wireless-controlled rocket bomb released from an aircraft and a gigantic rocket weighing nine tons were the forms which it was believed the secret weapon would assume.

British propaganda had adopted a contemptuous tone in referring to what it had assumed was a propaganda device for keeping up German morale and carrying out a 'war of nerves'. Once, however, the possibility of there being effective secret weapons in existence, the matter became one of great significance to our Political Warfare.

Unfortunately owing to the large measures of divorce between PWE Planning Directorate and PWE Intelligence, it did not occur to anyone to ask Mr Walmsley to analyse German propaganda on the secret weapon before November. Thus the first statement of PWE views[1] was that belief in a secret weapon was an important support of German morale and that dispelling this belief was a constant preoccupation of PWE. It would thus be a major reverse for our propaganda against the Germans if anything were done in this country to show that we were reacting to the 'War of Nerves'. Goebbels would quote to his home front with resounding effect any publicity or currency given to the threat of the secret weapon.

In other words, PWE had 'committed' itself to the view that the secret weapon was only a German propaganda device and could not recede without loss of face.

During the first week of November, 1943, a sub-committee of the JIC was set up[2] to sift the evidence available from all sources and PWE was invited to nominate a member who would also attend meetings of another committee of which Sir Stafford Cripps was chairman. Major General Brooks nominated Mr Walmsley at the invitation of the JIC Sub-Committee.

Mr Walmsley put forward his views on Bodyline,[3] advocating a warning

1. Major General Brooks to Minister of Information, 28.10.43.
2. Major General Brooks to Minister of Information, 11.11.43.
3. The code name for the indiscriminate bombardment of Britain from fixed ramps in the Pas-de-Calais area.

through media of Black and Grey propaganda that the British intention was to use gas if the Germans used Bodyline. To convince the German High Command it would be necessary to provide evidence of preparations for the use of gas and for defence against gas and to 'convey to them through high-grade channels' that the British Government knew the nature of Bodyline, had no qualms against using gas but welcomed the opportunity to shorten the war by its use.

In a covering note, Mr Walmsley informed Major Powell of the War Cabinet Offices that the Minister of Information had seen the memorandum and raised no objection to its going forward at that level but stated that he would state his objections to the project on the Ministerial level should it come to be considered.

A decision to bomb the ramps and other constructions from which it was believed rockets would be launched was taken and the French Region was asked to prepare a leaflet warning the workers engaged in their construction.

Lt Colonel Fairlie stated[1] in a covering minute that he did not believe such a warning would have much effect as the workers were undoubtedly impressed men working under machine guns and unable to take to the Maquis. He asked that there should be a time lag of at least twenty-four hours between dropping the leaflets and bombing and that whatever intelligence might come to hand the targets should be attacked once the warnings had been dropped. He also urged that we were more likely to be successful if we relied upon bombing. The warning leaflet (F157) stated that the Germans were carrying out certain military constructions which we should bomb until they had been entirely destroyed. It ordered the workmen to take to the Maquis if there was the slightest chance of doing so and recommended the local population to evacuate the district.

As is well-known, the bombardments were carried out on such a scale and with such effect that a new method of launching rockets had to be invented by the enemy.

A decision to bomb French factories working in the production of certain kinds of war material, even in built-up areas, was taken early in November. Certain of these factories were believed to be working in the production of German secret weapons. PWE was accordingly asked to prepare *Avis* No. 19 to warn the population.[2]

The industries in question were tanks, guns, lorries, aircraft, aero-engines and locomotives and thirteen major cities of France were listed as liable to attack, the particular districts frequently being specified. This *Avis* must be regarded as only partly concerned with enemy secret weapons, but there is little doubt that the inclusion of targets in heavily built-up areas in France was partly owing to our anxiety with regard to the manufacture or assembly of secret weapons.

---

1. Lt Colonel Fairlie to DDG (through DPW(O)), 28.10.43.
2. Text approved by Secretary of State for Foreign Affairs, 17.11.43.

Mr Walmsley's proposals to make threats of retaliation could not be held to commit PWE and, in any case, the threat to use gas in retaliation had been found unacceptable by higher authority. The question came up again[1] in a discussion of Crossbow. PWE was invited by the Defence Committee to consider and to report on the advantage of sowing fear of retaliation in Germany by subterranean methods on the postulates that no public denunciations of 'Crossbow' as a form of indiscriminate warfare should be made, and that there should be no threat of retaliation by the use of gas.

PWE reported[2] that the German High Command was protected against our subversive propaganda threatening retaliation by their own intelligence. Our problem would therefore be to cause such widespread fear among the population in Germany as to infect the High Command in spite of the absence of any corroborative evidence. The means at our disposal were short-wave clandestine stations, infiltrated subversive leaflets and verbally disseminated rumours.

Our short-wave clandestine stations alone could reach an audience quickly, but the German High Command would only be convinced that we were seriously alarmed at the threat of Crossbow by such transmissions. The infiltration of Black leaflets and the dissemination of rumours was slow and imprecise and would be unlikely to have any influence in time. Building up a threat which we do not intend to carry out would damage us and raise German morale still more. The morale-sustaining effect of Crossbow depended on whether it could change the course of the war and bring our bombing to an end. The most effective retaliation was therefore that there should be no deflection of the course of the war and that bombing should continue.

This paper was communicated to the Minister of Information and the Foreign Secretary[3] and endorsed by the Minister of Information: 'Threats of retaliation will encourage the rocketeers and Nazi propagandists. I agree with your paper. Alas it is starchy and long. B.B.'

The Chairman of the Defence Committee, Sir John Anderson, felt that the minutes of the Committee had not done justice to a suggestion which he had made and which had consequently not been taken into account by PWE. He therefore asked PWE to report on his suggestion to him personally in order to save the time of the Committee.[4]

The Chancellor's proposal was that a leading article should be inspired in a secondary Sunday paper, implying that the use of blind terrorism in the shape of 'Crossbow' would be a 'mad-dog' act, would not affect our capacity to win and would justify drastic treatment of Germany after the war. The article should be represented as a spontaneous outburst of mass opinion.

PWE reported that the article would find its way to Germany via Lisbon

1. Meeting of Defence Committee (Operations), 22.12.43, to discuss 'Crossbow'.
2. Operation Crossbow, 29.12.43.
3. Major General Brooks to Minister of Information, 28.12.43.
4. Major General Brooks to Minister of Information, 14.1.44.

ad be evaluated by German Intelligence, and it could be quoted on the BBC and/or used in leaflets.

No trained evaluator would accept an article in a Sunday newspaper as evidence of spontaneous mass opinion and that by the BBC would destroy the illusion of spontaneity. Moreover, if Germany were told that it would be treated like a mad dog if Crossbow were used, and this weapon were then employed, the threat would produce desperation which would work against Rankin and increase the difficulties of Overlord. This paper appears to have convinced Sir John Anderson.

Mr Walmsley was asked to begin quantitative analysis of German propaganda in November 1943 in order to draw deductions as to the date when the Germans were likely to use their secret weapon. These deductions were extremely accurate, but not much attention was given to them by the military authorities. It is therefore worth putting the results of Mr Walmsley's technique on record as a guide for the future. Walmsley's analyses are here compared with the facts as given in 'The German long-range rocket programme 1930–1945 by MI4/14, 30.10.45' and Oberst Max Wachtel 'The Flying Bomb and Flakregiment 155 by ADI (K) Report No. 411 1945'.

The Facts as later Ascertained	***Mr Walmsley's Deductions***
'In May 1943 the Fuehrer was for the first time completely persuaded of the practicability of the use of V2.'	'It is highly probable that by the end of May preparations for the use of this weapon were past the experimental stage.'
Report No. 411 On 7th January, 1944, it was stated that the original site system would have to be abandoned if the present rate of damage continued.	*Mr Walmsley, 8.11.43* 'There was an indication that after about 10th January, there was a decline of confidence that Crossbow would be launched with sensational results at all.'
Report No. 411 'Dornberger hoped to begin V2 operations early in May.'	*Mr Walmsley, 27.1.44* 'It is unlikely that Germany's leaders expect to launch Crossbow with sensational results within about the next six weeks.'
The German long-range rocket programme The Flying Bomb was employed as an anti-invasion measure on 6.5.44 admittedly prematurely.	*Mr Walmsley, 23.3.44* 'There is nothing to confirm or to refute the previous evidence that Germany's leaders consider the use of Crossbow on a small scale as a counter invasion measure to be reasonably probable.'

On 29th August the Fuehrer decided operations must begin at once.

'The use of V2 on a *large* scale is most unlikely in the near future. If sites, material and organisation are available however, small scale attack is likely to occur at any time.'

The German long-range rocket programme
The first V2 fell on Paris on 6th September and in Britain on [the] 8th.

Mr Walmsley, 31.8.44.

Effect of Flying Bombs on Work in the Department

During the height of the flying-bomb bombardment on London, instructions were issued that all personnel must seek refuge in the bomb-proof shelter in the basement on an alarm being sounded. Had this been generally observed, working hours would have been greatly curtailed and the order was consequently almost completely disregarded. There was at one time a certain trooping to and fro into the central halls of each floor which were comparatively safe from flying glass. But most officers and their secretaries remained at work.

A number of flying bombs fell extremely close to Bush House, but the only damage was caused by one which, after grazing the roof of the East Block of Bush House, fell into Aldwych in front of the Post Office killing, it is said, all its occupants and the occupants of two buses [30.6.44]. Fortunately it fell just before the end of the lunch hour, when most of the PWE heads of departments were outside the building. Practically all windows and partitions on the 6th, 7th and 8th floors in the North Wing of Centre Block were wrecked and many windows and skylights elsewhere. A few members of the staff were injured by flying glass and many had very narrow escapes. Practically all partitions and windows in Ingersoll House were wrecked, but the staff carried on work with very little interruption.

[18.2.44] An incendiary raid destroyed four or five detached villa residences held by the Department in Brondesbury. The damage would have been much greater but for the courage of a caretaker, Mr Wall, who dealt with a large number of incendiaries single-handed and whose action was strongly commended by the School Commandant, Colonel Johnston.

Scheme for Evacuation to Woburn Abbey

An emergency scheme for the evacuation of Bush House was prepared shortly before the enemy began using the V2, the effects of which were then anticipated to be far more devastating than those of the V1. Accommodation for 153 members of PWE with chauffeurs and domestic staff and for six members of OWI and twelve members of ABSIE was found in PWE country establishment at Woburn.

The priority personnel to be evacuated consisted of the Intelligence directorate distribution office, the Regional staffs for the Daily Digest, and the staff engaged in writing the German Zone handbook. In addition there was accommodation for a further thirty people. Further accommodation was to be met by equipping a tented camp for 100 persons. The proposal received the Director General's approval[1] on 11.8.44. The schemes would have housed a total of 205 persons out of the total London staff of 764.

Personnel Requirements and Training

The personnel sub-committee of the Reoccupation Committee in an interim report[2] recommended that a nucleus of staff should be earmarked for each country some of whom would remain on the job through all phases of liberation.

> . . . urgent steps must be taken to improve the necessary medium for selection namely a PWE/MoI/CCAO interviewing board and the appointment of an officer for talent scouting. . . .
>
> A Director of Studies and ten instructors will be required in addition to the Commandant . . . the instructing staff will ultimately become available themselves for employment in the field.

The sub-committee suggested a course of *three months' duration* including two weeks' attachment to troops of the countries in which they were destined to serve.

The Directors General of MoI and PWE approved the recommendation of the Reoccupation Committee that a Joint Selection Board should be immediately set up to choose suitable candidates for training and that a 'talent scout' should be employed to find them in the first place. In addition to PWE and MoI, DCCAO was represented on this board by Major R. F. Lethbridge.[3]

The provisional estimate of the British personnel that would be required made by the Reoccupation Committee was forty-five officers at Force Headquarters and 140 at Regional Headquarters and fifteen liaison officers with the US Forces – a total of 200.

At the first meeting[4] instructions for Major Armitage were approved and he was informed that he was to seek candidates among civilians including those in reserved occupations whose release it might be possible to obtain, and in the Services. He was to assume that no Service candidate

1. Major General Brooks to Director General, 11.8.44.
2. SCR 2(b) RC paper 10, 2.6.43.
3. Afterwards a member of PWE Mission Middle East.
4. 11.6.43.

under thirty-eight would be released. It was shortly afterwards agreed that he was to find candidates suitable for PWE Mission Middle East as well as for Western Europe. It was considered desirable on grounds of security that Major Armitage should interview candidates outside Bush House and an office was therefore taken for him at Brettenham House.

Certain other difficulties at once arose on the 'vetting' of candidates for security. This work was in the hands of Colonel Chambers and was carried out through MI5. But Colonel Chambers, though unwilling to delegate responsibility for officers who became members of PWE, would take no responsibility for officers who might be wanted for work by MoI or Civil Affairs. Colonel Chambers also imposed a ban on any direct approach by Major Armitage to Service officers or men.

Applications for the employment of civilian candidates had to be made through the Ministry of Labour.

By 31st August, 1943, Major Armitage had nevertheless interviewed 150 officers; the Selection Board had interviewed eighty-four and recommended fifty-seven for training.[1] In the selection of these officers the qualifications insisted on were those of language and experience of the country in which they were to be employed. Less attention was paid to age, physical fitness and press, cinema and radio experience.

A preliminary course of training was started in September 1943 at CHQ under Lt Colonel Sedgwick. The pupils were paid at the rate of £425 per annum for the duration of the course and the Joint Selection Board informed them that subject to their proving satisfactory in training they would be commissioned with the rank of captain.[2] This commitment was to prove a source of considerable trouble later on and was quite unjustified since the Joint Selection Board was not in a position to make any such promises and could not be certain that they would be carried out. In October the terms of reference of the Joint Selection Board were extended to Germany.[3] First estimates were that between 600 and 700 German-speaking persons would be required.

The first hint that more scientific methods of selection might be employed is contained in a report[4] on a visit to the SOE Selection Board which carried out its work with the assistance of professional psychiatrists. Candidates lived with the members of the Board for a period of three to four days in a country house. The tests were carried on the normal WOSB lines.

Major Armitage reported that 'I am inclined to recommend that this Department should adhere to the old rule of thumb methods which under the correct thumb, seems to continue to produce adequate results.'

---

1. This number included the pool of officers initiated by Air Commodore Groves and held on the strength of the French Region.
2. Minute of Director of Training to Air Commodore Groves, 9.9.43.
3. Mr Ritchie Calder to Lt Col Gielgud, 4.10.43.
4. Major Armitage to Lt Col Gielgud, 9.10.43

This recommendation was accepted, a decision which proved unfortunate, since OWI regarded the passing of a modified WOSB test as essential for PWD personnel, and it became impossible for PWE to refuse to allow its nominees chosen by 'correct thumb' to be tested by modern scientific methods. It was found that only a small proportion of the 'correct thumb' men were physically fit enough to satisfy the WOSB acting for OWI/PWD. Not infrequently they were temperamentally or psychologically unsuitable, and in several cases[1] candidates who had successfully passed the Joint Selection Board were unsuitable for reasons which should have been obvious under any system of selection.

Nevertheless, some of those chosen did brilliantly. It is only fair to Lt Colonel Sedgwick, PWE Director of Studies, to put on record that in practically all cases his private reports were conformed by the OWI/PWB WOSB and that his forecasts in regard to his pupils were almost always confirmed. In view of his experience as a teacher and army 'coach' and in training and observing pupils for work in PWE, it is regrettable that his knowledge was not made use of by the Joint Selection Board.

The methods employed by Major Armitage and the Joint Selection Board did at all events produce bodies with the necessary linguistic qualifications for France, the Low Countries, Scandinavia and the Balkans. They failed to produce German speakers. The obvious reason, as Major Armitage stated, was that from the outset of the war the Intelligence Services and other branches had employed all suitable German speakers. In practically all cases any German speaker who was unemployed in 1943 was unemployed for some very good reason which disqualified him from employment by PWE.

Major Armitage,[2] considering his work was done, asked for other employment. As from 13.12.43 the Joint Selection Board was adjourned sine die, as civilian sources of candidates seemed to have been exhausted and it had been decided that personnel required for Germany should be nominated by the War Office.[3]

The total numbers of persons interviewed and selected by the Joint Selection Board in the six or seven months of its existence was 137, of whom twelve were rated as above the average as regards qualifications.

Before leaving the subject several factors must be taken into account in any comparison with American officers selected by OWI for PWD. In the first place British manpower was rapidly becoming exhausted by the end of four years of war, whereas American manpower was at its peak. Secondly, the United States could draw upon an immense supply of persons who were either recently naturalised native speakers, or whose parents had been

1. Personal observations. The writer was PWE Director of Training from 1.1.44 until the Directorate was wound up in November 1944.
2. Major Armitage to Air Commodore Groves, 17.11.43.
3. 30th Meeting Joint Selection Board, item 162, 29.11.43.

native speakers of the countries for which they were wanted. Finally the difficulties put in the way of recruitment by security considerations would appear to have been quite excessive, and dictated more by a fear of possible publicity in the press than by any real danger to security.

PWE Training School

The first 'training' of an officer for Political Warfare in the field was the forty-eight-hour visit of Lt Colby to CHQ on 18/19 March 1942, before sailing with the Force engaged in the occupation of Madagascar.

Experience with Lt Colby was made use of by the French Region in training officers for 'Torch' which was conducted under the direction of Lt Colonel Sedgwick at CHQ and lasted for about three weeks. It was a purely French 'regional' course and for security reasons the officers taking it were not informed that they were proceeding to North Africa.

When the first course of twenty-four officers and eleven o.r.s for Torch was completed, a second course was held of four persons who were being trained for Political Warfare to Italy from North Africa. A full report on the course was submitted by Lt Colonel Sedgwick on 14.11.42.

Lt Colonel Sedgwick's appointment as Commandant PWE Training School was signed by the Director General on 1.1.43 in order 'to train personnel in Political Warfare for contingencies which may arise in the future'. The Staff and students were to live at Wing House. A course for nine men and four women selected for the PWE Mission to West Africa was given between 12.1.43 and 7.2.43. Lt Colonel Sedgwick delivered thirty-two out of sixty-one lectures. There were also practical demonstrations, voice tests and actual broadcasts. A further course in advanced propaganda was given apparently entirely for SOE personnel or PWE agents. The Policy and Planning Committee stated that training would be necessary for the actual expansion of PWE itself, for staff going to PW Missions abroad and for PW duties following the liberation of Western Europe.[1] In the same paper it was recommended that the school should be not more than half an hour distant from Central London and that the posts of School Commandant and Chief Instructor should be kept distinct.[2] Both these recommendations were contrary to the views of Lt Colonel Sedgwick, who had been strikingly successful in the courses hitherto held.

The recommendation that the School should be moved from the existing premises to London was due to the increasing pressure of work in London upon the chief regional experts and planners of PWE who would not have time to give many lectures at CHQ and to the recognition that lectures by regional experts, occupied with the conduct of actual Political Warfare was

1. Political Warfare Training School, Provisional Summary of Requirements, 29.5.43.
2. Item (VI), *ibid.*

the only way to provide the best training possible and to ensure that the lectures were in line with the developments of PWE policy.[1]

These recommendations were submitted to the Ministers[2] and CAO recommended that the School should be established in premises at Brondesbury.

These proposals were agreed by the Ministers and a committee was appointed by the Director General with Air Commodore Groves as Chairman to 'plan the organisation, training and administration requirements of the School at Brondesbury and prepare for front-line propaganda courses at CHQ' until the Brondesbury School opened.[3]

A number of sub-committees were at once set up to draw up syllabi, and Colonel A. C. Johnston DSO, MC, who had unexpectedly returned from an unfruitful PWE Mission to India, was appointed Commandant of the School. His duties were not only 'the command, administration and discipline of the school'[4] but also 'to ensure that the policy in regard to the directives which he will receive from the Director of Training is carried into effect'.

Lt Colonel Gielgud, MBE, was appointed Director of Training[5] having recently been succeeded as French Regional Director by Lt Colonel Fairlie. His duties included issuing directives to the School Commandant and the Director of Studies who were responsible to him for carrying out the policy of his directives.

Lt Colonel Sedgwick was appointed Deputy Commandant and Director of Studies.[6]

The School Commandant, however, took exception to the designation Director of Studies and persistently referred to Lt Colonel Sedgwick as 'my Chief Instructor'. He also took exception to direct communication between the Director of Training and Lt Colonel Sedgwick and to School Instructors visiting Bush House which was essential for them to obtain material for lectures.

A preliminary course for officers chosen by the Joint Selection Board or drawn from 'regional pools' was given at CHQ from 6.9.43 to 25.9.43. A secondary object of the course was to select instructors for later courses from the students.

The opening of PWE School Brondesbury at the appointed date in November 1943 was rendered impossible by a protracted inter-departmental battle over the necessary domestic staff. The details of this

---

1. Considerable uneasiness was felt by the Director of Plans and the German Regional Director as the policy of some lectures given at former courses in Political Warfare had not been in line with that of the Department. For example, in one lecture, the students had been told: 'No direct attacks on Fascism.'
2. Minute to Minister of Information from the Director General, 18.6.43.
3. To Air Commodore Groves from Sir Robert Bruce Lockhart, 11.10.43.
4. PWD/AN/88, 17.8.43.
5. PWD/AN/89, 17.8.43.
6. PWD/AN/90, 19.8.43.

dispute would be tedious and the historian would willingly pass them over in silence if the preoccupations of the War Cabinet with scullery maids, necessitating the personal intervention of the Prime Minister himself during the months of vast preparations, involving the movements of millions of men and millions of tons of material for the purposes of Overlord, did not indicate an extraordinary absence of mutual accommodation over a very small matter. Upwards of fifteen letters on this subject passed either to, from or between the Minister of Information, the Secretary of State for Foreign Affairs, the Secretary of State for War and the Minister of Labour between the beginning of September and the end of January 1944, and matters having reached a deadlock, the matter was brought before the War Cabinet whereupon 'on the suggestion of the Prime Minister[1] the War Cabinet invited the Lord Privy Seal to decide which department should be responsible for providing the necessary staff'. Further delay was caused by the reluctance of the Lord Privy Seal to arbitrate and it was twenty-five days before he arrived at the decision that the ATS should provide the domestic staff.

The refusal of the War Office and of the Ministry of Labour to provide domestic staff had delayed the opening of PWE training school for over four months. It must, however, be added that the first estimate presented by PWE of 120 ATS to look after the needs of 200 students was much too large. In point of fact, partly owing to the lack of co-operation of 21 Army Group in providing British officers for training, there were never more than seventy-seven students at any of the Brondesbury courses.

PWE Training School Brondesbury

As the Brondesbury School could not be opened at the date fixed, a second course was given at CHQ for officers chosen by the Joint Selection Board. This was followed by two courses for British Commando officers given at CHQ during December 1943. They were attended by about twelve officers headed by Brigadier Leicester. These courses were followed by two courses for intelligence officers destined for Norway.

The first course held 13.12.43 to 21.12.43 at CHQ was attended by nine British officers. Instruction for the first three days was given entirely by Major Bodington, Lt Van Dierem and Mr Maclaren, and for the remainder of the course by Major Petch, Mr Kenney and Mr Brinley Thomas of the Northern Region PWE. Lt Colonel Sedgwick was absent on sick leave.

A second Norway course for CIO's was held at CHQ from 31.1.44 to 5.2.44 and was attended by thirty-two British and two American officers and included three lt colonels and seventeen majors. The course was planned and organised by Major Petch of the Northern Region and only four lectures were given by members of the School staff, including Major

1. Item of minutes of War Cabinet Meeting held 14.2.44.

Gallie, head of the SOE School Wallhall, who attended three days to give lectures and instruction in Fact and Opinion Research in a liberated country. The course was most successful and certainly influenced the subsequent attitude of Scottish Command to PWE problems in Norway.

After Lt Colonel Sedgwick and the instructors had taken up residence at Brondesbury, a 'refresher' course was given from 8.2.44 to 18.2.44 to those persons who had attended either the first or second courses for Joint Selection Board candidates and could find accommodation in or near London. The Director of Training was also able to arrange for lectures to be given by the staff to OSS personnel who would not have been able in any case to be residential students. These lectures were given at OSS premises in London. Lectures were also arranged for officers and men at the large American Civil Affairs training camp at Shrivenham and the British Civil Affairs training school at Wimbledon. A large proportion of these lectures dealt with the political conditions which would be met with in France, Belgium and Holland, and at all these lectures the PWE view of British relations with Allied Governments and Resistance movements after liberation was firmly insisted on.

Meanwhile the plans put forward by the Reoccupation Committee and by Brigadier Lee had had to be reconsidered in the light of the appointment of General Eisenhower as Supreme Allied Commander.

The delay in opening [the] PWE School at Brondesbury enable[d] syllabi to be agreed with OWI and PWD and for adjustments to be made in the Staff and to some extent in training so that the instruction at Brondesbury must be regarded as completely 'integrated' with OWI.

The presence of the OWI Director of Training, and the establishment in Britain of a large American training camp for the military and technical training and physical hardening of Press and Psychological Warfare personnel at Clevedon under Colonel Powell, US Army, and later the opening of a PWD school at Rushton Hall, Northants, and the 'screening' of all PWD officers by a special WOSB at Watford, enabled the training given at Brondesbury to take its place in a co-ordinated scheme. For these purposes a PWD training committee was set up with the PWE Director of Training as Chairman.[1] The flexibility in these matters, looked for by the Americans, was greatly assisted by the appointment of Colonel Thornhill as Commandant in the place of Colonel Johnston.[2]

The flexibility referred to was on the whole advantageous as it enabled outside lecturers with experience in different fields to be brought in when they were available, and it enabled lectures and exercises to be scrapped and remodelled at short notice. The drawback of the system was that it resulted in real authority being transferred from the Director of Studies (Lt Colonel

1. 29.2.44.
2. 7.5.44.

Sedgwick) to the Director of Training (Mr David Garnett)* as the latter was at first Chairman of the PWD Training Committee and was continually having to make new arrangements with his fast moving American opposite number. Though this had the advantage that complete control of policy was in the hands of an officer in Bush House who was in the closest touch with Air Commodore Groves, the Director of Plans and Regional Directors, it had the disadvantage that the man who was doing the work of actual teaching, and who was a most brilliant lecturer, was continually being interfered with by something very like an Anglo-American Soviet.

The entire organisation of the PWE School at Brondesbury with a Commandant as its titular head and an Anglo-American Committee working through a Director of Training at Bush House exercising detailed control was not altogether fair to the man to whom the greater part of the credit for the excellence of PWE training was due – who was Lt Colonel Sedgwick, the Director of Studies.

Nevertheless, so long as Lt Colonel Sedgwick remained, the success of the School was most marked, and the courses gained immensely from the Director of Training's being able to call upon expert lecturers from all sources and the help given him in particular by members of the French, German and Low Countries Regions, and by M. Mayoux, Chef du Service des Informations at Carlton Gardens. It was these regional lectures backed by Lt Colonel Sedgwick's personality which made the courses the great success they were, profoundly modifying the outlook to Western Europe of all the students who took part in them.

An inevitable difficulty of courses which drew their star lecturers from outside the School was that continual change had to be made in the syllabus to suit the convenience of extremely busy men, who were not always able to keep engagements made some time in advance. These changes upset the logical presentation of the subjects and were usually at the expense of the school staff. There were thus factors which made the school instructors resent such a system in favour of running the whole course themselves. The advantages, however, of having the men who were actually carrying out Political Warfare, and who had worked with or even in resistance movements as lecturers, was enormous, particularly when it came to answering questions, and the results achieved could not have been obtained by any other means.

In all, nine Anglo-American courses were given at Brondesbury, the first beginning on 13th March and the last ending on 23rd September. The pressure was naturally greatest before D-Day, 6th June, both because the OWI Director of Training had not by that time organised his school at Rushton Hall, Northants. Between 13th March and 9th June five courses were held, 290 students attended the courses of which 221 were American and 69 British.

---

* [David Garnett (1892–1981); see Introduction.]

Lt Colonel Sedgwick resigned his post as Director of Studies after the conclusion of the fifth course and this coincided with a break in the flow of American officers and men who required training. He was replaced by Major Burnett who was appointed Chief Instructor. During the interval – from 19th [to] 22nd June, a small course was carried out under the directions of Major Hazan, the lecturer on French subjects, for five officers under Major Gwynne who were to carry out a Political Warfare special mission in France.

Courses were resumed on 17th July and ended with the ninth course beginning on 10.9.44 and ending on 23.9.44, after which the School was wound up, as the necessary work had been done and the premises were required for other purposes.

The last four courses were attended by 158 officers and men of whom six were British, five being senior officers from the British Civil Affairs training centre at Eastbourne.

The Director of Training's responsibility ended with the sixth course as he was absent on sick leave from early August until November. In all 444 officers and men and four women members of OWI attended the nine Anglo-American courses at Brondesbury, the great majority being trained for PWD functions.

A Typical Syllabus

An analysis of the syllabus of the third Anglo-American course (23.4.44 to 5.5.44) which 'turned out to be the most successful ever held here'[1] shows of approximately forty-eight lectures, apart from exercises, the numbers given respectively were:

20 by School staff.
7 by lecturers from OWI and PWD (including 3 lectures by a British instructor from the OWI school).
12 by Bush House experts.
4 by outside lecturers (M. Mayoux, head of the Service des Informations, Colonel Dillard, Head of American Civil Affairs training and Lt General Martel*).
2 by SOE instructors.

OWI and PWD contributed more to the exercises than to the lectures

1. Lt Colonel Sedgwick's Report on the Course.
* [Lieutenant-General Sir Giffard Le Quesne Martel (1889–1958) was commissioned in Royal Engineers 1909; served in France 1914–16; at tanks HQ 1916–18; Imperial Services welterweight champion 1921–2; Assistant Director, mechanisation, War Office, 1936; Deputy Director 1938–9; commanded 50th Northumbrian division 1939–40; improvised Arras counter-attack May 1940; commander, Royal Armoured Corps, 1940–2; head of military mission to Moscow 1943–4.]

especially to those in leaflet writing. SOE instructors Major Hackett, Major Gallie, Captain Waddicor and Mr Jaffé were responsible for teaching of Fact and opinion research. Sunday afternoon was devoted to a field exercise in which students collected opinions of members of the public on a particular subject by entering into conversations on the tops of buses, in Hyde Park, etc. Lt Colonel Sedgwick and the school staff were responsible for exercises in interrogation impersonating different types of Germans and Frenchmen, Belgians and Dutchmen, etc.

An analysis of lectures by subjects shows that they may be roughly divided into Political Warfare 8, General 8, Germany 10, France 12, Low Countries 4, Russia 1.

Assessment of the Work of Brondesbury School

A provisional assessment of the value of Brondesbury School is contained in a paper[1] submitted to the Tripartite Committee for PWE/OWI/PWD by Brigadier General McClure.

> The great accomplishments of Brondesbury are fully appreciated. Without its assistance the field work now being undertaken, could not even have been begun. It is realised that if all training is concentrated in the PWD School[2] it will be impossible to obtain anything like the present standard of political expertise which has made Brondesbury such a success.

Leaflet Dissemination in Preparation for D-Day

A detailed leaflet programme in Preparation for D-Day was prepared by Mr Frank Kaufman and Mr Harold Keeble.[3]

It stated that the equivalent of 320,000,000 leaflet units (i.e. single sheets 5¼ × 8¼") was produced in March 1944 and that it was proposed to keep production at that monthly figure until D-Day.

Approximately 265,000,000 leaflet units were disseminated in March by the RAF and USAAF. It was proposed to keep dissemination at the figure of 320,000,000 units a month, of which 270,000,000 would be addressed to the civilian populations and 50,000,000 directly to German troops. The 60,000,000 lag between production and dissemination in March was expected to decrease. The quotas for the civilian populations [were] as follows:

1. Brigadier General McClure to Sir Robert Bruce Lockhart and Mr Robert Sherwood, 24.6.44.
2. Rushton Hall, Northants, is referred to.
3. Inter-office memo from Mr Kaufman and Mr Keeble to General McClure, Sir Robert Bruce Lockhart and Mr Sherwood, 22.4.44.

	March 1944	Proposed Monthly till D-Day
Germany	105 million	100 million
France	130 million	114 million
Belgium	11 million	20 million
Holland	15 million	20 million
Denmark	800,000	3 million
Norway	practically none	9 million
Poland	None	4 million
	265 million	270 million

It was planned to distribute 5,250,000 copies of Nachrichten für die Truppe per month, 16,800,000 leaflet units.

The following monthly schedule was suggested for German troops, exclusive of Nachrichten für die Truppe:

Germany	15 million
France	8 million
Belgium	3 million
Holland	3 million
Denmark	1 million
Norway	2 million
Poland	1 million

The programme was approved and superseded the PWE/OWI plan approved for Overlord of 22.1.44.

PWE Leaflet Policy

The policy which was followed by PWE in regard to leaflet dissemination in the spring of 1944 was an impossible one. For PWE was at this period determined on the one hand to take the fullest advantage of the new dissemination facilities offered by the leafleting squadron of USAAF Fortresses while at the same time taking no steps to alter the system by which RAF Bomber Command 'loaded leaflets automatically as though they were as essential as petrol'.[1]

Supplies of Paper for Political Warfare

The paper shortage in Britain was acute and the demands of the programme up till D-Day and after it, the demands for stockpiling printed matter for the Western seaboard countries after liberation, and the attempt to continue RAF disseminations could not all be met.

1. Mr Keeble, meeting of Leaflet Committee.

Mr Keeble's anxiety to print periodicals on rotogravure had made the situation particularly bad with regard to rotogravure paper. Moreover, Britain was exporting rotogravure paper to Cairo at this period because nobody had countermanded the order. When two new periodicals, *Arc-en-Ciel* for Belgium and *Vliegender Hollander* for Holland, were started for dissemination by the USAAF squadron of leafleting Fortresses, Mr Keeble insisted on their being printed by rotogravure[1] although the Chairman of the PWE Leaflet Committee had gained Mr C. D. Jackson's[2] consent to their being produced on newsprint and although in order to print the new ventures on rotogravure, Mr Keeble had to produce one of the French periodicals, *Revue de la Presse Libre*, on newsprint 'with a Germanic-looking heading' without notice and without informing the French Region. Mr Keeble, however, urged that operational leaflets should be produced by letter press on newsprint. In spite of the fact that the Germans could fake operational leaflets far more easily if they were printed on newsprint, Mr Keeble successfully carried out this policy against the ruling of the Chairman of the Leaflet Committee and of the French Regional experts. The reason for what seems arbitrary behaviour was that both he and the Americans with whom he worked disliked showing what they regarded as 'an inferior job' of printing to the USAAF officers of the Leafleting Fortresses which had to disseminate the two new newspapers. Extraordinary efforts were made to find the paper required. Thus an attempt was made to borrow paper from the stocks which were believed to be imported for the American Army periodicals, *Stars and Stripes* and *The Yank*.[3] It was found, however, that both were printed on British paper.

The Joint Production Unit's estimate of requirements for the period was 1,300 tons of paper in[4] excess of the 2,200 tons allocated by the Ministry of Supply and the Stationery Office, i.e. it was a total of 3,500 tons. The greater part of this had to be disseminated by air, at a time when the maximum demands were being made on the RAF for bombing. Yet at no time did any high officer of PWE attempt to reduce this enormous weight of paper by a proposal that the RAF should used the Munroe bomb to obtain an *equivalent* coverage. When, five months after D-Day, the RAF adopted the Munroe bomb, PWE sought to obtain the same numerical disseminations of leaflets by bomb as had previously been given by package which was quite unjustified. In retrospect, it is obvious that had the leaflet bomb been introduced early in 1944, the paper crisis would have been less since an equivalent coverage could be obtained with a much smaller number of leaflets. As this was not done, the paper crisis was only surmounted by the provision of special stocks shipped on high priority from the USA, at a

1. 13th Meeting of the Leaflet Committee, 28.2.44.
2. 12th Meeting of the Leaflet Committee, 21.2.44.
3. Tripartite Committee Meeting, 9.5.44.
4. Tripartite Committee Meeting, 9.5.44.

time when shipping space across the Atlantic was all allocated for war materials. These shipments of paper can only have been made at the expense of other munitions of war, yet there was no attempt at economy in the use of paper by securing the most efficient dissemination of leaflets owing to the laissez-faire policy still prevailing in the Military Wing of PWE.

The policy which had been followed by Mr Keeble in printing all periodicals as far as possible on rotogravure had not allowed for the production of 'bookstall' publications for the post-liberation period. The production of these, though the need for them was obviously going to be urgent, was still being held up a month after D-Day.

A paper from Mr Keeble[1] pointed out that if the OWI magazine *Voir*, the MoI magazine *Aspect*, and one of the Paniguian series per fortnight were to be produced it would involve *Luftpost*, *Sternebanner* and almost all tactical and strategical leaflets being printed on newsprint by letter press or brought to an end. Mr Keeble's proposal of using rotogravure for Liberation bookstall publications and stopping publications of *Luftpost* and *Sternebanner* were accepted by PWD and OWI.[2]

In spite of shipments of paper from the USA, the shortage of paper continued as a major difficulty and it was this factor which really brought to an end the system of automatic loading of leaflets by the RAF. By August, there was only enough paper for the current month and it was decided to allocate paper in the ratio of 50% PWE–SHAEF and 25% each to PWE and OWI.[3] The shortage of paper had resulted in limiting the dissemination of Nachrichten in favour of the dissemination of Surrender leaflets,[4] the figures being 4 million copies of Nachrichten to 70 million Surrender leaflets in June and 5 million Nachrichten in July to 51 million Surrender leaflets.

The transfer of leaflet writing for Germany to Paris in September 1944 was followed by a shortage of leaflets for dissemination by the RAF. It was accordingly agreed[5] to increase the dissemination of Nachrichten which became an RAF responsibility. But this was not immediately possible owing to the paper shortage again becoming acute.

A Joint Policy with the Americans

The policy of temporising with OWI enjoined on Major General Brooks, and the resulting policy of drift in regard to methods of leaflet dissemination, was finally reversed, after the return of the Director General from sick leave, thanks to the initiative of Mr Crossman who had been appointed

1. Re-adjustment of Airborne publication to accommodate bookstall programme for liberated Europe.
2. Minutes of Tripartite Committee, 11.7.44.
3. Minutes of Tripartite Committee, 10.8.44.
4. Meeting of Tripartite Committee, 10.8.44.
5. Meeting of Tripartite Committee, 20.11.44.

Brigadier General McClure's deputy for Planning, after he also had recovered from a serious illness.

A preliminary meeting of PWD/PWE/OWI was held with Mr Ritchie Calder in the chair on 23.3.44 to discuss the subject of leaflet policy and distribution, at which a plan drafted by Mr Crossman and C. D. Jackson was discussed and approved. The proposals were put up to Brigadier General McClure, approved by him and communicated by him to Sir Robert Bruce Lockhart[1] and Mr Hamblet, then Deputy Director of OWI.

These proposals were accepted though they were formally redrafted and certain alterations made in them by Sir Robert Bruce Lockhart who sent them back[2] to Brigadier General McClure with a covering letter.[3] The redraft nominated Sir Robert Bruce Lockhart, Mr Sherwood and Brigadier General McClure as members of the Leaflet Co-ordinating Committee, with power to nominate deputies. The terms of reference of the Committee would be to agree on a common leaflet policy, to agree on leaflet priorities and to decide which leaflets could be released to the press.

PWE and OWI were to continue to be responsible for strategic, i.e. long-term, leaflets and magazines.

PWD were to be responsible for tactical leaflets. PWD would submit all such leaflets to PWE and OWI.

So long as aircraft utilised for tactical leaflet dissemination [were] based in Britain PWD–SHAEF would be responsible for them.

When the tactical leaflet operation moved overseas responsibility was to rest with 21 Army Group and First US Army Group.

PWD agreed not to set up Regional Desks as the Regional Desks of PWE and OWI would be placed at their disposal.

Mr Keeble would be considered Anglo-American Production Chief.

Mr Kaufman would be Chief of PWD Leaflet Section responsible to Mr Crossman.

All arrangements with USA Air Forces and those under the command of SHAEF would be made by PWB. Distribution of leaflets by the RAF would continue to be handled by PWE.

Brigadier General McClure accepted the alterations.[4]

The first meeting was proposed for 18.4.44 with [an] agenda which included the subject of radio co-operation. The deadlock had been solved though with little time to spare. Though originally constituted as a 'Leaflet Co-ordinating Committee', this Committee rapidly became the deciding authority on all Political Warfare questions during the SHAEF period and was always afterwards referred to as the PWE, OWI, PWD–SHAEF Tripartite Committee.

---

1. Proposals for Leaflet Co-ordination between PWB, SHAEF, PWE and OWI. From Brig. Gen. McClure to Sir Robert Bruce Lockhart [and] Mr Hamblet, 27.3.44.
2. Draft Agreement between PWE, OWI and PWB (G6) for the Co-ordination of Leaflets so far as the area of SHAEF is concerned, 3.4.44.
3. Sir Robert Bruce Lockhart to Brig. Gen. McClure, 3.4.44.
4. Brigadier General McClure to Sir Robert Bruce Lockhart, 14.4.44.

Tripartite Committee

The Tripartite committee, a perfect example of Anglo-American integration, thus became the real policy-making authority for the last weeks before D-Day and during the earlier part of SHAEF period of liberation.

The first task of the Committee was to consider and ratify the proposals for leaflet disseminations up till D-Day. The second task was the approval of a paper on Directive Procedure during Operations. This memorandum provided for the setting up of a Tripartite Duty Room with all the intelligence resources of PWE, OWI, OSS which should be available twenty-four hours a day to PWD. It also provided for PWD to issue daily and weekly directives forward to PWD men in the field. For the preparation of these directives daily and weekly meetings of PWD–SHAEF/PWE and OWI representatives in order to ensure that they confirmed to the PWE, OWI overall weekly directive. The daily meetings should be held at 9.30 and 4 p.m. so as to be ready for the BBC daily directives prepared at 11 a.m. and 5 p.m. The PWD/SHAEF representative at these meetings was one of the civilian Deputies, usually either Mr Jackson or Mr Crossman. Their responsibility would be to represent the Psychological Warfare requirements of the Supreme Commander. PWD requirements in personnel were frequently raised. PWE not only met General McClure's requests for seconding[1] personnel, but also continued to carry such personnel on its establishment until PWD was able to obtain the War Establishment necessary.

Responsibilities of PWE in Regard to D-Day

A summary of the D-Day responsibilities of PWE for Overlord gives a general view of much of the work undertaken. The immense development of Political Warfare activities since Torch is shown less by a comparison of PWE responsibilities for each of these operations than by a comparison of PWD–SHAEF largely staffed by PWE and OWI experts, with the almost non-existent organisation at the time of the North African landings.

Leaflets

PWE Regions had been allowed to draft leaflets for normal requirements before D-Day, in the interests of security so as to excite no suspicion among staff who were not ticketed. Unknown to the Regions these draft leaflets were not printed. Nine special leaflets, amounting to forty million all told, were prepared in their place. PWE arrangements with regard to drafting and printing of leaflets were submitted beforehand to the Inter Services Security Board which approved of them. The position with regard to leaflets on 30.5.44 was as follows:

1. Meeting of Tripartite Committee, 2.5.44.

German Leaflets

1. A leaflet (Code No. ZG1) with German on one side and Polish on the other, 3,200,000 copies packed in forty bombs for dropping by USA aircraft only.
2. A leaflet in German (Code No. ZG2), 2,400,000 copies packed in thirty bombs to be dropped by USA 8th Air Force during their second sortie on German troops outside the assault area but in areas to be bombed on D-Day.

French Leaflets

1. A leaflet (Code no. ZF1), Eisenhower statement on one side and De Gaulle statement on reverse, 320,000 copies in eight bombs, to be dropped late in the afternoon of D-Day on places in France being bombed by Allied Air Forces.
2. A leaflet (Code No. SF2), a message to French transport workers 1,200,000 copies, thirty bombs, to be dropped during D-Day on communication centres in France.

In addition to the above distributed by 8th and 9th USAAF Bomber forces on D-Day itself the following were to be distributed on D-Day night and D + 1 morning.

1. Special edition of Nachrichten für die Truppe with special map. 1,000,000 copies, forty bombs to be dropped on German troops in and behind the assault area by 422nd Bomber Squadron.
2. 2,680,000 copies, 335 packages of French leaflet ZF1 to be dropped, 135 packages by 2nd Tactical Air Force on places in France outside the bombing areas.

Belgian Leaflets

1. A leaflet in French and Flemish (Code No. ZB1) with Eisenhower's statement on obverse and M. Pierlot's statement on reverse, 100,000 copies (twenty-five bombs) to be dropped on principal cities and transports of Belgium by 422nd USA Bomb Squadron.
2. A leaflet (Code No. ZB2) message to Belgian Transport Workers, 600,000 copies (fifteen bombs) to be dropped on transport centres by 422nd Squadron.

Dutch Leaflets

A leaflet (Code No. ZH1), Eisenhower's statement on obverse, Queen Wilhelmina or Gerbrandy's statement on reverse, 800,000 copies (twenty bombs) to be dropped on the principal cities of Holland by 422nd Squadron.

Very similar plans had been worked out in detail for dissemination for D + 1, D + 1 night and D + 2 morning (leaflets included Norwegian leaflets), D + 2 night and D + 3 morning. The leaflets in this period included a Danish leaflet.

Broadcasts

On D-Day the BBC broadcast two special programmes, announcing the beginning of the operations and containing a proclamation by General Eisenhower. The first programme was destined for Europe, the second for the Home Services and relaying to the Empire and America. The first programme would be relayed by US foreign-language transmissions and United Nations radio stations in the Mediterranean. Special messages would be broadcast to Norway by King Haakon, to Holland by Mr Gerbrandy, and to Belgium by M. Pierlot.

By arrangement with SHAEF the BBC European Service would provide a medium-wave transmission for an Anglo-American entertainment for the troops, a six-hour service for airborne troops and special arrangements had been made for SOE and SIS needs so as not to conflict with propaganda programmes.

Grey Broadcasts

The main themes of Soldatensender Calais and Kurzwellensender Atlantik for D-Day were that:

1. The OKW plan for the defence of the West involved the deliberate sacrifice of the Coastal Divisions.
2. There could be no relief for the West owing to the engagement of all Divisions on other fronts and guarding the Atlantic wall.
3. The defensive task allocated to the German Navy was suicidal.
4. The menace of airborne troops and secret armies in the rear.
5. The unreliability of foreign elements in the German Army.
6. The glaring inferiority of the Luftwaffe.
7. While the troops fight in the West the situation on other fronts and in Germany grows worse.

Full military intelligence had been arranged with SHAEF to be used in a policy worked out day by day with Operations.

Pocket Guides

Pocket Guides for France, Belgium, Holland, Denmark and Norway with vocabularies had been prepared by PWE Regions for issue to the troops. 300,000 pocket guides for France had been printed with a special edition for Canadian troops.

Basic and Zone Handbooks

Handbooks of all Western seaboard countries containing political, administrative and economic organisations and detailed supplements with maps for special areas had been prepared by PWE and were supplied to the Armies.

Production

The whole of the printing requirements for Overlord, which included leaflets, handbooks for troops, handbooks for countries, publications and posters for liberated areas, were carried out by PWE.

Duty Room News

PWE was providing SHAEF with a twenty-four hour service of monitored news, together with a daily appreciation of the value of that news.

Directives

PWE would issue jointly with OWI and PWD SHAEF

1. A special directive for Europe for D-Day.
2. A special directive for the Forces for D-Day.
3. Directives twice daily from D-Day onwards, as long as required.

Deception

PWE output for several weeks had conformed to the deception and cover plans for Overlord, including such naval plans as Fabius and Neptune which were represented as naval exercises.

Bombing of Railway Targets

PWE issued a daily summary of reactions to this bombing of enemy propaganda and of the populations concerned.

Lack of Machinery to Counter Enemy Rumours

Amid these multifarious activities certain elementary precautions for countering enemy Political Warfare were totally neglected. Thus in the weeks following the landing in Normandy the British and American newspapers were filled with stories of French women snipers. Whatever the origin of these stories, it is clear that they were likely to undo the work of the PWE booklet on France, given to each of the troops before the landing.

There was a complete failure to censor the dispatches of war correspondents in the interest of Political Warfare, nor were correspondents set on their guard against spreading enemy rumours. Almost equally damaging to British and American relations with France were the true reports of the abundant food supplies found in Normandy. Neither the British or

American public could realise that dairy farming is the chief industry in Normandy and that owing to the dislocation of French transport it was bound to be full of milk, butter, eggs and cheese. Powers for Censorship in the interests of Political Warfare and Political Warfare guidance for correspondents should have been provided as a routine measure, and a warning against enemy sibs with illustrations of the forms they can take should have been included in booklets for troops.

The D-Day Directive

The Special Directive on Operations against Western Europe issued by PWE and OWI was written by the PWE Director of Plans and was prefaced by an admirable exhortation to those who were to carry it out.

> The issue of this solemn hour is the liberation of Europe and the freedom of mankind . . . meaning is given to the waiting years. . . . The Supreme Allied Commander calls upon Political Warfare, the Fourth Arm in this combined operation, to reduce not only for our fighting men, but for the peoples of Europe the cost of ultimate victory. Though the peoples may not shrink from sacrifice, we shall neither wantonly nor unwittingly make vain that sacrifice.

The Directive itself emphasised that the 6th of June was not the D-Day for popular uprisings, but stated that a special directive was being issued for transport workers to encourage sabotage of transport between Antwerp and Nantes. General resistance could help to immobilise enemy communications by undetectable methods.

Propaganda to foreign workers in Germany should be given a sharper edge and should convince the Germans that there were armies fighting against them behind their lines and in their midst.

No greater justification for the policy of giving instructions to the populations of Europe over the BBC could be found than this wholly admirable directive.

Part VI
The Chief PWE Activities from the Landing in Normandy till the German Surrender

Reorganisation in PWE

The Director General returned from sick leave on 23rd February, 1944, and soon realised the need for strengthening the department, and for delegating much of his own work. He therefore asked the Governors of the BBC to release Mr Kirkpatrick as a Deputy Director General PWE and appoint Mr J. B. Clark Controller of the BBC European Services in his stead. The Governors agreed[1] and the Director General divided the work of the department under two deputies, Major General Brooks remaining responsible for the Country Establishment, Training, Security, Overseas Directorate, relations with SHAEF and service matters and Mr Kirkpatrick becoming responsible for Directorates of Plans, Political Warfare Intelligence, Production, Editorial Unit, Regions, and relations with the BBC.[2]

Mr Kirkpatrick, however, was not able to remain long as DDG as he returned to the Foreign Office, preparatory to taking up the position as head of the Control Commission.

The Director General thereupon appointed Sir Percy Loraine as responsible for the work of the Production Directorate and Editorial Unit and Mr J. W. Wheeler-Bennett responsible for the Directorates of Plans, Political Warfare Intelligence, and Regions.[3]

Mr Kirkpatrick did not accept the position of British representative on the Control Commission in Germany and became head of FORD.

---

1. Mr Haley to Sir Robert Bruce Lockhart, 31.3.44.
2. PWD/AN/164, 11.5.44.
3. PID/AN/209, 31.8.44.

Mr. Wheeler-Bennett was sent on three months' special duty to the United States at the end of 1944 and Mr Walter Adams, who had returned from the USA, was appointed to act as ADG with the same duties.

Leaflet Dissemination and the Paper Shortage

By July 1944, the paper shortage no longer permitted the holding of sufficiently large stocks of leaflets necessary to ensure that suitable leaflets would be available for RAF bombers for whatever operational mission was decided. The system, wasteful and inefficient at its best, was breaking down as paper supplies could not keep pace with the increased airlift available.

The need to bring RAF methods of dissemination up to the level of those which had been achieved by OWI and the USAAF in a period of six months or so, was expressed in a paper[1] put forward by the PWE Leaflet Committee to Major General Brooks. It reflected the views which had long been held, and frequently put forward, by Major Ryder, and Squadron Leader Taylor, but which had received no serious consideration either in PWE Military Wing, or at the Air Ministry, since Major General Brooks was anxious not to disturb arrangements with the Air Ministry.

The paper asked for regular dissemination to reduce the time-lag between production and distribution; means of ensuring that a certain type of leaflet reached an appropriate target area in the right quantity and at the right time; restriction of supplies of German leaflets to a small number of stations from which one or two aircraft with a primary leaflet load would operate with the main bombing forces on the latter's missions thus ensuring distribution anywhere required between base and bombing target; further consideration of the desirability of leaflet disseminations by leaflet bombs.

Mr Duncan Wilson stated 'there seemed to be some objections to the leaflet bomb on a high level within PWE'.[2] And Squadron Leader Hodgkin pointed out that until unanimity existed within PWE on the necessity of representing its requirements no progress could be hoped for.

Such was the background for a request which seems farcical considering the date when it was put forward. For over three months, PWE had relied entirely on the Munroe bomb for the dissemination of *Nachrichten für die Truppe*[3] which was dispatched ready packed into the Munroe Bomb to the 422nd Squadron. Sixteen million copies had been successfully disseminated and it is less surprising that Major General Brooks should have acquired 'a perfectly open mind on its merit'[4] than that Air Commodore Groves remained unconvinced that the Munroe Bomb was more useful than package dropping.

1. Minute to Major General Brooks from PWE Leaflet Committee, 16.7.44.
2. 22nd (and last) meeting of the Leaflet Committee, 27.7.44.
3. Minute to Director General from Harold Keeble, 6.4.44.
4. Minute of meeting with Group Captain Rose, 10.7.44.

Discussion at a meeting between Major General Brooks, Air Commodore Groves and Sir Percy Loraine for PWE and Group Captain Rose and Squadron Leader Horner for the Air Ministry was inconclusive, but it was agreed that a technical report on the possibility of the RAF using the leaflet bomb should be furnished. This was a great advance. A proposed meeting between the Director General and the Deputy Supreme Commander, Air Chief Marshal Sir Arthur Tedder,* was replaced by an exchange of letters, which revealed that Sir Robert Bruce Lockhart was well aware of the need for a change of methods:[1]

> The present policy for leaflet dropping by Bomber Command is that except in special cases, it is incidental to bombing operations, consequently our leaflets can only be disseminated when and where operational missions happen to have been planned which are by no means necessarily when and where they are likely to be most effective . . . this policy does not meet the propaganda needs for which I am responsible and the loss of effectiveness is frankly causing me some embarrassment because the American methods are by contrast much more suited to my needs.

Air Chief Marshal Tedder replied[2] that the calls on Bomber Command, owing to the opening of the Invasion and the emergence of Crossbow, made it inopportune to press for a revision of Air Ministry policy with regard to a special squadron being allocated for leaflet dropping. In a P.S. he added that 'when special emergencies (such as the present) arise, I have found C. in C. Bomber Command most ready to be helpful'.

The 'special emergencies' in question were the attempt upon Hitler's life on 20.7.44 and PWE's difficulties were enlarged upon in a further letter[3] from Sir Robert Bruce Lockhart to the Deputy Supreme Commander. In this he pointed out that the leaflets specially prepared for dissemination over the Ruhr on the night of 22/23 July in connection with the attempt on Hitler were not disseminated as arranged but were dropped on the following night, 23/24 July, on Kiel, a target which had already been well saturated with the same leaflet by the Americans the previous day.

The Director General proposed that although routine disseminations by

---

1. Sir Robert Bruce Lockhart to Air Chief Marshal Sir Arthur Tedder, Deputy Supreme Commander, 19.7.44.
2. Air Chief Marshal Tedder to Sir Robert Bruce Lockhart, 25.7.44.
3. Sir Robert Bruce Lockhart to Air Chief Marshal Tedder, 28.7.44.

* [Marshal of the RAF Sir Arthur William Tedder (1890–1967) joined the Colonial Service 1914; commissioned in RFC 1916; commanded No. 70 Fighter Squadron 1917; squadron leader 1919; group captain in command Air Armament School 1931–3; air officer commanding, Far East 1936–8; Director General, research and development Air Ministry, 1938; Deputy Commander, Middle East, 1940; Commander-in-Chief 1941; Air Chief Marshal 1942; Commander-in-Chief, Mediterranean Air Command, 1943; Deputy Supreme Commander, Allied Air Forces in Europe, 1943–5; Chief of Air Staff 1946–9.]

the RAF should be unaffected, PWE should be able to apply to Air Chief Marshal Tedder through General McClure for a special leaflet operation by Bomber Command.

The Deputy Supreme Commander agreed[1] to this course giving the assurance that he would do all he could to help in the event of an emergency.

In spite, however, of Air Chief Marshal Tedder's warning, the Director General of PWE decided to take the matter to the Chiefs of Staff Committee and submitted a memorandum on the methods of dissemination of the leaflet bomb for Air Chief Marshal Portal's consideration.

The memorandum, forwarded with a letter to the Chief of Air Staff,[2] capitulated American methods and existing British methods of dissemination and stated the disadvantages of existing British methods.

The paper then recommended that failing the provision of a special leafleting squadron, a specified number of operational aircraft at a limited number of Bomber Command stations be set aside exclusively for leafleting and that these aircraft should operate wholly or partially with the leaflet bomb similar to that used by the USAAF.

Adequate and more accurate disseminations could thus be provided not only over all bombing targets but also over all propaganda targets en route. There would still be little or no coverage over enemy-occupied countries and areas of enemy territory which were not being subjected to bombing attacks. But the advantage over the existing methods of covering German industrial towns would be considerable.

No reply was received to this communication for six weeks, when a letter was received from Air Marshal Sir Norman Bottomley[3] but the time of waiting had not been wasted. For the first time the Air Ministry admitted the merits of the Munroe bomb and the defects of the existing system.

> It is generally agreed that we should make every effort to avoid scattering leaflets over areas where they will be of little or no value. The Munroe bomb . . . is certainly one of the best instruments to avoid wasteful distribution and a trial installation has now been carried out in our heavy bombers. From this it is clear that we shall shortly be able to stow as many of these in our aircraft as can be stowed by the American Fortresses. We are now arranging for a supply of these bombs from America.[4]

In addition, the Air Ministry agreed that the system whereby leaflets were distributed to all Bomber Command stations for ultimate dropping was wasteful both in paper and administrative services. The Chief of

1. Air Chief Marshal Tedder to Sir Robert Bruce Lockhart, 31.7.44.
2. Sir Robert Bruce Lockhart to Air Chief Marshal Sir Charles Portal, 14.8.44.
3. Air Marshal Sir Norman Bottomley to Major General Brooks, 28.9.44.
4. It will be remembered that 'Nickel' was the RAF code name for leaflet.

Bomber Command had therefore agreed that one base commander in each operational group should be responsible for leaflet droppings.

There were serious operational objections to specialising squadrons or even operational aircraft to be used exclusively for leaflet dropping. It would, however, be possible to arm operational aircraft either wholly or in part with leaflet-dropping bombs which could be dropped either on the industrial areas being attacked or industrial areas en route. Instructions were being issued to Bomber Command.

The promise of the last paragraph to attack industrial targets en route to the target was, however, withdrawn in a letter from Air Marshal Peck.

PWE decided not to fight this issue.[1] Air Marshal Peck had notified PWE at the same time that Bomber Command was prepared to drop 400 bombs per month. To obtain the same average dissemination as before Bomber Command should have dropped 520 bombs per month and a request for the larger number was raised by Air Marshal Peck himself. This, it must be pointed out, was a quite unjustifiable demand since the coverage of the leaflet bomb was so much better that Political Warfare would gain greatly by dissemination of the smaller number. The request indicated that Air Marshal Peck, like Major General Brooks and Air Commodore Groves, had formed the habit of thinking of leaflet disseminations in terms of statistics. But the statistics bore little relation to what really mattered which was the numbers picked up and read. Leaflets dropped by bomb were far more likely to be picked up.

PWD Leaflets for Germany

After the liberation of Paris, proposals were put forward by PWD for writing the leaflets themselves instead of receiving leaflets written by the civilian agencies; the reason being that PWD would shortly move its headquarters to Paris from Inveresk House which was within a stone's throw of PWE in Bush House.

After consideration, Sir Robert Bruce Lockhart sent General McClure[2] a joint OWI/PWE memorandum agreeing to the proposal. In a covering letter, the Director General informed General McClure that he had agreed to the proposal without reference to the Ministers who would have objected to one or two passages in the PWD paper.

The OWI/PWE Memorandum[3] agreed without prejudice to give a trial to the proposed arrangement whereby the writing of leaflets to German troops and civilians would, in general, be undertaken in Paris on the undertaking that such leaflets would be written within the framework of policy laid down in OWI/PWE directives.

1. Air Marshal Peck to Major General Brooks, 3.11.44.
2. Sir Robert Bruce Lockhart to Brig. General McClure, 15.9.44.
3. Of 15th September, 1944.

The production of Nachrichten für die Truppe would, however, continue to be written and printed in Britain as a PWE responsibility. In any case, PWD–SHAEF had neither the personnel, skill, or equipment to produce it.

The agreement did not debar OWI and PWE from writing and printing leaflets for Germany at short notice, if they were required. PWE agreed to consult the Air Ministry on the question of Bomber Command dropping Nachrichten. The Air Ministry would also be asked to accept SHAEF censorship of leaflets initiated by PWD.

OWI and PWE agreed that co-ordination of print orders should be established through Mr Keeble and the staff officers responsible for arranging airlift with the Air Forces concerned.

Brigadier General McClure intimated that these proposals were acceptable to him. The results of this new arrangement were not long regarded as satisfactory by PWE. The German Regional Director informed the Director General[1] that one of three PWD leaflets attached was highly unsatisfactory, written in bad German and that it was hard to believe Mr Crossman or Mr Anderson had passed it.

Moreover, the RAF stock of leaflets was down to about 1,000 packages and when they started dissemination by bomb the new arrangements of production and liaison would not meet their requirements.

The matter was raised inconclusively at the Tripartite Committee[2] and it was merely decided that PWD representatives should visit London more frequently. The logic of events, however, was to compel PWE to write leaflets, for as Major General Brooks pointed out as soon as the RAF started using the Munroe bomb they would be able to distribute eighty million leaflets a month.

The request that in future Bomber Command should accept responsibility for the distribution of Nachrichten für die Truppe was acceded to by the Air Ministry.

The leaflet bomb[3] had come into general use by aircraft of Bomber Command during December, and had been employed by aircraft of Nos 1, 3 and 5 Group to drop Nachrichten für die Truppe.

Policy Difference with OWI

The difficulties subsisting between PWE and OWI even after the high level of integration secured became apparent in the arrangements made for publication of a joint weekly newspaper, *Tous les Fronts*, for France by which PWE and OWI were responsible for alternate issues. General McClure complained[4] that the differences between the British and American Governments in regard to the French National Committee were thereby

1. Mr Duncan Wilson to Sir Robert Bruce Lockhart, 10.10.44.
2. Meeting of the Tripartite Committee, 18.10.44.
3. Leaflet operations for the month of December, '44, Air Ministry DDCP, 5.1.45.
4. Meeting of Tripartite Committee, 27.6.44.

underlined and asked that the newspaper be transferred to PWD–SHAEF. This request was refused but a Canadian PWE/OWI editor, Mr Placide Lebel,[1] was appointed to quell the storm that had arisen.

Weekly Newspapers Out-dated by Events

The value of airborne weekly newspapers as a propaganda and news medium was questioned owing to their becoming out of date owing to the rapid march of events,[2] and a proposal was made to replace them by undated leaflets concerned with news.

The PWE and OWI newspaper leaflets to France, *Courier de l'Air* and *L'Amérique en Guerre*, became unnecessary after the rapid liberation of France and ceased publication at the end of August.[3] *Luftpost* and *Sternenbanner* were, however, continued for another fortnight.

The Use of German Ps/W for Overlord

Mr Walmsley and Mr Duncan Wilson put up papers on this subject on 27.11.43 and 13.12.43 in which broadcasts by German Ps/W and leaflets were stated to be the principal propaganda media to make German troops surrender to the British and American Armies.[4]

The paper proposed that we should broadcast as many messages by Ps/W, recorded as soon as possible after capture, talks by recently converted anti-Nazis, technical talks on the military situation and descriptions of life in base camps particularly in Canada.

The plans were developed and led to the formation of a camp at Ascot for Ps/W likely to be useful for Political Warfare and to the Ascot–Brondesbury Scheme.

The Ascot–Brondesbury Scheme for Use of Ps/W for Political Warfare

The Ascot–Brondesbury Scheme was the result of an agreement reached between PWE and MI19 with DPW WO for a camp at Ascot to be shared between MI19 and PWE.

The procedure arranged was for the stream of Ps/W arriving at Kempton Park to be roughly classified for further interrogation or as not required and for those suitable for PWE to be sent to Lingfield Camp. At Lingfield a CSDIC staff officer working for PWE made a further selection who were sent on to Ascot Camp.

---

1. Minutes of Tripartite Committee, 18.7.44.
2. OWI/PWE Leaflet Plan to German Civilians, 26.7.44.
3. Meeting of Tripartite Committee, 31.8.44.
4. Overlord: The Use of Ps/W in Propaganda to the Enemy. Mr Duncan Wilson to Major General Brooks.

At Ascot parties of not more than eight prisoners willing to carry out propaganda were formed by a PWE officer and sent up to the PWE working centre at Brondesbury.

An Ascot–Brondesbury 'desk' was created in the German Region of PWE at Bush House to co-ordinate the needs of PWE, BBC, OWI, SOE and OSS and to make all arrangements for access to the prisoners and with MI19 and DPW.

The scheme was Anglo-American and the authorities concerned were PWE, OWI, OSS and SOE. PWE work was represented by both the German Region and the BBC and by Mr Delmer who selected those useful for MB purposes.

Ps/W groups from Brondesbury visited Bush House to record in the BBC studios.

Mr Marius Goring, BBC representative for prisoner arrangements, stated that the PWE organisation combined supplying a steady flow of new prisoners with making it possible to upset the agreed plan in times of emergency and he could not think of any improvement. Mr H. C. Hatfield of ABSIE stated that prisoner material was one of their most valuable resources and that it was fed to OWI for re-broadcast from New York as well as in the ABSIE programmes.

There is little doubt that the talks and songs of German Ps/W in the BBC German programme was the only material which could hope to rival the popularity of the Soldaten-sender West programmes at that time.

The contribution of German Ps/W to the BBC German Service increased steadily and continued not only until the surrender of Germany but until the autumn of 1946, by which time the Ps/W division of PID had been transferred to the Control Commission.

The latest report stated that the Brondesbury Hostel contained eighty-nine Ps/W, thirty of whom were periodically charged for work in the BBC Ps/W programmes.

Seven Ps/W were working on 'Visual re-education', i.e. producing pictorial propaganda.

The Ascot–Brondesbury Scheme and the Brondesbury Hostel were throughout a great success and were the means for making friendly German Ps/W contribute first to the defeat and then to the spread of democratic ideas in Germany and among Ps/W.

Bivouac

In the months before D-Day, Major Gwynne, who had joined PWE after having carried out SOE work with Royalist guerillas in Greece, put forward a plan for the infiltration of Political Warfare officers behind the enemy lines in France and Belgium in order to organise and control the civilian population during the period of invasion.

The plan stated that it would be necessary to provide leadership and ensure that the written instructions reach key places. It was therefore proposed to drop three American and three British officers at places selected by PWD/SHAEF. They were to wear uniform. The instructions for the Allied Liaison Officers concerned who were to be under SFHQ and attached to any SAS unit, if thought fit, contained the warning that 'having regard to the present delicate and explosive state of French politics, the utmost care must be taken not to allow the French to think that the Allied Liaison Officers are attempting to usurp the leadership of FCNL or to act as spies on behalf of the British Army'.

[10.4.44] The draft plan was sent to Brigadier Mockler-Ferryman of SOE asking if he had any objection to the plan being passed to SHAEF.

[4.5.44] Brigadier Mockler-Ferryman made criticisms but agreed to the plan going forward to General McClure. The plan was approved by PWE/SOE/PWD.

Major Gwynne, the author of the plan, had been actively recruiting suitably qualified officers and their training had already begun. The training was divided into four periods.

Group A	Toughening, field craft, weapon training.
STS 51	Parachute jumping.
Group B	Security, intelligence, propaganda communication.
Brondesbury	Political Warfare in the field.

The group originally consisted of Major Gwynne, Captain Ayer (SOE), Captain Gosling (PWE), Captain Fleetwood-Hesketh (PWE), 2nd Lt Merson (PWE).

Bivouac was the result of the fanaticism, physical courage and instinct for practical Political Warfare of Major Gwynne.

The unfortunate tendency to work in parallel water-tight boxes was particularly apparent in proposals for dropping officers, the use of agents, etc. Thus a PWD/SHAEF plan for the proposed use of agents for PW activities behind the enemy lines prepared by Major John Hackett (SFHQ), Major Gwynne (PWE), and Mr Rae Smith (OSS) was issued [29.5.44] by PWD without Major Gwynne having consulted Mr Dadson, or being 'in the picture' of what already existed in an advanced form in Belgium. The results of PWE experience were therefore not incorporated in the plan.

Plan Bivouac had been prepared at a time when no consultations on any subject concerning Overlord were allowed with the French.

The need for such a plan would indeed have been far greater if we did not take the French into our confidence than if we did. Although General Koenig had been appointed to a French Military Mission with SHAEF in April, full discussions were resisted on the grounds both of security and of the under-estimate of the military value of French civilian resistance.[1]

1. Brig. R. W. McLeod to Brig. General Brooks, 30.7.44.

Soon after D-Day, however, the picture changed owing to the importance of the French resistance becoming known. The enemy communications were being cut in hundreds of thousands of spots as forecast in the PWE/SOE plan for Overlord, and large parts of France were passing into French control.

As a result, General Koenig was appointed as SHAEF liaison with the FFI and entrusted with the co-ordination of all resistance movements in France, including SOEF and RF section and PWE.

The appointment was followed by what can only be described as considerable confusion. Bivouac could not be carried out as originally planned. Nevertheless it was decided that three of the officers should go and Captain Gosling, Captain Fleetwood-Hesketh and Lt Merson were applied for by Brigadier R. W. McLeod for attachment to SAS in order to assist SAS senior officers in contact with the Maquis. Lt Merson did not go.

Captain Gosling

[14.8.44] Captain Gosling was dropped in the forêt d'Yvoy, 45 kms north of Bourges and broke his arm and shoulder in mid-air. The SAS troops under Major Lepine, to which he was attached, were the first to be seen in the Cher.

There were at first only two Americans in the department and the British were by far the more popular.

Captain Gosling's chief problems were to restrain the FFI from shooting German prisoners as they were being shot or clubbed to death themselves if captured. He produced a number of photographs taken by members of the Gestapo of tortured Frenchmen and women. The Americans behaved with great tactlessness, arranging for 18,000 Germans who wished to surrender to march through the district with their arms and much stolen loot in order to surrender to an American general, and providing comforts for Germans only. Captain Gosling's chief effort at Political Warfare was not successful as he was unable to get a message through to the BBC. He did provide an opportunity for outbursts of enthusiasm for Britain, and lists of members of the resistance who had hidden British pilots and helped them to escape.

He provided evidence that as a result of our policy of refraining from attacking Pétain, the Marshal was surprisingly popular.

Captain Gosling and Captain Fleetwood-Hesketh returned to Britain in October and [on 5.10.44] Brigadier McLeod wrote to Major General Brooks to thank him 'for allowing them to come and them for the good job they did'.

The Landings in the South of France, Anvil and Dragoon

The success of Overlord was assisted by Anvil, the objects of which were to secure a major port in the South of France, to contain and destroy forces which might oppose Overlord, by advancing to the north to threaten the south flank and rear communications of the force opposing Overlord, and to develop lines of communication for the forces which would be introduced through the port in the South of France. These objects were to secure the port of Marseilles and to advance up the Rhone valley to Lyons.

Whereas command, administration and civil affairs remained in the initial stages with AFHQ, SHAEF was responsible for servicing the FFI.

> Para. 7. Control of resistance[1] in the agreed area of South of France will pass to SACMED at time suitable to you. SHAEF will retain responsibility for general co-ordination of resistance policy in France. SHAEF intends to furnish all practicable supplies to develop resistance in Southern France. As the bulk of the resources for supplies are located in the United Kingdom, SHAEF will act as your agent in making the necessary supply arrangements. . . .
>
> Para. 8. PWE policy of publicity and psychological warfare in the Anvil area should be co-ordinated by SHAEF promulgation.

General Maitland Wilson[2] telegraphed agreement but pointed out that he would be dependent on Overlord for Civil Affairs' personnel and civil supplies. SHAEF was, as Major General Brooks pointed out, the dominant partner.

PWE Mediterranean informed[3] Brigadier General McClure that

> French propaganda activities will be fully co-ordinated with our own. Security has prevented our discussing any propaganda plans with the French. Tyler will call personally on Henri Bonnet a short time before the announcement of the landings and will hand him the directive making it clear that it must be strictly followed by Radio France and the press. The application of the directive locally by the PWB combat teams will be carried out with the co-operation of 17 members of the French Service Metropolitan d'Information who have been fused into the PWB team. The rest of the SMI is going in separately and later than PWB.

The telegram added that a speech by De Gaulle would be discouraged if proposed.

PWB AFHQ forwarded[4] the text of General Maitland Wilson's proclamation which was to be released with the first communiqué. The most important passages were:

---

1. S 55130 General Eisenhower to AFHQ, 6.7.44.
2. General Maitland Wilson to General Eisenhower, FX 69883, 8.7.44.
3. F 77678 INC to McClure, 1.8.44.
4. McChrystal for McClure, F 80512, 8.8.44.

> The Army of France is in being again, fighting on its own soil, for the liberation of its country with all its traditions of victory behind it. All Frenchmen, civilians as well as military, have their part to play in the campaign in the South. Your duty will be made clear to you. Listen to the Allied Radio, read notices and leaflets, pass on all instructions from one man and woman to another.

Brigadier General McClure communicated his views[1] and PWE issued a special directive[2] underlining many points which Brigadier General McClure had not emphasised. The most important of these were:

> All prominence warranted by the news should be given to the FFI and to the French people.
>
> Emphasise the need for restraint and discipline and that all action must be co-ordinated through the FFI and comply with official instructions and repeat on lines used for Normandy instructions and advice as to how they can best help Allied military operations and minimise the risk of casualties to themselves, and explanations of the necessity for Allied bombing and the part it plays in speeding liberation.

By the time the landings took place the FFI was in control of very large parts of Southern France. British SAS officers who had been in the neighbourhood of Dijon since D-Day[3] found it possible to drive in their jeeps for 100 miles without likelihood of meeting Germans so long as they kept to second- and third-class roads. The SAS camp was even on the telephone, and the engineers at the power station supplying the area cut off electricity on orders from the FFI while parachute droppings were in progress so that there should be no danger from high tension overhead cables. These SAS officers were indeed withdrawn before the arrival of the Anvil forces, as the whole territory was then in the hands of the FFI.

Thanks to the far-sighted policy adopted by that date, one of the chief underlying Political Warfare objectives in regard to France had been achieved – the restoration of the self-respect of the French people by a sense of active contribution towards the defeat of the enemy. To this PWE's treatment of the news had powerfully contributed.

Military Results of PWE/SOE Activity in Belgium

The records of secret army and civilian group activity in Belgium are incomplete. But they include the cutting of upwards of 1,000 main railway

---

1. Guidance for propaganda concerning Operation Dragoon. From SHAEF to Director General, PID.
2. PWE/AH/44/2/47.
3. Information from Captain Trower, one of the SAS party and formerly and subsequently a member of PWE.

lines and an enormous amount of sabotage of the enemy's transport and communications. Moreover, the secret army acting under the orders of De Liederkerke[1] was largely responsible for saving the port installations at Antwerp, for which General Erskine tendered official thanks from SHAEF and the dock and transport workers, acting under instructions were available to man it. On 3.9.44 when Brussels was liberated General Horrocks* stated that Belgian resistance had been invaluable and that the rapid advance of the British Army would have been impossible without its help.

The Othello organisation set up by the PWE agent Othello was responsible, after liberation, for taking possession of and handing over the Ministry of Food and Agriculture in working order. (See p. 223.)

It is clear, even from SOE records alone, that a great deal of the credit for extending, supporting and directing resistance in Belgium must be given to PWE and in particular to the successive Low Countries Regional Heads, Mr Harman and Mr De Sausmarez.

Linnett. The Arnhem Operation

[7.9.44] A special directive in connection with the airborne operation at Arnhem was issued to PWE and OWI in the hope of focussing attention on General Patton's forces rather than on the Arnhem operations and in order to prevent speculations about the threat to Germany.

The operations were postponed and a second directive[2] issued in which the operations were to be treated as designed to liberate Holland and to trap German forces in Holland and Belgium.

A 'Voice of SHAEF' broadcast giving instructions to Dutch Resistance groups and the Dutch people accompanied the directive. The instructions to the Resistance groups were to avoid action against superior forces, to protect factories, mines and industrial installations, and to obey the orders of their local commander under Prince Bernhard. The population were asked to shelter fugitive members of the Resistance and to avoid road and railway junctions but otherwise to stay in their homes.

The failure of the operations showed that the special caution that Dutch Resistance groups outside the area of operations should stay underground was well-founded.

---

1. See p. 219 (Regional Aims and Media Agents).
2. Brig. General McClure and Sir Robert Bruce Lockhart, 16.9.44.

* [Lieutenant-General Sir Brian Gwynne Horrocks (1895–1985) was commissioned into the Middlesex Regiment 1914; prisoner of war 1914–18; MC 1919; captured by Soviets 1919–20; Olympic pentathlon competitor 1924; Staff College 1933; commanded 2nd battalion Middlesex Regiment 1939; brigadier during Dunkirk evacuation 1940; commanded XIII, then IX, then X Corps in Western Desert 1942; seriously wounded 1943; commanded XXX Corps in Normandy 1944; GOC Western Command 1946; Black Rod 1949–63; TV personality and board game promoter.]

Radio Luxembourg

In the D-Day plans, provision had been made for the use of Radio Luxembourg as a PWD–SHAEF station and this proposal was agreed by the Luxembourg Government in exile on 24.5.44.[1]

Radio Luxembourg was captured intact [on 11] September, 1944, Mr Pierce of PWD persuading the 5th Army Division to send a special force for the capture of the transmitter. On 22.11.44 the station began putting out a twelve-hour schedule including four 12th Army Group tactical programmes. The staff at that date consisted of William Hale with four PWD people and about fifty 'local people'. It was soon afterwards decided to use Radio Luxembourg as a key station from which stations which might be captured in Germany should relay the major part of their programmes. Time was divided between PWD for foreign broadcasts and G1 for the entertainment of the US Army. 3¼ hours going to PWD and the balance to entertainment. All time after 11 p.m. was available for PWD. The foreign broadcasts were in German (seven fifteen minute periods) and news in French, Dutch, Flemish, Polish, Czech and Italian.

On 20.10.44 four BBC men arrived headed by Patrick Gordon Walker. On 10.11.44 the schedule was increased to eighteen hours a day, with a corresponding increase in the number of language and PWD periods which included Luxembourgeois and English.

Four programmes a day were carried for 12th Army Group. Arrangements were made to give the station tactical intelligence from 21 Army Group and 6th Army Group. Mr Paley reported progress to the Tripartite Committee and it was agreed[2] that directive meetings in London should take place earlier so that cipher instructions in the form of a daily summary could be dispatched daily at 4.30 p.m. to Luxembourg.

Mr Newsome, who had been appointed assistant to the Chief of the Radio Section SHAEF, was appointed Chief of Broadcasts Radio Luxembourg in April 1945.

Although repeated assurances had been given by OSS and PWD–SHAEF that Black and Grey broadcasts should be carried out only from MB, OSS set up Black stations of their own, which were in some cases so bad that they endangered secret broadcasting altogether. The motives for these breaches of their agreement with PWE is believed to have been due to political considerations connected with Colonel Donovan's status with President Roosevelt, rather than to a genuine belief that they could either improve the Atlantik and Soldatensender West programmes or usefully supplement them.

After the capture of Radio Luxembourg, OSS started the Black transmission which was called 'Annie' on reduced power and with a different frequency, at times when Radio Luxembourg was not transmitting a 'White' programme.

---

1. Progress Report on Radio Luxembourg, 20.11.44, Tripartite Committee papers.
2. Meeting of Tripartite Committee, 20.11.44.

'Annie' was of limited range and covered the Ruhr and Rhineland. Lt Commander McLachlan, though nominally working under the deputy for Black, Mr Oechsner of OSS, was in fact largely independent and believed he could work most usefully as the PWD–SHAEF outpost for Mr Delmer and MB. For about a month after the establishment of 'Annie', Lt Commander McLachlan made use of its transmissions in a somewhat disingenuous manner.[1] He discovered that 'Annie' could be monitored at MB and therefore used the service to give Mr Delmer news from General Bradley's 12th Army Group which was otherwise not available for the Atlantik and Soldatensender West transmissions as the 12th Army Group PWD men, who were all American, wished to reserve it for use on their own Black output. This was not discovered until after the German Ardennes breakthrough when Lt Commander McLachlan returned to SHAEF HQ in Paris. Considerable annoyance was felt by OSS personnel at having been outwitted in this way. The character of the 'Annie' transmissions caused many complaints which led to its subsequently being closed down.

Braddock II

The original Braddock plan was largely a matter for SOE and consisted in the dropping of large quantities of very small delayed-action incendiaries, with instructions for use in seven languages, over the Reich in the hope that they would fall into the hands of foreign workers and persons hostile to the regime who would use them to commit arson; in any case a large proportion of them would fall into the hands of the German police and would force them to take extra precautions in guarding buildings, factories, etc. Such droppings were made sporadically. In the original plan 3½ million were to be dropped in one or two nights.

The subject was considered by the JIC[2] which decided that the Braddock plan should be launched when we had reason to believe that the desperation of the German people was such that Braddocks might be used by them. Five months later, the JIC recommended[3] that it should be launched when the Overlord landings had stimulated resistance among the foreign workers in Germany. But when the landings had been carried out, General Bedell Smith, C. of S. To General Eisenhower,[4] believed it would be better to postpone the use of Braddock 'until Germany began to disintegrate'.

By August, SHAEF thought the time had arrived[5] but pointed out 'the success of the operation would be enhanced if launched in conjunction with Black propaganda' and suggested that Aspidistra should be used to

1. Information from Lt Commander McLachlan.
2. JIC(43)439(0), 9.11.43.
3. JIC(44)188(0), 3.5.44.
4. SHAEF/17240/20/Ops/A, 29.5.44.
5. C. of S. to SHAEF to COS, COS(44)730(0), 16.8.44.

intrude on a German wavelength closed down by an RAF bomber raid, and to issue scare instructions as from the local police, asking the public in specified districts to turn out at night in their thousands to collect Braddocks. The Chiefs of Staff pointed out the authority to use Aspidistra was required from the Foreign Secretary *and the Prime Minister*. A letter from General Eisenhower with a letter supporting the proposal to use Aspidistra, subject to the approval of the Foreign Secretary, was considered by the Chiefs of Staff and a minute was sent to the Deputy Prime Minister by the Chiefs of Staff Committee (owing to the Prime Minister's absence from the country). Four days later the Chiefs of Staff considered a note[1] from the Foreign Secretary agreeing to the use of Aspidistra for Braddock II. In the middle of the meeting, however, General Ismay* was called to the telephone to speak to the Minister of Information who told him that he, Mr Bracken, was the sole arbiter as far as Aspidistra was concerned and that he had no intention of using it in conjunction with Braddock II. The Minister appears to have repeated these statements in a letter and to have added that Sir Robert Bruce Lockhart had never been consulted with regard to the Braddock plan. He also reflected on the procedure of the Chiefs of Staff Committee itself and referred to 'High Military Officers seeking to use Aspidistra for small operations'. This intervention by the Minister appeared to Sir Robert Bruce Lockhart likely to prejudice PWE's position with the Chiefs of Staff Committee. After consulting the Foreign Secretary, he addressed the following frank expostulation to Mr Bracken:

> There are two misstatements of fact in the first two paragraphs of your letter. I was consulted from the beginning. The PWE Ministers were referred to as soon as a question affecting PWE arose. . . . Indeed, the procedure of the British Chiefs of Staff who had nothing to do with planning the operation has been impeccable.
>
> I think it is a pity, from the point of view of PWE that you stated to General Ismay that you were 'the sole arbiter of the uses for which Aspidistra was to be employed'. This statement has caused some comment. Apart from other considerations affecting the past history of Aspidistra, it is surely imperative that the Foreign Secretary must be consulted about the political and moral consequences of the use of Aspidistra for an intruder operation in a foreign country. The whole structure of PWE's work in this way has been built on a close and, in

---

1. War Cabinet Office Summary, 23.8.44.

* [General Hastings Lionel 'Pug' Ismay, Baron Ismay (1887–1965), entered Indian Army 1905; seconded to King's African Rifles 1914; served in Somaliland with Camel Corps 1919–20; assistant secretary, Committee of Imperial Defence, 1925–30; military secretary to Viceroy (Lord Willingdon) 1931–3; War Office 1933–6; secretary, Committee of Imperial Defence, 1938–46; full general 1944; Baron 1947; chief of Lord Mountbatten's staff at transfer of power in India; first Secretary-General of NATO 1951–7. The oil in the machinery connecting Churchill and the Chiefs of Staff during the Second World War.]

> my opinion, successful co-operation with the Foreign Office and the Chiefs of Staff.
>
> Because they lack a similar co-operation with the American State Department and the American Chiefs of Staff and because they are also concerned with *publicity* matters, OWI are given no secret information in advance, are brought into operations only at the very last moment, and are therefore quite ineffective as an instrument of political warfare. If a similar situation were to be created here by the elimination of the Foreign Office the consequences to PWE's work would, in my opinion, be disastrous. . . .
>
> Control by two Ministers may not be a good system. It was never to my liking, but it has worked reasonably well and at this stage of the war it hardly seems practical to try and alter it.

During the successive absences of the Director General on sick leave, the Minister of Information had played a more important part in the affairs of PWE than at any period in its history. This was because Major General Brooks, Deputy Director General, had always been the Minister of Information's representative, and accustomed to referring problems to the Minister, often verbally. Mr Scarlett had not the same direct access to the Foreign Secretary.

The Minister of Information had thus decided many policy questions during the Director General's absence without reference to the Foreign Secretary. The most outstanding of his decisions, as we have seen, had been his veto on closer collaboration with OWI at a time when a policy of integration would have given PWE a far stronger position with regard to PWD.

There can be little doubt that the Director General's frank letter on the Minister's claim to be the sole arbiter of the use of Aspidistra did much to redress the balance and show from what quarter PWE derived its ultimate authority.

The Director General, however, realised that in view of the Minister of Information's long-standing dislike of the use of Aspidistra for counterfeiting enemy broadcasts, he might raise further difficulties to the execution of SHAEF plans. He therefore sought to obtain in advance an overall approval from the two Ministers for the use of Aspidistra in connection with future military operations.

Brigadier General McClure in a letter supporting such a proposal[1] suggested that 'when the Ministers had agreed in principle, Commander McLachlan and Mr Crossman should work out with G3 the precise application of Aspidistra in any particular operation; plans would then be submitted to the Director General PWE and Mr Delmer should be instructed to make the necessary arrangements'.

Such procedure was in fact the best way of carrying out Mr Delmer's

---

1. Brigadier General McClure to Sir Robert Bruce Lockhart, 12.9.44.

plans, which were usually arrived at in conjunction with Commander McLachlan and always discussed most fully with him. Sir Robert Bruce Lockhart, after obtaining the Foreign Secretary's approval, informed the Minister of Information that 'I have received an application from Brigadier General McClure for an over-all Ministerial approval for the use of Aspidistra in connection with future Military operations'[1] and strongly recommended that approval should be given. The Minister of Information signified his agreement.

In the meantime, however, General Eisenhower directed that Braddock II be launched by the US Strategic Air Force,[2] 200,000 Braddocks to be dropped. The following Political Warfare preparatory measures were taken in conjunction with the droppings.

The 'Voice of SHAEF' broadcasts were given on 5, 6 and 7 September on BBC and ABSIE in French, Polish, Dutch, Czech and Italian. In these there was no reference to Braddocks as they were a first 'Alerting'. Between 8 and 22 September, leaflets to foreign workers were scattered over twenty-four industrial districts. One the night of 25.9.44 200,000 Braddocks were dropped with leaflets, and after the return of the aircraft, 'Voice of SHAEF' broadcasts were addressed to foreign workers over the BBC and ABSIE making in all forty-six repetitions. Although no Aspidistra intrusion was used in conjunction with Braddock II, Calais-sender regularly reported the finding and use of Braddocks. Calais-sender included alarmist items on the Call to Arms of Foreign Workers in the Reich, and Brigadier General McClure was able to report that 'enemy reactions show that Braddock II has hit a sore spot'.[3]

The use of Braddocks was not, however, followed up, in spite of pressure from the Minister of Economic Warfare[4] and, later, from the Prime Minister himself.[5] Some droppings took place, but an order that the use of Braddocks be discontinued was issued by SHAEF at the end of April, 1945.[6] As a result, an enormous number of unused Braddocks had to be destroyed after the war. An official instruction of the State Criminal Police dated Berlin 3.11.44 was issued on the dropping of Braddocks, and the appeals to foreigners and traitorous elements to carry out sabotage.

Further Changes in PWE

Major General Brooks left PWE at the end of 1944, on taking up the position of Inspector-General, the Royal Marines. Pending the appointment of Major General Brooks's successor, Colonel P. R. Chambers was appointed

1. Director General to Minister of Information, 14.9.44.
2. SHAEF, 17240/20/Ops/C, 2.9.44.
3. Brigadier General McClure to Assistant COS G3.
4. Lord Selborne to Prime Minister, 28.11.44.
5. Minute No. M189/5, 3.3.45.
6. Brigadier General McClure to Major General Bishop, 26.4.45.

Assistant Director General (acting), responsible for Service matters and the work of the country establishment.

Under the new arrangement, Air Commodore Groves, the ADDG, head of the Directorate of Ps/W became responsible only to the Director General who was in fact absent, seriously ill.

Major General W. H. A. Bishop[1] was appointed[2] Deputy Director General of PWE as from 1.3.45 and took over his duties in the absence of the Director General and without having met his predecessor.

Mr Wheeler-Bennett returned from his Mission to the USA in April and resumed his position as Assistant General (Political). Mr Walter Adams continued, as Assistant Director General (Civil), to be responsible for the work of the Directorate of Intelligence and the Regions.[3]

Major General Bishop remained with the department for five months, leaving after the surrender of the German Armies to take up the position of Director of Information and Publicity Control Commission for Germany. He was succeeded as Deputy Director by Major General K. W. D. Strong.[4]

PWE Becomes PID Responsible to Foreign Secretary

With the defeat of Germany, the Director General submitted recommendations to the Ministers that PWE should come under the sole control of the Foreign Office and that the title Political Intelligence Department should replace that of PWE.[5] The changes were accepted by both Ministers and the new arrangement was initialled by the Prime Minister on 29.6.45.

The remaining commitments of PID at this date were Political Warfare against Japan, servicing of information to SHAEF and re-education of Ps/W.

The first and second of these commitments lie outside the terms of reference to this history, but the third, which was begun early in the history of the department, is dealt with up to November, 1946.

Mr Wheeler-Bennett relinquished his appointment as ADG at the end of July, 1945, and was succeeded by Mr Leonard Ingrams who was appointed ADG (Political).[6]

Six weeks after the appointment of Major General Strong as DDG, Sir Robert Bruce Lockhart resigned the post of Director General. He was succeeded by Major General Strong.[7]

As from 1.9.45 Air Commodore Groves had experienced great difficulties in carrying out the work of re-education of German Ps/W owing to

1. Military Sec SO to QMG, WO.
2. PID/AN/259, 28.2.45.
3. PID/AN/297, 25.4.45.
4. PID/AN/308, 19.7.45.
5. Director General to Foreign Secretary, 17.5.45.
6. PID/AN/315.
7. PID/AN/321, 21.8.45.

strained relations with DPW War Office. He was profoundly convinced that the work was essential if German militarism and National Socialism was not after a few years underground, to seize power and plunge Europe in a third world war. He had come to think that the importance of the work was not recognised either by the old or the new Director General, and that the only hope of its being carried out efficiently was if he were made the head of a separate department with direct access to the Minister of State, Mr Noel Baker.*

There was a measure of justification for his point of view. Sir Robert Bruce Lockhart had wished, in vain, to avoid assuming the responsibility for the re-education of Ps/W. Major General Strong, coming fresh to the department, was anxious to wind up its activities and naturally did not welcome proposals for increased expenditure and expansion.

Air commodore Groves was unable to secure the position which he wished and resigned on the same day as Sir Robert Bruce Lockhart left the department. As will be seen elsewhere, his departure, which coincided with that of Major General Gepp from the position of DPW resulted in a *détente* between the Division of Ps/W PID and DPW and the policy of re-education, for which Air Commodore Groves had fought consistently, was carried out with far better co-operation from the military authorities.

On the resignation of Air Commodore Groves, Wing Commander Hitch was appointed head of the Ps/W Division with the title of Controller.

Periwig

Plan Periwig[1] was largely SOE in conception and execution but required considerable PWE assistance and might well have had important political repercussions. It is an excellent example of the need for integration of Political Warfare and subversive action. It is arguable that as Periwig dealt with an imaginary rather than a real situation, it was really more a matter for PWE than SOE.

The plan was to behave as though we knew of the existence of a German resistance movement inside Germany which was willing to co-operate with us. The plan was therefore to dispatch stores and agents, to send code messages and to make open appeals to its members. It was obvious that the

1. The facts which follow have been taken from SOE History of the German Directorate, Part II, Section 1 (g).

* [Philip John Noel-Baker, Baron Noel-Baker (1889–1982), was educated at Quaker School in Bootham, York, and in Pennsylvania and King's College, Cambridge; served with Friends' Ambulance Unit 1914–18, decorated for valour; secretariat of the League of Nations; professor of international relations, London University, 1924–9; Labour MP, Coventry, 1929–31; published *The Private Manufacture of Armaments* (1936); Labour MP, Derby, 1936–70; Joint Parliamentary Secretary to the Ministry of War Transport 1942; Minister of State, FO, 1945–6; Chairman of the Labour Party 1946–7; Minister for Fuel and Power 1950–1; published *The Arms Race, a Programme for World Disarmament* (1958); awarded Nobel Peace Price 1959; peerage 1977.]

Gestapo would monitor the messages and a proportion of the stores and agents would fall into its hands and that it therefore might be convinced of the existence of a widespread resistance movement, and make wholesale arrests and take other measures which would help to break the German Will to Resist. The main object was to divert the energy of the police system into wasteful activity. But once a belief in a resistance movement became widespread in Germany it might soon become a reality. The experience of PWE with regard to the creation of such a myth as *Les Chevaliers du Coup de Balai* was encouraging in this respect.

Periwig was planned between 12.11.44 and 12.1.45. We were straining every nerve to break German morale by means of Political Warfare and Subversion. It was a moment when it appeared that the German Armies might continue to defend Germany ditch by ditch. The plan was considered by the German Will to Resist Committee, under the Chairmanship of Sir Robert Bruce Lockhart on 27.11.44 and on 12.1.45. The plan operated for about one month but was interrupted by SHAEF ban on air supply operations to Germany on 13.3.45.

Volunteers were asked for among anti-Nazi prisoners of war, but very few came forward. Those who did were given four weeks' instruction by instructors who were themselves deluded into the belief that the German Resistance movement existed.

The right Political Warfare background was effectively produced by BBC messages, by a W/T 'umbrella' that is to say a dummy W/T outgoing traffic to Germany was initiated by SOE signals to cover a real traffic which might come into existence after agents had been dropped. Morse code messages were also superimposed on the Soldatensender musical programme. Rumours and stories in newspapers in neutral countries contributed to the atmosphere. Owing to the overloading of PWE printing facilities, and flying-bomb damage, there was great delay in printing leaflets and Black propaganda material for Periwig. After 1.3.45 an effort was made to increase the Political Warfare character of the plan and a joint PWE/SOE operation was planned. But SOE's contribution was severely limited first by SIS and then by SHAEF and also by the fact that Periwig was the lowest priority in regard to PWE Black printing.

After the SHAEF ban on dropping supplies a few agents were dispatched but it was no longer possible to provide serious evidence and all that could be hoped was to cause a nuisance.

From 19.4.45 to 8.5.45 the chaos inside Germany had reached such a point that any contribution to it by Periwig was ineffective and unnecessary.

Materials dropped consisted of W/T equipment, propaganda, sabotage and incendiary materials, carrier pigeons.

On 31.3.45 the first two agents Bienecke and Kick were ready and were dropped near Wildeshausen in the Bremen area. On 18.3.45 Otto Heinrich and Franz Langmeh were dropped west of Chiem See with a parachute package and instructions to contact an anti-Nazi resistance movement in the Bavarian mountain redoubt.

A large number of carrier pigeons were dropped in order to deceive the Germans into the belief that we were using pigeons to obtain information from the German 'resistance'. Both genuine carriers and 'duds', that is to say stale birds, were dropped, the 'dud' birds carrying forged messages provided by PWE. Of 330 genuine birds dropped in April, nine homed to the UK and two were picked up in France. Five of these birds brought back genuine messages written by their German finders. Pigeons continued to be dropped until 27.5.45 owing to Mr Delmer's enthusiasm for the project.

Among other objects dropped was a German briefcase with incriminating documents indicating a clandestine organisation in a big industrial concern. This was dropped during a low-level Mosquito bombing attack on a German railway station.

SOE missions in neutral countries supplemented Periwig operations, e.g. a document was planted on a German traveller, in the hope that it would either be found in the German customs or given up to the police. All the four agents dispatched survived. Bienecke was recovered from the Russian Zone in August 1945. Kick shot a Gestapo man who was doubtful of his papers. He then remained in hiding until the arrival of the British forces, and gave himself up and returned to England on 30.3.45. The second pair gave themselves up to the American Army in May, 1945, and stated that they had succeeded in contacting [a] subversive group, as instructed. This is an excellent example of how the imaginary can crystallise into the real. In this respect, Periwig resembles the subject of many plays by Pirandello.

Plans which were not carried out included the smuggling of letters and propaganda pamphlets indicating the existence of German railway workers' cells and the dispatch of an agent personally acquainted with General der Flieger Kolle in order to incriminate him. The agent concerned, a P/W named Mattes, believed in the existence of the Resistance movement and that General Kolle was implicated in it, but refused to go after we had virtually won the war.

Opposition to Periwig on the part of SIS was due to the fear that the whole plan, which was to increase Gestapo measures and to bring about wholesale arrests, might endanger their agents. SIS in particular objected to any plans which would lead to closer guarding of German frontiers.

SHAEF objections were to droppings in the neighbourhood of camps containing Allied prisoners of war. There was at that time very great apprehension of a general massacre of Allied prisoners in Germany and any indication that we were arming or supplying Allied prisoners was vetoed. The Germans were moving Allied prisoners about Germany and it was impossible to be sure no such movement was taking place in a Periwig area.

There was opposition to any Periwig evidence of Roman Catholic resistance, owing to a belief that such resistance existed. Only rumours were therefore put out.

One objection to Periwig which does not seem to have been stated was that the extremely cynical exploitation of genuine German anti-Nazis would have caused a wave of indignation, in Britain and America and in Germany itself, if the facts ever came out. SOE German Section felt strongly that Periwig should have been an integral part of SHAEF operations.

The reason why it was not, was due to the fact that PWD–SHAEF was only able to operate through the civilian agencies, PWE OWI which jealously guarded their independence. None of the 'Black' work ever really passed into the hands of SHAEF. The chain of command was in practice at the low level of McLachlan (as head of the Special Operations Section of PWD) and Delmer. PWE never thought highly of Periwig – and rightly!

Plan Periwig, like many other plans was carried out too late in the day and on too inconsiderable a scale to have any real effect. It is, however, a plan of abiding interest since it is an example of Political Warfare carried to its furthest possible point.

Casement

General Templer of SOE, criticising Sir Robert Bruce Lockhart's report on methods of breaking the German Will to Resist, put forward a plan which involved the deception of friend and foe, and neutrals alike by revealing to the German Army that their leaders had made complete preparations for taking refuge in Eire on a given date, some by submarine and some by aircraft.

The plan involved an invitation by HMG to the Government of Eire to deny that it had any knowledge of the impending arrival of Nazi leaders couched in terms which were bound to result in the Government of Eire refusing to make such a denial or to give any undertaking. Further colour should be given to the story by patrolling the coast of Eire.

The Director General decided that owing to political reactions, it was unsuitable to make Eire the country chosen, and it was agreed that the Argentine was the next best country for the purpose.[1] It was proposed that PWE should produce a plan for providing 'hard evidence' which would force the Germans to give publicity to the story.

A German in Lisbon might be framed so that when arrested by the International Police, he should be found carrying documents proving the Nazi leaders had made preparations to reach the Argentine through Spain. Meanwhile questions relating to Eire had been asked in Parliament by Professor Savory[2] and General Templer accordingly asked that the FO objections to Eire should be waived and that Eire should be chosen. The proposal was not accepted[3] and it was decided to continue to carry out the plan with regard to the Argentine. The SOE experts reported that it was not possible to produce a convincing incident in Spain or Portugal.[4]

1. Minutes of meeting held 11.1.45. Colonel Chambers in the chair.
2. P. 116 *Hansard*, 16.1.45.
3. Minutes of meeting, 25.1.45.
4. General Templer to Sir Robert Bruce Lockhart.

The Director General informed General Templer that PWE was doing its best to carry out the plan without reference to Eire and without the hard evidence which had been asked for.

It may be justifiable to point out that though a considerable volume of such rumours on the subject of preparations for flight by Hitler, Himmler, etc., were disseminated and appeared in the Allied and neutral press, they contradicted a major theme of our Political Warfare to Germany – that Hitler was involving Germany in ruin by his decision to continue fighting after defeat was certain. The latter theme had the advantage of being true, and was supported by Hitler's declaration that he would fight until 'five minutes past twelve'.

Huguenot[1]

The object was to undermine the morale of the German Air Force by suggesting to the GAF authorities that German airmen were deserting in their machines, taking advantage of an Allied reception scheme, getting them to take action against German flying personnel which would undermine their morale and to encourage German pilots to desert in their machines.

The plan was yet another example of treating an imaginary situation as real and thus bringing it about.

Methods Proposed

By official radio channels and leaflets

1. dropped in leaflet bombs over German airfields would be stated that many German pilots had wished to desert in their machines but had been prevented by Allied AA defences; that pilots were therefore advised to desert singly and give the following signal: Lower undercarriage and jettison equipment; at night fire emergency signals, show navigation lights and lower undercarriage. The fact of a pilot deserting would be kept secret by the Allies unless he wished it made public.
2. Covert channels to be used to convey to the GAF authorities that pilots they thought dead had deserted and were in Allied hands and that the Allies were reporting deserters as prisoners.

   Radio telephone dramas of German deserters calling Allied stations and Allied voices replying with directions were planned.
3. Covert radio and rumours to suggest that deserting German pilots would find employment on Allied civilian air lines, and would be given administrative jobs in Germany after her surrender.

The Allied authorities were unwilling to give instructions to their anti-

1. Plan Huguenot, 18.1.45.

aircraft defences to cease fire. This, however, was not a serious objection to the plan as the object of the plan was not to capture live German airmen.

The plan was communicated to Brigadier General McClure, who asked that PWE should go ahead with the Black part of the operation[1] but pointed out that proposals for White might infringe the Geneva Convention by issuing false instructions on how to surrender. Mr Delmer accordingly went ahead with the Black side of the operation. Instances of GAF pilots following the instructions and safely landing on Allied aerodromes followed.

Capricorn

OSS proposed a Black radio programme[2] after Mr Delmer's agreement had previously been obtained. The plan was considered at a meeting held 15.2.45 by the PWE–OSS 'Black' Committee, and OSS was instructed to clear the plan with SHAEF.

The plan was submitted to Brigadier General McClure,[3] who was advised by Lt Commander McLachlan[4] that it would deceive nobody and could do no harm and that when the writer had got experience it might be good. McLachlan, however, advised that the supporting operations asked for in respect of White leaflets and references to the programme in Frontpost and in Nachrichten für die Truppe should be refused and also added a warning as to security.

Brigadier General McClure's consent having been given, the Capricorn programme was started on 26th February. Ten repeats of thirteen minutes each were transmitted daily six days a week from the PWE 7½ k.w. short-wave transmitter 'Pansy'.

On 27th March, the consent of the Wireless Telegraphy Board having been obtained, the programme was transmitted on a frequency of 9765 kc/s from the PWE 100 k.w. short-wave transmitter Aspidistra III.

Nature of Capricorn Programme

The programme consisted of a series of talks, given by a speaker who adopted a military tone and purported to be the mouthpiece of an underground movement within Germany. The talks were supported by inside and up-to-date information and advocated the overthrow of Hitlerism and unconditional surrender as the only way of avoiding annihilation, and the reconstruction of Germany under Allied control. Specimen scripts which have been preserved strike the present writer as tedious and lacking in a tone of authority.

1. Brigadier General McClure to Sir Robert Bruce Lockhart, 12.2.45.
2. Mr Howard Baldwin to Sir Robert Bruce Lockhart enclosing plan Capricorn, 14.2.45.
3. Chief MO Branch OSS to Brig. Gen. McClure, 16.2.45.
4. McLachlan to McClure, 18.2.45.

The OSS team of two were housed by PWE and recorded daily at Simpson's, and the records were then played by landline to the transmitter.

Matchbox

The first fruits of Ministerial agreement to use Aspidistra in connection with military operations were alternative plans prepared in PWD with Mr Delmer in the creative role [14.9.44] and approved by G3 SHAEF which were submitted to the Chiefs of Staff Committee for consideration on 19.12.44.[1]

The features of the plan were that Aspidistra should be used only at night, on enemy wavelength channels which had closed down owing to RAF activity. Incidentally, it may be remarked that the Air Ministry could find no explanation of why the Germans shut down certain transmissions during our raids as we did not use the beams in any way for navigational purposes.

The suggested uses were to give direct support to land operations causing confusion and uncontrolled movements of civilians in areas adjacent to the battlefield. Alarmist orders were to be issued purporting to come from official German sources.

At the time this alternative was put forward, it commanded no support in SHAEF as it was believed that it would have negligible military results. We shall see later that this assessment was completely wrong. The second possible method suggested was spreading a false story such as that Himmler had taken over command of all military forces and that Marshal Von Rundstedt had been arrested. This would have been directed at the German forces in the field. The third suggestion, made by G3 SHAEF, was that Aspidistra should broadcast news of Hitler's capitulation in the form of an official communiqué or a fake broadcast by Hitler himself. The latter proposal need not detain us as it was declared by Mr Delmer to be totally impossible of execution. Rundstedt was to be incriminated in two stages:

1. By linking his name with a new Black station which Himmler would believe was operated from England by Rundstedt's envoys.
2. When an Allied breakthrough occurred east of the Rhine Aspidistra should put out a counterfeit statement that OB West had sent emissaries to SHAEF. Soldiers would be ordered to continue fighting and reports of a cease fire would be denied. Four minutes later, the statement was to be withdrawn, but without an actual denial. This was intended to take the sting out of the German denial which would follow. It was hoped that the statement would be regarded by Himmler as a final proof of Rundstedt's treachery, for although he would know it originated in Britain, he would believe it was a prearranged signal.

---

1. COS(44)1039(O), 19.12.44.

The special Committee for breaking German Will to Resist considered the plan and reported favourably[1] although giving full weight to the dangerous results of failure and the post-war effect of providing Germans with the excuse that they had been defeated by a propaganda trick.

Before the British Chiefs of Staff Committee had made any decision, General Eisenhower[2] informed the Combined Chiefs of Staff Washington of the proposal and sought their approval and stated:

> Chief of Staff SHAEF is satisfied that dangers of ill effects on Allied troop morale in this theatre can be dealt with here. The whole problem because of its possible far-reaching effects is forwarded to the Combined Chiefs of Staff . . . so far as our own operations are concerned it appears to be promising and if other considerations do not outweigh this fact its approval is recommended.

Matchbox came up before the British Chiefs of Staff Committee three days later and the Committee decided to forward the proposal to the American Chiefs of Staff Committee giving their views in a confidential annex. In a covering letter to the Secretary of the Joint Staff Mission Washington, Major General Hollis* wrote: 'The Chiefs of Staff . . . are not attracted by it, since they feel that its usefulness is only likely to arise at a stage when military operations will already be about to cause the overthrow of the enemy . . . they are in no way committed to the proposal. If the United States Chiefs of Staff press for its adoption, it will have to be considered in this country at the Ministerial level since the political implications are serious.'

The United States Chiefs of Staff did not make a decision or reply for nearly two months and then reported that they thought it unacceptable and unwise, but that 'the Supreme Commander should consider submitting a specific plan based on Aspidistra technique when he could foresee that a collapse in Germany was imminent'.

The Minister of Information was informed by General Bishop[3] then Deputy Director General and Mr Bracken recorded his gratification in a marginal note in his own hand: 'I am glad that this silly plan has been scrapped. B.B.'

The attempt on Hitler's life four months later showed, however, that Mr Delmer's plan was not so silly after all.

---

1. GEN 52/2, 1.1.45. War Cabinet. Use of Aspidistra in final phase of military operations.
2. SCAF 166. S73848, 5.1.45.
3. General W. H. A. Bishop to Minister of Information, 22.3.45.

* [General Sir Leslie Chasemore Hollis (1897–1963), commissioned in the Light Marine Light Infantry 1915; at battle of Jutland 1916; attached to Plans Division, Admiralty, 1932–6; secretary, Joint Planning Sub-committee 1936–46; secretary, Chiefs of Staff committee, 1938; deputy secretary, Committee of Imperial Defence, 1940–6; deputy military secretary to the cabinet 1946–9; author *War at the Top* (1959).]

In the same paper, Mr Bracken was informed that Aspidistra would be used in an intruder role in order to help block the enemy communication east of the Rhine with civilian traffic. His consent was no longer necessary and he made no comment.

Aspidistra in Support of Varsity and Rhine Crossings

This use of Aspidistra which had been included in the original plan as an alternative to Matchbox had been revived by a SHAEF directive calling for efforts to effect the general evacuation by German civilians of the battle areas. The question was discussed at a meeting[1] with Major General Bishop in the chair and attended by Brigadier General McClure, Lt Commander McLachlan, Mr Crossman and Mr Delmer, etc.

The employment of Aspidistra in this way involved, however, priority for its use in the operation over the Air Ministry use of it for Dartboard. This was strongly resisted by both Chief of Bomber Command and the Chief of Air Staff, who stated that six or seven bombers a night would be lost if Aspidistra were not available for Dartboard.[2] The matter was considered before the Chiefs of Staff Committee,[3] and a telegram dispatched to General Eisenhower asking that the intruder use of Aspidistra should be restricted to two weeks from the commencement of Plunder and to a total of five intruder operations, each less than an hour in extent, the time to be selected by PWE, but that even so, the use of Aspidistra might lead to heavy losses in Bomber Command.

Mr Delmer, however, proposed to carry out intruder operations at a time which would lead to no infringement of Bomber Command's use of Aspidistra for Dartboard. Such use had already been authorised. The question was obviously one of timing. The first modified intruder operation accordingly was carried out on the night of 24.3.45. The plan was to broadcast short messages to the local German ARP authorities on ARP frequency of 599 k/cs stating that the German evacuation plans known as Aktion Siegfried, of which copies had been brought back by Lt Richard Wylly of the US Marine Corps who was attached to McLachlan for special duties by OSS, had had to be cancelled for the mass of the population owing to transport difficulties.

The two following programmes were carried out on the evening of 24.3.45.

I Operation ARP Channel. 20.19 hrs. Aspidistra went on the air on 599 k/cs with interval signal identical with that used by Germans to fill gaps in announcements about movements of Allied aircraft. Various

1. Minutes of meeting, 10 a.m. 15.3.45.
2. Major Gen. Bishop to Brig. Gen. McClure, 17.3.45.
3. COS(45)188(O), 20.3.45.

announcements of this type broadcast. 20.30. Special announcement read twice. This was followed by interval signal and various ARP messages. 20.52. Aspidistra off the air.

II Operation on Reichsender Cologne. 658 k/cs. Cologne closed down owing to the approach of Allied aircraft. The period during which it was off the air was used to relay the German programme, which Cologne should have broadcast on 658 k/cs, into which the announcement was inserted.

21.40. Cologne closed down and Aspidistra went on the air with Cologne programme.
21.44. Special announcement.
21.55. Special announcement repeated.
21.59. Aspidistra went off the air.
22.00. Cologne resumed transmission of German Home Service.

The ARP announcement was as follows:

> Here is an announcement from the Reich Defence Commissioner of Gau Dusseldorf for all Command posts of R. Aktion Siegfried in Gau Dusseldorf.
>
> Zone wise evacuation of Zones 4 and 5 on the established lines starts immediately. However unless I give express instructions to the contrary only folk comrades liable for military service and of the age groups 29 to 31 are permitted to take part in the evacuation. All necessary measures to counteract panic among the remaining population are to be taken immediately. Individual evacuation independent of the march columns should be suppressed as far as possible.
>
> All bridges and ferry crossings over the Lippe between Dorsten and Lünen are unusable for Aktion Siegfried. New approach roads and crossing points only after agreement with the senior P1 Leader of the Army Group.

Having in this ARP instruction limited evacuation to a minute fraction of the population, Delmer framed a special announcement calculated to produce the highest degree of panic. After stating that the British had crossed the river and that an immense battle was to be expected, an appeal for the utmost discipline was put out, ostensibly from the Gauleiters and Reich Defence Commissioners of Essen, Dusseldorf, Westphalia North and Westphalia South, in these terms:

> Folk Comrades. The enemy has reached the gates of our Gau. His intention to destroy the Reich and exterminate the German people will meet with fanatical resistance. . . . On account of the enemy penetration in the eastern side of the Rhine, our population is open to all the effects of modern weapons and threatened with complete destruction. The utmost discipline must therefore be maintained in this hour. Since the

> evacuation measures originally planned have become impossible . . . only those compatriots who are suited to carry on the decisive struggle . . . will be evacuated. The evacuation of a great number of our compatriots will, for the time being, be impossible. Their duty, therefore, is to stick it out and, if need be, to face death bravely.

As Reichsender Frankfurt was off the air throughout the evening and night of 25/26 March 1945, the opportunity was seized without consultation of SHAEF though General McClure was kept daily informed. Between the hours of 20.43 (25th) and 00.12 (26th), Aspidistra relayed the German Home Service on the Frankfurt frequency, interrupting the relay with fifteen separate announcements, some giving positions of Allied tanks and armoured cars, and others addressed to Red Cross workers, butchers and doctors, etc.

There was no immediate enemy reaction.[1] The fifteen announcements taken together and reproduced by Reuter make natural part of Frankfurt's military story as told in morning newspapers. 'It should be possible to continue tonight far to the rear of Frankfurt.'

The whole of the Allied public was of course deceived, including the vast majority of military intelligence officers. Indeed Major General Bishop informed JIC on each occasion that deductions about the collapse of German morale could not be drawn from these broadcasts and asked that no reference to them should appear in JIC minutes.

On the night of 26.3.45 Aspidistra again commandeered the Frankfurt wavelength[2] to put out instructions and messages in which evacuation columns were diverted to avoid imaginary Allied thrusts, all motor vehicles with certain markings were commandeered and local party leaders were informed of the arrival of relief trains stopping at various stations.

On the night of 30.3.45 Aspidistra commandeered the Hamburg and Berlin wavelengths at 20.30 and 21.10 respectively to put out a warning that the advancing Allies were trying to cause confusion among the German population by sending false telephone messages forward from occupied to unoccupied towns.

> To counter these enemy machinations once and for all, no action must from now on be taken on orders, instructions or reports received by telephone before they have been confirmed by ringing back. This applies to all State and Party authorities and to each individual German.

There was no immediate enemy reaction. If this message had been universally acted on it would have doubled the work of the Reich telephone service and have brought it to a stand-still. But on [the] 28th the German

1. No. 572 Pilot XL. To Scarlett for Hodgkin from Delmer.
2. No. 601 Pilot XL. To Scarlett for Hodgkin from Delmer, 30.3.45.

Home Service warned its listeners that an enemy transmitter was broadcasting misleading news on the Frankfurt wavelength and told listeners to rely only on news from the OKW.

But Delmer pointed out[1]: 'Such statements can only add to confusion in enemy ranks and we assume they are welcome reactions.'

On 29.3.45 Mr Delmer was able to report to Major General Bishop that the Aspidistra operation had forced the Germans to confine instructions to the civilian population to Deutschlandsender long-wave transmissions on which Aspidistra could not intrude. Mr Delmer informed General Bishop of the exact location of the Deutschlandsender transmitter and asked him to put it up as an immediate bombing target.

The whole system of carefully prepared channels for ARP and civilian instructions had been disrupted in four nights and very great confusion had been induced behind the enemy lines.

So, when Aspidistra was at last used, it was controlled by two or three individuals using their judgement and a small amount of special information, without any red tape of military control.

The announcer used in these operations was a German prisoner of war who had been an announcer on one of the German services programmes. He had the perfect official technique.

The accounts of the Allied advances given during this period were widely reproduced in the world and British press, and were broadcast to Germany as genuine by the BBC.

This small series of operations during the crossing of the Rhine were a vindication of the plans for which many leading spirits in PWE had fought for many years. They were the last important Political Warfare operation before the German surrender, and they may well prove the point of departure for the planning of Political Warfare as a branch of Military Operations in a new war.

Political Warfare to Prisoners of War

As has been made clear in earlier chapters, PWE was concerned with enemy Ps/W in many ways.

It prepared much of the material in broadcasts and leaflets which helped to bring about surrender by enemy troops; it derived much of its intelligence from Ps/W to carry out further propaganda to the enemy; it carried out propaganda to Ps/W in order to secure their co-operation in winning the war and to spread the beliefs useful to Britain after the war.

Propaganda to enemy troops in order to induce surrender permeated PWE output. Propaganda about Ps/W in our hands was carried out partly to induce further surrenders by showing that they were well treated; partly as listener bait to increase our audience.

1. Pilot XL. To Scarlett for Hodgkin from Delmer, 28.3.45.

Propaganda by enemy Ps/W proved particularly effective if they were carried out in the form of programmes apparently organised by Ps/W themselves and on a sufficiently large scale to dispel the belief that they were only being given by one or two notorious traitors. (See Ascot–Brondesbury Scheme.)

An early attempt to use Ps/W due for repatriation as a Political Warfare medium is dealt with here although it did not materialise.

Political Warfare to Ps/W outside Britain was the function of separate missions to ME and India, and it was also the object of the liaison officers with Canada.

Political Warfare to Italian Ps/W. The Camp Newspaper

A proposal for a newspaper for Italian Ps/W was put forward in February 1942 by the Movimento Libera Italia. It was strongly supported by Mr Greenlees and Mr Martelli of PWE and in May 1942 it was approved, and an experimental issue of four numbers was decided on, each to consist of 2,000 copies of a four-page sheet the same size as *France*. Circulation was to be restricted to Italian Ps/W, and subject to security supervision. Messrs Greenlees and Magri were appointed editors, and the paper became one of the activities of the Italian Section of PID with the title of *Il Corriere del Prigioniero*. The first number appeared during the first week of June 1942.

The *Corriere* gave all official war bulletins, including the enemy's, without any political slant. It consisted of the important news items – a page of sports, crosswords and light relief – a very simple course of English – short stories, light educational articles of every kind, and photographs. The paper was an immediate success, in spite of much suspicion among the prisoners and of the rabid enmity and opposition of Fascist elements. However, the lack of any blatant propaganda and the factual presentation of news soon overcame suspicion. As a result, the demand for the paper increased quickly, and circulation grew accordingly. In due time, the prisoners began to collaborate, and the paper became popular, so that it had to be expanded to six pages, when it changed its name to *Il Corriere del Saboto*. In the autumn of 1942, Mr Greenlees left, and Mr Magri became sole editor, until he was transferred to the Publications Department in November, 1943. Mrs Waterfield and Mr Rosenbaum were for a time joint editors, later Mr Rosenbaum alone edited it. The paper was increased to eight pages, and remained that size until February 1946, when it reverted to four pages.

During 1944 and 1945, after Italy became a co-belligerent, the *Corriere* adopted an openly anti-Fascist policy and was supported by the great majority of its readers. They sent in large numbers of contributions, often of a high quality; the paper thus developed into a forum of opinion, aimed at the political re-education of the Ps/W. In March 1946, the paper became only a source of factual information for the few Ps/W remaining in Britain, and in August 1946, it ceased publication, on the departure of the last Ps/W.

Political Warfare to Italian Ps/W in Britain

Political Warfare to Italian Ps/W in India has been described under the PWE Mission to India (see p. 139). A plan for Political Warfare to Italians in this country was drafted,[1] the long-term object of which was that Ps/W should become our best propagandists in post-war Italy after their return home. The methods included segregation of Fascists, special camps for anti-Fascists, English lessons, camp newspapers, etc. The plan crystallised into a proposal for an anti-Fascist Labour Italian Corps which was considered by the Cabinet.[2]

The Minister of Agriculture opposed the suggestion on the grounds that Italian Ps/W were already doing work of national importance and that there was no advantage in segregating anti-Fascists. Indeed by introducing controversy, segregation might do harm.

The effect of this ruling was naturally to debar the War Office from giving PWE the kind of facilities and co-operation needed and to prevent PWE carrying out its work.[3]

PWE hopes to carry out further Political Warfare to Italian Ps/W in Britain were thrown into confusion by the surrender of Italy and Italian adherence to the Allied cause as co-belligerent.

Though the numbers of Italian Ps/W who were anxious to resume fighting at the first opportunity was not large, all were anxious to improve their status and the great majority would willingly have co-operated whole-heartedly in order to achieve this end, had such action received encouragement from the Badoglio Government.

PWE realised that the possibilities of raising a Free Italian Force from among Italian Ps/W were very great and General Mesge, a fervent supporter of Badoglio, was anxious to undertake this work. There were, however, many interests to be considered and conflicting views as to what the status of Italian Ps/W should be.

The need for labour for agriculture in Britain, combined with the shortage of shipping, made it uneconomic to transfer Italian Ps/W from this country and the Prime Minister's dictum that Italy 'would have to work her passage' was held to preclude the recognition of Italian Ps/W as Allied Forces. It was clear that an alteration in the status of Italian Ps/W would result in the abrogation of the Geneva Convention in order to enable them to be employed in any way.

But the Directorate of Ps/W at the War Office, under General Gepp, saw in the abrogation of the Geneva Convention an opportunity to effect economies, not only in guards, but in the amenities to which Italian Ps/W were entitled. It was immediately suggested that they should be given inferior notepaper and that the free issue of cigarettes should be stopped. The

---

1. Plan for Political Warfare in Italian P/W Camps, 10.12.42.
2. WP(43)73, 18.2.43.
3. Minute and letters from Sir Percy Loraine to Director General, 24.3.43, 2.4.43, 6.4.43.

proposals put forward by DPW were that when serving in Pioneer Corps or other military formations, Italians were to rank as co-belligerents but of inferior status. When not so employed, they were to revert to the status of Ps/W but without the protection of the Geneva Convention.

These proposals were regarded as serious political and psychological blunders by PWE. The department represented that they would result in a grievance among Italian Ps/W against the Italian Government if it agreed to them, resentment against the British Government and people among all classes of Italians, a reluctance in Italy to co-operate with our troops, a danger that similar measures might be employed against our prisoners in Italian Fascist and German hands and unfavourable reaction in other satellite countries.[1]

PWE pressed its opposition at several meetings with the War Office authorities and tried to enlist Foreign Office support for its point of view. The Foreign Office, however, was more concerned with possible resentment among our Allies if Italian prisoners were recognised as Allied Forces than with the bad results of the proposals on the Italian campaign and on our relations with the Italian people.

Meanwhile General Eisenhower had already put Italian Ps/W in North Africa into military units under Italian Command and with British liaison, the Ps/W being released on parole but retaining their status as Ps/W.

As a result, further protests from PWE against the proposals became impossible.

Major General Gepp visited Italy to secure the agreement of Marshal Badoglio to the proposals, but he failed to do so. The Italian Government indeed declared that they were unacceptable even as a basis of discussion.[2]

The proposals were nevertheless put into force which the PWE Director of Plans described as 'a hole in the corner attempt to trick Italian Ps/W and to sneak past the refusal of Badoglio to sign the agreement'.[3]

As the quotation shows, the conditions under which Italian Ps/W were made to choose between volunteering as co-operators and remaining non-co-operators generated considerable heat and the matter resulted in permanently strained relations between Air Commodore Groves and General Gepp as a result of which the work of the Ps/W directorate suffered until the departure of each of these officers from their respective positions. Some 60% of the Italian Ps/W in this country volunteered.

PWE believed that at least 80% would have volunteered had the terms been such as to secure the approval of the Italian Government and that the men would have worked better with better status. The results of the new conditions were much as PWE had foretold. Strikes broke out in some

---

1. PWE considerations in regard to the future status of Italian Ps/W, 11.10.43.
2. No. 212. From Resident Minister Algiers to FO, 5.2.44.
3. Mr Ritchie Calder to Director General, 11.4.44. The Director General marked the paper 'I agree'.

camps, a recurrence of Fascist propaganda was reported. Anti-British feeling was reported to be on the increase and there was a serious decline in morale at a time when the military developments were such as to produce higher morale.[1]

The psychological effect of the enforced retention of Ps/W status on public opinion in Italy was very bad.[2]

The Commandant and Deputy Commandant of Byfield Camp were both reported the following October as declaring that the co-operator scheme was wrong in principle and that only an appeal from the Italian Government and visits from Italian officers would produce a change of spirits.[3] Articles in the British press at this period did much to increase the anti-British attitude of Italian Ps/W.

The Italian Government was fully alive to the welfare of the prisoners and of the importance of preventing a revival of Fascism amongst them.

In August 1944, it forwarded proposals for Italian Government sponsored broadcasts to the camps.[4] An official of the Italian Embassy was appointed to look after their interests and in February, 1945, the Italian envoy Count Carandini was able to visit camps in company with General Gepp.

Nevertheless conditions remained bad, the reason being that DPW War Office continued to regard Italian co-operators as prisoners of an inferior status. The attitude is exemplified in answer to five specific complaints of the treatment of Italians sent to Brigadier Blomfield by Mr Oliver Harvey.[5]

[10.8.44] An application for the visit of Italian journalists to the camps was refused on the grounds that if it were allowed British journalists would have a legitimate grievance, an argument which it is difficult to follow since the visit of the Italian journalists would be to influence opinion in Italy. No similar advantage would result from a visit of British journalists.

PWE nevertheless pursued their attempts to make Italian Ps/W friendly to Britain before their return, and put forward proposals for a mission of pro-British and anti-Fascist Italian officers to visit Ps/W camps on behalf of the Italian Government,[6] and for an increased number of PWE camp visitors of whom there were only three for 43,500 Ps/W.

Low morale continued throughout the summer of 1945, owing to the absence of any dates being fixed for repatriation. By November, PWE and the Italian envoy, Count Carandini, working closely together, had succeeded in securing acceptance of an Italian mission to Italian Ps/W[7] which had

1. Regional Director Italy to Director General PWE, 29.8.44.
2. Telegram from Sir Noel Charles to FO referred to by Sir Percy Loraine, 24.5.44.
3. Report by Mr Ashcroft, 6.10.44.
4. No. 7 Sir Noel Charles to FO, 10.8.44.
5. Oliver Harvey to Brigadier Blomfield, 30.6.45, and No. 0103/3811 (PWI), 3.7.45, to Mr Harvey.
6. Memorandum on re-education of Italian Ps/W in England, 30.9.44.
7. Foreign Office Paper ZM 5615/157/22, Nov. 1945.

been first put forward by PWE over a year before. The Mission was to inform Italian prisoners of the arrangements made for their future in Italy. The DPW Major General Blomfield raised objections to the Mission visiting labour camps but accepted that it should be based on the transit camps where Italian Ps/W were waiting to be repatriated. Count Carandini did not demur.[1]

Under these conditions the Italian Mission was allowed to carry out its work and undoubtedly did much to raise the morale of the prisoners before returning.

A last effort was made before repatriation to carry out work with the non-co-operators. They were not, however allowed to volunteer to become co-operators in the few months remaining before their repatriation.[2] The great majority of Italian prisoners were repatriated by the end of July 1946.

Political Warfare to German Ps/W Due for Repatriation

During the height of the German Blitz in 1941, a project was put up to use German Ps/W due for repatriation under the Hague Convention for 'projecting Britain' in Germany after their return. The proposal was to house them in hotels with sympathetic German speakers in charge, to dress them in civilian clothes and to arrange excursions to various entertainments, concerts, football matches, cinemas, to various factories, docks and ship-building areas before they were finally seen off with a Guard of Honour and a farewell speech by an officer of high rank.

It was believed that no action by the German authorities could prevent these men from spreading stories of their experiences. The scheme was strongly opposed by the Minister of Information on the grounds that it would excite indignation among the public and questions in Parliament. It was also opposed by the security authorities. The practical difficulty of providing civilian clothes appears also to have loomed large; it was one which for several years dogged Political Warfare experiments with Ps/W.

The scheme was finally vetoed. It may have been a little too obvious in conception, but the obvious is sometimes effective.

Propaganda to German Ps/W – Early Period

At the request of the JIC SO1 assumed responsibility for propaganda to German Ps/W in 1940 and a plan was drawn up which included publication of a weekly news-sheet for distribution in the camps, provision of libraries of German and English books, facilities for reception of BBC broadcasts and exhibition of films.

The scheme was approved by DPW. The Wochenpost was first

---

1. 0103/7454 (PW2), Major General Blomfield to Sir Oliver, 26.1.46.
2. 0103/7454 (PW1), Lt Colonel Chandler to W/Cdr Hitch, 25.1.46.

published [on] 8.1.41. It was at first refused by the inmates of two camps, but 1,800 copies were being produced by October, 1941. It was several months before suitable contributions from Ps/W were forthcoming.

Libraries were provided and serious books were read by officers with interests, books by émigrés and Jews being, however, rejected.

PWE censored all books suggested for libraries or bought by Ps/W.

BBC

Home and Forces programmes were listened to but up till the end of 1941, the prisoners refused to listen to the BBC German programmes.

The decision taken that German Ps/W should not, except in special cases, be retained in Britain, but be shipped to Canada, brought PWE attempts at re-education almost to an end.

The printed Wochenpost was reduced to a roneoed sheet, the Lagerpost.

Second Period

The situation in Britain was entirely changed by our re-entry into Europe, large numbers of German Ps/W consequently reaching Britain. A Cabinet decision to retain 17,000 of them in this country followed.

The Director General[1] advised the Ministers that PWE should refuse to accept the responsibility of re-education unless proper facilities were given. He would indeed have welcomed any legitimate reason for not accepting the responsibility. The Ministers sought a Cabinet decision on the matter, and the War Cabinet agreed[2] that PWE should undertake the work of re-education of German Ps/W and that all possible steps be taken to facilitate their work.

The decision also covered re-education of German Ps/W in the ME which is dealt with separately.

PWE took immediate steps to recruit personnel for work in the camps. The shortage of CSDIC trained officers, who were by far the best for the work of segregation, and of German speakers was acute and the work of re-education of Ps/W took a low priority. The difficulties at the outset were indeed so great that the Director General would have preferred to hand back the responsibility for re-education to the War Office. Earlier difficulties which had arisen between Air Commodore Groves and General Gepp, DPW, resulted in strained relations at a high level. Fortunately, there were excellent relations on the immediately lower level between Wing Commander Hitch of PWE and Colonel Chandler of DPW.

1. Director General to Foreign Secretary, 6.9.44.
2. War Cabinet Conclusions, 123(44), 18.9.44.

Policy and Methods of Re-education

The short-term aims of re-education were to gain the co-operation of Ps/W so as to enable us to:

1. Economise in guards and avoid trouble in the camps.
2. Obtain volunteers for labour purposes, for secret service and Political Warfare work.
3. Obtain intelligence. In addition to the intelligence useful for military or Political Warfare purposes during the war, we obtained an assessment of the political and social problems which would confront the controlling power on occupation.

The long-term aims were to:

1. Indoctrinate Ps/W with democratic views of life and convince them that National Socialist and Militarist ideologies have been and always must be disastrous to Germany.
2. Obtain politically reliable administrators for Germany.

Segregation

The presence of a secret Nazi hierarchy in a camp effectually prevented successful re-education of Ps/W. Nazis were frequently appointed as camp leaders as they were good disciplinarians.

Segregation was effected by:

1. Lists of hostile elements supplied by the camp commandants.
2. Posting agents who were ostensibly sergeant interpreters to the camps to mix with the Ps/W.
3. Censorship of incoming and outgoing mail.
4. Hidden microphones.
5. Agents visiting camps ostensibly as welfare officers.

When a list of 'Blacks' had been compiled, PWE recommended that they should be paraded without warning and removed to a camp prepared for them, after which no communication with their fellow prisoners should be allowed. A separate hospital for 'Blacks' was necessary.

When the Blacks had been removed, re-education of the Greys and Whites could begin.

Later, the Whites were sifted from the Greys. The camp newspaper could be used to provide information. A paragraph of indirect propaganda was occasionally inserted.

Any Ps/W who objected to such items were classed as 'Greys'.

English newspapers and periodicals, carefully selected German or Italian books, BBC classes in English, BBC broadcasts, to which prisoners need not listen and suitable films were used in the process of re-education. PWE 'welfare officers' helped to provide games, organise choirs, bands and debating societies.

Only in White camps was the political side of re-education ever carried out openly and even in them the machinery of re-education was kept as secret as possible.

Priorities in Repatriation of German Ps/W

A decision taken on 18th May, 1945,[1] on a paper put forward by the S. of S. for War [was] that while as many German Ps/W as possible in this country should be put to work, the extreme Nazis should be returned to Germany and that the numbers of Blacks so repatriated should be replaced by Whites or Greys sent from Germany.

PWE saw in this not only the end of all attempts at re-education, but disastrous political consequences in Germany. It would reinforce the Nazi Underground in Germany, take all heart out of the Whites and lead them to believe they had been deliberately misled. PWE sought to reverse this decision and fortunately found support from Field Marshal Montgomery who foresaw[2] the possibility of mass-escapes of Nazi extremists in Germany and that 'Whites' would learn that the easy way home was to abandon democratic beliefs for fervid devotion to National Socialism.

A long controversy followed and in October, a paper put forward by the Foreign Secretary[3] secured a reversal of the original paper and the decision that 'Whites' should be given priority over 'Blacks' in repatriation. PWE was for some reason not directly informed of the decision.

Resignation of Air Commodore Groves

Before this decision had been reversed, Air Commodore Groves resigned as he had failed to secure acceptance of his proposal that the Ps/W directorate should become an independent department and that he should have direct access to the Minister of State, Mr Noel Baker. He was succeeded as head of the Division by Wing Commander Hitch with the title of Controller.

PWE Third Mission to ME

The formation and dispatch of a para-military mission to the Middle East resulted from the War Cabinet decision.[4] Approval of the military

1. WP(45)292, 18.5.45.
2. HQ/1408/1, Lt General R. M. Weeks, Chief of Staff British Zone, 9.7.45.
3. C 6358, 23.10.45.
4. War Cabinet Conclusions, 123(44), 18.9.44.

establishment was asked for from the War Office and the Resident Minister was informed that the head of the Mission would be Colonel Thornhill, who would be given acting rank of Brigadier, and two officers would leave by air as soon as possible.[1]

The choice of Colonel Thornhill and of some members of the Mission was a result of the closing of Brondesbury School of which Colonel Thornhill had been Commandant. The specialists from the school had mostly gone to PWD or SHAEF but some of the staff remained. Thus Major Burnett, one of the instructors, and Major Makgill, Colonel Thornhill's staff officer at the school, were members of the Mission. But although German speakers were recruited to act as visitors for the camp, no specialist with a knowledge of Wehrmacht psychology or experience was included and the new men were untrained amateurs.

If Colonel Thornhill's record with PWE is examined, and it is remembered that he had been in poor health for two years, there can be no doubt that a younger officer of proved organising ability and drive would have been a better appointment. It is possible that some such criticism may account for part of the obstructive tactics adopted to the Mission both at GHQ Cairo and at the War Office.

But it is unlikely to account for all of it – since opposition in Cairo was based partly on the claim that the work of segregation was already being carried out,[2] partly owing to dislike of re-education as such by those who thought the 'only good German was a dead German'.

The departure of the Mission was held up for nearly three months pending formal approval of the Military part of the establishment. Colonel Thornhill's promotion to Brigadier was refused.

A telegram from C. in C. Middle East[3] to the War Office stated that he had informed the Resident Minister that he had no instructions regarding the Mission yet the Adjutant General had informed PWE that a telegram had been dispatched a fortnight earlier. Meanwhile the War Office steadily held up approval of the War Establishment though the majority of the officers were already members of PWE.

These obstructionist tactics were carried on in spite of the War Cabinet decision that 'PWE should undertake re-education of German Ps/W and that all possible steps should be taken to facilitate their work'.

Major Burnett, who formed the advance guard found the DAG GHQ Middle East critical of the establishment, averse to segregation being carried out by the Mission, and sceptical with regard to re-education. Major Burnett was only able to obtain accommodation owing to the courtesy of PWB.

Colonel Thornhill finally arrived in Cairo in March 1945. He was soon

---

1. No. 3670, Lockhart to Resident Minister, 31.10.44.
2. No. 4077, Lockhart to Sir Edward Grigg, 28.12.44.
3. No. A5/70996. C. in C. ME to War Office, 18.12.44.

successful in bringing about a different attitude on the part of the military authorities, and by July, from GOC downwards, the members of GHQ ME and GHQ BTE were all co-operative and friendly to the Mission, the Camp Commandants being especially so.

The first essential – that of gaining the good will of most of the military authorities – had been achieved almost entirely owing to Colonel Thornhill.

But there can be little doubt that the actual work of re-education could have been carried out if organisation had been better and if the staff had had more experience and knowledge of the work. Thus in August 1945, there were only seven camp visitors of whom four were ranked as good, two were not so good, and one lacked any interest in the work.[1] One of them was leaving shortly and two others contemplated departure if their wives could not join them. There were 91,000 German Ps/W, largely of the Afrika Korps, who had been left to stew in their own juice during the war. Some segregation had been carried out by the military authorities, but by August, the Mission's right to segregate was admitted and AG5 (DPW) was pressing the Mission to carry out the work.

As the Mission lacked suitable staff, segregation was carried out by selected teams of friendly 'White' Ps/W.

There were very few books and no broadcasting in the camps. A few lectures were given by 'Whites' under supervision; there was no PWE plan for teaching English, though some classes had been organised by the Ps/W themselves.

The publications section under Mr Manning (an alien) was one of the best features of the Mission and was producing 20,000 copies of a weekly newspaper to which the Ps/W contributed. Many more copies were wanted, but could not be produced with the machinery available. No one had been appointed in charge of films.

There was a crying need for work in all camps. None were dominated by Blacks. Many were badly sited, in one water had to be rationed; another site is alleged to have been deliberately chosen as sandstorms blew regularly there for some hours every day.[2]

There was therefore some basis for the allegations made by Colonel Curran, military advisor to the Resident Minister, in a personal interview with Sir Robert Bruce Lockhart.

Colonel Curran stated that Colonel Thornhill was 'neither mentally nor physically qualified to direct the Mission'. That the Mission had become something of a joke and that Colonel Thornhill's refusal to move the Mission to Ismailia, the headquarters of the Ps/W area, made it impossible for much concentrated work to be done in the [camps] 'since visits from Cairo necessitated a motor drive of some four hours'.

The Director General at once dispatched W/Cdr Hitch, an officer of

1. Report by W/Cdr Hitch on the Mission.
2. Wing Commander Hitch's Report on PWE Mission to ME.

considerable organising ability, to report on the work of the Mission and in particular on the truth of these allegations.

W/Cdr Hitch made a secret and personal report on his return, on which this history is largely based.

Wing Commander Hitch was able to show that some of the allegations made by Colonel Curran were without foundation. Thus the work of the Mission, in his opinion, would have suffered had its HQ been moved from Cairo, and 'whatever may be the faults of Colonel Thornhill, my opinion is that his perseverance and drive on high levels "opened the doors". The responsible members of his staff were the first to confirm this.'

Nothing, however was done to strengthen the Mission until after the resignations of Sir Robert Bruce Lockhart as Director General and Air Commodore Groves as head of the Prisoners of War Directorate.

Wing Commander Hitch, who succeeded Air Commodore Groves, applied for the services of a CSDIC trained officer Major Kettler and arranged for his promotion to Lt Colonel and sent him out to organise the work of re-education.

Lt Colonel Kettler undoubtedly achieved great improvements but he was however dissatisfied with the conditions imposed on him by Colonel Thornhill, under which he had to work.

Major General Strong, who had become Director General, decided to send out Lt Colonel Gordon to make an independent report. At this period, two libel actions were threatened by members of the Mission – one against Wing Commander Hitch by Sir Joseph Addison and one against Colonel Thornhill.

Major General Strong finally decided to visit the ME himself, and later Mr Stuart Roberts, Director of Finance, sent out a member of his staff to investigate the lavish expenditure of the Mission. Allegations of overspending and of improper expenditure had been made.

The present writer has not been asked to see this report as the period under review is really outside the limits of this history.

As Lt Colonel Gordon had recommended cutting down the establishment of the Mission considerably, Major General Strong took the view that an officer of Colonel Thornhill's rank and seniority was no longer required at its head. The Mission was left under Lt Colonel Moriarty and was still functioning in November 1946.

German Ps/W in Italy

No work on segregation and re-education of German Ps/W held by British forces in Italy was undertaken by PWB AFHQ as it was regarded as not one of its functions[1] though Major Colby and Major Taylor visited camps at the request of the British and American military authorities and advised on starting camp newspapers and radio broadcasts.

1. Mr Radford to PID, 22.7.45.

Brigadier Metherell recommended[1] that any mission set up should be a separate organisation unconnected with PWB which had not the staff to undertake the work.

While anxious to help, Wing Commander Hitch pointed out that the PID charter for re-education of Ps/W was limited to the UK and the Middle East and asked for an extension of the charter to Italy, if the Division was to undertake the work. Wing Commander Hitch was informed that the Director General was unwilling to extend PID commitments[2] until the Ps/W division was operating efficiently in Britain. The form of this communication was not such as to encourage further application. The need was urgent as the conditions in some of the camps in Italy were very bad.

In 215 P/W camp 900 boys were[3] segregated in a compound with no opportunity for recreation or study, no amenities, no books, in fact nothing but the mud of the compound and the tents where the boys lived, 'the place was a breeding ground for Nazi ideas since no other ideas could reach it' and for sexual perversion.

The obvious solution was repatriation as soon as possible since 'the harm they can do now would be trifling to that which another year or two of the present treatment would produce'. The 'obvious solution' was not adopted.

Owing to the Director General's ruling against new commitments, PID was only able to assist by advice and by providing stereos, lists of books and by offering to recruit two lecturers.

On the transfer of the Ps/W division PID to the Control Commission, the War Office requested[4] that the activities of the Division should be extended to operate in Italy.

Discussions on the salary, etc., of lecturers to be sent to the camps was still in progress at the end of October, 1946, but they had not been sent.

Re-education of German Ps/W in Canada

In the years following the decision to transfer the vast majority of German Ps/W to Canada, Air Commodore Groves made frequent attempts to persuade the Canadian authorities to initiate the segregation and re-education of German Ps/W, held in Canada. These attempts were largely fruitless. It is true that the Canadian authorities in London were interested, and a Psychological Warfare Committee was formed in Ottawa. Moreover, PWE appointed an officer, Colonel Skilbeck, as liaison officer between PWE and the Canadian Psychological Warfare Committee. But conditions in the Ps/W camps in Canada were bad and continued to get worse, owing to

1. PWB/M/G/33/3, 1.10.45. Brigadier Metherell to PoW Section PID.
2. Lt Colonel Keith to Wing Commander Hitch, 4.12.45.
3. Report by J. Blackie dated 12.12.45, and forwarded by Lt Colonel Chandler of Directorate Ps/W War Office to Wing Commander Hitch.
4. BM 3928 (PW4). Major General Blomfield, DPW, to C. in C. CHQ/CMF, 24.8.46.

the non-co-operative attitude of the Canadian military authorities from camp commandants upwards to the Canadian Adjutant General.

As a result, Nazi extremists dominated the Canadian camps, Hitler's birthday was publicly celebrated, anti-Nazis were bullied, and secret trials were carried out for disloyalty to Hitler and in one camp, in the autumn of 1943, two anti-Nazis were hanged.[1] The use of Nazi symbols and practices were not forbidden and were almost universal until after the defeat of Germany.[2] In the summer of 1944, the whole question of segregation and re-education was taken up on a high level with the Canadian authorities by the Foreign Office[3] and a simultaneous approach was made to the United States authorities. Particular stress was laid by the FO on the segregation of Austrian Ps/W from German. But the situation was still extremely unsatisfactory a year later.

By September 1945, some progress had been made in the creation of a special organisation in Canada to deal with re-education. A party of intelligence officers had been trained in the camps and a further party were undergoing training at Brondesbury. A segregation camp for Blacks had been prepared.[4]

But most important of all, Ottawa had at last decided to attach a Canadian Army officer to Canadian Military HQ in London to act as a liaison officer with PID on all matters concerning segregation and re-education of Ps/W, in place of Colonel Skilbeck.

A meeting followed between PID and the Canadian military and civil authorities. Procedure was agreed and from that time forward, progress was extremely rapid and co-operation between PID and the Canadian authorities all that could be asked for.

Thus when the decision was taken to transfer Ps/W in Canada to Britain, not only were full details supplied about all the Ps/W, so that those who had been allotted priority for repatriation could be included in the *Oberon* scheme,[5] but camp libraries and other equipment for re-education was shipped with them.

In spite of the excellent relations which subsisted between the Canadian authorities and PID it must be recorded that the Canadian standards did not come up to PID requirements.

Thus 183 Ps/W from the Canadian White camp at Sorel were screened by Captain Parry of PID after their arrival in this country. Under 50% fell into the PID White category, many were of the type that would never have any political ideas. Others were opportunists. PID therefore acted on its own screenings and not on the general recommendations of the Canadian authorities.

1. Director General to Foreign Secretary, 18.9.44.
2. Minutes 58 Meeting Psychological Warfare Committee, Ottawa, 18.7.45.
3. Telegram No. 5359, Washington, 13.6.44.
4. P(G)131. Air Commodore Groves to Director General, 16.9.44.
5. POW 1/H448, 20.12.45.

For good or evil, this meant that the same standards were being applied to all German Ps/W.

Co-ordination with US Authorities

In June 1944, Lord Halifax[1] had been asked to approach the US authorities and to impress on them the desirability of segregating Austrian Ps/W and of establishing co-operation between the US authorities and PWE.

But the simplest method of establishing co-operation, the disclosure of our methods to the Americans, and an invitation to them to disclose their plans, was not taken, because PWE was afraid that the secrecy of its work would be jeopardised by disclosure to OWI which had numerous contacts with the press,[2] and PWE had not direct contacts with the American Army authorities except through OWI.

After the collapse of Germany, Mr Harman, then head of the P/W Mission in [the] USA was authorised to show documents on re-education to OWI but was forced to ask for fuller information as he had not been 'kept in the picture' regarding PWE work in this field.

The first attempt at co-ordination of effort came from the American side when Colonel Powell, of USA Army of the Provost Marshal General's Office, called at Bush House and saw Wing Commander Hitch,[3] who welcomed the visit and gave him all available information on British methods of re-education.

Colonel Powell revealed that the US War Department had a secret plan for the segregation and re-education of German Ps/W in the US which had been in operation for some time. A special camp had been started for training 'Whites' for work in Germany in the American zone of occupation and a special camp for Whites was planned in France. He was anxious to establish reciprocal liaison between PWE and his Department.

As a result of this visit, PWE kept the US authorities supplied with information regarding re-education in Britain, but the close liaison which both Colonel Powell and Wing Commander Hitch would have welcomed was not established.

A feature of the American approach to the work of re-education was the insistence on teaching English. It was believed by the Americans that a new language brought with it a new set of ideas. No doubt familiarity with the transformation of German immigrants to the US into American citizens influenced the Americans in this respect. On the other hand, less attention was paid to a thorough system of segregation than in the United Kingdom. Although Mr Hitch regards the attempt to secure close co-operation with the US authorities as having failed, it should be mentioned that he was awarded the US medal of freedom for his assistance to the US authorities.

---

1. Telegram No. 5359 from FO to Washington, 13.6.44.
2. No. 6760 FO to Washington, 25.6.45.
3. Wing Commander Hitch to Air Commodore Groves, 22.5.45.

Co-operation with the French Authorities

In the summer and autumn of 1946, Mr Hitch was able to enter into close liaison with the French authorities who were much impressed by the evidence of results of PID methods of segregation and re-education, in securing economies in the guarding of Ps/W and increasing their usefulness as a labour force. As a result, in November 1946, the French authorities were enthusiastically introducing PID methods. The result may do something to bring about better relations between the French and German peoples. It is fair to say the adoption of PID methods by the French was due to Mr Hitch's initiative and to his thorough knowledge of the French people.

Ps/W Division – Third Period

The Prisoners of War Division owed a great debt, if not its existence, to Air Commodore Groves who had always recognised the importance of the work and in particular of the danger of repatriating well-fed and well-disciplined Ps/W dominated by Nazi extremists. Air Commodore Groves had fought long, both inside and outside the Department, for ideas for which the Department stood and which he had done much to formulate. Nevertheless his resignation, which was closely followed by the departure of General Gepp from the position of DPW at the War Office, was followed by a great improvement in the relations of PWE and the War Office and in the scale of the work done.

It was not long before General Blomfield, the new DPW, realised the great assistance which PID was able to give to such practical matters as the selection of Ps/W who could be safely billeted on farms, the reduction in the number of guards needed in White and Grey camps, etc.

Organisation of Directorate of Ps/W

Ps/W Division was organised under a Headquarters Staff and divided into two sections. The Field Section was responsible for all the work carried out in the camps. The officers of the Field Section were divided into segregation, training advisers and English instructors.

The Re-education Section was responsible for the supply of the books, lectures, and training material of all sorts. It was divided into a literature sub-section which was responsible for selection, supply, and censorship of books, pamphlets and newspapers in English and German. It also supervised and controlled 190 weekly or fortnightly newspapers written and edited by Ps/W themselves in the camps.

The publication sub-section edited and produced the weekly Ps/W newspaper, the Wochenpost. During the Nuremberg trial it sent out a daily news-sheet giving a report of the trial.

The section was also responsible for educational supplies, stationery, wireless grants, etc.

The English teaching sub-section was responsible for organising English teaching in camps.

By October 1946, there were 45,000 English students in the camps and 3,000 had sat for examinations in English.

Special Camps

In addition to the Brondesbury Hostel, the Ps/W Division set up two special camps.

The Training Centre, Wilton Park, provided a six weeks' course under Dr Koeppler for 300–350 Ps/W selected from among the 'Whites' for intelligence and ability. The object was to equip them for work as re-educational instructors after their return to their camps, to influence opinion in Germany in favour of the Allies after their return to Germany.

The syllabus covered the study of German history from Bismarck to the present day, of the relationship of the individual and the State and the nature of the democratic way of life. The Training Centre was opened in January 1946 with an address by Major General Strong and many prominent persons have lectured to the students.

The Youth Camp was agreed to in June 1946 and organised at Wimbish as a special measure for the re-education of 'Black' youth among Nazi Ps/W.

Upwards of 1,000 Ps/W were drafted to the camp, all Blacks under twenty-seven years of age. The camp was unwired. The occupants were employed in agricultural work, the hours being staggered so that each P/W devoted one day a week to attendance at re-educational classes, etc.

Oberon

The value of having politically reliable Germans trained as lawyers, administrators, doctors, etc., ready to fill posts in the administration of Germany, was realised at an early date by the German Region of PWE and by Air Commodore Groves. Plan Oberon was accordingly drawn up for the priority repatriation of selected White Ps/W.

Austrians

The plan worked well with regard to Austrians owing to close liaison being arranged between the Labour Division, Allied Commission for Austria, and PID. At a meeting between Mr Kirby[1] of the Labour Division and Wing Commander Hitch, it was agreed that PID would provide lists of specialists giving all details possible, and bulk lists of other White Ps/W.

The Control Commission agreed to make a selection of individual Ps/W for its requirements. Owing to the acute shortage of labour in Austria, the

1. POW 1/H/jdh/458, 27.12.45.

Control Commission was willing to accept all screened Austrian Ps/W who were 'White' or 'Grey', a month later.

Germans

The Oberon scheme did not work so well in Germany as in Austria.

The basic reasons for the failure[1] were the different conditions and a difference in interpretation of the Oberon scheme.

In practice the Oberon scheme only worked for the higher posts for which there were many professionally qualified Germans available. The minor posts were filled by German local officials to whom the lists prepared by PID were not made available.

Moreover, the ruling that Ps/W should be sent to Britain to replace those repatriated made the Control Commission authorities reluctant to accept Ps/W under Oberon.

Lt Colonel Faulk therefore recommended that the Oberon plan should be scrapped and merged in those of 'Seagull'.

Seagull

Oberon was therefore superseded by Seagull which covered the repatriation of all classes of Ps/W.

Bulk repatriation of White and Grey Germans was in progress during the summer and autumn of 1946 starting with 2,000 Whites a month in July. Selection of Ps/W was made by PID. Special priority was given to Whites, and to miners, volunteers for the mines and timber workers.

So far as possible priority within these groups was given to those who had been longest in captivity.

Transfer of PID Ps/W Division to Control Commission

A letter from the Director General to Sir Arthur Street[2] invited the Control Commission to take over the Ps/W Division, as it was the intention to close down PID.

Negotiations followed and the Ps/W Division was transferred as a going concern with Mr Hitch as Controller, to the Control Commission as from 1st July, 1946.

Summary of Work done by Ps/W Division PID. War Office. Segregation

The system of screening enabled guard companies to be withdrawn from most of the camps and thus effected a substantial saving in manpower. The

1. Report by Lt Col Faulk, 30.4.46.
2. 22.2.46.

process of screening enabled dangerous elements to be sorted out and concentrated in the few Black and base camps where they could not create unrest.

Labour

The selection of all Ps/W billeted on farms was a PID responsibility. Such advances were made in segregation and re-education that all Ps/W in working camps could be put out to work without considering political grading and in the vast majority of cases without escort.

Morale

PID contributed towards raising and maintaining morale in all camps and in that respect assisted labour output.

Camp Problems

Innumerable special visits were paid by Field Workers to camps at the request of War Office, Commands, Districts and Commandants themselves, to deal with political and other problems.

Discipline

All camp and hostel leaders were either appointed by PID or such appointments were checked by PID. Most cases of indiscipline in camps originated either from political trouble inside the camp, from misunderstandings with the British staff or from low morale. In nearly all cases PID officers settled the matter satisfactorily.

Interpreter Staff

PID work was carried on in close conjunction with the British Interpreter staff of camps. PID was thus able to keep the War Office informed of the quality of this staff.

Liaison with IPW

PID maintained close liaison with Inspectors of Prisoners of War and at their instance paid many special visits to camps to deal with various problems. IPW in their turn reported on matters of interest to PID.

Repatriation

The programme of repatriation for Ps/W held in the UK was organised in close consultation with the War Office, the cardinal factor being political grading of Ps/W. Priority screening of many individual Ps/W was carried out at the request of the War Office.

Nationalities

PID was responsible for the separation, screening and repatriation of Austrian Ps/W which involved the examination of all cases of Ps/W claiming Austrian nationality, and also advised in numerous cases of dual personality.

Documentation

The documentation of Ps/W awaiting repatriation to Germany was very largely a PID responsibility, working in the closest possible collaboration with the War Office.

RAF

On nearly all points noted above a similar close co-operation was carried out with the Air Ministry. PID segregators and re-educators visited the many RAF units where Ps/W were held.

CCG

PID approved of direct assistance to CCG in their repatriation of selected Ps/W required for specialist and other responsible posts in Germany and Austria and was also of much assistance to legal division.

Letters from Repatriated Ps/W

A result of the repatriation of German Ps/W in progress as this history is being completed, is that numbers of letters have been received in the Ps/W Division PID from 'Whites' after their return to Germany.

Extracts from two of these letters form fitting testimonials to the spirit which has animated PID throughout its existence.

> During the past weeks I had an opportunity to talk[1] to men who returned from American, French and Russian captivity and inquired about camp activities, treatment and educational training. I do not exaggerate when I say that Great Britain has thus contributed most to the reconstruction of Germany by treating her prisoners as human beings. . . . Never was I forbidden to speak freely and express my

1. Letter from Max Muehldorfer, transferred from Ascot Camp to 92 Camp, 2.2.46; repatriated 19.6.46. To the Commandant 92 Camp Tiverton, Devon.

> views. . . . I have taken the liberty to express my thanks to you, Sir, and should like to extend thanks to all who have participated in your endeavour to make life behind barbed wire comfortable, free, and worthy of human beings.

The writer of the following extract was a P/W who had given himself up at the first opportunity as a result of our broadcasts and leaflets.

> Looking back I have to stress again and again that the Germans who at an early stage have put their confidence in you, the Press, the Radio, the Propaganda, have trusted you and have finally made up their mind to make their way to you as Prisoners of War at the earliest opportunity can be regarded as the most lucky people. The time they have spent in the British Isles has not been wasted for anybody who thinks honestly. . . .[1]

It is difficult to imagine a better testimonial to the effectiveness of Political Warfare in all its stages.

1. Letter from Karl Buehl, 25.8.46.

Select Bibliography for Further Study of PWE

Aldrich, Richard, *The Hidden Hand* (2001)

Briggs, Asa, *The History of Broadcasting in the United Kingdom vol. 3: The War of Words* (1970)

Bruce Lockhart, Sir Robert, *Comes the Reckoning* (1947)

—— *Giants Cast Long Shadows* (1960)

Cruickshank, Charles, *The Fourth Arm: Psychological Warfare 1938–1945* (1977)

—— *Deception in World War Two* (1979)

Dalton, Hugh, *The Fateful Years: Memoirs 1931–45* (1957)

Delmer, Sefton, *Black Boomerang* (1962)

Dorril, Stephen, *MI6: Fifty Years of Special Operations* (2000)

Duff Cooper, Alfred, *Old Men Forget* (1953)

Foot, M.R.D., *SOE in France* (1966)

Hesketh, Roger, *Fortitude: The D-Day Deception Campaign* (1999)

Howard, Anthony, *Crossman: The Pursuit of Power* (1990)

Howe, Ellic, *The Black Game* (1982)

Mackenzie, William, *The Secret History of SOE* (2000)

Stuart, Sir Campbell, *Secrets of Crewe House* (1920)

West, Nigel, *MI6*: *British Secret Intelligence Service Operations 1909–45* (1985)

—— *Secret War: The Story of SOE* (1992)

West, Nigel (ed.), *British Security Co-ordination* (1998)

Young, Kenneth (ed.), *The Diaries of Sir Robert Bruce Lockhart vol. 2 1939–1965* (1980)

Index